at the Council Chamber at Quebec
on Monday, November 9, 1789...

" His Lordship intimated to the Council that...it was
his wish to put a mark of honour upon the families
who had adhered to the Unity of the Empire, and
joined the Royal Standard in America before the
Treaty of Separation in the Year 1783."

This book is a tribute to the courageous men and women who first settled the Niagara frontier. Their spirit lives on to this day along storied Portage Road, the first King's Highway in Upper Canada. May we never forget those brave pioneers.

William S. Smeaton
Mayor
City of Niagara Falls, Ontario

The Niagara Portage Road

A History of the Portage on the West Bank of the Niagara River

The Niagara Portage Road

A History of the Portage on the West Bank of the Niagara River

BY

George A. Seibel
City of Niagara Falls Historian
Niagara Parks Historian

Olive M. Seibel, B.A.
Editor

Published by
The City of Niagara Falls Canada
1990

Seibel, George A. (George Alfred)
  The Niagara Portage Road and the history of water and rail transport between Lake Ontario and Lake Erie

Includes bibliographical references.
ISBN 0-9690457-4-3

  1. Niagara Portage Road (Ont.)--History.   2. Niagara Peninsula (Ont.)--History.   3. Roads--Ontario--History--19th century.   4. Railroads--Ontario--History--19th century.   5. Waterways--Ontario--History--19th century. I. Seibel, Olive M. (Olive Marguerite)   II. Niagara Falls Heritage Foundation (Ont.)

FC3095.N5S44 1990   971.3'38   C90-090024-5
F1059.N5S44 1990

Book Design and Layout
George A. Seibel

Typesetting and Finished Layout
Just Your Type, Niagara Falls, Ontario

Colour Separations
Ainsworth Press, Kitchener

End Papers Sketch
George Balbar

Printed and bound in Canada by
John Deyell Co., Lindsay

OFFICE OF THE MAYOR

It is with pleasure that I recommend this very fine work, *The Niagara Portage Road,* by our City Historian and long time friend, George Seibel. This publication serves to highlight a piece of Canadian history which has all too often been forgotten, a piece of history which is now properly presented.

Our Portage Road carries a storied past on to Niagara's history stage. The ghosts of the wagon and stage coach drivers can be found along its winding path from Queenston through to Chippawa. Stalwart, innovative engineers created this, the first King's Highway in Upper Canada. The roadway has witnessed the War of 1812 and the players on that stage, and has seen the birth of our present City.

George Seibel has brought to life in a vivid picture, the living story that is Portage Road. I take special interest because the Smeaton family's original holding, now part of the present site of the Ontario Hydro Reservoir, once had Portage Road as its access. My great-grandfather, James Gordon Smeaton, settled his family on land above the escarpment in the late 1800's, and saw his sons, including my grandfather, travel daily on the old Portage Road to school and to work.

Now properly we highlight for future generations this rich fabric of Canadian history, and on behalf of my Council and all Niagara citizens and historians, I salute George Seibel for this wonderful story.

William S. Smeaton
Mayor

1990 City Council

Back Row – left to right: Bruce Ward, Mark Hopkins, Charles Cheesman, W.A. Hinsperger, Patrick Cummings, Bruce Cowan, Judy Orr, Ed Sherar.
Front Row – seated: Norman Puttick, Wayne Campbell, Mayor William S. Smeaton, Margaret Harrington, Paisley Janvary.

The Falls of Niagara, 1697.

An engraving by J. Van Vienan, from Father Louis Hennepin's ''Nouvelle Découverte''. This hand coloured copy originally belonged to King William III of England to whom the book is dedicated.

On the morning of December 7, 1678, an advance exploration party of Robert Cavelier, Sieur de la Salle, led by Lieutenant La Motte, made a landing on the west bank of the Niagara River, at what is now Queenston. They proceeded overland, climbed the escarpment and travelled along the bank of the Niagara Gorge, and in doing so, were the first white men to portage there. They came upon the Falls of Niagara later that same day, and went on to the mouth of the Chippawa River, where they set up camp for the night. Father Louis Hennepin, a Recollet priest who was with the party, later published a book in which he included his description of the Falls of Niagara, and this engraving, by J. Van Vienen, which the artist drew in Holland, from Hennepin's written description of the Falls.

AUTHOR'S PREFACE

"History is Bunk". These words are attributed to Henry Ford, the American engineering genius who pioneered mass production in the automobile industry. Mr. Ford denied that he used this actual phrase, though he did not disavow the sentiment.

For another and different opinion I quote Winston Churchill: "History with its flickering lamp stumbles along the trail of the past, trying to reconstruct its scenes, to revive the echoes, and kindle with pale gleams the passion of former days."

This book concurs with Winston Churchill's sentiments. It encompasses the history of the Niagara Portage Road on the west bank of the Niagara River, the pioneer settlers who came to this area, and some of the history of water and rail transportation between Lake Ontario and Lake Erie. Scenes are reconstructed, events are recalled as the story of the early days in our area is told.

I have included biographies of some of the people, past and present, who have helped to record and preserve history in this area. While their writings were consulted and information from them used in this book, I alone am responsible for what is written.

My hope is that in reading the chapters of this book, the reader will come to appreciate the achievements of these pioneers in re-establishing themselves in a new land, and in developing the portage and the communities, industries and services associated with it. *The Niagara Portage Road* is about all of these.

George Seibel
Chairman, Niagara Falls Heritage Foundation
City of Niagara Falls Historian
Niagara Parks Historian

ACKNOWLEDGEMENTS

A book such as this, which attempts to recount the history of our area, is made easier because of the research and writing on the subject which was done by others. These people, beginning with Ernest Cruikshank and Ernest Green, are acknowledged in the appendix of this book and their biographical sketches outline the part they played in preserving our local history.

There are some who deserve special mention. It was Mrs. A.H. Walker, (Isabel), who first piqued my interest in the Portage Road and pointed out in 1971 the dilapidated condition of Old St. John's Anglican Church. Mrs. Walker more than anyone else is responsible for my interest in celebrating the 200th Anniversary of the Portage Road by the compilation of this book and the displays of historic material in locations along the Road. Mrs. Walker allowed us to copy many of the original documents from her collection of the Thompson Papers and contributed her information on the historic houses along the Portage Road. She was a reliable source of information in many areas.

Mrs. A.E. Huggins, (Jean), was a willing source of pictorial and written information on Queenston. It was my privilege to visit and get to know Mrs. Huggins in the three years since my work on this book began. I regret that she did not live to see the results of her efforts as Queenston's unofficial historian, reproduced in this book.

As most of this book deals with historical events which took place before the advent of photography, it was necessary to rely on artists' sketches, watercolours and oil paintings, to depict the events. Photographs and colour transparencies of works of art were obtained from museums and archives in Canada, the United States and England.

We received colour transparencies on loan from: National Archives of Canada, Martha Marleau, Art Acquisition and Research Section; Royal Ontario Museum, Mrs. Karen Smith, Departmental Assistant; Environment Canada, Canadian Parks Service, Woodside National Historic Park, Barbara Hoover, Chief of Visitor Activities; Metropolitan Toronto Reference Library, Robert Cupido, Librarian, History Department; the United States Department of Transportation, Washington, D.C., Colonial Williamsburg Foundation, Suzanne Brown, audiovisual librarian; Public Library, Manchester, New Hampshire; Old Fort Niagara, Brian Leigh Dunnigan, Executive Director; William L. Clements Library, the University of Michigan, John C. Dann, Director; National Gallery of Art, Washington, D.C.; New York State Parks, Recreation and Historic Preservation, Bureau of Historic Sites, Waterford, New York; New York Historical Society, New York.

Hallmark Cards, Michael Chortyk, Creative Director, Toronto, provided the colour separations for Captain Levigne's *The 43d Light Infantry at the Falls of Niagara;* Willowbank Estate Wines, Patricia Carter, provided colour separations of Alexander Hamilton's house, "Willowbank"; Mrs. Rilla J. Hewer, Information Officer, Niagara Escarpment Commission, lent us colour separations for the sketch of the Battle of Queenston Heights, which was drawn by cartographers R. Pepper, J. Novostad and C. Mandy, and which appeared in the Commission's magazine *Cuesta.* Dr. Richard Merritt and James Campbell, curator Weir Gallery of Art, provided Sebron pictures.

The National Army Museum, London, England, gave us permission to reproduce Henry de Berniere's *View of Fort Erie,* and waived the reproduction fee. Brian Dunnigan, Executive Director of Old Fort Niagara, lent his photographic copy of the de Berniere view so that a copy could be made.

Public Libraries are the custodians of much of our local history, with historical books and documents available for research. Their micro-films of newspapers provide a fertile source of historical material. The Reference and Local History librarians, Christel Haeck in St. Catharines, and Lorne Featherston in Fort Erie, provided information on request.

In particular our own Niagara Falls (Ontario) Public Library, Dorothy VanSlyke Chief Librarian, Joe Longo, Deputy Chief Librarian, was a valuable source of information. The Research Department staff – Claire Beckermann, Betty Beam, Mary Jocelyn, Andrew Porteous, Bev. Rodman, Inge Saczkowski and Milly Willson – were most co-operative. They answered telephone enquiries and saved many hours of research and travel. Margaret Anne Tabaka, Administrator/Curator of the Lundy's Lane Historical Museum, provided photographs and information.

Donald Loker, Local History Consultant at the Niagara Falls (New York) Public Library was most helpful. John Burtniak, Brock University, Special Collections Librarian, kept us advised of his most recent acquisitions of early travellers' narratives, and made researching easier by allowing us stack privileges in Brock's Rare Book Room. Dwight Whalen, who has researched and written articles on local history, was a source of information.

The Niagara-on-the-Lake Public Library where Gerda Molson is Chief Librarian, and Mrs. Linda Gula is Reference Librarian, is a source of prime material on the history of early settlement in this area. It is a rare experience to sit at a desk in the old police station's prison cell to do your research. Because the barred iron door has been removed you are not locked in with the rare material you are examining. Walter Haldorson, Superintendent Niagara Niagara National Historic Sites, Fort George, was very co-operative.

The photographs of historic houses were taken by: Mike Aceti, George Bailey, Ron Kitchen and John Walker. While the book was in progress several people called to offer special photographs.

Many of the pen and ink sketches were done by Carol Breton and Ian Graham over ten years ago during one of several Canada Works Grants to the Niagara Falls Heritage Foundation. Astrid Akkerman who did pen and ink sketches for *Our Romantic Niagara,* sketched once again for this book. We used some of Audrey Johnston's fine sketches from the 200th Anniversary publication of Stamford Presbyterian Church.

We appreciate Valerie Robinson's contribution in researching the land title records at the Welland Registry office, to provide us with information on the former owners of historic houses. Marv Kriluck of Bench Keough Barristers, St. Catharines, provided title searches on two of Queenston's historic houses. Helen Oberlein provided documentation tracing the ownership of the Dee-Hawken house on Portage Road.

The Heritage Group of Stamford Presbyterian Church, Audrey Johnston, Allan Brand and Don Millar, gave permission to reproduce the chart and list of burials in Stamford Presbyterian Church Cemetery. This material originally was part of the Stamford Historic Sites Tour brochure, published June 20, 1985, by Stamford Presbyterian Church, as a project of their Bicentennial Celebrations.

We thank the Ontario Historical Society for giving us permission to reprint Ernest Green's *Family Notes* which appeared in the Society's Papers and Records Volume 25, 1919. Esther Summers provided additional material which has come to light since Ernest Green first compiled the material, and she contributed information on families not mentioned in the original *Family Notes.* Dorothy VanSlyke co-ordinated the bibliography from this section from titles provided by Mrs. Summers. Inge Saczkowski compiled the index.

Doreen Gervais at Just Your Type in Niagara Falls did the typesetting, and Mari-Lynne Eastland deciphered my written instructions on the rough layout, to produce the final layout, preparing the pictures and copy for the printer. George Bailey made my task easier by working out the specifications for the printing of the book. I thank Jack Collinson, the City's Chief Administrative Officer, who was our liaison with the City.

This book is a project of the Niagara Falls Heritage Foundation of which I am chairman. The directors of the Foundation are Jack A. Sampson, secretary-treasurer; Robert L. Coombe; William Sauder; Robert F. Smith. I appreciate and thank them for their support and encouragement.

My wife, Olive, and I worked on this book as a partnership, the third book in four years. She was again responsible for editing and proofreading. Not enough can be said about her contribution. Her willingness to endure another book project which is so time consuming – the subject of our conversation for months and months on end – cannot be fully understood by those who have not gone through the ordeal.

Finally I would like to thank Mayor William S. Smeaton and the members of the Niagara Falls City Council for their approval of the expenditure of the money required to publish this book. Mayor Smeaton in particular has shared my enthusiasm for the celebration of the 200th Anniversary of the Portage Road, and has encouraged and supported me in my efforts to have this book published.

George A. Seibel
City of Niagara Falls Historian

DEDICATION

This book is dedicated to those people,
past and present, who have preserved our history
by their research and writing.

TABLE OF CONTENTS

The Falls of Niagara and the East Bank Portage

The Falls of Niagara became known to Europeans through the writings of the early French explorers, beginning with René Bréhant de Galinée who explored the shores of Lake Ontario and reached the Niagara River in 1669. He heard about the Falls of Niagara from the Indians, but did not take the time or trouble to visit them. He nevertheless described them as "one of the finest cataracts or waterfalls in the world."[1] It was Father Louis Hennepin's description and the subsequent depiction of the Falls in Hennepin's book *New Discoveries,* that aroused the curiosity of Europeans.[2] It was published after Hennepin's visit to the area as part of the French explorer La Salle's exploration party in 1678.

Those who came after Hennepin left graphic descriptions which further intrigued the Europeans. One of these visitors, Lord Edward FitzGerald, wrote in 1789: "I am just come from the Falls of Niagara, to describe them is impossible. I stayed three days admiring and was absolutely obliged to tear myself away at last. As I said before, to describe them would be impossible; Homer could not in writing, nor Claude Lorraine in painting; your own imagination must do it.

"The immense height and noise of the Falls, the spray that rises to the clouds - in short, it forms all together a scene that is worth the trouble coming from Europe to see them. The greenness and tranquility of everything about, the quiet of the immense forests around, compared with the violence of all that is close to the Falls - but I will not go on, for I should never end."[3]

Explorers had another concern - how to get around this awesome obstacle with their canoes. This concern was later shared by the merchants and fur traders who were interested in opening up the interior of North America to the fur trade, and the military men who had to transport material and supplies to build and maintain the fortifications needed to protect the fur trading posts. In an era when water transportation by canoe or bateau was the only means of travel, the Falls of Niagara, awesome and beautiful, were a formidable natural barrier which had to be overcome if they were to carry out their business.

Canoes carrying goods could be pulled up minor rapids, such as those of the St. Lawrence. When formidable rapids or falls were encountered, the explorers and the fur traders had to portage (portage, carrying of boats or goods between two navigable waters). The traveller, whether fur trader or explorer, put his canoe and goods ashore at the last point of safe navigation, and then carried them on his back, along a trail through the woods beside the rapids or falls, until he reached another navigable water. He then put his canoe back in the water, reloaded it and paddled on. The portage around the Falls of Niagara was the longest portage in the St. Lawrence-Great Lakes system.

The North American Neutral Indians probably made the first portage route on the east (American) bank of the Niagara River because it was shorter. The portage route on the east bank was 12.9km (8 miles) long, whereas the portage route on the west bank was about 4.8km (3miles) longer.[4] The French explorers

1

Portage Around the Falls of Niagara, January 22, 1679
An oil on canvas by George Catlin, 1827.

George Catlin was an American artist who painted a number of Niagara Falls scenes in 1827. At about the same time he did two or three other oil paintings which depicted his conception of the La Salle Expedition of 1678 when Europeans made the first recorded sighting of the Falls of Niagara. This highly imaginative view shows the Horseshoe Falls in an even sheet of falling water, with very little mist. Catlin has included a group of Indians, in the bottom right, and other figures dressed in European garb along the bank. While the Indians are resting the others are looking at the Falls. Of course Catlin is incorrect in placing the portage on the west bank, or Canadian side of the Falls, as at that time it was on the east bank or American side.

The Portage Path - 1679
An oil painting by Carl Rakeman.

Carl Rakeman's depiction of the Niagara Portage, was painted only thirty years ago. The Europeans looking at the Falls of Niagara are identified as Father Zenobe and party, with the explorer LaSalle. The artist's imaginative, but incorrect depiction of the landscape on the west or Canadian bank of the River, shows a large hill, with a pack laden portager labouring as he climbs the slope. The two men carrying the canoe are also a figment of the artist's imagination, as the portage in 1679 was on the east or American bank.

then followed this Indian trail when they climbed the escarpment above the present site of Lewiston, New York, on their way to the upper river. However, according to Francis Parkman, a recognized authority on Hennepin, who wrote *LaSalle and the Discovery of the New West,* the exploration party Hennepin was with travelled to the Falls of Niagara along the west (Canadian) bank of the Niagara River.

The portaging of goods is the second oldest economic activity, next to fur trading, engaged in by Europeans in North America. The importance of the Niagara River, the main route for the transfer of military supplies, fur trading items, and the return shipments of furs, made portaging the chief economic activity at Niagara.

The French, led by explorer René Robert Cavelier, Sieur de la Salle, were the first white men to use the portage, when they carried tools and supplies over the portage, to be used in the building of the *Griffon,* the first ship to sail the Great Lakes. The *Griffon's* keel was laid on January 22, 1679, at the mouth of a Creek the French named Cayuga, just above the Falls of Niagara, on the east (American) bank of the river.

The fur trade was the dominating reason for the European interest in North America. The French and the English both wanted to trade with the Indians. They fortified the fur trading outposts not only to protect them from the Indians but from one another. Each wanted a monopoly and they felt that this could only be achieved if one drove the other from this part of

North America and the Niagara Frontier. It was clear that whoever controlled the Niagara River, controlled the western fur trade.

In early January 1679 La Salle's carpenters constructed a stockade on the bank of Cayuga Creek, at the site where they wanted to build the *Griffon*. It was to be a temporary structure, to protect the shipbuilders and supplies, while the boat was being built. Then, on January 14, 1679, the expedition's second in command, Henry de Tonti chose a position on the east bank at the mouth of the Niagara River, for a fortification. In two weeks a log blockhouse was built, and named Fort Condé. [5] Later in the year it was destroyed by the Seneca Indians.

Ten years after La Salle, another Frenchman, the Marquis de Denonville erected a new fortification on the present day site of Fort Niagara, at the mouth of the Niagara River. He named it after himself, Fort Denonville. The garrison ran out of food in the winter of 1687-88 and was prevented from hunting by the hostile Senecas. Plague broke out and when the Fort was relieved in the spring only twelve men were left alive. The Fort was abandoned.

The French had an ally in Chabert Joncaire, [6] a Frenchman who was married to a Seneca woman and so had influence with the Senecas. Through Joncaire's intervention, the French were allowed to erect a Magazin Royal, a "Cabin of Bark", near the site of present day Lewiston, New York. Under Joncaire's direction the fur trade flourished and at one time as many as two hundred Senecas were employed as porters, carrying goods along the portage.

Joncaire's influence enabled the French to strengthen their hold on the Niagara River and in 1726 they built the French Castle, or House of Peace, a building which stands overlooking Lake Ontario, a part of present day Fort Niagara. [7] Every effort was made to convince the Senecas that the building was no more than a trading post. The British protested to the Iroquois councils, and did everything in their power to bring about the dismantling of the French Castle, but failed.

There is reason to believe that pack ponies were first used on the Niagara Portage about 1700. [8] A village of Senecas sprang up adjacent to Joncaire's cabin, with most of the villagers, including the women and children, employed to carry goods. Women and children carried the bundles up the steep bluff for almost 2km (over a mile). The climb was so difficult that they called if Duh-jih-heh-oh, or "The Crawl-on-all-Fours". At the top, the men and ponies took over, carrying the goods along the portage to the bateau landing at Fort Schlosser.

A traveller described the portage in 1755: "On this carrying place I saw about two hundred Indians, most of them belonging to the Six Nations, busy carrying packs of furs, chiefly of deer and beavers over the Carry-Place. It is surprising to see what quantities of these goods are brought every day to this carrying place. An Indian has twenty pence for every pack he carries, and he dearly earns it, for the distance is nearly three leagues." [9]

In 1750 Joncaire was appointed Master of the Niagara Portage. He arranged for a fort to be built 2.5km (a mile and a half) upstream from the Falls, midway between present day Grass Island and the mouth of Gill Creek. Fort du Portage, or Fort Little Niagara was built between the fall of 1750 and 1751. It included a warehouse, stable, barn, shed, log house, all surrounded by a stockade. The portage equipment included 36 goods carts, 12 horse sleds, 4 "drags with wheels and chains" and a caleche or carriage. [10]

The French and British vied with each other in showering the Indians with gifts. The Senecas were the object of their attentions as the other members of the Five Nations hated the French, because French explorer Champlain had joined forces with their enemies the Hurons. This action of Champlain's angered the Iroquois and Mohawk tribes, leaving the Senecas who inhabited the Niagara Frontier as their only possible allies. Before long it was obvious to the English that the French had won control of the fur trade, not only in the Niagara area but as far west as the Ohio valley.

It was in 1759, after the British recaptured Oswego, which had been taken from them by the French in 1756, that a strong army led by Brigadier-General John Prideaux moved against Fort Niagara. Prideaux laid siege to the Fort. The defenders' only hope was a relief force of about 1200 volunteers, coureurs-de-bois and Indians, who were hurrying from western outposts, to relieve the Fort. Prideaux was killed during a bombardment of the Fort, when a small cannon exploded near him, and command fell to Sir William Johnson. He continued the siege of the Fort and blockaded the road leading from Lewiston to Fort Niagara at La Belle Famille. [11]

The French relief force made a frontal assault on the entrenched British troops and within an hour the French were defeated. With the defeat of the French forces who were to relieve Fort Niagara, there was no alternative for the Fort's commander, Captain François Pouchout, but to surrender. The British Union Jack replaced the French fleur-de-Lis, ending France's control of the Fort, and with the victory of the British under Wolfe over Montcalm and the French at Quebec later that same year, French power and control came to an end in Canada. [12]

The British Portage on the East Bank

After the French capitulated to the British, Fort Little Niagara on the Niagara River above the Falls, which had been evacuated and burnt by its garrison in July 1759, was not rebuilt by the British until July 1760. When the new fortification, also named Little Fort Niagara was completed and garrisoned, boats, animals and carts could once again be protected when they were not employed in portaging goods along the road.

The British took over the French forts on the Upper Lakes and moved their troops and supplies to their new outposts. Later in 1760, Little Niagara was improved with the addition of a log building which served as a barracks and a storehouse with a capacity of two hundred barrels of portage goods. [1]

The British improved the portage by grading the long steep slope up the Niagara Escarpment from the low land above the Lower Landing, now the town of Lewiston, New York. The original trail ran almost straight up the escarpment and was called *Crawl-on-all-Fours* by the Seneca Indians who had carried or pushed and rolled portage goods such as barrels of salt pork and flour, and carried boxes of ammunition on their backs, up the steep slope for the French. The French used wagons drawn by draft animals, oxen and horses, to carry the bulk of their portage goods, but employed the Indians to carry a portion of their portage business, perhaps as a way to keep on good terms with them.

When the British took over the portage they transported all of their goods by wagon, and did not employ any Seneca Indian porters. Soon after the British had restored the portage, British private traders became interested in the profitable fur trade. By 1760 the volume of their business was so great that storage facilities for their trading merchandise were built at Fort Niagara.

French influence was still strong in the Ohio and Illinois Valleys, and Indian tribes, under the leadership of the Ottawa chief, Pontiac, rebelled against the British in the spring of 1763. [2] Anticipating trouble with the Indians along the Niagara Frontier, the British Army command ordered Captain John Schlosser to improve Fort Little Niagara's defenses. He completed the work in record time and as a reward for his services the fort was renamed Fort Schlosser. For many years after, the Falls, now known as the American Falls, were referred to in travellers' accounts as the *Schlosser Falls.* [3]

The Seneca Indians whose territory encompassed the Niagara Portage, joined Pontiac's rebellion and were assigned the task of attacking the British supply line to the western outposts, to cut off the supply of goods and ammunition. The Niagara Portage was the most important but vulnerable land link in the British supply system. The Senecas prepared to attack and disrupt the Niagara Portage.

On the morning of September 14, 1763, a twelve wagon train of provision carts was ambushed by a Seneca war party at a point where the portage passed a notch in the gorge above a cave called the Devil's Hole. [4] Five hundred Seneca warriors hid in the

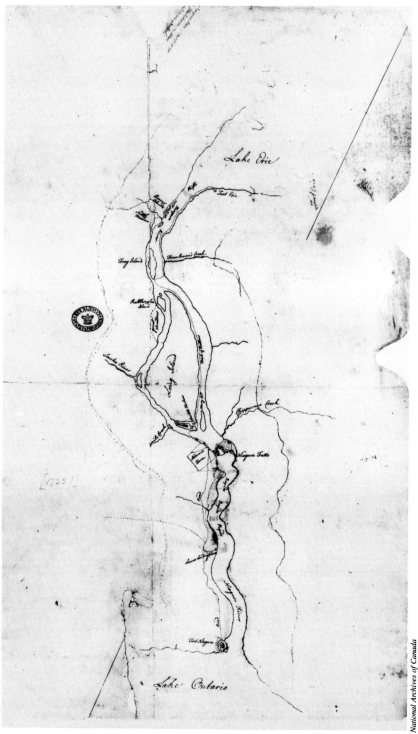

The Niagara River and the Portage, a map circa 1775-81.
Map No. 8869, National Map Collection.

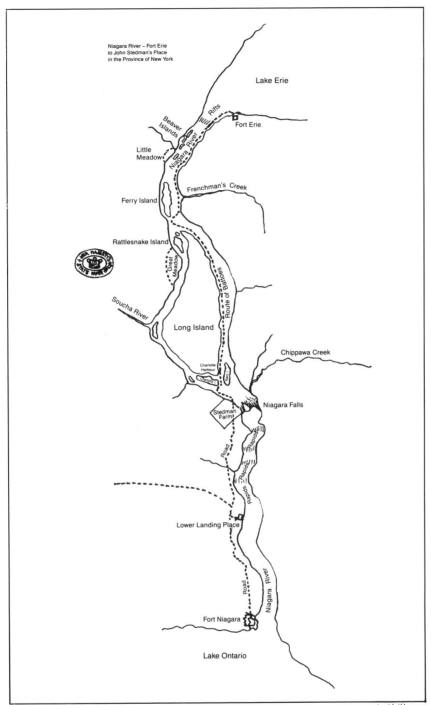

Niagara River – Fort Erie
to John Stedman's Place
in the Province of New York

Lake Erie

Rifts

Beaver
Islands

Fort Erie

Little
Meadow

Niagara River

Frenchman's Creek

Ferry Island

Rattlesnake Island

Great Meadow

Route of Battoes

Soucha River

Long Island

Chippawa Creek

Charlotte
Harbour

Niagara Falls

Stedman
Farm

Rapids

Road

Rapids

Road

Rapids

Lower Landing Place

Road

Niagara River

Fort Niagara

Lake Ontario

Astrid Akkerman

The Niagara River and the Portage, circa 1775-81.

This sketch of map No. 8869, is one of the earliest depictions of the portage on the east bank of the Niagara River. John Stedman's ''farm'', the land Stedman received under a ''Seneca patent'', is shown. The Senecas gave Stedman this land as a reward for his courage and for escaping from the Seneca ambush of Stedman's portage wagon train on September 14,1763. The dotted line leading from the Upper Landing, at Stedman's Farm, is the route of the bateaux - battoes is the spelling used on this map. It shows the route the bateauxmen took, taking advantage of the shorter, straighter western channel, and how they crossed to the western bank of the river as they got close to the rapids. At the rapids the bateaux had to be pulled by ropes attached to a windlass on shore, to get them past these rifts or rapids where the waters of Lake Erie tumble over the rock ledge, before they could reach the wharves south of Fort Erie.

a. The Place where a Piece of Rock was broken from, which while standing turn'd the Water of Obliquely across ye Fall as in Popple's Map.

b. Two Men passing over ye east Stream with Staves.

c. The Indians reascending their Ladder

A View of the Fall of Niagara.

A View of Niagara Falls.
An engraving from ''Gentleman's Magazine'' (February, 1751) by an unknown artist.
This view was published with Peter Kalm's: ''A letter from Mr. Kalm, a gentleman of Sweden, now on his travels in America, to his friends in Philadelphia, containing a particular account of the Great Fall of Niagara'', in ''Gentleman's Magazine'' February, 1751. This is the first picture after Hennepin to be based on a sighting of the Falls. The artist based his work on Kalm's description, using artistic license in depicting the large feathery trees. The figures, artistically referred to as image clusters, include a number of well dressed explorers and a dog at the left. Other figures are shown at the right, walking along what looks like a well travelled road. Kalm evidently wrote about the incidents which are noted in the legend:

a. The Place where a piece of Rock was broken from, which while standing turn'd the Water obliquely across the Falls as in Poppell's Map - Kalm records that a piece of what was later Table Rock broke off, and the third Falls which appeared in Hennepin's view, no longer flowed over the bank at that point;

b. Two men crossing over the east stream with staves - a novel way to get to Goat Island without going by boat or getting your feet wet;

c. The Indians descending or reascending their ladder - no explanation is given as to why the Indians would want to reach the lower river at this point between the two Falls.

dense forest alongside the road. When the slow moving wagon train was completely surrounded, with Seneca Indians on one side of the portage trail and the steep gorge bank on the other, the Indians struck. In the ensuing melee, the surprised and outnumbered soldier wagon drivers and the small escort of accompanying foot soldiers were all killed.

Only John Stedman, the civilian wagon master who organized and conducted the wagon trains along the portage, survived. Stedman was riding on horseback in front of this wagon train when he was surrounded by Indians and taken prisoner. While being led into the woods by an Indian who had seized his horse's reins, his captor's attention was diverted long enough to allow Stedman to cut the reins with a knife. He spurred his horse and sped off outdistancing his Seneca pursuers.

The garrison at the Lower Landing heard the gunfire from the ambuscade and a party of troops hurried to the scene. They ran into a second ambush and in the ensuing action all but eight of the relief party were killed. Tradition says that one of those who survived was a drummer boy named Matthews, who jumped or was pushed over the gorge bank, where he landed in the branches of a tree growing from an outcrop in the gorge wall. He hung there undetected by the Indians, until he was rescued by other British troops. Eighty British soldiers were killed in these Indian attacks. [5]

The Cataract of NIAGARA, some make this Water-Fall to be half a League while others reckon it no more than a hundred Fathom.

The Falls of Niagara , 1732.
An engraving from "A New and Exact Map of the Dominions of the King of Great Britain
on ye Continent of North America", Herman Moll.

This sketch accompanied Moll's Map, and characteristically depicted the North American wilderness, and an abundance of beavers. The beavers are shown as being fierce, almost lion-like, many of them upright, looking like prairie dogs and as if they were walking on their hind feet. Beaver skins were the mainstay of the fur trade and were used in making felt for beaver hats which were in fashion in Europe for many years, long enough for the "inexhaustible" supply of beaver pelts to dwindle when beaver were trapped nearly to extinction.

*View of Niagara Falls with the Biblical Scene of the Prophet Elijah on his Chariot of Fire.
Engraving by Sebastian LeClerc. (circa 1790)*
*This engraving by Sebastian LeClerc is the second known engraving of Niagara Falls. J. van Vienen's engraving
for Hennepin's 1697 Dutch edition of "New Discoveries", the first. A definite adaptation from the Hennepin view,
but with higher cataracts and more rugged rocky cliffs, the Falls seem to be only a background for LeClerc's religious
message. Of the many Hennepin-like engravings which appeared over the next 150 years, this is the only known
engraving to have a Biblical theme included. LeClerc did not explain his reason for including Elijah ascending
to heaven in this view.*

The Senecas were thorough in destroying the captured draft animals and in throwing the wagons and harnesses into the Niagara Gorge. It took the British two weeks before they were able to replace the portage equipment and once again move military supplies over the portage. [6]

After the Seneca ambush, the British decided to construct small fortified posts, called redoubts, along the portage road to discourage further Indian attacks. Captain John Montressor, an Engineering Officer, was ordered to supervise the building of these redoubts - nine picketed enclosures - spaced strategically along the length of the portage. [7] The redoubts were completed by the beginning of August 1764. At the top of the escarpment Montressor also built a fortified post consisting of a storehouse surrounded by a log picket. This was called the *Principal Entrenchment on Mount Pleasant.* Mount Pleasant was the name given to the Niagara Escarpment.

During the winter of 1763-64 work began on an ingenious device, a *machine* to move boats and supplies from the Niagara River at the Lower Landing, 106.7m (350 feet) up to the top of the escarpment. This device called *The Cradles,* actually an inclined tramway, was built in three stages. The first stage carried goods from th river level to the top of the lower bank. The second ran up the steep face of the escarpment to a point about halfway to the top where there is a ledge of Clinton Limestone. The third and last section was steep, ending at the top of the escarpment.

Captain John Enys in 1787 described the device as "a Cradle like that from which they launch a ship on which is laid a kind of Cart on Small Iron Rollers, which run in Grooves. At the top is a capstern or windlass by which they hoist the Cart Up, with a great weight of goods on it, with a very small number of men. This is in general done by soldiers quartered here, for which they are paid by the proprietors." [8]

FALLS OF NIAGARA.

Above, below, where'er the astonished eye
Turns to behold, new opening wonders lie,

With uproar hideous first the *Falls* appear.
The stunning tumult thundering on the ear.

There the broad river, like a lake outspread,
The islands, rapids, falls, in grandeur dread.

This great, o'erwhelming work of awful Time,
In all its dread magnificence, sublime.

The Falls of Niagara, 1825 , undated.
Oil on wood panel, Edward Hicks.

Abbey Aldrich Rockefeller Folk Art Collection

This view is one of two companion works, the other an oil on canvas, dated 1825, is in the Metropolitan Museum of Art, New York. On the left the artist has depicted an eagle, a rattlesnake, a beaver and a moose, creatures which were common to the wilderness adjacent to the Falls of Niagara. There are three figures on the right, viewing he scene with different reactions. The figure in the centre with arms upraised could be exclaiming the last lines from Alexander Wilson's poem "The Foresters" : "This great o'erwhelming work of awful Time, In all its dread magnficence, sublime."

Montressor has mistakenly been given credit for designing and building the Cradles. Credit should go to several other officers and engineers who were stationed at Fort Niagara that winter, before Montressor arrived in the area. One of them, Lieutenant George Demler, had constructed a similar machine to move provisions up the bank at the Lower Landing in early 1762.[9] Montressor, for his part, expressed his doubts about the device, "I imagine that the Cradles will not answer the purpose intended...as

it must labour too much, particularly in the upper one."

He was wrong in his assessment of their capability. They were built to handle the large amount of supplies needed by General Bradstreet's Army in suppressing Pontiac's rebellion, and performed satisfactorily, avoiding the long climb up the escarpment.

One accident caused by rotten rope, sent the lower cradle carrying fourteen barrels of provisions, into the river. Montressor wrote in his diary after this mishap

American Fall from Goat Island.

National Archives of Canada

Coloured aquatint painted and engraved by W.J. Bennet, printed by John Neale, circa 1830.
Goat Island, is an area of 28.3ha (70 acres). Archer Butler Hulbert in "The Niagara River" wrote that the island
was named Iris on the map accompanying the Treaty of Ghent, when the international boundary line between
Canada and the United States was set. Bennet has depicted two goats on the island, one white and one black.
He was responding to local folklore in recognition of an incident involving John Stedman, the British contractor
for the east bank portage. In 1769 Stedman planted a crop of turnips on the island. Then in the autumn of 1770
he placed a "number of animals, among them a male goat", on the island, to keep them out of the reach of the
bears and wolves on the mainland. Only the goat survived the severe winter. In recognition of the goat's har-
diness, the island became known as Goat Island. All attempts to revert to the name Iris Island were unsuccessful.
It is fortuitous that the goat did not die, otherwise the island would probably have been called "Turnip Island".

on May 26, 1764: "Sent up Rope for the Cradles, the white rope rotten." In spite of this the device was a success and it was often mentioned in travellers' accounts of the period.

Joseph Hadfield in 1785 saw the Cradles and wrote: "The bateaux discharged their cargoes by means of a cradle which is turned by 8 or 10 men and is a kind of sledge in which the goods are placed, to the summit of the bank...From whence they are conveyed to Fort Schlosser in waggons, drawn by 8 oxen or horses." [10] It is possible that the lower section of the Cradle was still being used when the British abandoned the East Bank Portage in 1790.

The British decided in 1765 to transfer the operation of the portage to private contractors. Ralph Izard who visited Fort Niagara during that year, wrote that M. Pfister had a contract from General Gage "to carry all stores, bateaux, etc., belonging to the army..." [11]

The next year the British turned over to Pfister all the draft animals, wagons and equipment on the Niagara Portage. [12]

John Stedman became Pfister's agent, arranging for the transfer of goods. His experience as a wagon master at Fort Niagara since 1760, where he was involved in the maintenance of wagons and teams, and the actual cartage of goods along the portage, qualified him for the job. The private operation of the portage became a lucrative business, and for many years the system worked to the satisfaction of both the British military and the merchants.

A Quebec merchant, John Lees, described the operation of the portage as he saw it during his visit here in 1768: "We dined at Little Niagara, at Mr. Physters, now an officer in the Royal Americans; who with one Mr. Stedman hires this Portage from the King and is paid £100 Stg. and Seventeen Rations of

Buffalo and Erie County Public Library

View of the Fall of Niagara.
An engraving by an unknown artist, circa 1790.
The artist has the Falls in a subtropical setting, with palm trees as well as evergreen trees. The figure standing in the centre foreground with arms outstretched is black, wearing a white loin cloth.

Provisions for carrying over all the King's Stores, Provision, and Officer's Baggage; it is reckoned that this did not Cost the Government formerly, less than £1200 a year, but what makes the contract valuable (to Pfister) is, he has the privilege of Carrying over all Traders Goods, which come to something very considerable; for an empty Batteau he is paid £3 York Currency, for each pack 3/0 NYC Crcy…A Cart load going up is £5 Nyc..* The Portage was formerly Dearer than this…" [13]

Pfister became a half pay officer but continued to serve at Fort Niagara where he remained until 1773. Pfister and Stedman became partners at some time. Their business grew, and they were able to take over the facilities at the Lower Landing and Fort Schlosser when the garrisons were withdrawn in 1766.

In 1773 Lieutenant Francis Pfister, once again a full pay officer, left Niagara and was killed four years later in the Battle of Bennington. When he left Niagara, John Stedman became the chief operator of the portage, and obtained renewals of the government contract. The Pfister family still kept an interest in the operation after Lieutenant Pfister's death. John Stedman continued to pay his widow an annual sum of £500. [14]

A provision in the peace treaty that Sir William Johnson negotiated with the Six Nations Indians after the end of the Seneca Indian uprising, granted John Stedman 2023.4ha (5000 acres) of land. This was all the land that he had galloped over in his flight to safety after the Devil's Hole ambush. John Maude who visited the area in 1800 wrote about Stedman's grant, saying that he got the information first hand from the Senecas. The Senecas considered Stedman's escape so miraculous, that his gift was said to be in atonement to him and the Great Spirit who protected him, for their guilt in trying to kill him. [15]

Stedman had already built a house in 1762 close to Fort Schlosser and he now chose additional land nearby. He cleared the land adjacent to the Fort's barracks where he pastured his draft animals and raised crops of grain. When John Lees visited Stedman in 1768, he stayed at John Stedman's as did an increasing number of travellers who came to see the Falls of Niagara.

Originally Stedman's agreement with the Senecas allowed him only to clear enough land to raise forage for his oxen and horses. As he cleared more and more acreage and planted an orchard of apple trees, the Indians became apprehensive and expressed their displeasure by raiding his crops and livestock. "I beg leave to observe also that the Indians not only make free with the Corn Gardens but often with the Cattle belonging to Mr.Stedman and sometimes even with those under the Cannon of this Fort." [16]

An inventory of Stedman's assets prepared in 1779 gave some idea of the scope of the portage business. Stedman not only had houses, stables, barns, a sawmill, and cleared farm land, but as well, fifty oxen, twenty-four draft horses and twenty wagons and carts. The value of his property, which also included, in addition to the assets listed above, "1 fine healthy negro man", totalled £7,500. [17]

14

Vue Du Cataracte De Niagara, Au Pais Des Iroquois.
A water colour by Antoine du Loup.
Another fanciful interpretation of Hennepin's sketch. The figure seated in the foreground has his hands clasped about his ears, to shut out the roar of the Falls.

John Stedman retired to England in 1781 after having accumulated a fortune from the portage operations. He turned over the portage business to his younger brother Philip. The Niagara Portage became more and more important as a vital link with the Upper Lakes. The Montreal merchants who got their furs from the Upper Lakes estimated in 1787 that 40 per cent of their furs came along this route. As well in 1785, slightly more than 45 per cent of all private goods by value, moving west from Montreal, passed over the portage. Philip Stedman, through his influence with the British Military enjoyed a monopoly on the Niagara Portage. [17]

Dissatisfaction with the operation of the portage grew and the Montreal merchants began a campaign to get the portage out of government control. They charged that Stedman was partial to certain merchants and overcharged others for his service. When the Stedman portage lease came up for renewal in 1787, as part of their drive to free themselves of military control, the merchants worked to have the portage controlled by someone more sympathetic to their interests. They asked the government to limit the time of a renewal of the Stedman lease to three years, after which time they foresaw that the portage would be transferred to the west bank of the Niagara River. They were successful and the Stedman lease was renewed for only three years as the merchants had recommended.

The British held on to control of the east bank of the Niagara River for thirteen years after the American War of Independence ended, claiming that the Loyalists, the refugees who were loyal to the British Crown, should be compensated for their losses before a border settlement could be made. In 1795 Britain and the United States signed Jay's Treaty, without any settlement being made to the Loyalists. This treaty made the Great Lakes (except Lake Michigan) and the Niagara River the International Boundary. The British were then required to withdraw from their forts along the Great Lakes, with the exception of Fort Erie, and the Americans took possession of these outposts in accordance with the terms of the Treaty of Paris signed in 1783, which ended the American Revolution [18]

When Jay's Treaty made the Niagara River an international boundary river, the British were required to withdraw from the east bank of the Niagara River. As early as 1788 the first goods were portaged along the west bank of the river. It would not be long before the portage of British Military supplies and British merchants' goods would be transferred to the west bank.

The West Bank Portage

In 1790, realizing that the inevitable transfer of the east bank and its portage to the United States was near, Lord Dorchester decided that the transport of British goods on the west bank, should be officially established without delay. Accordingly he ordered the Land Board for the District of Nassau to "open the portage on the west bank of the Niagara River." [1]

There were only two tenders for the contract, one Robert Hamilton and his associates, the other by Philip Stedman Jr., supported by his uncle Philip Stedman Sr. The group of traders led by Robert Hamilton had been carrying goods on the west bank of the Niagara River since 1788. The Stedmans, anticipating the transfer of the carrying place to the west bank, had already settled on a large tract of land near Black Creek and had moved their herd of cattle over from the east bank. It was there that they expected to raise and care for the oxen that they would need to pull the portage wagons.

The Stedmans offered to have draught oxen and horses available to carry 9.8 tonnes (10 tons) of goods and to have one extra large wagon on hand strong enough to carry 1814kg (4000 pounds) of bulk cargo, or a large bateau. Their price to carry goods, in wagons pulled by their oxen and horses, was to be 1s, 8d, New York Currency per gross hundredweight plus a 2 pence tax per hundredweight for road upkeep.

Robert Hamilton's group included George Forsythe, John Burch and Archibald Cunningham. In their tender they asked for a three year contract and their price was 1s. 9d. New York Currency per gross quintal - a quintal weighed 50.8 kilograms (112 pounds) - and a further 2 pence per quintal for road maintenance. The two tenders were almost alike, they differed only in the manner in which the goods would be hauled over the portage.

Since they began their west bank portage in 1788 the Hamilton group had employed local settlers with their wagons and teams, paying them to haul the goods. The Hamilton group's tender read: "For these two years the merchandise and peltries of the Upper Country have all been transported by the inhabitants on this side without the least delay, with advantage to the undertakers and with satisfaction to their employers.

"The plan adopted was allowing every person who thought proper, if of respectable character, who had taken an oath of trust, to join in this business, only securing at all times, when wanted, the services of those who thus joined. In no one instance has it yet been found necessary to complain of want of attendance. The encouragement offered the settlement by this has been so great that two teams are this season in employ for every one of last year and more are preparing. If not constantly employed, still what little they gain assists them much, and the oxen they must necessarily keep for this purpose enables them to go on with their farms with spirit and advantage. To increase this encouragement the subscribers, having fully secured themselves in the portage of double the quantity of wagons and teams daily required by the advertisement, now make the following offer..."

What followed was the difference between the

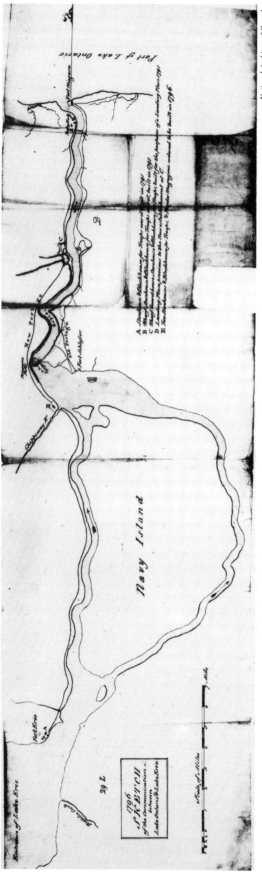

Sketch of the Communications between Lake Ontario and Lake Erie, 1796. Map No. 15447, National Map Collection.

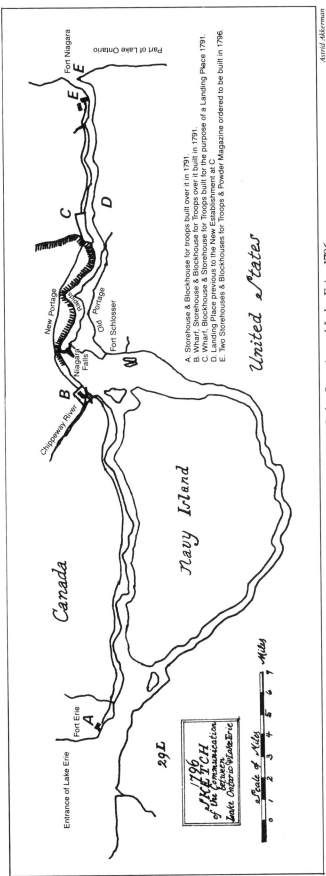

Astrid Akkerman

A. Storehouse & Blockhouse for troops built over it in 1791.
B. Wharf, Storehouse & Blockhouse for Troops over it built in 1791.
C. Wharf, Blockhouse & Storehouse for Troops built for the purpose of a Landing Place 1791.
D. Landing Place previous to the New Establishment at C
E. Two Storehouses & Blockhouses for Troops & Powder Magazine ordered to be built in 1796.

Sketch of the Communications between Lake Ontario and Lake Erie, 1796.
Map No. 15447, National Map Collection.

This map shows the route of the New Portage on the British west bank, with the locations of the military storehouses and the blockhouses that were built to protect them. The large island is of course incorrectly named Navy Island, as it is Grand Island and the small island at its northern tip is Navy Island.

Stedman and the Hamilton group's tenders: "We will adopt a similar plan to the one at present established of employing every inhabitant of a fair character, who shall offer his services regularly in turn. To render the good as general as possible, we will not permit any person to employ more than two teams at any one time, unless the hurry of business shall absolutely require it."[2]

The settlers who had been employed by the Hamilton group over the past two years wanted their employment to continue and they presented a petition supporting the Hamilton tender. Those who signed the petition were: Benjamin Canby, Thomas Cummings, James Forsyth, Adam Kreisler, John McEwan, David Secord, Timothy Skinner, Adam Vrooman, Charles Wilson, and Irish John Wilson. The Land Board, after examining the witnesses, unanimously recommended the Hamilton group's tender. Then the Committee for Inland Navigation and Commerce approved the decision. The contract was awarded when the Hamilton group agreed to adjust their price to the 1s 8d. per hundredweight tendered by the Stedmans.

The farmers who were employed to drive their teams, carrying goods along the portage, were not paid in cash. Paper money and coin were scarce and the settler drivers were given a Portage Account Credit for the loads they delivered, redeemable at the store operated by the particular member of the portage company for whom they carried goods. In this way they bartered their labour for their portage of merchandise.

James Thompson of Whirlpool Farm was one of those farmers who was employed on the portage when the "hurry of business" required that additional teams be hired to transport goods. A bill for merchandise Thompson bought from Thomas Clark in Queenston during 1809 - Clark joined the Portage Company in 1798 - shows a Portage Account debit, for hauling done. Thompson very skilfully spread out his purchases against his Portage Account throughout the whole year, so that at the end of the year, after paying 9s, 8d, interest on what he had charged for the whole year, he had to pay only 18s. 1d. on £40, 16s, 1d, of purchases. James Thompson had built up a Portage Credit of £41, 4s, 6d, and from this was deducted £2, 16s, 6d, for road maintenance.[3]

The official granting of the portage lease over a road that had been in use for two years, moved the Nassau District Land Board to establish regulations for this new highway. The Land Board appointed Commissioners of Roads, on March 31 1890, to set down regulations for roads in the District. The Commissioners appointed were: Jacob Ball, Andrew Butler, Robert Lottridge, John McNabb, Robert Nelles, Charles Pettit, Elijah Phelps, John Powell, Jacob Tenbroeck, Gilbert Tice and John Warren.

The Commissioners' only road or highway was the road that had been followed by the portage wagon drivers as they made their way from the New Landing on the west bank to the banks of the Chippawa River, following the most suitable high ground, 10.5km (6 and a half) miles of its 12.9km (8 mile) length across private land. The Military Reserve along the gorge bank was impracticable for a road as it was cut by ravines from the many creeks that drained the countryside. These were obstacles which would have had to be bridged. The wagon road took the easiest route through the forest, skirting the ravines, and keeping on the high ground above the swamps.

Governor Simcoe permitted the settlers of Upper Canada to build local roads under their own authority and supervision. The Road Commissioners had to provide statutory labour to maintain the roads. A Pathmaster was appointed to supervise the settlers, who were required by law to work six days a year on the roads, using their own equipment. Fines were levied against any who did not do their allotted share and the Pathmaster himself was fined if the road was neglected.[4]

It was more than ten years after the first wagons had been pulled over the Portage Road before it was given legal status. The settlers had established their own roads by taking the most suitable and least difficult route between two points. Present day Mountain Road, St. Paul Avenue, Warner Road which led from St. David's to Thorold, and the Portage Road were all travelled routes, used without regard to the surveyors' lines.

In 1802 two of the Road Commissioners, John Reilly and John McKerlie, officially examined the route and found that the owners of the private land through which it ran were willing to give up their title to the land for the advantage of having this important thoroughfare pass close to their homes. On March 5, 1803, the Council of the Township of Stamford ratified the Road Commissioners' decision made on September 14, 1802 specifying the route of the Portage Road.[5]

Our Early Settlers

The Loyalists who had fled from the Mowhawk Valley in present day New York State, after being persecuted and losing their homes and possessions because they were loyal to the British Crown, were camped outside of Fort Niagara during the years 1778 to 1780. There were from 800 to 1000 of them and here they were protected and fed by the British garrison. While the American Revolution had long since ended, the British were retaining possession of some areas in the new United States until a satisfactory arrangement was made to compensate the Loyalists, some 40,000 of them, who wished to remain loyal to the British Crown. Their indemnity claims totalled more than 9 million pounds. [1]

Lieutenant-General Frederick Haldimand who was Governor-in-Chief of Canada, decided to try to relieve the pressure on British Military provisions. He was an avid gardener and he devised a "plan of agriculture". Allotments of land were to be "distributed to such Loyalists who are capable of improving them and desirous of procuring...a comfortable maintenance for their families until such a time as by peace they shall be inclined to quit their situation at Niagara." [2]

The Crown would provide the Loyalists with vegetable and grain seeds, plows and "necessary agriculture equipment" for gardens planted outside the forts and for the development of homesteads on adjacent Crown Lands. For the Loyalists camped outside of Fort Niagara, the Crown Lands were on the west bank of the Niagara River.

Governor Haldimand's "plan of agriculture" became *The Niagara Plan of Edible Annex to the Fortresses.* This was soon shortened to *The Niagara Plan for Edible Annex.* The settlements on the west bank were considered to be temporary, as the Governor held the opinion that a satisfactory settlement of repayment for losses and the restoration of property would be made to the Loyalists by the United States Government. They would then return to their homes and resume their lives in the new United States. The Loyalists for their part were realistic and adamant that they would stay loyal to the British Crown.

Colonel John Butler was ordered to negotiate with the Mississaugua Indians, whose land included the west bank of the Niagara River. Settlement began before Butler's negotiations with the Indians were completed. The area marked for settlement lay between Lake Ontario and Lake Erie. It is equally divided into plain and plateau, with the escarpment rising midway between. [3]

Haldimand asked Lieutenant-Colonel Mason Bolton who was commandant of Fort Niagara to choose three or four families from those around the Fort, who were "good husbandmen" and who wished to settle on the west bank. In July or August of 1780, James Secord, Michael Showers, Samson Lutes and Isaac Dolson moved to the west bank. [4] Others who followed soon after were the Fields, Depues (Depews) and the Phelps.

Township Number 2, Plan, 1797.

This plan shows the allocation of Crown Grants in what was to be become the Township of Stamford. Cook's Bog, west of present day Dorchester Road, is at No. 1, with Muddy Run leading from the bog to the bank of the Niagara River. This stream must have been muddied from the runoff after a heavy rain when the surveyor saw it, as the water was usually clear. In the mid 1920's the stream was diverted into a large concrete conduit which was laid along its course. Then the roadway for present day Valley Way was laid over it. The large marshy area shown at No. 2, was filled in during the excavation for the intake structure for the Hydro Electric Power Commission of Ontario's Chippawa-Queenston Canal. Over the past ten years John Holer, of Marineland, has re-excavated much of this former swamp, to make a canal waterway through the property. The excavated rock was used to build the "mountain" on which his roller coaster runs.

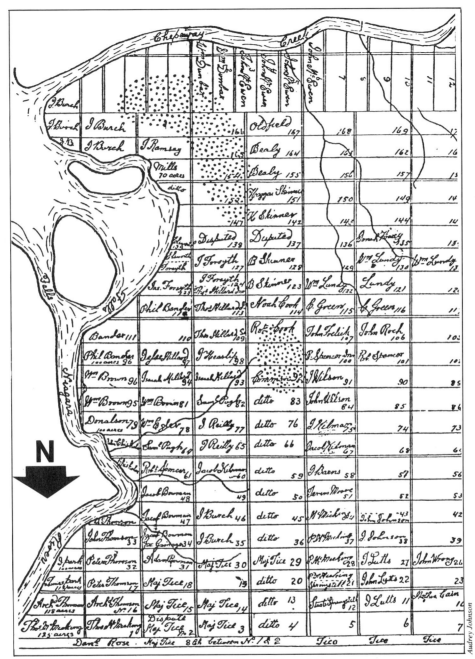

Partial Re-drawing of the Plan of Township Number 2,
original circa 1791

This map was drawn from the original which is in the National Map Collection of the National Archives of Canada.

National Archives of Canada

General Sir Frederick Haldimand.
Oil painting, by M.B. Messer,
after a painting by L.P. Abbott.

General Haldimand was Governor-in-Chief of Canada 1778-1786, succeeding Sir Guy Carleton. Born in Switzerland, he joined the British Army in 1754 as a mercenary soldier and came to North America in 1756 as a Lieutenant-Colonel of the Royal American Regiment. Haldimand instituted a ''plan of agriculture'' as a means of relieving the pressure on British Military provisions. He accomplished this by allowing Loyalists to settle on the west bank of the Niagara River, so they could grow grain and vegetables, to supply themselves and the other Loyalists camped outside of Fort Niagara.

The first settlers on the plateau, or as they called it, *The Mountain,* arrived in 1782. They were Philip Bender, his wife and three children; Thomas McMicken (McMicking), his mother, a sister with two children and a negro slave. In 1783 eight more men arrived with their families: John Reilly, John Coon, Peter Thompson, John Burch, James Forsyth, John Chisholm, Francis Ellsworth and Thomas Millard. Following soon after were the Lundy, Cook, Durham, Biggar, Ramsay, Pugh (Pew), Rowe, Tice, Rose and Corwin families. [5]

The settlers, some of whom had come to America eight years before, began again the task of clearing the land to establish farms. Their land on the Mountain, while it had no access by water, had advantages over land on the lower level. It was above the swamps which created a constant dampness which brought on malaria, which they called fever and ague. As well there were fewer trees to be cleared away. The land was described in 1785 as being "thinly timbered with lofty oaks, which at first view, one would be apt

to think were artificially transposed". [6]

Patrick Campbell, who visited the area in 1791 wrote: "the land on the Mountain appears to me to be the fittest I have yet seen for a poor man to begin upon, as it requires scarce any clearing, there being no more wood upon it than a sufficiency for rails, enclosures, and the necessary purposes of farming; so that if he chooses he may plough down the land the moment he acquires possession of it. Clearing land of heavy timber is both expensive and tedious." [7]

Under Governor Haldimand's plan, the new farmers were allowed half rations, until they raised enough food to support themselves. One full ration included a daily issue of one pound of flour, and twelve ounces of beef or pork. At the end of 1783, the first year of farming, Thomas McMicking had cleared 3.2ha (8 acres) of land and harvested ten bushels each of potatoes, oats, and Indian corn. Daniel Rose had 2.4ha (6 acres) cleared and a harvest of forty bushels of potatoes and thirty bushels of oats. He also had two cows, one "steer or heifer" two horses and three hogs. [8]

The settlers needed to get across the countryside, and they used the trail that led from Isaac Dolson's tract at the Lower Landing, (Queenston) up the escarpment and then wound along the edge of the high ground bordering the wet swampy areas. It ran through Mcmicking's, Rose's, Tice's, Rowe's, Pugh's Reilly's and Millard's, along the bottom of the big sandy hill, (Drummond Hill) through Forsyth's by the Falls, then Ellsworth's, Ramsay's and John Burch's tract on the banks of the Chippawa River. It was this trail that was widened, that became the Portage Road.

Only a rough laying out of the land was possible, though some basic lot lines had been run by Allan Macdonell as early as 1783. It was not until June of 1787 that Philip Rockell Frey, Deputy Surveyor for the Upper District of the Province of Quebec, made the first survey of the new township. As each man's holdings were marked out, he was given a ticket stating the number of the lot on the plan, and warned that the ticket was not in any sense a title-paper to the property. Paper was short and Jones used the white backs of playing cards as land tickets. Frederick Smith received a land ticket signed *P.R. Frey,* written on the back of a six of diamonds. [9]

This card with Frey's signature was the only document the settlers had attesting to their ownership of the land they had been settled on, until 1791 when actual ownership of their land was confirmed. District Surveyor Augustus Jones, Frey's former assistant, was directed to supply the Deputy Surveyor-General at Quebec with a map of the township with the names of the settlers on the lots. Since Frey's survey there had been some selling and exchanging of land, which had been approved by the Nassau Land Board.

On this survey a reserved strip of one chain, 66 feet, called the Military, or Chain Reserve, was set out, running all along the river bank. Some of the settlers had fenced their property right to the gorge edge and they were ordered to remove these fences and end their enclosed property at the edge of the Reserve. The new Township was called Township No.2 in the French tradition. It was soon called Mount Dorchester in honour of Sir Guy Carleton who had been made Lord Dorchester, but this was changed by

Governor Simcoe to Stamford.[10] It was not until 1796 that patents, or Crown Grants were issued confirming the settlers' ownership of the land. The Portage Road, the only road through the settlements was not shown on this map.

Brief biographies of four of our early settlers on the Portage Road, Philip George Bender, Thomas McMicking, John Burch and John Thompson have been included in this chapter.

Philip George Bender

Philip George Bender, Niagara Falls first settler, a native of Germany, and his wife, who was born in Holland, came to North America in the second half of the eighteenth century. They settled in New Jersey, and a short time later took up 320 acres on the Susquehanna River, close to Philadelphia. During the American Revolutionary period, he remained loyal to the British Crown and was subject to persecution by the American rebels, and the loss of his property. In the Fall of 1776 rebels and Indians carried off his livestock and grain and attempted to remove his household furniture. Realizing that he and his family were in grave danger he left the area, abandoning everything.

Bender and his family were part of a group of fifty-three Loyalists who started out along the wilderness trails towards Fort Niagara. Only seven of the party arrived, Bender and his wife were among them. Others found refuge with sympathizers along the way, or with the Indians, while some died from the exertion of the trip. Philip Bender enlisted in Butler's Rangers in 1778 and served for five years. Upon his discharge, as a reward for his service, he was given the opportunity of selecting land on the west bank, on which he was to settle. He chose land just north of the Falls.

As Bender's location was on a slope it was well drained. It was not long before he planted grain and vegetable seeds. On August 25, 1782, when Colonel John Butler took the first census, under instruction of Governor Haldimand, the Benders were listed as having three children, a boy and two girls. The Benders had three other children by the end of 1789.

He had two horses, two cows, one head of young cattle, 19 sheep and 10 hogs. He had raised 10 bushels of corn, 20 bushels of oats and 30 bushels of potatoes on the 4.85ha (12 acres) of land he had cleared. As

impressive as this was for a beginning, the Bender family still depended on Government rations and two years later, in July 1784, they were still listed as being entitled to receive rations from the King's Stores at Fort Niagara.

Bender must have been impressed by the beauty of the Falls, he chose a site with a superb view of the Falls on the east bank, the present day American Falls. His property extended from present day Seneca Street, to the south side of present day Robinson Street, which is south of the present Niagara Parks Police Headquarters. It then extended west to Stanley Street in the southern section, and Victoria Avenue in the northern section.

It was not long before Bender built a stone house, the first of its kind in the area. This house was destroyed during the War of 1812 and Bender claimed and received £400 for its value in his War Losses Claim. While the Bender house which was located south east of present day Maple Leaf Village, was demolished years ago, the family is remembered in the street names in the area of their farm. They are Bender Street (Bender Hill) and Hiram, John and Philip streets, named after the three sons.

There was an exposed ridge of limestone at the gorge bank edge on his property and Bender quarried this for building stone for his stone house and stone from this quarry was used in many of the buildings in Elgin and Clifton. The stone towers and retaining walls of the Railway Suspension Bridge were made of stone from Bender's Quarry. Some of this stone work is still in evidence at the Canadian entrance of the Whirlpool Rapids Bridge at the foot of Bridge Street in Niagara Falls. The depression left by the quarrying of the limestone is still evident today, and the Niagara Falls Museum, with its parking lot and the adjoining lot to the south of the building are built where the limestone was taken out of the cliff.

Early travellers, including Mrs. Simcoe, visited the Bender home. She wrote in her diary for Monday August 17, 1792: "This evening we drove to a farm inhabited by Painter. It is just opposite Fort Schlosser Fall. I was so delighted with the sight of the Falls from this spot, just above what is called the *Indian Ladder* which gives so different a view of them from what I saw at Table Rock that I am determined to return here again." [11]

Philip Bender sold off some property and acquired other sites. such as the Donaldson grant, to the south of present day Bridge Street. The Great Western Railway purchased land for their tracks and the Bridge Street station from the Bender family. When Philip and his wife died, they were buried on their Falls property. Then, when the *Erie & Ontario Railway* was built, the graves were on the railway right-of-way and their remains were moved to Drummond Hill Cemetery. No stone was erected and the exact location of their graves is not known.

When we consider the activity that takes place in the area today, the hundreds of hotel rooms, with the parking lot and the crowds of people who mill along Clifton Hill and around the entertainment complex and amusement park at Maple Leaf Village, it is hard to visualize that two hundred years ago this was Philip Bender's farm, with sheep grazing on the hillside pasture, and crops ripening in the fenced in fields.

John Burch

John Burch was one of our area's most prominent settlers. He was born in London, England in 1741 and emigrated to New York City in 1772. He was a tinsmith by trade and advertised his services in the *New York Gazette and Weekly Mercury,* on May 3, 1773. His advertisement read: *Tin-Plate Worker and Japanner...* he has by him a large collection of tin ware of all kinds, both plain and japan'd...Many block-tin articles for kitchen use, warranted to stand the fire..."

Burch soon built up a thriving business, as there was a great demand for his skills. He trained others, and soon had enough money to buy land in the countryside. He bought three tracts of land on the east branch of the Delaware River and one at Papacunk, New York, which became his country home. In 1775 he moved from New York City to Albany, where he established his principal residence, tinsmithing workshop and a dry goods store. He was in the process of building a saw and grist mill when, as he described it, "the Rebellion broke first out."

Burch at first did not take sides in the American Revloution, but the revolutionaries took their inspiration from the Bible and the gospel of Luke 11:23, "He that is not with me is against me." Political neutrality was not tolerated, and they denied freedom of expression to those who disagreed with them. When the rebels pressed Burch to sign a declaration of association and support of the revolution against the Crown, Burch refused. He then "retired to Albany to avoid it." Disturbances at Albany in 1778, forced him to take refuge at his country home and farm in Papacunk. [12]

It was these attempts to intimidate him and the mob violence which made Burch into an active loyalist and in 1778 he sent a letter to Colonel John Butler, offering his help. Burch offered to supply Butler's Rangers and their loyalist Indian allies with cattle, provisions and men. Later, Burch and forty others who were encouraged by his stand, delivered two hundred and six head of cattle to the Rangers. He later told the Commissioners who were investigating Loyalist claims for compensation, of how he was persecuted for this action.

"The Rebels having information of the part he had taken came in a large Party, surrounded his House & plundered his effects." They burned his crops and took away as much of his other possessions as they could carry. Burch went on "He was attacked in this manner three different Times". He was particularly distressed at the loss of three purebred English horses.

Burch's Delaware property consisted of 202ha (500 acres) buildings, live stock and grain. He had a sawmill and grist mill under construction at Marble Town and Woodstock. When his housekeeper and some friends, one of them being Hugh Alexander, attempted to remove the contents of his dry-goods store and tin shop, the goods were seized on the road and his friends were imprisoned. Burch's Delaware losses exceeded £2,500 and his Albany losses were in excess of £1,000. Burch, who in the words of a friend "reckoned himself as a rich man", lost everything. His total losses were to exceed £4,500. [13]

Everything that Burch owned became subject to confiscation. In the third attack on his farm, the rebels set his house on fire. Burch escaped through a window and ran into the woods. He became a fugitive and set out on foot through Indian territory for the safety of British held Fort Niagara. There he volunteered for service with Butler's Rangers, but he was not fit for active duty. He was appointed keeper of the Indian stores at the Fort and sutler (provisioner) for Butler's Rangers in March 1779.[14]

While he was at Fort Niagara he met and later married Martha Ramsey who was a Loyalist widow from the Cherry Valley. At the end of the war, John and Martha Burch settled on the west bank, taking up land at the mouth of the Chippawa River. Thomas Cummings who had been Burch's farm manager, and Cumming's mother who had been Burch's housekeeper, settled nearby on the opposite bank of the Chippawa.

In 1786 he received permission from Major Campbell, commandant at Fort Niagara, to build a saw and grist mill on the upper rapids above the Horseshoe Falls. Here he made the first industrial use of the waters of the Niagara River on the west bank, and his mill was one of the first in present day Ontario. His mill was prosperous until 1794 when Governor Simcoe granted John McGill, the Quartermaster in Simcoe's Queen's Rangers, and Benjamin Canby, a tanner from Pennsylvania, a 999 year lease on a mill site upriver from Burch's (where the waters of the Niagara River entered the embayment now known as Dufferin Islands). This new mill took away much of Burch's business.

He was dealt another blow when the British Military took over much of his property at the mouth of the Chippawa, as a location for Fort Chippawa. His service with Butler's Rangers entitled him to 202ha (500 acres) of land. He applied for an additional 289ha (700 acres) citing his service to the Crown as a member of the Land Board until its dissolution and as a magistrate. His request was approved and his land holdings increased to 485.6ha (1200 acres). His wife, Martha, was awarded 161.8ha (400 acres) as the wife of a magistrate.[15]

In spite of his setbacks as a result of his loyalty to the British Crown during the American Revolution, John Burch rose from an immigrant tinsmithing craftsman to become an entrepreneur, one of the four original members of the Portage Syndicate, a government official, and magistrate in just twenty years. He was recognized as a "gentleman" and visitors to his home at Chippawa, left written accounts of his hospitality, and remarked on his intelligence, breadth of knowledge and curiosity. Hector St. John de Crèvecoeur enjoyed Burch's hospitality and described him as "a very sensible, well-informed character, his conversation pleasing and instructive and his communications very novel."[16]

Robert Hunter, a visiting merchant, wrote that Burch was "a most sensible, agreeable, well-informed man... His land is the finest without exception in the best order of any Loyalist's that I have yet seen."

Burch was recognized by the government for his loyalty and achievement. In June 1786 he was appointed Justice of the Peace and he then became Squire Burch.

On August 1, 1793 he was appointed Magistrate and in 1794 he was named to the Land Board of Nassau, the district which would later be named Lincoln. Burch's stature with the government is better appreciated when it is understood that he, along with Gilbert Tice, and Hendrick Nelles were among the first of the settlers to be appointed government officers in the upper region of the Province of Quebec, of which present day Province of Ontario was then a part.

John Burch died on March 7, 1797 in his 55th year. He was survived by his wife Martha Ramsey Burch, and his son John Jr. who was a land surveyor and was married to Elinor, one of Philip Bender's daughters. After his death his mills were sold to Thomas Clark and Samuel Street. John Burch was buried in Drummond Hill Cemetery. His gravestone, which has long ago disintegrated, stated that his was the first burial in the cemetery. For many years his grave has been unmarked, except for a wooden marker which was often removed to allow the grass to be cut. The Niagara Parks Commission is marking John Burch's grave and that of his wife and son, with a bronze plaque embedded in a granite block.

The first part of the inscription follows the wording on Burch's original gravestone, and reads:

> In memory of John Burch, Esq., who departed this life March 7th, 1797, in the 55th year of his age. The first interment in this yard.
> John Burch, Jr., who departed this life August 15th, 1822, aged 38 years, 5 months.
> Martha, wife of John Burch, Senr., Esq., who departed this life Nov. 28th, 1823, aged 77 years.

The second part of the inscription was added by The Niagara Parks Commission and reads:

> John Burch was one of the earliest Loyalist pioneers in this area. In 1785 he made the first commercial use of Niagara power by erecting saw and grist mills on the shore of the Upper Rapids.

John Burch, as Ernest Green wrote, "...may fairly be said to have been the leading man in Stamford during the first fifteen years of the settlement."[17]

Thomas McMicking

Thomas McMicking who settled at the same time as the Benders, took up land closer to the edge of the escarpment, just at the northern boundary of the present City of Niagara Falls, in Township No.2, later called Stamford Township. McMicking was born in the parish of Stranraer, Scotland and as a young man he apprenticed as a mason. After spending three years at his trade, splitting, shaping and dressing free stone, he became dissatisfied with the this method of making a living. He and his brother John, who was also a mason, emigrated to America in 1771.

McMicking and his brother worked one month for a farmer in a Dutch settlement in northern New York. He then took up virgin land on the west branch of the Delaware River, in Kortright Township, not far from the Catskill Mountains. McMicking was a bachelor. Two years after he settled in Kortright Township, his mother and two sisters, Sarah and Janet, a widow with two sons, left Scotland to come to live with him. Sarah died during the sea voyage.

When the American Revolutionary War broke out he joined the Loyalist cause and fought against the rebels. This made him a marked man and he and his family were subsequently imprisoned by the rebels. On his release he compromised himself further by furnishing supplies to the British raiding parties, Butler's Rangers, and the British Indians led by Chief Joseph Brant. McMicking and his family were taken away in 1776 and imprisoned by the Seneca Indians.

As a result of an incident in which several Indians were killed, but in which McMicking had not taker part, he was chosen as one of three prisoners who would be killed in retaliation. He was condemned to run the gauntlet. He was a speedy runner and outran his pursuers, but was injured by a thrown tomahawk which hit him a glancing blow on the head, causing him to stagger but not fall. Having no place to hide, he was recaptured. The Indians, as was their custom, acknowledged his courage and rewarded him by sparing his life and by keeping him prisoner, without further molestation.

After holding McMicking for four months the Senecas set out for Fort Niagara, with him and the other captives, to collect a ransom for their prisoners. It was a ten day journey and each member of the party had only a sock full of parched corn for food. They killed small animals along the way and ate them. They arrived at Fort Niagara in a destitute state. Here McMicking was exchanged for a ransom of £4 and given new clothing. His mother arrived at Fort Niagara after he did in 1781.

He enlisted in Butler's Rangers and joined Colonel Johnson's Foresters. He remained with them for a little over a year. On his discharge in 1782, he was given land in reward for his loyalty to the Crown. He chose what were to be Lots 1 and 2 of Stamford Township. McMicking paid a ransom for his sister and her sons who were still held by the Senecas and they joined him in late 1782. A list of settlers in 1783 gives the McMicking family, with ages as follows: Thomas 33, his mother Jane 66, Jane Cooper 43, Thomas Cooper 14, James Cooper 11, and Harvey Alexander 3.[18]

To help him in clearing the land McMicking employed "A Young or Hired man" and he owned the only slave, in the community, a male Negro.[15] Using the oak logs from the felled trees he built a log house to shelter his "family". The oak trees were so large that their branches shut out the sun and thus prevented the growth of any underbrush, so the work of clearing was confined to cutting down and burning the trunks that weren't used for houses and barns.

In 1787 Thomas McMicking went back to Scotland where he married Isabella Gass, the daughter of William Gass, grain merchant. She was seventeen years younger than McMicking and was twenty when he brought her to Niagara. He built a larger log house and converted the smaller house into a cattle shed. Thomas McMicking served as county warden and in 1794 when the Nassau Militia was formed in anticipation of American attacks on forts still held by the British, he enlisted and was commissioned as a Lieutenant. Mickmicking and his wife died in 1830, and they are buried in Stamford Presbyterian Cemetery.

Gravestones in the McMicking family plot in Stamford Presbyterian Cemetery.

Ron Kitchen

John Thom(p)son

The Thompsons, Archibald, John and James, were other prominent pioneer settlers. John and his son James are best remembered because many of their original documents have been preserved and are in the care of John Thompson's great-great-grandaughter, Isabel Walker. It is from her history of the Thompson family, *The Thompsons of Whirlpool Farm* that the following account was taken.

In 1773, Archibald Thomson of Hawick Scotland emigrated to America, and settled along the Delaware River. He was one of four sons and three daughters of a mercantile family. He came to this area as a Loyalist in 1779 when his New York State property was confiscated because of his loyalty to the British Crown. He served with Butler's Rangers and when the Rangers were disbanded in 1782, Archibald was granted land along the Niagara gorge north of Twenty Mile Pond, the present day Whirlpool.

In 1785 John and James Thomson joined Archibald and received grants of Crown Land near their brother. On Frey's map showing the original Crown Grants, Archibald's grant is adjacent to and south of Thomas McMicking's, James next to Archibald's and opposite the Niagara Glen, while John's was the land now occupied by the Niagara Parks Whirlpool Golf Course, extending to the edge of the Whirlpool Ravine where Jacob Bowman's Crown Grant began.

When land title papers were prepared an official in the Registry Department spelled the Thomson name Thompson on all of the Crown Grants. To avoid confusion the family accepted their new family name Thompson. That is Archibald and James accepted it, but not John. Every time John made and signed a contract he adhered to the old spelling of his ancestors by erasing the objectionable "p" and signing his name Thomson.

John returned to Scotland in 1785 and married Jeanett Nixon, returning immediately to Canada with his bride. They lived with Archibald and his family while John built their log house. As their property was adjacent to the Whirlpool they named it Whirlpool Farm.

John was engaged as a private contractor by the Portage Syndicate, to haul goods from Queenston to Chippawa along the Portage Road. The road proved a boon to those who were employed on the road. They were able to use their farm animals and equipment for both farming and hauling. The extra money they earned enabled them to have more oxen and horses, and more equipment to assist them in clearing and cultivating their land.

The Thompson Homestead at Whirlpool Farm.
The Thompsons had moved from Whirlpool Farm when this photograph was taken. William Sutherland, a mason who was also a joiner (carpenter), contracted to build this house for John Thompson. The design was copied from Thompson's brother Archibald's house. John was canny, he saved money on the design of the house by doing this. The houses were the same with the exception of the gables. Those on Archibald's house were only 30 cm (1 foot) thick and John specified that the gables on his house were to be 60 cm (2 feet) thick. The house was constructed of stone quarried from the quarry on the farm, and Thompson lime was used in the mortar. The house was demolished in 1929.

Niagara Parks Archives

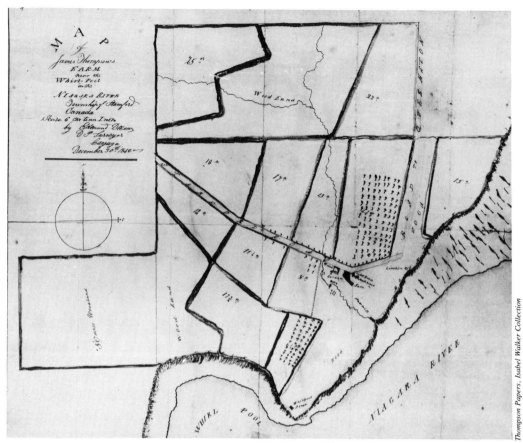

James Thompson's Farm near the Whirlpool in the Niagara River, 1842.

This map, drawn by Edmund DeCew, Deputy Surveyor, Cayuga, shows the location of James Thompson's property at the exit of the Whirlpool. The sawmill, with the small stream which provided water to power the saws, is shown at the edge of the gorge. The lime kiln is conveniently located beside the road to Queenston, which is the same route taken by today's Niagara Parkway. This road connects with the road to Stamford, which passed to the north of the house. This road, later called Thompson Road was cut off when the Hydro Electric Power Commission built the Chippawa-Queenston Canal. The west end of this road, where it joined with the Portage Road is still in use today. At the point by the Whirlpool exit, the building marked Whirlpool House was a shelter and refreshment stop for travellers who turned off the Portage Road and went along Thompson Road, past the farm, to see the Whirlpool. For a time there was a stairway here, down to the water's edge. Visitors from all over the world signed their names in the guest book kept at Whirlpool House. Mrs. Simcoe first saw the Whirlpool in the early 1790's from this vantage point.

John Thompson showed his entrepreneurial abilities when he took advantage of the resources on his farm. A small stream on his property made it possible for him to operate a small saw mill, where he cut logs into boards. There was an exposed outcropping of limestone close to the edge of the gorge at the Whirlpool. Realizing that masons would need lime for mortar and plaster, Thompson built two lime kilns and quarried the limestone. He processed it by burning it in the kilns, then sold or bartered it to merchants in the area for food, clothing and household goods. Bartering, or payment in "kind" were the usual ways of doing business.

Thompson contracted in 1803 with William Sutherland, a mason-joiner, for a stone house. Sutherland was to do the work, with Thompson helping him as his other duties allowed, for £46, 17s, 6d

worth of "good merchantable Lime". Sutherland was to take delivery of the lime over a period of three years. If he could not use that much lime in that period of time, he could take the balance in wheat. While the house was under construction he could also take some of his payment in "victuals, drink and clothing."

Thompson's wife Jeanett died on January 21, 1813 and John Thompson died on March 30, 1814 at the age of fifty-six. His son James who was twenty-eight years old, took over Whirlpool Farm and the lime business. Whirlpool Farm was sold to the Hydro Electric Power Commission of Ontario before they built their Chippawa-Queenston Canal in the 1920's. There are remains of the foundations of the Thompson house still visible in the woods adjacent to the thirteenth fairway of the Niagara Parks Whirlpool Golf Course.[19]

The Portage Road

Philip Bender, Francis Ellsworth, and John Burch had to find their way through the forest to reach the locations where they settled on the Niagara River - Burch at the mouth of the Chippawa Creek, Bender and Ellsworth adjacent to the Great Falls. They and the McMickings and the Roses are shown on Surveyor Allan Macdonnel's plan of the "New Settlement - Niagara River Line", March-April 1783. Other settlers who came soon after were the Ramsays, Forsyths, Millards, Reillys, Pughs, Rowes and the Tices. Historian Ernest Green wrote about these early settlers, describing how their settlement had progressed in 1789. "The Loyalists have established themselves all along the Niagara River and their clearings and buildings are rapidly increasing. Little by the way of road building has been attempted but blazed trails and bridle paths led through the forest from clearing to clearing.

"Very probably one of the first of these trails led from Burch's at the mouth of the Chippawa, past Ramsay's, Ellsworth's and Forsyth's near the Falls, by Millard's on the side of the big sand hill (Drummond Hill), near Reilly's, Pugh's, Rowe's, Tice's, McMicking's and Rose's and on down the steep face of the escarpment to the navigable waters of the lower river. This trail, the only route from...the region of the Chippawa towards Niagara (Niagara-on-the-Lake) was, of necessity, quickly improved, and soon assumed the character of a public highway. Within a few years it was destined to become 'the new portage road'." [1]

This "road through the settlements" was in use as early as 1789 and over it the ox-drawn wagons carried Robert Hamilton's goods, when he and other merchant traders received permission to portage on the west bank and to build storehouses at Queenston and Chippawa. Their storehouses were small and made of logs. When the British Military built a wharf, guardhouse and two-storey storehouse and blockhouse at each of Queenston, Chippawa and Fort Erie in 1791, the merchants shared these facilities with the Military and did so until 1794.

The importance of the road was apparent soon after portaging began. Lord Dorchester ordered the Land Board of Nassau "to open the Portage on the west side of the river above Niagara" and on March 31, 1790 the Portage Road on the west bank was given official status. [2] The British officially moved their portaging to the west bank, from the east bank, or United States side of the River in 1791.

At first the Portage Road ran almost straight up the steep rocky face of the escarpment at Queenston, taking advantage of whatever natural features there were to make the climb less arduous. It was a very difficult climb for the teams of oxen who had to pull the heavily loaded wagons. A yoke of oxen - two oxen side by side, secured by a wooden yoke around their necks - could pull a wagon holding as much as .984 tonnes (one ton) on level ground. Four and even six oxen were required to pull the heavy loads up the escarpment.

From the top of the escarpment the road went along mostly flat terrain. Here, if the weather had been dry, the sandy roadbed was packed hard with deep ruts made by the wagons which had gone that way before. But, if it had rained, the low areas along the road were pools of mud. Heavily laden wagons carried barrels of flour, salt and salt pork destined for the military outposts on the Upper Lakes, and on their return journey from Chippawa, hauled bales of furs, called peltries, which were destined for the European fur markets. They also carried maple sugar. The wagon wheels sank deep into pools of mud on the road, often up to their axles. The oxen had difficulty in keeping their footing as their hooves slipped on the bottom of the mud pools. It took much longer to get the loads to their destination when the road was wet.

Travellers, military officers and fur traders also rode along the Portage Road to reach Chippawa where they could board a boat again, and continue their journey to the Upper Lakes. There is no record of who built the first rest stop for travellers along the Portage Road - an inn or tavern -but it would not have been long after the first wagons travelled the road. These pioneer inns were the highway rest stops of the day, where the wagon drivers and travellers would stop to refresh themselves and give their oxen or horses water.

The Duke of Kent, Queen Victoria's father, visited Niagara Falls in 1791 and ''The only place of accommodation, was a log-hut for travellers of the day to refresh themselves. There the Royal Party alighted, and partaking of such refreshments as the house afforded, followed an Indian path through the woods to the Table Rock overlooking the Falls.''[3] This is the first written account of an inn or tavern along the Portage Road.

Elizabeth Simcoe, the wife of Upper Canada's first Lieutenant-Governor, kept a diary whose entries give us some graphic descriptions of the Portage Road. She and the Governor made many trips over the Portage Road during the time Governor Simcoe had his headquarters at Niagara, from July 1792 until 1796. One of Simcoe's first acts was to change the name of his new headquarters from Niagara to Newark.*

After visiting Robert Hamilton at The Landing (Queenston) on July 30, 1795, she and the Governor left by horse and carriage and ''ascended an exceedingly steep road to the top of the mountain…from thence the road is entirely flat to the Falls.'' Again on August 13 they drove to the Falls, ''…and returned by starlight, tho' the road has many stumps of trees on the sides, of which I was a little afraid.''

Mrs. Simcoe Driving Francis Over the Portage Road in a Caleche

On September 30, 1792, Governor Simcoe left Mrs. Simcoe at Fort Chippawa, while he went on to Long Point on Lake Erie. Mrs. Simcoe who wanted to return to Mrs. Tice's on the Mountain Road, wrote in her Diary: ''but having no gentleman with me I was obliged to drive the carriage myself, which I had never done, and the roads were excessively rough till after passing the Falls. I tied Francis into the carriage and drove him very safely, altho' he complained of being much bruised and shook.''

Astrid Akkerman

The Simcoes' Tents at Mrs. Tice's on the Mountain Road
The summer of 1793 was oppressively hot, and Mrs. Simcoe decided to "Camp on the Mountain", hoping that it would be beneficial for her son, Francis. "I shall have an Establishment of Two marquees & two sentries." The camp was three miles from Mrs. Tices on the Mountain Road. In 1795, they camped on Mrs. Tice's property.

On August 30 she and the Governor were returning from a trip to Detroit, and stopped at Chippawa. From there the Governor went on to an Indian Council, leaving Mrs. Simcoe and their four year old son to find their way back to Mrs. Tice's on the Mountain Road, just west of the Portage Road. "I was obliged to drive the carriage myself, which I had never done, and the road was excessively rough...I tied Francis into the carriage and drove him very safely, tho he complained of being much bruised and shook."[4]

Many of the travellers who came this way wrote accounts of their experiences, and it is from their books and journals that we learn of the early days along the Portage Road. Isaac Weld visited the area in 1796 and left this account of what must have been an inn near the Crossroads - as the intersection of Portage Road and Lundy's Lane was called. "On the part of the road leading to Lake Erie which draws nearest to the Falls, there is a small village consisting of about half a dozen straggling houses; here we alighted and having disposed of our horses, made a slight repast."[5]

According to travellers' reports there were two hotels in Chippawa in 1796, One was the Fairbanks House, built by J. Fairbanks who also built hotels at Queenston and Niagara. Surveyor John Stegmann's map of 1797 has the Fairbanks House marked, but John Fanning's Hotel which was farther inland from the mouth of the Creek was not shown on the map.

John Milton Holley wrote after visiting here in 1796: "Left Buffalo...arrived about one o'clock at Chippewa, dined at Fanning's."[6]

In 1796 the Road Commissioners, acting on a request made by the Portage Company, undertook improvements to the road leading up the escarpment. It was "to benefit the commercial intercourse of the country and add to the beauty of the place."[7] George Heriot who visited here in 1801 found that "the road that winds up...is so steep that it is absolutely necessary for the traveller to leave his carriage, if he should be in one and proceed to the top on foot."

This road up the escarpment was in use until the mid 1920's when the Queen Victoria Park Commission built the Niagara Boulevard extending from the Whirlpool to the junction of present day York Road. A 1920 air-survey map shows the Portage Road as going to the east as it climbs the escarpment, whereas the present day Niagara Parkway runs down the escarpment in a westerly direction.

It was not long after the road was improved that a stagecoach service began along the Portage Road. When George Holley visited in 1796, his baggage did not arrive with him, an experience which many a modern day air traveller has also had. After dining at Fanning's in Chippawa, he "found our goods were not in Chippawa, and was obliged to go to Queenston after them - as I could not get a horse, was obliged to walk."[8]

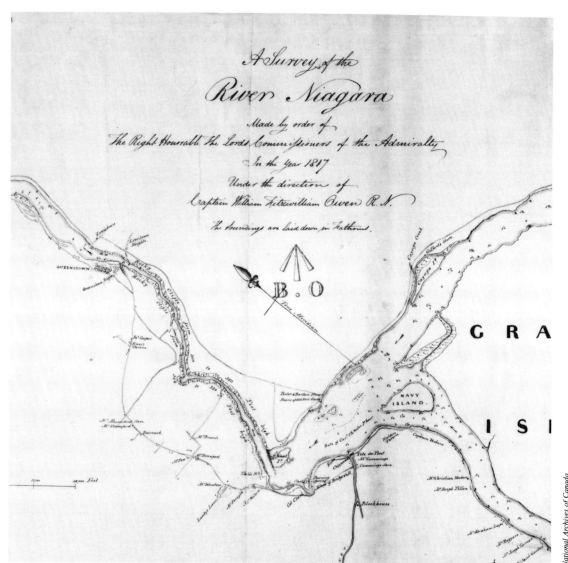

A Survey of the River Niagara by Captain William Hamilton Owen R.N., 1817.

*A Sketch of a Part of A Survey of the River Niagara
by Captain William Hamilton Owen R.N., 1817.*

Captain Owen has drawn the Niagara River accurately. This is remarkable because he was restricted to looking at the river from ground level. He has shown the Portage Road, and the roads which intersected it. The area at No. 1 where Knox's Tavern is shown, is present day Stamford Halfway; No. 2, at the Barracks, shows a number of dots to indicate houses near Stamford Green; No. 3, where Mr. Davenport was located, is the intersection of present day Thorold Stone Road which at that time continued east, past Mr. Brown's property and ended at the edge of the gorge where John Donaldson's saw and grist mill was located (present day Leader Lane).

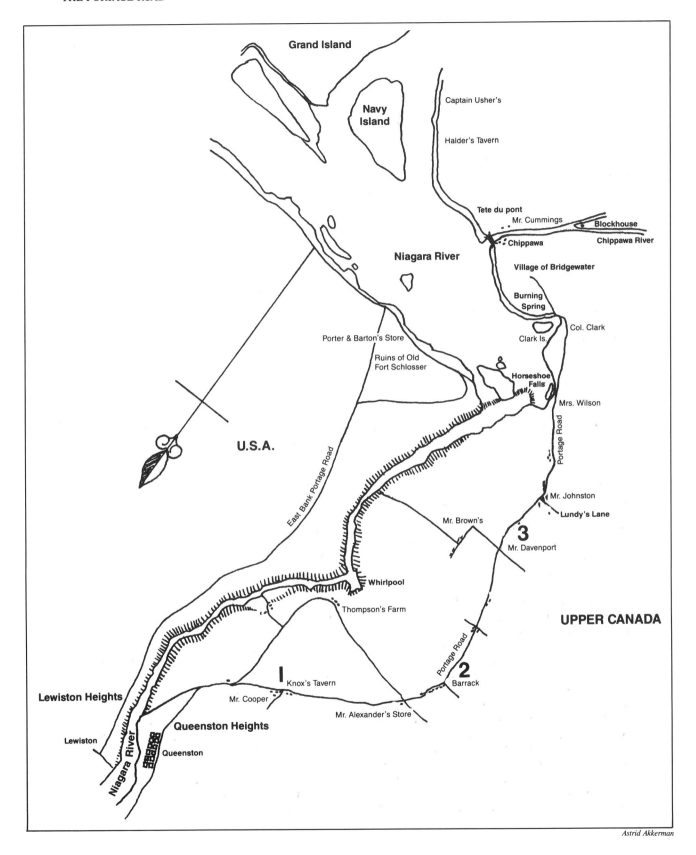

Grand Island

Navy Island

Captain Usher's

Halder's Tavern

Niagara River

Tete du pont

Mr. Cummings

Blockhouse

Chippawa

Chippawa River

Village of Bridgewater

Burning Spring

Porter & Barton's Store

Clark Is.

Col. Clark

Ruins of Old Fort Schlosser

Horseshoe Falls

Mrs. Wilson

U.S.A.

East Bank Portage Road

Portage Road

Mr. Johnston

Lundy's Lane

Mr. Brown's

3

Mr. Davenport

UPPER CANADA

Whirlpool

Thompson's Farm

Portage Road

I

Knox's Tavern

2

Barrack

Mr. Cooper

Lewiston Heights

Mr. Alexander's Store

Queenston Heights

Lewiston

Niagara River

Queenston

Astrid Akkerman

Two stagecoach lines began operation in 1798. John Fanning, proprietor of Fanning's Hotel in Chippawa, advertised in the *Niagara Herald* for his stagecoach service, which ran between Newark (Governor Simcoe's new name for Niagara), and Chippawa. "My stage coach is as easy as any in the province and the goodness of the horses and the carefulness of the drivers are exceeded by none. And customers will not be overcrowded in my coaches, for generally four, not exceeding five passengers will be admitted while, for the better accommodation of aristocratic passengers, way passengers will not be taken up but by the request of the passengers."

Even in pioneer times there was first class travel. In this case, if you were waiting along the route to board the stagecoach - that is, a way passenger - you could be left standing, with the dust of the passing stagecoach swirling around you, if the other passengers decided that they didn't want you to ride with them. Under this arrangement they simply ordered the driver to drive on.

Also in 1798 J. Fairbanks and Thomas Hind advertised their stagecoach service in the May edition of the *Upper Canada Gazette*. "J. Fairbanks and Thomas Hind acquaint friends and the public that their Stage will continue to run between Newark and Chippawa on Mondays, Wednesdays and Fridays; to start from Newark at 7. A.M. on each day and return the same evening, provided four passengers take seats by 4 in the afternoon. Otherwise to start from Chippawa at 7 o'clock the following morning and return the same evening. Each passenger is allowed fourteen pounds of baggage, and to pay one dollar. Way passengers to be taken up at sixpence a mile York currency. Good horses and careful drivers are provided and that attention and despatch which are necessary to the ease, satisfaction and convenience of the passengers may always be expected. Letters fourpence each."

The service offered by Fairbanks and Hind was more democratic than the "aristocratic" service advertised by John Fanning. The offer to pick up way passengers, was sure to bring this new stagecoach line extra business. It is not known how the waiting passengers distinguished between the two lines, but there must have been long periods of waiting for a stagecoach to appear, and when they wondered whether or not it would stop for them. Modern day bus riders, may still have similar experiences.

The carrying of letters is the first mention of postal service, and the indication given is that the stagecoach operator received the 4 pence per letter for carrying it from one point to another. Fairbanks received extra business at his hotel whenever there was not the required number of passengers to fill the quota. The travellers then had to stay overnight at his hotel, and he had three of them, one each at Niagara, Queenston and Chippawa. They had to pay for a room, eat and drink before the next stage left.

The inn known best by present residents is the Whirlpool Inn, now a private residence on the northwest corner of the Portage Road at the intersection of Church's Lane. In 1799 Andrew Rorbach, a saddler, came from New Jersey and settled on the Portage Road, where he built the present day Whirlpool House. He chose his location wisely, as it became a stopping off place for wagon and coach drivers, who needed repairs to their teams' harness. It would not be long before he was providing them with liquid refreshment, water for their horses and oxen and the sanitary facilities required by the travellers in attending to their natural needs - all in all the forerunner of a modern day highway rest stop with restaurant, washrooms, automobile servicing and repair facilities put there for the convenience of today's travellers.

John Maude visited the area in 1800 and stayed three days at a new tavern in Chippawa, Macklem's. He paid $4.62 1/2 for his three days' lodging. Then while spending two days at Fairbanks' in Queenston, his bill came to $1.37 1/2. This money was New York Currency. A York shilling which was the coin of the realm, was 12 1/2 cents in New York Currency, while a pound was $2.50. To make things more confusing, Provincial or Halifax currency was often presented as payment for lodging accounts. A shilling was twenty cents and a pound $4.00 in Halifax currency. [9]

James Macklem, the proprietor of Macklem's Inn entered into partnership in 1801 with Abraham Markle and William Hamilton at Niagara to establish another stagecoach line, called the *Niagara and Chippawa Stages*. The stages started at 8 a.m. from both Macklem's in Chippawa and Niagara (now that Lieutenant-Governor Simcoe was no longer in the country, the name Newark was dropped in favour of the former name Niagara), and they met at Fairbanks' at Queenston, exchanged passengers and returned. The fare was four shillings to Queenston from either Chippawa or Niagara. The baggage charge for 150 pounds was the same as the charge for one passenger, and each passenger was allowed to carry along 14 pounds free. The company assured their prospective customers that: "The proprietors have, at great expense procured easy carriages, good horses and careful drivers." This stagecoach line was short lived as in 1802 Markle and Hamilton dissolved their partnership. [10]

The stopover at Fairbanks' in Queenston annoyed some travellers. John Fowler was one of those who expressed his annoyance in his *Journal of a Tour*. He wrote: "At five in the afternoon, two coaches from Forsyth's started for Niagara, and at six we arrived at Queenston. A considerable delay ensued here, which the passengers did not at first comprehend; but, at last, they began to fancy it a plan calculated to make them weary of sitting in the coach, and by this means go into the tavern to spend a few shillings.

"However the gentlemen in the coach in which I was were determined not to spend a single cent, on account of such treatment; and, at last gave the milksop driver to understand, that, if he did not start presently, they would take personal satisfaction of him. He now intimated, that we had to leave the coach we were in, and go into another which stood besides, as the coaches from Crysler's at Niagara and those from Forsyth's at the Falls, meet at Queenston to exchange passengers, and then return to their own place. They presently went into the other coach, expressing their indignation at the driver for not informing them of this arrangement when they arrived.

"The gentlemen instantly cheered till the uproar was heard all over Queenston; and the villagers ran to the doors and windows to see what was ado...after we had lost sight of Queenston, one of the gentlemen sang Scotch songs till we arrived at the Niagara Hotel." [11]

Fowler and his "Scotch" friends returned to Queenston and once again ran into trouble with stagecoach scheduling. After having breakfast at Queenston and waiting patiently for the stage, he wrote, "At ten o'clock no stage had arrived, but four of us from Scotland were unwilling to stay longer, so we procured a post chaise in the village. As we were seating ourselves at the tavern door, some of the gentlemen who were standing there were pleased to compliment us with their unasked for opinions. These wiseacres discovered by their penetration, that the chaise had a weakness, but where we never learned, and began to make their observations thus, 'That vehicle is not sufficient to carry you - the crazy thing will come down with you'. However, we gave them to understand that we were of a different opinion, and at all events were determined to try; so off we set, and a pleasant drive we had. After ascending the heights by a circuitous route, the road is pretty good and level." [12]

Ray Corry Bond described another type of horse-drawn vehicle used on the Portage Road. "If one wished to travel over the Portage Road in a more private fashion, one could hire a calèche, or 'calash'

as it was commonly spelled. This was a gig on grasshopper springs with a seat for two passengers. The driver sat where the dashboard would normally be, with his feet on the shafts. These were frequently used by the ladies of a party while the gentlemen rode with them on horseback, or, if necessary, walked." Mrs. Simcoe often used a calèche when she travelled on the Portage Road.

There was a regular stagecoach service along the Portage Road for twelve years before any stagecoach service was inaugurated in 1808 to run between Kingston and Montreal. Eighteen years after the first stagecoach began to run on the Portage Road, the first stagecoach began to run from York in 1816. It ran between York and Niagara and the fare was $5.00. Due to the poor condition of the road the trip took over 17 hours, considerably longer than and not as comfortable as a steamboat trip across the lake. The next year a regular stagecoach service began between Kingston and York. [13]

Evidently the taverns in Upper Canada, as the English and American travellers called the inns and houses which provided accommodation, were superior to those generally found along the stagecoach routes in the United States. Tavern life was harsher, less hospitable and less palatable than the refined institutions - hotels, and motels - which serve today's tourist.

"There were three major rooms in most taverns. A large public room with a great open fireplace on one side; a kitchen serving as a dining room that may have been included in the public room; and a bed chamber. The early tavern was distinguished by its smells, sounds and experiences. The smells of baking bread or venison roasting, sweaty wagon drivers and stage drivers, horses, stale alcohol and cigar smoke. The sounds were of a dinner bell and a crackling fire. The experience of having to sleep on a barroom floor or with a stranger in the same bed, spoiled food, dirty sheets and towels, little privacy." [14]

Louis Philippe, the man who became King of France from 1830 to 1848, visited North America in 1796-7 and saw Niagara Falls. His account of a tavern in Abington, Virginia, where he stayed on April 26, 1797 tells of a problem he encountered. "Nowhere there are chamber pots; we asked for one at Mr. J. Campbell's and were told that 'there were broken panes in the windows'... There were indeed many broken panes, and it is a rare thing to sleep in a hermetically sealed room. The other day being in a loft, we were looking for a window, or opening that should do service for a chamber pot. We found it 10 feet up, so we insisted on some sort of receptacle; they brought us a kitchen kettle!". [15]

We picture in our imagination arriving at the tavern's door by stagecoach on a cold winter's evening, and going into the tavern where the main room is warmed by a roaring fire. The fireplace was light and warmth , and often the place where the food was cooked. To get a place close to the fire on a cold night took creativity. One new arrival finding the space around the fire crowded, ordered oysters for his horse. Curiosity overpowered everyone and they went out to witness a horse eating oysters, while the stranger staked himself a spot close to the fire at little expense. [16]

There are no travellers' accounts which complain of similar conditions in the public accommodation establishments along the the Niagara Frontier. A traveller, known only as T.C. wrote in 1808: "...Chippeway there are two good taverns, one kept by Stevens and the other by Fanning ...Each has a new part connected with old buildings and each has eight windows in front. The dining-room at Stevens' is twenty by thirty feet, carpeted. The attendance is good and the people civil. For a pint of tolerable Tenerife, a gill of rum, supper, breakfast, bed, and feed for my horse, I paid only thirteen shillings and sixpence, York money." [17]

There were problems of course. DeWitt Clinton in 1810 had an experience at Stevens'. "A traveller engaged a room with two beds, and then another traveller coming later got a room which he could not reach except by going through the room with the two beds." In spite of this Clinton gave Stevens' his stamp of approval, "...Stevens keeps a tolerable inn here."

The log hut, the traveller's rest, where the Duke of Kent stopped for refreshment in 1791 was in business during this time. While there is only the occasional mention of a tavern at this spot, it came into prominence during the War of 1812. Charles Wilson was the proprietor, as early as 1797, according to a notice in the *Upper Canada Gazette* on December 4, 1797. In this notice an inhabitant of Stamford gave notice that he would no longer be responsible for his wife's debts, as she had "eloped from my bed and board, and improperly resides with Charles Wilson of this town, inn-keeper." [18]

T.C. mentioned Wilson's in 1808. He was returning to the high bank above the Falls, after visiting Burch's and the other mills on the Flats (the area now occupied by the Niagara Parks Greenhouse, Canadian Niagara Power and the Toronto Power Generating Stations). As he came to the top of the hill and on to the Portage Road he saw: "... about a hundred yards before you a house, with a field before it, fenced with a worm fence. It is now occupied by Charles Wilson, but has been lately sold to a Mr. Shannon." [19]*

During the War of 1812 Wilson's was used as a British command post. On July 12, 1812, Lieutenant-Colonel Myers chose the garden in front of Wilson's as the location of one of the warning beacons which were set up to pass the alarm in case of an American invasion. These beacons consisted of an iron basket, filled with firewood, hung from a pole. When an invasion occurred the beacon closest to the scene was to be set afire and when the sentinels at the next beacon saw the glow, they set fire to their beacon and others were to follow suit. There is no record of these beacons having been used. [20]

Another early inn on the Portage Road was Forsyth's. It served as headquarters for the British general staff during the War of 1812, and many despatches from this area were addressed as being from *Forsyth's.* Its location is unknown although others historians have assumed that it was in what was the James Forsyth home on the east side of the Portage Road, near the present St.Mary's Ukrainian Catholic Church. James Forsyth was the original owner of the lot on which the *National Hotel,* later named the *Prospect Hotel* was built. He sold it to J. Buchner in 1799 and Buchner sold it to Harmanus Crysler in 1827. Forsyth could have had his inn close by, near the Crossroads.

Another inn which is mentioned in one incident related to the War of 1812, was run by a Mr. Denfield, and a more detailed account of what happened at this Portage Road inn is told in the chapter on The Portage Road and the War of 1812. The war brought an end to travel, and at the end of the war, Fanning's and Macklem's property, which would have included their inns, had been burned. Other men would become prominent in the business of providing accommodation to the travellers, who would be called tourists.

* Lanty Shannon later said that he was only considering the purchase of Wilson's.

Early Pioneer Life

Some of the earliest settlers, James Park, Archibald Thompson, and his brothers James and John, Peter Thompson, Jacob and Adam Brown, Gilbert Tice and John Burch settled along what was the portage path, soon to become the road that became the vital link in the transportation route between Lake Ontario and Lake Erie.

These Loyalists who settled in our area were accustomed to the hardships of pioneer life, and some of them had spent many months camped outside Fort Niagara. Here they had been provided with basic military rations of flour, salt pork, and dried beef. When they crossed the Niagara River and settled on the west bank, they were given a ration allowance consisting of these staple foods for a period of up to three years, until they had enough land cleared and they were able to grow their own crops.

When the settler arrived on his land his first task was to build a shanty for shelter. This was a log structure that was little more than a glorified tent. The earth was the floor and a hole was left in the roof to let smoke out from the fire, but this hole also let in the rain and the snow. With this basic shelter finished, the settler then could start to clear the land and plan to work as soon as possible on a more permanent house.

Trees were obstacles to the pioneer. He had to cut them down and remove the logs before he could plant his crops. The land had to be cleared of trees so that seeds could be planted. The first logs cut were used to build a log house. The "land above the Mountain" was an oak forest, with trees so large that their branches shut out the sun and thus prevented the growth of any underbrush. Lieutenant-Governor Simcoe noted this lack of undergrowth and wrote: "There was little more for a farmer to do, than cut a sufficiency of timber to fence his fields, girdle or ring the remainder, and put in the harrow, for in a few places only is it necessary to make use of the plough, to till and plant, there being little underbrush. [1] After the trees were cut, wheat, oats and Indian corn were planted between the stumps, so that as soon as possible a crop could be taken off the land for food. The soil was so fertile that the settlers got an average yield of forty bushels to the acre, and continued to do so without any fertilization with manure, until after 1800.

As there was an abundance of logs, it made good sense to build a log house, as the logs would otherwise have to be burned. The loghouses were usually eleven or twelve logs high, with dovetailed corners, and the spaces between the logs were chinked with moss or mud. There was no time to allow the logs to dry, and the green logs warped and twisted when they dried out. Spaces for windows and doors were cut out after the log walls were up, and the openings were covered with blankets until the doors and windows were available. Leather was used for door catches and hinges, and windows were without glass in the very early days.

Fireplaces and chimneys were built of boulder stone which was abundant throughout the area. There

Sir Guy Carleton, Lord Dorchester.
An engraving by A.H. Ritchie.

Sir Guy Carleton was an Irish soldier, who rose to the rank of Quartermaster-General. For his part in the defence of Quebec during the American invasion of Canada in 1775-76 he was created K.C.B. and became Sir Guy Carleton. He was appointed commander-in-chief of the British Forces in North America in 1782, with headquarters at New York, where he held control of the city, refusing to give it over to the Americans until compensation was paid to the Loyalists for their confiscated property. In 1783, realizing that no compensation would be paid, and that the Loyalists could not stay in New York, or return to their homes outside of the City, his superiors ordered Carleton to evacuate the Loyalists and the British troops. He held control of the port of New York until all of the Loyalists were safely away. In 1786 he was created Baron Dorchester and became Governor-in-Chief of British North America. It was he who ordered in March 1790, that a portage be established on the west bank of the Niagara River. The area of present day Niagara Falls was once called Mount Dorchester and Dorchester Road is named in his honour.

were no separate rooms, and the bottom floor served as general living quarters and kitchen, while the second floor which was a loft, was an all purpose bedroom, and generally without windows. Bedbugs and vermin were a problem, no matter how carefully the log house was built. It was difficult to keep the log house warm in winter. Wood fires had to be tended several times during the night, and wood added, or the fire would die down and the temperature would

drop to an unbearable level. There was always the danger of fire from an overheated stove or chimney.

Pumpkins were among the first garden crops, along with corn, potatoes and peas. The settlers also ate the green leaves of plants they found in the woods and swamps, such as fiddleheads, dandelion, lamb's quarters and watercress. They learned how to tell the safe greens from those that were poisonous by watching what their hogs ate when they were left to forage in the woods. If the hogs didn't like the greens, or if they became ill after eating a certain plant, it was certainly unsuitable for human consumption.

There was an abundance of wild fruit, strawberries, gooseberries, raspberries, cherries, plums and grapes, to be found in the forest. The fruit that wasn't dried for winter eating was eaten after picking. Maple sap was gathered each spring and boiled down to provide maple sugar.

Until John Burch and John Donaldson built grist mills, the wheat the settlers grew was either pounded or ground by hand in a crude mill, which gave them a very coarse flour and equally coarse bread. They found that Indian corn was the indispensable food which could be boiled or roasted. When the corn was ground the cornmeal could be cooked to make a porridge, which was eaten with maple sugar sprinkled over it. Cold cornmeal porridge was cut into slices and fried. Cornmeal was also combined with meat, or mixed with water, then placed on a board or shingle in front of the fire to bake and then eaten hot. Eggs and milk could be added to produce a cake, which the Indians called *Johnny Cake.* [2] The Loyalists were using knowledge which they had acquired more than ten years before when they settled in the Mohawk Valley in present day New York State.

The first official census taken by Colonel John Butler in August 1782 recorded that there were sixteen farmer settlers and their families on the west bank of the Niagara River, Two of the families were settled in the area of Township No.2, later called Mount Dorchester, then Stamford. They were Philip Bender and his wife, with four children, and Thomas McMicken's (McMicking) family of six with one black slave. Allan Macdonell's *Plan of a New Settlement - Niagara River Line,* dated March-April 1783, shows that Francis Ellsworth had taken up land south of Philip Bender, and directly opposite the Falls of Niagara. Daniel Rose is also shown as having settled north of and adjacent to Thomas McMicking.

The present area of the City of Niagara Falls includes part of the former townships of Willoughby and Crowland. In these parts of present day Niagara Falls, Michael Gonder and his son are believed to

Niagara Falls New York Public Library

Horse – Shoe Fall, Niagara.
An engraving by R. Sands from a sketch by T. Allom, circa 1840.

The men shown with staves, are catching eels which were plentiful at the base of the Falls, where they sometimes crawled out among the wet stones in their attempt to pass up the river. Peter Kalm, the Swedish naturalist, who visited Niagara Falls in 1750, observed: "Below the Falls in holes of the rocks, are a great plenty of Eels, which the Indians and the French catch with their hands, without other means; I sent two Indian boys, who directly came up with about twenty fine ones."

have settled on the Upper Niagara River in the former Willoughby Township area, as early as 1779 and Peter and Henry Buchner are believed to have taken up land in the part of Crowland Township that is within our City limits, as early as 1778.[3]

The settlers brought seeds for apples,cherries and peach trees, and as soon as their seeds grew into small trees, orchards were set out. Thomas McMicking grew the first apples in this vicinity. His son wrote in his memoirs that McMicking brought apple seeds with him from the Catskills. Someone told him that the apple seeds would sprout faster if they were steeped in milk and left overnight. He put the seeds in a cup, and then placed it high up on top of a cupboard. The family cat must have watched this procedure with interest, and during the night it climbed up to the top of the cupboard and drank the milk, seeds and all. [4] This set back his orchard planting for a year, until he could get more seeds.

The settlers complained that they had not been provided with the services of a blacksmith, or a grist and saw mill. It was John Burch who in 1785 received permission to build a grist and saw mill on the banks of the Niagara River a kilometre (about a mile) above the Horseshoe Falls. The mill went into service in 1786 and the settlers were able to have their grain ground into flour, by "paying" Burch, one-twelfth of the grist as his "miller's dues" and " a moiety" (one half) of the lumber sawn as his share for cutting logs. Several years later John Donaldson built a saw and grist mill at the outlet of Muddy Run Creek, just north of present day Whirlpool Rapids Bridge, near the corner of Ferguson Street and River Road.

According to the 1782 survey these pioneer families also had horses, cows, sheep, hogs and a steer. Philip Bender is listed as having a flock of sheep. Forage for these animals was usually dried leaves and stalks of corn. They were left to roam in the nearby forest for

Carol Breton

Thomas McMicking puts his precious apple seeds, brought all the way from the Mohawk Valley, in a bowl of milk, to soak overnight so that they may germinate faster.

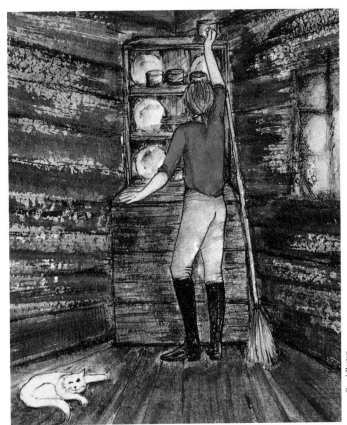

He puts the bowl of milk and apple seeds in a safe place, on top of the cupboard. His cat, snoozing on the mat beside him, has one eye open, watching with interest.

McMicking awakens and discovers that the cat has eaten his precious apple seeds. It will take him a year to get another supply of apple seeds, thus delaying the planting of his apple orchard. It is not known what happened to the cat.

food, and the cattle developed a taste for the tender leaves of trees, maple leaves in particular. They soon ate all of the foliage they could reach and kept on the lookout for fallen trees. One observer, commenting on their appetite for tree leaves wrote: "On hearing a Tree fall, the Cattle set off full scamper towards it." [5] This sound was to them like the ringing of a dinner bell.

The settlers' hogs were also left to forage in the woods. Their food was the mast - the layers of nuts fallen from the trees, mostly acorns from the oak trees which made up much of the forest in our area. They thrived and grew fat eating these nuts. The hogs were also used for other than their meat. The "land on the Mountain", as the land on the upper level of the escarpment was called, was infested with rattlesnakes. The snakes hibernated among the fallen blocks of limestone in the lower gorge, gaining access by way of the ravine at the end of the Whirlpool. When they emerged from hibernation, they came back up the ravine and spread throughout the countryside, where they posed a threat to the settlers as they worked the land.

The Indians had a simple way of dealing with the threat of the rattlesnake, they set fire to the leaves on the forest floor, smothering the snakes after they had come up from the gorge in the spring.

The settlers had a different method. They used their hogs to hunt down the rattlesnakes. Hogs were not affected by the bites inflicted on them as the snakes' fangs could not penetrate far enough beyond the hogs' thick skin to insert their venom. The settlers organized an attack on the snakes, taking their hogs into the lower gorge by way of the Whirlpool ravine, to strike at the snakes before they left their hibernation hideouts. In one afternoon some five hundred Timber rattlesnakes, some 1.8m (6 feet) in length, were killed by the hogs. [6]

The abundance of deer and small game in the forest was a source of meat the year round. Those who lived near the Niagara River could vary their diet with fish. Whitefish, herring, yellow and blue pike, white, rock and black bass, salmon, trout, muskellunge and sturgeon were common. Fish were caught with seine nets, or hook and line. George Heriot, on his visit to the area observed people spear fishing, "The spear in use is a fork with two or three prongs, with moving barbs, and fixed in a long handle. The fisherman takes possession of a prominent rock, from whence he watches his prey, and when it approaches within his reach, he pierces it with his instrument, with an almost inevitable certainty." [7]

The year 1788 was disastrous for the settlers. A late spring snow and heavy frost followed by a summer dry spell and hail, ruined many of the crops. Many

---

An Unusual Snake

Joseph Hadfield, an Englishman, visited America and the Falls of Niagara in 1785. The account of his visit included this snake story. "There are a vast variety of snakes in America as well as reptiles and insects, of the former the most curious I have heard of is called the Horn Snake. It is seldom more than 8 to 10 inches in length and very rarely found. It has a small horn on the top of the head, like the spur of a dunghill cork. It ascends trees which it selects near a path frequented by animals. It coils itself in a circle and suspends itself on a projecting bough which is perpendicular to the path. When the animal is passing, the snake by a sudden jerk, pounces on its prey, and by the same act forces the horn or tube into the flesh. A subtle poison is emitted through the tube which soon insinuates itself into the blood vessels and causes the death of the animal." This fanciful story is from "The Diary of Joseph Hadfield 1795".

---

of the families faced starvation. The winter of 1788-89 was to become known as the Hungry Year. Game was scarce, but there were fish in the river. Many of the families were able to survive only because they were issued additional military rations to tide them over.

Tea and coffee were not available in the early years. The pioneers found substitutes. For tea they could boil down herbs and barks such as sage, thyme, chocolate root, spice wood, hemlock boughs and sassafras. For coffee they roasted peas and barley, acorns and dandelion roots, rye and carrots, or they toasted bread and made a decoction of the crust.

When the grist mills were built, the grain that was damp, or otherwise unsuited to be ground into floor, was distilled into whisky. As a supply of water was essential to the distilling process, still houses were located beside one of the many fresh water springs which flowed out of the ground. There were two still houses in what is now Queen Victoria Park, one at the bottom of present day Murray Hill and the other in the Table Rock area.

Whisky was cheap, selling at twenty-five cents a gallon and it was potent. Every family had a supply on hand. James McMicking, born in Stamford in 1811, Thomas McMicking's son, wrote in his memoirs: "There was a habit at the time that is quite worthy of deprecation - that was that every family kept spirituous liquors in the house and gave to everyone that came, it was considered an insult if they refused to drink it. The consequence was that many drunkards were reared in such neighbourhoods". [8]

Isabel Walker, John Thompson's great-great-granddaughter, has in her possession a collection of documents, some dating back before 1800. This collection includes a school exercise book from 1799, various other documents and particularly, merchants'

View of the Horseshoe Fall of Niagara 1798.
An engraving from a sketch by I. Weld.

Buffalo & Erie County Public Library

The Indians on the rock at the edge of the river are spear fishing. George Heriot who visited the Falls of Niagara in 1802, described these spears as ''a fork with two or three prongs, with moving barbs, and fixed in a long handle. The fisherman takes possession of a prominent rock, from whence he watches his prey, and when it approaches within his reach, he pierces it with his instrument, with an almost unbelievable certainty.'' A leather thong is attached to the end of the spear so that the spear can be retrieved and the fish can be hauled in.

A Fish Story

Paul Dudley, an Englishman with the Royal Society of London, related this account of the size of fish in the Niagara River, after a conversation in 1721 with a Mr. Borassaw, a French trader who had been to the Falls of Niagara several times. ''He confirms Father Hennepin's account of the large trouts of those lakes, and solemnly affirmed that there was one taken lately, that weighed 86 lb., which I am rather inclined to believe... he saw a pike taken in a Canada river, and carried on a pole between two men, that measured five feet ten inches in length, and proportionately thick.'' Paul Dudley, ''An account of the falls of the River Niagara, taken at Albany, October 10, 1721.''

---

accounts with John Thompson and his son James dating from 1806 until 1843. It is presumed that John and James saved every piece of paper and record of their purchases. At some time someone must have sorted through the accumulation and had the foresight to keep what he or she thought most important. Of particular interest and benefit to this book, there is one invoice from each of the merchants with whom the Thompsons did business. It is from these invaluable papers that we know what general stores stocked for sale, what the doctor, shoemaker, tannery, harness maker, and others charged for their services.

Tailors were among the earliest merchants to set up shop. Mathias Steel and Hugh McCollum settled in Queenston and advertised in the *Upper Canada Gazette* for business in 1799. The Thompson papers include an 1810 account from John Tench, a tailor at Niagara, which includes only items of clothing for men. Listed in the account are: "a pair of pantaloons for Jimmy, 2 pair drawers for Mr. John", and something we might find unusual for the time,

Niagara Falls from Above.
A water colour by Thomas Davies, circa 1762-1766.

*Thomas Davies' training as a draughtsman is evident in this unusual view of the Horseshoe Falls, with an eagle soaring over the crest as the predominant feature. The two Indian figures at the extreme left are almost undetected. DeWitt Clinton, writing after his visit to the Falls of Niagara in 1822 observed: "In various places I have seen the **falco lancocephalus,** or bald eagle, the **falco ossifragus,** or grey eagle; and the **falco haliatus,** or osprey." William Barham commented on the eagle's aggressiveness: "the splendid gyrations of the gulls... attract much attention. But the eagle, fierce, daring, contemplative and tyrannical, takes his stand upon the point of some projecting rock or the dry limb of a gigantic tree, and watches with excited interest the movements of the whole feathered tribe below. Standing there in lordly pride and dignity, in an instant his eye kindles and his ardour rises as he sees the fish-hawk (osprey) emerge from the deep, screaming with exultation at his success. he darts forth like lightning, and gives furious chase. The hawk, perceiving his danger, utters a scream of despair, and drops his fish; and the eagle instantly seizes the fish in air, and bears his ill-gotten booty to his lofty eyrie."*

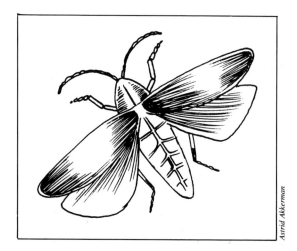

Firefly

Harriet Martineau found an abundance of fireflies during her visit in 1838. "In the dark woods on the Canada side we made ourselves visible to each other by catching fireflies and sticking them in our bonnets. They sat very still among our rows of ribbons, and really served our purpose very well."

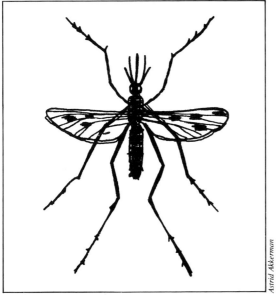

Astrid Akkerman

Mosquito
Duncan Ingraham, wrote in 1792: "I rode... through swarms of mosquitoes, gnats, moths, etc., beyond all description." Isaac Weld wrote of his experiences at Niagara Falls in 1796: "In the summer season you meet with rattlesnakes at every step, and mosquitoes swarm so thickly in the air, that to use a common phrase of the country, 'you might cut them with a knife'." Robert Burford in 1838 had a different experience. He wrote: "The heat of summer here can be borne with pleasure, while at the same time the annoyance of mosquitoes and other insects is unknown."

"making a walking coat   1 4s". There were a number of other notations for findings: thread, tape, linen, moulds, buttons, buckram padding, perhaps indicating that they were to be used by Mrs. Thompson when she made dresses for herself and her daughters.

Thomas Hardy, in 1787, established a tannery and a carding and weaving business in the Hollow, the area along the bank of the Niagara River, about 380m (half a mile) upriver from the Horseshoe Falls. The Thompsons took their raw hides there to be processed into shoe leather - soft and supple for the uppers and hard and wear resistant for the soles. There is also an item in Thompson's account with Hardy for carding 40 lbs. of wool and for weaving 45 lbs., presumably from the wool which had been carded into yarn.

James Thompson ran an account with John Hardy, Thomas Hardy's successor, who had moved the business to St. David's. This account which ran from August 28, 1835 until June 1, 1840, and was not settled until December 9, 1842, shows that James provided Thomas Hardy with sheep and calf skins as well as lime. Against the credits for these items Thompson charged not only processed leather, but leather products. Hardy was also in the harness-making business. There are items for: 1 pair horse collars, 1 set lines, 1 pair halters, and 1 set harness. Thompson had a debit of $69.07 against a credit for goods supplied of $68.14, leaving only 93 cents owing to Hardy. Whether by design or coincidence, this was characteristic of James Thompson's purchasing habits. It is assumed that James kept a running record of his accounts, all of this without the aid of a pocket calculator.

Jesse Cole in Stamford was the shoemaker to whom James Thompson took his shoe leather hides, to be made into shoes. Thompson's account with Cole for the last six months of 1829, included amounts for making "Grils (sic) and boys boots at $1.00 each; woman's calfskin boots, $1.25; making coarse boots (work boots) $1.25 and patching and soling boots." Once again James skillfully judged the amount of his bill, because after his credits were applied for supplying leather, and butter in 4 and 8 pound lots, at 8 pounds for $1.00, and flower (flour) there was only 18 cents to pay on a total bill of $14.37

Dr. John Lefferty settled in Stamford in 1800 on Lundy's Lane, and his former residence and office remained on Lundy's Lane, on the southwest corner of the intersection with Dorchester Road until it was demolished in 1975. Dr. Lefferty made house calls, a time consuming and difficult undertaking, when you consider that he travelled by horse and buggy, over very rudimentary roads.

Dr. Lefferty's account with James Thompson for the period of July 21 to September 28, 1832, was for £8,15s. This included 19 visits charged at 7s 6p each and other charges in the doctor's handwriting, which are written much like a present day doctor's prescriptions - indecipherable except to a pharmacist. Dr. Lefferty was fortunate in that the Thompsons paid him in currency, where it was not unusual for him to receive his fee in produce.

Isabel Walker wrote in *The Thompsons of Whirlpool Farm* that: "In the period from 1796 to 1879, there were more than twenty harness makers, blacksmiths, wagon makers and carriage makers along the Portage Road. An additional five or more were in St. David's and vicinity."[9]

James Thompson D[r]
To John J. Lefferty Surg[eon]

1832

(Feby) 21	To visit viij Pulv. Diaphont: for Hir[ed] man	=	=	=	=	10	=
22	To visit & Directions — Do	=	=	=	=	7	6
Augst 6	To visit Dos Cal: cum Rhei (for Duncan)	=	=	=	=	8	9
	To Dos Ol: Ricini - vj P. Febris: Do	=	=	=	=	3	9
	To Dos Cal: cum Rhei (for son)	=	=	=	=	1	3
7	To visit Dos Pulv: Ipeca: for Duncan	=	=	=	=	7	6
	To ir P. Alterat: Dos Ol: Ricini Do	=	=	=	=	3	9
8	To visit ir Pulv: Alterat: Do	=	=	=	=	7	6
	To Empl: Epispast: Parv: — vj P. Febris: Do	=	=	=	=	5	=
9	To visit vj Pulv: Alterat Do	=	=	=	=	8	9
10	To visit vj Pulv: Febrif: ij Pulv: Diaphont Do	=	=	=	=	8	9
	To xij Pil: Antibil: for (self	=	=	=	=	2	6
12	To visit Dos Ol: Ricini for Duncan	=	=	=	=	7	6
	To Dos Cal: et Rhei — iv Pil: Diaphont: Do	=	=	=	=	2	6
15	To visit ir P. Tonica Edp Med: Sulph: Dilut	=	=	=	=	8	9
	To 3i Syrp: Pro Infus: Tonica Do	=	=	=	=	2	6
16	To visit ij P. Febrif: Dos Ol: Ricini Do	=	=	=	=	8	9
17	To visit & Directions Do	=	=	=	=	7	6
19	To visit viij Pulv: Tonica Do	=	=	=	=	10	=
20	To two visits iv P. Astring - 3i Ol: Ricini Do	=	=	=	=	12	6
21	To visit & Medicine Do	=	=	=	=	8	9
22	To visit & Advice Do	=	=	=	=	6	3
Septem 27	To visit & Advice for wife	=	=	=	=	10	=
28	To visit Dos Ol: Ricini Do morning	=	=	=	=	7	6
	To visit Dos S. Magnes: cum Tol: Senna Do (evening	=	=	=	=	7	6
1833 Jany 9	Hlf: Cry	=	=	=	8	15	=
	Amt. of Duncans ac/c $25.25 £6.8.9	=	=	=			

James Thompson's Account with Dr. John J. Lefferty, 1833

Dr. Lefferty lived on the southwest corner of present day Lundy's Lane and Dorchester Road. When Dr. Lefferty made a house call to the Thompson farm it was a long trip, and a slow trip by today's standards, by horse and buggy. The individual entries are for house calls, and medicine in some cases. It is unusual that there are only two calls near the end of February, then nothing until August, when there were fourteen calls. After August 22, everyone was healthy and Dr. Lefferty's services were not needed for another five weeks, September 27.

Thompson Papers, Isabel Walker Collection

The Portage Road and the War of 1812

The United States of America declared war on Great Britain on June 24, 1812, but until Americans invaded Canada at Queenston on October 13, 1812, business was carried on as usual along the Portage Road. During the Battle of Queenston, the warehouses belonging to Robert Hamilton, James Kerby and Thomas Dickson were severely damaged or destroyed. This meant that goods arriving by ship at Queenston had to be immediately transhipped along the road. The war disrupted the fur trade and soon the traffic along the road consisted only of military supplies, and essential food items.

With the threat of invasion imminent, General Brock had ordered a series of beacons to be installed along the Road. They were iron baskets kept full with dry wood, ready to be ignited as soon as word of an attack was received. Then the beacon closest to the source would be lit. Those on guard at the next beacon who saw the flare, would light their beacon and so on until the word was spread and the defending forces were alerted.

There was a beacon at Chippawa, and one at Wilson's Tavern at the Falls, where the path ran down to Table Rock, near the present intersection of the Portage Road and Buchanan Avenue. Another was put on the "rising ground at Lundy's Lane (the school house)" and this beacon was expected to provide a warning flare for those watching from the heights at Fonthill. Other beacons were placed at intervals on the Road all the way to Queenston. There is no record of this alarm system being used. [1]

Artillery emplacements were installed at intervals along the river. The *New York Gazette* reported on July 12, 1812 that a rifleman had deserted the British forces, by crossing the river below the Falls on a pine log, and had provided the Americans with intelligence on the British gun locations. In addition to the guns at Fort Chippawa, a battery with two heavy guns was set up along the river, downriver from the Fort and opposite the storehouses and mills at Manchester on the American side.

Below the Falls a small gun battery protected by a wall of piled stones was installed, where the ladder (known as Mrs. Simcoe's ladder) went down to the site of the present Maid of the Mist landing. There were two 18 pounder guns directly above this battery on the high bank. The ladders leading to the lower river were removed on both sides of the river, in case someone else chose to swim across the river. [2]

The Portage Road was the route used to move troops and supplies from Lake to Lake. It was also used to transfer prisoners of war. After General Brock's victory over the Americans under Major General William Hull at Detroit, the General and his army were taken prisoner and put on British naval ships and taken to Fort Erie. Here they disembarked, and were then marched down the river road, and along the Portage Road to Niagara. John Lovett watched with dismay from Lewiston as the procession passed. "I saw my countrymen stripped of their arms...marched by the hundreds...the line, including waggons, pleasure carriages, etc., was half a mile long, scattered." [3] The soldiers estimated to number 500 walked, while General Hull and the officers rode in carriages.

When the Americans were established on the heights at Queenston on October 13, 1812 awaiting reinforcements from Lewiston, the British reinforcements were rushing to the scene. It was along the Portage Road that Captain Bullock led his Chippawa detachment of 200 men of the 41 st and two flank companies of the Lincoln Militia. They arrived before General Sheaffe's force which came from Fort George, and they immediately engaged the Americans, harassing them until Sheaffe arrived.

Sir Howard Douglas wrote to Lord Bathurst on December 20, 1812 commenting on the need to take over Fort Niagara from the Americans. The guns of the Fort commanded the mouth of the Niagara River and without shipping, the line of communication with Lake Erie by Queenston over the Portage Road to Fort Chippawa and Fort Erie would have to be abandoned and a new route opened. Douglas suggested a route by the River LaTranche, or Thames. [4]

During August of 1813, when the Americans again invaded Canada the portage was abandoned. Sir George Prevost, reported to Lord Bathurst "...the occupation by the enemy of our frontier territory on the Niagara River having interrupted our usual mode of communicating with Lake Erie, I had great difficulty to continue supplying the posts at Amherstburg and Mackinac....I have although at considerable expense been able to transport by a circuitous route by the Grand River...a small supply of Indian arms and ammunition." [5]

After the American landing, the outnumbered British garrisons at Fort George and Queenston retreated by the Portage Road, and established a base at DeCou's (DeCew's) at the Beaverdams. From here they harassed the Americans by attacking their patrols. During the next eight months, until December 19, 1813 the Stamford settlers along the road were plundered and robbed by a roving band of Americans led by a Buffalo doctor Cyrenius Chapin.

Dr. Chapin began as a medical adviser to General Van Rensellaer, then when he became impatient with what he considered a lack of resolve in carrying on the war with Canada, he formed his own group of volunteers and Indians. He and his men took part in several actions, and he was commissioned a Captain. In May 1813 the *Buffalo Gazette* reported "The public stores at Queenston were removed or destroyed. Dr. C. Chapin of this village was in the vanguard." [6]

By March 1813 he had about 300 volunteers including Indians under his command. He attached his corps to the American forces. After they invaded Canada in May of that year he took them out on forays

into Canada in an attempt find a fight with the British patrols who roamed the countryside. The inhabitants of Stamford were terrorized by these random raids, and in constant fear of being injured or plundered.

There was no provision made to pay Chapin's men, and General Porter wrote to General Wilkinson asking that they be paid for the time spent assisting the military. Wilkinson replied "I have no authority to pay volunteers. It is however my decided opinion that all the enemy's property should be good prize for any of our citizens who may take it." With this permission to plunder, Chapin's men now took what they wanted from the citizens as they rode along the Portage Road.

Stories of Chapin's exploits reached Buffalo and on September 21. 1813, the *Buffalo Gazette* found it necessary to explain that the 34 barrels of flour and a bale of blankets taken on a recent raid were the property of the enemy government. Then went on to say "The conduct of Major Chapin in all his incursions into enemy territory has been strictly honourable...This is not said to flatter ....we hope it will tend to counteract the scandalous stories respecting Major Chapin's corps being an organized set of marauders." [7] The farmers along the Niagara River and the people of Stamford Township along the Portage Road had a different opinion.

The intersection of Lundy's Lane and the Portage Road, called the Crossroads, was the scene of several incidents with Chapin's men. The *Buffalo Gazette* on June 29, 1813 reported this incident: "On Sunday, (20th June) the mounted men under Major Chapin passed down to Queenston. When they passed the foot of Lundy's Lane, (a place principally settled by the Rangers who fought under Butler in the Revolution,) they were fired upon by a small party of the enemy concealed. One of Chapin's group was taken prisoner.

"For several days previous to this small parties of the enemy had been lurking about the Lane...On Monday, (21st June) a detachment of 150...from Fort George with Chapin's corps marched for the Lane. When the advance came near the place where Ransom was taken prisoner, they were fired upon by the enemy and Sloot was killed, 5 balls and a buckshot took effect. The guard retired and the enemy retreated before the infantry came up." [8]

Lieutenant James FitzGibbon had an encounter with Chapin's corps in 1813 which almost cost him his life. FitzGibbon heard that the infamous Dr. Chapin was leading a raiding party, and was on his way from Fort George to Chippawa, on June 19. 1813. FitzGibbon brought his men from De Cew's at the Beaverdams, up Lundy's Lane, planning an ambush. When he got close to the Crossroads he left his men in the woods, while he went ahead to reconnoitre. A

Mrs. Kerby who lived at the inn on the southwest corner of the Crossroads, signalled FitzGibbon with a handkerchief, and ran out to tell him that Chapin with two hundred to three hundred men, had just passed by.

FitzGibbon saw a U.S. Dragoon's horse tied up outside the inn, and he went inside, to find two American soldiers. One of them pointed his rifle at FitzGibbon, who then proceeded to throw the soldier off his guard by walking forward with his hand outstretched, claiming that he was an old acquaintance. When he got close enough he seized the gun and a struggle ensued. Several inhabitants standing nearby refused to help FitzGibbon in spite of Mrs. Kerby's begging. Only a small boy, the son of Dr. Fleming, diverted their attention by throwing rocks at them.

During the struggle, one of the soldiers drew Fitzgibbon's sword from its sheath and was about to thrust it into Fitzgibbon's chest when Mrs. Denfield, (also called Denfeld, Duffeld) the wife of the proprietor, who was standing by the door with a baby in her arms, knocked the sword out of the soldier's hand. When the soldier bent to pick it up, she quickly put her baby down and grabbed the sword, wrenching it from his grasp. She ran with the sword and hid it in the back of the inn. Her husband appeared to see what the commotion was, and helped FitzGibbon disarm both men, taking them prisoner. He then quickly left, taking them with him, to join his party in the woods, and he had no sooner left the scene than the whole Chapin party returned. [9]

Another incident that gives an indication of the tension that the people of Stamford were living under took place on June 29 and was related by Captain W.H. Merritt: "On the 29th we were sadly alarmed at Decoo's by a report...that the whole American Army was advancing by the Queenston and Chippawa road. We were all drawn up under the command of Col. Dennis, 49th, in order of battle, expecting them on momentarily. I was sent ahead to reconnoitre with a few men. The report had spread through every house in Stamford; the people were all at their doors looking out for them, each saying they were at their neighbour's house.

After finding my way as far as Kilman's by by-roads (present day Dorchester Road at Thorold Stone Road) a fellow told me they were at McCartey's he had seen them. After cautiously approaching the house through the wood I found they had not been that far. I proceeded on to Knox's (present day Portage Road at the Halfway) and heard of them being at St. David's. crossed over to Mr. Smith's and found by him that they had not left their entrenchments that day. I returned in the evening after riding 60 miles in the

greatest suspense imaginable, either at a slow cautious walk or full gallop." [10]

Mrs. George Green who was born in 1826 told of her mother's experiences with "plunderers" during the war, obviously Chapin's Corps. "The women and children on the farms were most afraid of the white plunderers and the Indians and the Van Wycks did not escape them. Somehow they got a warning ... and they decided to hide whatever they could. There was a field of buckwheat in bloom near the house, so they took bags of flour, hams and sides of bacon, and other things and threw them as far as they could into the tall buckwheat, where they sank out of sight.

When the Indians came they rushed all through the house stealing mirrors, knives, clothing and whatever took their fancy. They found some drained honey in jars and dipped it out with their hands and filled their mouths full as one might fill a hole with putty. It made some of them sick." [11]

During the course of the war boats of many sizes ranging from batteaux to brigs and schooners were carried over the Road. In June 1812, Lieutenant-Colonel Robert Nicol wrote "...there may be some difficulty in getting teams at Chippawa prepared to carry boats. ..You will of course pay every attention to their being loaded on the carriage, so that they may not be injured." [11] Major-General Vincent had a number of batteaux transported from Chippawa to Queenston in the spring of 1813. [12]

A despatch written by General Drummond, in August 1814, to Sir George Prevost, reveals that vessels larger than batteaux were carried over the Portage Road. Drummond wrote "...I have omitted to express to Your Excellency the very great assistance which this division of the army has received from the detachment from H.M. Squadron on Lake Ontario, consisting of the brigs *Star* and *Charwell,* and *Netley* and *Magnet* schooners. Drummond went on to say that without these ships he could not have attempted offensive operations against the Americans who were then occupying Fort Erie.

Batteaux were also tramsported over the Portage Road for this action. When Captain Dobbs made his report to Sir James Yeo of the incident described above when the American ships *Ohio* and *Somers* were captured he wrote "Having succeeded in getting my gig and five batteaux across from the Niagara River to Lake Erie, a distance of eight miles by land, I last night attacked the three enemy's schooners that had anchored close to Fort Erie. [13]

Lieutenant-Colonel Robert Nicol "furnished and transported seven miles by land the boats employed on that service." It must have been quite a sight to see those ships, set on wheels, pulled by what must have been at least twelve yoke of oxen, along the Portage

Road. Brigs or Brigantines were about 27 feet long with a 7 foot beam, while Schooners were 22 feet by 6 ft. They were sailing vessels, and had masts over fifty feet high. As there were no overhead wires to contend with, it probably only required some tree trimming, to cut off branches that extended over the road. The ships were carried over the road in summer, when the sandy road surface would be dry and hard. The names of these vessels appear in despatches of Lake Ontario action in July, and by the middle of August they were on Lake Erie. [14]

Another incident which had a bearing on the outcome of the Battle of Lundy's Lane involved Mrs. Wilson, the widow of Charles Wilson, who kept a small tavern on the Portage Road, above the Table Rock and the Horseshoe Falls. On the evening of July 25 when General Winfield Scott's brigade was approaching the tavern, along Portage Road, several British officers were seen to leave the building and mount their horses. Several of them rode off along the road, but one elderly officer halted in the middle of the road, watching the approach of the Americans. When they were a musket shot away, he saluted the advance party and rode off toward Lundy's Lane.

Mrs. Wilson was nervous and apprehensive when the Americans arrived, but she told them with feigned regret that if they had come a few moments sooner they would have captured her former British guests. When asked for information, she very liberally estimated General Riall's force on the Lundy's Lane heights at more than twice its strength. At the same time the sound of bugles was heard from the woods directly in front, along the road. General Scott, stopped his brigade and sent out a small advance party to reconnoitre. Scott was afraid of an ambush and so he held back while he despatched a rider to bring reinforcements from the camp above Chippawa.

At the same time, General Riall had decided that his force was no match for the Americans, so he ordered his guns off the hill, and soon had his troops marching at the double down the Portage Road toward Queenston. General Drummond was in the meantime proceeding up the Portage Road from Queenston, to reinforce Riall's force, which he thought was still on Lundy's Lane Hill. The two columns came together at some point two to three miles down the Road toward Queenston. When his column stopped, Drummond galloped up to the front to see what was wrong, and on finding that Riall had abandoned the hill, he ordered Riall's column to about face and the they all marched on the double back to the hill, where they had only sufficient time to regain the hill and position the artillery with included two 24 pounders from Drummond's force and other 6 pounders and a howitzer before the Americans attacked. Mrs. Wilson's deception, whether deliberate or accidental,

made it possible for the British to stand and fight at Lundy's Lane.

The Battle of Lundy's Lane which began at twilight on July 25, 1814 and ended around midnight, was the most fiercely fought and the bloodiest battle of the War of 1812. The action centred on the heights at Lundy's Lane, now known as Drummond Hill, where the British artillery was set up. The battle began with the Americans attempting to get behind the battery, but they were turned back in the area of present day Culp St. and Drummond Road. They then sent their forces through the woods east of the Portage Road and came out north of the Crossroads, near North St. and the site of our Hospital. They pushed the British forces back from the Portage road, and when their force increased, they attacked the hill from the north of Lundy's Lane, up the heights, all through what is now the Morse Misener subdivision, Morse, Hanan and Summer Streets. When the British were driven off the hill, they moved around from the west, and began their counterattack against the Americans who were now entrenched on the hill.

The fighting was carried on at close quarters. Dr. E.L. Allan of the U.S. 21 st Regiment wrote later "For two hours the two hostile lines were within twenty yards of each other, and so frequently intermingled that often an officer would order an enemy's platoon. The moon shone bright, but part of our men being dressed like their Glengarrian Regiment, caused the deception. [15] One American officer, crouched behind a hedge as he made his way up the hill, heard sounds of movement on the other side of the hedge. "What Regiment are you" he asked; "The Royal Scots, Sir" came the reply. So close was the action that soldiers on both sides often fired at their own comrades.

The difficulty in distinguishing between friend and foe in the darkness, resulted in an embarrassing incident for British General Phineas Riall. General Riall was severely wounded and his aides were leading him to safety behind the lines, when they came upon a body of men on horseback. One of Riall's aides, assuming that the men were British, commanded "Make way for General Riall". The men on horseback obliged and parted so that Riall's party could pass between them. When the General and his aides were surrounded by these cavalrymen they found to their dismay that they were Americans. The General and his aides were taken prisoner. [16]

U.S. Colonel James Miller, who led the daring cavalry charge which captured the British guns and drove the British off the hill described the guns as "seven pieces of elegant brass cannon, with eight horses and harnesses, though some of the horses were killed...ammunition and wagons" [17] Two of the cannon were 24 pounders and the rest 6 pounders and 5 1/2 inch howitzers.

The British made repeated unsuccessful attempts to recapture the battery, with the last charge ending about midnight. Then, with both sides exhausted, the British withdrew and slept in the area north of the heights, over a mile north along the Portage Road. The exhausted Americans tried to take away the British guns but did not have enough horses to pull the artillery carriages. Consequently only one British 6 pounder was removed. In the confusion the Americans left one of their 6 pounders, and the howitzer which was lost earlier in the fighting when "the horses being on full gallop towards the enemy to attack them the riders were shot off and the horses ran through the enemy's lines." Thus the Americans who were tired and thirsty, unaware that water was available from an artesian well just east of the Portage Road, at the site of our present South End Farmers' Market, retired to Chippawa, taking the one British gun, leaving two of their own in British hands.

Before the Americans left the hill for their camp in Chippawa, they gathered their wounded, taking them back to camp in forty wagons which they had brought to the battle carrying ammunition. From about midnight until after dawn the heights were silent, only dead soldiers and dead horses lay on the battlefield. Dr. E.W. Bull, U.S. Hospital Surgeon wrote on July 31 "I understood that General Ripley was ordered to move early in the morning of the following day to the scene of action of the day previous for the purpose of burying the dead, securing all trophies captured (artillery), and driving back the enemy should they appear...In consequence I rode to the battleground about daylight without witnessing the presence of a single British officer or soldier. The dead had not been removed during the night and such a scene of carnage I have never beheld, particularly at Lundy's Lane, red coats and blue and grey were promiscuously intermingled, in many places three deep, and around the hill where the enemy's artillery was carried by Colonel Miller, the carcasses of 60 or 70 horses disfigured the scene. I went forward more than a mile beyond this point and saw no enemy. [18]

The British returned to the battle scene early in the morning, and found the hill deserted. They moved their artillery from the hill and repositioned it on both sides of the Portage Road, south of the hill, in the present day Delaware Street area, where the Portage Road curves toward Falls View. Here they awaited the Americans return. When the Americans came back along the road, and found the British established in force ahead of the hill, they retreated to their camp in Chippawa, setting fire to the Falls Mills on the river bank and Bridgewater and the mills at present day Dufferin Islands.

British losses were 878 killed, wounded and missing. American losses were acknowledged as 860 killed, wounded and missing, while an eye witness account of the action published in *Poulson's American,* estimated their loss in killed and wounded at 1200. The British 8th or King's Regiment lost 80 per cent of its roster. Hundreds of the dead were piled and burned in a funeral pyre on the hill. Sir J.E. Alexander visited the battleground in 1843 and recounted this conversation with a veteran of the battle, "We thought it unchristianlike of our General to order our dead to be burnt but as he said it was the custom in Spain and Portugal, we fancied it was all right. There were about 900 dead bodies and sixty horses." [19]

Others were buried in two mass graves on the north side of the hill, where they fell in battle.This area, now occupied by the playground and baseball field on Summer Street, was at one time a gravel pit operated by one of the Morse family. In 1856 he had the job of filling the potholes on the Portage Road with gravel from his pit. He was crticized for having too many bones in the gravel he used. As he dug deeper into the gravel bank, the graves were undermined and the bones came down with the gravel and went into the cart for distribution in the potholes on the Portage Road. In the 1880's people came from Toronto on an outing, and spent time on the hill and in the gravel pit, picking out the regimental buttons and badges, which they carried away as souvenirs.

Mrs. George Green's mother, Abigail Van Wyck told her that just before the battle of Lundy's Lane most of the people along the frontier left their homes and went back to the Short Hills, near Fonthill. All the good horses and wagons had been taken for the army but the Van Wycks had a couple of old horses that the British Army felt weren't worth taking for heavy work. These were hitched to a wagon with patched up harness and some feather beds and other household possessions were put in the wagon along with the children. The older children and her mother walked and drove the cattle.

When they returned after the battle, everything around the hill where the battle had been fought was in ruins - houses, fences, trees - and there were spots of dried blood in the sand where the dead and wounded had fallen. Several years later people came to visit the battlefield and old soldiers who fought in the battle would show them around and sell them bullets and buttons. The school boys used to dig up lots of relics on the battlefield. [20]

The Lundy's Lane Historical Society was formed in 1888 and they took an interest so that the remains from any graves that were accidentally uncovered

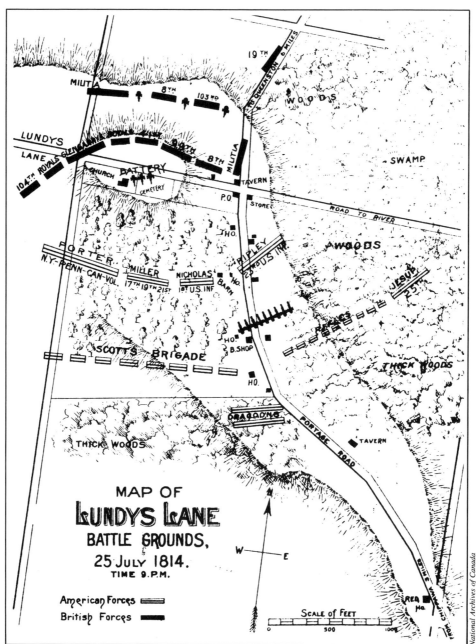

MAP OF
LUNDYS LANE
BATTLE GROUNDS,
25 JULY 1814.
TIME 9. P.M.

American Forces ▭
British Forces ▬

SCALE OF FEET

would be reinterred. During the 1890's when excavations were made for buildings in the area, many graves were uncovered. The remains were carefully removed and reburied in Drummond Hill Cemetery with appropriate re-interment ceremonies held in 1891, 1893, 1899 and 1901.

The inhabitants along the Portage Road had to contend with the Militia who were often obliged to find food and shelter as they could. In September 1813 when the British had their headquarters at Four Mile Creek (St. David's) there were soldiers billeted all over the northern end of the Township. Thomas G. Ridout writing to his father recounts this experience in 1813; "We came to Thompson's (John Thompson) the day before yesterday and met with rather an ungracious reception. The old fellow said he could not take us in as his family occupied the whole house, but that we might go into an old house a little distance off, which was inhabited at an early period of the world. Accordingly we cleared it of rubbish, made a fire and fried a little beef we brought with us. In the evening we made a straw bed on the floor. We collected balm in the garden for tea and carried on an extensive robbing of peas, apples, onions, corn, carrots etc., for we can get nothing except by stealing, excepting, milk which is carefully measured. Bread and butter is out of the question...We have an iron pot which serves for teapot, roaster and boiler, and two window shutters put upon three barrels form the table. We have three servants who eat the remains of our feasts. [21]

Portage Road Industries – Bridgewater Mills

Wheat was the first grain planted by the United Empire Loyalist settlers. Once they had cut down the trees and cleared a plot of land, they planted wheat seeds between the stumps, not waiting until the stumps were removed. According to Ernest Green, the resulting crop of grain was crushed and ground in hand mills supplied by the government, or pounded in hollowed stumps with wooden pestles. As the population grew, and more grain was harvested, there was a need for water-powered mills to process the grain.

The government, in response to a memorial presented by the settlers that private grist mills be built, agreed to build a government grist and saw mill near Niagara, but the "non-arrival of machinery delayed their completion."[1] Until mills were built, if they did not hand grind their wheat, the settlers were able to take it to Fort Niagara and exchange it for flour.

The first mill built was built in this area by Lieutenant Brass in 1794. This mill and one built at about the same time at Kingston, were known as the King's Mills, because they were built by the military with government money. This mill was built on the property known as Palatine Hill, on the Two Mile Creek just west of the settlement at Niagara. The settlers on the Mountain, who did not have horses to carry their bagged grain to the Palatine Hill mill, petitioned for a mill closer to their farms.

In 1786 the military issued a memorandum in response to the settler's petition: "On the petition of many of the settlers, the Lieutenant-Governor recommended that they be allowed to build necessary grist mills at their own expense and in order to indemnify them, they should be granted the right of Banalité." This was a French word which came into the English language when the feudal system was introduced.* It meant the custom of tenants being required to have their corn or grain ground at their lord's mills.

This memorandum was approved by the Legislative Council in Quebec, and regulations were drawn up authorizing the erection of a grist mill in any township or seignory, on or before the first of November 1786. The mills were to be kept in constant repair and were to be attended to by persons necessary to grind the settlers' grain. Persons building and operating them would be granted the enjoyment of the rights and privileges which the King held as Seigneur or Lord with respect to mills, by the laws of the Province, for a period of 15 years, at the expiration of which period the mills would become the property of the Crown.

One bateau, properly manned, would be allowed, at his Majesty's expense to make one trip to bring mill stones and other materials for the use of each mill. The localities selected under this regulation for the construction of mills within the settlement of Niagara

---

* *Banal Rights.* feudal privileges (banalities) in France that compelled tenants to have their grain ground at the seignoir's mill, their bread baked at a common oven provided by him and their grapes pressed in his wine press. In New France, only the milling was insisted upon, and this proved to be to the advantage of the colonists, since it forced the seignoir to provide a grist mill in the seignory. Encyclopedia Canadiana, Vol. 1, p.290.

View of the Falls of Niagara, From the Bank Near Birche's Mills .
An engraving by F.C. Lewis, from a water colour by George Heriot, circa 1806.
This hand coloured engraving was one of the colour plates accompanying Heriot's "Travels in the Canada's"
published in London, England, in 1807. John Burch's Mills are shown at the right, and his house is at the left.
The figure in the foreground is walking down the Mill Road to the Hollow, the lower level where the two men are
shown herding the cattle. Long Island (later known as Cedar Island) is shown at the right.

were: at the Falls of Niagara, one above the Twelve Mile Pond (Whirlpool), one 29km (18 miles) from Lake Erie (Black Creek), one 26km (16 miles) from the Garrison (Fort Erie), and one between the Great Falls and Chippawa Creek. [2]

John Burch, who had taken up land along the Niagara River between the Falls and the mouth of the Chippawa River, asked Major Campbell, the British Commander at Fort Niagara for permission to build a mill at the head of the rapids. Lieutenant Tinling, the Fort's engineering officer, inspected the site and recommended a site further down the river. Burch was given a permit to build a mill on condition that he built in the area Lieutenant Tinling specified, and Burch chose the site for his mill, the location of present day Ontario Hydro Toronto Power Generating Station.

He cut a channel for his mill race, to bring water from the northern shoreline where the water returned to the main river after flowing around the embayment, now known as Dufferin Islands. His mill was built on the bank of the river, with the water wheel located on

the west or land side of the building. After the water passed his water wheel, it re-entered the Niagara River, downriver from the mill. Burch created an artificial island, which became known as Sumac Island.

John Burch's mill was unapproachable by water. Settlers had to bring their grain and logs to the mill by horse or ox-drawn wagon. They came along the Portage Road, to a point at about the end of present day Livingston Street, north of Loretto, where a road known as the Mill Road ran down to the lower level. T.C. in his *Ride to Niagara,* observed: "…as you pass along at about two miles distance from Chippeway, you observe a wagon road descending to the right into some flats, washed by the rapids of Niagara. The descent may be eighty or ninety feet." [3]

The settlers found Burch's mill inconvenient, and Burch once again sought permission to build on the site originally chosen at the head of the rapids, where logs could be brought to the saw mill by water. Now, he had to "slay (sleigh) the logs in winter". He had

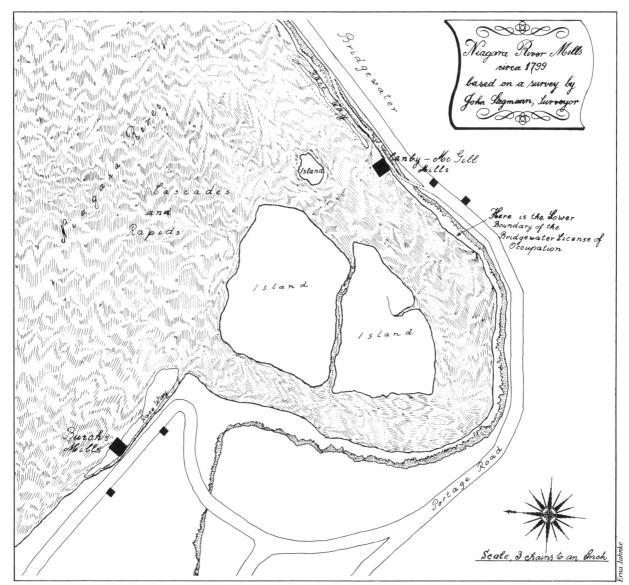

Within the map:

Niagara River Mills
circa 1799
based on a survey by
John Stegmann, Surveyor

Bridgewater

Race Way

Niagara River

Cascades and Rapids

Island

Island

Island

Canby – McGill Mills

Here is the Lower Boundary of the Bridgewater License of Occupation

Race Way

Burch's Mills

Portage Road

Scale, 3 chains to an Inch

Erna Jahnke

Niagara River Mills, circa 1799,
from a map, based on a survey made by John Stegmann.
The Canby - McGill Mills, located on the southern bank of the Niagara River where it entered the embayment
around the islands we now know as the Dufferin Islands. Burch's Mills are also shown, with the cut made for
the mill race, to bring water to the mill's water wheel. The road along the river, leading to Burch's Mills is incor-
rectly marked, ''Portage Road''. It is the Mill Road.. The course of the road leading down from the high bank
to Burch's Mills is still visible today.

at that time over £3000 worth of logs, of which he feared only one third would reach his mill that winter because of a lack of snow. He went on to complain that the deep declivity of the hill behind his mill was a liability to his business. His petition was refused, and the settlers had no choice but to haul their grain and logs to Burch's Mills, until 1793, when Benjamin Canby and John McGill were given permission to build on a mill site upriver from Burch's.

John McGill was Quartermaster in Governor Simcoe's Queen's Rangers and his wife often dined with Mrs. Simcoe. When Simcoe went on an extended trip, Mrs. McGill came from York to Newark (Niagara) to stay with Mrs. Simcoe while the Governor was away. These close associations gave John McGill an advantage when he applied for permission to build a mill to compete with John Burch's. McGill's partner was Benjamin Canby, a Quaker from Philadelphia, a tanner by trade, who had settled at Newark.

While John Burch had received a lease for 15 years, the Canby-McGill lease was twenty-one years. They built their mill in 1794 on the southern bank of the river, where a branch of the river flowed around the

56

Imagined Aerial View of Niagara Falls, 1827.
A water colour by George Catlin.

Elizabeth McKinsey, in *"Niagara Falls, Icon of the American Sublime"*, wrote that *"Catlin, who was a serious artist and ethnographer... capitalized on Niagara's popularity by constructing a scale model of the Falls and the surrounding area."* It was from this scale model that he painted the scene depicted on this page. The model was displayed in London, England, and advertised as *"representing in perfect relief, proportion, and colour, every house, tree, bridge, rocks..."*

The picture Catlin painted is as he visualized it would appear if he looked down on the scene from above. The area adjacent to the Falls appears well settled; the forest has disappeared, replaced by fenced fields and surprisingly extensive orchards with neatly planted rows of trees. The Niagara Portage Road runs along the right hand side of this view, and from it a road runs down the ravine, present day Murray Hill, to the edge of the gorge bank. This was the first road leading into what is now Queen Victoria Park.

It is possible to locate Forsyth's Pavilion and John Brown's Ontario House, both of them adjacent to the Horseshoe Falls. The Mill Road is shown just above left centre, leading down to the Hollow and the cluster of water powered mills. The buildings depicted at this time would include not only Street's Mills, but also Hardy's tannery, Zeba Gay's nail factory and H. Utley's woodworking shop where he made clock cases.

So successful was this exhibit that P.T. Barnum built an elaborate model of Niagara Falls, complete with running water, and added it to his American Museum and exhibited it in Boston in 1842. Barnum's model was about 6 m (20 feet) in length. The newspapers of the day praised it for its *"mechanical ingenuity"* and perfect illusion.

View of Niagara Falls. Oil on canvas by John Vanderlyn, 1804.
John Vanderlyn made the Falls and the rapids secondary features in this oil painting. A man leading a pair of
oxen pulling a cart is visible at the left, at the top of the Mill Road. Another man on horseback is seen at the right,
travelling down the Mill Road going toward the Hollow, where Burch's Mill - the building on the bank of the river
- is located. There are two Indians, barely discernible at the right, and the eagle perched on the branch of the
dead tree appears ready to take off in search of food.

New York State Office of Parks, Recreation and Historic Preservation, Senate House State Historic Site

embayment we now call the Dufferin Islands. On August 14, 1795 they petitioned the Legislative Council, asking for an extension of their lease to ninety-nine years. They said: "…the Petitioners at a very great expense erected a grist mill and saw mill…and finding that the 21 years lease allowed them will not be time sufficient to indemnify them and praying for a Grant of the fee simple in their tenure or a lease of 999 years."[5] Their request was granted.

François La Rochefoucault-Liancourt, visited the area on June 22, 1795 and left this description of the Canby-McGill Mills in his journal: "About a mile above the falls, two corn-mills and two saw mills have been constructed in a large bason (sic), formed by the river on the left. We examined, with peculiar attention, the most distant of them. It is the most remarkable, chiefly on this account, that the logs that are cut into boards (here), are thrown into the Chippaway Creek near its mouth, and by means of a small lock conveyed into a channel, formed within the bed of the river by a double row of logs of timber, fastened together and floating on the water.

"The breaking of these is prevented by other large balks floating at a certain distance from each other, which form, as it were, an artificial canal. The water retains in this canal the rapidity of the current, and conveys the logs into the lower part of the mill, where by the same machinery that moves the saws, the logs are lifted upon the jack and cut into boards. Only two saws are employed in this mill… On the same principle he has built his corn-mill, which has at present only four courses. The miller's dues for grinding, as fixed by the legislative power, amounts to a twelfth throughout all Upper Canada, and for sawing logs a moiety of the wood sawed."[6]*

Canby and McGill were not interested in staying in the milling business, and soon after they received the outrageous extension of their lease to 999 years, they sold their lease to Phelps and Ramsay. Canby and McGill went on to become land speculators. McGill used his influence with Governor Simcoe to obtain grants of land, which he then sold at a profit. John Burch lost his saw mill business to the more conveniently located Canby-McGill saw mill. Burch

---

* A moiety was one half. The sawmill operator was entitled to one half of the sawn lumber, the product of the sawn logs, as his payment. The miller received one-twelfth of the grist as his share in exchange for grinding the grain.

View of Niagara, The Rapids 1815.
A water colour by William Dunlap.

The artist painted this view from an island in the Niagara River, which was part of the group we now call the Dufferin Islands. Street's Mills, rebuilt after being burned by the American Army in July 1814, are at the left. These Mills were located on the site of Ontario Hydro's present day Toronto Power Generating Station. The building to the right of Street's Mills is John Hardy's Tannery.

sold his mills to Samuel Street Jr. shortly before he died in 1797. Street was in partnership with Thomas Clark, but the mills became known as Street's Mills.

At the same time as La Rochefoucault-Liancourt wrote about the Canby-McGill and Burch Mills in 1795, he noted the presence of an iron mine: "An iron mine too has lately been discovered near Chippawa creek. A company has associated for the working of this mine, and resolved on erecting an iron-forge in the vicinity of the falls."[7]*

A small community consisting of workers' houses grew along the Portage Road, on the high bank above the mills, and Governor Simcoe named it Bridgewater. Phelps and Ramsay soon transferred their lease on the mill site to Maitland McCulloch, who passed it on to James McCulloch, who in turn transferred it to James Durand.[8]

In the fall of 1798, Robert Randall, who had emigrated from Maryland, petitioned the Executive Council for permission to establish an iron works "at or near the waters of the Niagara River, close to the

Austin Morse's Account with General Merchants Ewart McNeilledge and Alexander Richardson, Falls Mills, February 12, 1826.

Falls Mills was the name given to Street's Mills, and the adjacent area in the Hollow. This is the only record of a General Merchant having a store in this area. This store precedes anything that we have on record for Drummondville -the Main and Ferry area. When Morse received this account in late September 1825, he paid 5 shillings on the amount of £2, 4s, 1 3/4 d. McNeilledge and Richardson billed him again almost five months later.

* The iron ore was bog iron or limonite, varying in colour from brown to yellow. This mineral, called hydrated oxide of iron, was present in the marshy, boggy areas along the banks of Chippawa Creek.

*James Thompson's Account with the estate
of the late John Hardy.*

This account begins on May 28, 1818 with one shilling, four pence owed to Hardy. The first item on September 30, 1818, is for tanning a side of Upper hide; in 1820 there was a charge for tanning a side of Sole ''taken not away''. Other items on January 4 and November 12 were for tanning, and dressing skins, with other tanning charges in 1821 and 1822. Of particular interest is the charge in 1826 for processing wool.

According to Ernest Green, ''John Hardy served for eight years as a sergeant in the 84th Regiment, a sergeant of grenadiers.'' He was granted 202 ha (500 acres) of land. He was one of five brothers, and had a wife and four children. After he settled on the west bank he became a lieutenant in the Lincoln Artillery in 1803, and a captain in the 3rd Lincoln Militia in 1809. In 1808 he established his tannery and wool carding mill on the bank of the Niagara River above the Falls, on the site of present day Canadian Niagara Power Rankine Generating Station. He is buried in Drummond Hill Cemetery.

Canby-McGill Mills.''[9] He also asked permission to mine the ''iron ore''. His request was denied at the January 14,1799 meeting of the Council.

Not to be deterred, Randall made an agreement with James Durand, to take over the Bridgewater Mills. Randall, upon fulfilling certain conditions, after a stated period of time,was to become a partner with a one third share in the works. Randall added an iron works with clay furnaces, to the Bridgewater Mills. Randall made what he claimed were the first wrought iron products in Canada. [10] George Heriot, writing in *Travels Through the Canadas* in 1806, said: ''Between the village (Chippawa) and the falls are three mills, the lower for the manufacture of flour; the two upper mills which are near each other and adjoining the road are for the purpose of sawing timber into boards and for manufacturing iron.''

The upper mills were Randall's and at some time after Heriot's visit he added a flour mill and claimed to have ground the first flour in Upper Canada for export. According to Ray Corry Bond, Chippawa's historian, Robert Hamilton of Queenston wrote a letter in 1800 stating that flour ground at Street's Mills, the former Burch Mills located closer to the Falls, had been too moist for export because of the humidity caused by the spray from the Falls. [11]

A map dated 1807 in the National Map Collection in Ottawa, shows a plan for another mill, to be located at the head of the rapids, the site which John Burch had asked for in 1786 and had been refused. Benjamin Hardison of Fort Erie, James Macklem and John Fanning of Chippawa were the petitioners. The petition was granted and a mill was built which became known as Fanning's Mill. It was in operation for only a few years, and the only record we have confirming its existence, was a newspaper item in the *Buffalo Gazette*, Wednesday February 12, 1812 which read'' ''We are sorry to state that the valuable mills of John Fanning Esquire, of Chippawa, were destroyed by fire on Sunday evening last.'' [12]

There is an intriguing mention of a mill at or near this location in Colonel Landmann's journal of his visit in 1798. The bateau which brought Landmann downriver from Fort Erie grounded on a sand bar at the entrance to Chippawa Creek, swung around in the current and drifted downriver toward the rapids. The bateau had a rope with a bar of wood fastened to it, which dragged behind. Fortunately the wood caught between some rocks and became an anchor which stopped the craft from drifting further downriver. Landmann wrote that it had drifted beyond a mill on the shore, and towing it back against the current was a difficult undertaking. [13]

Bridgewater Mills, and Street's Mills operated during the War of 1812-14, until July 26, the day after the Battle of Chippawa, when the Americans occupied the area. The workers left and the mill machinery was shut down, never to be restarted. An article in the *Buffalo Gazette* of August 2, 1814 which summarized the Battle of Bridgewater - the Americans gave the Battle of Lundy's Lane this name,

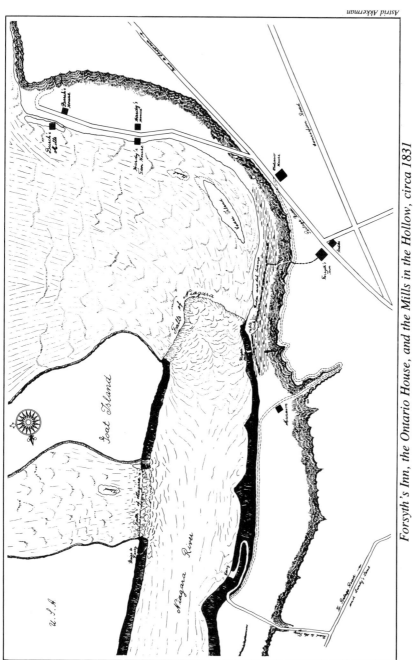

Astrid Akkerman

Forsyth's Inn, the Ontario House, and the Mills in the Hollow, circa 1831

This sketch shows the Portage Road, the Mill Road, Concession Two Road – present day Stanley Street – and the Ferry Road in 1831. Burch's Mills and Hardy's Tan House are shown where they were before the War of 1812-14. Samuel Street purchased Burch's Mills before the war, and they were known as Street's Mills when they were burned by the Americans on July 26, 1814, after the Battle of Lundy's Lane. The pathway leading from Forsyth's Inn – the Pavilion – down to Table Rock is shown. The carriage road along the high bank, leading from John Brown's Ontario House, through Forsyth's property, and down the ravine – present day Murray Hill – to the Ferry is also shown. This 1831 map is the earliest record of the Ferry Road, seen at the far left. The Ferry Road ran from the Portage Road, down the high bank by way of the ravine which is present day Clifton Hill, to the Ferry Landing. The Ferry Road would have been used after 1817 when Clark and Street completed the road identified by the hairpin turn, running down the gorge bank to the Ferry Landing.

Label and instructions on a clock-case manufactured by H.Utley & Co.
Niagara Falls, Upper Canada.

H. Utley & Co. had a water-powered woodworking shop on the bank of the Niagara River, where it flowed around Long Island, near the site of present day William Rankine Generating Station of the Canadian Niagara Power Company. Wooden cases were made here for clock mechanisms imported from Connecticut. The rod with a hook on the end for the pendulum is seen at the top of the picture. The label is almost obscured when the clock's pendulum is in place. Utley Clocks were "Warranted, if well Used". This clock is on display at the Lundy's Lane Historical Museum, Niagara Falls, Ontario.

because Bridgewater was the nearest settlement - contained a paragraph which read: "On the morning of the 26th our forces under Generals Ripley and Porter reconnoitered the enemy near the battle ground, returned and burnt Bridgewater Mills and all the enemy's barracks and the bridge at Chippawa and passed up the river to Fort Erie." [14]

The Bridgewater Mills were not rebuilt after the War of 1812. Randall submitted a War Loss Claim for what he claimed was his one third share of the destroyed mills. Thomas Clark challenged Randall's claim, saying that he had not fulfilled the terms of the agreement. Clark bought the mills from Durand, and

he wrote: "The only shadow of a claim Randall has or can show, is his agreement with Mr. Durand, in whom he ought to apply to if he thinks he has any claim." [15] Randall did not receive any compensation for War Losses.

Just north and downriver from where the branch of the river left the embayment (Dufferin Islands), the river again veered to the west. In times of high water it overflowed its banks and washed against the high bank, eroding it and, bringing down the glacial sand and gravel. When the river's level returned to normal, this soil which it had torn from the high bank, was left spread out evenly, leaving a flat surface. This area

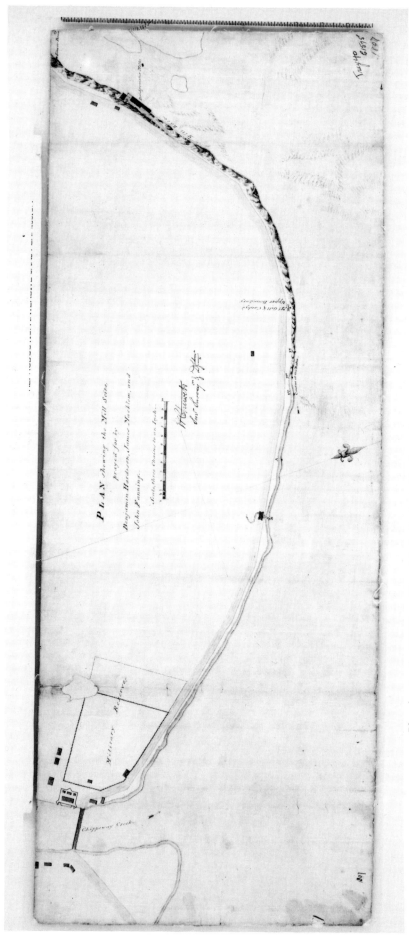

Plan showing the Mill Site petitioned for by Benjamin Hardison, James Macklem, and John Fanning, 1807. NMC 21726

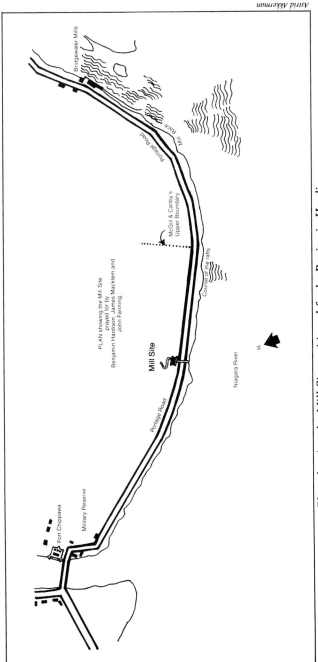

Plan showing the Mill Site petitioned for by Benjamin Hardison,
James Macklem, and John Fanning.

Their petition was granted and the mill was built on the Portage Road, to make use of the water from a small creek which drained the swamp land to the west. The swamp encompassed the area now occupied by the Niagara Parks Rapids View Parking Lot, Marineland, and the land extending west to the Queen Elizabeth Highway. The notation "course of the rafts" indicates that logs for the Bridgewater Mills, shown at the right of the map, were floated down the river, chained together to form a raft. This mill, which was known as Fanning's Mill, was probably only a grist mill. It burned to the ground in February 12, 1812 and was not rebuilt. 1812 and was not rebuilt.

which extends from the northern tip of today's Dufferin Islands, to the Table Rock, was called the Flats, or the Hollow, because it was on a lower level than the land on the high bank.

In the Hollow a branch of the river ran around a small island, and the presence of this constant supply of swiftly running water, available for water power, attracted other pioneer industries. According to historian Ernest Green, "a considerable village grew up on the flat land...populated almost exclusively by the workpeople of the mills and other water-powered industries which were located there." [16]

Around 1808 John Hardy established a tannery, and a wool carding and weaving mill along the banks of the river, opposite the island, which was then called Swayze's Island. In 1826 Zeba Gay established a nail factory near Hardy's Tannery. Here nails were cut from hoop iron at the rate of 270 nails per hour. H. Utley who was a cabinet maker, established a clock factory, where he made wooden clock cases into

Niagara Falls - River and Rapids Above Falls from Street's Road, Canada Side.
From a stereograph by Notman & Fraser, circa 1870.
This stereo view shows Cedar Island - formerly Long Island, (Swayze's Island) - at centre left. The narrow strip of land extending from the southern end of the island, and the Gap are shown. At times of high water, the river inundated this strip of land. The forebay of the Canadian Niagara Power Company's Generating Station was built where the River passed through the Gap. The roadway barely discernible in the bottom of the picture is Street's Road, earlier called the Mill Road.

Niagara Falls Heritage Foundation.

WOOL CARDING

AND

CLOTH DRESSING

THE LEASE of the FALLS FACTORY heretofore granted to Preserved Smith having determined, and the Premises having thereby reverted to the Subscriber as the Proprietor thereof, Notice is hereby given, that the business of the said Factory will be carried on by the undersigned in all its various branches, and under the superintendence and management of JOHN SPENCE, an experienced workman, who will be prepared to execute all orders with punctuality and despatch.

The Subscriber will pay the highest CASH PRICE for good MERCHANTABLE WOOL, delivered at his Factory, and will supply the trade with CASSIMERES, SATINETTS, TWEEDS & FLANNELS, of the best quality and on the most reasonable terms.
                                    THOS. C. STREET.
Niagara Falls, March 19, 1849.

Niagara Chronicle

The Falls Factory - Street's Mills.
This advertisement which appeared in the March 19, 1849 edition of the "Niagara Chronicle", gave notice that Thomas C. Street was once again the proprietor of his mill, which was no longer a water-powered saw and grist mill, but a steam driven wool carding and weaving mill. This mill remained in operation until it was destroyed by fire in 1874 The ruins were not removed until 1894.

which he inserted clock works imported from the United States.

Street's Mills, called the Falls Mills in the mid 1820's, were, according to a statement made by William Hamilton Merritt, "the only Mills from Long Point (on Lake Erie) around to Dundas capable of doing a merchantable business." [17] Samuel Street moved into John Burch's former house, opposite the mills. A fulling and cloth mill were added to Street's Mills. Thomas Clark lived in his house (Clark Hill) on the high bank above the mills built in 1805.

When steam power replaced water power, the mills in the Hollow went into decline. The Falls Mills became known again as Street's Mills, and were leased out to a succession of entrepreneurs, who worked the fulling, cloth weaving and milling operations. In 1874, the mills were known as Walker's Grist Mill and Gillett's Woolen Factory, when on the night of September 30, they were destroyed by fire. Only the blackened ruins of the mills remained when the Queen Victoria Niagara Falls Park Commissioners took over the property in 1885. The ruins were not cleaned up until 1894, thus removing all evidence of the industrial activity which took place in this area which is now parkland.

The Portage Road
Travel, Hotels, Tourism
after the War of 1812

After the end of the War of 1812 travel between the United States and Upper Canada was resumed, but it was a long time before there was a noticeable increase in stagecoach passenger traffic along the Portage Road.

Tourists began to come again to Niagara Falls. Captain Richard Langslow of the East India Company visited here in 1818 and noted that the burning spring was still bubbling up through the water at the former site of the Bridgewater Mills.* James Strachan, Bishop Strachan's brother, toured Upper Canada in 1819 and wrote that he crossed on the ferry below the Falls and that he was a guest at Forsyth's Hotel. This was the first mention of William Forsyth, a man who would make his mark as Niagara Falls' first entrepreneur in the burgeoning tourist business.

Forsyth was not only a hotel owner, but called himself a Coachmaster,with a stagecoach line which in 1820 ran from Buffalo to Black Rock on the American side, then by ferry to Waterloo (present day Fort Erie), then down the river road to Chippawa, and alongthe Portage Road to his hotel at the Falls, then on to Queenston and Niagara.

He was also one of the organizers of the first promotional event carried out at Niagara Falls - sending a derelict sailing ship over the Horseshoe Falls with a cargo of "wild" animals, a promotion conceived as a means of bringing tourists to Niagara Falls in the off season.

Another of Forsyth's achievements was to raise nineteen children, the product of two marriages. But it was his attempt to monopolize the tourist industry at Niagara Falls that brought him into prominence and later brought notoriety.

William Forsyth acquired Wilson's Tavern from Mrs. Wilson in 1817. Not satisfied with providing accommodation for visitors to his establishment, he began to cater to their sightseeing needs. In 1818 he built a covered stairway down the steep gorge cliff at the foot of his property, at the Horseshoe Falls, and the Table Rock. This enabled tourists to reach the river's edge and from there walk behind the sheet of falling water.

* It was Duc de la Rochefoucault-Liancourt who first wrote about the burning spring in 1795. " In the course of last year a sulphurous spring was discovered a few yards distant from the bank of the river, which was, however, filled up by the fall of earth crumbling from its verge. This spring has again shown itself...A stone laid over the spring, prevents its water from being mixed with that of the river. On the approach of a fire-brand the vapour or steam, assumes the colour of burning spirit of wine, and burns down to the bottom. Much time will probably elapse,before an enquiry shall be established, whether this spring be endowed with any medicinal powers." Captain Richard Langslow in 1817 observed that the burning spring was bubbling up from the ruins of the Bridgewater Mills, and added that the flow of gas "was used while the mills existed to light the works below." This is considered to be the first use made of gas for illuminating purposes in Upper Canada. John Goldie, on July 12, 1819 noted that the burning spring had been enclosed. From that time it became a tourist attraction and was from then on mentioned in every guide book.

Royal Ontario Museum

Brown's and Forsyth's Hotels, Niagara, circa 1827.
Water colour over pencil by Lieutenant-Colonel James Pattison Cockburn.
"Brown's Hotel" is on the left and William Forsyth's "Pavilion" is in the centre of this view, taken from the river
bank at the entrance to present day Dufferin Islands. The frame building on the left at the river's edge is the Falls
Mills, or Street's Mills. John Burch built his mill on this site (present day site of the Toronto Power Generating
Station) in 1786, but it was burnt by the American Army on July 26, 1814, after the Battle of Lundy's Lane.

He also began the first row boat ferry service in 1818. He "provided a boat with a constant attendant for the purpose of crossing such visitors and travellers over the River immediately under the Falls." [1] He undertook both of these projects without government approval, and he acknowledged that he had no lease for the ferry and that his "stairs are erected on the chain reserved for military purposes."*

Forsyth's establishment was called the *Niagara Falls Hotel.* In 1820 he advertised in the *Niagara Patriot* of Buffalo: "The subscriber returns his thanks to his friends and the public generally for their patronage, and hopes to merit a continuation of their favours by a strict attention to their accommodations, informed that unfounded reports are in circulation as to his charges, calculated to injure th reputation of his house, to prevent misapprehension, the following list of prices is annexed:

Board - Dinner 50 cents
Breakfast 37 1/2 cents
Lodging 12 1/2 cents
Post Coach Rates of Fare: From Black Rock to the Falls for more than one passenger, $1.50 each - a single passenger $2.00 -Return passage - single passenger $2.00 - for more than one $1.00 each. William Forsyth, Niagara Falls U.C., June 24, 1820." [2]

This advertisement set the tone for future advertising printed under Forsyth's name. He repeated this theme over and over - that rumours were circulating about his charges, etc., and he wanted to answer these scurrilous comments by quoting his prices or giving his side of whatever the current rumour might be. He always gave the impression that someone was maligning him,and that he was innocent of the charges made against him.

* The Chain Reserve also known as the Military Reserve and the Crown Reserve was a strip of land 20 m (66 feet) wide extending inland from the bank of the river. It was set aside for military communication and transport between the lakes. Government ownership of this strip of land along the river, gave the government jurisdiction over who landed a boat on the shore adjacent to the Reserve: over anyone who might encroach on the Reserve's boundaries with a building or fence. There was no military road built along the length of the Reserve and there was no controversy over the ownership of the Reserve until William Forsyth encroached on it beginning with the erection of the stairway and the establishment of the ferry in 1818.

Royal Ontario Museum

Brown's and Forsyth's Hotels, Niagara 1827.
Water colour over pencil by Lieutenant-Colonel James Pattison Cockburn.
The artist used the same title for two different views of the hotels. He was standing at the bottom of the Mill Road, which turned east off the Portage Road opposite "Brown's Hotel" and led down to the Flats, the area below the high bank where Street's Mill, Hardy's tannery, Zeba Gay's nail factory and Utley's clock factory were located. A portion of the Mill Road leading to the Queen Victoria Park area, north of the Canadian Niagara Power Generating Station, is still in existence. It can be reached by the stairway adjacent to the parking lot in front of Our Lady of Peace Roman Catholic Church.

In 1821 Forsyth purchased the land on which the *Niagara Falls Hotel* (formerly Wilson's Tavern) stood, from Thomas Dickson.[3] He made improvements to the facilities he bought from Mrs. Wilson. Dr. John Bigsby stayed there in 1822 and left this assessment of the Forsyths as hosts and their establishment. "They were primitive folks, but being very careful and shrewd they passed the world as rich. They paid their guests small worship and could be exceedingly harsh or bitter to the highest; but the gentle and quiet had good entertainment, old fashioned talk or none, according to the humour, wholesome food and white sheets. Their place might have been an old farm house in Worcestershire. The house was low, with little windows and lozenge shaped panes. It has been small but had been added to as the family increased and therefore showed a deal of roof. Cowhouses, stables and pigstyes hung close around. There it stood with an orchard of mossy fruit trees on one side and large forest trees on the other, the public road (Portage

Road) in the rear."[4]

When you visit the Falls View area again try to visualize Forsyth's *Niagara Falls Hotel* and its outbuildings in the area of Oakes Drive and the Minolta Tower. The reference "…it has been small but has been added to as the family increased" is understood when we remember that the Forsyths had nineteen children to care for in addition to their guests.

William Forsyth had no competition in the hotel business until 1820, when John Brown, who had previously operated *John Brown's Mansion House* in Niagara, built the *Ontario House,* located on the high bank, just south of Forsyth. The *Ontario House,* also known as *Brown's Hotel* was on the southwest corner of present day Livingston Street and Oakes Drive, on the Loretto property. The threat of this competition forced Forsyth to tear down the *Niagara Falls Hotel* and on the site, in 1822, he built a new hotel which he called the *Pavilion.*

Pavilion Hotel at Niagara, circa 1830.
Water colour over pencil by Lieutenant-Colonel J.P.Cockburn.
William Forsyth built the "Pavilion Hotel" in 1822-23 on the former site of Wilson's Tavern. (Today this site is occupied by the Minolta Tower). Forsyth had recently added the rear wing, with galleries, called piazzas, which ran along the east side of the hotel, overlooking the Horseshoe Falls and the Upper Rapids. The road visible at the right is the Portage Road. Across the road from the "Pavilion", Forsyth had stables where he kept riding horses for hire.

For the next ten years until 1836 the *Pavilion* was the foremost hotel at the Falls, a centre where entertainments and community activities such as election meetings, town meetings and dances were held, as well as a place of public accommodation. Today Oakes Inn on Buchanan Avenue and the new hotel presently under construction (1989) located on the northeast corner of Livingston Street and Oakes Drive, occupy the locations overlooking the Horseshoe Falls and the Upper Rapids which the *Pavilion* and the *Ontario House* did then.

The *Ontario House* with its colonnaded front and the three-storey white clap-boarded *Pavilion* stood out on the high bank above the Horseshoe Falls.* The *Pavilion* had galleries, called piazzas, which ran along the east side of the hotel, overlooking the Falls and the Upper Rapids. The pillars supporting these galleries were covered with graffiti - quaint devices written in pencil, original thoughts and impressions in rhyme and prose. Many newly married couples had carved their names,entwined in love knots on the pillars. Evidently Forsyth tolerated this age old impulse of tourists to leave their mark for posterity.

For a time there was nothing comparable to the *Ontario House* and the *Pavilion* on the American side. According to Ernest Green, Niagara Falls historian, "All travellers of respectability arriving at the Falls on either side became guests of the *Ontario House* or the *Pavilion.* [5]

John Brown was a worthy competitor. He advertised that "A new and convenient pathway has been made from his House to the Table Rock, and

* A letter signed *Notes from a Traveller,* which was really an anonymous letter from William Forsyth, appeared in the *Colonial Advocate,* on May 11, 1827. It described the *Pavilion.* "Mr. Forsyth's elegant house, or rather his castle, (for it is in size and splendour far beyond any house in the colony) is built on the highest and most commanding ground in the immediate neighbourhood of the Falls, its roof, on which the stranger may walk with safety, towers a full 350 feet above the level of the waters under the cataract.

"In one of the rooms of this immense building 100 persons may dine with ease. In the front and rear of each story (sic) are piazzas supported by massive pillars; the wings built last season are chiefly filled with bedrooms. There is ample accommodation at the Niagara Falls 'Pavilion' for noblemen and gentlemen...The gay and happy may here spend many a cheerful hour, and the best physicians have prescribed the high and healthful air of this neighbourhood to the invalid with much success. I saw à billiard table fitting up, in a large well lighted apartment. "A Letter from a Traveller", *The Colonial Advocate,* May 31, 1827.

Niagara Falls from Brown's Hotel, 1821.
Watercolour on paper, by Ralph Gore.

There is traffic, a carriage and two men on horseback travelling along the Portage Road in this water colour. The Mill Road to the Flats on the lower level, turns off and is visible at the bottom right. There are no close-up views of "Brown's Hotel" as it was impossible for an artist to get the hotel in perspective as the distance from its verandah to the edge of the high bank was too short. "Brown's Hotel" was located on the southwest corner of Livingstone Avenue and present day Oakes Drive, where the Loretto lawn is now.

The New York Historical Society

thence to the Stairs." The "Stairs" were no doubt Forsyth's stairway built in 1818. He went on to say "...this improvement will save some distance, in crossing from his House to the American Shore." He began a stage coach service in competition with Forsyth and offered: "Good Carriages and careful drivers, will at all times, be in readiness to convey his customers and others, to any part of the country on as low terms as any others. A stage will run regularly every day, from his House to the *Mansion House at Niagara. Niagara Falls U.C.''*[6]

Forsyth's main stagecoach line ran from Buffalo to Niagara Falls, but Brown's competition on the Niagara Falls to Niagara route obviously didn't affect Forsyth's business, because Ernest Green wrote in *The Niagara Portage Road:* "At this period (1821) the passenger carrying business on the Portage Road was so profitable that enterprising citizens of the States came over to participate in it. In 1822, after a petition by Forsyth and others, the Provincial Legislature prohibited aliens from engaging in such traffic."[7]

Forsyth made improvements and added amenities to match Brown's. He had riding horses available. His establishment grew in size and value. He estimated "the value of the whole being, perhaps not less than fifty thousand dollars, included in the hotel, coaches, stages, horses, etc." Forsyth's business began to suffer as a result of Brown's competition, and in 1823, Forsyth cut off the access road along the top of the high bank, along which Brown's guests had travelled by carriage to the Ferry - he built a blacksmith shop at th edge of the high bank, astride the road.

This blacksmith shop did not cut off Brown's access to the Table Rock, as Brown built a path down the high bank in front of his hotel, and laid out a plank walk

- single broad planks supported by rocks, - which led over the swampy terrain on the lower level, to the Horseshoe Falls and Table Rock. As Table Rock and the crest of the Horseshoc Falls were directly in front of Forsyth's *Pavilion* property, Forsyth's next move was to erect a high rail fence enclosing the Chain Reserve in front of his property, This fence prevented the public from approaching the bank at the Horseshoe Falls, except to those persons Forsyth permitted to go through his premises, to reach the bank of the river.

John Brown complained to the Lieutenant-Governor, Sir Peregrine Maitland, that the fence was on the Chain Reserve and that Forsyth therefore had

Brown's Hotel circa 1830.

This sketch by Carol Breton, a contemporary artist and sketcher, is her conception of "Brown's Hotel" circa 1830. Details are based on several existing but very distant views of the Hotel.

Carol Breton

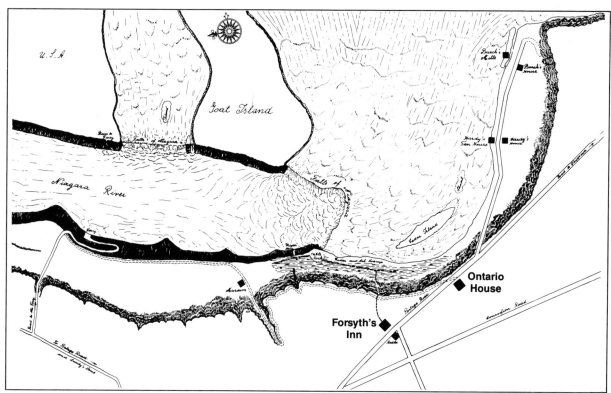

Map Of The Falls Of Niagara, circa 1830.
A combination of two early maps from the Archives of Ontario.

The "Ontario House" formerly John Brown's hotel, and "Forsyth's Inn" usually called the "Pavilion" are located on this map. The path to the Table Rock leads down the high bank from the "Pavilion" and then through the cedar and ash swamp, where a plank walk was laid, to the Table Rock. This swampy area was inundated during periods of high water. A carriage road begins at the "Ontario House", runs along the high bank, down the ravine, then along the top of the gorge to the ferry landing. From 1818 to 1827 this road was the only route to the row boat ferry to the United States. In 1827, Clark and Street built a carriage road down the gorge bank, to the ferry dock. It was then that the Ferry Road, leading from the intersection of the Portage Road and Lundy's Lane to the ferry, came into use. The stairway at Table Rock was being managed at this time by Mr. Wright. Thomas Barnett's Museum, established in an abandoned distillery, is at the bottom of the ravine.

A View From An Open Window Of The "Pavilion Hotel".
From "Aussich Auf Den Niagara Falls", pub. 1850, Winckelmann & Sohne, Berlin.

A weary tourist rests in his room at the Pavilion, oblivious to the beauty of his surroundings. The Horseshoe Falls is seen in the distance.

no right to cut off access to the Horseshoe Falls. Maitland agreed and Forsyth was warned to remove the fence, which he refused to do. What happened next provided the basis for a civil action with Forsyth suing the Provincial Government for the destruction of his property.

Lieutenant-Governor Sir Peregrine Maitland, instead of resorting to legal means, ordered Captain Philpotts of the Royal Engineers to remove the fence. Philpotts, with a fatigue party of engineers (an unarmed work party) on May 18, 1827, went on Forsyth's land, and in spite of his protests, tore down the fence "leaving exposed his growing crops and destroyed his blacksmith's shop". [8]

Forsyth had the fence rebuilt and a second time, Captain Philpotts and his men, under orders from the Lieutenant-Governor, tore down the fences. For these two acts of trespass Forsyth brought civil actions against the Government.

This turmoil had an adverse effect on Forsyth's business, and on May 10, 1827, using a pen name, in his *Notes from a Traveller* in the *Colonial Advocate,* he gave this account of the affair. "Major-General Maitland and Lord Dalhousie, truly appreciating Mr. F.'s unceasing endeavours to improve and adorn the environs of the great natural curiosity, are very liberal and kind to him, and while I was at the Falls, Mr. Philpot (sic) a British military engineer was, by his Excellency's orders, measuring the grounds and affording every possible facility to the owner of the *Pavilion* to put down a new flight of stairs leading below the Falls on the unoccupied government reservation, free for the use of the public. This is generous, and in perfect unison with General Maitland's conduct on all occasions." [9] This was a self serving account concocted by Forsyth to obscure what really happened.

Forsyth's challenging authority, worked against Forsyth's interests. The ferry rights were taken away from him, and he lost his right to the stairway when in 1827 Clark and Street were given an exclusive lease to the Chain at the Horseshoe Falls.

At the same time, his rival John Brown was having difficulty. On February 27, 1827 Forsyth wrote another skilfully crafted *Letter from a Traveller* to the *Upper Canada Gazette.* The editor was not deceived and carried it as an advertisement.

The letter read in part: "Brown's House was burnt last fall (1826) by some accident while occupied by a son of F.'s (William Forsyth Jr. was evidently managing the hotel). The building was insured as I understand for $8,000 and Forsyth's son was the great sufferer, having lost much of his furniture, etc. Since that time Brown has built an elegant house, also called *Ontario House* on or near the same place where his former one stood, which could not discredit any place on either frontier... but the most ungenerous, unjust, and infamous reports have been circulated, (by some malicious evil minded person, or persons as yet unknown) throwing out insinuations, that he (Forsyth) was privy to the burning of the house of Brown and subsequently destroyed his harness, etc." [10]

In spite of this controversy, Forsyth and Brown joined with Parkhurst Whitney Keeper of the *Eagle Hotel,* on the American side in staging the first stunt, organized and promoted with the avowed purpose of attracting tourists to Niagara Falls. On August 2,1827 they advertised "that on September 8 th 'The Pirate Michigan' will pass the Great Rapids and the Falls with a Cargo of Ferocious Animals." The event was a huge success in as much as it attracted thousands of visitors who would not otherwise have come to Niagara Falls.

Through all these controversies the *Pavilion* continued to be not only Niagara Falls' premier hotel, but also the centre for local events. William Lyon Mackenzie, the publisher of the *Colonial Advocate* reported on the election held at the Pavilion during the period of July 24 to 31, 1824, where four representatives from the County of Lincoln were chosen for the Upper Canada Legislative Assembly.* "The splendid hotel of Mr. Forsyth with its luscious signboard, was the central point of attraction" wrote Mackenzie.

He characterized the electors as "an assemblage as motley, as varied in its materials, as the four quarters of the world could afford to send together." He classified them by religion, race and personalities, occupations, equipages and hats. Not wanting to say anything complimentary, he ended by saying that "The speeches had nothing extraordinary, either in matter or manner...they fairly drowned out the cataract." [11]. Mackenzie was a great supporter of Forsyth, as both of them were fighting the government.

In October 1829, Forsyth participated in another promotion, organized to entice visitors to Niagara Falls in the off season. "The landlords of the hotels got up a 'variety of shows'." Forsyth, for his part, received permission to blast off overhanging ledges

* After six days' polling, four candidates were elected as representatives of the County of Lincoln. They were John Clark, Robert Randall, Bartholomew C. Beardsley and John J. Lefferty. Until 1856 Lincoln County encompassed the whole of the Niagara Peninsula. That year, it was split into two counties, the southern half of the peninsula became Welland County, and the remainder in the northern part of the peninsula remained as Lincoln County.

View of Niagara, 1815, from the Banks above the Stone House.
Water colour by William Dunlop.

It is this old distillery at the bottom of the ravine, in present day Queen Victoria Park, where Thomas Barnett established his first museum in 1826. The stone building had been abandoned. A distillery was located here because there was an abundant supply of water from a spring which came out of the base of the high bank at this point. John Maude wrote in his "Visit to the Falls of Niagara in 1800": "Descending a very steep and difficult road, I came to a deserted distillery, where I stopped to recover my breath, and to allay my thirst at an excellent spring." This spring continued to flow for many years after the establishment of Queen Victoria Park.

The American Falls as first seen from the Ravine near Forsyth's Inn, Niagara Falls.
Brown wash over pencil, John Elliot Woolford, circa 1830's.

The unspoiled natural beauty of the ravine (present day Murray Hill) leading to the lower level at the gorge bank, is shown in this sketch. The wooden, fence-like structure is probably associated with the stairway down the gorge wall, which Thomas Barnett built after he established his museum in 1826, just to the left at the end of the ravine. A carriage track is visible in the centre foreground. Carriages travelled along the edge of the high bank from "Brown's Hotel" and the "Pavilion", down the ravine and then along the edge of the gorge wall, to the ladder above the ferry landing, before the Ferry Road (present day Clifton Hill) was used.

of rock along the top of the gorge. William Leete Stone who witnessed the event wrote: " It was a sorry affair". [12] The main attraction for this three day program took place on October 10 when Sam Patch leapt from a 33.5m (110 foot) ladder placed on the river bank below Goat Island, into the river. This is acknowledged to be the first Niagara stunt performed by a human.

James Morden wrote about an unusual event which occurred during a dance held at the *Pavilion* in the early 1830's. The event was reported in the local newspaper. "A gay dance was in progress and the music arose with its voluptuous swell and all went merry as a marriage bell, when suddenly the windows of the dance hall crashed in and the lamps were extinguished by the incoming gusty winds. The hall was plunged into darkness. The revellers were suddenly seized with consternation and alarm, not having the slightest idea as to the cause. Doubtless many a one in his imagination detected the 'handwriting on the wall'.

"What was the cause of this sudden pandemonium? Merely this - a flock of ducks in their migration were attracted by the bright lights and swerved from their course. Dazzled by the glare, they struck the windows with sufficient force to smash them, the noise of which and the sudden darkness terrorized the merrymakers." [13]

Carol Breton (from an earlier sketch)

Sam Patch and his LEAP at the FALLS, 1829.
Sam Patch became Niagara's first stunter on October 10, 1829, when he jumped from the 33.5m (110 foot) ladder depicted in this sketch, into the Niagara River below Goat Island. Sam described his talent for jumping as an Aero-Nautical Feat. He jumped at Niagara Falls again on October 17. The next year he set up a higher platform at Rochester, New York, beside the Genesee Falls. He made one successful jump, then tried another but this time he did not surface. His body was never found.

Ontario Archives

Sam Patch's Leap.
An advertisement of Sam Patch's intended leap at the Falls of Niagara. From the "Colonial Advocate" October 15, 1829. This advertisement was reproduced from William Lyon Mackenzie's own copy of his newspaper. The "X" marks are to inform the compositor that the ad was to be removed from the next issue.

Sam Patch and His Leap

Sam Patch and his Leap - A Variety of Events.

In the Fall of 1829, William Forsyth asked Lieutenant-Governor John Colborne's permission to set off a series of explosions along the edge of the gorge, to blow off pieces of rock which extended, unsupported, out over the gorge and so were unsafe. Part of the ledge of Table Rock was included in this plan. This "blasting-off fete" was to be part of a "variety of events" planned to bring visitors to the Falls. It was another promotion like that of "The Pirate Michigan".

William Leete Stone was visiting at the time and wrote: "It was during the sixth of October, that the landlords, on both sides of the river got up a variety of shows...supposed to collect a multitude of people together on both shores, and thus give them some additional business...For this purpose several rocks were blasted off at various points of the rocks overhanging the gulf. But it was a sorry affair...Several thousands of people however, collected on both sides, many of whom probably had never before had curiosity enough to see the Falls themselves - if even they saw them now." While Stone looked with disdain on this "stunt" he remarked: "The descent and wreck of the vessel among the rapids was an interesting spectacle." Perhaps another "Michigan" was sent over the Falls?

On Wednesday October 7, however, the first stunt involving a human being took place, when Sam Patch jumped from a ladder into the Niagara River below Goat Island. William Lyon Mackenzie reported the event in the "Colonial Advocate". "The celebrated Sam Patch (he became a celebrity when he jumped into the Passaic River, in 1827) actually leaped over the Falls of Niagara into the vast abyss below." This statement casts doubt as to whether Mackenzie was present, as the facts tell us otherwise.

A ladder 27.4m (90 feet) high was set up along the bank of the river below Goat Island, with a short platform extending out from it. At the appointed time, Sam, dressed in white, climbed a ladder, walked out with great deliberation to the end of the platform, and putting his hands close to his sides, jumped into the river. According to Mackenzie, who still didn't have the stunt in proper perspective: "Sam Patch has immortalized himself - he has done what mortal never did before - he has propelled himself eighty-five feet in one leap into the cavern of Niagara's Cataract; and survives the romantic feat, uninjured!!!!"

At least Mackenzie got the height of the jump correct, but jumping into the Niagara River below Goat Island isn't the "Shoe of the Horseshoe - ...the mighty cavern of Niagara's Cataract." Sam did "immortalize himself" as he is on record as Niagara's first stunter. His mortality surfaced, when after repeating his Niagara jump successfully, he drowned later that October after leaping into the Genesee River at Rochester, New York. This sketch originally appeared in "The Niagara Daredevils" by Karl S. Brong.

"Superior"

In September 1831, an attempt was made to repeat the "Michigan's" trip over the Horseshoe Falls. An old hulk called the "Superior" was purchased by a group of promoters and it was advertised that she would be sent over the Horseshoe Falls. The "Superior" was launched in 1822, and outfitted with the steam engine from the "Walk in the Water" – the first steamboat to sail on Lake Erie – making the "Superior" the second steamboat on the Niagara River and Lake Erie.

This time there were no animals on board.

On the appointed day, with a large crowd gathered to see the event, the ship was set adrift in the upper river. The "Superior" struck one of the islands a short distance from the brink and grounded. The crowd left, disappointed. No one was around when high water refloated the "Superior" and she went over the Falls, and was smashed to pieces.

The Pirate, MICHIGAN,

WITH A CARGO OF FEROCIOUS ANIMALS, WILL PASS THE GREAT RAPIDS AND THE FALLS OF

NIAGARA,

8TH SEPTEMBER, 1827, AT 3 O'CLOCK.

THE first passage of a vessel of the largest class which sails on Erie and the Upper Lakes, through the Great Rapids, and over the stupendous precipice at Niagara Falls, it is proposed to effect, on the 8th of September next.

The *Michigan* has long braved the billows of Erie, with success, as a merchant vessel; but having been *condemned* by her owners as unfit to sail longer proudly "*above;*" her present proprietors, together with several publick spirited friends, have appointed her to convey a cargo of Living Animals of the Forests, which surround the Upper Lakes, through the white tossing, and the deep rolling rapids of the Niagara, and down its grand precipice, into the basin "*below.*"

The greatest exertions are making to procure Animals of the most ferocious kind, such as Panthers, Wild Cats, Bears, and Wolves; but in lieu of some of these, which it may be impossible to obtain, a few vicious or worthless Dogs, such as may possess considerable strength and activity, and perhaps a few of the toughest of the Lesser Animals, will be added to, and compose, the cargo.

Capt. *James Rough*, of Black Rock, the oldest navigator of the Upper Lakes, has generously volunteered his services to manage this enterprise, in which he will be seconded by Mr. *Levi Allen*, mate of the Steamboat *Niagara*—the publick may rest assured that they will select none but capable assistants. The manager will proceed seasonably with experiments, to ascertain the most practicable and eligible point, from which to detach the Michigan for the Rapids.

It is intended to have the *Michigan* fitted up in the style in which she is to make her splendid but perilous descent, at *Black Rock*, where she now lies. She will be dressed as a *Pirate*; besides her *Menagerie* of Wild Animals, and probably some tame ones, it is proposed to place *a Crew* (in effigy) at proper stations on board. The Animals will be caged or otherwise secured and placed on board the "*condemned Vessel*," on the morning of the 7th, at the Ferry, where the curious can examine her with her '*cargo,*' during the day, at a trifling expense. On the morning of the 8th, the Michigan will be towed from her position at *Black Rock*, to the foot of Navy Island, by the Steamboat *Chippewa*, from whence she will be conducted by the Manager to her last moorings. Passage can be obtained in the Michigan from *Black Rock* to *Navy Island*, at *half a Dollar* each.

Should the Vessel take her course through the *deepest of the Rapids*, it is confidently believed, that she will reach the *Horse Shoe*, unbroken: if so, she will perform her voyage, *to the water in the Gulf beneath*, which is of great depth and buoyancy, entire; *but what her fate may be, the trial will decide.* Should the Animals be young and hardy, and *possessed of great muscular powers*, and *joining their fate* with that of the Vessel, remain on board until she reaches the waters below, there is great probability that many of them, will *have performed the terrible jaunt, unhurt!*

Such as may survive, and be retaken, will be sent to the Museums at New York and Montreal, and some perhaps to London.

It may be proper to observe, that several Steamboats are expected to be in readiness at *Buffalo*, together with numerous Coaches, for the conveyance of Passengers down, on the morning of the 8th. Coaches will leave *Buffalo*, at 2 o'clock, on the afternoon of the 7th, for the Falls on both sides of the River, for the convenience of those who may be desirous of securing accommodations at the Falls on the 8th. Ample means for the conveyance of Visitors, will be provided at *Tonawanta*, at *Lockport*, at *Lewiston*, at *Queenston*, and at *Fort George*, to either side.

As no probable estimate can now be made, of the numbers which the proposed exhibition may bring together; great disappointments, regarding the extent of our accommodations, may possibly be anticipated by some; in respect to which, we beg leave to assure our respective friends and the publick in general, that, in addition to our own, which are large, (and will on the occasion be furnished to their utmost limits,) there are other Publick Houses, besides many private ones, at which comfortable entertainment can be had, for all who may visit the Falls on the present occasion—an occasion which will for its novelty and the remarkable spectacle it will present, be unequalled in the annals of *internal* navigation.

August 2, 1827.

P. WHITNEY, *Keeper of Eagle Hotel, United States Falls.*

WM. FORSYTH, } *Keepers of the Ontario House and*
JOHN BROWN, } *Pavilion, Canada Falls.*

The Pirate Michigan, a broadside advertisement.

Buffalo and Erie County Historical Society

The Pirate Michigan

William Forsyth of the ''Pavilion Hotel'' and John Brown of the ''Ontario House'' were arch rivals in the hotel business. They co-operated when they participated, along with General Parkhurst Whitney of the ''Eagle Hotel'' on the American side, in the first stunt at Niagara Falls - planned as an event that would bring visitors here, just to see the event.

The ''Niagara Falls Gazette'' on January 6, 1875, reprinted the reminiscences of a correspondent of the Louisville ''Courier Journal'' who wrote to that newspaper with an account of the event, the day after it occurred. The letter was printed in the ''Courier Journal'' on December 10, 1874. The following is taken from the letter.

''A Mr. Frazier was the owner of the largest schooner sailing the lakes, the 'Michigan'. The schooner was old and 'being somewhat decayed in her upper works', Frazier wanted to get rid of the vessel. He hit on a novel idea - that of 'testing the fate of a vessel, that by accident might approach too near the stupendous cataract of Niagara', and to add interest to the event, 'the fate of animals that might be caught in the rapids of these swift rolling waters and carried over the Falls.'''

It was a cruel and unfeeling plan, one that could only have been contemplated at a time when there was no respect for animal life. Frazier, who was from New York City, persuaded Forsyth, Brown and Whitney to purchase the ''Michigan''. Frazier convinced them that they would be well repaid by the business from the people who would be attracted by the event. They did not underestimate the intelligence of their potential audience, the event was to become a huge success.

William Lyon Mackenzie came to see the event and wrote in the ''Colonial Advocate''. ''The day was very favourable, and every steamboat, schooner, and stage coach, which could be had within many miles of the Falls were in motion, as well as waggons and other vehicles beyond calculation - the roads to the Falls in very direction were like the approaches to Yorkshire Fair and perhaps there were eight or ten thousand persons on the spot by one o'clock, including show men with wild beasts, gingerbread people, cake and beer stalls, wheel of fortune men, etc.''

The ''Courier Journal'' correspondent wrote: ''On Saturday morning Buffalo itself seemed to be moving in a mass towards the grand point of attraction.'' Five steamboats, the ''Henry Clay'', ''William Penn'', ''Pioneer''. ''Niagara'' and ''Chippawa'', being all the steamers on Lake Erie, except the ''Superior'' were pressed into service. The ''Chippawa'' towed the ''Michigan'' as far as Yate's landing on the Canada shore, ''within three miles of the Falls''. The ''Chippawa'' and the ''William Penn'' landed their passengers there. The other three steamers landed their passengers at Schlosser on the American side.

Then at 3 o'clock the ''Michigan'' was towed by a yawl manned by ''five oarsmen of stout hearts and strong arms''. She was cut loose one quarter of a mile from the first rapids, and the oarsmen had to ''pull for their lives to effect their own safety.'' The ''Michigan'' with: ''...an American ensign flying from her bowsprit and the British Jack displayed at her stern'' navigated the first rapid. On passing over the second rapid ''her masts went by the board...affording those who had never witnessed a shipwreck, a specimen of the sudden destruction of the spars of a ship at sea in case of a wreck.'' On passing over the third rapid she bilged (filled with water when her bottom was holed) and turned broadside, then was swung around by the current, and went over the Falls stern first. In the fall the ''Michigan'' was ''dashed into a thousand pieces.''

What of the animals? It would be interesting to know how many of those witnessing this sick event came to see the destruction of the ship and how many came to see the animals go to their deaths. The correspondent wrote about them, almost as an afterthought: ''They consisted of a buffalo from the Rocky Mountains, three bears...two foxes, a raccoon, a dog, a cat and four geese.''

When the ''Michigan'' was cast off the animals were loose on deck except for the buffalo which was in a pen. Two of the bears, not liking the situation, left the vessel after it hit the first rapid and swam to the Canadian shore, where ''they were taken''. Taken was a euphemism for shot. The buffalo was seen to go over the Falls and was not seen again.

What became of the other animals is not known. One of the bears was seen climbing the ''Michigan's'' mast as it entered the rapids. The foxes, raccoon, dog and cat were seen to be running up and down the deck as the vessel went over the Falls. Two of the geese were the only living things that passed over the Falls and were retrieved unhurt.

There was some criticism of this wanton display of cruelty to animals, but the defenders of this promotion explained that "...the brutes were vicious, and had to be killed anyway." The event was a huge success. The estimate of the assembled crowd ranged from 10,000 to 30,000 people. The "Courier Journal" correspondent wrote: "...you may judge the situation of affairs, when I assure you that I stopped at Forsyth's ('Pavilion') about 4 p.m., and was unable to obtain a cracker or a glass of water."

Theodora Vinal in "Niagara Portage" wrote of an event on the American side, in which one of the potential profiteers got his just deserts. "One tavern keeper had anticipated a big profit from that day. So many were to be fed that he had spread tables along the river bank - at least that is how the tale goes. The 'Michigan' being a bit late, and dinner ready, the host urged his guests to be seated. He neglected to collect his fifty cents in advance. Just as the diners were finishing their meal and before they had settled their checks, loud huzzas announced that the schooner was riding the rapids. Every single person, all full of nice unpaid-for food, stampeded to the river's edge, and never came back. The hotel lost money that afternoon."

Horseshoe Fall from the Canadian Side .
Pencil drawing by Edwin Whitfield, circa 1834.

Barnett's Museum

Thomas Barnett's Museum at the Table Rock, is in the bottom centre of this sketch. One of Niagara Falls oldest attractions, the present day Niagara Falls Museum, was founded by Thomas Barnett in 1826. Thomas Barnett was born near Birmingham, England in 1799 and at the age of 25 emigrated to the United States. It is not known under what circumstances, but he was induced by Sir Peregrine Maitland, then Lieutenant-Governor of Upper Canada, to settle in Niagara Falls, on the Canadian side.

In 1826 he established a museum which he called Barnett's Museum, in a stone building located on the north side of present day Murray Hill in Queen Victoria Park. The building had been a distillery and in 1826 was deserted. The area from a few hundred yards south of the ravine, past the crest of the Horseshoe Falls was a cedar and ash swamp and it was impossible to reach the Falls from that point. For that reason Barnett laid out a road along the top of the gorge bank, (from the ravine) to a point just beyond the crest of the Horseshoe Falls.

The next year, 1827, he erected a stone building about 91m (300 feet) south of the Table Rock. The building had a broad verandah that extended across the front and an outside stairway which led to the roof where there was a covered observation deck, with open sides. His intention was to use the building as a residence, and a museum, but he found the location too damp for a residence. It was used as a museum and an observation point. He obtained permission to cross the Chain Reserve and built a stairway down the gorge wall, just south of and adjacent to, the stairway built by William Forsyth, at that time operated by Clark and Street and managed by a Mr. Wright.

In Barham's ''Descriptions of Niagara'' there is a description of Barnett's Museum at this location, circa 1840. ''A few yards from this staircase (Wright's), and very beautifully situated, is Mr. Barnett's Museum of natural and artificial curiosities - an establishment well worthy of patronage. The rooms are arranged tastefully, so as to represent a forest scene, and contain upwards of 5,000 specimens of various kinds and descriptions. There are bipeds and quadrupeds; birds, fishes, insects, reptiles, shells, minerals and Indian curiosities; all regulated to delight the eye and improve the understanding and mend the heart. Of the birds, beasts, fishes and insects, several hundred species were caught in the vicinity of the Falls. The noblest eagles of the land delight to hover around the Falls, and here they are frequently killed, stuffed and offered for sale. A large collection of living rattlesnakes may also be seen here. Mr Barnett also keeps an excellent house of refreshments, and a large assortment of Indian curiosities and geological specimens for sale, and is very polite and attentive to visitors. One of the very best general views of the Falls is to be obtained from the piazzas of this Museum, and a view through a prism, which is kept here, is extremely beautiful and interesting.''

He was well regarded in the community and his museum was always praised in travellers' accounts. A visitors' register was kept at the museum so that impressions and comments could be reported. One entry read:

''The best remark is silence. - G.
Then pray, why do you 'break it'? - H.
For the same reason that you do;
Because, 'tis hard to speak it. - Y.
On memory's page two things will never fade -
Niagara Falls and Barnett's 'lemonade'.''
''Table Rock Album'', Buffalo, New York, 1859

Barnett built a new museum in 1859 on the site of present day Victoria Park Restaurant and moved his exhibits there. The specimens and exhibits which were in his museum have been on display ever since Barnett's time and are to be found today in the Niagara Falls Museum on River Road in Niagara Falls, Ontario, just north of the Rainbow Bridge. Barnett's was the first museum in North America, predating such museums as the Smithsonian and the Royal Ontario Museum. Thomas Barnett died at Niagara Falls, New York in February 1899, at ninety years of age.

Niagara Falls
MUSEUM.
Near Table Rock.

The Proprietor, most grateful for the liberal support he has received from the Ladies and Gentlemen visiting the Falls, begs leave most respectfully to announce to them, that his collection has undergone an entire alteration this Spring, and a numerous variety of fresh specimens have been added to the rooms, the arrangement of which gives the highest satisfaction to the most learned from all parts of the world. The GALLERIES are classically arranged with the rarest and finest specimens the Country can produce. The Collection contains

AN ENTIRE FOREST SCENERY,

Arranged with such taste as to display the nature of every object; exhibiting most of the native Birds and Animals, with their nests and young ones; and showing the voracity of others when seizing their prey. In this splendid collection of natural and artificial curiosities will be found upwards of five thousand interesting specimens, principally collected in this vicinity; and it must be gratifying to visitors to become acquainted with the Birds, Quadrupeds, Reptiles, Fish from Lakes Ontario and Erie, Lake Shells, Insects, Plants, Minerals, Indian Curiosities, &c. that are found in this part of America, including the finest specimens of the Bald Eagle, with all the Falcon order, an extensive variety of rare and beautiful specimens of the Duck and Diver tribe, a great Family of Owls, and a vast variety of other species of rare and fine-plumaged Birds.

QUADRUPEDS,

Comprising the Moose (the largest species of the Deer tribe,) a white Virginia Deer, a Pied Deer, with a large specimen of the common color, the Lynx, Wild Cat, Red and Grey Wolves, many different varieties of Foxes, Porcupines, Oppossums, Otters, Beavers, Marmots, Skunks, Racoons, Muskrats, and a great variety of Hares and Rabbits, Martins or Sables, Ermines, Squirrels of all colors, radiated Moles, White Rats, Mice, &c.

RATTLE SNAKES, AND A NUMBER OF BIRDS AND ANIMALS, ALIVE.

Some very interesting skeletons;—the Eagle, Humming Bird, Rattle Snake, Ducks, Divers, Birds and Animals, of various kinds. Many singular deformities;—a calf with a large protuberance from the head, a Lamb of the same nature, a Chicken with four legs, and one with four legs and four wings, a Goslin with four legs, and many deformities of the Deer's Horn. Bark of trees worn by the natives in different parts of the world. Fine specimens of the saw of the sawfish, and sword of the Swordfish; jaws of a Shark, the Whip of a Sea Spider. A number of different species of Foreign Fish.

A rich collection of Roman, Greek, Egyptian and Polish Coins, some of them upwards of three thousand years old.

A numerous variety of rare and beautiful Birds, Animals, Reptiles, Sea Shells, Minerals, Fossils, Indian Curiosities, &c. from all parts of the world; among which are worthy of notice, a fine specimen of the Barbary Lion, the largest ever imported to this country, a Jackal, (the Lion's Provider,) the Glutton, Civet, Antelope or Gazelle, Agouti, Coatimondi, Leopards, Badger, Duck-billed Platipus, the Alligator, and Crocodile, from the river Nile, Greenland Dog, various kinds of Monkies, Seal, Guana, Green Lizard, the Boa or Ox Serpent.

Also some of the most beautiful of the Feathered race;—the Argus Pheasant, Himalaya Pheasant, the Horned Pheasant, English Pheasant, Pied Pheasant, Pencilled Pheasant, White Grouse, Black Grouse, Wood Grouse, Red Grouse, the Ostrich, Lyre Bird, Bird of Paradise, Toucans, Macows, Cockatoo, Parrots, Pengun, and Albatross which measures 12 feet across the wings, with a numerous variety of interesting objects, both Native and Foreign.

Visitors will find the best general view of the Falls from the verandah of the Museum.

BIRDS, INSECTS, MINERALS, CANES, INDIAN CURIOSITIES, ETC., FOR SALE.

The following extract, written by a scientific gentleman (PROFESSOR SILLIMAN, of *Yale College, U. S.*), is from the Register kept at the Museum, and bears date Niagara Falls, Sept. 13th, 1838 :—"I take the liberty to say, that I have been greatly delighted with this Museum, arranged and prepared as it is, with science, taste and skill. In my judgment, it richly deserves encouragement, and adds an important feature to the attraction of this most interesting region."

The Museum will be open all hours through the day.—Admittance 25 cents, children half price.

THOMAS BARNETT.

CHRONICLE.   NIAGARA.

An advertisement for Thomas Barnett's Niagara Falls Museum which appeared in the "Niagara Chronicle", circa 1838.

Niagara - View of the British Fall from the Table Rock.
Lithograph by Tazewell, York, Upper Canada, circa 1830.
This simplistic depiction of the Horsehoe Falls exaggerates the notch at its centre. Table Rock is in the foreground, and the Americans have constructed a walkway at Terrapin Point, opposite Table Rock, to give their visitors the same close up view of the Falls that can be had from Table Rock.

In the meantime, Forsyth lost the lawsuits in which he asked for compensation for the damage done to his property. He appealed to the Legislative Assembly; a select Committee reviewed his case and said that he should be compensated. The Provincial Government stonewalled and refused to pay Forsyth the compensation that was due him. In 1832, disgusted and financially drained by his legal costs, he sold his holdings which by then included the *Ontario House* to the "City of the Falls" promoters and moved to Bertie Township, settling along the Niagara River at what is now Fort Erie. His holdings also included the *Pavilion* and 161.8 ha (400 acres) of land.

Lieutenant E.T. Coke of the 45th Regiment wrote about the transaction in 1832 and gave his opinion of the *Pavilion:* "The hotel, which is to be pulled down, may well be spared without loss in any respect. It is not only dirty but an uncomfortable place." [14] Forsyth's decision to sell in 1832 may have been influenced by the "prevailing sickness", a cholera epidemic which swept the northern United States and Upper Canada bringing travel to a halt. He claimed that he sold his holdings for $15000 less than their market value.

The "City of the Falls" promoters rented the *Pavilion,* "partly furnished" for five years at $2000 or £500 a year. The *Ontario House* was also rented out for five years at $800 or £200 a year. In the prospectus announcing these rental opportunities, a hotel, the *Red House,* of which nothing is known, was offered for sale at $1500. [15]

By 1833 tourists came again, so many that the Niagara *Gleaner* on August 3, remarked about the heavy travel between that place and Fort Erie. "A number of coaches pass up and down every day. We believe there are few places in America where there is so much travelling." Previously, in the June 29 edition of the same paper it was reported that six steamers were running weekly trips from the Niagara River to the ports at the foot of Lake Ontario - Kingston and Prescott - and one steamer ran daily to Toronto. The fare by stage from Niagara or Queenston and along the Portage Road to Fort Erie was nineteen shillings. Baggage was carried from Queenston to Chippawa over the Portage Road, by wagon for 12 s 6 d to 15 s per load. A steam towboat plied between Chippawa and Fort Erie every other day. [16]

New York State Office of Parks, Recreation and Historic Preservation. Senate House State Historic Site

Horseshoe or Western Branch of the Falls of Niagara.
Oil on canvas by William Goodacre, engraved by F.C Lewis, 1824.
When the patrons of "Brown's Hotel" and Forsyth's "Pavilion" went down the path from the high bank, the only clear spot from which they could view the Horseshoe Falls was the Table Rock. Sightseers were the same then as they are today, two figures are seen out on the Table Rock, one is shown at the very edge. The overhanging ledges of rock are shown. These are the ledges that William Forsyth got permission to blast off, in 1829, as part of the "variety of shows" promotion.

The glory days were over for the *Pavilion*. Patrick Shirreff, visited the Falls during a tour in 1835 and wrote: "The 'Pavilion House'...was greatly inferior to the hotels in the States." [17]. The hotel which had been praised by travellers since 1821 was now relegated to the status of a second class or even a third class hotel. During the Mackenzie Rebellion of 1837, it was taken over by the military and used as a barracks. Tradition has it that Colonel McNab's officers climbed to the observatory on the roof of the *Pavilion* and from there, with the aid of glasses (binoculars) saw Mackenzie's chartered supply ship the *Caroline* passing to and fro between Schlosser on the American side and Navy Island. [18]

Other travellers in 1837, and there weren't many of them in that year not only because of the political upheaval caused by the Mackenzie Rebellion, but also because of an economic depression in the United States, reported the *Pavilion* was closed. The next year, 1838, was a better year and the *Pavilion* was once again open. It was during 1838 that honeymooners were first observed staying at the *Pavilion*.

An officer of the 43d Monmouthshire Regiment who was billeted at the *Pavilion,* under the pen name *Bugle,* wrote: "At the present genial season, this beautiful spot is a favourite resort of lately married pairs. I have counted several cooing couples, both Canadian and American fulfilling the fleeting period of their 'honey-lunacy' at the great staring 'Pavilion'." [19]

Newly married couples usually went on trips to visit relatives in the early 1800's and if they visited Niagara Falls while they were travelling, it was only another point on their itinerary. It was not until the late 1830's - 1836 to be precise - that there are references that would support dating the beginning of the Niagara honeymoon, that is making Niagara Falls the main destination of the honeymoon trip. Then Caroline Gilman, visiting the Falls, noted "a young married couple who had come to pay true homage to nature, by consecrating their new happiness at this shrine.". [20]

Bugle wrote about the rates at the *Pavilion*. "Living is very reasonable here - one may board and lodge...for one dollar, or four English shillings, per diem, of course paying extra for wines; and a pair of horses may be very well kept for one shilling and sixpence a day." During *Bugle's* stay at the *Pavilion* the 43d Regiment was camped on the common just north of the hotel - the present day site of Ontario Hydro's Ontario Power Distribution Centre, at the corner of Buchanan Avenue and Murray Hill.

The 43d was posted to Niagara Falls in response to a threat of invasion by American forces, over the tension caused by the destruction of the *Caroline* and the general unrest caused by the Mackenzie Rebellion of 1838. From time to time, to keep the troops active, and to impress the Americans who could observe the 43d's parade ground from their side of the river, parades and mock battles were held on the grounds. A grand review was held there on July 17, 1838, with more than 200 persons attending dinner after the affair, at the *Clifton House,* hosted by Governor-General Lord Durham.[21]

Bugle commented on the two hotels on the high bank, the *Pavilion* and *Brown's.* "Sensitive travellers have bewailed the sacrilegious erection of huge hotels on a spot that should be sacred to the sublime and beautiful; and I must admit that, in my previous dreams of Niagara, there, places of public carousing rose up as nightmares of horror. The neighbouring country is for full dress, that these tall columned and terraced edifices are not incongruous to the scene as might be imagined.

"I doubt even whether one of the dark solemn castellated ruins of the Rhine would better suit the character of Niagara than the huge white clapboarded, or to use the term more intelligible to insular ears, clinker-like 'Pavilion Hotel', which perched on the high dry pinnacle above the Falls, looks like Noah's ark, left high and dry on Mount Arrat (sic). The antiquity of either edifice is but a day in the eternity of Niagara."

As if to fulfill *Bugle's* prophecy, the *Pavilion* caught fire at five o'clock in the afternoon of February 19, 1839. The *Pavilion* was made entirely of wood, and the fire was soon out of control. The spectacle was grand and solemn.

Samuel DeVeaux saw the fire and wrote: "The light of the fire reflected upon the rising spray from the Falls and upon the trees covered with congealed ice. The cloud of mist appeared like another conflagration, and to a person at a distance was taken as such. The ice of the trees reflected back the blazing light and shone brilliant in the keen pure air like burning coals. Though, thus dazzling, yet it was a sad and painful sight."[22] When it was all over there was only "the burnt fragment of the bullding…to tell travellers of its recent destruction by fire."

A new *Pavilion* was erected on the site at a cost of 6000 guineas. No description of this hotel has been passed down, but an inventory of its furnishings taken when it was requisitioned as a barracks in 1843, shows that the *Pavilion* had twenty-two bedrooms and two parlours with sleeping facilities; a dining room, a barroom, a saloon and a sitting parlour. It was not nearly as large as its predecessor.

Party at the Falls, 1843.
Pencil sketch with grey wash,
by Sir James. E. Alexander.
In this sketch the artist has taken a light-hearted view of a party of tourists standing on the Table Rock, looking at the Falls, He has included himself, wearing his officer's dress hat, and is seen at the far right, sketching the scene. Sir James Alexander was a member of the 14th Regiment, and included this sketch in the note book where he recorded his observations during a winter trip through Canada West (present day Southern Ontario). An account of his trip entitled ''A Sleigh Ride in Canada West'' was published in the August 1843 edition of ''Godey's Lady's Book''.

In order to show what a first-rate hotel of the 1840's was like, what amenities it had to make the traveller's stay comfortable and memorable, some items from the inventory are listed here.

The dining room had one dining table on casters, 21 chairs, 42 tumblers, 7 best quality wine glasses and 4 dozen white handled knives and forks, for a total value of $50.50.

The barroom had 10 arm chairs, a writing desk and chair, 1 wall map, 4 fine cut glasses, 37 tumblers of first quality, 3 jars, 2 pitchers and 1 register. The total value of this was also $50.50. This amount of money would not purchase much of what would be required today by a hotel owner, who was complying with Liquor Control Board of Ontario specifications for setting up a lounge where liquor could be served to the hotel's guests.

The Cutting Out of the Caroline.
A sketch by Henry J. Morgan in ''Sketches of Celebrated Canadians...'', Quebec 1862.
This depiction of the ''Caroline'' incident is from a Canadian viewpoint. The ''Caroline'' is shown as she actually was, a steam driven, side-paddle wheel boat. Built for Commodore Cornelius Vanderbilt in 1822, she passed through the hands of several owners before she reached Buffalo in 1836. Through 1836 and 1837 she made daily trips between Buffalo and Chippawa, with her team mate the ''Victory''. In mid December of 1837 she was sold and her new owner let the vessel out on charter to transport arms, munitions and supplies from Buffalo to the Mackenzie rebels on Navy Island. This sketch shows three of the boatloads of Canadian Militia leaving the scene after having cut the burning ship loose from its moorings, to drift downriver and over the Horseshoe Falls.

The Caroline Steam Boat Precipitated over the Falls of Niagara, circa 1838.
Coloured engraving by an unknown artist.

The "Caroline" incident, as it was called, brought out the creative talents of a number of artists in the United States, who depicted the incident from newspaper accounts as they imagined it to have happened. In reality the action took place at night, there were only a few men on watch on board the "Caroline", and one of them was killed. The boat was set on fire, set adrift, and went over the Falls. This imaginary daylight view is particularly interesting as it shows four men who have fallen out of a lifeboat going over the Falls and another figure, just to the right of the "Caroline's" bow, who has fallen off the ship as she dropped over the crest. Goat Island is depicted at the left with only one tree. The artist must have used one of the many Hennepin-like depictions of Niagara Falls, which had been replaced more than a hundred years before by more accurate pictures of the Falls.

Parlour D was the *Royal Suite* if there ever was the opportunity to entertain royalty. It had 6 yellow rush-bottom chairs, 1 bedstead, 1 straw palliasse, 1 pair cotton sheets, 1 pair blankets, 2 feather pillows and a bolster, 1 pair pillowslips, 1 counterpane, 4 pairs window curtains, 31 2/3 yards of carpeting at .69 cents, 1 gilt mirror, 1 wall map, 1 ewer, basin and chamber pot, 1 soap dish, a stove, stove pipes and a stove pan. These furnishings were valued at $93.01.

The ordinary traveller who might be assigned Bedroom No. 22, would find: a bedstead, straw palliasse, mattress, and 2 pillows, a counterpane, window curtains, an ewer, basin and a chamber pot, for a total value of $33.75. [23]

The saloon, but not the dining room or the barroom, was carpeted. It had a carpet that cost 63 cents a yard. The first hall carpet cost 28 cents a yard. The saloon also had 17 cane-bottomed chairs at $2.50 each, 5 pairs of window curtains, wall map and 7 pictures under glass.

The best rooms in the hotel were called parlours. Parlour C was luxurious. It had a featherbed, 2 pillows and a bolster, 1 straw palliasse, 1 pair pillow slips, 1 pair cotton sheets, 1 pair wool blankets, 1 counterpane and 1 pair window curtains. There was also a washstand, a basin, an ewer, and a chamber pot. It had a fireplace with a fender, a pair of andirons and a fire shovel, and 6 green rush-bottom chairs. All of this was worth $61.75.

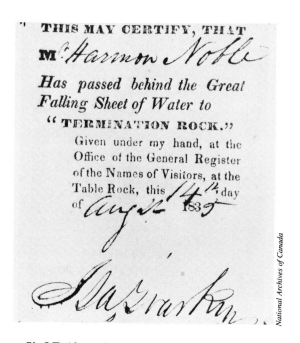

Termination Rock Certificate.

In 1827 Captain Basil Hall walked for 46.6m (153 feet) behind the sheet of falling water at the Horseshoe Falls when he was stopped by a huge piece of limestone which had broken off from the crest and come to rest on a ledge of Clinton Limestone. Later, guides took tourists behind the "Sheet of Falling Water" - (a named tourist attraction) - and those who persevered, reached and touched this rock, which was named Termination Rock, were given signed certificates of achievement when they returned to the top of the bank. These certificates were signed by Isaiah Starkey, who managed the stairway and guides for Thomas Clark and Samuel Street.

Sir J.E. Alexander was a visitor in 1839 when the *Pavilion* was a barracks. " We walked toward the *Pavilion,* now a barracks of the newly-embodied Canadian Rifle Corps, composed of volunteers from various regiments stationed in this country. Their winter dress was...high and flat caps of black fur, gray great-coats, black belts and long boots. We asked several men who had lately worn the red jacket if they were pleased with their change of service and they said that they were happy and contented. A man lately of my company, who married a wife with £100 had also joined a Temperance Society and was doing well." [24]

During all this time little news was heard about Brown's Hotel - the *Ontario House.* J.W. Orr's *Pictorial Guide to Niagara Falls* in 1842 noted that the former *Ontario House* was then occupied as barracks by the 67 th Regiment. On June 18, 1845 an advertisement in the *Niagara Chronicle* announced that Isaiah Starkey was the new proprietor of the *Canada House.** This was Brown's former *Ontario House* with a new name.

Starkey advertised that he had "A great variety of Albums and Registers, formerly kept at Table Rock, where he had been the manager of the stairway for 11 years. He evidently felt that the registers would attract patrons. A tourist, who had just returned from a trip to Termination Rock, in 1838 examined these registers before he signed his name and made these comments. "Having reached upper earth, and resumed terrestrial attire, I was gravely furnished with the customary certificate of my aquatic feat and requested to inscribe my name - with appropriate remarks. A large table was literally covered with a host of ledgers, scrap books, and alba.

*Isaiah Starkey was well known as the keeper of the stairway at Table Rock. He worked there for eleven years, from 1834 until 1845, managing it for Clark and Street, who had obtained the rights to have the stairway, after it was taken away from William Forsyth in 1827. Harriet Martineau, visiting here in 1838 was one of the thousands of tourists who received a certificate bearing Isaiah Starkey's name and who signed the Table Rock Register.

When Starkey took over there was a "shantee" described by Major Heath in his *Morals and Manners,* 1833, as: "a log cabin tavern where brandy is attainable by gentlemen of sluggish temperament who, surrounded, by such objects, still require the stimulus of alcohol."

Starkey, in an effort to stimulate business, made the use of the stairway free, but you had to pass through the barroom to get to the stairs. Sir Richard Bonnycastle, commented that it was a very profitable venture and that it made £200 a year. Not content, Starkey added a cabinet of minerals, to educate his visitors. He was a "practical Confectioner and a Pastry Cook" and he also began to sell ice cream and light refreshments. In 1838 *Bugle* wrote, complaining: "British Officers escort their ladies down to the ice shops near Table Rock...Finger post signs point 'To the Falls' and placards 'To Starkey's Refreshment Rooms' set the teeth of the romantic tourist on edge. Yet, after all, making due allowance for the incongruity of these things with the glories of Niagara, an ice cream or a goblet of iced lemonade is not amiss after a ramble under a temperature of 90 (degrees) in search of the picturesque." Starkey was summarily dismissed as a result of a trifling disagreement with Thomas Street, and left the area for New Berlin, Wisconsin where he was in 1844 when he wrote to Street claiming that compensation was due him. He returned to the area in 1845 and took over as proprietor of the old *Ontario House* renamed *Canada House.* He advertised that he had "a great variety of Albums and Registers, formerly kept at Table Rock."

Francis Petrie Collection Niagara Falls Public Library

The Stage Coach Between Buffalo and Niagara Falls.

In this satirical sketch the cartoonist has given us his idea of stage coach travel along what is now the upper Niagara River Parkway. Road conditions were so bad that the passengers got out of the stage, to make the load lighter for horses as they strained to pull the vehicle over the rough ground. Whenever the horses were able to pull the stage faster than a walk, the revolution of the wheels stirred up dust which floated in on the passengers. When it was wet, the wheels shot out slugs of mud and muddy water. The seats were hard, and there were very simple if any, springs to cushion the shock of passing over uneven ground. At the end of the trip from Buffalo, which had been accomplished at an average speed of two and seven-elevenths miles per hour, the passengers were ready for a bath and sleep.

"I passed a very amusing half hour. Such straining after the sublime, and such inevitable downfalls into the ridiculous, I never encountered. The frothy and forced rhapsody of the would be poet is instantly followed by the slashing attack of some bitter satirist; and the canting and ranting outpourings of the ultra-sanctimonious is immediately assaulted by the still more disgusting ribaldry of the ruffian scoffer." These albums were probably of more interest to his prospective guests than the "cabinet of minerals" which he kept on display when he was at the stairway.

Canada House was purchased in 1861 by Archbishop Joseph Lynch, the Roman Catholic Archbishop of Toronto, to become the Loretto Convent at Niagara Falls. [25]*

Nor was there much news of the *Pavilion*. It was no longer the favoured hotel, having since 1836 relinquished its position to the *Clifton House*. In the early 1840's a man named Moxley was the proprietor. In October 1848 an advertisement announced that Adam Crysler, "had secured the Hotel *Pavilion* for a term of years. The Larder is supplied with every

*John Joseph Lynch when a small boy in Ireland, saw a picture of Niagara Falls. "The awe inspiring Cataract and its surroundings; the beauty and majesty of the scene impressed him." This was in 1820. He became a priest in the Roman Catholic Church, and always held the memory of Niagara Falls and became convinced that it was the ideal place to build a Roman Catholic institution. He came to this area in 1856 and founded the seminary on the American side, which later became Niagara University. When he became Archbishop of Toronto, he was able to carry out his long held dream and purchased the *Canada House* with its spectacular view of the Horseshoe Falls and the upper rapids. He had it repaired and remodeled and deeded it over to the five sisters of Loretto who formed the Loretto Community at Niagara Falls.

delicacy of the season, the Wines are of the choicest qualities…while the charges are as reasonable as at any other Hotel in the vicinity of the Falls." [26]

However the *Pavilion* still had a clientele, as local people used it as a community and social centre. In 1855 a notice in the *Niagara Falls Gazette* advised "The Drummondville Fire Co. are making preparations to give a ball and concert at the *Pavilion* in that village on February l st. Delvecchio's Band is to be present. It is given to raise funds for the purchase of a new engine." [28]

The end came on April 26, 1865. "The old Pavilion Hotel - lately used for a dwelling on the opposite side of the river, was destroyed by fire last Wednesday. It belonged to Mr. Saul Davis, and was uninsured."

To stay at either of the *Pavilion Hotels* was a memorable event for the travellers of the day. There isn't a present day hotel in Niagara Falls that would evoke the comments today, made by William Leete Stone when he visited Niagara Falls. "As we reached Forsyth's Hotel, near the Falls, for some time previously to which our ears had been filled with the heavy sound of the rush of the waters. Without looking at the river, however, we took supper and retired to our apartment, which we found to overlook the famed cataract.

"I repressed my curiosity and did not lift a curtain, being resolved not to dissolve the charm of the first look upon the mighty, the glorious whole! But the roar of the tumbling torrent long banished sleep from my pillow; and when all was quiet and still in the house, I could distinctly feel that the earth, and the whole building and my whole body trembled, and when some fitful slumbers stole over me, it was only to dream of whirlpool, cliffs and crags and cataracts." [27]

Royal Ontario Museum

Table Rock, View of Niagara Falls, 1850.
An oil painting by Hippolyte Sebron.
Sebron did several oil paintings using this same general view of Table Rock and the Horseshoe Falls. This view shows a canal boat on the edge of the Horseshoe Falls. This boat was loaded with pork and whisky. It broke loose from its tow boat when it was entering Chippawa Creek. There was no one on board as it was carried downriver, where it grounded on the edge of the Horseshoe Falls. It was a great attraction for the tourists who saw it during the six weeks it remained in this precarious position. It was eventually swept over the Falls, without any of the cargo having been recovered. This oil painting has darkened over the years, otherwise it would be possible to read the sign, which says TABLE ROCK. The Falls Mills are on the bank of the river at centre right.

City of the Falls

William Forsyth sold his hotels and land to *The Niagara Falls Company* composed of a group of prominent men: Lieutenant-General John Murray, Thomas Clark Street,Honourable Thomas Clark, James Buchanan, Honourable William Allan, John Henry Dunn, Thomas Dixon and James Robinson.* This prestigious group was the predecessor of a modern day real estate developing consortium.

The company announced two goals: the first, to make money; the second, to preserve the Falls from "vandalism and commerical enterprises that would detract from the natural beauty of the surroundings". These were high sounding words. What the members of the company did was to survey and divide into lots, the land in what is now Queen Victoria Park.

They began at the extension of present day Robinson Street (Jolly Cut), which enters Queen Victoria Park just south of the Niagara Parks Police Headquarters building. They continued south, past present day Murray Hill, where they allocated larger lots to themselves, until the survey reached the extent of the property, south of the crest of the Horseshoe Falls. The northern half of present day Queen Victoria Park was not involved as it was part of Captain Ogden Creighton's *Clifton* estate.

Their optimistic sales projections for the lots in the project, which they called *The City of the Falls* depended on the Americans who would buy the lots and put up, what we would today call summer cottages, on the property. At that time American visitors to the Falls came by way of Buffalo, then across the Niagara River by ferry then down the Canadian side in four-horse stagecoaches, to Niagara Falls. Then they would find accommodation at one or the other of the three hotels on the Canadian side, the *Clifton, Ontario House* or the *Pavilion*. They crossed the Niagara River on the ferry below the American Falls to visit Goat Island and then returned to their hotels on the Canadian side. The success of this real estate devlopment venture depended on these travel patterns remaining as they had been.

The scheme was doomed when railroads replaced horse-drawn stagecoaches beginning in the mid 1830's as the means by which tourists came to Niagara Falls. As early as 1836, there was a railroad on the American side, running from Lockport to Niagara Falls. But when railroad service began between Buffalo and Niagara Falls, New York, the travellers who formerly came down the Canadian side, now came down the American side. The tourists then found

*Lieutenant-General John Murray ret. British Army 3 shares; James Buchanan, His Majesty's Consul ᴉᴜ New York 2 shares; the Honourable William Allan, President of the Bank of Upper Canada 1 share; the Honourable Thomas Clark 1 1/2 shares; the Honourable J.H. Dunn Receiver-General of Upper Canada 1 share; Thomas Dixon, President of the Society of St. George, New York, 1 share; Samuel Street 1 1/2 shares; James Robinson who was the resident agent for the Company 1 share.

Astrid Akkerman

Niagara's Visitors Arrive by the Steam Railway.
The artist has taken considerable artistic license in depicting the Falls as a background for this scene which shows travellers who have just arrived at Niagara Falls on the American side after travelling on one of the early steam railways. The sketch was made from a sketch which appeared in "Greater Niagara - All the Beauties of this Great Watering Place - How to See Them" by Mrs. S.D. Morse, printed by "The Record", Niagara Falls, Canada, 1896.

accommodation at hotels on the American side, crossed on the ferry to visit Table Rock and the Horseshoe Falls, then returned to their hotels on the American side. This change in the mode of travel dealt a death blow to the *City of the Falls* project.

The project began in 1832, but was held up by litigation, and surveying did not begin until 1833. There was a further delay and it was May 1834 before the first advertisements, offering lots for sale, appeared in newspapers. The *City of the Falls* is today identified by the street names which are still in existence: Buchanan, Clark, Allandale, Robinson, Dixon, Dunn, and Murray, all named after the shareholders. Stanley Street was probably named after E.G. Stanley, then Secretary to the Colonial Office, London, England. [1] Other street names in the survey, lost when the project was abandoned were Hay's Mount, Royal Terrace, Colborne Crescent, Washington Crescent and Point Turnagain.

Stanley Street was surveyed 30 m (100 feet) wide, while all the others were 24.3m (80 feet) wide with stable lanes - roadways along the back of the lots - 6m (20 feet) wide. Fronting along the river and the high

bank was a 15m (50 foot) wide carriage road. The company appealed to the speculative nature of their prospective buyers. "Taking into view the lots fronting on the river, as also the lots in the market square and Stanley Street, it is not hazarding too much to say that from 300 to 400 lots, at an average are worth at this hour $400 each, and in a very short time every lot (even those most remote from the Falls being not a mile) may be confidently expected not only to improve but to become a valuable investment." [2] The lots were on average 42.6m (140 feet) deep, and 9m (30 feet) wide.

The sale of lots was to be in the form of a lottery. Shares in the company were offered at £5 or $20 each and shareholders would be issued a ticket for each share purchased. The books were closed on August 1, 1834. After that date the shareholders would receive "a ticket duly numbered, securing the holder the lot which such number may be entitled to".The drawing was scheduled for the second Wednesday in September. The advertisement appeared in newspapers in New York City, Buffalo, Toronto, London, Hamilton and Niagara.

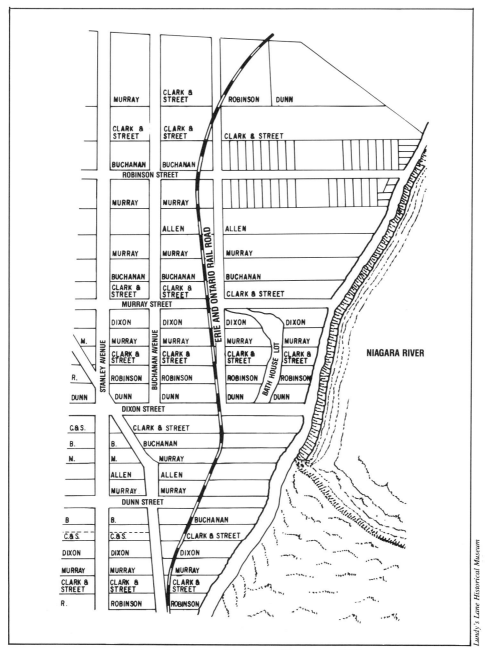

Portion of the City of the Falls Plan, circa 1835.

This is the original lot arrangement of the City of the Falls project, in what is now Queen Victoria Park. The Town of Clifton, incorporated 1856, is shown on the map.

Of particular interest is the Bath House lot, with what looks like a road allowance leading out to Clark Street. Clark Street ends at Robinson Street, so where the road allowance enters Murray Street, is the present entrance to the Ontario Hydro property, off Murray Hill, opposite the Holiday Inn By The Falls. The route of the horse-drawn Erie and Ontario Railway is shown as it curved to avoid high points of land. Until 1947 the remains of the stone abutments, which carried the railway over the Murray Hill Ravine, were still standing, just west of the abutments for the present Canadian Pacific Railway bridge. The small lots laid out at the right are along the extension of Robinson Street, including the rose garden, just south of the Niagara Parks Police Headquarters These lots were meant for ''summer cottages''.

*Lookout Tower on the Canadian Shore,
Niagara, circa 1835.
Pencil drawing on grey paper by
Lieutenant J.R.Coke Smyth.*

*The lookout tower is a standpipe - the water storage
reservoir - into which water was to be pumped up from the
Table Rock area. There are four or five figures in the lower
part of the sketch and it appears as if they are carrying or
working with a length of pipe. There was an undershot
water-wheel set in the rock at Table Rock, and wooden
pipes, bound with iron wire ran from the wheel pit to the
standpipe above. When the system was put in operation, the
pressure of the water being forced through the wooden pipes
was too strong and they burst. The water system was a
failure.*

To encourage prospective buyers to make a decision quickly, the promoters advised "The proprietors, in holding over a number of shares for distribution in Great Britain, Ireland, and the West Indies, reserve the right to raise the price of shares from and after the 1st of August." High pressure sales tactics haven't changed much, and we can recognize in their sales pitch, many of the devices in use today, refined, but still basically the same. The advertisements were a failure. Very few sales were made and only a few buildings were erected.

Prospective buyers were advised that a waterworks would be built "to furnish a supply of not less than 80 gallons a minute, on the summit level."* This was the area at the top of the high bank above Table Rock. The water would be stored in a standpipe and then distributed under pressure to the lots in the *City of the Falls* and to the Bath House.

As early as 1826 bathing in mineral water which emanated from springs, became popular, because the sulphurous water was claimed to have curative powers. Saratoga Springs in New York State was one of the first of these mineral springs to attract tourists, who then "took the baths". St. Catharines had its own baths that same year, when Wm. C. Chace the owner of the St. Catharines Salt Works, fitted up a temporary Bathing Room adjacent to the Salt-Works, for showering, and cold or hot salt water bathing. [3]*

Niagara Falls, with all its water, had no bathing beach, and the promoters of the *City of the Falls* realized that they had to provide a place where the visitors could bathe as much as they wished - in spacious bath tubs if not in the river. The Bath House was conceived as a hydropathic cure-all, a sanatorium for the sick and a resort for the water-loving healthy visitors to Niagara Falls. [4] This project was doomed to failure when the water system's wooden pipes burst under pressure, and there was no way to get water from the Table.Rock level to the standpipe on the upper bank. The burst pipes were never replaced and the Bath House never operated.

* A mill dam and an undershot water wheel,set in a pit 3.6m (12 feet) cut in the rock was erected at Table Rock. Water entering the pit turned the water wheel which would then force water through wooden pipes, bound with iron hoops,to a standpipe tower on the high bank,at the rate of 346 litres (80 gallons) a minute. The water stored in the standpipe would provide the pressure required to distribute water to the far corners of the "City of the Falls", and to the Bath House. The water wheel was put in operation but the wooden pipes burst under the pressure of the water being forced through them. The project, and the Bath House were left without water.

* Mrs. Simcoe, writing in her diary reported a "spring of water whose vapour is highly inflammable" located about 4.8 km (3 miles) from Chippawa in Willoughby township. This was not only a mineral spring, but surpassed the "Burning Spring" at the Bridgewater Mill site in its force. "If collected within a narrow compass, it is capable of supporting combustion for nearly 20 minutes." This spring was offered for sale in the May 14, 1845 edition of the Niagara *Chronicle*. The advertisement read " The springs.....have been found on examination by scientific and professional gentlemen as well as of the many extraordinary cures which they have effected, to possess efficient medicinal qualities. They are held to be superior to the celebrated Saratoga Springs by the many who have visited them...The water of these Springs is notably efficacious in the cure of many diseases, particularly those of the cuticle of all descriptions." There is no trace of this spring today.

National Archives of Canada

The 43d Encampment at Niagara Opposite the American Fall Aug. 9th, 1838.
Water colour over pencil by Lady Caroline Bucknall Estcourt.

The 43d Monmouthshire Regiment was camped here in 1838-39 as a show of British force. War with the United States seemed imminent as a result of public indignation there over the incident involving the burning of the "Caroline" while docked on the United States side. The Americans demanded redress from Great Britain for this violation of United States territory. During sporadic raids into our area, carried out by American groups calling themselves Patriots, houses, a church and barns were burnt. During these troubled times the troops of the Canadian Militia were unable to maintain the peace and the British sent in regular troops, the 43d Monmouthshire Regiment. This view by Lady Caroline Estcourt shows the encampment, with tents pitched on the present site of the Ontario Hydro Ontario Power Distributing Station at Buchanan Avenue and Murray Hill. The waterworks standpipe, cleverly camouflaged as a lookout tower, is at the right. Of particular interest is the building at the top left, the Bath House - built as a hydropathic institution, where visitors were to relieve their aches and pains by bathing in the huge zinc bath tubs located in the basement. The Bath House never received water for bathing, as the waterworks system did not work. At this time the Bath House was being used as officers' barracks and as an infirmary.

Cout's Hallmark

The 43d Light Infantry as they Turn Out in Their Sleighs at the Falls of Niagara 1839.
By R.A. Levigne, from a colour lithograph published by Ackermann & Co., London, 1839.
The 43d Monmouthshire Light Infantry Regiment arrived in Niagara Falls in August 1838. Every Regiment in the British Army had an officer who was an artist. While at the Royal Military Academy in Woolwich, these officers had taken instruction in water colour sketching from Paul Sanby R.A. We are indebted to these artists for the thousands of water colours and sketches done during their tour of duty in Canada. Without them we would not have the pictorial record we have today, because they were here before the advent of photography. The Monmouthshire Regiment had two artists, Lieutenant-Colonel Sir James Bucknall Estcourt, and Captain R.J.A. Levigne.. This winter scene, with the 43d turning out, was another of the full dress parades, demonstrations and mock battles which they carried out regularly, to impress the Americans who could watch from their side of the river. This turn out took place on present day Ontario Hydro property, directly opposite the Ramada Falls View Hotel.

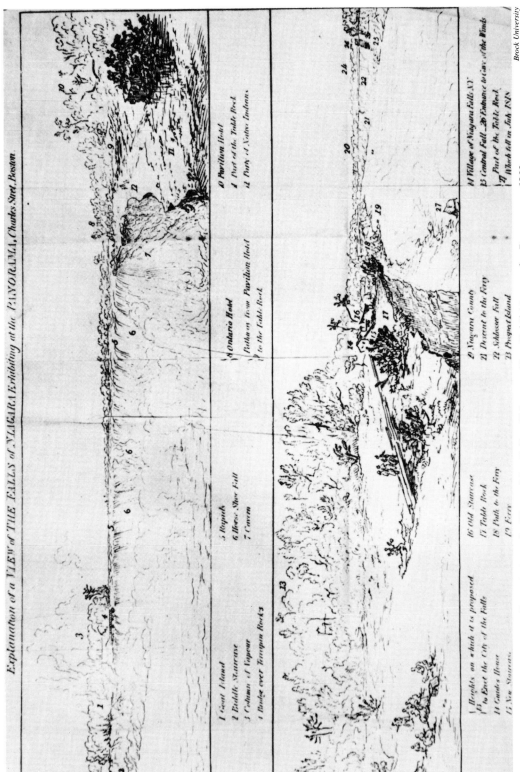

Description of a View of the Falls of Niagara Now Exhibiting at the Panorama, 1832.

Robert Barker the Scottish inventor of the Panorama, a 360 degree picture show, accepted a painting done by Robert Burford as the only panoramic view which met his requirements. This is a sketch of the painting which was exhibited in the rotunda-like Panorama building in Leicester Square, London, England. The spectators stood in the centre of a darkened room at eye level with the horizon in the picture. The painting was hung around them, covering 360 degrees, giving them the sensation of standing in the centre of the scene. The effect was enhanced by addition of the sound of falling water. Today's version of Barker's panoramic theatre features a 360 degree moving picture with stereophonic sound.

This sketch with the points of interest numbered, was included in the program which was given to those who came to see the Panorama.

Clifton House, Niagara Falls.
Pencil sketch on light grey paper, by Lieutenant J.R. Coke Smyth.

The Pagoda

When the City of the Falls project failed, the good intentions of the promoters "to protect from vandalism and commercialism" the area adjacent to the Horseshoe Falls were abandoned. One of the principals in the company, trying to salvage some of his investment, built this wooden, lattice-work, viewing tower, just north of Table Rock. Sir Richard Bonnycastle was so distressed when he saw it that he wrote "...the crowning glory of "the City" is the reflecting Pagoda, a thing perched over Table Rock bank, very like a huge pile engine, with a ten-shilling mirror, where the monkey should be." The Pagoda also housed a camera obscura. The building remained into the 1870's, but does not show in an 1880 photograph of the area.

Clifton House

Harmanus Crysler still had the "National Hotel" on the Portage Road, just a few hundred yards south of its intersection with Lundy's Lane and the Ferry Road. when he began to plan the erection of the "Clifton Hotel". Thomas Fowler visiting here in 1831, wrote: "Mr. Crysler who at the present has the inn at Drummondville, is making preparation for erecting a comfortable hotel in Clifton at the very verge of the cliff." Crysler sold the "National Hotel" to Richard Woodruff in 1833 for £ 1000, so that he could devote his efforts to the building of the "Clifton". The "Clifton" was under construction when Patrick Shirreff noted in 1833 that two rival companies were building villas on the Canadian side. The "Canadian Correspondent" of Toronto carried an item dated October 1, 1835, saying: "...the building is made of stone and will open on May 1, 1836."

Tyrone Power saw the "Clifton" in 1836: "Here directly at the top of the ferry road stands the 'Clifton House', erected by Mr. Crysler, which contains 60 rooms, and will accommodate nearly one hundred guests." The "Clifton House" opened at a time when travel patterns were changing. Up until this time travellers to Niagara Falls from the United States, came by stagecoach along the Canadian side of the Niagara River.

By 1836, there were three railroads which terminated at Niagara Falls, New York - formerly called Manchester - and where there had formerly been only one hotel, the "Eagle", now there was also the "Cataract" and the foundation for the "Rathburn Hotel" was being laid. In spite of this change in the mode of travel and the increased competition, the "Clifton House" continued to get its share of the accommodation business.

In 1837 there was an economic depression in the United States and Mrs. Anna Jameson, visiting Niagara Falls in June of that year, noted that the "Clifton Hotel" was almost empty and the "Pavilion" was closed. Business must have improved considerably because in 1840 Harmanus Crysler added a wing to the north of the hotel, along Front Street, now River Road. It was nearly 30m (100 feet) long and the same height as the main building.

Then in 1843, Sir James Alexander stayed at the "Clifton House" because the "Pavilion" was being used as a barracks. He expressed pleasure about the mattresses which were filled with "wholesome horsehair", an innovation in Canada West, and a welcome change from what he called the "abominable feather beds". He had "good service, excellent fare and moderate charges". On a return visit, however, he complained of the charge - $3.00 a day for three adults, a child and two horses.

Orr's "Pictorial Guide" in 1842 described the "Clifton House": "It is a noble structure, with triple colonnades of ample length and area...Mr. Crysler, a fine old English gentleman is proprietor and landlord...Are you fond of hunting?...he keeps a pack of hounds and has a passion for the chase. You could not wish for a better sportsman or a more jovial companion, and cannot fail to like him in either capacity - as host or hunter."

Harmanus Crysler, the "fine old English gentleman" was born in New York State and was only a few months old when his family settled in Canada as United Empire Loyalists. He lived forty-two years after Orr's tribute to him and was well known and respected by the travelling public and was a prominent citizen of Clifton -present day Niagara Falls. His home, "Hunter's Lodge", was located at the corner of Victoria Avenue and Morrison Street, where the Niagara Falls Public Library is now located.

Lieutenant E.T. Coke, while visiting here learned of the *City of the Falls* proposal and made his own environmental study: "The company of speculators intend erecting grist mills, store houses, saw mills and all other kinds of unornamental buildings, entertaining the most sanguine hopes of living to see a very populous city. The die is then cast and the beautiful scenery about the Falls is doomed to be destroyed. Year after year it will become less attractive... 'Tis a pity that such ground was not preserved as sacred in perpetuum." [5]

Sir Richard Bonnycastle spoke disparagingly of the whole enterprise, and his remarks were widely publicized. When the scheme failed, and only a few lots were sold, those who lost their investment blamed Bonnycastle for their misfortunes. Bonnycastle, for his part was nonplussed and when he returned to the area in 1849 he wrote a disparaging account of what the promoters had done to the area around the Falls. When it came time for them to try to salvage some of their investment, they abandoned their previously announced goal - "to protect from vandalism and

Astrid Akkerman

Waterpipe
This sketch is of a section of the wire-bound wooden water pipe, which is preserved in the Lundy's Lane Museum.

commercial enterprise". James Robinson who owned the lot just north of Table Rock erected a lattice-work viewing tower. Bonnycastle describing the structure, wrote sarcastically: "But the crowning glory of "the City" is the Reflecting Pagoda, a thing perched over Table Rock bank, very like a huge pile engine, with a ten-shilling mirror, where the monkey should be".

Bonnycastle went on: "...The Company of the *City of the Falls* - a most enlightened body of British subjects, who first disfigured Table Rock, by putting a water mill on it, and now are adding the horror of gin-palaces, with sundry ornamental booths for the sale of juleps and sling, all along the venerable edge of the precipice, so that trees of unequalled beauty on the bank above, trees which grow no where else in Canada, are daily falling before the monster of gain.

"It is the greatest wonder of the visible world here below, and should be protected from the rapacity of private greed and not made a Greenwich fair of; where pedlars and thimble-riggers, and barkers, the lowest rulls and the vilest scum of society, congregate to disgust and annoy visitors from all parts of the world, plundering and pestering them without control."[6] These were the conditions, perhaps a bit exaggerated, as Sir Richard Bonnycastle saw them in 1849, thirty-six years before the formation of the Queen Victoria Niagara Falls Park Commission in 1885, when the property and the commercial

enterprises in the area adjacent to the Falls, below the high bank were bought or expropriated, and present day Queen Victoria Park came into being.

The Bath House remained one of the forlorn relics of the project. It served for a time as a hotel, and then as a boarding school for girls, with an Irish Headmaster named Ditty. Tradition says that the school's servants slept in the zinc bath tubs on bundles of straw. During the Mackenzie Rebellion of 1837-38 the Bath House became a barracks for men of the 43d Monmouthshire Regiment and others, with the government paying the owners £100 a year.[7] It also had an infirmary during the time it was used as a barracks.

In September 1951 four boys from Falls View, Paul Plamendon, Cyril "Ronny" Chevers, George White and Frank Beauty, were playing on the bank behind the Refectory - now the Victoria Park Restaurant - when they found a button with the numeral 43 on it, an old clay pipe, several flints, a coin with a Queen's head, razors, knives, forks, an iron ball and a leg bone with knee cap. The bones were no doubt from a leg amputation performed in the infirmary. Others soon dug over the whole area and unearthed several other buttons.[8]

The Bath House was destroyed by fire, but there is no record of the date of its demise.*

The Bath House was located on the south side of the Murray Hill Ravine, directly above present day Victoria Park Restaurant. It was a three storey frame building, and Ernest Green interviewed an old resident who remembered being in the building: "the main corridors on each floor ran from side to side and from front to rear of the building. The mammoth zinc bath tubs were located in the basement rooms, and there was provision for heating the rooms and supplying hot water as well." It had large verandahs and contained a big ballroom. All of this was heated from central hot air furnaces.

The Erie and Ontario Rail Road

By 1830 most of the transport of goods and supplies formerly carried over the Portage Road, was carried by sailing ships using the New Welland Canal. The merchant traders, and others who had benefited from the portage, felt the loss of business and took steps to counteract the effect of the Canal. In 1831 they formed a company called the *Erie and Ontario Rail Road Company,* and applied to the Provincial Legislature for a charter.

This application was vehemently opposed by William Hamilton Merritt, who had spearheaded the promotion and eventual construction of the Welland Canal. Merritt was at the time a member of the Provincial Legislature and he used his influence to denounce the plan on the floor of the House. The business people of Niagara were also opposed. They fought an unsuccessful battle against the canal, and they felt that this plan to build a railroad would bring added complications to their businesses. They made their displeasure known, claiming the railroad would lead to a monopoly situation, leaving them out. [1]

The Military authorities at Niagara were also opposed, and would only consent when they were assured that the new railroad would not interfere with their defence plans. The opposition managed to delay the granting of a charter, and the Provincial Legislature turned down this application for a railway charter in 1832 and 1833. The negotiations with the Military continued through April 1834 until April 1835. Finally, when the Military gave their approval, the Legislature in late April 1835, granted the *Erie and Ontario Rail Road Company* its charter, but Royal Assent was held up until the Board of Ordnance obtained a commitment from the Company not to intrude with railway tracks closer than 914m (1,000 yards) to any military fortification. Royal Assent was given on April 16, 1835.

Those who were listed as incorporators were: Alexander and John Hamilton (sons of Robert Hamilton one of the original Portage Road contractors); Thomas Clark, another of the original Portage Road contractors; Robert Grant of Grant & Kerby; David Thorburn, a Queenston merchant; Humphrey J. Tench of Queenston; James Cummings of Chippawa; Samuel Street; James Gordon and Malcolm Laing.

Shares of this railroad which became known locally as the *Queenston-Chippawa Rail Road* or the *Chippawa-Queenston Rail Road,* sold for £12, 12 s with a limit of 6000 shares, providing the company with £75000 (about $375,000 at that time) in working capital. Provision was made for the issuing of more shares, if the rail line was later extended to Lake Erie.

The *Erie and Ontario's* Board of Directors, at a meeting held at the *Whirlpool House* on the Portage Road on September 7, 1835, passed a resolution which read: "Resolved: That John B. Jarvis Esquire, Civil Engineer, who originally made a survey of the practicability of making this railroad, has recommended to the highest manner, Mr. James Archibald, Civil Engineer, at Carbondale, Luzerne

County, in the State of Pennsylvania, as a person in every manner qualified to grade, estimate and carry on to completion the intended double or single railroad with steam engine, carriages, etc." [2]

The line was to be completed in five years. The company experienced financial difficulty and asked for and received a Provincial loan of £5000 to carry on. Early travellers accounts confirm that the line was operating between Chippawa and the Falls of Niagara in 1839. This section of the line, carrying passengers who arrived on the side-paddle wheel steamboats from Buffalo, would be used most, and so would be put in service first. Coventry's Guide Book in 1839 has a map which showed the rail line. Ernest Green suggests that probably some sections were finished and used before the others were ready. There is no record of an official opening, and work was still being carried out in 1841.

Queenston, at the northern end of the railroad, was anticipating an influx of passenger traffic, which was to be the railroad's chief source of revenue, as the ships using the canal would carry the freight. A wharf was to be built at Queenston, at the river's edge and passengers arriving by boat would be transported in horse-drawn carriages to the rail depot which was located on the northeast corner of present day Front Street and York Road. The rail line ended there on the glacial Lake Iroquois shore line because the grade from the river's edge to this level would be too steep for the horses to pull the rail carriages loaded with passengers.

This provision was necessary because the original intention to power the railroad with steam engines was abandoned, and horses were used to pull the rail carriages, trotting horses for passenger carriages, draught horses for freight. The Queenston portion of the line was completed last. According to Sir Richard Bonnycastle, the wharf was still not finished in 1841. [3]

Orville L. Holley in 1844 described the Queenston terminus: "The railroad to Chippawa terminates on the south of Queenston village, near the monument. Passengers are taken from the depot and arrive several times daily during the summer months. Stages leave Queenston daily at 8 a.m. for St. Catharines, London, Windsor and return from Windsor 8 a.m. each day." [4]

It wasn't impressive by today's standards, but it was the first railway in Upper Canada. The rails were made of wood, with lengths of strap or band iron fastened along the top, to protect the wooden rails from being worn away. The railcars were pulled by horses, one, two and perhaps three hitched in tandem, depending on how many cars were being pulled.

From the depot (See No.1 on Map) the railroad ran

west along the south side of present day York Road, then it turned south toward the escarpment and climbed on a sloping grade to the top. The grade was very gradual, from 3 to 5 degrees, and the roadbed is still visible in many places and can be reached through the rear of the properties on the south side of York Road. [5] At the top of the escarpment the rail line turned south along the road allowance for the Second Concession Road, running through the quarry, and then along the west side of the Second Concession Road, present day Stanley Avenue, all the way to the Ferry Road. (See No. 2 on Map).

A traveller left this account of his experiences on this horse-drawn railroad: "I found myself seated in a railway carriage, which was drawn by three horses in a string, none of whom appeared to derive their pedigree from Eclipse (a famous race horse of the time in England)." [6] He went on to describe the ride up the escarpment as "sufficiently tedious". The horses found it very difficult to pull the rail carriage with passengers up this long slope.

The rail line then continued south along the west side of the Second Concession Road, until it intersected with the Portage Road.(See No. 3 on Map). At this point passengers would leave the carriages while the horses were changed. The three horses which had pulled the car or cars up the escarpment from Queenston, were unhitched and one or two fresh horses, mostly just one horse, were hitched to the "train" as the route from then on to the Falls and Chippawa was more or less level. From this point on not as much horsepower was required to pull the cars.

This stopover at the intersection of present day Stanley Avenue and the Portage Road, became known as the Stamford Halfway. It was the halfway point not in distance but in effort - the amount of energy that the horses would have used - between Queenston and Chippawa. A small settlement sprang up around the corners. It included a tavern, appropriately called *The Halfway House,* a bakery, a general store and a blacksmith's shop.

From the Halfway the rail line ran along the west side of the Second Concession Road to the intersection of present day Thorold Stone Road. The topography in this area was later changed radically during the excavation for the Hydro Electric Power Commission of Ontario's Chippawa-Queenston power canal. Evidently there was a ravine or gully there then, as there was a bridge there which carried the railroad over the road, a road which ran from present day Leader Lane in Glenview, to Thorold. When the Great Western Railway line was built, a tunnel was constructed and the road went under the

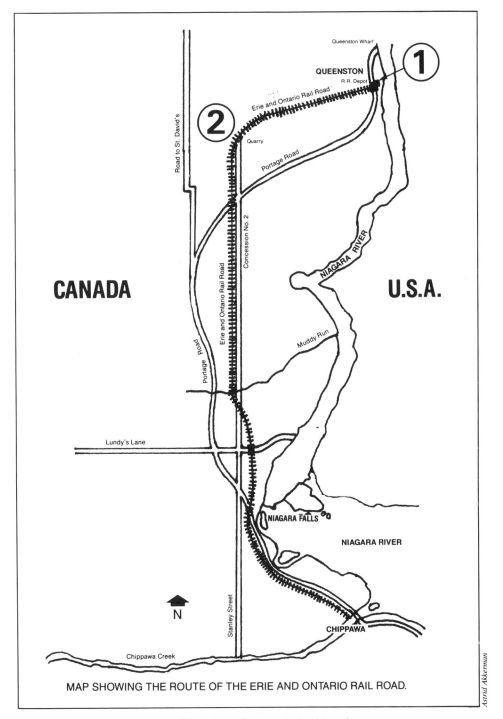

MAP SHOWING THE ROUTE OF THE ERIE AND ONTARIO RAIL ROAD.

Map of the Erie & Ontario Rail Road .
This map of the route of the Erie and Ontario Rail Road , was adapted from a map by Ernest Green. It shows only those those roads which were in use at the time the railroad began operating.

The Three Horse Railway
This sketch shows a carriage of the Erie & Ontario Rail Road, being drawn by three horses in tandem.

tracks through this tunnel. This road was cut off when the North American Cyanamid Company located here in 1907.

The *Drummondville Reporter* of September 29, 1853, carried this report of an accident to the railroad at this point. "On Saturday last whilst the Chippawa and Queenston horse-cars were crossing over the St. Catharines and Suspension Bridge Road, on their way to Queenston, a loose pin which rose above the level of the rail caused the cars to run off the bridge, dragging the shaft-horse with them; the leaders having extricated themselves from their harness, were not carried over; and, strange to relate, that although they fell a distance of some 20 feet, only one person, a lady, received any damage, and that only the breaking of a collar bone, the rest escaping nearly scathless. The car was smashed up a good deal, but with the exception of a few bruises, the horse had a miraculous escape, falling on top of the car. Dr. Mewburn, of Stamford Village, was fortunately near the spot at the time of the accident, and rendered to the sufferer surgical aid." [7]

The line continued along Stanley Street through the forest. This would be the area adjacent to present day Fairview Cemetery, past Oakes Park to Valley Way. In October 1931, the Township of Stamford, at the request of the Lundy's Lane Historical Society, erected a memorial cairn to commemorate the *Erie and Ontario Rail Road*. Constructed of glacial boulder stone, gathered when the grounds of Oakes Park were graded, this memorial stands on the southwest corner of Stanley Avenue at Morrison Street, adjacent to Oakes Park. The granite plaque, which has withstood the ravages of weather over the years, was donated by the City of Niagara Falls, and cost $50.00. [8]

The inscription on this plaque reads: "To Commemorate the Erie and Ontario Railway between Queenston and Chippawa, The First Railway in Upper Canada, Built 1831-41. This cairn erected 1931 on the original line." The 1831 date as the start of construction is in error, but it is the year in which the company was formed. An interesting and appropriate addition to the plaque's wording could have stated that it was a horse-drawn railroad.

The railroad crossed a bridge over the Creek which drained Cook's Bog. This stream was called Muddy Run, and present day Valley Way in Niagara Falls is the channel of this stream, running east toward the edge of the Niagara Gorge, just south of the Niagara Parks Commission's Great Gorge Adventure elevator building.

At the Ferry Road, now Ferry Street, there was another stopover. Here passengers destined for the United States would transfer to a stage coach, which would then carry them either to the Clifton House or the Ferry Landing. Sir Richard Bonnycastle wrote about this stopover in 1844: "The railroad (three horse power) takes you to the Falls or Chippawa. If you intend to visit the former, and desire to go to the Clifton House, the best hotel there, you are dropped at Mr. Lanty Mc Gilly's, where the four roads meet, one going to the Ferry, one to Drummondville, a village at Lundy's Lane now cut off from the main road; the other you came by, and the continuation of which goes on to Chippawa, where the steamer *Emerald* is ready to take you to the city of Buffalo."

An Erie & Ontario Rail Road Carriage
This is a sketch of a railway carriage used on the Stockton & Darlington Railroad in England. The cars on the Erie & Ontario were exactly like this, according to H.J. Cambie, of Vancouver, B.C. who described them to Ernest Green in the 1930's. Mr. Cambie, who was eighty-five years old at the time remembered a trip he had on the horse-drawn rail road, when he was a young boy.

The Remains of an Abutment Where the "Erie & Ontario" Crossed the Murray Hill Ravine.
This sketch made from a photograph, shows the remains of the stone abutment from the "Erie & Ontario Rail Road" bridge, built about 1854, to cross the Murray Hill ravine. This abutment was located about 30m (100 feet) west of the present Canadian Pacific Railway Bridge. It was originally higher, but was partially buried when the ravine was filled in to lay out the grade for Murray Hill leading into Queen Victoria Park.

The Clifton House, built by Harmanus Crysler between 1833 and 1835, had a horse-drawn omnibus which met the *Erie and Ontario* to pick up passengers destined for the hotel. Other passengers destined for Canboro, London and points west would also make their stage coach connections at this stopover.

A tavern or hotel, the Railroad Hotel was built on the northwest corner of this intersection to cater to the travellers who stopped over, transferred, or boarded the railroad at that point. Lanty McGilly ran this hotel,and it was a busy place,because, not only did the railroad run along the Second Concession but the traffic on the Portage Road turned along the Second Concession Road at the Halfway, and used this more direct route to the high bank above the Falls at present day Falls View. The present stucco finish building at the northwest corner of Stanley Avenue and Ferry Street now occupied by the Napoli Pizzeria, is the modified *Railroad Hotel.*

Bonnycastle got off at this stopover and went to see the Falls. he was disappointed and disgusted with the commercialism which had increased since his last visit in 1835. He wrote: "I was so disgusted to see the spirit of pelf, that concentration of self, hovering over one of the last great wonders of the world, that I rushed to the Three Horse Railway, and soon forgot all my misery in scrambling for a place: for there was no alternative. There were only three carriages and one open cart on the rail; the three aristocratic conveniences were full; and the coal box - for it looked like one - was full also, of loafers and luggage." [9]

After crossing the Ferry Road the rail line turned southwesterly toward present day Clark Avenue, then south toward the Murray Hill Ravine, where a bridge carried the tracks over the gully. It then ran along somewhat the same route as the present day Canadian Pacific Railway roadbed. There was another stop at the Pavilion Hotel, just south of present day Oakes Inn.

The only picture of this railroad's horse-drawn cars - a partial view - is in a watercolour by J.B.B. Estcourt. This watercolour is a view from the Pavilion Hotel, showing the Horseshoe Falls with spray rising towards the sky, and a horse-drawn car of the Queenston-Chippawa railroad at the bottom left of the view.

Ernest Green provided a description of the passenger cars, from a conversation he had with someone who remembered a trip on the *Erie and Ontario.* He wrote: "It has been my rare good fortune to discover a gentlemen of eighty-eight years, H.J. Cambie of Vancouver B.C., whose alert memory gives an excellent picture of the old railroad as it was when he - then a boy of fifteen, travelled over it from Chippawa to Queenston on May 28, 1852. The passenger cars he says,were exactly similar to those used by the *Stockton & Darlington Railroad* in England ten years earlier. They had a box-like body, divided into compartments, with doors along the sides and a 'running board' to assist in mounting and

*The Horseshoe with Spray rising on a cloudy day from the
Pavilion Hotel with the rail omnibus to Chippawa, waiting at the gate.
A water colour by Sir James B.B. Estcourt, 1838.*

*A car of the horse-drawn "Erie & Ontario Rail Road" is visible in the bottom left hand corner of this watercolour.
This is the only known depiction of the rolling stock of this the first railway in Upper Canada.*

dismounting.

"The cars were lighted by glass panels in the upper parts of the doors. The seats were crosswise of the carriage and about a score of passengers might find accommodation. Baggage was carried on the roof. The car rested upon a single truck, having four wheels. While the English railway used locomotives and ran its cars in trains, that upon which the informant made his trip over the portage was drawn by a single horse, the driver having an outside seat at the front, at the level of the roof. The speed was probably about five miles an hour. There were only about a dozen passengers on this occasion and, a good part of the run from Chippawa to Queenston being down grade, the single horse was sufficient." [10]

From the Pavilion the roadbed ran along the high bank, following it around the curve through what is now the Par Three Golf Course north of Oak Hall, The Niagara Parks Administration Headquarters. After rounding the bend, it went straight to Chippawa, parallelling present day Portage Road, then a plank road, to its southern terminus, a dock on the Chippawa Creek at about the intersection of present day Front and Norton Streets.

Steamboats from Buffalo running daily during the season brought passengers for the railroad, many of them making trips to view the Falls from the Canadian side, some travelling through to Queenston, after they visited Table Rock at the Falls. One of these steamboats was the *Emerald,* built in Chippawa in 1844. Service was suspended during the winter months, coinciding with the cancellation of steamboat service on the river and on Lake Ontario because of ice. Clearing the railroad right-of-way of snow would

have been an impossible task.

The development of steam-driven locomotives which were able to pull heavier railway cars, and therefore carry more passengers and heavier loads of freight, brought the era of horse-drawn railways to an end. The *Erie and Ontario Rail Road Company* applied for and received a revision to its charter, in 1852, allowing it to change to a steam operation. Construction began immediately on a new rail line.

The new route ran from a point west of the carriage bridge at Chippawa, running in a straight line, along the right-of-way which still exists today. It crossed the cut off portion of present day McLeod Road and ran past Mount Carmel and Loretto. After bridging the Murray Hill Ravine - the bridge was about 30m (100 feet) west of the present day Canadian Pacific bridge over Murray Hill - it ran directly toward the north end of present day City of Niagara Falls along the same route as the present Canadian Pacific Railway line. At Huron Street, behind and to the east of City Hall, it turned to the left and ran along Erie Avenue and crossed Queen Street. There is a railway spur line in the same location today, and it follows the old route, northwest from Queen Street, to cross Park Street, then turns west behind the houses on the north side of Park Street and along the south side of Muddy Run Creek. Near the end of Park Street it turned toward the north and crossed the intersection of Victoria Avenue and Bridge Street. This line now ends at the Cyanamid Company of Canada yards.

The old line crossed Bridge Street and turned north to run on the west side of Victoria Avenue, before entering a junction with the tracks of the Great

S.S. Zimmerman.

The "Zimmerman" was a wooden hull side-paddle wheel steamer, 60.9m (200 feet) long, with a 8.5m (28 foot) beam and 2.7m (9 foot) draft, weighing 467.4 tonnes (475 tons). This vessel was built for the Erie & Ontario Rail Road, by Louis Shickluna, at the Niagara Dockyards. Oliver T. Macklem was listed as the owner and the ship was named in honour of Samuel Zimmerman, who had a financial interest in the railroad. Launched in 1853, she ran between Toronto and Niagara, making connections with the Erie & Ontario Rail Road , and the "Clifton" which ran from Chippawa to Buffalo. This service was discontinued in 1858 when the steamboats lost most of their passengers to the new steam railways, and there was also an economic depression. On the night of August 21, 1863 while she was tied up at her Niagara dock, fire broke out on the main deck between the smoke stacks. She was cut adrift,and despite the efforts of the firefighters, the fire raged all night, out of control. Dr. Scadding, in his "Toronto of Old" gives a vivid description of the loss of the "Zimmerman": "The long shrieking of the whistle, the resounding moans and convulsive sighs in a variety of keys from the tubes of the boiler, gave the onlookers the painful impression of some gigantic creatures suffering pangs, protracted and inexpressible." The "Zimmerman's" vertical beam engine made by the Macklem Iron Works, Chippawa, was salvaged and put into the "City of Toronto", the "Zimmerman's" successor.

Western Railway. It ran west on the tracks of the Great Western Railway for about 3.2m (2 miles). When it reached the St. David's embayment where the Whirlpool-St.Davids buried gorge ends at the escarpment, also known as St. David's Hill, it ran down the eastern side of the hill, on a gentle grade around the bend of the escarpment and east toward Queenston.

A kilometre or so (a mile or so) from Queenston, opposite Niagara Township Concession Road No. 2, it crossed the former King's Highway 8A, now York Road, on a bridge - a stone abutment of this bridge still stands on the south side of York Road at this point. There was a station on the north side of the bridge. The rail line then ran down the short grade to the lower level, where it went directly to Niagara (Niagara-on-the-Lake), along the east side of present day Concession Road No.2.

The President of the Great Western Railway proposed to his Board of Directors in 1854, that they purchase the assets and rights of the *Erie and Ontario Rail Road*. He foresaw that the rail line to Niagara, which he thought would be completed in 1855, would be profitable, because of the travellers who would use the railway, after crossing Lake Ontario from Toronto on their way to Niagara Falls.

"Niagara being the nearest point the Steamers on Lake Ontario touch at, would secure for the 'Erie and Ontario' line a large proportion of traffic to and from the Falls; and these two items of traffic alone would be quite sufficient to yield a handsome return." He went on: "The line is 17 miles in length, and will be completed to the satisfaction of the Engineer of the Great Western Company. The purchase money includes a Steam Vessel (the *Zimmerman*) now

The Erie & Ontario Makes a Stop at Falls View, circa 1879.
This is an early photograph of the locomotive "Clifton" and two passenger cars of the Erie & Ontario Rail Road. Falls View, at a point just below present day Minolta Tower was a regular stop for this train.

building... at a cost of £20,000."[11] The English shareholders who controlled the Great Western Railway did not approve the purchase.

Samuel Zimmerman of Clifton (Niagara Falls) who made a fortune as a railway contractor for the Great Western Railway, took over control of the *Erie and Ontario.* He was in charge of constructing the rail line. His influence is evident as his name was used on the 467 tonnes (475 tons) wooden hull, side-paddle wheel steamer being built for the railroad company at Niagara, and the *Clifton,* another steamboat being built at Chippawa. The rail road had only one engine and they named it *Clifton* also. It was a 4-4-0 engine built by the Amoskeag Company of Manchester N.H., in 1854. It was number 169 on their list. This locomotive had 40.16cm by 50.8cm (16 inch by 20 inch) cylinders and 152.4cm (60 inch) drivers.[12]

According to Ray Corry Bond, Chippawa's historian, the railroad's Chippawa terminal and steamship dock was near present day Front and Norton Streets. A turntable was located here and the *Clifton* was driven on to it and turned around for the return trip to Niagara.[13]

Samuel Zimmerman died as a result of a railway accident on the Great Western Railway, at the Desjardins Canal, near Dundas, Ontario, on March 1857. The *Erie and Ontario Rail Road Company* had just changed its corporate name to the *Fort Erie*

Railroad Company, with the authority to build a line from Fort Erie to Chippawa and to purchase or lease that portion of the *Erie and Ontario Rail Road* between Chippawa and Clifton. With Samuel Zimmerman's death, his financial empire collapsed - the *Fort Erie Railroad Company* and the *Erie and Ontario Rail Road Company* included.

In 1862 the railway was purchased by William A. Thompson, and the next year a consortium bought it from Thompson. The various lines and charters were amalgamated in a new company, the *Erie and Niagara.* Construction on a lake to lake railroad continued while service was maintained on the core line.[14] The extension to Fort Erie was not complete in 1866 according to Alexander Somerville, who wrote in his narrative of the Fenian Invasion: "As the Fenians approached Waterloo Village (now Fort Erie) the Shore Road on which they marched, crossed the railway track of the *Erie & Niagara* line, a track not yet regularly in service."[15]

The *Great Western Railway* made another unsuccessful attempt to purchase the railroad. In 1878 the *Erie and Niagara* became part of the *Canada Southern Railway,* which took over its right-of-way through what is now the City of Niagara Falls. Then in 1904 the *Canada Southern* was acquired by the *Michigan Central,* and in 1929, the *New York Central* leased the line from the *Michigan Central.*

The Canada Southern Railway at Niagara Falls.

An oil on canvas by Robert Whale, 1883. Woodside National Historic Park, Kitchener, Ontario.
Robert Whale, born in England March 13, 1805, studied art at the National Gallery, in London. He became a
successful painter of portraits and landscapes. He came to Canada in 1864 and settled at Brantford. Niagara
Falls was a convenient and obvious choice of subject for several of Whale's oil paintings. In 1883 Whale painted
this view of a Canada Southern train at the Falls View stopover. He thought so much of the perspective from this
vantage point that he did another oil painting, which is in the National Gallery of Canada, of this same view,
except that the train is headed in the opposite direction. In both views he omitted Street's Pagoda which appears
in the ''Niagara Parks Illustrated'' sketch made from the same location. The Clifton House and the wooden towers
of the Upper Suspension Bridge are visible in the distance at the upper left.

Within the memory of our older citizens, the train which ran from Fort Erie to Niagara-on-the-Lake was affectionately known as the *Paddy Miles Express,* named after Paddy Miles the popular and beloved conductor who worked on the run for many years. The *Paddy Miles Express* ran its last run when the *Michigan Central* discontinued service on the Fort Erie to Chippawa line in 1925. This abandoned section of rail line was used to store surplus box cars until about 1940, when the rails were removed. [16]

Freight service continued on the line from Niagara Falls to Niagara-on-the-Lake, but passenger service had been discontinued - the use of automobiles and buses had taken away the railroad's passengers. Then in July, 1959 the *New York Central* announced that it was discontinuing the rail service, as the freight business was inadequate to support the line. The area

through which it ran was mainly a fruit growing area, without a manufacturing base to support a freight business.

This railroad which had carried millions of passengers in its time - tourists travelling from Toronto to see Niagara Falls, soldiers, regular troops and militia in peacetime as they travelled to their summer Military Camps at Niagara-on-the-Lake, and soldiers of both Great Wars, going to training camp - was no more. This railroad, beginning with the horse-drawn service, had been an extension of the Portage Road which began in 1788. With its demise, there was no longer a transportation link connecting the lower Niagara River below the escarpment with Chippawa and Fort Erie, bypassing the Falls of Niagara.

Bird's Eye View of Niagara, 1886.
A plate from "Niagara Parks Illustrated",
W.T. Hunter.

This view of the Falls of Niagara has a Canada Southern train in the foreground, making a stopover at Falls View. The Canada Southern bought out the Erie & Ontario and in 1883 upgraded the roadbed running through Niagara Falls, to make it strong enough to take heavier trains. The lattice-work tower at the right is Street's Pagoda, erected in 1860 on Cedar Island, in time for the visit of the Prince of Wales. This stopover, known as Falls View Station, was a popular feature of the Canada Southern and its successor, the Michigan Central Railway, until the 1930's.

1858. **SUMMER ARRANGEMENT.** 1858.

ERIE & ONTARIO RAILWAY.

TIME-TABLE.

BETWEEN NIAGARA, SUSPENSION BRIDGE AND CHIPPAWA.

ON and after **MONDAY**, the 17th **MAY**, 1858, and until further notice, (Sunday's excepted), Trains will run as follows :—

STATIONS.	Going South.	STATIONS.	Going North
	A. M.		A. M.
Leave NIAGARA,............		*Leave* CHIPPAWA,............	11.15
(on arrival of Boat from Toronto).	10.00	CLIFTON HOUSE,............	11.25
QUEENSTON,............	10.15	SUS. BRIDGE............	11.35
STAMFORD,............	10.25	STAMFORD............	11.50
SUS. BRIDGE,............	10.40	QUEENSTON............	12.00
CLIFTON HOUSE,............	10.50	*Arrive* NIAGARA............	12.15
Arrive CHIPPAWA,............	11.00	(Connecting with boat for Toronto.)	

CONNECTIONS GOING SOUTH.

At Suspension Bridge with Great Western Railway, and with N. Y. Central Railroad, East, and for Buffalo.

CONNECTIONS GOING NORTH.

At Suspension Bridge with the Great Western, and N. Y. Central Railways, arriving at Niagara in time for

STEAMER PEERLESS,

For Toronto, connecting there with the Grand Trunk Railroad and Royal Mail Line of Steamers for Montreal.

FARE FROM BUFFALO TO TORONTO, - - - $2.00
SUS. BRIDGE, " - - - - 1.50

J. B. ROBERTSON,

Lessee.

NIAGARA, May 14th 1858.

Erie & Ontario Railway Timetable.

Niagara River Ferries

In 1792, Governor John Graves Simcoe issued a proclamation authorizing ferry service across the Niagara River at Niagara, Queenston and Fort Erie. He imposed regulations on the standards of equipment, service and ferriage charges. The ferry was to be free during the six day annual Fair held at Niagara, beginning on the second Monday in October.

He set up a system whereby those who wished to provide ferry service would be required to submit tenders and obtain government approval. As ferrying - the transportation of people and goods across the Niagara River - was a link in the Niagara Portage, the history of the Niagara River ferries along the portage, beginning at Queenston, and at Niagara Falls and Fort Erie, is included in this book.

QUEENSTON FERRY

There is nothing in the Upper Canada State Records in the National Archives about the granting of ferry leases during the period from 1792 to 1816.. We do know that Thomas Dickson, who was Collector of Customs for the Port of Queenston, also had the ferry lease there before 1816, from the details of his petition for a renewal of his lease. He wrote: "...that the ferry at Queenston was leased to your Petitioner during the administration of Governor Hunter, (Lieutenant-Governor of Upper Canada, 1799-1805) and that lease expired during the late war, that the ferry house belonging to your Petitioner worth one hundred and twenty five Pounds currency was burned by our own troops to prevent it from being a cover to the enemy, for which your Petitioner can claim no remuneration, it having been built on the Military Reserve and his base of occupancy being conditioned to this effect." Dickson finished by saying that he had made a great investment in the ferry by building a new ferry house, provided a scow and boats. On April 2, 1816, he received a seven year renewal of the ferry. [1]

Samuel Lewis petitioned on August 8, 1818, that he be allowed to establish a second ferry. He said that his wharf, which was located at the Deep Hollow, at a dock "commonly known as Hamilton's Wharf", was more convenient as it was directly opposite Lewiston, whereas the established ferry docked on the Canadian shore nearly a mile upriver from Lewiston. He graciously conceded that "...in making this application...it is neither the wish of myself or the intention of the Petitioners that the said ferry (Dicksons's) should be entirely abolished. His request was not granted. [2]

The ferries in use were scow-like vessels which accommodated horses and wagons. They were rowed across the river, with the oarsmen taking advantage of the back eddies in the river, to get the ferries to a position where they could make a dash across the current, and then float downriver to the ferry dock on the opposite side.

When Thomas Dickson petitioned for a further seven year renewal of the lease in 1823, he asked that it be granted to "him or his Successor in Office", evidence that he did not expect to continue as Collector of Customs. He also wanted to sub lease the rights to the American ferryman who would build a horseboat. There is no record as to whether his request was granted, but there was no horseboat ferry operating on the river at Queenston during the next seven years. [3]

When the lease came up for renewal in 1830, Robert Hamilton submitted a petition for the ferry lease. He made what he thought was a strong case, in wanting to establish a horseboat ferry between Lewiston and the Deep Hollow before the Americans did. Thomas Dickson died in 1825, two years after the renewal of his lease, and according to the conditions of the lease Robert Grant who succeeded him as Collector of Customs, took over the ferry lease. Grant objected to Hamilton's submission, and in making his own petition he wrote: "The Queenston Ferry as at present established…is an easy, safe and expeditious ferry at all seasons, capable of doing, with the present means, much more business than others, and being opposite the centre of the Town is more convenient for the public than if it would be removed downriver to the Deep Hollow." [4]

The agitation for a change in the location of the ferry landing was not successful, but the Executive Council acknowledged that there was a need for a change from manpower to horsepower, and on June 2, 1829 ordered that an advertisement be placed in the newspapers asking for tenders for the ferry lease, to operate from the same location, but with a horseboat ferry.

Five men submitted tenders for this ferry, all of them offering to provide a horseboat. There was a horseboat operating at both Niagara and Fort Erie by this time. The tenders were from David Thorburn, James Humphrey, Oliver Smith, William Wynn Jr., and Joseph Wynn. The ferry was leased to Joseph Wynn, an innkeeper, at £106,5s per annum on condition that he use a horseboat. The Executive Council concurred that… "The best place of departure for the horseboat ferry is at the present place of departure of the scows and ferry boats, because access to the water's edge is much better and the eddy (in the river) running some distance, facilitates crossing and the location is under the view of the Collector of Customs." [5] Robert Grant, the Collector of Customs did not submit a tender.

David Thorburn, one of the unsuccessful bidders, provided an estimate of the cost of operating a horseboat, as compared to operating a rowboat ferry. His estimate reads: "First the cost of Horse, Boat and Outfit, say £250, other boats in addition, £250, 2 men's board and wages for seven years, £110 per annum, keeping 3 horse 7 years to work the boat

£770; interest and miscellaneous costs £239.8" This totalled £1644 8s and he estimated the cost of operating a rowboat ferry for the same period of time as £1240 8s. [6]

In 1831, soon after he received the ferry lease, Joseph Wynne asked for a reduction in the annual rent. He had counted on the co-operation of the lessee of the American ferry, Jerrard H. Randall, to help in the cost of building a horseboat. When this co-operation did not materialize Wynn wrote: "For the past seven years I have at considerable expense procured a fast running, decked boat, which is propelled by horsepower." Wynn's "fast running, decked boat" was a scow with paddle wheels along each side. A pair of horses, wearily marched on a disc which rotated as the horses kept up their monotonous, steady pace. As the disc turned, its gear-toothed edge meshed with the paddle wheels. The paddle wheels revolved, pushing the scow through the water. [7]

Once again there was an attempt to have a second ferry established to run from the Deep Hollow. John Niven was the petitioner. His request was not granted. Wynn also asked the Executive Council to take into consideration the likelihood that "The projected magnificent suspension bridge will in a very few years supersede the necessity of a Ferry at this point." He asked that the term of the ferry lease be for only five years, to become void if the bridge "shall have been completed." [8] The proposed suspension bridge was not built until 1851, so the horseboat ferry had many more years before it would go out of business.

Thomas Trumble appears to have received the ferry lease when it came up for renewal, replacing Wynn. On February 12, 1841, he wrote to the Executive Council complaining that he was being harassed by the American ferry. Wynn had joined forces with Job Chubbuck who held the American lease, and according to Trumble they were preventing his ferrymen from landing at Lewiston. He wrote: "…my boats can no longer run as Wynn and Chubbuck have on both sides in a lawless fashion…fined my ferry man twice in the sum of £5 10s…I have no alternative but to appeal to a Just and Benevolent Government, for protection or remuneration." [9]

The Executive Council was also having trouble with the ferry lease at Fort Erie, and passed the matter over to the Inspector of Frontier Ferries for his recommendation, When the Inspector made his report, he recommended a change in the method of awarding ferry leases. From then on ferry leases were awarded to "such persons as shall be nominated by Your Excellency (the Lieutenant-Governor), during pleasure. There are no further records of ferry leases being granted along the Niagara River in the Upper Canada State Papers after 1841.

The November 15, 1848 edition of the *Niagara Chronicle* carried a notice which read: "New 8 horsepower STEAMBOAT *ODDFELLOW,* Has lately been placed on the route, and plies regularly between QUEENSTON and LEWISTON." This marked the end of the era of the horseboat ferries. It is not known if the *Oddfellow* continued on the ferry service after the opening of the Lewiston-Queenston Suspension Bridge in 1851. No doubt, ferry service once again was resumed after this bridge was destroyed in the spring of 1864. A ferry service was in operation up until the 1920's according to photographs of the river which show a ferry dock and a ferry building.

NIAGARA FALLS FERRIES

While government leases had been awarded for ferry service at Niagara, Queenston and Fort Erie as early as 1792, there was not the same need for a ferry over the Niagara River at the Falls. At those locations, the ferries provided a transportation link between communities on both sides of the river, while there were only small settlements on both sides of the river at the Falls.

With the establishment in 1791 of the British Portage on the west bank of the Niagara River, most travellers began to use this route along the Portage Road between Queenston and Chippawa, because of the availability of stage coach service. By 1805 a town plan was laid out for a community at the Falls on the American side, which was called Manchester,while on the British side settlement was still spread out along the Portage Road, with no discernible concentration of people adjacent to the Falls.

For travellers who wanted to visit the other side of the river, the prospect of crossing the turbulent, swift flowing river below the Falls presented a formidable challenge. The depth of the gorge, and the long climb down to the river's edge and the arduous climb back up to the top of the gorge on the opposite side was another deterrent to the crossing.

As the number of travellers along the Portage Road increased the need arose for a ferry service for those adventuresome and curious who wanted to view the Falls of Niagara from the United States side.

There is no record of who made the first crossing of the river below the Falls by boat. In 1807 Christian Schultz, an inquisitive and hardy visitor, descended

Royal Ontario Museum

The Stairway and the Path to the Foot of the Gorge near Table Rock, Niagara, circa 1830.
A watercolour by Lieutenant-Colonel J.P. Cockburn.
The people shown in this watercolour are walking along the Clark and Street road to the ferry landing, completed in 1827. The remains of two stairways, one an open, inclined stairs, and the other enclosed spiral stairs, are visible. The open space between the trees on the left gives a view of the Horseshoe Falls.

Niagara River.
A brown wash on wove paper attributed to W.H. Barlett.
The road to the ferry dock on the American side dominates this view. The first "Maid of the Mist" is shown in
the centre of the river, heading toward the Falls. This watercolour is dated 1840, which is incorrect as that is six
years before the "Maid of the Mist" was launched.

to the bottom of the gorge using a borrowed ladder after finding the one in place " a poor ladder...by some accident or other had lost four of its rounds...added to its constant tremulous action..."[1]

When he reached the river's edge, Schultz noted "Immediately below the falls is a small space in the river, over which a boat might cross with the greatest safety...What led me to this reflection was the manoeuvres of some wild ducks, which I observed swimming backwards and forwards across this space, and who carefully avoided every place which I should have thought dangerous for a boat. Could I have obtained a canoe or a skiff, I should not have hesitated a moment about trying the experiment."

There were ladders down both sides of the gorge before the War of 1812-14. These were probably used by those who crossed the river here by boat as well as by fishermen. A report in the *New York Gazette,* dated Buffalo, July 14, 1812, read: "Below the Falls there is a small stone battery near the bank of the river where the lower ladder formerly stood. On Thursday

evening last a rifleman deserted from the other side and crossed the river below the Falls on a pine log...The ladders on both sides of the river are taken up." The rifleman who deserted took what was probably a route well known to local people, in defecting to the United States.[2]

William Forsyth, the proprietor of the *Niagara Falls Hotel* on the Canada side and Parkhurst Whitney, proprietor of the *Eagle Hotel* on the United States side, began the first regular ferry service across the Niagara River below the Falls in 1818. Forsyth on the Canadian side and Whitney on the American side, built stairways down the steep gorge wall to the top of the talus slopes, and then cut winding pathways along the slopes, leading down to the river's edge. From there guests at Forsyth's and Whitney's hotels were able to board a small row boat, to be rowed across the river.

It was an arduous trip on the Canada side, beginning with a walk or a carriage ride from Forsyth's hotel. The rudimentary carriage road ran

General View of Niagara Falls.
An oil painting on canvas by Robert W. Weir, circa 1840.
The rowboat ferry in the centre is depicted much larger than life. Clark and Street's road down to the ferry dominates the foreground and the lower right of the painting. The birds flying overhead are passenger pigeons which were abundant here at that time.

Ferry on American Side crosses to Canada, 1856.
A pencil sketch by Ferdinand Richardt.
This close-up view shows a rowboat ferry about to land its passengers at the base of the incline railway on the American side. The man holding the umbrella is shielding the passengers from the spray coming from the American Falls.

View of the Horseshoe Falls from Snail Road leading to Clifton House, Canada, 1856. A pencil sketch by Ferdinand Richardt.

along the top of the high bank to the ravine (present day Murray Hill), then down the ravine to the edge of the gorge. From there the roadway ran along the exposed rock which had a few centuries earlier been the river bed, to the top of the stairway. Baggage had to be carried down the stairway and along the talus slope path to the ferry landing.

At the ferry landing the passengers got into a row boat, and stowed their baggage as they could. After being rowed across the river, there was another climb up the talus slope path on the American side, and the stairway leading to the top where a carriage would be waiting. Some of the travellers of the day left written accounts of their experience crossing on this ferry. One account read "The passage of the ferry is most interesting...one steps into a small but staunch looking boat...At first the ferryman hugs the Canadian shore, taking advantage of the strong backwater, then suddenly turning the head of the cockle-shell, he abandons her to the current, and dancing merrily over the eddying billows, she is quickly stranded within a few yards of the American Cascade. After feasting his eyes on the Falls the craft is guided to the landing place...He looks in vain for the expected 'cad' to carry his luggage. With a sigh as heavy as his portmanteau, and a face as long as the stair he is about to ascend, he shoulders the former and proceeds to climb several scores of steps, spray sprinkled and therefor slippery steps... until he reaches the summit." [3]

Another account read: "A neat well-built boat about sixteen feet in length, lay drawn up on the rocky beach. In attendance on her stood a most uncouth looking lad, whittling to keep his fingers from being idle. As we gazed at the white mass of raging foam hurtling down the cliff before us, and the whirling eddying water which must be crossed before we could reach the opposite shore, we felt that had we not seen the same slight lad rowing backwards and forwards many times in the day, we should have hesitated long indeed before we had ventured with the power of the fearful vortex...

"We set out and a back eddy enabled us to get up the stream toward the great Fall without difficulty, and then thrusting forth into it, we were whirled downwards again many fathoms in the direction of the whirlpool, while the clouds of spray, driven by the wind from both Falls, showered down upon our waterproofs, till we looked as if we had been diving under the very cataracts themselves. Our surly Charon pulled right sturdily across the troubled tide, when much to our satisfaction, another eddy caught our boat, and took us up to a rough stage at the foot of a perpendicular cliff." [4]

William Forsyth had begun his row boat ferry service without government permission. His stairway down the gorge bank was built on the Military Reserve. When he petitioned in 1818 for the ferry lease, he explained in detail how he was already operating a satisfactory service. His aggressiveness was not appreciated, and he was not given the ferry rights. Thomas Clark, used his influence to keep Forsyth from getting the ferry lease and it was awarded to Christopher Boughner whose farm adjoined the gorge at the ferry landing. As well, the road to the ferry "ran about 1000 yards through the centre of Boughner's farm." [5]

Christopher Boughner was granted the ferry rights across the Niagara River below the Falls on October 18, to begin on December 25, 1820 for a period of seven years. [6] Forsyth, not to be deterred, found another way to get the ferry rights and the way he went about it is explained in Thomas Clark's petition to the Secretary of the Executive Council on December 9,1821. Clark wrote: "I intended to have spoken to you yesterday, representing the ferry across the Falls. This, about eighteen or twenty months ago, I recommended should be given to some person on lease, principally to keep Forsyth from extorting enormous ferriage from passengers and at the same time to be a check on smuggling.

"As the road leading to the Ferry passes through the centre of Christopher Boughner's farm and he a civil and obliging man...I with some others recommended him as a proper person to keep the ferry and an Order-in-Council was made on his favour for the lease of the Ferry for seven years and last April the rates of ferriage were established at the Niagara Quarter Session.

"When Boughner commenced his ferry he built a flight of steps down the precipice adjoining those formerly built by Forsyth. Boughner had not ferried long before Forsyth began to harass Boughner in the following manner, viz, knowing that he (Boughner) owed several debts in the neighbourhood which he could not pay without sacrificing his property, Forsyth went around and paid the full amount of the different notes or debts of Boughner to the creditors, upon which he immediately commenced action against Boughner in the court of the King's Bench.

"Boughner, from this, seeing certain ruin staring him in the face was coerced into Forsyth's terms and agreed to assign to Forsyth his leases for a term of six years - upon which Forsyth withdrew his suits, and is I understand to allow a sum to Boughner for the privilege of the ferry - the sum to be fixed by arbitrators. Forsyth from his late purchases at the Falls, engrosses all the country around them with his large capital and extensive buildings now erecting, intends driving down all opposition in business, more especially Brown (John Brown of the "Ontario House"), whose civility has taught Forsyth to behave somewhat better to his visitors. Now, knowing Forsyth's character and former conduct, I should be sorry to see him have more to say about the Falls, of access to them, than his neighbour. His conduct to Boughner which has been immoral, is perhaps unsuitable.

"The lease for the Ferry is (I believe) not yet out - at least it has not yet been paid for. I should therefore most gladly see it in other hands, say Brown, Bender, or old Leach, or indeed any other decent person about the place. If you, upon consulting the Attorney-General and other Gentlemen of York, are interested to prevent imposition on the public, think it could be done, any of the previous named by me would go over to make application to take on the lease, signed Thomas Clark." [7]

The old Ferry House (Canada on other side), 1856. A pencil sketch by Ferdinand Richardt.

On January 22, 1822, the Executive Council after considering all aspects of the matter, rescinded the Boughner lease, taken over by Forsyth. Their reason for the cancellation was that Forsyth had neglected to pay the £1, 5s rent. [8] The ferry lease was advertised as being open to the highest tender.

On April 30,1822, George Milmine was granted a three year lease of the Niagara Falls ferry. The row boat ferry service was carried on by Milmine until 1825. Thomas Clark and Samuel Street applied for the ferry lease, offering to build a carriage road down the side of the gorge bank, to the ferry landing. Their offer was accepted and they were granted a lease beginning April 15, 1825. [9] The lease was for a term of twenty-one years.

Clark and Street built a cobble-stone road down the side of the gorge wall, with a sharp hairpin bend about two thirds of the way down. This road is still in use though the cobble-stones have been covered with asphalt. The hairpin bend still exists, but it has been widened by the Maid of the Mist Steamboat Company, to allow easier access by vehicles driving to the landing.

This road connected with the Ferry Road which ran along the ravine (present day Clifton Hill), until it reached a point close to the upper level, where it turned to the south, and continued until it joined with the road which connected with the Portage Road. This is the same route taken by Ferry Street today. With the coming of the Erie & Ontario Rail Road, and the subsequent re-alignment of the railway right-of-way for the present day Canadian Pacific Railway tracks, the direction of the part of the road which is now Victoria Avenue was changed to run west of the railway tracks.

Ferry service was at times sporadic because the ferrymen were away from their posts for one reason or another. During the term of the Clark and Street lease different ferrymen were employed to operate the boats. In February 1842, the "residents of the neighbourhood of Niagara Falls" (on the American side) signed a petition which they addressed to the Executive Council, complaining about the ferry service and asking that "there be a change in the individuals who have the Immediate care of the Ferry below the Falls."

They wrote: "...the principal ferryman and his subordinate (John Shutterburgh and Levi Hammond were the ferrymen) are both addicted to habits of intemperance and are from that cause unfit many times, when their services are required to take charge of a boat in crossing the Stream when entire self possession is so indispensable a requisite. We have also been informed and some of us know the facts that due to their indulgence in strong drink they are often

unaccommodating and uncivilized to passengers and as we are informed are in the habit of extorting from persons larger sums for ferriage than they are permitted by their agreement with you to exact for their service.

"In making this representation we beg to be understood as disclaiming any wish to interfere with your private affairs but in the wish to promote the public convenience have deem'd it our duty to submit to you the foregoing statement containing facts which we believe you must be ignorant of." The names of some of those who signed the petition were: B.H. White, H. Woodruff, H. Marsh, Alfred Manger, J.A. Robinson, John Quig, R.S. Page, James M. Pierce, Nathan Robinson, H.W. Clark, Robert H. Pease, C.B. Griffen, T.S. Hulett, James Pierce, G.P. Shiver, G.S. Porter, and George W. Sims. [10]

However John Shutterburgh received an endorsement from a different group of inhabitants on the American side. On March 10 ,1842, they described John Shutterburgh as "a very competent, experienced, obliging and safe man in his capacity as Ferryman, and believe that any objections or complaints brought up against him, to be of an obvious and malicious nature, calculated to injure him in the eyes of the public as well as those by whom he is employed." Among those signing this petition were: John Adams, Daniel Kelly, T.W.Lanning, G.S. Ware, C,K, Clark, Robert Burris, B. Eurins, M. Walsh, B. Talmodje, Stephen Morris, D. McKenzie, G.H. Smith, H.M. Johnson, Wm.Lyon Webster.

On March 15, 1842, the inhabitants on the Canada side of the river rose to the defence of their ferrymen. Actually their petition named Levi Hammond, but did not mention John Shutterburgh. They wrote: "We believe...Levi Hammond to be a civil, obliging, competent and experienced person and will cheerfully give him our support and patronage, believing any complaints got up against him or the Ferry are of a malicious tendency calculated to injure him..." Among the names of those who signed this petition were: Thomas Barnett, Collier Skinner, James Gastin, James McGarry, Thomas Morty, S. Falconbridge Jr., John Creighton, Hanson Rop, Robert R. Hubbard, C.R. Rop, William Prouse, Richard P. Woodruff, Joseph Woodruff, Austin Morse, Thomas Robertson, William Powell, Henry Spence, James Skinner, L. Falconbridge, George Bender, John Prouse, James Oswald, William Woodruff, William Woodruff Jr., John McMicking, and John Simpson. [11]

There is no record of what action was taken, but these petitions were received by the members of the Executive Council at about the same time that they had become disenchanted with conditions at both

General View of Niagara Falls.
A lithograph by Deroy after a sketch drawn from nature by August Köllner, 1848.
The rowboat ferries are seen in this view. Two are at the left crossing the river, and the slips where they were drawn up on shore at night, are visible at the bottom right. The first "Maid of the Mist" is seen in the distance in the shoe of the Horseshoe. At the top of the gorge at the left of the Horseshoe Falls is Terrapin Tower, built in 1833 to provide sightseers with an exciting view of the Falls. At the right is the enclosed spiral stairway down the gorge wall at Table Rock. The structure on the gorge wall at Goat Island, between the Horseshoe and American Falls, is the Biddle Stairs erected in 1827 with money provided by a tourist by that name, to provide access to the lower gorge. At the bottom of the stairway there are paths along the talus slope leading to the base of both the Horseshoe and the American Falls.

Queenston and Fort Erie. The Clark and Street twenty-one year lease, granted in 1825, did not run out until 1846. In 1845 Adam Fralick was operating the ferry when Thomas C. Street petitioned that he be allowed to "continue in possession of the ferry without the same being put to public competition."

His request was not granted and tenders were called. Upper Canada State Book E in the National Archives of Canada has several pieces of correspondence on the granting of the ferry rights at this time. On November 6, 1845 Adam Fralick's tender, at a rent of £345 a year, was granted and the limits of the ferry were extended 4 km (2.5 miles) below the Falls. T.C. Street was ordered to surrender the old lease as his tender was for only £100 a year.

Adam Fralick was required to keep the carriage road down to the landing in repair, and soon after taking over the lease the stone wall supporting the embankment around the hairpin curve needed repair. Fralick applied for and was granted half the cost of erecting a new wall, £112, 10s in August 1847. On May 5, 1848, he was allowed a deduction of £140 on his rent, after petitioning that the expense of the wall had made the ferry unprofitable. The Executive Council, on granting him the deduction, cancelled his lease.

The lease was offered to James Chubbuck on March 2, 1849, but he declined and tenders were advertised for. There is no record of who received the ferry rights at that time. On January 11, 1850 the management of the ferries was transferred to the Customs Branch of the Inspector-General's Office with authority to sell the ferry leases either by auction or by tender. Gilbert Mickmicken was awarded the lease on April 29, 1853 with Samuel Zimmerman and James Oswald as his guarantors. HIs lease was extended for five more years in 1858.

When Clark and Street built the carriage road down to the landing on the Canadian side, the Porter brothers who owned land adjacent to the American Falls replaced the American stairs with a spiral stairway. It was used until 1844 when a water-powered incline railway was built. From that time on travellers found the trip down to the ferry landing less difficult on the American side.

Anthony Trollope wrote his impression of the trip across to Canada: "The readiest way across to Canada is by the ferry: on the American side this is very pleasantly done. You go into a little house, pay 25 cents, take a seat on a wooden car of wonderful shape, and at a touch of a spring, find yourself travelling down an inclined plane of terrible declivity, and at a

very fast rate…Below, the boat is generally ready…looking at the rapidity of the river, you will think that the passage must be dangerous and difficult. But no accidents ever happen and the lad who takes you over seems to do it with sufficient ease. The walk up the hill on the other side is another thing. It is very steep…in full season, however, carriages are generally waiting there… Having mounted the hill on the Canada side, you will walk on toward the Falls." [12]

In April 1846 the Niagara Falls Ferry Association received a charter from the State of New York, authorizing it to operate a steamboat ferry across the Niagara River. It is assumed that permission was also received from the Canadian authorities, In May 1846, the clumsy barge-like vessel with two smoke stacks was launched at the new ferry dock located on the American side about 0.8km (half a mile) upstream from the present Railway Arch Bridge. A carriage road was built down the side of the gorge wall to the boat landing, to accommodate the stage coaches and carriages which the Ferry Association thought would

Landing on Canada Side, road leads to Clifton House, 1856.
A pencil sketch by Ferdinand Richardt.
There are three carriages waiting at the ferry landing in this view and another pair of horses is tied to a tree. Judging by the number of the people and the vehicles congregated here, it was a busy day. The plank walk in the foreground led to the rowboat ferries docking area. The flat rock, set at an angle at the right, is still in this location.

Dr. and Mrs. F. Keller

The Ferry Landing on the Canada Side, circa 1857.
A stereograph by an unknown photographer.

The windlass used to pull the rowboat ferries out of the water is shown in the centre of this view. A carriage is standing by with a seated passenger. The waterfall shown on the American side is the overflow from the new hydraulic canal which was built to supply water for industry. Water first flowed through this canal and dropped over the bank on July 4, 1857.

use the new ferry to take passengers to and from the Canadian side. The new ferry, christened "Maid of the Mist", was expected to become a vital link in a proposed new stage coach route from New York City to Toronto.

Although the stage coach route was never established, the *Maid of the Mist* took over most of the ferrying from the rowboat ferries. In 1848 the ferry business lost the majority of its business to Ellet's Suspension Bridge which had just been built across the gorge at the head of the Whirlpool Rapids. The *Maid of the Mist* then began carrying sightseeing tourists upriver to the Horseshoe Falls.

There was still a rowboat ferry for those who found it more convenient to take the ferry than to travel the extra distance to cross on theSuspension Bridge. The Canadian ferry rights allowed the rowboats to travel downriver to the Maid of the Mist dock on the American side. A new *Maid of the Mist* was launched on July 14, 1854. She was a single stack, steam-driven, paddle wheel boat, 22m (72 feet) long. This boat was used primarily for sightseeing and the rowboat ferries continued in business.

When the tourist business declined because of the American Civil War, the second *Maid of the Mist* was sold in 1861. Captain Joel Robinson and two other crew members sailed her down the river through the Whirlpool Rapids to Queenston. From there she sailed to Quebec City to serve as a ferry across the St.Lawrence River between Quebec City and Orleans. The rowboat ferries again took over providing transportation for those who wanted to cross the river at the Falls, and for sightseers on the river.

George W. Sims, who had the ferry lease on the American side in 1864 "was the successful bidder at the late letting of the Canada side of the Niagara Falls Ferry for the term of five years". [13] He had been sub-leasing the Canadian ferry for some time and was not only ferrying passengers but taking sightseers on trips upriver to the Horseshoe Falls.

The rowboat ferry business continued to prosper, with Sims as the lessee, until 1869 when the New Suspension Bridge was built near the Falls. The *Niagara Falls Gazette* carried this report on June 16, 1869: "Although the New Suspension Bridge is in close proximity, many visitors will take a trip over on the Ferry for variety and to get a close and fine view of the Falls. Carriages are always in readiness on the other side if parties wish to ride, and the railway on this side is in good condition." [14]

During the twenty-four years between the sale of the second *Maid of the Mist* in 1861 and the building of the third *Maid of the Mist* in 1885, the rowboat ferries continued to ply the river, ferrying and taking tourists sightseeing. It was only after the third *Maid of the Mist* began to take over the sightseeing business that the rowboats left the river.

FORT ERIE FERRIES

The Duc de la Rouchefoucault provided the first description of a ferry operating between the American shore and Fort Erie in his *Travels in Canada in 1795.* On Saturday June 29, 1795 he wrote: "The vessels, in which we crossed the river Niagara belong to the English, and are, for this reason, in a better condition than the major part of the American vessels or ferries, which are entirely left to the will and pleasure of the owners, without any public office taking the least notice of their condition, and providing for the safety of the travellers.

"The ferry consists of a vessel of considerable capacity, sides of which are one foot and a half high, it was tolerably staunch, and sufficiently large to contain five horses without any apparent danger. The master of the vessel is directed to write down the names of the passengers; ours were already known. Governor Simcoe, Governor of Upper Canada, informed of our journey by Mr. Hammond, the English ambassador to the United States, had long ago given notice by the post, of our expected arrival.

"The passage from the American to the British side requires four to five minutes, and from the English to the American shore about a quarter of an hour. Fort Erie stands on the shore of the lake, about two miles above the ferry."[1] The ferry was a scow-like vessel, which was rowed across the river, not in a direct line, but on a circuitous route, taking advantage of the river's eddies and currents.

DeWitt Clinton in *Letters on the Natural History and Internal Resources of the State of New York* wrote in 1810, locating the ferry landings on the United States side: "There is an upper and a lower landing there about a mile apart...a ferry and a tavern are kept

at the upper landing by B. Miller and a store by Porter and Bartow." Barton was the correct name of Porter's business partner.

A writer in *Port Folio,* a literary publication in New York, wrote in 1810 that he "came to Millar's (sic) ferry and there were three wagons of emigrants waiting to cross to the British side from Scohaire, New York State, and Buffaloe (sic) in Northumberland County in Pennsylvania... They expected about 100 acres of land to cost them $50.00... The crossing cost half a dollar for a man and a horse."

Charles D. Norton, in *The Old Ferry at the Black Rock,* a paper read before the Historical Society Club, Buffalo, in December, 1863, gave information on the names of some of the ferrymen on the Canada side in the early days. He wrote: "The earliest name I can find among the ferrymen is that of Gilmore...he is a highly respectable man, and amassed property in Canada, but his house and barns were burned during the war, and Gilmore returned to Pennsylvania. Windnecker, or Decker was ferryman for a time there, and then Hardison.

According to Norton, there was a short time at the beginning of the War of 1812-14 before actual fighting began in this area when it was still safe for Americans to "venture upon business along the river." At that time a Mr. Brace and Mr. St. John, Americans, bought Hardison's ferry boats, and attempted to carry out a ferrying service. This venture ended in tragedy, when some American passengers landed after crossing under a flag of truce. Several were taken prisoner, two escaped into the woods, and the "British party then fired into the boat, which had moved from the shore into the river; Merrill, the ferryman, was

View of Fort Erie.
Left half of a pencil sketch by Sempronius Stretton, 1803.
The portage merchants' warehouses are shown in this half of Stretton's sketch. According to Gother Mann's map of June 1798, the warehouses belonged to Robert Hamilton, Thomas Clark, John Warren, Robert Dickson, Henry Warren and A. Nichols.

Royal Ontario Museum

View of Fort Erie by Henry de Berniere, 1773.
This work of art combines early views of The Falls of Niagara with sketches of Fort Niagara and Fort Erie. The View of Fort Niagara shows a sailing ship docked alongside the Provincial Marine Dock at Navy Hall.

View of Fort Erie.
Right half of a pencil sketch by Sempronius Stretton, 1803.
The first Fort was built close to the water's edge in 1764. This Fort was severely damaged by high water and river ice which was hurled against the pickets by high winds, in 1779 and 1803. The dock where the portage goods were unloaded is seen at the left.

killed; his body, stripped of boots and watch was afterwards recovered by a flag of truce. One of the passengers was taken prisoner and was never heard of; another was carried away as a prisoner and subsequently released at Halifax."

This reprehensible deed, outraged the people of Fort Erie. The wartime ferry was discontinued. The ferry boats purchased from Hardison, which were on the American side, were "taken by the British in one of their maurauding expeditions, and carried over to Canada. They were subsequently retaken by the Americans and used by the U.S. Army." [2]

The records of ferry leases granted in Canada beginning in 1818, are to be found in the Upper Canada State Papers, in the National Archives of Canada. The first mention of ferry leases at Fort Erie is in a letter, dated York, March 28, 1817, from John Smith, Secretary of the Executive Council, to Lieutenant-Governor Gore. Smith advised him that the Fort Erie ferry lease would expire in June, 1818. A notice appeared in the *Niagara Spectator* advising that the Fort Erie ferry lease would expire in June 1818, and that tenders would be accepted for a new lease. [3]

The lease was not awarded until March 25, 1821, when John Warren Jr., who was Collector of Customs at the Port of Fort Erie, and the current holder of the lease, was granted a seven year extension. Warren submitted a tender on December 21, 1820, offering to pay £25 a year and he was requested to increase this to £75 a year before he received his renewal.

John Warren Sr. was Robert Hamilton's shipping agent at the Fort Erie terminus of the Niagara portage. He was a retired Colonel of the Militia, having served in the Commissariat during the War of 1812-14, and was a Justice of the Peace. In 1798 he was appointed the first Collector of Customs for the Port of Fort Erie. He died in 1815, and his son John Warren Jr., succeeded him as Collector of Customs, and as lessee of the Fort Erie ferry.

The Warren ferry ran from his wharf which was at the end of the Garrison Road south of the Fort. The ferry had to contend with a river current of 11.2km (7 miles) an hour, with the river running over a rocky bed estimated to be not less than 6m (20 feet) deep. That ferry dock was not convenient for those who lived further downriver. Warren, on taking over his father's duties as Collector, moved the ferry landing downriver to a point opposite his house and office in the growing community of Waterloo. From there the ferry crossed the river and docked at Black Rock.

The moving of the ferry dock was recorded much later, in 1840, in a deposition from Robert Campbell, "an inn keeper at the Lower Ferry and a respectable man." The deposition read: "Doctor B. Hall, our medicine man of long standing at this place, and William B. Smith, magistrate, both of them have personal knowledge of the late Col. Warren having removed the Port of Entry at the Old Fort Erie, down to his residence at the lower ferry to suit his convenience and that the construction of the ferry wharf in front of his said residence was with the sanction of the government." [4]

For the next twenty years there was a continuing series of depositions to the Legislative Council, asking that ferries be established at two other locations. Those who had previously found the ferry at the end of the Garrison Road convenient, asked that it be re-established. Others who lived farther downriver from Waterloo, asked that a ferry be established with its terminus at Squaw Island on the American shore.

To counter those who wanted a lease for a second ferry, John Warren Jr. entered into an agreement with Henry Penfit, who had the American ferry rights, to co-operate in a ferry which would operate from the old location at the end of the Garrison Road. Warren did not carry through with this arrangement. In October 1825,William Powell and E. Riselay petitioned the Legislative Council that they be allowed to work with Edward and Penfit, but their request was not granted.

John Fowler, a traveller in 1830, wrote about the change in the method of propulsion of the ferries crossing the upper Niagara River. In his *Journal of a Tour in the State of New York in the year 1830,* he wrote: "Over this (the Niagara River) we ferried in a boat, with paddles worked by horses. On the Canadian side, just as you land, are a few houses, christened Waterloo, very near the site of the Old Fort Erie…"

This new ferry technology was brought about by the increase in travel after the opening of the *Great Western Canal,* later called the Erie Canal, in 1825, This canal now called the New York State Barge Canal, brought passenger traffic to what became a new ferry landing on the American side, at the foot of present day Ferry Street in Buffalo. At first a scow rowed by four men was used, but it was inadequate. The horseboat ferry was invented in 1826, and the State of New York made it a condition of the renewal of the lease on their side in 1827, that a horseboat, or a steam ferry be used to replace the traditional scow.

Brace and Fraser who held the American lease at the time, put a horseboat ferry on the river. Mr. Brace made a trip to Albany where the first horseboat ferry was in operation, to ascertain the merits of this novel invention. He brought back the machinery for his horseboat. Charles Norton describes this machinery: "it was nothing more than a wheel on a horizontal

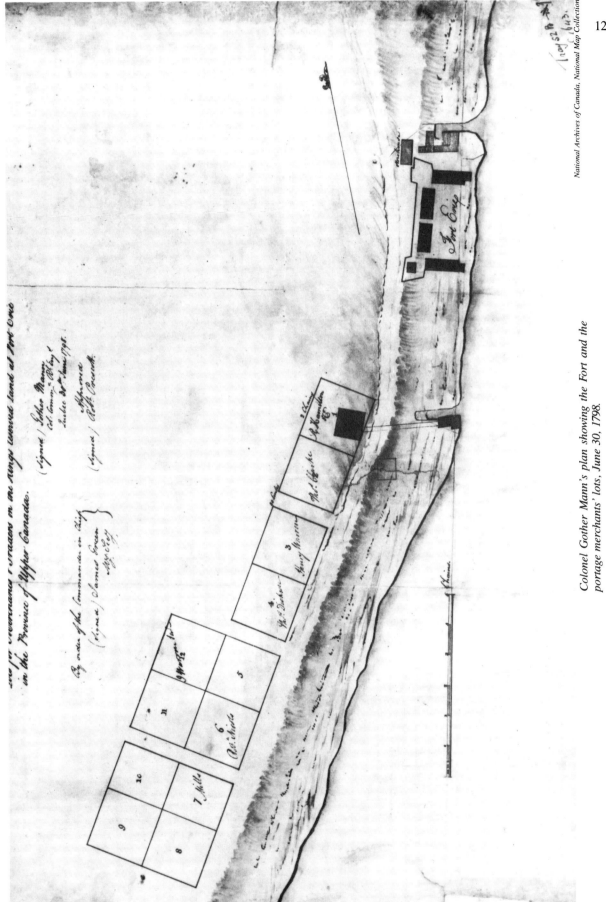

Colonel Gother Mann's plan showing the Fort and the portage merchants' lots, June 30, 1798.

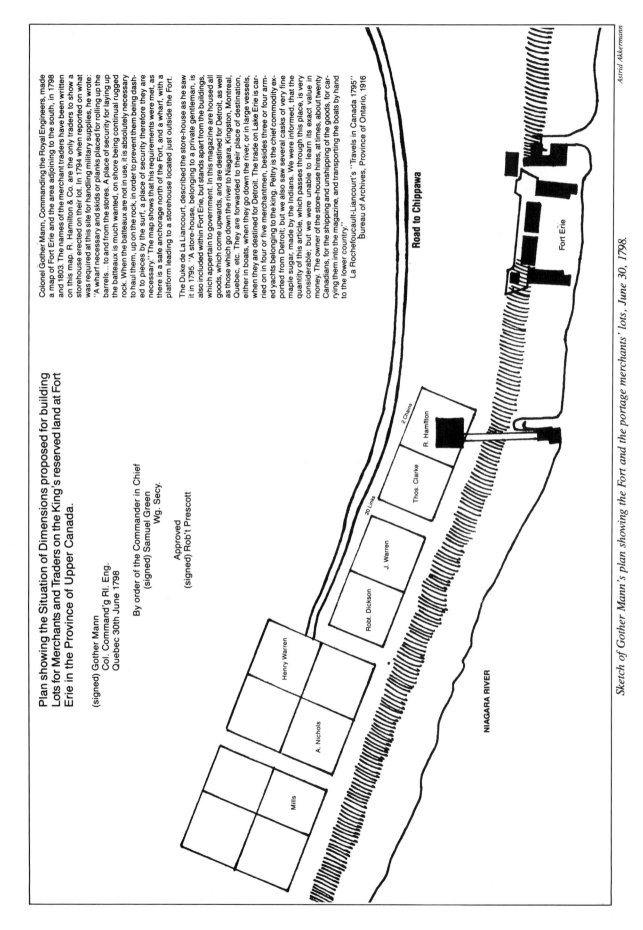

Plan showing the Situation of Dimensions proposed for building Lots for Merchants and Traders on the King's reserved land at Fort Erie in the Province of Upper Canada.

(signed) Gother Mann
Col. Command'g Rl. Eng.
Quebec 30th June 1798

By order of the Commander in Chief
(signed) Samuel Green
Wg. Secy.

Approved
(signed) Rob't Prescott

Colonel Gother Mann, Commanding the Royal Engineers, made a map of Fort Erie and the area adjoining to the south, in 1798 and 1803. The names of the merchant traders have been written on this map. R. Hamilton & Co. are the only traders to show a storehouse erected on their lot. In 1794 when reported on what was required at this site for handling military supplies, he wrote: "A wharf necessary and skids or planks placed for rolling up the barrels... to and from the stores. A place of security for laying up the batteaux is much wanted, on shore being continual rugged rock. When the batteaux are not in use, it is absolutely necessary to haul them, up on the rock, in order to prevent them being dashed to pieces by the surf, a place of security therefore they are necessary." The map shows that his requirements were met, as there is a safe anchorage north of the Fort, and a wharf, with a platform leading to a storehouse located just outside the Fort.

The Duke de La Liancourt, described the store-house as he saw it in 1795. "A store-house, belonging to a private gentleman, is also included within Fort Erie, but stands apart from the buildings, which appertain to government. In this magazine are housed all goods, which come upwards, and are destined for Detroit, as well as those which go down the river to Niagara, Kingston, Montreal, Quebec, etc. They are forwarded to their place of destination, either in boats, when they go down the river, or in large vessels, when they are destined for Detroit. The trade on Lake Erie is carried on in four or five merchantmen, besides three or four armed yachts belonging to the king. Peltry is the chief commodity exported from Detroit; but we also saw several casks of very fine maple sugar, made by the Indians. We were informed, that the quantity of this article, which passes through this place, is very considerable; but we were unable to learn its exact value in money. The owner of the store-house hires, at times, about twenty Canadians, for the shipping and unshipping of the goods, for carrying them into the magazine, and transporting the boats by hand to the lower country."

La Rochefoucault-Liancourt's "Travels in Canada 1795"
Bureau of Archives, Province of Ontario, 1916

Road to Chippawa

Fort Erie

R. Hamilton

Thos. Clarke

J. Warren

Robt. Dickson

Henry Warren

A. Nichols

Mills

NIAGARA RIVER

2 Chains

20 Links

Astrid Akkermann

Sketch of Gother Mann's plan showing the Fort and the portage merchants' lots, June 30, 1798.

Royal Ontario Museum

Old Fort Erie and the migrations of the Wild Pigeons in the Spring, 1804.
A watercolour by Edmund Walsh.

Walsh was the 49th Regiment's Surgeon, and when he did this watercolour the Fort had been repaired after having been damaged by a winter storm on January 6, 1803. According to Fort Erie historian David Owen, the gale winds and crashing waves of water tore out the pickets and washed away one of the barracks with its furniture. The wild passenger pigeons which fill the sky at the top left were abundant at this time. It is estimated that they numbered one and a quarter billion and consumed eight million bushels of mast, seeds, etc., in one day. The birds were so plentiful that it was possible to hit and kill them with sticks. Lieutenant-Governor Henry Hope wrote on November 5, 1785: "The quantities of wild pigeons...taken in abundance...will contribute towards their (the Loyalists) support." They were subsequently hunted into extinction and the last known living passenger pigeon died at the Cincinatti Zoo in 1914.

plane, resting on a main shaft, which it propelled by means of cogs upon the shaft; four horses treading the wheel being the propelling power. It was a great invention for the time...it (the Brace and Fraser horseboat) was the second boat of that kind ever used in this country (U.S.A)..."⁵ This was the horseboat named *Cossack,* that William Forsyth's stagecoaches used in crossing the river, on their way from Buffalo to the Falls of Niagara in 1827.

In September, 1831, the Collector's Office of the Port of Buffalo granted permission for a ferry between Buffalo and Fort Erie. On September 23, the Secretary to the Executive Council in Upper Canada gave notice that tenders were open for the right to operate a ferry in conjunction with this American lease.

Richard Moon, described as "brave Richard Moon, resident for 32 years," joined John Warren and Benjamin Prescott Hall in submitting a tender. As it was the only tender received they were granted the

lease for this upper ferry, for a term of seven years, at the sum of £3 per annum. Richard Moon was to run the ferry. The Executive Council approved this new ferry because Moon wrote in his deposition: "...a ferry has been established by the American Government between Buffaloe (sic) and Fort Erie, about two miles above the Upper Ferry held by Mr.Warren the Collector."

There were now two ferries, one landing south of the Fort and the other downstream at Waterloo. John Warren Jr. died in 1832, and John Douglas applied immediately for Warren's ferry lease. His application was refused in spite of his offer to upgrade ferry service by instituting a "Steam Boat Ferry" in co-operation with the American ferry owners.

John Warren's widow, Charlotte, applied also and was not only allowed to continued her late husband's lease, but was granted a three year extension, to commence from the expiration of her husband's lease. Charlotte Warren was supported in her petition by

James Kerby who had succeeded her husband as Collector of Customs; John Anderson, Missionary at Fort Erie; James Cummings, J.P.; James Macklem; and Thomas Clark.

They asked that special consideration be given her request because of her husband's service to the country. She wrote that her late husband "...had been engaged in rendering public services, the emoluments from which were not of great amount, with the numerous family to support (she was left with six children), and limited means, he depended in great measure on the proceeds of the Public Ferry at Fort Erie, of which he had been the lessee for the last fourteen years."

She wrote further to say that her husband had incurred considerable expense in the construction of a proper conveyance for passengers and goods, thereby affording prompt and safe communications from shore to shore. The downturn in travel due to the "prevailing sickness" had materially decreased the proceeds from the ferry so that they scarcely covered the expense of rent, and charges of men and horses for its maintenance. From this correspondence we learn that there was a horseboat ferry operating from the Waterloo ferry landing. The prevailing sickness was an epidemic of cholera.

Tyrone Power, wrote of his trip across the Niagara River in 1833, by horseboat ferry; "The vessel was a large horseboat, that is a flat boat, propelled by paddle wheels similar to those of a steamboat, only wrought by horsepower - an animal treadmill in fact. Whether the horses working this were on their good behaviour or not, I could not rightly ascertain, but certainly they were scampish looking steeds, their physiological expression was low and dogged, such as one might expect from the degrading nature of their unvarying task." [6]

On February 10, 1834, William Forsyth, the former owner of the Pavilion Hotel at Niagara Falls, applied to Lieutenant-Governor John Colborne, asking for permission to establish a ferry across the Niagara River, to run from a point in front of his residence, to Black Rock. Where Forsyth wanted to build a ferry dock was about 1.6km (one mile) below the Waterloo ferry dock. This application was refused as was another he made on September 27, 1835.

Forsyth was very persuasive, offering to operate a steam ferry. He explained that he wanted to supply ferry services to those on the Canada side who wanted to travel to the flourishing village of Lower Black Rock on the opposite shore. Forsyth wrote: "...Lower Black Rock has a very extensive Mills and other manufacturing establishments carried on by means of water power, which from the locality of our frontier we are deprived of and consequently obliges most of the inhabitants from this section of the Country to cross over in order to get their grinding, carding. fulling, etc., etc., done and (they) often complain from the want of an established ferry for their accommodation. There is also a foundry at Lower Black Rock." The Executive Council on reading this petition, recommended that a ferry be established at the "place prayed for within" and that it be advertised in the usual way. James Kerby , the Collector of Customs interceded saying that Mrs. Warren was giving satisfactory service, and as he had his office "near the place of Mrs. Warren's ferry landing", it would put him to much inconvenience to have it moved, if a new ferry location was granted.. No new ferry lease was granted.

Charlotte Warren's lease was to end in 1836 and twelve people responded when an invitation to tender was advertised in the *Upper Canada Gazette* in March 1836. Those tendering were Duncan Warren, Thomas Hardison, John Francis Smith, Job Chubbuck, John W. Lewis, John B. Chubbuck, Barnett Ulman, William Forsyth, Francis A.B. Clench, Benjamin G. Pound, Alex Douglas and Charlotte Warren. The Chubbucks and Clench were from Queenston.

The closing date for the tender was May 1. Once again Charlotte Warren played on sympathy to get a renewal. To be certain that her tender would be given special consideration, she ignored the instructions and sent her petition directly to the Lieutenant-Governor, Sir Francis Head, on the very last day. She wanted to be sure that he read it.

She wrote: "As the daughter of an old and faithful inhabitant and a servant of the Government and the widow of a respectable inhabitant of the Country, left with a family of Six Young Children dependent upon her exertions for their support and further prospects in life..." She went on to ask his Excellency's gracious consideration and said that she would pay an annual rent "as will exceed by two per cent per annum above any other offers" for the lease. The total was not exceed £300 per annum, and she further asked: "Your Excellency to extend indulgence to her under peculiar circumstances." Her tender was included, even though she did not abide by the rules, and it did reach the proper office, with the Lieutenant-Governor's instructions that it be considered.

While the tenders were being considered, Alexander Douglas petitioned the Lieutenant-Governor on July 7, 1837, saying that the Upper Ferry, the horseboat ferry at Fort Erie Rapids, was inadequate, and asked permission for the ferry lease at this location, so he could establish "a Steam Boat there." He was supported in his application by William Hamilton Merritt. William Smith also petitioned for this ferry lease.

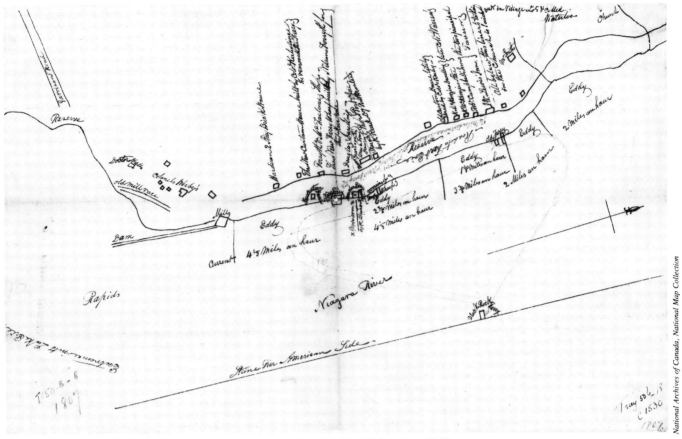

The Niagara River at Fort Erie, circa 1840.
This map was sketched by M.D. Miller, Inspector of Ferries, to accompany his report to the Executive Council of the Legislative Assembly of the Province of Ontario dated January 11, 1841.

There was a delay in awarding the Waterloo ferry lease, until March 15, 1837, when the Executive Council passed the matter back to the Lieutenant-Governor, saying that they had no objection if His Excellency saw fit to grant the ferry lease at this point to Charlotte Warren. She was granted a renewal, over the other eleven submissions. The Douglas and Smith petitions for the *Upper Ferry* were also turned down.

The Executive Council evidently became disenchanted with this system of awarding ferry leases, and with the recurrring petitions complaining of poor service, in an attempt to have the existing leasees cancelled. Soon after receiving yet another application, for a third ferry, at the same location downriver from Waterloo which William Forsyth, without success, had twice petitioned for, the Council asked the Lieutenant-Governor to change the method of awarding ferry leases.

They wrote to the Lieutenant-Governor: " On taking into consideration the various petitions for the Establishment of ferries on the Frontier Waters of this Province adjacent to the United States, the Council are respectfully of the opinion that the present system of Leasing the same to the person making the highest tender, without regard to Character, or qualification is essentially wrong and is likely to be productive of disadvantageous results to the Revenues of the Province to a greater extent than the rents of the respective ferries.

"The Council would therefore respectfully recommend that Ferries established, or to be established...shall be at the disposal of the Government, shall be granted to such person or persons as shall be nominated by your Excellency during pleasure and on payment of such rents and

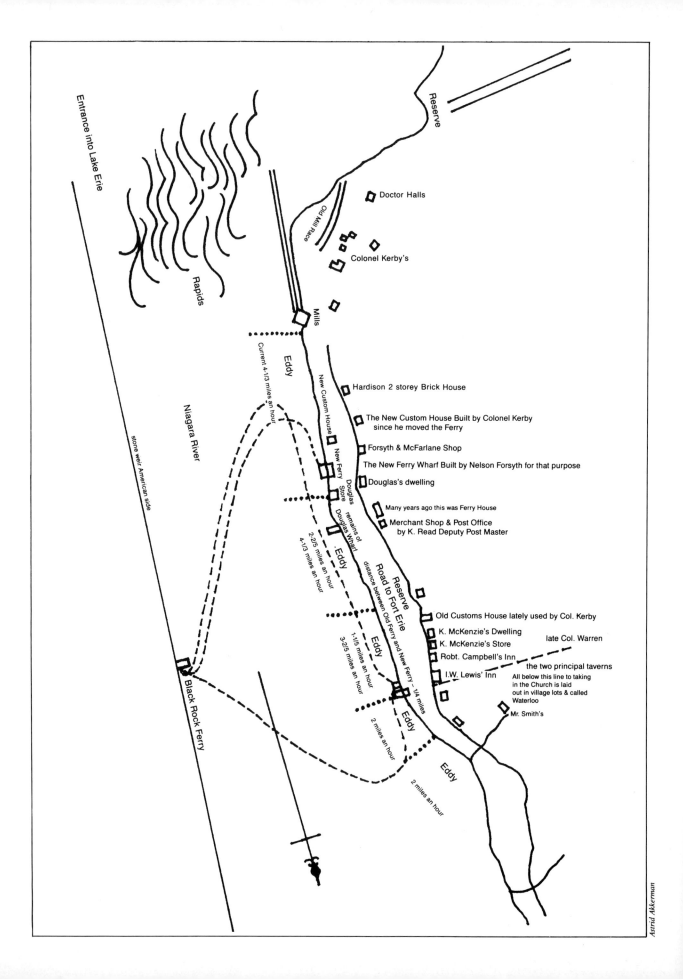

Entrance into Lake Erie

Reserve

Doctor Halls

Colonel Kerby's

Old Mill Race

Rapids

Mills

Eddy

Niagara River

Current 4-1/3 miles an hour

stone weir American side

New Custom House

Hardison 2 storey Brick House

The New Custom House Built by Colonel Kerby
since he moved the Ferry

New Ferry

Forsyth & McFarlane Shop

The New Ferry Wharf Built by Nelson Forsyth for that purpose

Douglas's dwelling

Douglas Store

Many years ago this was Ferry House

Merchant Shop & Post Office
by K. Read Deputy Post Master

remains of
Douglas Wharf

.Eddy

2-2/5 miles an hour
4-1/3 miles an hour

distance between Old Ferry and New Ferry – 1/4 miles

Reserve
Road to Fort Erie

Old Customs House lately used by Col. Kerby

K. McKenzie's Dwelling

K. McKenzie's Store   late Col. Warren

Robt. Campbell's Inn

the two principal taverns

I.W. Lewis' Inn

All below this line to taking
in the Church is laid
out in village lots & called
Waterloo

Mr. Smith's

1-1/5 miles an hour
3-2/5 miles an hour

Eddy

Eddy

2 miles an hour

Eddy

2 miles an hour

Black Rock Ferry

Astrid Akkerman

> *The Niagara River at Fort Erie, circa 1840.*
>
> *This is a sketch of the map which accompanied the Inspector-General of Ferries report. In the Fall of 1840 he was ordered to "...go immediately to Fort Erie and make a full report into the grounds and causes of the difficulties which have arisen between Hon. James Kerby Collector of the Port and also lessee of the Ferry and certain individuals in the ferry on the opposite side of the Niagara River and in the wharf upon the Crown Reserve at which during many years the ferry boats have landed, and to report on same."*
>
> *Besides providing us with the names of the settlers and businesses located along the bank of the river, the map shows the location of the mill race for the Dunbar Mill. According to the "Report of the Mills in the Home District" made by Augustus Jones on November 7, 1792, item 15: "A saw mill now Erecting near Fort Erie on the west shore of the River St. Lawrence at the Rapids by William Dunbar on a lot of land granted to John Gardner."*
>
> *In 1822 the firm of Grant & Kerby acquired an interest in the Dunbar Mills. James Kerby, who emigrated to Canada from Scotland when he was 21 years old, went to work as a clerk in Thomas Clark's store in Queenston. In 1811, at the age of 26, he formed a partnership with Robert Grant and they leased Clark's storehouses at Queenston and Fort Erie. In the spring of 1822 Kerby moved to Fort Erie and petitioned Lieutenant-Governor Sir Peregrine Maitland for permission to "occupy military land at Fort Erie and to make an enclosure...for the accommodation of goods being transhipped at Fort Erie."*
>
> *John Cousens Ogden in his book "A Tour through Upper and Lower Canada..." in 1799, described the shipment of goods over the portage and Fort Erie's place in it. "From Montreal, boats called by the Canadians, batteaux, containing twenty-five barrels bulk are worked by four men to Kingston, a distance of nigh two hundred miles up the river (from Montreal) in the course of six or eight days, and again return in three, loaded with furs, potash, and other produce of the country. Vessels, generally schooners, receive the goods at Kingston, and convey them in a short time, to the landing at Queenston...Here the portage gives employment to a number of teams in transporting them to Chippawa...They are received again at Fort Erie in vessels of the same burthen as formerly, which navigate Lakes Erie, Huron and Michigan. The expenses incurred during all this route are comparatively trifling, as you will observe there is but one portage, and that only ten miles in the course of this communication."*
>
> *In 1823 Grant & Kerby sold a one third interest in the Dunbar Mills to Benjamin Hardison who had been managing them for some time. The "Stone Pier on the American side" was part of the channel of the present New York State Barge Canal.*

under such regulations as shall be imposed in that behalf." [7] No further references concerning the awarding of ferry leases along the Niagara River appear in the Upper Canada State Papers in the National Archives of Canada.

The first steamboat on the Upper Niagara River, the *Walk in the Water,* was actually a sailing ship with auxilliary steam power. It was launched at Black Rock on the American side on May 28, 1818. The *Walk in the Water* sailed for three years on Lake Erie until 1822, when her steam engine was removed and installed in the *Superior.* [8] In 1840 James Haggert became the lessee of the American ferry and the successor to Brace and Fraser, and he placed a steamboat ferry on the river, in accordance with the provisions of an Act of the New York Legislature which granted him the right to maintain a ferry. [9]

In the information filed in January, 1841, detailing a complaint against James Kerby, the Collector of Customs, is found the first Canadian reference to a steamboat ferry. At that time the 96.4 tonnes (98 ton)

steamboat *Waterloo* was sailing between Black Rock and Chippawa and also operating at times, between Black Rock and Fort Erie.

In 1853 the *International,* a 466 tonnes (474 ton) wooden hulled steamboat, built at Chippawa, for the Brantford & Goderich Railroad Company went into service as a ferry between Buffalo Harbour and Waterloo. The advertisement for this ferry service stressed that the trip across the river on their ferry was more speedy, to say nothing of being safer, than a trip over the Suspension Bridge at Niagara Falls. The bridge at Niagara Falls was Charles Ellet's carriage bridge built over the Niagara gorge at the head of the Whirlpool Rapids.

The *International* ran until December 3, 1854, when a fire broke out while she was tied to her dock at Black Rock. She was cut loose and drifted downriver, where she grounded and burned to the waterline. The *International* was replaced by the *Sandusky* which was replaced the following year by the *Troy.* [10]

Canadian Illustrated News

Brock's Monument

This is an artist's interpretation of the ceremony which took place on October 13, 1857, when the present Brock Monument was dedicated

Queenston

In the summer of 1780 Isaac Dolson, James Secord, Peter Secord, Michael Showers, Samson Lutes, along with one or two others, settled on the west bank of the Niagara River below the escarpment. Peter Secord settled where the waters of Four Mile Creek ran down the ravine (present day St. Davids), James Secord adjoining him to the east under the escarpment, Michael Showers along the river bank a few miles toward the river's mouth and Isaac Dolson, at the lower end of what was to become the west bank portage, at the west landing. Dolson became the first to settle the land occupied by present day Queenston.[1] It was also where the Iroquois trail leading westward along the high ridge to the interior, began.

In the first census taken by Colonel John Butler, dated August 25, 1782, Isaac Dolson had cleared 12.1 ha (30 acres); James Secord 8.1 ha. (20 acres); Peter Secord 9.7 ha (24 acres); and Michael Showers 4.8 ha (12 acres).[2] In 1784 after Niagara Township, then called Township No.1, was surveyed, Samuel Street was shown as the owner of Lot No. 4, the land where Isaac Dolson had settled. Samuel Street petitioned Peter Hunter, the administrator of the Province of Upper Canada, on August 25, 1787, asking that he receive title to Lots No. 2, 3 and 4, stating: "That your memorialist having been for many years in possession (of these lots)…" On October 15, 1796, his request was granted.[3]

George Field came from the State of New Jersey in 1785 and settled on Lot 15 along the Niagara River. He built a house in what is now Queenston, where he lived and carried on a blacksmith and wagon-making business. He did not work at the trade, but employed men to do his work while he supervised the business. He put his sons Gilbert, Nathan and Daniel on the farm. He was already well established when Robert Hamilton and his partners received permission to establish the portage on the west bank in 1788, while the east bank portage was still under Stedman's control.

The banks of the river near Queenston are 15m (50 feet) or more in height with only a few areas such as gullies where streams flowed into the Niagara, where landing places with access to the top of the bank were possible. It was in 1788 at the end of one of these gullies, just north of Queenston, called the Hollow or Deep Hollow, where Robert Hamilton first unloaded goods and transferred them to ox-drawn wagons for transhipment over the trail that was to become the west bank portage, the Niagara Portage Road. In 1789 he received permission to build storehouses at Queenston, Chippawa and Fort Erie and the next year he wrote: "we did at very considerable expense erect wharves and storehouses along this communication."[4]

Establishing a new portage was a costly enterprise. Fortunately the cost was borne by the British Military. In 1790 Lord Dorchester, in preparation for the British evacuation of the east bank of the Niagara River and the portage there, ordered the Land Board for the District of Nassau - as present day Southern Ontario

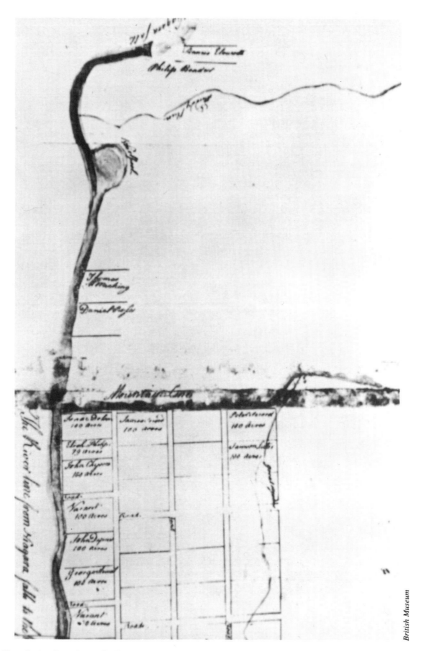

The Southern Portion of Alan Macdonell's "Plan of the New Settlement – Niagara Line, March-April 1783", from the original in the British Museum

This map shows the names of the early settlers along the west bank of the Niagara River, with the size of their land allotments. Isaac Dolson, James and Peter Secord, Michael Showers and Samson Lutes settled there in the summer of 1780. Isaac Dolson settled on land now occupied by the Village of Queenston, but by the mid 1780's Samuel Street was in possession of Dolson's tract. In 1796 Street received title to it, along with two adjoining lots.

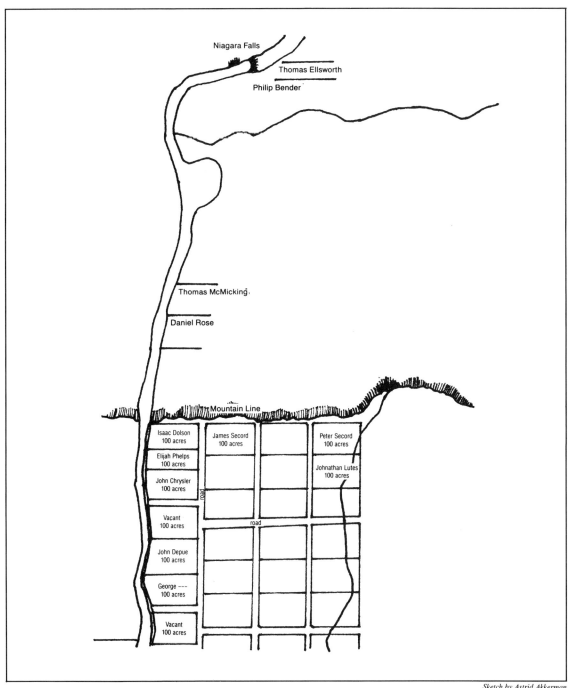

Niagara Falls

Thomas Ellsworth

Philip Bender

Thomas McMicking

Daniel Rose

Mountain Line

Isaac Dolson 100 acres	James Secord 100 acres		Peter Secord 100 acres
Elijah Phelps 100 acres			Johnathan Lutes 100 acres
John Chrysler 100 acres			
Vacant 100 acres			
John Depue 100 acres			
George --- 100 acres			
Vacant 100 acres			

road

road

Sketch by Astrid Akkerman

Alan Macdonell's "Plan of the New Settlement – Niagara River Line, March-April 1783"

Hamilton Wharf and Landing.
Water colour after Mrs. Simcoe, circa 1795.

Robert Hamilton was the first merchant trader to land goods on the west bank of the Niagara River, as early as 1788. In 1789 Hamilton and others received permission to build storehouses and wharves on the military reserve along the bank of the river. This close-up view of the wharves and storehouses was taken from Mrs Simcoe's sketch of 1795. These buildings were destroyed during the War of 1812-14.

was then called - to establish a portage on the west bank. Robert Hamilton and his associates, George Forsyth, John Burch and Archibald Cunningham - known as the Syndicate - were the successful bidders. [5]

There were only two tenders, theirs and one from Stedman. The Hamilton syndicate had been operating the portage on the west bank since 1788. "For these two years the merchandise and peltries of the Upper Country have all been transported by the inhabitants on this side without delay." The settlers were using their wagons to carry the goods and were being paid by the Portage Company. A petition supporting the application, carrying the names of eleven of the settlers who were benefiting, accompanied the tender.

The Land Board unanimously recommended the syndicate's tender, based on the provision that the portaging would be carried out by the west bank settlers. However, before the portage contract was awarded they had to reduce their price to match the Stedman tender of 1s 8d per quintal (112 pounds). [6]

In 1791 when the British gave up the east bank to the Americans, they built a wharf, guardhouse and a two-storey storehouse, the lower portion in stone, and the upper of logs, on the west bank of the river a half mile south of the Hollow. At the same time they built storehouses and wharves at Chippawa and Fort Erie.

The storehouses held the military supplies - barrels of salt, flour, salt pork and boxes of ammunition, etc.- destined for their outposts on the Upper Lakes. As there was no other storage space available, the merchants were allowed to store their merchandise there - trade goods which would be exchanged with the Indians for their furs.

Robert Hamilton moved to the west bank in 1790, to be close to his portaging business. He built a "very good stone house, the back rooms looking on the river. A gallery, the length of the house, is a delightful covered walk, both above and below, in all weather", as Mrs. Simcoe wrote in her *Diary*. [7] He prospered and by 1795 he had opened a store, from which he sold or bartered merchandise for the settlers' produce - grain, pork, and beef - which he in turn sold to both the British and American Military. The Duc de la Rochefoucault-Liancourt in 1795, wrote: "Mr. Hamilton possesses a very fine house..also a farm, a distillery and a tan-yard." [8]

The population of the new settlement - first called The Landing, then the West Landing, to distinguish it from the Landing on the east bank - increased rapidly as people were drawn to the area to service Hamilton's businesses and the wharves and storehouses. It was Lieutenant-Governor John Graves Simcoe, who would "name" the new settlement, in

Robert Hamilton (1749-1809).
From a water colour in the John Ross Robertson Collection
Robert Hamilton was born in Dumfries Scotland. He served his apprenticeship as a trader based at Fort Niagara during the American Revolution. His experience gained there gave him an advantage at the end of the Revolution, when he became a supplier for the British Military. Generally considered to be the founder of Queenston, Hamilton, in the words of Duc de la Rochefoucault-Liancourt was by 1795: "...an opulent merchant, who is concerned in the whole inland trade of this part of America...This merchant bears an excellent character. He is the most valuable kind of man for a new country".

an indirect way. When he came to Canada in 1791, he chose Niagara at the mouth of the Niagara River for his capital, and immediately renamed it Newark.

He had a series of barracks built along the lower bank of the river at the West Landing, for a detachment of his regiment, the Queen's Own Rangers. This encampment included twenty-eight log barracks, 7.3 m by 3 m (24 ft. by 10ft.) in size. Eight of these were for officers, three for a hospital, two for the mess and cooking facilities, one a bakery and the rest for the troops. The Queen's Rangers were not quartered there long as the location was damp and many of the garrison became ill, and some of them died, before they could be moved. These barracks became known as "The Queen's Town", and the adjoining settlement soon took that name. This soon became Queenstown

and then Queenston. The first recorded, unofficial use of the name Queenston was a November 4, 1792 dateline on a letter written by Robert Hamilton - from "Landing - now Queenston". [9]

Samuel Street, a merchant trader, had built a storehouse on the Military Reserve on the river bank, adjacent to one of the lots he had acquired from Isaac Dolson. Governor Simcoe chose this location for the Queen's Rangers' encampment and it was with great difficulty that Simcoe had him moved off the land. The Governor in a letter to Lord Dundas wrote: "Mr. Street, an inhabitant of this place, chose to dispute the right of land, but judgement was given in favour of the Crown". [10] Street had originally been a fur trader

John Graves Simcoe. Oil on canvas, by John Wycliffe Lowes Forster.
John Graves Simcoe, the first Lieutenant-Governor of Upper Canada, was born in Cotterstock, England on February 25, 1752. He entered the British Army and commanded the Queen's Rangers during the American Revolutionary War. He was appointed Lieutenant-Governor of Upper Canada in 1792 and made Niagara, present day Niagara-on-the-Lake, his capital, after changing its name to Newark. In 1794, at Lord Dorchester's insistence he moved to York, present day Toronto, which then became the seat of government. He built roads in an attempt to open up the province to settlement. Under his guidance, the Parliament of Upper Canada passed a law in 1792 abolishing slavery. He is best known for renaming every geographical feature, township and settlement with English names, replacing all of the Indian names.

Hamilton House.
Water colour, after a sketch by Mrs Simcoe circa 1795.
Robert Hamilton's house in the village of Queenston, built in 1790. Lieutenant-Governor Simcoe and Mrs Simcoe
visited the Hamilton's and Mrs Simcoe described the house in her diary: "a very good stone house, the back
rooms looking on the river. A gallery, the length of the house, is a delightful covered walk, both above and below,
in all weather". There was a skirmish here in the garden during the Battle of Queenston Heights. When the British
dislodged the Americans from their position here, they set up their artillery close to the house. In the ensuing
exchanges of artillery fire, the house was destroyed. Robert Hamilton received £ 2000 compensation for its loss,
after the war, it having "been burned by accident by our troops".

at Quebec and a land speculator on the Connecticut Frontier and by 1789 he had moved his operations to the Niagara Frontier. He and Robert Hamilton were major traders, but it was Hamilton who would make the greater impression through his commercial and land speculation activities.

Bruce G. Wilson in *The Enterprises of Robert Hamilton* wrote that by 1784 Robert Hamilton was confident enough of his own success as a merchant trader that he began to build a network of his Scottish relatives - men who would apprentice with him, then later begin business along the Niagara Frontier, in direct and indirect competition with him. Over the next seven years he sent home to Dumfries, Scotland for four of his relatives, Thomas, William and Robert

Dickson, and Thomas Clarke. Thomas Dickson was the youngest at 14 years of age and Thomas Clarke the oldest at 21 years. They all served their apprenticeship as clerks in his store, or as agents in Hamilton's forwarding business along the Niagara Portage. [11]

Thomas Dickson and Thomas Clarke spent four years working for Hamilton in his Queenston store. In 1793 Thomas Dickson opened his own store in Fort Erie - his brother William had the year before opened a store at Niagara. In 1796 Thomas moved his store to Queenston, where he was to remain for many years. Thomas Clarke, after completing his apprenticeship in 1796 opened a store in Queenston. Dickson and Clarke were now in direct competition with Robert Hamilton.

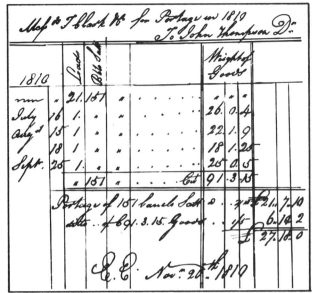

Thompson Papers, Isabel Walker Collection

John Thompson's Portage Account with Thomas Clark, 1810

Shortly after Thomas Clarke opened his store, he went into partnership with Samuel Street Jr., operating as Clark and Street and dropped the "e" from his name. Robert Hamilton guaranteed the success of this partnership in 1798 by allocating the firm a share of his military and fur trading contracts. The next year, 1799, Street left the partnership and Clark took Robert Nicol as partner. The firm built a storehouse and wharf at Queenston, at a cost £3000.

Eleven years later Clark sold his share in the store and portage company to Nicol. Then he went into partnership for the second time with Samuel Street Jr. Clark invested the proceeds of the sale in the new firm, which entered the milling business, purchasing Burch's Mills and the Bridgewater Mills at the Falls of Niagara. [12]

Clark rented his storehouse at Queenston to his clerks, Robert Grant and James Kerby, who formed another trading company, Grant & Kerby. In 1793 another Scot from Dumfries arrived, John Muirhead, and he became a merchant in Chippawa. Clark personally arranged for a relation of his sister's husband, Robert Kirkpatrick, to come to Queenston to work for him in 1809. Then by 1816 Robert's brother John came to Queenston. The Kirkpatricks would later set up shop in Chippawa. This "old boy network" co-operated as well as competed, and dominated business in Queenston in those early days of our country.

Queenston's rapid growth during the early years is well documented by travellers who left journals, or published books telling of their visits to the area. The

Duc de la Rochefoucault-Liancourt wrote of his visit in 1797, describing Queenston: "The different buildings, constructed three years ago, consist of a tolerable inn, two or three good storehouses, some small houses, a block-house of stone, covered with iron, and barracks, which should be occupied by the regiment of General Simcoe, but which are now unoccupied, the regiment being quartered in another part of the province." [13]

In January of 1797, Samuel Street had his land-where the present village of Queenston is situated - surveyed and marked off in lots. He advertised them for sale in the January 1, 1799 edition of Upper Canada Gazette. The firm of Clark and Street were his agents for this sale and lots were sold for from £20 to £60 per lot - $100 to $300. Tradesmen could rent a number of lots set aside for a commercial area, for 900 years, at an annual fee of six per cent of the purchase price. Subsequent advertisements in this newspaper confirmed the success of this offer to sell land to tradesmen. Tailors Mathias Steel and Hugh McCollum, a shoemaker and another general merchant W. Robertson, were established there over the next few years following the notice of the lot sale.

J.C. Ogden in 1799 was particularly interested in the activity around the wharves. He wrote:"At the lower landing, Queenston, the vessels discharge their cargoes, and take on furs brought from 300 to 1500 miles back. I have seen four vessels of 60 to 100 tons unloading at once and 60 wagons loaded in a day for the Upper Landing at Chippawa. Each wagon was drawn by two or more yokes of oxen and carried from 2000 to 3000 pounds. The portage is a source of wealth to the farmers, who carry from 20 to 30 hundredweight at 1s. 8 pence, N.Y. currency per hundred weight and load back from Chippawa with furs." [14]

Janet Carnochan, Niagara-on-the-Lake historian, wrote in *Queenston in Early Days:* "In 1805, Darcy Boulton, another traveller, says 60 waggons loaded every day from Queenston to Chippawa." Boulton must have visited on the occasion when there had been several ship arrivals, and all available drivers and wagons were called into service.

John Maude in 1800 made an unusual comment: "Queenston contains twenty to thirty houses, whose fronts are east and west, the worst possible aspect, but which has been regulated by the course of the River, which is S. by E. to N. by W. and very Rapid, and full of eddies." [15] In 1808 Christian Schultz visited Lewiston "a settlement of about a dozen houses" and on looking across the Niagara he saw: "...Queen's Town a village of Upper Canada, containing about a hundred houses, and a small

National Archives of Canada

Queenston, or the landing between Lake Ontario
and Lake Erie. Water colour, by an unknown artist, circa 1812.
This view shows Robert Hamilton's house, and the barracks of the Queen's Rangers - four buildings in a row
on the river bank. The artist has incorrectly depicted the cliffs of the Niagara Gorge on the American side, as
sloping, and the river below as placid, with a sailing boat heading upstream.

garrison of twenty-eight men". [16] He must have been blinded by looking into the setting sun, as the community had not grown that much.By 1808, when T.C. visited , he found "...a pleasant village of about sixteen or eighteen houses." [17] DeWitt Clinton counted more by 1810: "Queenston contains about 40 houses. I saw two square rigged vessels taking in salt."

The portage business and the travellers visiting the area, pausing to visit the Falls of Niagara before they continued their journeys, required a stagecoach service to transport them and inns to accommodate them. As early as 1796 a stagecoach service operated between Niagara and the Upper Landing (Chippawa) with a stopover at Queenston to pick up passengers. Two inns are mentioned in early writing, Bannister's and Fairbanks.

T.C. in his *Ride to Niagara* stopped at Bannister's in 1808 and left these observations: "Queenston... I stopped at Bannister's, a civil man from Massachusetts. I got a pint of excellent port, which I find to be the fashionable wine among Canadians. This is a place of trade, being the commencement of the portage around the Falls. Bannister pays about twelve shillings sterling a year in direct taxes of all kinds. The military and judiciary are paid by the Crown. Judge Hamilton, who died lately, and had a

very large property, was assessed at no more. The imported goods come by way of Montreal. For tea they give a dollar and a half, loaf sugar three shillings (New York Currency). For my wine he charged me five shillings, but it was good. At Batavia I got Mr. Ellicott to change my Pennsylvania notes for the notes current in New York State; but I found notes of no current kind in Canada. They trade for coin. They have no bank and they dislike our notes. No wonder." [18]

As T.C. noted in his *Ride to Niagara*. Queenston was a "place of trade" because of its location at the beginning of the portage around the Falls. But it was also the place where the Iroquois Indian Trail from the area of Burlington crossed the Niagara River to continue east along what is now Ridge Road (U.S. 104) in the United States. As the trail became a road, there was increased traffic from the United States to destinations in Canada, and Queenston at the junction of the two roads, became a busy place.

One of Lieutenant-Governor Simcoe's first acts when he arrived at Niagara in 1792 was to establish, officially, ferry services across the Niagara River, to Youngstown and Lewiston. He established a schedule of tolls and provided an interesting fare exemption to help attendance at the Niagara Fair which was held

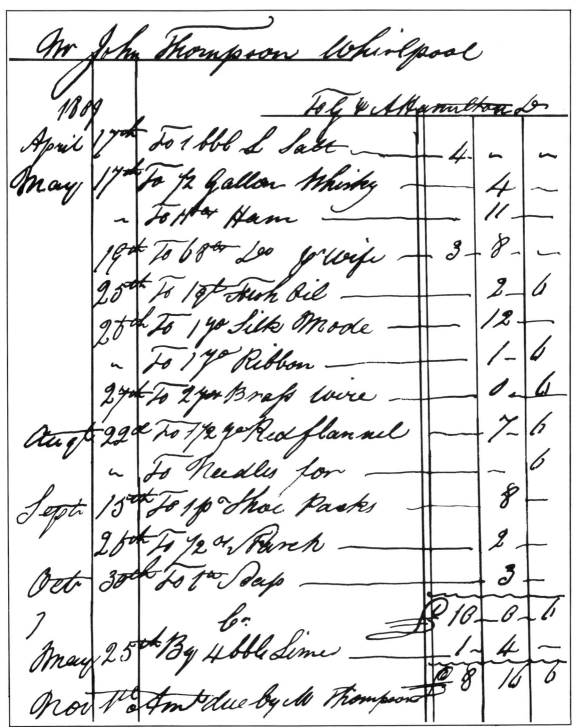

John Thompson's Account with G. & A. Hamilton

This is an account of John Thompson's purchases during the period April 17, 1809 until October 30, 1809. The items Thompson purchased were: 1 barrel of Salt on April 17; 1/2 gallon of whisky and 11 pounds of ham a month later. Then on May 19, there is a coded entry, "To 6 pr Dr. for wife". Dr. was probably an abbreviated entry for drawers. These were pioneer ladies' lingerie which were purchased. Mrs. Thompson needed some sewing supplies, and 1 yard of Silk Mode and 1 yard of Ribbon were added to the account, along with 2 yards of Brass Wire. More sewing supplies on August 22, 1/2 yard Red flannel and needles. On September 15, 1 pair of Shoe Packs, possibly liners for boots, and an indecipherable item on September 26, which must have been potent, only 1/2 oz. was purchased. The last item charged on October 30 was one pound of soap. When John Thompson came to settle the account, he brought 4 barrels of lime, for which he received a credit, and he paid the balance which was £8, 16s, 6p.

during a six day period beginning the second Monday of October each year. The ferry service would be free during that period. [19] In 1799 a Niagara newspaper carried this ad: "In 1799 the annual fair at Queenston 9 th Nov. A park provided to show the animals". [20]

The British traders, merchants operating from Queenston, were still supplying the American southwest with goods and the American Government moved to exclude them by establishing customs houses in 1799 along the border. In this way they restricted the transhipment of trade goods through American territory. The British countered, after a delay, by establishing Ports of Customs at Queenston, Niagara and Fort Erie in 1801, and at Chippawa in 1802. From that time on, what had been an informal arrangement, allowing people and goods to pass freely between the two countries, now became subject to government regulation and control, with customs duties imposed on imported goods. Thomas Dickson became the first Collector of Customs at Queenston.

At the same time Queenston got a postoffice. Colin Troup, postal historian, wrote in *Postal Villages in the Niagara Peninsula* that the Niagara Peninsula's postal service began with the opening of the first post office at Niagara in the year 1798. In 1801 post offices were established at Queenston, Chippawa and Fort Erie, and a network of official mail distribution began, replacing the previous system where merchants, lawyers and others who wished to forward mail, dealt with the stagecoach owners, who carried letters at 4 pence per letter. Beginning August 1,1801, official postmaster's stages carried mail only, no passengers, between Niagara and Queenston and then along the Portage Road to Chippawa.

In 1789 there were only four merchant shops in the Niagara Peninsula. By 1803 there were twenty-seven, and by 1810 only seven of the twenty-seven were still in business. Merchants starting out in business tended to try to attract customers by granting credit. In most cases of business failure, they had overextended themselves with credit sales and were unable to pay for their goods. [21]

Original merchants' accounts of James Thompson presently in the possession of Isabel Walker, Thompson's great-great-granddaughter show those still in business in 1800 included Thomas Clark, Thomas Dickson, R. Hamilton, William Robertson at Queenston; William and James Crooks at Niagara; Thomas Cummings, and Grant & Kerby at Chippawa. [22] Robert Hamilton's relatives are well represented in the list of surviving merchants.

Queenston was a "shopping centre" for the Niagara Peninsula because of the variety of merchandise offered for sale by its merchants. While merchants in other communities would stock only the necessities of life, the merchants of Queenston, who had a greater market, were able to stock luxury items - things that one would not expect to find in a pioneer town.

Robert Hamilton of Queenston died in 1809. An inventory taken after his death to establish the value of his estate, shows the wide range of merchandise offered for sale. The necessities of life were there - sugar, salt, molasses, liquor, crockery, knives, tools, combs, buttons, cloth and ammunition. What surprises us are the luxury items, goods that we might not expect to be available for sale to a pioneer community. He stocked fine silver, gilt paper, gentlemen's fur hats, pewter basins and snuffboxes. Hamilton's stock of cloth would do justice to a modern fabric shop as he carried a wide range of materials. There were calico, corduroy, jean, cotton, linen, fustian, sheeting, canvas, dowlas, madras and osnaburgh to satisfy domestic needs. For those who were fashion conscious there were Pink Burant, Brown Florentine, Black Shallorn, Swansdown and Bengal Stripe. All together this amounted to 3097m (3,387 yards) of cloth.

Hamilton and the other merchants did not sell their goods cheaply. The executors of his estate, Thomas and William Dickson and Thomas Clark, merchants themselves, estimated that Hamilton's profit on his stock was 40 per cent. [23] He offered credit and even in those days people bought more than they could afford. He and other merchants employed bill collectors, called outriders, who travelled throughout the area calling on debtors to collect past due accounts. They covered the whole of the Niagara Peninsula as far west as Ancaster. In 1803, one of these outriders who serviced 443 accounts, reported that 18 debtors could not be found and 7 could not pay. [24] When Hamilton's business was audited at the time of his death, 1,218 people owed him money.

If you couldn't pay a merchant's account, he would accept a mortgage on your land. In this way many of the settlers got themselves into difficulty, made worse when they bought more merchandise on credit. Hamilton acquired property all over the Peninsula when these mortgagees defaulted. After Robert Hamilton's death his merchandise empire declined while his estate was being disputed. Two of his sons, Robert and John would use their inheritance to found a lake shipping enterprise which benefited Queenston. Queenston's prominence as a retail and distribution centre was disrupted by the War of 1812. It was never to recover as its retail trade was lost to Niagara and St. Davids.

Queenston and the War of 1812

Throughout the early months of 1812 tension mounted between Britain and the United States over the interception of American shipping on the high seas - the British were ostensibly looking for British citizens among the American crews. If they were found, they were transferred to the British vessel. The United States was also carrying on trade with France, while Britain and France were at war. The British Navy blockaded American ports to prevent ships from leaving for France and the United States considered this a violation of their neutrality. The people of the Niagara Peninsula and in Queenston were aware of the possibility of war, but they carried on business as usual with the people of Lewiston.

There were isolated incidents that disturbed the peace. Around April 15, 1812, someone in Queenston fired three shots toward the American shore, one of which narrowly missed a Lewiston businessman who was walking along the street. An exchange of letters took place between Benjamin Barton, Rufus Spalding and Joshua Fairbanks of Lewiston who wrote complaining of the incident. They were answered by Thomas Dickson, Robert Grant and James Kerby of Queenston, who expressed their regrets and gave assurances that the person responsible would be punished.[1] They also assured their correspondents that they would encourage "the disposition which unanimously exists here for the promotion of uninterrupted harmony between the two countries."

Colonel John Clark in his *Memoirs* recalled an incident involving a cow, which occurred just before war was declared. He wrote: "Mr. Phelps (Elijah Phelps) a large farmer at Queenston sold a cow to a Mr. Fairbanks over the river at Lewiston, on the American side, which was sent over in the ferry boat. The next day, cowey, as if not liking her quarters, or preferring the Loyalty of the British Government for her headquarters, strolled down to the water side, and altho the current was swift there, she plunged into the stream and swam over to her old quarters where she remained until after the war was over, being taken care of by her old master, then she was honourably restored to her American owner."

The inhabitants of Queenston and Lewiston were unaware that war had been declared on June 11, 1812. It was not until June 20 that Thomas Clark received a letter by courier, along with his business correspondence, advising him that a state of war existed between Great Britain and the United States. The news was unwelcome to people on both sides of the river, and these two communities who "were in the habit of friendly intercourse, connected by marriage and various other relationships", would now be enemies. It would be more than three years before hostilities would end, and normal communications and relationships would be resumed.

With the possibility of invasion by the American forces, many families left the area or removed their

Sir Isaac Brock.
A water colour, by an unknown artist.
Isaac Brock was born on the island of Guernsey in 1769.
He entered the British Army when he was 15 years old. In
the early days of the War of 1812-14 his inspired and
audacious leadership quickly brought about the surrender
of Detroit, where an entire American Army Brigade was
taken prisoner. At the time of his death on October 13, 1812
at the Battle of Queenston Heights, he was provisional
Lieutenant-Governor of the Province of Upper Canada.

valuables. The *New York Gazette* on July 24, 1812 reported; "...at Newark, Queenston and other villages along the river there are no inhabitants except a few civilians, soldiers and their officers. It is said that an immense quantity of specie, plate, etc., from various parts of the Province had been taken up, destined for Quebec."[2] Some of the inhabitants who left Queenston for points inland, returned after a few weeks when there was no military action.

The British set about fortifying the Heights at Queenston and on July 3, 1812 the Americans suddenly realized that a stone redoubt, known today as the Redan Battery, had been erected on the Heights, and was armed with two or three long range cannon which were pointed toward Lewiston. The presence of this battery which could shoot into every area of Lewiston, and which could destroy everything within its range, alarmed the Americans and they countered with a battery on the heights on their own side, overlooking Queenston.

United States Army Inspector-General Gray who supervised the construction of this battery, boasted: "The battery at Lewiston has a powerful command, is intended for two or three large guns, and keeps the inhabitants of Queenston in perfect subjection. Its elevation above the one-gun battery of the enemy is nearly forty-five feet and can sweep it off the surface of the field, distant from it about four hundred yards and from Queenston about six hundred, and elevated above the village about sixty-eight feet, has command of the Niagara River."[3]

He was premature in his announcement, as the Americans did not have long range cannon to arm this battery, which was named Fort Gray in honour of the man who built it. For some time the United States Army had no cannon available of sufficient range to counter the British Redan Battery on Queenston Heights.

The Americans felt that their only solution to the threat of the Redan Battery was to invade Canada and take it over by force. They assembled a large force of soldiers near Lewiston, many of them members of the Militia. The Militia were not professional soldiers, but mainly farmers who served as soldiers, joining the Militia when they were not looking after their crops. By October 1812, thousands of men were assembled around Lewiston, and there were problems feeding and housing them. Many of them left the service, deserting and returning to their farms. In one instance over one hundred men stacked their muskets and went home, and another large group threatened to do likewise. The mutiny was stopped when the men were persuaded to return to duty on the promise of "better quarters in a few days."[4]

In September, with a truce in force, the sentries on both sides of the river kept up a constant firing back and forth. A resident of Lewiston reported: "On the bank of the river musket balls are almost as thick as whippowills on a summer evening." A shot fired from the American side "put a ball so quick thro' a lad's head on the other side that he fell dead without winking."[5] The British protested these outrages, breaches of the truce.

The American plan was to invade Canada, destroy the Redan Battery on Queenston Heights, and then retain possession of the village of Queenston, where they would quarter their disgruntled troops in the village's houses. With this in mind they laid plans to cross the Niagara River by boat, beginning at 3 a.m. October 11. Major-General Stephen Van Rensselaer, in reporting to William Eustis, United States Secretary of War, wrote: "To avoid any embarrassment in crossing the river, what is here a

Ian Graham

Lieutenant Sim absconds with the oars for the rowboats meant to carry the American Army across the Niagara River on the morning of October 12. This caused the invasion to be delayed for a day, so that other oars could be obtained.

sheet of violent eddies, experienced boatmen were procured to take the boats across."[6]

In spite of his precautions, he did suffer a major embarrassment when a Lieutenant Sim, delegated as the man with the greatest knowledge of the river, deserted, carrying with him most of the oars required for the boats. This forced the postponement of the attack on Queenston for twenty-four hours and disheartened the American troops who were prepared to board the boats for the crossing.

Major-General Isaac Brock had his own problems with mutinous troops. Major Thomas Evans reported on the evening of October 11, that he had been advised by Captain Dennis, commander of the flank companies of the 49th Regiment stationed at Queenston, that the soldiers were in a highly mutinous state, some having deliberately threatened to shoot their officers. General Brock replied "Evans, you will proceed and investigate and march here as prisoners a half dozen of those most culpable and I will make an example of them." General Brock no doubt intended to have a firing squad shoot the mutineers. Major Evan arrived at Queenston on October 12 and found most of the company confined to a burned out guardhouse. The American Army invaded Canadian territory at Queenston in the early morning of October 13 and the mutinous troops of the 49th were released from confinement and pressed into service as every able bodied man was required to counter the American attack.

There are other accounts of the Battle of Queenston Heights, to which the reader can refer, so only that part of the battle that concerns the village is written about here. The American boats made landings all along the shore of the river at Queenston, with the main party landing below the high bank by the ferry landing. Here they were pinned down by the defending British regulars. John Lovett wrote after the battle: "Three of the batteaux carrying troops landed at the Hollow below Mr. Hamilton's gardens where they were met by British regulars." Some of

the American troops had to be "dislodged from behind a stone guard house and they took refuge behind Judge Hamilton's storehouse, where our 18 pounder cannon raked them from there and what could fled."[7]

When British reinforcements arrived from Fort George, they met spirited opposition from these American troops. "We were halted a few moments in Mr. Hamilton's garden, where we were exposed to shot from the American battery at Fort Gray."[8] When the British dislodged the Americans from the Hamilton property, they set up their artillery close to the house, so that they could return artillery fire from Fort Gray. During the ensuing action the Hamilton house was badly damaged by cannon-fire.

The American forces at the landing were for the most part confined to the lower shore. They were not making any progress until a party led by Captain John Ogilvie and Captain John Wool, went some distance upriver, along the shore, where they found a fishermen's path leading up the escarpment. They climbed to the top of the Heights and soon were positioned above and behind the British gunners manning the Redan Battery. From this advantageous

Before dawn on the morning of October 13, American soldiers set out to cross the Niagara River and invade Canada at Queenston.

Ian Graham

Ian Graham

American soldiers, led by Captain Ogilvie and Captain Wool, climb the heights, undetected, by way of a fishermen's path. They are soon above and behind the gunners of the Redan battery.

Ian Graham

Major-General Isaac Brock, mounted on his horse Alfred, leads his British troops in a charge against the Americans who now are firing from the Redan battery. Brock's horse Alfred is killed and Brock is forced to end the assault and retire on foot.

position, they charged down on the surprised British artillery men, who barely had time to spike their guns oefore they retreated down the hill into the village of Queenston.

General Isaac Brock arrived in Queenston soon after the loss of the Redan Battery. He immediately led a detachment of troops in a charge up the Heights in an attempt to retake the battery. His horse, Alfred, was killed and he was forced to turn back. He organized a second charge, and though suffering a musket ball wound to his sword arm, he pressed on. An American sniper, using a tree trunk for cover, shot Brock in the chest. He barely had time to murmur a few words before he died. "His lifeless body was immediately conveyed into a house in Queenston unperceived by the enemy", wrote J.B. Clegg in a letter to Brock's brother.[9]

After Brock's death the British forces withdrew from the village and the American troops took over. The American forces augmented by reinforcements crossed over the river without opposition from the British guns. Then, in spite of the orders the soldiers had received forbidding plundering, the houses in Queenston were plundered for whatever possessions there were. An American newspaper later reports "…of the prisoners taken by the British on the

Major-General Brock regroups his men and leads a charge on foot, against the Americans entrenched around the Redan battery.

Ian Graham

Ian Graham

An American Army rifleman from Kentucky, using the trunk of a tree as cover, suddenly steps out into the open, takes aim and fires, hitting Brock in the chest.

Heights, the militia were permitted to return home, under the promise that they would not take up arms again during the war, an indulgence they do not deserve, as it appears that during the time they were in possession of Queenston, they plundered the houses of everything they could conveniently carry away, indeed it appears they were allured over by the hopes of plunder.'' [10]

Major-General Roger Hale Sheaffe brought a relief force from Fort George down a back road, now Concession Road No.2, and took his men up the escarpment, along a narrow path, and brought them in a wide flanking movement to a position in the rear of the now stranded Americans on the Heights. It was 2 p.m., and already a detachment of British troops under Captain Bullock and a party of two hundred Indians who had marched along the Portage Road from Fort Chippawa, had been harassing the Americans with a series of hit and run raids. The Indians' war cries demoralized the Americans, who had little battle experience, and the sporadic attacks greatly hindered their attempts to build defences. When Sheaffe ordered the British forces to attack, the forces were about equal, with a thousand men each. After a single volley of musket fire, accompanied by the Indian war cries, the British advanced. The American line was shattered. Their commander, Colonel Winfield Scott, tried to organize an orderly retreat to the landing, but to no avail; his force was being cut to pieces. After half an hour of battle he called for surrender and the fighting gradually ceased.

Brock staggers and slumps into the arms of two British soldiers. He dies and is carried off the battlefield.

Ian Graham

Battle of Queenston Heights.   *Royal Ontario Museum*
A chromolithograph by J.D. Kelly, circa 1896.

The artist painted his conception of the Battle of Queenston Heights in 1896, eighty-three years after it took place.
Major-General Isaac Brock is shown at the bottom left, with the inscription "Push on York Volunteers" at the
bottom of the picture, to the right of Brock's left foot. From actual reports we know that Brock died without issu-
ing any memorable words. The British charge, with colours flying, is highly dramatic and unlikely. As well, the
depiction of Indians fighting with tomahawks against American musket fire lacks credibility. The Indians were
equipped with the same muskets which the British troops and Canadian Militia used.

The Americans landed about 800 regular troops and about 400 militia. Their losses according to United States Colonel Mead were about 100 killed, 200 wounded and 725 taken prisoner. George Heriot who was taken prisoner, wrote a letter from Quebec on October 24, to F. Freeling in which he said: "..,in the last attempt (at Queenston) between two and three hundred were drowned in crossing the river (these are casualties not listed in the battle losses) and at the conclusion of the combat many precipitated themselves into the river to avoid the bayonet." The British losses were 110 killed, wounded and missing.

Major-General Isaac Brock and his aide-de-camp, Lieutenant-Colonel John Macdonell, were two of the one hundred and ten British casualties. The Americans were unaware that Brock had been killed on October 13. On October 14, General Van Rensselaer wrote to Brock, proposing that a detachment of American soldiers sufficient for the purpose, be allowed to bring the dead bodies of American soldiers over the river in boats, and also that he be allowed to send his officers who were prisoners their baggage and cash. [11]

The Battle of Queenston, Oct. 13th, 1813.
Drawn by Major Dennis, engraved by T. Sutherland, 1836.
The inscription reads: "Which ended in a complete Victory on the part of the British, having captured 927 men,
killed or wounded about 500. Taken 1400 Stand of Arms, a six pounder, and a stand of Colours." Major Den-
nis' interpretation of the battle includes all of the events of the day, beginning with the boatloads of American
troops crossing the river and being pinned down below the river bank. To the left, Captain Ogilvie's and Cap-
tain Wool's men are shown scaling the Heights by the fishermen's path. The final battle on the Heights shows
the British troops pushing the Americans towards the edge of the gorge. Major Dennis was present during the
battle. A Captain then, he was commander of the flank companies of the 49th Regiment stationed at Queenston.
The evening before the battle most of the company were confined to a burned out guardhouse, because they were
in a mutinous state and had threatened to shoot their officers. They were released before dawn to fight the in-
vading Americans.

Brock's death was a severe blow to the morale of the people of Upper Canada. While a monument was erected on the Heights in Brock's memory, no recognition was made of the part that Major-General Sheaffe played in gaining the victory. British Prime Minister Churchill paid a brief visit to Queenston Heights during his 1943 visit to Canada and Niagara Falls. He surprised everyone with his knowledge of Canadian history. After criticizing General Brock's irrational dash up Queenston Heights, in his attempt to retake th Redan Battery, he expressed surprise that no monument had been erected, no recognition made of the part that Major-General Sheaffe - the real victor of the battle - had played. Someone in the party said: "I believe that there is a plaque somewhere." Churchill musing on the tactics of the battle, replied: "Perhaps it is because he wasn't killed." [12]

Major-General Sheaffe was ignored when the monument was erected to commemorate Brock's death and the British victory over the Americans at Queenston Heights because of the animosity of the people of York. When York was attacked by the American Fleet in April 1813, General Sheaffe and his small force of British regulars were ordered to retire towards Kingston, as his force was hopelessly outnumbered. The Americans found no resistance and burnt the public buildings and many of the houses in York.

At that time General Sheaffe was Administrator of the Province and his position made it necessary for him to consider his personal safety as both a political and a military necessity. The people of York felt that he had "betrayed them to save his own skin". When they raised the money for Brock's first monument, they expressed their lingering resentment by excluding General Sheaffe from any recognition of the part that he played in the victory.

The British would later burn Washington in retaliation for the destruction of York. Sheaffe, unable to carry out his duties as Administrator of

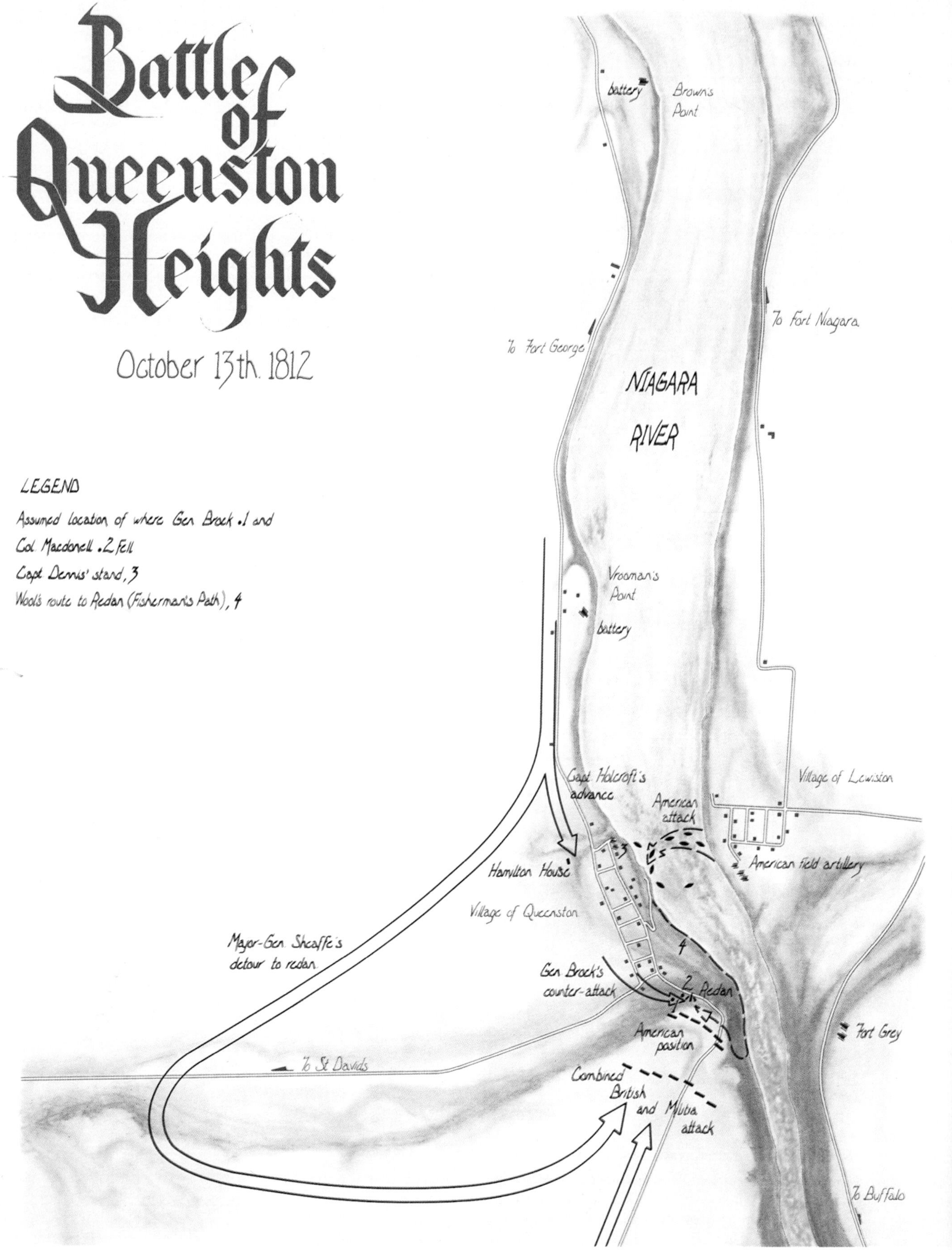

Battle of Queenston Heights

October 13th, 1812

battery   Brown's Point

To Fort Niagara

To Fort George

NIAGARA

RIVER

Vrooman's Point

battery

Capt Holcroft's advance

American attack

Village of Lewiston

American field artillery

Hamilton House

Village of Queenston

Major-Gen Sheaffe's detour to redan

4

Gen Brock's counter-attack

2 Redan

American position

Fort Grey

To St Davids

Combined British and Militia attack

To Buffalo

Battle of Queenston Heights, October 13, 1812.

This map of the battle appeared in the May 1984 edition of "Cuesta" – a Niagara Escarpment Commission Publication. R. Pepper, J. Novostad and C. Mandy were the cartographers.

Niagara Escarpment Commissic

Upper Canada because of this animosity toward him, was recalled to England in June 1813. The British, recognizing that he acted under orders, made him a baronet for his services at the Battle of Queenston Heights. It was the Women's Literary Club of St. Catharines, founded by Mrs. J.C. Currie, who erected the stone marker - "Sheaffe's Path to Victory" - in 1892. While it is several miles from the battle site, it marks the path where Sheaffe led his relief force up the escarpment to outflank the Americans on Queenston Heights.

It was 146 years before the old animosities were forgotten and Major-General Sir Roger Hale Sheaffe was given the recognition due him. In 1959 the Archaeological and Historic Sites Board of the Province of Ontario erected a plaque on the north side of Brock's monument recognizing his part in the Battle of Queenston Heights.

The inhabitants of Queenston returned to their homes after the battle and tried to resume their lives, using what was left of their possessions. The village was under constant scrutiny from the opposite shore and the British began to take advantage of this, to distract the Americans by sending troops marching through the village in full view of the American observers. On February 23, 1813, the *Buffalo Gazette* reported: "Last Wednesday an express from Lewiston brought news that 160 sleighs with troops aboard had passed upriver by Queenston (as was said) bound for Fort Erie."

Soon the Americans saw through the ruse and the *Buffalo Gazette* wrote: "…we consider deceptive manoeuvres on the part of the enemy. The British commander at Fort George is in the frequent practice of sending out detachments from that place to Queenston in the night and on the next morning would march them down again to the Fort in sight of our garrison at Niagara. At other times he would march forces to Fort George at night and the next morning return them in plain view of our troops."[13]

In December 1813, when the Americans retreated from Fort George, they set fire to Newark, reducing it to rubble. The American General McClure who

was responsible for this outrage, wrote to the United States Secretary of War on December 12, 1813, saying that the British had appeared at Queenston and were observed fortifying the Heights. He planned to counter their actions "… have detached Colonel Grieves and about 100 of his Regiment of Artillery, to Lewiston to open a fire of hot shot on Queenston from Fort Gray and deprive them of quarters there also: you will observe from my despatch of yesterday that every building in Newark is reduced to ashes."[14] There is no record of this hot shot barrage having been carried out and Queenston was spared the ordeal of a hot shot cannonade.*

Queenston had been a centre of action beginning with the American invasion in October 1812 and the Battle of Queenston Heights. Then after a quiet winter the Americans crossed the Niagara River on May 27, 1813 and captured Fort George. The British withdrew from the Niagara Frontier and the Americans occupied Queenston and the Heights. After the Battle of Stoney Creek on June 6, 1813, the Americans withdrew to Fort George, and on June 8 they left Queenston. The British meanwhile had a force led by Lieutenant James FitzGibbon at Decew's (also called Decou's) at the Beaverdams, from which point they sent out patrols to harass the Americans.*

On June 23, 1813, an American force commanded by Colonel Boerstler left Fort George, with the intention of attacking the British force stationed near the Decew house.* They set up camp that night at Queenston. The American officers took over one of the few houses left in a habitable condition, the home of James and Laura Secord, and bivouacked there. During the evening Laura Secord overhead their plans for the attack which was to take place the next day.

Intent on warning FitzGibbon and the British force of the impending attack, she set out on foot before dawn the next morning and walked to the Decew's at the Beaverdams. Tradition says that she drove a cow in front of her to allay suspicion as to the intent of her mission, but there is no historical evidence of this. It is also said that FitzGibbon already knew of

---

* *Hot shot*

   Cannon balls were heated until they were red hot, in a "shot furnace". They were taken out of the furnace with tongs and loaded into the cannon. They were effective against wooden buildings, as they set fire to any building that they hit. They were used by the British and American artillery in their frequent cannon fire barrages against each others Forts - British Fort George at Niagara, and Fort Niagara opposite on the American shore.

* *Lieutenant James FitzGibbon was commander of a special group of the 49 th Regiment, composed entirely of Irish soldiers. They were all trouble makers and had either been court martialed, or had joined his unit to escape being court martialed. Their assignment was to roam the countryside and harass the Americans with hit and run raids.*

* *Captain John Decou was a Loyalist settler. He built a stone house and a mill where the water from the Beaverdams fell over the escarpment, This waterfall now bears his name and is called Decou Falls, or Decew Falls. His house became a British headquarters at various times during the War of 1812-14. In 1813 it was the base for Lieutenant James FitzGibbon's raiding party.*

Laura Secord overhears American plans for a surprise attack on the British forces at the Beaverdams.

the impending attack and her information only provided confirmation. Nevertheless she made the journey and was subsequently recognized for her bravery. The American force was defeated in this engagement and those not killed were taken prisoner.

Some business was carried on in Queenston during the war. Thomas Dickson's store was open in 1814 as Lieutenant-Colonel Harvey writing to Major T.G. Simons on January 1, 1814, said: ''I enclose a requisition for articles of clothing, etc., required for the American prisoners of war. You will get them at Mr. Dickson's at Queenston.''[15]

Queenston was to be occupied by the American forces once more before the war would end. On July 4, 1814, the Americans crossed in force at Fort Erie, capturing the Fort and then advancing some 6000 strong down the river road to Chippawa. On July 5, they met and defeated a British force commanded by Major-General Phineas Riall south of Street's Creek, now called Ussher's Creek. This battle is known as the Battle of Chippawa. After this battle the British withdrew to Fort George, leaving the rest of the Niagara Frontier undefended.

United States Major-General Jacob Brown marched his American Army along the Portage Road, took over the undefended Heights at Queenston and established his headquarters in the village. He installed his artillery around what was left of the Hamilton house, and remained in the village until July 9, when without attacking Fort George, he withdrew his whole force to Chippawa. The Americans left Queenston on July 24, 1814 and that was the end of the war for Queenston.

While the American Army was encamped at Queenston, foraging parties were sent out to obtain food for the troops. The farmers were victimized as the troops "requisitoned" their grain and livestock without making any payment. The farmers around St. Davids took exception to this and fired on the foraging parties. In retaliation, on July 19, 1814, the Americans set fire to St. Davids, burning every building to the ground. According to a report by Sir George Prevost to Vice-Admiral the Honourable Alexander Cochrane on July 24, 1814, "The villages of St. Davids and Queenston were committed to flames and totally destroyed when General Brown withdrew to his camp above Chippawa."[16] The report was correct only for St. Davids - Queenston suffered major damage but was not totally destroyed. However Queenston was in ruins at the end of the war of 1812-14. Homes, businesses and storehouses had either been burnt or damaged by cannon fire. The War Losses Claims filed by those who had property destroyed, plundered or burnt, during the war, give an indication of the loss suffered by Queenston's residents and businessmen. One account lists the warehouses of Robert Hamilton and Co.; Robert Hamilton's barns and stables; his house was listed as having been "burned by accident by our own troops."[17] The Hamilton loss was estimated at £2,000.

Before dawn the next morning she sets out to walk through the woods to warn the British of the impending attack.

Battle of Queenston, a print.

This rather fanciful depiction of the American invasion of Upper Canada at Queenston on October 13, 1812, gives a very dramatic, but incorrect interpretation of the actual landing. The invading Americans did not land into cannon fire, but were strongly opposed by British troops who occupied the high bank above the shore of the river.

Battle of Queenston Heights.
An oil on canvas attributed to Major James B. Dennis.

Brock's Memorial in St. Paul's Cathedral, London, England.
Brock's courage and leadership was recognized by the British people soon after his heroic death at the Battle of Queenston Heights. The British House of Commons, on July 20, 1813, voted the sum of £1575 for the erection of this monument, which is located in St. Paul's Cathedral.

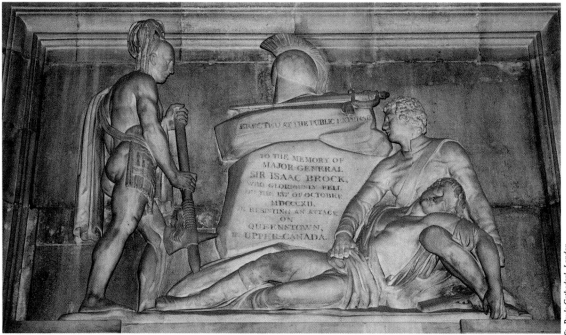

Queenston After the War of 1812

Ten or more years would go by before the damaged and destroyed buildings in Queenston were repaired or rebuilt. Commercial activity resumed as soon as war was over, but Queenston would never regain the prominent position it held before the War, as a centre of commerce for the Niagara District.

William Hamilton Merritt, who opened a store after the war at Shipman's corners (St. Catharines), branched out and moved part of his stock to Niagara, where he opened another store in 1815, and "the same at Queenston - that being the principal rendezvous for traders."[1] His assessment of his business prospects was in error as he evidently did not attract enough trade to stay in business. By September 1816, he had closed both his Niagara and Queenston stores and concentrated his commercial activities in the area around what is now St. Catharines.

Merritt left us a record in his diary of the difficulties he had with the postal service. According to him, the Canadian Postal service was expensive and slow. It cost him four dollars and "other sundry expenses before I could mail my letter." The letter went by ferry to Lewiston, then on to New York. Overseas letters could only be interchanged once or twice a year.[2]

Captain Richard Langslow of the East India Company passed through Queenston in 1817 and called it "a poor town in a hollow".[3] The portage was still operating, and stagecoaches passed through on their way from Niagara to Chippawa, or began their runs from Queenston, taking passengers to Chippawa.

Conditions had improved by the 1820's when E.A. Talbot reported "sixty houses and three hundred people" in Queenston. This was countered by John Howison, another officer of the East India Company who detected an "air of depression and inactivity".

In spite of the air of "depression and inactivity" which Howison found in Queenston, he was optimistic for the future of the place. Unduly optimistic as it turned out. Howison wrote: "Queenston must infallibly acquire magnitude and importance when the province becomes populous and flourishing, for it is situated at the commencement of a portage that can never be evaded by any improvement in the navigation. It being rendered necessary by the Falls of Niagara...Even now a good deal of this carrying business goes on during the summer months".[4] When Howison was visiting Queenston and making these observations, a project was getting underway, which would doom Queenston's warehousing and portaging business. Construction on the Welland Canal had begun, and the "evasion" of the portage which Howison said was impossible was soon accomplished.

In 1823 there came to live in Queenston for a short time a man who would to go down in history as one of Queenston's most famous citizens, William Lyon Mackenzie. After selling out a successful bookselling business in Dundas, he invested his savings in Queenston by building a stone house at the top of Front Street. In it he opened a store where he sold

View from Queenston Heights, Upper Canada 1816.
Water colour by Francis Hall.

Francis Hall took a bird's eye view in this depiction of what you can see from Queenston Heights. An apt title would be "On a Clear Day you Can See Forever". The Niagara River is shortened, to make it appear that it is not very far to Niagara (Niagara-on-the-Lake) and Lake Ontario is shown as being only a few miles rather than forty miles wide. His depiction of sailing ships on the river, and a much larger than life ferry dock on the American side, add interest to the view. Hall was the architect who designed the first Brock's Monument.

patent drugs and books, and did job printing as a sideline. To provide an outlet for his political views - he was a vociferous opponent of the ruling clique of prominent people, called the Family Compact, and a promoter of the cause of self government - he established Queenston's first and only newspaper, the *Colonial Advocate.*

His job printing press was too small to print the newspaper, and it is presumed that he had it printed in Lewiston. He published the first edition of his newspaper on May 18 1824. The radical views, which he expressed in the newspaper, caused great consternation, and encouraged his readers in their desire for responsible government. Suddenly, with only one week's notice, in November of that year, Mackenzie sold his book and drug business and moved his printing press and newspaper to Toronto.

Another significant event which took place in 1824

was the erection of the first monument to the memory of Major-General Sir Isaac Brock. Francis Hall, a civil engineer and architect who had recently emigrated from Scotland, to live in Queenston, was commissioned to design the monument. Limestone from the quarry on the heights above the village was used in the 19.8m (65 feet) high structure. It had a circular inside stairway which led to a viewing area at the top. A trip to the heights, and a climb up th monument to view the surrounding countryside became an attraction for visitors. [5]

Queenston's economy received a boost in 1824 when John Hamilton brought in shipbuilders to build a steamboat. It was built on the river bank south of the Hollow - also called the Deep Hollow. An ice jam in the early spring of 1825 nearly destroyed the shipyard and it was only with strenuous effort that the unfinished boat lying in the stays could be moved

James Thompson's Portage Account with Grant & Kerby merchant traders and portage operators at Queenston, for December 1816.

The account was for portaging services carried out by James Thompson. Thompson carried 3 loads of goods from Queenston to Chippawa, and received £7, 7 shillings 8 pence. He also portaged 1 load of 2 barrels of salt, "up" - that is from Queenston to Chippawa for which he received £1,16 shillings.

farther up the river bank and out of range of the ice. It was 1828 before the 350 ton side-paddle wheel steamboat, christened *Queenston,* was launched. It was the first ship built on the lower Niagara River. It was not until 1831 that the Niagara Dock Company was formed and the next year their shipyard was constructed at Niagara.

An advertisement in the *Niagara Herald* in 1828 carried this message: "STEAM BOAT NOTICE The first sailing steamboat *Queenston*…Niagara-Kingston-Brockville-Prescott, every Thursday 8 a.m. throughout the season." This steamboat became part of Robert and John Hamilton's *Lake Ontario & Lake Erie Steamboat Line,* also known as the *Hamilton Line* which was formed in 1833. The main steamboats of this line were the *United Kingdom* and *Adelaide.* The *United Kingdom* ran from Prescott to Niagara, making direct connections via stage from Niagara to Chippawa along the Portage Road. At Chippawa the travellers boarded the *Adelaide* for Detroit. The *Hamilton Line* continued to provide service on Lake Ontario in later years, with the paddle wheel steamers *Canada, Niagara, Alciope,* as well as the *Queenston.*

There were other steamboats built at Queenston at various times over the next twenty-five years. John M. Mills in *Canadian Coastal and Inland Steam Vessels 1809-1830,* lists Queenston as the building port for the following ships: *Queen Victoria* 1838; *Gore* 1839; *Chief Justice Robinson* 1842; *Admiral* 1842; *Magnet* 1847; *Peerless* 1853. Of these the most famous was the *Chief Justice Robinson* which maintained year round service between Toronto and Niagara for ten years. The *Peerless* which made two daily trips across Lake Ontario during ten months of the year was an iron ship. She had been put together at Dunbarton, Scotland, then taken apart, sent out to Canada, and put together again, at Queenston, according to John Mills.

Brock's Monument at Queenston 1831.
Water colour over pencil by Lieutenant-Colonel J.P. Cockburn.
Lieutenant-Colonel James Pattison Cockburn of the Royal Artillery was in the Niagara area at various times between 1827 and 1832, during which time he made numerous sketches and water-colours of the Falls and the surrounding area. This view is the only one he did of Queenston. The stone storehouses which dominate every view of Queenston made over the next one hundred and fifty years, are much evident at the right of the picture. The buildings on the lower bank are probably associated with the ferry to Lewiston.

National Archives of Canada

Brock's Monument at Queenston, near Niagara 1828.
Water colour over pencil by Lieutenant-Colonel J.P. Cockburn

Lieutenant-Colonel Cockburn made this sketch on the Heights in 1828. He has depicted the Tuscan column of Brock's Monument as being square, while the traditional Tuscan column is round. The small openings in the column are windows, to provide light for the inside stairway which wound to the top, where there was a viewing area. Construction on this monument began in early 1824. Sir Peregrine Maitland, Lieutenant-Governor of Upper Canada, laid the cornerstone. The masonry work had been done on the base to a height of about 14.5m (48 feet) when the Lieutenant-Governor learned that William Lyon Mackenzie, the publisher of the "Colonial Advocate", and a vociferous critic of the government, had surreptitiously placed a copy of his newspaper inside the cornerstone. Maitland ordered that the work already done be dismantled so that the cornerstone could be uncovered and the offending newspaper removed.

General Brock's Monument, above Queenston.
W.H. Bartlett, eng. by R.Wallis. In "Canadian Scenery"
London, 1840, Vol.1

This view shows the first monument to Major-General Sir Isaac Brock, erected in 1824. The notch in the bank at the right is where the Portage Road came out at the top of the escarpment. At this time, according to "Smith's Gazeteer", Queenston had a population of 300. Now that the Welland Canal had taken over the bulk of the freight business that had formerly been carried over the Portage Road, Queenston was relying on the steamboat passenger business. One of these steamboats is seen in the river at Lewiston.

Mackenzie House.
Water colour in the John Ross Robertson Collection.

The Mackenzie House, as John Ross Robertson's artist envisioned it. William Lyon Mackenzie was born in Scotland on March 12, 1795 and emigrated to Canada in 1820. He opened a drug and book store in York (Toronto) in partnership with James Leslie. Mackenzie soon moved to Dundas to manage a branch store. He was a prodigious reader and was deeply interested in politics, and developed an all consuming obsession - a hatred of the Family Compact, the clique of influential citizens and members of the Provincial Cabinet, who ran the government of Upper Canada. In the autumn of 1823 Mackenzie moved his family to Queenston and invested his savings in this house, where he established a drug and book store, doing job printing as a side line.

To provide an outlet for his political views, and to further his agitation for responsible government, he published a newspaper called ''Colonial Advocate and Journal of Agriculture Manufactures, and Commerce'', which he shortened to ''Colonial Advocate''. The first edition appeared on May 18,1824 and Mackenzie in an effort to make his cause known, addressed the front page of the first edition to prominent people in Britain, Europe and the United States. He promised to send them subsequent editions, ''free of any expense whatever'', in the hope of promoting his view of responsible government for Upper Canada.

He had only a small press suitable for job printing and it is assumed that he had his paper printed in Lewiston. He gained immediate notoriety with his published views, and felt that he had to move to York where his newspaper had its largest following. It was a sudden decision, characteristic of Mackenzie's volatile temperament, when in the November 18 edition he announced that he was moving to York, and the November 24 edition was published in York. He lived in Queenston for a little more than a year, but he made an indelible impression and his stay in Queenston is commemorated in the restored Mackenzie House.

In 1830 Queenston replaced Niagara as the border crossing point for the transfer of mail to the United States. The roads leading into Queenston were the best maintained in Upper Canada and there was a year round ferry service to Lewiston. For the next fifteen years the steamboats of the United States Mail Line, *Cataract*, *Bay State*, *Ontario* and *Niagara* brought mail to Lewiston and the Royal Mail Line steamers, *Eclipse* and *Chief Justice Robinson* brought mail to Queenston.

Alexander Hamilton, one of Robert Hamilton's sons, became postmaster in 1830, when the volume of mail increased dramatically. The staff of six mail clerks was increased to eighteen when the steamboats arrived with overseas mail. Two and sometimes three wagons, drawn by teams of oxen were required to transport the bags of mail from the wharf to the postoffice. There the staff sorted and redirected the mail. Some was sent west toward Hamilton for western destinations in the Province, some put back in mail bags and sent by ox-drawn wagons along the Portage Road, destined for the Upper Lakes. The mail destined for the United States was sent by ferry across the river to Lewiston. The Queenston Post Office kept up this busy pace until the cross-border system was discontinued in 1851. When the steam railways began operating, the mail was sent by train rather than by boat.[6]

Patrick Shirreff, writing in *A Tour Through North America Together with a Comprehensive View of the Canadas and the United States* complained of the overseas mail service in 1835. "My friend D....... found letters at the post office of Niagara, but like fortune did not attend me, although our letters are said

Brock's Monument (From the American Side).
W.H. Bartlett eng. by Willis, N.P. In "American Scenery"
London, 1840, Vol. II

This view which shows Queenston across the River, and Brock's Monument on the Heights in the background, is particularly interesting because of the steamboats and the activity around the Lewiston dock area in the foreground. The steamboat at the dock is the "Great Britain", owned by the Honourable Robert Hamilton, a son of Robert Hamilton, who was Upper Canada's pioneer steamship owner. The "Great Britain" was a ship of 738 tonnes (750 tons), 99m (162 feet) long with an 18m (60 foot) beam. She was propelled by two low pressure engines, each having its own smoke stack.

A luxurious boat for her time, she had twenty-four ladies' cabins, forty-six men's first class, and twenty six second class cabins. She carried a crew of 35. Her main route was between Niagara and Prescott. The "Great Britain's" best time for a run across the lake from Niagara to York was 3 hours and 20 minutes, achieved in July 1834 during a race with the steamboat "United States". The "Great Britain" lost.

National Archives of Canada

to have been put into the same post office in Scotland, and similarly directed. I did not receive a letter from Britain while across the Atlantic, but my communications reached their destinations in Scotland." Perhaps his moving from place to place after only a short stay, had something to do with his lack of mail.

The residents of Fort Erie were not happy that their mail for Buffalo, just 4.8 km (3 miles) away, had to be sent to Queenston then across the river to Lewiston before it was sent on to Buffalo, a distance of 78.8 km (49 miles). They wanted to eliminate the delay and asked for the power to forward letters direct to Buffalo by ferry, but were refused. We have a modern day example, as this system has been perpetuated. A letter sent from Niagara Falls, Ontario, in 1989, goes to St. Catharines, then Mississauga, then on to Buffalo and finally to Niagara Falls, New York, 0.6km (1 mile) away.

Immediately after the war, the residents of Queenston and Lewiston renewed their associations; the ferry across the river was their only means of transportation. With the establishment of Ports of Customs on both sides of the river it was necessary to intercept goods being brought into Canada, to levy the proper customs duties. To facilitate inspection, the ferry lease was granted to the Collector of Customs, Thomas Dickson. He had been in charge of the ferry before 1816, possibly from as far back as 1809, for on April 2, 1816 he "received a 7 year renewal of the ferry lease at Queenston". Being the astute businessman that he was he paid the Government £5 and promptly leased the ferry rights to a second party for £10. [7]

In 1823 he applied for a further seven years, implying that he might built a "steamboat, to be propelled by horses". It is not clear if he obtained the renewal, but in 1829 when the seven year ferry lease time was up, Robert Hamilton petitioned for the ferry rights, making what he thought was a strong case, in wanting to establish a horseboat ferry, between Lewiston and the Deep Hollow, before the Americans did. [8] As Hamilton wanted to dock the ferry at his wharf, Robert Grant who was then the Collector of Customs, objected: "The Queenston Ferry as at present established...is an easy, safe and expeditious ferry at all seasons, capable of doing, with the present means, much more business than others and being opposite the centre of the Town is more convenient for the public than it it would be removed down river to the Deep Hollow." [9]

The ferry lease was to expire on July 24, 1830 and the Executive Council advertised that it was to be given to the highest bidder - the expiring lease was for £83 a year, and the condition was that it would be a horseboat ferry and operate from the same point

as the present ferry. Robert Grant's objection to the proposed new location was upheld. The Executive Council wrote: "...best place of departure for the horseboat ferry is at the present place of departure of scows and ferry boats, because access to the water's edge is much better - the eddy (in the river) running up some distance facilitates crossing and the location is under the view of the Collector of Customs." [10] On July 23, 1830 the Lieutenant-Governor-in-Council awarded the ferry lease to Joseph Wynn, Innkeeper, at £106 5s per annum, on condition that a horseboat ferry be used.

A year later Wynn asked the government to adjust his tendered sum, as he had applied, expecting the ferry owner on the American side to co-operate with him in constructing a horseboat. The deal fell through and Wynn was left to construct the horseboat on his own. The Executive Council, after substantiating his claim, gave him an allowance of one year's rent. Wynn built his horseboat, and when he re-applied in 1837 in his petition he said "For the past 7 years I have at considerable expense procured a safe, fast running, decked boat, which is propelled by horsepower." [11] Wynn's "fast running, decked boat" was a scow with paddle wheels along each side. A pair of horses, wearily marched on a horizontal disk which turned as the horses kept up their monotonous pace; as the disk turned, it operated the paddle wheels, moving the scow through the water. [12]

It is not clear if his extension was formally granted, but he continued to operate the ferry. He asked for only a five year extension , which would "become void, when the said Bridge shall have been completed". Wynn was referring to a proposal which was being made to build a bridge across the gorge at the Iroquois trail level. As early as 1824 a bridge was

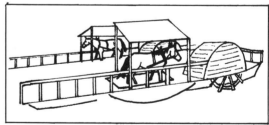

Astrid Akkerman from an original sketch by Paul Kane

HORSEBOAT FERRY

Paul Kane, noted Canadian artist, famous for his paintings depicting Indian life, sketched the horseboat ferry at Queenston, when he visited this area in the mid 1840's. A horseboat was a scow with a paddle wheel along each side. A pair of horses walked a treadmill on a horizontal disk, which was connected by gears to the paddle wheels. As the horses moved the disk, the paddle wheels were turned, moving the scow through the water.

Ralph Greenhill and Thomas D. Mahoney

Suspension Bridge Bank Note
A five dollar bank note issued by The Niagara Suspension Bridge Bank. October 18,1840

suggested over the Niagara Gorge, "located at the narrow strait which commences just above Queenston".[13] A chain bridge, where the bridge deck would be suspended by large chains strung between towers - cables had not yet been invented - was proposed by Francis Hall, a Scottish civil engineer and architect. Hall's parents had emigrated to the Canadas in 1820 and settled in Queenston. In 1824 Hall and his wife left Scotland and joined his parents in Queenston. Here he was soon retained to design a monument to the late Major-General Sir Isaac Brock.[14] There was no action taken on Hall's design for the bridge, but the ferrymen were aware of the possibility of a bridge putting them out of business.

In 1836 there was another proposal to erect a suspension bridge at Queenston. The Niagara Falls, New York *Journal* on August 3, 1835 carried a reprint from an earlier issue of the *Buffalo Journal* announcing the opening of the books for the subscription of capital stock for a suspension bridge at Lewiston. The promoters stated that about $60,000 had already been subscribed. Evidently the balance required was not raised as the bridge project was not carried out.

The promoters kept the idea of a bridge before investors, and in 1840, using the contacts that they had made in raising capital, funds were collected for the establishment of a bank in Queenston. The "Niagara Suspension Bridge Bank" as it was known, opened for business. The bank issued bank notes in denominations of $10.00 or fifty shillings, $5.00 or twenty-five shillings and $1.00 or five shillings. Each

bank note had a sketch of the proposed Lewiston-Queenston Bridge and carried the signatures of Joseph Hamilton, President and G. McMicken, Cashier. The bank failed after one year in business, with losses to the investors.[15]

There had also been bad news for the villagers of Queenston in 1838. On Good Friday, April 17, Benjamin Lett, an Irish-Canadian rebel, who was acknowleged to be a Mackenzie sympathizer, surreptitiously placed a charge of gunpowder within the base of Brock's Monument. The resulting blast damaged the monument beyond repair. Public indignation over this outrageous act led to a massive public gathering of concerned citizens, mostly from Toronto, who came to Queenston and met on the Heights on July 30, 1840.

They came to Queenston in a fleet of steamboats led by the *Traveller* with Governor-General Lord Sydenham and staff on board. Then the *Transit, Queen Victoria* and the *Gore* which crossed the Lake from Toronto together, were met at the mouth of the Niagara River by *Burlington* and *Britannia* coming from Hamilton and the *Gildersleeve* and *Coburg* from Kingston and points east. After the rendezvous, the flag-decorated steamboats, led by *Transit* proceeded up the Niagara River to Queenston. No such flotilla of steamboats was ever again seen on the river.[16]

Walter Haldorson, of Parks Canada, in his article *Sir Isaac Brock's Four Funerals* wrote about the meeting that day on Queenston Heights beside the ruined monument. "Despite the solemn purpose of the campaign, good cheer, merry dining and wining

General Brock's Monument Damaged.
Pencil sketch by T.H. Hibbert.
The remains of Major-General Sir Isaac Brock and his aide-de-camp Lieutenant-Colonel John Macdonell, rested beneath this monument from October 13, 1824, when it was dedicated until April 17,1840. Then their rest was disturbed by Benjamin Lett, an Irish-Canadian Mackenzie sympathizer, who destroyed the monument with a massive blast of gunpowder. The handwritten inscription on the sketch reads: "10th Oct. 1844 from Brock's Monument Queenston, near Niagara after the recent injury it had sustained from a gunpowder blast by some Yankee."

characterized the inaugural function. A temporary pavilion 192 feet long and 55 feet wide was built and a local innkeeper was contracted to supply among other things, 12 wild turkeys, 30 wild geese and 200 chickens, and to furnish 'good help'. The innkeeper and his staff, which included 50 waiters, fed the gathering who paid seven shillings sixpence each for the banquet. There were over one thousand people from Toronto alone.[17] This auspicious gathering notwithstanding, the campaign to raise money for a new monument dragged on until 1853 when the present monument to Brock was erected."

Ferry crossings were a common occurrence between Queenston and Lewiston, they were made year round, only a winter ice jam would stop the service. The hazards of a winter crossing are

dramatically depicted by William Hamilton Merritt in his Diary, relating how he and his family experienced a most melancholy and heart-rending shock. "Mr. Gordon, his eldest sister and her daughter, aged 13, in company with a Miss Stephens, went crossing the ferry from Queenston to Lewiston, when a large piece of ice was driven by the force of the current against the boat, capsizing it, and throwing the ladies and the ferryman into the water. Miss Stephens and the child sank, never to be seen again. Rescued by a passing scow, Mr. Gordon, his sister and the ferryman returned to shore." The men recovered, but Mr. Gordon's sister died.[18]

Not every crossing of the river was made on the ferry. During the War of 1812 there were desertions from both sides, using logs and planks, in fact anything that would float, to help them across. A news item in the *Niagara Mail* on August 10, 1823, showed how the Niagara River at Queenston was one of the crossing points into Canada for escaping black slaves. "The Steamer *Chief Justice Robinson* picked up a 'coloured man' about twelve miles from Niagara floating on a raft made of a gate. He escaped from Tennessee and came to Lewiston but was afraid to go on one of the steamers to cross and tried to cross the river on a gate but the current being strong he was drifted out into the Lake. He said when rescued: 'Thank the Lord...I am a free man now'."

Ferry traffic was brisk in the 1830's when large numbers of families from the Eastern United States, migrating to Michigan and beyond, chose Lewiston-Queenston as their border crossing. The barge-like ferries carried many of the canvas-topped wagons across the river. The more adventuresome took the wheels off their wagons and floated them over the river, no doubt taking the precaution to load their goods and transport them by the ferry. From Queenston the wagons took the road to St. Davids and St. Catharines, to reach points west, on their way to Michigan.

These travellers, called Overlanders, stopped at Queenston and bought supplies from the merchants. It was welcome business for David Thorburn one of the merchants in the early 1830's. According to James Thompson's account with Thorburn, from February 1 to December 30 of that year, Thorburn not only sold general merchandise, but also cashed loans - presumably the cheques of the day - and was the postmaster. There are a number of entries "To postage of a letter 7d". Thompson's accounts also show that he used Thorburn as a broker for lime, and there are several transactions for lime that was delivered to Colonel FitzGibbon - the same Lieutenant FitzGibbon of the Battle of the Beaverdams.

Willowbank Seen from the Landing at Queenston.
Pencil sketch on light grey paper, J.R. Coke Smyth, 1838.
Alexander Hamilton's home, ''Willowbank'', was built in 1834. The figures on horseback are moving through the Hollow toward the beginning of the Portage Road. The horse-drawn cart at the bottom has picked up a load of goods from a ship docked at the wharf.

Thompson bought a mixed lot of goods from Thorburn: sugar, salt, tea, tobacco, whiskey, a scythe, Blue Calico, Black Bomba, Black Muslin, ribbon, bell buttons, buck skin mitts, window glass, putty, and nails. Thorburn also lent James Thompson money, with the amounts ranging from 25s to £31.

The *Niagara Gleaner* in 1833 gives an account of the heavy traffic between Niagara and Fort Erie all of which passed through Queenston. "We believe there are few places in America where there is so much travelling" they wrote editorially. There were six steamers running weekly trips from the Niagara River to the end of Lake Ontario, one steamer ran daily to Toronto. The fare from Prescott to York, Niagara or Queenston was 19s , then by stage from Queenston to Fort Erie 5s. Baggage was carried from Queenston to Chippawa by wagon for 12s. 6d. to 15s. per load. At this time there were seven stagecoaches a day passing through Queenston.

All was not well with the ferry service in 1841. Thomas Trumble who evidently had obtained a second license to operate a ferry, wrote to the Executive Council on February 12: "My boats can no longer run as Wynn and Chubbuck (Joseph Wynn of Queenston and Job Chubbuck of Lewiston who were in the ferry business together) have on both sides in a lawless fashion, fined my ferryman twice in a sum of 5 pounds 10s. for landing at their wharf on the American shore...For the past six months I have borne every expence (sic), inconvenience and trouble, still hoping the Government would extend to me the protection I require". [19] There is no record of what action was taken, the records from then on were lost. In 1848 the Queenston-Lewiston Ferry changed to steam, when the 8 hp steamboat *Odd Fellow* was put in service.

In 1831 after the Welland Canal had taken away much of the former portaging business from Queenston, an alternative form of transport, relatively new to Canada, was proposed. Merchants who had lost business since the Welland Canal opened in 1829, spearheaded by John and Alexander Hamilton, Thomas Clark, David Thorburn, Robert Grant,Samuel Street, and James Cummings applied for a railway charter. Opposition from the Welland Canal Company and Niagara held up approval.

Finally in 1835, the *Erie and Ontario Rail Road Company* got its charter.

Queenston was in economic decline now that the portaging of merchandise and supplies was taken over by the Welland Canal. *Smith's Gazeteer* in 1841, reported Queenston as having a population of 300,with three stores, eight taverns, one wagonmaker, two blacksmiths, one baker, four shoemakers, one tailor. There was evidently enough business from the travellers arriving by boat, and then going by coach over the portage, to provide trade for eight taverns. The Queenston merchants were anticipating increased business from the railway and they were waiting impatiently for it to begin operating. The December 1845 edition of the Niagara *Chronicle* carried an advertisement for a "New Cheap Store". William Brown, Baker and Confectioner was opening in enlarged quarters, in a store the "2nd door north of Mr. Wynn's Hotel". This would be a discount store in today's terms, and Brown carried a complete line of groceries, provisions, glass and tinware, drugs, books, woodenware, stovepipes, etc.

There is no record of when the *Erie and Ontario* was completed, but the section between Niagara Falls and Chippawa, running over terrain that required minimum grading for the roadbed, was in operation by 1839. It took more time and manpower to lay out the inclined roadbed up the steep slope from Queenston to the top of the escarpment. The railway depot, which was its southern terminal, and a warehouse, were built near the corner of present day Front Street and the York Road in Queenston. This eliminated a steep climb from the dock.Passengers and freight were brought up to the depot by carriages and horse-drawn wagons.

O.L. Holley wrote about the railway and Queenston in 1844: "At Chippawa commences a railroad extending to Queenston, a distance of ten miles. Steamboats continue the line of travel from both ends of this road,thus furnishing an interesting and speedy conveyance between the Lakes Erie and Ontario...The railroad... terminates on the south of Queenston village, near the monument. Passengers are taken from the depot in carriages to the steamboat landing, a short distance below, where steamboats depart and arrive several times daily during the summer months. Stages leave Queenston daily at 8 a.m. for St. Catharines, London, Windsor and return from Windsor 8 a.m. each day." [20]

The "Queenston-Chippawa (Rail)Road" as it was called, also the "Chippawa-Queenston (Rail)Road"- the name seemed to change depending on where you were when you used it, was a horse-drawn railway. It ran on wooden rails,which were topped with iron bands. It was not impressive by today's standards, but it had the distinction of being the first railway in Upper Canada.

Travellers coming from York and points east, to Niagara, and from points west, came by steamboat rather than overland on stagecoaches. It was easy to make a choice. In 1837 the stage service between York and Niagara, which travelled over the rudimentary roads, operated three days a week, cost five dollars and took eleven hours. That was eleven hours of jostling and discomfort as the stagecoach rode over the bumpy roads. Schedules were only an estimate - a rough calculation of when you might arrive at your destination. There was always the caveat - that you would arrive "God Willing" as close as possible to the declared time. Delays were caused not only by the condition of the roads, but by the drivers. At the frequent stops, where horses were watered, and passengers made a restroom visit, then had a drink in the tavern, the trip was often delayed when the driver stayed in the tavern refreshing himself, long after his passengers were seated in the coach and ready to resume the journey. It is no wonder that travel by steamboat was preferred.

In 1840 there were as many as fifty steamships operating on Lake Ontario. Many of those well known at the time crossed Lake Ontario and landed at Queenston - *Transit, Great Britain, Queenston* and *Chief Justice Robinson* built at Queenston in 1842. Sir Richard Bonnycastle in 1846, found the *Chief Justice Robinson* to be a luxurious boat. "The fare is five

Lewiston-Queenston Suspension Bridge. Frederick Knight, artist.   *Royal Ontario Museum*

In the "Colonial Advocate" of May 12, 1824, William Lyon Mackenzie wrote about a plan prepared by Queenston architect Francis Hall, to erect "a Chain Bridge across the Niagara River, at the narrowest strait which commences just above Queenston". No more was heard of this plan. Then in 1836 an attempt was made to raise money for a suspension bridge across the gorge. The money was not raised and it was not until 1850 that a bridge was built. Designed and built by Edward W. Serrell, Civil Engineer, it was the "Largest in the World" at the time. It was 257m (849 feet) long, with a 6m (20 foot) roadway. The ten cables which held up the bridge were 379m (1245 feet) long and were strung from stone towers set in each bank, a distance of 317m (1040 feet) apart.

dollars in the cabin, or about £1 sterling; and two dollars in the steerage. Cabin passengers have tea and breakfast. By paying a dollar extra you may have a stateroom on deck...where you find a good bed, a large looking glass, washing stand and towels, and a night-lamp if required... The ladies' cabin has generally a large cheval glass (mirror) and a piano, with a white lady to wait, who is always decked out in flounces and furbelows and usually good-looking. All you had to do on embarking or on disembarking is to see personally to your luggage; for leaving it with a servant unacquainted with the country will not do." [21]

The fare was the same, $5.00 and the steamboat took only five hours, while the stagecoach took eleven or more. There was no comparison in the relative comfort, the stagecoach's hard ride, or the luxurious accommodations of the lake boat. It is no wonder that travellers chose to go by steamship. They could do this for nine or more months of the year, before ice conditions on the lakes would force the steamboats to tie up for the winter. Only then would the stagecoaches have the travel business to themselves. From 1842 to 1852 The *Chief Justice Robinson* carried on a winter service, to Niagara town. Travellers going west then had to take stagecoaches to reach their destinations.

Queenston, more than Chippawa, was counting on providing services to travellers, as a way of revitalizing the village. By 1851 Queenston had prospered. W.H. Smith writing in *Canada, Past, Present and Future* reported 200 houses there and mentioned the Telegraph Co. office which had opened in 1848 when service began between Queenston and Niagara. The road along the bottom of the escarpment was now macadamized and a toll road operated by the Queenston - St. Catharines Toll Road Company. No mention was made of how many taverns, but there were in 1848 three churches - Baptist, Episcopal and Presbyterian - in Queenston.

Queenston's pride and joy then was the new "Lewiston and Queenston Suspension Bridge - The Largest in the World". Designed and built by Edward W. Serrell, C.E., it opened in 1851. Built two years after Charles Ellet's Suspension Bridge over the gorge at the head of the Whirlpool Rapids, which was the first bridge over the Niagara Gorge, Serrell's bridge was longer and larger. The 6m (20 foot) wide bridge roadway accommodated the heaviest of the immigrants' wagons. No longer was it necessary to load the wagons on the horseboat ferry and make the slow, perilous trip over the Niagara River. Business was booming, the *Erie and Ontario Rail Road* was still operating in 1853, but there was trouble ahead. Once

Wreck of the Suspension Bridge Over the Niagara River at Queenston.
From a sketch by A.W.R.R., in the Buffalo & Erie County Historical Museum.

There was a heavy spring run of ice in the river in 1864 and the bridge's guy wires on the shore were unfastened so that they would not be torn out by the ice. They had not been refastened when on April 1 a heavy gale set the bridge in motion. The gale raged on through the night and when daylight came, the centre section of the roadway of the Lewiston & Queenston Suspension Bridge, lay in pieces on the river ice. The bridge was damaged beyond repair.

again progress would overtake Queenston, this time it would bring about changes that would bring Queenston's business to a halt.

The era of steam railways began in the 1850's. The *Erie and Ontario Rail Road Company's* directors decided that they had to change with the times and in 1852 they obtained a revision to their charter allowing them to reconstruct the rail line and change to steam locomotion. Queenston was not to be part of the new rail line, as the revision to the railroad's charter allowed them to extend the rail line to Niagara, by-passing Queenston. Despite vigorous protests from Queenston's businessmen, the route of the rail line was changed.

The rail line was laid down the east side of the St. Davids embayment, which provided a longer, less steep grade, thereby eliminating the steep climb up the escarpment taken by the horse-drawn railway. From the bottom of the escarpment, the line headed east toward Queenston, to Concession Road 2 (Progressive Avenue), here it crossed present day

York Road, wound down the bank there and headed straight along the east side of the roadway to Niagara-on-the-Lake. The stone abutments of the bridge over York Road are still standing on the south side of the road west of Queenston. The first steam train ran over this line, from Chippawa to Niagara on July 3, 1854. This was the end of the haulage of goods over the portage and Queenston also lost the steamboat passenger traffic, as the boats docked at Niagara and their passengers then took the *Erie and Niagara Railway* (formerly the *Erie and Ontario*) to Niagara Falls.

The *Great Western Railway* line around the bend of Lake Ontario, completed rail connections from Toronto to Niagara Falls in 1853. Then travellers went by train rather than by steamboat, and by 1855 many of the steamboat lines were bankrupt. Shipbuilding came to a halt, and to make matters worse, there was an economic depression in the United States in 1857, which brought about a reduction in travel.

Queenston would suffer another blow when a

Astrid Akkerman

Brock's Cenotaph

This cenotaph was dedicated by the Prince of Wales in 1860 to mark the spot where Brock died. At the time it was located on private property. In 1896, the Queen Victoria Niagara Falls Park Commission acquired the small plot of land surrounding the cenotaph and enlarged the area by purchasing adjoining land. On October 3, 1976 a bronze statue of "Alfred", Brock's horse, mounted on a sandstone base and encased in a safety glass case, was installed, to the left of the cenotaph. Then on October 12, 1981 a plaque set in a granite boulder commemorating the part played by Indians fighting on the British side during the Battle of Queenston Heights, was installed to the right of the cenotaph.

severe gale in April 1864, destroyed the Lewiston and Queenston Suspension Bridge. The bridge's guys, which were attached to anchors along the river's edge, had been unfastened when a larger than usual ice jam threatened to tear them out. They had not been replaced when on April 1, gale winds blowing down the gorge set the unguyed bridge in motion. When daylight came, the horrified residents of Queenston saw what was left of their bridge. The centre section of the bridge's roadway was gone, with the planking strewn on the ice in the gorge below. All that remained was a section of the roadway extending out from each bank, and in the centre there was nothing but the stringer cables dangling in the wind. After 14 years the residents of Queenston and Lewiston were once again required to use the river ferries to cross the Niagara River The remains of the bridge hung forlornly from the suspension cables for 34 years. Bit

by bit pieces of the railing and roadway broke off and dropped into the gorge, leaving only the stringers hanging from the suspension cables, a mournful reminder of the bridge's past glory.

The wharves and boat docks rotted, the only boats that called at Queenston were the steam ferries. Ferry service resumed when the bridge fell and a steamboat ferry transported travellers who landed at Lewiston and wanted to continue their journey on the Canadian side. There weren't many travellers who took this route. It would not be until 1892 when the *Niagara Park and River Railway* was built, running from Queenston to Chippawa, that steamboats would return to dock at Queenston. Then the larger and more powerful steamships, the *Corona, Chicora, Chippewa* and *Cayuga* would return to Queenston a small vestige of its former glory as a destination for lake boats.

Niagara Falls from the Canadian Side, 1850.
An oil on canvas by Hippolyte Sebron.
This is one of several similar oil paintings by Hippolyte Sebron which show the Horseshoe Falls and the Table Rock. This painting can be seen at The Weir Library of Art, Queenston, Ontario.

The Horseshoe Falls.
An oil painting by Hippolyte Sebron, circa 1852.
Sebron painted at least four versions of this view after he visited Niagara Falls to make his sketches. This oil painting which is owned by Richard D. Merritt M.D. FRCSC differs from the others in that the storm which dominated the sky in the other views, has passed. The Table Rock area in the right foreground is shown in a wilder, more natural state, without horses and carriages. The Horseshoe Falls is depicted in a more turbulent manner and the Maid of the Mist is dimly visible in the river below.

Queenston and the Lake Boats

When the Erie and Ontario horse-drawn railway became the Erie and Niagara steam railway, the tracks were extended to Niagara (Niagara-on-the-Lake), by-passing Queenston. The *Zimmerman* and other lake boats then disembarked their passengers bound for the Canadian side of the Falls, at Niagara, and they then took the train to Niagara Falls.

The lake boats carrying passengers bound for Niagara Falls on the American side continued upriver to Lewiston. Here the excursionists disembarked and took the Niagara Falls and Ontario Railway which began operating between Niagara Falls and Lewiston in 1854. This new American railway connected with the New York Central Railway going to Buffalo and from there to New York and Chicago. Niagara and Lewiston benefited from being the terminus of these railroads by having the lake boats dock there, while Queenston lost its steamboat docking and passenger transfer business.[1]

This flurry of business was shortlived as the completion of the Great Western Railway from Niagara Falls to Hamilton in 1855 and to Toronto in l856, drew passengers away from the steamboats. Most of the shipping lines went bankrupt, and during the next fifteen years, steamboat traffic on the Niagara River was minimal. What steamboat passenger service there was used the Lewiston docking facilities, with the travellers going on to Niagara Falls via railroad.

In 1878 the Niagara Navigation Company began a regular steamboat passenger service across Lake Ontario and up the Niagara River to Lewiston with the *Chicora*, the company's first steamship. The *Chicora* was an iron hulled steamboat which had sailed as a blockade runner in the American Civil War, under the name *Let Her B*. The *Cibola* became the company's second steamship in 1887, and joined the *Chicora* on the Lake Ontario run.

By 1887 there was sufficient demand from passengers who wanted to dock at Queenston for the Niagara Navigation Company to begin ferrying passengers across the Niagara River from Lewiston to Queenston. It acquired the ferry rights and chartered a small steamer called *Kathleen* for the purpose. In August 1889 it purchased a "smart little steamer to specially fill these services", as Barlow Cumberland, the head of the company, described their new acquisition, the *Ongiara*.

With the creation in 1885 of public parks on both sides of the Niagara River at the Falls, more people used the Niagara Navigation Company's boats on their way to see Niagara Falls. To the consternation of the Queen Victoria Niagara Falls Park Commissioners, these visitors most often disembarked from the lakeboats at Lewiston and went on to the Niagara Reservation, the public park on the American side, where they did their sightseeing.

The Commissioners felt that an electric railway, operating from Queenston to Queen Victoria Park would provide a convenient and economical means of reaching the Park. It would divert the excursionists from Lewiston to Queenston, where they would board

The "Chicora" under full steam entering the Niagara River,1908, with the Queens Royal Hotel, Niagara-on-the-Lake in the background.The "Chicora" was a side-paddle wheel coal burning steamboat, 67.4m (221 feet) long, 916 tonnes (931 tons). She was built in 1864, at Liverpool, England. First named "Let Her B" she was used as a blockade runner during the American Civil War. The Niagara Navigation Company purchased her in 1877 and after a refit she became their first boat on the Toronto to Niagara and Queenston-Lewiston lake run. Her first trip was on June 23, 1878. She sailed this route until after Labour Day,. the end of the season, in 1914 when she was retired, and cut up for scrap.

Ontario Hydro Archives

The "Chicora" at Queenston Dock, circa 1903.

The gangplank has been drawn up and the lines have been cast off as the "Chicora" moves away from the Queenston Dock. Going to the dock to watch the arrival and departure of the steamboats was a pleasant pastime for the residents of Queenston. The two young women are sitting on the bulkhead which just moments before held the cable which tied the boat to the dock.

Jean Huggins

"Ongiara"

In 1887 the Niagara Navigation Company acquired the ferry rights between Queenston and Lewiston and chartered a small steamer named "Kathleen" to ferry passengers.

On August 13, 1889 the "Niagara Falls Gazette" reported that the Niagara Navigation Company had purchased a steamboat called "Queen City", to ferry passengers over the Niagara River from Lewiston to Queenston. The company renamed the boat "Ongiara", a name which Barlow Cumberland, the company's president, thought "a name appropriate to her Surroundings, and to her duties between the original portage routes of Indian and historic periods at the landings at Lewiston and Queenston." The "Niagara Falls Gazette", in September 1895, reported that the "Ongiara" was still operating and "At the August term of Niagara County Court at Lockport (N.Y.), a license was granted Captain Hugh J. McIntyre (of Lewiston) to operate a ferry over the Niagara River from the wharf of H.G. Cornell, to Queenston for two years, beginning September 1, 1895.

"The ferry service is to be performed by the Niagara Navigation Company's steamer "Ongiara" during the months of June, July, August and September and by rowboats during the balance of the year, during the time of the license. The "Ongiara" will leave Cornell's wharf for Queenston at intervals of 90 minutes during the daytime, beginning at 7.30 a.m. The rates of ferriage will be 10 cents by steamer and 15 cents by rowboat. The "Ongiara" is licensed to carry not exceeding 250 passengers per trip and to maintain a crew of five men. The steamer will continue to make the usual daily trips to Niagara-on-the-Lake, connecting with the observation trains as heretofore. The ferry service between this point (Lewiston) and Queenston has for many years been conducted in a very irregular manner and this new departure in having a steam ferry during the summer months will be hailed with great satisfaction by the residents of these two frontier towns and the travelling public generally."

There is no record of when the "Ongiara" was taken off this ferry service, but the opening of the Lewiston-Queenston Suspension Bridge in 1899 would make the steamboat ferry service redundant.

the electric cars and be carried along the west side of the gorge to the Canadian park. On December 4, 1891, after extensive negotiations they entered into an agreement with the Niagara Falls Park & River Railway Company. The company agreed to pay a $10,000 yearly fee for the forty year term of the franchise.

Construction began in early 1892, and before long the railway company's engineers realized that they had a voltage problem in their electrical system. The company's powerhouse at Table Rock generated direct current at 600 to 660 volts, but this voltage was not strong enough to reach the northern terminus of the rail line at Queenston. The Park Commissioners refused the suggestion that they use a steam engine to pull the cars up Queenston Heights and to the Whirlpool, where the electric rail line would begin.

Instead the company built a steam driven, electric power generation station on the bank of the river just south of the Queenston Dock. The rail line began at dockside and ran through the village of Queenston with several zig-zag curves until it reached the base of the escarpment on the south side of present day York Road, just west of the intersection with the Niagara Parkway. From there it made a steep climb to the top of the escarpment at Queenston Heights Park.

In 1887 the Niagara Navigation Company had only the "Chicora" crossing Lake Ontario to Lewiston. A new ship was ordered from the E.W. Rathbun Company's shipyard at Deseronto. This steamboat, named "Cibola", was launched on November 1, 1887. and went into service on June 10, 1888. The "Cibola" was 76.8m (252 feet) long with an 8.8m (29 feet) beam and 946.6 tonnes (962 tons) burden. Her compound engines with two large cylinders developed 2,000 horsepower. She was called the "Buffalo Boat" because of the painting of a rampant buffalo on the sides of her paddle boxes. She sailed on the Toronto to Queenston-Lewiston lake run until 1895. In June of that year, she caught fire while docked at Lewiston. She was set adrift and floated down the river, where she went aground at Youngstown, opposite Niagara-on-the-Lake. Only her blackened hull was left after the fire, and it was towed to Toronto and cut up into scrap. The "Cibola" sailed only seven seasons on the lake route.

Metropolitan Toronto Public Library

Clifford Marsh

*Niagara Falls Park & River Railway Car No. 584
going downhill on the Queenston grade, circa 1900.*

The trees were cut down on the railway right-of-way along the escarpment at Queenston Heights to provide an unobstructed view of the river. The actual distance between the Heights and Queenston Dock was 762m (2500 feet). However the rail line from Queenston Heights to Queenston Dock was 2286m (7500 feet) long as it wound its way down the Heights to the river's edge. The first cars were built by Patterson & Corbin of St. Catharines, but in later years cars were built in the company's own shop which was located just south of the Niagara Spanish Aero Car.

Niagara Falls Park & River Railway Observation Car.

This photo shows one of the ten 8.5 m (28 feet) long open-sided observation cars which were built at the Niagara Falls Park & River Railway's Whirlpool shop. The Whirlpool shop and car barn complex was also the headquarters for the Canadian Division of the International system. Here were located the machine shop, electric wiring department, blacksmith shop, paint and woodworking shops, all fully equipped with machinery driven by electric motors. The cars built here were mounted on McGuire trucks (wheels). On February 12, 1906 the Whirlpool shop and car barn, which was located opposite the Aero Car, was destroyed in a fire. The morning after the fire there was only one car left to go into service. The loss was estimated at $125,000. The shops were never rebuilt, and repair work was transferred to the United States side. A small shed covered with sheet metal siding replaced the burnt out facilities.

W. Gordon Collection

General View looking from Queenston Heights, circa 1900.

Clifford Marsh

The steam powered electric generating booster plant of the Niagara Falls Park & River Railway is seen at the river's edge at No. 1. This plant was built here to provide direct current to maintain voltage. Coal was burned to heat water to provide steam for the two 150 horsepower Wheelock steam engines built by Goldie & McCulloch, Galt, Ontario. They drove the two 250 horsepower Canadian General Electric generators which provided the direct electrical current for the rail line. This plant operated from June 1st until September 10th each year, when the railway did 75% of its business. This booster station was used until 1898 when improved electric transmission techniques made it possible for voltage to be maintained all along the line from the company's powerhouse located south of Table Rock. The "Chippewa" is at Lewiston dock, and the boat approaching Queenston dock is the "Ongiara", ferrying boat passengers from Lewiston to Queenston. The "Wadsworth House", present day "South Landing Inn" is at No. 2. The connecting line with the Great Gorge Trip, leading to the Lewiston-Queenston Suspension Bridge is seen coming out of Kent Street just this side of the "South Landing Inn", and continues to the right and out of the picture. The white poles at No. 3 indicate where the line coming along Dumfries Street crosses Front Street, and then turns north, before it enters the last curve in the line, at No. 4, where the accident occurred on July 7, 1913. On Partition Street, No. 5, one of the many stables which lined this street is visible. As late as 1920 the dilapidated remainders of these stables, where the stage coach horses were housed between trips, lined both sides of this road, which was then a laneway between Kent and Dumfries Streets. The "Ivy Block" as it was called in more recent times is at No. 6.

This route provided a splendid view for the excursionists who came by the thousands after the electric line began operations on May 24, 1893 with a single track line. The Niagara Navigation Company had the foresight to have purchased the Queenston Dock property many years previously, and they improved the facilities to handle the passenger traffic which now was landed on the Canadian side.

Barlow Cumberland, in *A Century of Sail and Steam on the Niagara River*, writing about the new railway line running from Queenston to Chippawa, described it as "…but the revival of the old Portage Route on the Canada side, which had so long existed between Chippawa and the head of navigation at this point (Queenston)…"

The arrival of the first boatload of excursionist on May 24, 1893, - 345,000 people would use this route to Niagara Falls before the season was over - was the beginning of a new era for Queenston. It would not regain its previous prominence, but it was once again a destination for travellers and over the next forty years Queenston and Queenston Heights Park would greet millions of excursionists.

The Niagara Navigation Company anticipated this increase in business and in 1892 the company changed from a family business, and took in new capital. The

*Niagara Falls Park & River Railway cars at Queenston Dock waiting to take
on passengers from the "Chippewa", circa 1900.*

*In this picture trolley poles are visible on only two of the cars, indicating that they are motorized. The other cars
on the siding are trailers. Each car usually pulled one trailer and together they carried a total of 150 passengers.
The company had four closed motorized cars 5.5m (18 feet) long, ten open-sided motorized cars 8.5m (28 feet)
long, one motorized express car, sixteen assorted size open and closed trailers, and ten double-truck observation
cars. The extra trailers are being held in readiness on the dockside siding here waiting for a boat load of pic-
nickers bound for Queenston Heights. The "Chippewa" had a capacity of two thousand passengers and had a
light load when this picture was taken.*

money raised was used to finance the construction of
another ship to sail the lake route. The two thousand
passenger boat *Chippewa* was built at Hamilton, and
in May 1894 took her place on the Niagara Route.
There was almost continual activity at Queenston
Dock with five lake crossings and arrivals each day.
They were at 7:00 a.m., 9:00 a.m., 11:00 a.m.,
2:00 p.m. and 4:45 p.m.

Sections of the Niagara Falls Park & River Railway
were double-tracked in 1894 and the track was
extended 2.4km (a mile and a half) south of Chippawa
to Slater's Dock. Here the Richelieu & Ontario
Navigation Company's steamboat *Columbian*,
working in conjunction with the electric railway,
disembarked excursionists from Buffalo.

Lake boat passengers could now sail from Toronto
to Queenston, take the electric railway to Slater's
Dock, board the *Columbian* for Buffalo and from
there make connections by train with New York or
Chicago. In 1894, 499,015 passengers travelled on the

Niagara Falls Park & River Railway, the great
majority of them had crossed Lake Ontario on the
Niagara Navigation Company's lake boats before
landing at Queenston, where they went on to
Queenston Heights Park and Niagara Falls on the
Niagara Falls Park & River Railway.

One night in June 1895 the *Cibola* caught fire while
tied up at the Lewiston dock, and was a complete loss.
The company immediately ordered a replacement and
on May 26, 1896 the *Corona*, a steamship with
capacity for two thousand passengers was launched
and put in service on the Toronto to Queenston route.
Excursion business had kept pace, and the new
electric railway which ran along the water's edge, on
the American side of the Niagara River, took its share
of the excursionists. Now the excursionsts had two
electric railways from which to chose, and this variety
helped to entice people for a return visit to Niagara
Falls.

Niagara Falls Heritage Foundation Collection – Valentine & Sons

The "Chippewa" entering the Niagara River at full steam, with a large complement of passengers. The "Chippewa" was designed by Frank Kirby of Detroit, and built by the Hamilton Bridge & Shipbuilding Company, She was 93.9m (308 feet) long with a 11.6m (38 feet) beam, and 1549 tonnes (1574 tons) burden. Launched on May 2 1893, she was named after H.M.S. "Chippewa" the ship on which Major-General Isaac Brock sailed on Lake Erie. There was a carving of an Indian head in the centre of each of her two paddle wheel boxes. The "Chippewa" had a capacity of two thousand passengers and was easily identified by the upper works of her vertical beam engine which operated her paddle wheels. She was in service on the Toronto to Queenston route until the end of the 1936 season and was broken up for scrap in 1939.

Laura Secord House in Queenston, circa 1915

This postcard view shows the Laura Secord house in Queenston, some 60 years before its restoration. Laura Ingersoll Secord was born in 1775, the daughter of Thomas Ingersoll who founded the town by that name. She married James Secord in 1802 and they had five children. The Secords were living in this house in 1813, during the War of 1812-14 when Laura walked to Beaverdams to warn Lieutenant James FitzGibbon of an impending American attack. The house has been restored, and is open to view during the summer season. It is owned by Laura Secord Inc.

Historical VII. Modernized residence of Laura Secord, heroine of War 1812-14, Queenston, Ontario. Leaving this house, she tramped 20 miles through the woods to warn the British troops of the approach of the American forces, June 23rd, 1813.

(Jean) Huggins

Jean Huggins

Queenston from the Top of Brock's Monument, circa 1900.

The ruins of the William Lyon Mackenzie House are at No. 1; a car of the Niagara Park & River Railway is seen going along the Kent Street right-of-way in No. 2; present day South Landing Inn is at No. 3; the approximate location of the 1913 accident is at No. 4; the merchants' warehouses, later known as the Ivy Block, are at No. 5; Queenston Dock is at No. 6; the boarded up former Baptist Church is at No. 7; the former Methodist Church, later the United Church, is at No. 8; Lewiston dock, with one of the Niagara Navigation Company's steamboats docked there, is seen at No. 9.

Queenston Canada, interior oldest printing shop in Ontario,
Brock's Monument in the distance.

This postcard view of the ruins of William Lyon Mackenzie's home dates to the 1920's. The building was reconstructed by the Niagara Parks Commission in 1936-37 "from available original drawings and from data relating to construction in the particular period." On June 18, 1938 when William Lyon Mackenzie's grandson, the Honourable William Lyon Mackenzie King, Prime Minister of Canada, opened the reconstructed building, he read a letter written by Mackenzie, referring to the planting of locust trees in front of his home. One of these trees is at the left in this view. The original house was constructed of field stone, whereas the reconstructed house has cut stone.

In 1901 Queenston had a Royal visit, no matter how brief a visit it was. Their Royal Hignesses the Duke and Duchess of York (later King George V and Queen Mary) using the *Corona* as their private yacht, arrived at Queenston on October 10 on their way to visit Niagara Falls. The residents of Queenston had an opportunity to see them when they disembarked at Queenston dock to take the specially outfitted private electric car to Niagara Falls, and again when they returned to board the *Corona* for the return trip to Toronto.

A new ship was added to the route in 1907 when the *Cayuga*, the best known of all the Niagara Navigation Company's *C* boats, made her first trip to Queenston. She was a powerful boat, her engines generated 4300 horsepower, and were able to push the ship through the lake water at an average speed of 36.2km (22.5 miles per hour). Because of the *Cayuga's* speed, the company changed her early morning departure time from Toronto, from 7:00 a.m. to 7:30 a.m.

In 1908 there was competition for passengers, when the Hamilton Steamboat Company put the *Turbinia* and the *Northumberland* on the Niagara route, docking at Lewiston. The *Turbinia* and the *Northumberland* made two trips a day, but could not compete with the Niagara Navigation Company's three *C* boats which provided the convenience of six trips a day. The *Turbinia* could not match the *Cayuga's* speed, and did not attract enough business to pay her way. In mid season she and the *Northumberland* left the Toronto to Queenston-Lewiston lake route and were returned to their former Toronto to Hamilton route.

The lake boat era was a time when people took great enjoyment out of simple pleasures. The annual church picnic was eagerly anticipated, and thousands of Sunday School children in Toronto looked forward to the boat trip across Lake Ontario to Queenston. During the crossing the lunch boxes were often opened to appease a child's sudden pangs of hunger. When mother and father weren't looking some of the sandwich was offered to the audacious seagulls which swooped low over the heads of the passengers, demanding to be fed.

When the lake was calm, it was a pleasant, relaxing experience to sit on the deck and be lulled by the regular "pat-pat" of the feathered paddles as they drove through the water. The *Coronoa* and the *Cibola* were quieter than the *Chippewa* whose wallking beam engine drove the paddles by its vigorous up and down pumping action. This resulted in a motion and sound reminiscent of that of an old fashioned agitator-action washing machine.

Jean Huggins

In 1907 the Hamilton Steamboat Co.'s "Turbinia" was placed on the Toronto to Queenston-Lewiston run across Lake Ontario, in competition with the Niagara Navigation Company's "Cayuga".

The "Turbinia" at Lewiston Dock, 1907, with her sister ship the "Northumberland" visible in the centre of the river. The "Chippewa" is unloading at the Queenston Dock.
The "Turbinia" was a 76.2m (250 foot) long propeller driven steamboat built by Hawthorn, Leach & Co., Newcastle-on-Tyne, England in 1904. She was the first boat powered with steam turbines, which drove her triple propellers, to operate on the Great Lakes. She was beaten in an unofficial race with "Cayuga", but her sister ship, the "Northumberland" restored the Hamilton Steamship Company's pride, when in July 1907, according to a report in the "Niagara Falls Gazette", "The 'Northumberland' is victor over the 'Cayuga' in the Great Lakes Race." The "Turbinia" and the "Northumberland" were not able to compete with the Niagara Navigation Company's "C" boats, and after only two months on the Toronto to Queenston-Lewiston run, were returned to their usual Toronto to Hamilton route.

Niagara Navigation Co.'s Steamer "Corona"

Valentine & Sons

The "Corona" was launched May 25, 1896, at the Bertram Engine and Shipbuilding Company's shipyard in Toronto. This steamship was 83m (272 feet) long with a 9.8m (32 feet) beam, had a capacity of two thousand passengers. Her paddle wheels were powered by 2,000 horsepower engines. She was built to replace the "Cibola". She sailed on the Toronto to Queenston-Lewiston route until 1930 when she was taken to Buffalo. She was cut up for scrap in 1936.

Jean Huggins

The "Coronoa" leaving Queenston Dock and heading upriver to make the turn downriver to Lewiston. Circa 1920.

The "Corona" and the Royal Party at Queenston Dock, 1901

This picture was made from a frame of film taken from a movie made by the Edison Company on October 10, 1901, when the Duke and Duchess of York (later King George V and Queen Mary) used the "Corona" as their private yacht in a trip from Niagara-on-the-Lake to Queenston. The Royal Party has just disembarked from the ship and is preparing to board the "Ongiara", a specially outfitted Niagara Falls Park and River Railway car. The Duke and Duchess visited Niagara Falls, and returned to Queenston where they reboarded the "Corona" for the return trip to Niagara-on-the-Lake.

After the boat entered the Niagara River and proceeded upriver towards Queenston, there was the anticipation of being the first to see Brock's Monument on Queenston Heights, the destination. When the boat docked there was a rush for the waiting electric cars, and soon the trip to the Heights began. The railway line ran through Queenston across Front Street, then by way of Dumfries and Queen Streets, then north of the ruins of the William Lyon Mackenzie House and across King Street (present day Niagara Parkway). Here it made a one hundred and eighty degree turn as it crossed King's Highway No. 8A (present day York Road), after which it climbed the escarpment. [2]

On a Sunday afternoon in October 1901 there was a power interruption and the cars stopped running. There were cars spread out along the line between Niagara Falls and Queenston, and all were filled to capacity. After waiting impatiently for the electric current to be turned on again, people got off and began to walk. As many as one thousand people plodded along the tracks, hoping that they would soon be picked up. They walked all the way to Queen Victoria Park. They were fortunate that power was restored to the line in time to take them back to their boat that night.

When a boat docked as many as two thousand passengers would disembark and the electric railway was required to transport this number to and from the dock four or five times a day during the summer season. Each electric car with two 25 horsepower Canadian General Electric motors, pulled a trailer up the Heights on a 5.7% grade.

Barlow Cumberland described the trip up the escarpment: "As the cars wind up and approach the summit, a splendid and far distant landscape is opened to the view, one which the Duke of Argyle considered to be one of the 'worthy views of the world'. Below are terraces and fruit orchards of this 'Garden of Canada'. Through these variegated levels the Niagara River curves in its silvered sheen to Lake Ontario where the blue waters close in the far horizon."

This scenic trip down the escarpment on the electric railway turned to tragedy on Wednesday July 7,1915 when fifteen people were killed and between sixty and seventy people were injured when car No. 685 ran off the tracks in Queenston, crashing into a tree. The passengers were members of St. John's Presbyterian and Woodgreen Methodist Churches of Toronto, who were holding their Sunday School picnics on Queenston Heights.

A sudden storm followed by steady rain, and the lack of shelter on the picnic grounds, abruptly ended their picnics. There was a sudden rush of people to board the first electric car which would take them back to the shelter of Queenston Dock. One hundred and fifty-seven people crowded on board the eighty-four seat capacity open car. The grossly overloaded car proceeded down the escarpment, with people packed inside, and others hanging on the side running boards.

The extra weight sent the car down the hill at a speed higher than normal. When the motorman tried to apply the brakes to slow the car, the brakes would not hold on the wet, slippery tracks. The car careened down the hill, making the first turn, at present day York Road. Many of the passengers, unaware of the danger, and unmindful of the impending tragedy, appeared to enjoy the sensation. The car made the turn at Queen Street (present day Queenston Street), and the turn into Dumfries Street. After crossing Front Street the car approached the fourth and last curve, as it hurtled onward toward the river's edge and the dock. As it entered this curve the car suddenly left the rails, turned over and crashed into a tree located on the side of the small ravine which parallelled the track. [3]

The roof on one half of the car collapsed on the passengers. Ten people were killed outright and five others died of their injuries. The most severly injured were taken by ambulance to the Niagara Falls General Hospital. The remainder were taken on board the *Chippewa* on stretchers, for the return trip to Toronto. This was a tragic day for Queenston. Queenston's citizens responded, taking charge of the rescue operation and comforting the injured, many of whom they took into their homes while they waited to return to Toronto.

An inquest was held in the Wadsworth House (later called the Riverview Inn, and currently the South Landing Inn), which was also serving as a temporary morgue. Toronto Mayor Church was angered by what he thought was negligence. "Fancy no emergency brakes coming down a hill like that! The conductor had no sand to put on the rails. It was wilful murder." The motorman of the car and the General Manager of the railway were arrested on August 4 and charged with "slack observance of the rules". The charges were, however, not pressed and they were released.

The International Railway Company which had taken over the electric line in 1902 was reprimanded by the Ontario Railway and Municipal Board, and held responsible for the accident. The Board found that many spikes were loose or missing, rails on curves were badly worn and in some cases lacked guard rails, drainage was faulty and many ties were rotten. The cause of the accident was found to be a broken brake rod. [4]

Niagara Parks Archives

The front half of International Railway Company Car No. 685, which collapsed, crushing the passengers underneath, when the car left the track, turned over and hit a tree broadside.

The rear section of International Railway Company Car No. 685. Many of its passengers were thrown out, falling through the open sides of this car when it left the tracks and turned over. This electric car had a capacity of eighty-four passengers. There were 157 passengers on board when the accident occurred.

Niagara Parks Archives

Astrid Akkerman

The International Railway Company's tracks at the Deep Hollow, circa 1930.
This pen and ink sketch was made from a photograph provided by Jean Huggins. This is the route of the electric cars to and from the Queenston Docks. The single track on the left with the wider curve was the spur line which the Hydro Electric Power Commission of Ontario laid down before 1920. This line went west up the Deep Hollow, and through the countryside to connect with the Erie & Niagara Railway which ran along the east side of Concession 1. This railway line was used to transport the generators and other heavy equipment for the power generating station. The double tracks were the International Railway Company's tracks leading to and from the Queenston Dock. From there the tracks went up Queen Street (present day Queenston Street) and turned west toward present day York Road, just north of the ruins of the William Lyon Mackenzie House.

When the Hydro Electric Power Commission of Ontario began construction of the present Sir Adam Beck Generating Station No.1 it co-operated with the Niagara Falls Park & River Railway in building an improved line to Queenston Dock. Instead of turning east at Dumfries Street, the line continued north on Queen Street (present day Queenston Street), past Laura Secord School and on to the Deep Hollow. Here it turned east, running down into the Hollow and then south along the river bank until it reached Queenston Dock.

In June 1913 the Niagara Navigation Company became part of the Richelieu & Ontario Navigation Company, which was later to become the Canada Steamship Lines. Many of our readers will have memories of the *C* boats when they were sailing under the Canada Steamships flag. The *Chicora* sailed for one more year after the two companies merged, and was retired after Labour Day 1914, leaving the *Chippewa*, *Corona* and *Cayuga* to carry on. By 1930

the lake passenger business had declined due to the beginning of the Depression and the *Corona* made her last run, then she was taken to Buffalo and scrapped.

A boat trip to the Canadian National Exhibition at Toronto was an experience many of our readers experienced during the 1930's. A book of five round trip tickets cost $6.00. The trip to Queenston Dock in one of the open-sided cars was a delight, with the ground flitting by at what seemed a tremendous speed, just beside your seat, Only a wooden bar, set shoulder high, kept you from falling out. There was always the anticipation of wondering which of the boats would be waiting at the dock. The *Chippewa* with its walking beam engine, and its thrashing paddle wheels seemed to be favoured over the more modern propeller driven *Cayuga*.

After a full day at the Exhibition, and the trip back on the boat, the open-sided cars waiting at the dock were not quite as welcome as they had been in the morning. It was dark, and much cooler, and the blinds

Niagara Falls Heritage Foundation Collection

Niagara Navigation Company's Dock at Lewiston, New York.

The Lewiston Dock was owned by George Cornell, who also owned the large hotel seen in the upper centre of this view. There were two docks, an upper and a lower dock. In 1878 Mr. Cornell repaired the lower dock which had not been in use since 1864-65 when all of the large lake steamers were withdrawn from the Lake Ontario and Niagara River route to be employed in service during the American Civil War.

The upper dock was being used by the Richelieu and Royal Mail Lines steamboats, the ''City of Toronto'' and the ''Rothesay''. Donald Milloy who was agent for these steamship lines also owned the dock at Niagara-on-the-Lake. He had agreed to co-operate with the Niagara Navigation Company in a joint venture with his ''City of Toronto'' and the ''Chicora'', but backed out of this agreement. The Niagara Navigation Company then had to make hurried arrangements for alternate docking at Toronto, Niagara-on-the-Lake and Lewiston.

A spirited and at times vicious competition arose between these two companies. Where they had tentatively agreed to divide the lake passenger business between them, they now became bitter rivals. Their boats left Toronto at the same time and raced across the lake to Niagara-on-the-Lake, where they both tried to tie up at the same time. This manoeuvre was like two automobiles trying to get into the same parking space. They engaged in a ticket price war, and at one time the fare for a return trip from Toronto to Lewiston was as low as twenty-five cents.

Both companies lost money, but it was the Niagara Navigation Company which had the staying power. The ''Chicora'' used the lower dock during this time. When ''Turbinia'' and ''Northumberland'' competed on this route, they used the upper dock. After these steamships were returned to their former Toronto to Hamilton run, the Niagara Navigation Company purchased the Lewiston Dock from Mr. Cornell at the end of the 1908 season. The dock needed repair and modernization. The work had only begun when one of the largest ice jams on record engulfed the dock in 18.3m (60 feet) of ice.

The dock facilites shown in this view were built in the early spring of 1909. Barlow Cumberland wrote in ''A Century of Sail and Steam on the Niagara River'': ''In reconstructing the dock (after the ice jam) we were able to introduce improvements which would not have been previously possible.'' At the far left is a gravity fed coal bin, from which the ''C'' ships refilled their coal bunkers.

Queenston from the Heights, 1925.

The "Chippewa" is seen making the turn in the river, on her way to the Lewiston Dock. An International Railway Great Gorge Route car is visible at the bottom left at No. 1. The car is crossing Queen Street (present day Queenston Street), about to go along Kent Street, cross Front Street and then along the connecting line, No. 2, which leads to the Lewiston-Queenston Suspension bridge, which is at the far right, out of the picture. The Ivy Block is at No. 3. St. Saviour's Anglican Church is at No.4.

Jean Huggins

The "Cayuga" was the largest and most powerful of the "C" boats operating on the Toronto to Queenston lake route. Built by the Canadian Shipbuilding Company of Toronto in 1907, this steamship was 97m (317 feet) long, with a beam of 10.9m (36 feet). She was propeller driven and her engines generated 4,300 horsepower. She had a capacity for twenty-five hundred passengers. She began with coal-fired boilers, but was converted to two oil-fired water tube boilers in 1946. Retired from service in 1952, she was tied up for two years when she was purchased by group of interested citizens, led by Alan Howard. After a refit, she set sail again in 1954 on the Toronto to Queenston run, but was unable to pay her way. After three unprofitable seasons, she was again taken out of service and remained tied up until 1961 when she was cut up for scrap.

The "Cayuga" approaching Queenston Dock, with an International Railway Company car waiting to make the last run from Queenston on September 10, 1932.

The "Cayuga" docking, June 1937, with two motor buses waiting to pick up passengers going on to Niagara Falls. The two little girls in the right foreground are Betty and Ruth Huggins.

Astrid Akkerman

The Queenston Dock and the Ice Jam of 1938.

The lower Niagara River does not freeze over due to the strength of the current, but it is subject to sporadic and spectacular ice jams when unusual weather conditions, accompanied by southwest winds, try to empty all of Lake Erie's ice into the Niagara River in a short time. Such an ice jam occurred in 1825, when the ''Queenston'', a ship which was under construction in a ravine close to the river's edge, had to be moved further up the bank, to escape destruction. Another occurred in 1883. The ice jam of 1908-09 blocked the mouth of the river at Niagara-on-the-Lake, stopping the river's flow and backing up the river water so that it rose 6m (20 feet) above its normal level. The ice level was even higher. For many years there was a sign on a tree, placed 9m (30 feet) above high water level indicating the height of the ice jam. In 1883 and in 1908-09 and again in 1912 the dock shelter and ticket office were destroyed. This view shows the damage to the dock and buildings during the January 1938 ice jam. It was the most spectacular on record, when the river filled with ice in less than twelve hours, from the base of the Horseshoe Falls down to Lake Ontario 22.5 km (14 miles). Another ice jam in 1955 demolished the shelter and ticket office on Queenston Docks. That was the last ice jam of its kind because of the installation of the Ice Boom across the entrance of the Niagara River at Lake Erie.

The Ferry dock and boathouse, at Queenston, circa 1919. Mrs. Huggins remembers renting a rowboat at this boat house from John Humphrey, the Queenston Dockmaster. She and Hazel Corman, then principal of Laura Secord School, where Mrs. Huggins also taught, went out on the river. Both of the young ladies knew how to row, but they had difficulty coming back up river against the current. They were late in returning to the boathouse, and there was some concern as to their safety. The rowboats kept here were used to ferry people across to Lewiston, and were rented out when there was no ferrying to be done.

Jean Huggins

*The Riverview Inn (South Landing Inn)
and Front Street, circa 1950.*
The old stone merchants' warehouses which were built in
the early 1800's are in the centre of this view.

Front Street, Queenston, 1921.
The old stone merchant's warehouses, which appeared in
sketches as early as 1828, are seen in this view.

Mrs. Jean Huggins

The Ivy Block, circa 1935

This stone building which appeared in sketches by Lieutenant-Colonel J.P. Cockburn in 1831 and by W.H. Bartlett in 1840, was originally built to serve as a storehouse for one of the Portage Syndicate's merchant traders. Over the years it housed a wide variety of tenants. In 1840 the Niagara Suspension Bridge Bank had its office there. When the telegraph line came to Queenston in 1848, the telegraph office was in this building. Known in contemporary times as the Fisher building – Carl Fisher bought it in the 1880's – Dainty's General Store was there. Charles Lowrey later took over this store and when long distance telephone service was established between St. David's, Queenston and Niagara Falls, Lowrey was the only subscriber. By 1907, the telephone exchange which was in Lowrey's store, had seven subscribers. Frank and Walter Sheppard were the owners when it housed a sub branch bank of the Canadian Imperial Bank of Commerce at St. David's. Gasoline was sold from the old style pump seen in the front of the bank. The gas pump in the picture had a cylindrical glass storage tank, so that you could see how much gas had been put in your gas tank. The round globe at the top of the pump had the brand name of the gasoline displayed on it. The building also housed a boarding house, and it was here that Laura Secord School teachers Miss Hazel Corman and Miss Jean Hill (Mrs. Jean Huggins, Queenston's historian) stayed when they first came to Queenston. The building became vacant in the 1950's and when the new owner abandoned his plans for its restoration, it was demolished in July 1968.

PLATE 7.

Queenston Heights and the Village of Queenston from the Air, 1920

This "Aero Photo" was taken by Bishop-Barker Aeroplanes Ltd., the aerial photo company operated by Canadian World War 1 fliers William A. "Billy" Bishop, and W. George Barker. They were Canada's most decorated aviators, both recipients of the Victoria Cross. The Queen Victoria Niagara Falls Park Commission hired them to take aerial photos of the land along the Niagara River from Lake Ontario to Fort Erie. No. 1, is the road up the escarpment, which was first laid out in 1796, replacing the original road up the escarpment which was steeper. This new road was to "benefit the commercial intercourse of the country and add to the beauty of the place." It was the only road up the escarpment from Queenston until the Parks Commission built the present road in 1923. No. 2, the Portage Road cutting across to the Stamford Halfway. The Larkin Farm which is shown in the picture was inundated in the Ontario Hydro Reservoir. No. 3, Village of Queenston. No. 4, Brock's Monument and Queenston Heights Park. No. 5, tracks of the International Railway (former Niagara Falls Park and River Railway). The Niagara River Recreation Trail is laid out along this roadbed. No. 6, the track is shown leading to No. 7, the Lewiston-Queenston Suspension Bridge and from there it went on to Lewiston, New York, where it connected with the Great Gorge Route.

Queenston and the Dock from the Deck of the Cayuga, 1954.

This photograph was taken as the Cayuga was on her way upriver from Niagara-on-the-Lake. The South Landing Inn is at No.1; the former merchants' warehouses of the early 1800's, later known as the Ivy Block, are at No.2; Saint Saviour's Anglican Church is No. 3; Niagara Parks Queenston Heights Restaurant is No.4; the sand dock is No.5.

195

which were drawn beside your street car seat, were only a minimal protection from the cool breeze which blew in on you on the return trip to Niagara Falls. At the foot of Bridge Street you got off and boarded a local street car, an enclosed car, and were carried to your destination - the closest street car stop from your house. You still had several blocks to walk before you reached home, tired, and chilled, after having had a never to be forgotten experience.

During the fruit harvesting season there were dozens of hand truck loads of fruit, cherries, plums, peaches, pears, apples and grapes in six quart baskets. When the boat arrived, the fruit was loaded on board for the trip to Toronto, where it was sold at various markets.

It was an inexpensive evening's entertainment to drive to Queenston Dock to see the boats come in. Those who had an automobile during the Depression were the lucky ones who could have this experience.

The electric railway also carried local passengers. The fare in 1909 was five cents for any distance not exceeding 4.8km (3 miles) between Queenston and Chippawa. Children under 10 years were charged three cents. School pupils could buy eight tickets for twenty-five cents, for 8km (5 miles), to be used during school hours. By the 1930's adult fares had risen to ten cents and children paid five cents for any distance between Chippawa and Queenston.

The International Railway Company chose not to renew its charter when it expired in 1932, and made its last run on September 10 of that year when one street car met the *Cayuga* for the last time. After that boat passengers disembarking at Queenston were transported to Queenston Heights and Niagara Falls by motor bus. At the end of the 1936 season the *Chippewa* was taken out of service and was tied up for three years before she was cut up for scrap in 1939. After the *Chippewa* was taken off the route, the *Cayuga* sailed alone, until 1952. After a number of unprofitable years the company put her up for sale.

A group of interested lake boat enthusiasts, headed by Alan Howard of Toronto, purchased the *Cayuga* and refitted her to comply with the more stringent safety regulations which were imposed after the disastrous and tragic *Noronic* fire in 1949. The *Cayuga* set sail again in 1954, but after three unprofitable years, she was retired for the last time, and in 1961 she too was cut up for scrap, bringing an end to the lake boat era.

When the lake boats no longer called at the Queenston Docks, the docks became a storage area for sand which had been mined from the huge sand bar at the mouth of the river - sucked up by a ship with sandsucking equipment.

Over the years many of the old buildings deteriorated beyond any possible restoration, and were torn down. During 1936, William Lyon Mackenzie's house, which had been a ruin for almost fifty years, was reconstructed using architectural data relating to the period.

The former Baptist Church which was built between 1842 and 1845 was bought by Dr. Djamal Afrukhteh in 1970. He donated the building to the Town of Niagara-on-the-Lake. The Queenston Community Association raised the money required for renovations and in December 1972 it was officially opened as the Queenston Library and Community Centre.

The Laura Secord Candy Company purchased Laura Secord's Queenston home, had it restored, and opened the house for public viewing. Its furnishings relate to the period when she lived in Queenston. *Willowbank*, Alexander Hamilton's stately home was purchased by Willowbank Estate Wines, and is at present undergoing a complete restoration.

By-passed by the majority of the motorists who drive on the Niagara River Parkway, on their way to visit Niagara-on-the-Lake, Queenston has become a quiet, out of the way, retreat. While there are some reminders of Queenston's past glory which give it a place in history alongside Halifax, Kingston and Niagara-on-the-Lake, there is scant evidence of the bustling commercial, postal, and shipping community that it once was.

Alfred, Major-General Brock's horse. A statue in bronze by Ralph Sketch, located beside Brock's Cenotaph, a few hundred yards west of the Mackenzie House in Queenston.

Queenston's Historic Houses

George Bailey

South Landing Inn

This frame building on Front Street at the corner of Kent Street, was built by Thomas Dickson, and it appears in a water colour painted by Lieutenant-Colonel J.P. Cockburn in 1831. It is Queenston's oldest building, having been built before 1827. Dickson sold the property in 1841. In 1883 it was owned by the Wadsworth family and was for many years operated as a hotel, and known as the "Wadsworth House" or the "Wadsworth Hotel". The Wadsworths had been in the hotel business at Queenston for many years. According to "Mitchell & Co.'s General Directory and Gazetteer of Lincoln and Welland County for 1856", Daniel Wadsworth was the proprietor of the "Suspension Bridge Hotel" and John Wadsworth was the proprietor of the "Traveller's Home".

James Wadsworth who was the proprietor of the Inn at the turn of this century was notorious for his bootlegging activities during Prohibition. He sold liquor to anyone who was willing to meet his price. He was also accused of smuggling aliens across the Niagara River to the United States at fifty dollars a head.

The building was sold to Margaret Dressell in 1910 for three thousand dollars and renamed the Riverview Inn. It served as a morgue and a resting place for the injured in July 1913, when the Niagara Falls Park & River Railway car went off the tracks as it rounded a curve just a few hundred yards away, east of the Inn. At that time, it was still generally referred to as the "Wadsworth House". It was purchased by Mrs. Rie Bannister, a weaver, who changed its name to South Landing Craft Centre.

Mrs. Bannister, her son William, his wife Carol and family, began the restoration of the building, while operating a weaving and craft business. In 1981 Tony and Kathy Szabo bought the building, and renamed it South Landing Inn. They modernized the second floor to accommodate overnight guests, and converted the spacious loft into their living quarters. Its former weatherbeaten clapboard has been enhanced by two coats of paint, without affecting the building's "majestic air of tranquility" as Terry Boyle described its appearance in "Under This Roof."

197

Ron Kitchen

Dickson House and Stone Barn

The property on which this house and barn are located was purchased from Samuel Street in 1799 by Thomas Andrews and John Butler. In 1800 it had evidently reverted to Samuel Street, and was purchased by Philip Stedman. In 1807 it became the property of William and James Crooks, who were prominent merchants in Niagara, and it could have been during their ownership of the property that the stone barn was built.

The age of the house is not known. It is the barn which creates the most interest, as it was probably used as a store and warehouse in the days before the War of 1812-14. Tradition says that this barn was the ''stone building where Major-General Isaac Brock's body was housed overnight after he was killed at the Battle of Queenston Heights.''

Owners of the property through the intervening years have been: Elijah Phelps 1817, David Secord 1819, Joseph and Adam Brown (who were also merchants), Joseph Hamilton 1842, James Humphries, Lewis Willson, Charles B. Secord, Thomas Humphries, Anna M. Hamilton, Joseph Wynn and Joseph Walker. Other owners who were prominent in Queenston, were William Mitchell, John Crawford, George Robson, John Rankin, David Thorburn, Edward M. Hodder and Carl E. Fisher.

Matthew C. Lowrey purchased the property from Carl Fisher in 1895. The Lowreys operated a grocery store there for many years and sold out to Thomas H. Clifford who operated a fruit distributing business from the barn, from 1931 until the 1950's. Mr. and Mrs. Ken Pifher bought it and operated an antique business there for about fifteen years, until 1977 when it was sold to Richard D. Merritt. M.D. FRCSC.

Dr. Merritt used the premises as a residence and during his occupancy he carried out a program of restoration. Mr. and Mrs. Ralph Peck purchased the property in 1981. During renovations and restoration work, the Pecks discovered that a number of the original small windows, 1.8 m (4 feet) square on two levels of the barn had been stoned in some time ago. This discovery was made when a corner of one window was opened temporarily in 1987.

It was revealed that the boards forming the inner and outer frame were secured by irregularly-shaped wooden dowels which were evidently hand-whittled. Between the frames were pieces of tree limbs, 7.6 cm to 10 cm (3 to 4 inches) in diameter, with bark attached. Mr. and Mrs. Peck have researched early methods of construction and have been told that hand-made dowels, and the use of limbs with bark intact date the barn to around 1805.

The stone barn has an interesting history, not only as the overnight resting place for Brock's body in October 1812, but according to the Niagara Historical Society publication, ''Freedom of Worship in The Town and Township of Niagara 1640-1962'', it was for a few years used by the Episcopal Church for ''occasional services'' after 1827 when the first Episcopal chapel fell into disuse and was demolished. This house, and the barn with its rich history, are being well cared for by the current owners, Meg and Ralph Peck.

John Walker

The Dee House

This red brick house was built by Robert Hamilton in 1807 as a wedding present for Robert Hamilton Jr., and his bride. It was occupied by four generations of the Hamilton family, until June 1954, when Mrs. Reginald Stewart, the fifth generation owner, sold it to George A. Allen. There are no transactions recorded in the Lincoln County Registry Office indicating that the house was sold at any time during that 147 year period, it was transferred from one Hamilton relative to another.

Jimmy Simpson, a "Globe and Mail" reporter wrote about the house in the June 1, 1954 edition, before Mrs. Stewart gave up possession. According to Mr. Simpson, Colonel Hamilton passed it on to his daughter Jane, who was Mrs. Sidney Mewburn. Mrs. Thomas Dee who was Mrs. Mewburn's daughter Jane was the next owner and it is from her residency that the house took its present name. Another of Mrs. Mewburn's daughters, Jessie, who was married to James Young, became the next owner. They had a son Fred C. Young, who inherited the house and lived in it from 1917 until his death in 1948. Mrs. Stewart was Fred C. Young's daughter, the fourth and last of the Hamilton family to own the house.

George A. Allen of Niagara Falls bought the house from Mrs. Stewart and then sold it to Ernest Smith and he in turn sold it in 1960 to Jonathan Kormos the present owner. Mr. Kormos has repaired and restored portions of the house, and while excavating in the basement of one wing used as servants' quarters, a sterling silver spoon engraved with the initials "R.H." was found. It's interesting to speculate if this piece of silverware was part of the Hamilton family's silver tableware which might have been temporarily buried in this basement at the time of the Battle of Queenston Heights, to prevent it being carried away as loot.

The house is at the northern end of the village, and while it would have been damaged during the Battle of Queenston Heights, its location and its sturdy construction would have contributed to its survival.

Ron Kitchen

"Glencairn".

"Glencairn", located on the lower Niagara River Parkway about 1.6 km (one mile) north of Queenston, was built by John Hamilton another of Robert Hamilton's sons at about the same time as "Willowbank" was built by Alexander Hamilton. John Hamilton was born in 1802 and educated in Edinburgh, Scotland. When he received his inheritance from his father's estate he entered the shipping business and in 1824 had the steamboat "Queenston" built at the Deep Hollow in Queenston.

The "Queenston" ran between Queenston and York. Barlow Cumberland, in "A Century of Sail and Steam on the Niagara River" wrote that: "... from his fine residence... he could watch the movements of his own and other steamers... it stood on the edge of the high bank overlooking the Queenston Dock." In 1830 when Hamilton built the "Great Britain" to replace the "Queenston" on the Queenston to Toronto to Prescott run, his company's headquarters was at Prescott.

Hamilton's shipping business prospered and in 1841 he formed the "Royal Mail Line" with boats running between Toronto and Kingston, and a secondary line which ran between Niagara, Hamilton and Toronto. The names of the steamboats which sailed under his flag included: "Traveller" 1835-38, "Constitution" renamed "Transit", "Great Britain", "Niagara", "St. George", "City of Toronto", "Brockville" and "Gildersleeve". John Hamilton's Company evidently weathered the depression of the mid 1850's which forced many other companies into bankruptcy. "Passport" was the last ship listed in his company's name, and was in operation from 1847 until 1861.

He was appointed to the Legislative Council of Upper Canada in 1831, and the Legislative Council of United Canada in 1841. In 1867 he was called to the Canadian Senate and became the Honourable Robert Hamilton. For 15 years he was the senior member of the Senate. He died at Kingston on October 10, 1882.

"Glencairn" is a two storey Colonial style house. In more recent years, its original wooden clapboard exterior has been replaced with white aluminum siding. The front of the house faces the Niagara River and its distinctive lower and upper galleries, supported by fluted wooden columns, capped with hand-carved capitals, are out of public view. It was owned by the Hamilton family until 1866 when it was purchased by William A. Thompson. Around the turn of the century, in the early 1900's it was sold to John B. Larkin and was then owned by Mr. Larkin's son-in-law, James Robb, Dr. Djamal Afrukhteh is the present owner.

George Bailey

Brown-Bassil House

This house with its "salt box" shape which is generally associated with houses found in New England, is owned by Dr. Brian M. Bassil. While it has undergone extensive renovations and restoration over the years, it retains many of its original attributes.

Research was carried out by the Heritage Branch of the Ministry of Culture and Recreation in 1976. Through a search of the Upper Canada land petitions, it was ascertained that in 1820 the property was owned by Thomas Helmer, the son of John P. Helmer, U.E. and a Revolutionary War veteran. Thomas served in the War of 1812, and in 1817 he petitioned for land on the basis of his war service and Loyalist descent. He was at that time an innkeeper at Niagara (Niagara-on-the-Lake), but the location of his inn there is not known.

Helmer sold the property in 1820 to John Johnson Brown, a merchant, who occupied it until his death in 1848. It was willed to his wife Mary Susan Brown, "with all and singular the buildings and improvements there on erected." According to Dr. Bassil there is an invoice extant from John Brown, merchant, which gives credence to the opinion that there was a store on the premises during Brown's occupancy.

After Mrs. Brown died, William G. Church and Archibald Wray became the owners of the property, then Joseph Wray, then his wife Mary Jane Wray and next their daughter, Emma Wray. When Emma Wray died in 1933, the house was willed to Rubie Powner, then in 1936 to George Wray. Other owners have been Helen Goring Robinson, Lillian Wray Boring, Charles Oswald Mortimer Lailey, Margaret Isobel Lailey, Rita Joyce Cudney, Jack Niven, John Kormos and John Ghetti. Dr. Bassil acquired the property in 1975.

This house has been designated as an historic house by the Town of Niagara-on-the-Lake, and listed as the Brown-Bassil house, circa 1820. An architectural description done by Graham W. Owen in September 1976 said: "The...interior has undergone drastic alteration over the years, however, there is a certain amount of apparently early detail surviving inside, and a sympathetic renovation (by Dr. Bassil) is under way at the present."

Ron Kitchen

McClosky House

This white clapboard house located on the northwest corner of Dumfries and Queenston Streets is one of the oldest houses in Queenston. Memorial Number 9826 in the Lincoln County Registry Office records the sale of this property "on which is erected a dwelling house and house intended for and occupied as a merchant shop". While the transaction was recorded on March 14, 1859, the date of sale was October 25, 1821. At that time Adam Brown bought the property from Elijah Phelps. There is no indication of when the house was built, but it was prior to 1821. There is an account in the Thompson Papers, Isabel Walker Collection showing that James Thompson did business with Adam Brown at Queenston.

Adam Brown sold out to Charles Livingston Bradley on December 8, 1855. The property remained in the Bradley family until 1923 when it was sold to Eliza Rolph. Jean Huggins remembered that Eliza Rolph and her sister operated a type of bed and breakfast rooming house, where visitors who came to Queenston on the lake boats found accommodation for a few days or a week. In 1940 the property was purchased by Rose Price, the present owner's grandmother. In 1950, when Rose Price died, the house was transferred to her daughter, Ruth McClosky and in 1966 her son, John, became the owner.

John Walker

Dr. Trimble's House

Dr. Robert J. Trimble came to Queenston to practise on September 29, 1877. Not long after he built this house as a residence and also as an office from which he took care of the medical needs of the community. His practice extended beyond the boundaries of the village of Queenston, as W.A. Lorne Robinson recounts in the following family story revolving around the birth of his wife Jean Milling. Lorne Robinson tells of the difficulties that doctors faced in the early days.

"Old Dick", a horse owned by Stewart Milling, is the villian in this story. Milling lived at the southwest corner of the Portage Road and the Mountain Road. "Old Dick" was used to till his market garden of several hectares (acres) and also as a means of transportation for the Milling family.

The first week of December 1906 had been very disagreeable with almost continual rain and near freezing temperatures. On December 6, upon returning from work as darkness fell, Stewart Milling found his wife in labour for their third child. He was dispatched by Mrs. Amelia Young, U.E., mother of Mrs. Milling, to bring Lydia Thompson, a midwife, to attend at the birth.

"Old Dick" was hitched to the buggy and driven to the Thompson home on Portage Road, near present day Church's Lane. Mr. Milling then set off along the Portage Road for Queenston, in order to bring Dr. Trimble. Earlier Dr. Trimble had been accosted during the darkness in the ravine tunnel north of St. David's. He was able to use his horse-whip on the villians and he and his horse escaped without further incident, but thereafter Dr. Trimble requested transportation to attend a patient at night.

All went well until Milling reached Smeaton's Creek near the Larkin Farms (now inundated by the Ontario Hydro Reservoir). The creek had risen and was flowing over the planking of the wooden bridge. "Old Dick" shied and refused to cross. Mr. Milling dismounted and was obliged to use the horse's halter to turn the horse and buggy around. He then headed back on the Portage Road, the way he had come, passing his own home on Mountain Road before going north to go down the ravine hill to St. David's.

Mrs. Milling heard the clippity-clop of "Old Dick's" hooves and wondered what had happened. Milling headed "Old Dick" east on the Grimsby Road (present day York Road) from St. David's to Dr. Trimble's home on Walnut Street in Queenston. Here Dr. Trimble was picked up and driven back along the same route to the Milling house.

At 2 a.m. on December 7, 1906, Jean Stewart Milling was born. She was given the second name Stewart, her father's name, because he had wanted another boy. Dr. Trimble remained for breakfast after which "Old Dick" was hitched up for the return trip. In spite of his recalcitrance "Old Dick" received an extra feeding of oats for his efforts. No mention is made in the story of any special recognition to Dr. Trimble. What he did was "all in a day's work."

Willowbank Estate Wines

"Willowbank"

"Willowbank" was built in 1834 by Alexander Hamilton, Robert Hamilton's fourth son. It was named after the grove of willow trees which filled the end of the Deep Hollow at the front of the house. When you see "Willowbank" from the Niagara Parkway, you are looking at the rear of the house. The front, which is visible through the trees, as you drive along Queenston Street, has "Willowbank's" outstanding feature, the eight wooden Ionic columns, cut from solid logs, two storeys high. The columns are topped with hand-carved capitals.

"Willowbank" was occupied by the Hamilton family until 1934, when J.M. Bright purchased it from the A.E. Boultbee estate. The Sisters of Christian Charity acquired the house from the Brights in 1966. The Sisters put the building up for sale on September 1, 1980 and it was purchased by Arthur Appleton in late 1982. In the spring of 1983 Mr. Appleton established a school for boys with learning disabilities which he carried on for several years. In 1985 "Willowbank" was sold to Tony Boyle who planned to establish a winery, Willowbank Estate Wines, on the premises.

"Willowbank" is presently undergoing extensive renovation and restoration. What the facilities will be used for is still under consideration.

Chippawa

Queenston has retained its general geographic shape over the years, with its topography much the same as it was when it was first settled, while the Chippawa of two hundred years ago would be barely recognizable to someone coming back from the past. The Chippawa Creek which then flowed eastward, emptying into the Niagara River, now flows westward bringing the waters of the Niagara River to the Ontario Hydro Sir Adam Beck Generating Stations at Queenston.

Chippawa is supposed to have been named after a tribe of Chippewa Indians who had a village nearby as late as 1788. After the Iroquois annihilated the Neutral Indians, who occupied the west bank of the Niagara River in what we now know as Southern Ontario, the Chippewas, a tribe of the Mississauguas, crossed what is now the St. Clair River, to occupy this vacant territory. The Iroquois made no objection, and so the Mississauguas became the dominant tribe in this area.

The name "Chippawa" is supposed to translate to "people without moccasins", though it is difficult to imagine why anyone would go without moccasins or other foot protection in our climate. An early writer in describing this Chippewa tribe, wrote that "they were short of stature, gay ,lively and filthy". [1] Early travellers who left valuable accounts of this area called it by various names: Chippawa, Chippeway, Chippaway, Chippewa, and Cheapway.

Because the settlement had no formal name at the time when Governor Simcoe changed all the Indian names to English names, it escaped his attention. The Chippawa Creek he renamed the Welland River. To her credit, the Governor's wife, Elizabeth, when writing in her diary, usually called the stream "the Chippawa" - never "the Welland". To this day, when the stream is mentioned in written accounts it is more often than not referred to as Chippawa Creek. Local inhabitants without exception refer to the stream as Chippawa Creek. When the Ontario Provincial Department of Travel and Publicity erected a commemorative plaque at the site of the Fort in 1960, it was in commemoration of Fort Chippawa, not Fort Welland.

Father Louis Hennepin, a member of French explorer La Salle's advance exploration party, wrote about the party's exploration of this part of the country in December 1678. After seeing the Falls of Niagara "On the 7 th...we lay that night near a River which runs from the Westward, within a League above the Great Falls of Niagara." Historian Francis Parkman, writing in 1890, interpreted Hennepin's reference to the "River which runs from the "Westward" as being the Chippawa River. [2]

The French were the first Europeans to occupy the west bank of the Niagara, and according to early reports they had a clearing and perhaps a storehouse at the mouth of the creek before 1759. When the Indians on the east bank became hostile to them hampering their shipbuilding there, the French moved their shipbuilding to present day Navy Island. From

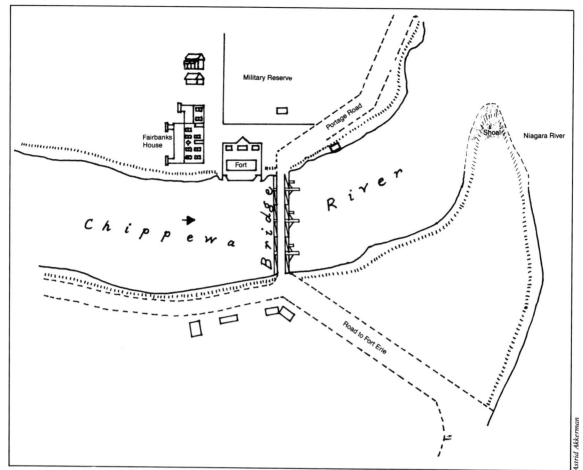

The Fort, the King's Bridge and Early Settlement at Chippawa,
from Surveyor John Stegmann's Map of 1797.

Fort Chippawa and the King's Bridge over the Chippawa River are the prominent features of this map, which was drawn from the original. "Fairbanks House", operated by John Fairbanks, was mentioned in travellers' reports as early as 1795. John Burch had originally settled on the land on the north bank of the Chippawa, but was forced to give it up to the British Military, for the Military Reserve. The buildings on the south bank are merchants' storehouses. The Chippawa River is seen to curve to the north, and downriver, as it enters the Niagara River. The peninsula jutting out from the south bank, has a shoal at its tip which was often under water, posing a hazard to boats trying to enter Chippawa Creek.

there they were assumed to have come to the west mainland, to cut timber for the ships, and perhaps even to cultivate the land to grow vegetables. [3]

Present day Chippawa owes its origin to Captain Gother Mann, Commanding Engineer to the Governor-in-Chief, Lord Dorchester. In 1788 Dorchester ordered Gother Mann to report on the establishment of a public road, a portage, on the west bank of the Niagara River. Mann wrote, pointing out that the mouth of the Chippawa would be a suitable replacement for Fort Schlosser, the southern terminus

of the portage on the east bank which the British would have to give up to the Americans, under the terms of the Treaty of Paris in 1783 and Jay's Treaty of 1795 which completed the process.*

Travellers' accounts described the Creek unfavourably. The Duc de la Rochefoucault-Liancourt in 1795, wrote: "...the stagnant water of the creek renders it very unhealthy and to this circumstance are imputed the endemic fevers which every year afflict the inhabitants of this place". Isaac Weld in 1796 said:

*

"The situation above the Falls to be chosen instead of Fort Schlosser ought I imagine to be the Chippeway Creek; it is indeed nearer the Falls than Fort Schlosser, and there is a very strong current (that) passes it, but there is no difficulty to get into the Creek, and there is then still water, boats may lye there in great safety and such buildings as are requisite may be erected. The Creek is about 80 yards across and has 7 or 8 feet depth of water; it would be necessary to have a bridge as likewise a good road; the first would not cost a great deal as there is a good bottom and no current; but the latter would be attended by some expence as the ground is very wet to a mile and a half from each side of creek."

National Archives of Canada

View of a Settlement on Both Sides of the River, Joined by the Bridge.
Water colour on pencil by George Heriot, 1806.

The barracks of Fort Chippawa and a pillory are on the north bank - left side of the sketch. A pillory consisted of a wooden frame with holes through which a person's head and hands were placed and the frame was then locked in place. They were the "penalty boxes" of pioneer days. If a soldier misbehaved he was assigned to the pillory, and forced to stay there for an undetermined time. The buildings on the south bank were Thomas Cummings' and Grant & Kerby's storehouses. The King's Bridge was a simple structure, with wooden planking supported by timbers driven into the bed of the Chippawa Creek. There is no indication of a draw-span, which could be raised to allow boats to pass through upriver, so all loading and unloading of cargo took place at the wharves downriver from the bridge. George Heriot, was the Deputy Postmaster General of British North America at the time he visited this area and made this sketch.

"...the water of the creek is so bad that it cannot be drank, and the garrison (of the fort) is obliged to draw water daily from the river". Mrs. Simcoe was not impressed and wrote in her diary: "The Chippawa is a dull, muddy river, running through a flat swampy country."

It was a traveller, identified only as T.C. who explained the creek's colour: "The waters of the Chippeway are dark coloured owing to its running for near 30 miles through a swamp". An article in the *National Intelligencer* of Washington D.C. described the Creek and its military significance. "The Chippawa, though a considerable stream, cannot effect to mingle its dark waters with the pellucid current of the majestic Niagara for one mile and a half. It is confined to a narrow path along the shore and the line is as definite between the waters as between the land and water. The passage of this creek

in a hostile manner, except on ice, may be disputed. Nature opposes no other obstacle in a march to Fort George on this road." [4]

Several accounts describe the mouth of the Creek and how the strong current of the Niagara affected the Creek's discharge. Captain Enys, who visited in 1787, wrote: "Mr. Birch (sic), who lives at the mouth of the Chippaway Creek, said he had perceived a regular flux and reflux in the Creek resembling the tide of the Sea."

"Mr. Hamilton (Robert Hamilton of Queenston) says it is not a regular flux or reflux at all, but that occasionally the current runs up instead of down, and what appears at first more extraordinary is, that the Creek has its source to the West and runs to the Eastward, yet it is a Westerly or a wind directly down the Creek which occasions the Current to run up it to the Westward. This he accounted for in some measure to my satisfaction". [5]

Colonel Landmann, R.E., wrote in his journal, describing the topography at the mouth of the Chippawa, and the procedures necessary for a successful entrance into the Creek from the Niagara River: "...the two currents of the Niagara and the Chippawa, uniting at this place caused a long shoal of sand to extend from the upper side of Chippawa Creek over which the water was too inconsiderable to allow a boat to pass upon it so as to enter the creek - thus rendering it necessary to follow the Niagara to some distance across the mouth before there would be sufficient water for the boat to turn into the creek without touching".

Joseph Hadfield who visited in 1785, wrote of his experience in crossing the Niagara River from the east bank to the west bank at Chippawa:"Captain Jones, who was the senior officer commanding Fort Schlosser...ordered a military bateau with six soldiers to convey us to the opposite bank of the river. The current is too strong to permit passing in a direct line, for fear of being drawn into the rapids, where many have perished by imprudence and temerity. The soldiers, besides oars, were furnished with long poles, with iron ferrals or spikes, with which they ascended some miles the river Erie (Niagara). Then from a certain point of land they take their oars, which they pull with all force, and then with difficulty made the entrance of Chippaway Creek." [6*]

These conditions lasted until a channel was made in the peninsula, at the edge of the northern bank, in the late 1820's when the first Welland Canal was built. This channel allowed sailing ships to go directly into the Niagara River, and head directly upstream as they do today. Before this channel was made, some of the boats were unable to make the sharp turn into the Creek and were swept over the Falls.

* Fort Schlosser was originally called Fort Little Niagara. When it was taken over from the French, the British ordered Captain John Schlosser to enlarge and strengthen it. When the work was completed in record time, as a reward for Schlosser's's services the Fort was renamed Fort Schlosser. For many years the Falls, which we now call the American Falls was called the Schlosser Falls. The docking area near the Fort continued to be called Schlosser and was the destination for Niagara River ships coming to the east bank above the Falls, well into the 1850's.

The Road to Fort Erie, Chippawa Creek, a part of the town of Bridgetown.
Pen and ink drawing on grey wash by Sempronius Stretton, 1804. (actually circa 1812).
Lieutenant-Colonel Stretton mistakenly named the settlement he sketched, Bridgetown, when he meant Bridgewater, Bridgewater was the settlement above the mills at the head of the Islands (present day Dufferin Islands). This is actually a view of Chippawa, with Thomas Cummings' and Grant & Kerby's warehouses shown in detail. The presence of the basket-like object hung from a pole dates the sketch as at least 1812. This device was one of the warning beacons installed by order of Major-General Isaac Brock, to warn of an American attack. These beacons were installed at strategic points along the Niagara River. The iron baskets were filled with dry firewood and kindling, so that they could be set on fire quickly. If the Americans crossed the Niagara River in a surprise nightime attack, the nearest beacon would be set afire. Sentries would notice the blaze, set their beacon on fire, and others along the river would follow. There were beacons along Lundy's Lane and as far west as present day Fonthill. They were meant to alert the military and the settlers that an invasion was in progress. There was never a need for the fires to be lit.

National Archives of Canada

The arrival of Chippawa's first settler, Thomas Cummings, predated the first use of the west bank portage by five years. Cummings, a Scot who had settled in Albany, but had to flee because of his loyalty to the Crown, came to the west bank in 1783 and settled at the mouth of the Chippawa River. John Burch, also from Albany settled on the northeast side of the river. Burch had been a prominent merchant in Albany and Cumming's mother was his housekeeper. Their land acquisitions were confirmed in 1797 when they received Crown Grants of 80.9 ha (200 acres) each in the area in which they first settled. Burch's land was on the north side at the mouth of the Creek, and he had to give up part of it for the Military Reserve.

Squatters settled on lands that had not been surveyed and assigned to their rightful owners. On January 25, 1797 the *Upper Canada Gazette* carried this notice from Thomas Cummings: "All persons whom it may concern are hereby cautioned not to purchase from John Gardner, the house wherein he now dwells, at the mouth of the Chippawa Creek, the same being built upon the freehold of the subscriber, and, as yet not alienated." The *Upper Canada Gazette* carried lists of people to whom land titles were granted, as they were processed and it was later in the year when Cummings received confirmation of his grant.

James Macklem from County Tyrone, Ireland, came to the area in 1791, after two years in Pennsylvania. He established Macklem's Tavern, which is first mentioned in a traveller's report in 1800 and a year later he joined in partnership with Markle and Hamilton in the "Niagara Chippawa Stage Coach Line". These enterprises were the beginning of the Macklem commercial and industrial undertakings, which were to include a foundry, tannery and distillery. They brought prosperity to Chippawa and made the Macklem name most prominent in the village's history.

Captain Gother Mann's recommendation of 1788, stating "there is then still water (after entering the Creek from the Niagara River), boats may lye there in great safety and such buildings as are requisite may be erected", established it as a good docking area for boats. As early as 1788 merchant trader Robert Hamilton and his associates were carrying goods over the Portage Road, to Chippawa and transhipping them by York boats to Fort Erie. In 1789 they received permission to build a log storehouse and a dock on the banks of the Chippawa.

When the British transferred the portage of their military supplies to the west bank of the Niagara River in 1791, the north bank of the Chippawa was chosen as the site for the King's storehouse and a stockaded fort to protect it. In 1791 the British Military built a stone storehouse with a second-storey log blockhouse for troops. This fortification was called Fort Chippawa.

Isaac Weld in 1796 wrote about the new fort and the settlement which had sprung up nearby: "The fort, which occupies about one rood of ground only, consists of a small blockhouse, enclosed in a stockade of cedar posts about 12 feet high, which is merely sufficient to defend the garrison against musket shot. Adjoining the fort there are seven or eight farm houses, and some large store houses, where goods are deposited preparatory to their being conveyed in carts, to Queenston". [7]

This combined storehouse and blockhouse at "Cheapway" was near the mouth of the river. As time passed the post was improved and its garrison increased. When Governor Simcoe changed all of the Indian names to British names, in 1792, the "official" name for the Chippawa River became the Welland River and the Fort became Fort Welland.*

Mrs. Simcoe wrote about the fort in her diary and depicted it in a sketch. "Tuesday July 25, 1792 - The Governor and I and Francis went in a carriage to Fort Chippawa, but finding the baggage had not arrived, could proceed no further: dined and slept at Capt. Hamilton's who commands here. We walked this evening, and I made some sketches. Weather excessively hot. We slept in a room in the Block House where the logs were some distance apart. Without this contrivance, used as loopholes in the case of attack, as well as for admitting air, I think the heat would have been insufferable; as it was, I left my bed and lay on the floor". [8]

The Fort was garrisoned by a small detachment. Though the purpose of the Fort was the accommodation and preservation of government stores in transit, the garrison was available for other duties. La Rochefoucault-Liancourt in 1795 wrote: "The duty of the soldiers, who form the garrison, consist of standing sentries: but they are also obliged to serve on board the ships which belong to the government." They manned the batteaux and using

---

* In 1791 Governor John Graves Simcoe arrived at Niagara and set up the government of Upper Canada. He showed his authority by giving English names to every town, river, and lake within his jurisdiction. Niagara became Newark. He ran out of names when he was assigning names to three townships in Simcoe County and Mrs. Simcoe helped him out. She suggested the names of her three lap dogs, *Tiny, Floss* and *Tay* and the townships were given those names. *Places in Ontario* Nick and Helma Mika, Vol II ,III, pub. Mika Publishing Co. 1983

210

FORT CHIPPAWA, ON THE RIVER WELLAND, 1795.
(From a Drawing by Mrs. Simcoe.)

poles or oars, navigated their fully loaded charges upstream, from Chippawa to Fort Erie. La Rochefoucault-Liancourt also reported that " for this extremely difficult and laborious task, they were allowed only fifteen shillings, to be distributed among five men, who compose the crew." [9] This it is assumed was in addition to their regular pay as soldiers.

A small detachment was stationed at the Fort, but the structure was allowed to become rundown. Various reports attest to this. One of them by Erastus Granger, a United States Government Indian Agent, reported to Henry Dearborn, the American Secretary of War, in 1807 "Fort Chippawa...merely a wooden blockhouse, the pickets mostly rotted down, not capable of any defence". [10]

The British command shared this opinion and considered that the Chippawa was the only legitimate barrier behind which British forces could dig in to hold back an American force advancing from the direction of Fort Erie.

The Fort, even in its dilapidated state, still fared no worse than the bridge built by the British Military, over the Chippawa Creek. The first record of a bridge here, appears on John Stegmann's map of 1791. As it was built with government money it was called the "King's Bridge". It consisted of a wooden plank roadway, supported by stringers or beams which were fastened to timbers which had been driven into the mud bottom of the stream. It was narrow and only one way traffic was possible.

The British Military did not keep the bridge in good repair, Ernest Green wrote that by 1807: "...the bridge across the Chippawa at its mouth had become decayed and unsafe and the magistrates and principal inhabitants along the road from Niagara to Fort Erie petitioned the Legislature for authority to appropriate £200 of county money for the purpose of rebuilding it." Nothing was done because in 1810 T.C. noted: "There had been a handsome bridge over the Chippeway, but the middle part was broken down and they now ferry across." [11]

Thomas Cummings became Chippawa's first general merchant, beginning business on a small scale. He exported wheat and flour which he bought or obtained by barter from the nearby settlers, to the Montreal merchants, and received food stuffs, and general merchandise in payment. These items he then sold to or bartered with his customers.

His list of goods received from the Montreal merchants - all of which had to be imported from England - included: gunpowder, iron bars, loaf sugar, salt, Bibles, spelling books, men's, women's, youth's and children's hats and stockings, shoemaker's supplies, table and pocket knives, shears, snuff boxes, brass padlocks, shaving boxes, carpenter's tools, bread baskets, tea trays, spectacles, household utensils and crockery of all kinds.

He also carried a line of yard goods and cloth accessories: black silk and bandana handkerchiefs, yellow chintz shawls, white, yellow and red flannel, checked and striped calico, black callimancoe and Irish dowlas. In 1807 Thomas Cumming's son James managed his father's business, but by 1811 James was in business for himself as both of them were buying goods from merchants in Schenectady, New York, rather than from the Montreal merchants. [12]

Chippawa and
The War of 1812

With the outbreak of the War of 1812, Fort Chippawa's garrison was increased and stood ready behind the natural barrier of Chippawa Creek, to prevent the advance of any United States forces which would cross the Niagara River to the south and attempt to proceed north toward Queenston. Detachments of famous British regiments, including Major-General Isaac Brock's 49th, the 6th and 8th (King's) Regiments were garrisoned at Fort Chippawa during the war.

American Major-General Stephen Van Rensselaer in October 1812, considered the Chippawa River a major check to any attempt to invade Canada by way of the upper Niagara River. He preferred an invasion across the lower river, and to support his proposal he wrote that "...by taking up the bridge at Chippawa they might greatly embarrass us...the cleared country is but a mile or two wide." [1] The United States War Office accepted his argument and he was allowed to mount the first American invasion of Canada later that same month, at Queenston.

On October 13, 1812, when the Americans invaded at Queenston, Captain Bullock and his troops left Fort Chippawa and marched along the Portage Road to join Major-General Roger Hale Sheaffe's troops from Fort George. Together they successfully attacked the American position on Queenston Heights and brought an end to this enemy incursion into Canada.

The Lincoln Militia, under the command of Lieutenant-Colonel Thomas Clark, was posted to Chippawa. As there was no room at the Fort, other accommodations had to be found. "You are not to expect tents and must endeavour to shelter your men in the adjacent houses and barns" the Quarter-Master of Militia wrote to Colonel Clark. Thomas Cummings owned two storehouse, and twenty houses which he rented out, and Clark took over the storehouses as barracks for the Militia troops and the officers were billeted in the private homes.

Mostly farmers were recruited to serve in the militia, usually on the assumption that they would serve their time in uniform during the crop growing season, after seeding and before harvest. There were long periods of inactivity resulting in boredom, and they became frustrated when they were away from their families for extended periods. As well, they were often left to their own devices to find their food, and they were not paid on time.

All of these incoveniences combined to make the men of the Lincoln Militia stationed at Chippawa in 1813 vent their frustrations. What they did was reported in the American newspapers. The *New York Statesman* reported in the March 29, 1813 edition: "Two very handsome buildings were some time reduced to ashes in the town of Chippawa on the Canadian side of the river, opposite Fort Schlosser by an exasperated Militia, who had been detained from their homes for a length of time, without being permitted to see their families, who were suffering behind them. We are informed that those militia were soon afterward permitted to retire." [2] The "handsome buildings" were Thomas Cummings' warehouses.

Chippawa became involved in the war when the Americans sent an expeditionary force across the Niagara River at Niagara on May 27, 1813. By the end of the next day they had 6000 troops on the west bank and they marched south, along the river road capturing Queenston. They then went along the Portage Road, where they occupied Chippawa before moving on to take Fort Erie. When the British withdrew from Chippawa, they burned the government storehouses filled with supplies, the blockhouse and barracks at the Fort, to prevent the Americans from taking the supplies, or finding shelter at the Fort. [3]

The tedious periods of inaction for the Militia were some times alleviated, as on July 5, 1813 when Lieutenant-Colonel Clark led a force of fourteen men across the Niagara River, below the mouth of the Chippawa in three boats, to attack Fort Schlosser. Arriving just before daybreak they surprised the Fort's

guard and collected what booty they could find and returned to the Canadian shore, and "No damage was done to any person in the boats and I believe little hurt was done to the people on shore." A bronze marker, commemorating this raid, stands at the embarkation point, north of King's Bridge Park.

The booty they brought back with them included "one brass six-pounder gun, 57 stands of arms, two and a half kegs of musket ball cartridge, 16 musket-proof curtains for boats, one gunboat, two batteaux, two anchors, twenty barrels of salt, twelve cases of tobacco, eight barrels of pork, one barrel of whiskey, with some spades, oars and axes." [4]

The Americans again invaded Canada on July 3, 1814, at Fort Erie, where the outnumbered British garrison surrendered. Only a small British force escaped to carry out a rearguard action as they retreated north, along the river road toward Chippawa, taking up the planking on the bridges as

The Battle of Chippawa.
An engraving from a sketch by an unknown artist.
Brigadier-General Winfield Scott is shown commanding his American troops at the Battle of Chippawa, July 5, 1814, in this artist's impression of the action. The British force, commanded by Major-General Phineas Riall, represented by the fallen soldiers, one from a Scottish Regiment, the other from an English Regiment, were put to rout by Scott's revitalized corps. Scott's men were dressed in grey, the traditional dress of the Militia, and the British underestimated their ability to fight. When the Americans not only stood their ground, but attacked with force, Riall was heard to say, as he ordered his men to retreat, ''My God! these soldiers are regulars.''

The U.S. Army in Action at the Battle of Chippawa, July 5, 1814.
An oil painting by a unknown artist.
Brigadier-General Winfield Scott is shown in this painting leading his grey clad brigade of U.S. Army regulars. They wore grey, because there was a shortage of blue cloth, and British General Phineas Riall, believing them to be only militia – troops who were not considered to be good soldiers – treated them with contempt. It was a costly error. Riall and his British troops were defeated at the Battle of Chippawa, July 5, 1814. The Americans were so pleased over this victory that in one city, Atlanta, Georgia, there is a Chippawa Square, named after this battle.

Stamford Kiwanis Photo Collection. Niagara Falls Public Library

they retreated. The American force under Major-General Jacob Brown, halted and set up camp on Samuel Street's farm, on the south side of Street's Creek, now called Ussher's Creek.

The Battle of Chippawa took place in a field on the south side of the Creek, on the next day, July 5, 1814. In the ensuing action, the British forces under Major-General Phineas Riall were defeated and forced to make a hasty retreat to the northern bank of the Chippawa. As the British rearguard withdrew over the King's Bridge, they removed the wooden plank bridge deck, rendering the bridge impassable.

The British dug in on the north bank. positioning their artillery, and aiming it toward the southern side and the road leading along the river to Fort Erie. They were affirming Captain Gother Mann's assessment in 1788, followed by subsequent military opinions, that: "The passage of this creek in a hostile manner, except on ice , may be disputed". Events would prove this incorrect. The Americans circumvented the fortified crossing and brought their army across the stream, where it joins Lyon's Creek. They had a large force on the north bank, ready to outflank the British dug in at the mouth of the creek, before the British were aware that they had crossed to the north bank. The British withdrew hurriedly to avoid being trapped.

During Major-General Riall's retreat to the north bank of the Creek on July 5, he ordered all of the houses and other buildings on the southern bank to be burnt. Then, after the Battle of Lundy's Lane, when the Americans retreated toward Fort Erie, the Americans set fire to any remaining structures. No buildings were left standing in Chippawa after the Americans retreated south along the river road toward Fort Erie.

The War Loss Claims submitted by Thomas Cummings and John Muirhead in 1815 give details of the losses they suffered and an interesting comment on the conduct of the militia, and how they contributed to the destruction.

Thomas Cumming's petition read: "That your memorialist lived at the mouth of the Chippawa since the close of the American Revolution, and made very large improvement on his lands, besides a number of buildings, which is now all destroyed by fire and the farm laid waste and is now a common, which by that means your memorialist is unable to support himself and his family. The first two buildings were destroyed by fire on the 13th of December 1812, whilst occupied by the 2nd and 4th Regiments of the Lincoln Militia…About the beginning of last July your memorialist had twenty more houses, large and small burnt by order of Major-General Riall at the same place, which buildings I got appraised by two

carpenters previous to their being burnt, one of whom was master carpenter in the Royal Engineering Department, which buildings they appraised at £1,570 15s Halifax currency,making the whole buildings, including the two former occupied by the 2nd and 4th Regiments of the Lincoln Militia,to the amount of £ 2,480 4s 1 1/2d currency, which sum is a very serious loss for me to lay out of at this time when I have every article to purchase at the highest rate for myself and family". Cummings went on to relate his record of service: "Your memorialist has spent the prime of his life in His Majesty's service, to wit: seven years in the late American Revolution and twenty-one years in the Commissariat Department, and is so advanced in years and unable to labour to support himself and his family." [5] J.J.Lefferty's house which was on the south bank of the Creek was also "Burned by Order of the Commanding General."

John Muirhead's War Loss Claim tells of damage done to his property by the troops stationed at Chippawa. His claim read: "Enclosed you have an account of the damages which two respectable neighbours think I have sustained during the late War with the United States of America. My dwelling house was burned by the enemy, the morning after the Battle of Lundy's Lane, the remainder by the British Troops and as far as respects the store house and stables, barns and fences, it is out of my power to say what Regiment destroyed them. You have seen it and will know that when a soldier draws his rations he wants fuel to cook them and will take picket fences to cook them or whatever comes first". [6]

Muirhead claimed £ 400 for the losses inflicted by the American forces and £118 8s for losses attributed to His Majesty's Forces. He received £ 382. Grant & Kerby's storehouse, James Macklem's buildings and John Fanning's Inn on the north bank of Chippawa Creek were also burned by the retreating American forces after the battle of Lundys Lane. Macklem received £ 750 and Fanning received £ 700 to compensate for their loss.

At the end of 1814 and the beginning of 1815 Fort Chippawa was greatly strengthened. There was a square redoubt with a blockhouse built for one hundred men. It mounted four twelve-pounder guns, and a twenty-pounder and a howitzer were emplaced nearby. A contemporary report states that by February 1815, barracks were being built for seven hundred men, around which field work in a polygonal form was to be prepared in the spring. There were also to be officers' quarters, a commissariat store and a hospital. When the war ended these plans must have been forgotten as by the end of 1815 the Fort seems to have been abandoned. [7]

Chippawa After The War of 1812

After the war there was little left of what DeWitt Clinton saw in Chippawa during his visit in 1810. He wrote: " Chippeway is a mean village of twenty houses, three stores, two taverns, a windmill and a distillery". [1] The two taverns mentioned by DeWitt Clinton and described by T.C, in his "Ride to Niagara" in May 1809 "one kept by Stevens and the other by Fanning" were probably not rebuilt as they were not mentioned in travellers' reports after the war. Chippawa suffered more than Queenston from the ravages of the war, but it was Chippawa, not Queenston which would not only recover its former prominence, and would also become a thriving industrial and shipbuilding centre; Chippawa's prominence would extend into the 1850's, while Queenston would gradually decline in importance.

The Portage Road where it ran along the river bank, above the rapids, was within sight of the American shore. Because all troop movements and the transport of military supplies would be under enemy scrutiny, a new road was cut through the swamp, running directly from Bridgewater - the bend of present day Dufferin Islands - to the Creek. It is not certain when this road - the road allowance in use today - became a legal road. As it was laid over swampy terrain, it was a corduroy, or log road.

At the end of the war there was no King's Bridge and the government did nothing to replace the bridge. Money was allocated for roads, it seems, but none for bridges. For a time the only way to cross the Creek was by ferry. Samuel Street, who owned the Falls Mills, lost business because there was no bridge. The settlers south of Chippawa could not bring their grain to be ground at his mill. In 1816 he built a wooden bridge over the Chippawa, at his own expense, and "threw it open to public use." In 1817 Captain Langslow wrote of the existence of two bridges at Chippawa, "the lower (near the mouth of the river) called King's Bridge."

At about the same time Street formed "The Niagara Falls and Chippawa Plank Road Company" and made the portion of the Portage Road, from the bend at the islands to Chippawa, a toll road. Samuel Street soon began to petition the Legislature to be repaid for what he spent on the bridge. Three times he submitted his appeal, but there is no record of his having been reimbursed. However the bridge was in the care of the Village of Chippawa in 1856.

John Howison, another officer of the East India Company, visited the area in 1824. Noting the need to transport goods overland around the height of the Falls, he declared "...a portage which can never be evaded by any improvement in the navigation, it being rendered necessary by the Falls of Niagara". He was unaware of Robert Gourlay's comment in his "Statistical Account" of 1817, where he said: "Locks may be made to pass the great falls and connect Lakes Ontario and Erie, but many years must elapse before the province is rich enough to meet the expense".

As well, he was also unaware that after years of promoting the idea of a canal to bypass the Falls, in

Linking the Great Lakes of Canada - Opening of the first Welland Canal, November, 27, 1829.
Oil Painting by J.D. Kelly.

On November 27, 1829, the 78.7 tonnes (80 tons) schooner, "Ann and Jane", and the "Broughton", entered the
northern terminus of the new Welland Canal at Port Dalhousie and were towed through 38 canal locks to Port
Robinson. After passing through locks No. 39 and 40 the vessels entered the Chippawa Creek and were towed
to the southern terminus of the Canal at Chippawa, and then on to Buffalo, arriving on November 29th. These
were the first boats to bypass the Falls of Niagara without being carried overland. From that time on bulk cargo
was carried on canal boats, and freight traffic on the Portage Road dwindled. The era of the Niagara Portage
Road had come to an end.

1824 the very year that Howison made his statement, William Hamilton Merritt and his associates in the Welland Canal Company, were beginning work on what was to become the first Welland Canal. Chippawa, which then was described as "a small village of a dozen houses, several store-houses, and two or three taverns", was to benefit from this canal, as the mouth of the Chippawa River was to become the southern terminus of the canal.

It took five years to construct the locks and other facilities for the canal. To allow sailing ships to enter and exit the mouth of the Chippawa River with greater ease and safety, it was necessary to cut a channel through the peninsula-like sand bar which extended from the north bank. A cut, beginning from the north bank, made the peninsula an island. This passage, which allowed ships to enter and leave the Niagara River by heading directly upstream, was 120.7m (396

feet) long. The canal's course ran from what is now Port Dalhousie, along the course of the Twelve Mile Creek. A series of 34 wooden locks lifted the sailing ships up to the top of the escarpment. From there a canal was cut to present day Port Robinson, where it intersected with the Chippawa River. The sailing ships were pulled through the canal by horsepower, with the horses walking on a tow path along the shore, with ropes from their harnesses attached to the boats.

Engineer Hiram Tibbet in his May 10, 1823 report to the stockholders projected how boat traffic would pass through the canal."Boats from 20 to 40 tons will Navigate this stream with ease & 2 men & a horse will take one from Lake Ontario to the Chippawa (at Port Robinson) in One day, or to the Mouth of the Chippawa in a day & a half at farthest."

Towing the ''Ann and Jane''
Along the Chippawa Creek
This is an artistic depiction of the schooner ''Ann and Jane'' being towed along Chippawa Creek in November 1829. The section of the Creek from its mouth at the Niagara River to Port Robinson, was part of the first Welland Canal. At Port Robinson there was a lock which provided the entry into the Canal proper.

Carol Breton

In November 1829, a schooner of 78.7 tonnes (80 tons) burden, named *Ann and Jane* and a smaller vessel entered the southern terminus of the canal - the mouth of the Chippawa River - and proceeded to Port Dalhousie. This was the beginning of a period of prosperity for Chippawa, which would extend into the 1850's. The canal business would last only four years, because, no sooner had the canal opened than plans were being made to extend the canal from its intersection with the Chippawa River at Port Robinson, straight through to Lake Erie. This was accomplished by 1833, and a lock was installed at Port Robinson to allow ships to enter or leave the canal at this point, to proceed by way of the Chippawa to the Niagara River. The remains of this stone lock are still to be seen at Port Robinson.

There was still some traffic on the Portage Road, because it was faster for travellers to come by boat to Niagara or Queenston, then by stagecoach to either Chippawa, or Fort Erie, where they could again board boats, than it was to take passage through the canal.

The sailing ships coming out of Chippawa Creek, heading for Lake Erie, had to be towed upriver against the current of the Niagara River. The roadway along the river bank became a tow path by the removal of trees, brush and anything else on the river side of the road that would obstruct the tow ropes. Looking back to those days it is easy to take a romantic view of passage through the canal and up the river, but it was anything but romantic for the men and animals who towed the boats.

Barlow Cumberland has left this description of conditions along the tow path of the Welland Canal: "The canal bank and tow paths were a sticky mush, which in those autumn months were churned and stamped into a continuous condition of soft red mud and splashing pools. From two to six double teams were employed to haul each passing vessel, dependent upon whether it was light or was loaded, but in either case there was the same dull, heavy, continuous pull against the slow-moving mass, a hopeless constant tug into the collars, bringing raw and calloused shoulders.

"Poor beasts, there was every description of horse, pony, mule forced into the service, but an all prevailing similarity of lean sides and projecting

bones, of staring unkempt coats, gradually approaching similar colour as the red mud dried upon their hides. Rest! they had in their traces when mercifully for a few moments the vessel was in lock, or when waiting her turn at night they lay out on the bank where she happened to stop. It was the rest of despair.

"The poor devils of "drivers", boys or men, who tramped along the canal behind each tottering gang, were little better off than their beasts. Heavy-footed, wearied with lifting their boots out of the sucking slush, they trudged along, staggering and half asleep, until aroused by the sounds of a sagging tow line, with quickened stride and volley of hot-shot expletives, they closed upon their luckless four-footed companions. What an electric wince went through the piteous brutes as the stinging whip left wales upon their sides! A sudden forward motion brought up by the twang of the tow line as it came taut, sweeping them off their legs, until they settled down once more into the sidling crablike movement caused by the angle of the hawser from the bow to the tow path." [2]

Sailing boats were later towed by steamboats, as the *Buffalo Journal* reported on August 11, 1831: "For the first time in our history,...the steamer *W. Peacock* Wednesday last towed a schooner of 60 tons from Port Robinson to Buffalo in 3 hours and 50 minutes." [3]

There was boat traffic on Chippawa Creek into the 1840's as this announcement confirms: "It is understood a steamer will ply daily from Buffalo to Port Robinson this season from whence a packet boat will run to Dunnville and a steamer thence to Cayuga." [4] The opening of the Welland Canal brought about the decline of the the Niagara Portage. It was less expensive and faster to transport bulk cargo by canal boat. There was only one loading and one unloading from a canal boat. Transport over the Niagara Portage required additional costly handling of the goods, unloading from ships, loading on to wagons, unloading at the Chippawa dockside, loading on to batteaux or York boats, rowing or poling the boats up the Niagara River to Fort Erie, unloading on to the dock, then loading on to a sailing ship for delivery to the Upper Lakes.

Erik Heyl

"Canada"

The "Canada" built at the Niagara Harbour and Dock Company's Chippawa shipyard, was the largest and most luxurious steamboat to be built there. Built of wood, it was 60.7m (199 feet 2 inches) by 9.1m (29 feet 9 inches) by 4m (13 feet 6 inches) with a displacement of 726 tonnes (738 tons). She had an upper cabin 54.8m (180 feet) long, with forty-two staterooms. This cabin was sumptuously decorated with ornate mirrors and oil paintings which were views of scenery along the Canadian shore from Quebec westward. Included were scenes of Brock's Monument, and Navy Island as seen from the Canadian shore. The "Canada" was launched on June 1, 1847 and cleared Buffalo on June 3, under the command of Captain Van Allen, bound for Detroit. The captain was not satisfied with her speed, and while he was at Detroit he had alterations made to the smokestacks - he had them changed from a horizontal alignment, to a side by side alignment. This unorthodox arrangement of the smokestacks produced more draft for the engine's fires, which produced more steam and a higher speed resulted. The "Canada" had a short life, ran aground near Detroit, and although apparently undamaged, her engine was removed in the winter of 1849-50 and she was converted into a barge.

Chippawa Becomes A Shipbuilding and Industrial Centre

As you drive from Niagara Falls along the Niagara Parkway past King's Bridge Park on your way to Chippawa, you see a grassy parkland and trees all along the banks of the Chippawa River, until you reach the Weightman Bridge. It was a different scene one hundred and sixty years ago; then it was a thriving industrial area.

For almost thirty years Erastus Parson's Iron Foundry, later the Chippawa Steam Foundry, dominated the landscape. When Chippawa's industrial era was at its height, clouds of acrid smoke poured from the foundry's smoke stack, and mingled with the aromas given off by the brewery, the distillery, the tannery and the potash works, to produce a pungent odour which permeated the atmosphere.

In late 1825 Erastus Parsons, whom Ernest Green called an "enterprising genius...who had revolutionized the plough-making industry of the province with his invention", operated an iron foundry on the north bank of the Chippawa Creek, about opposite present day Macklem Street. Parsons was further described as "a founder casting a variety of useful machinery, particularly mill machinery and plough irons."[1]

The bog iron which Robert Randall is said to have used in his Bridgewater Mills Foundry, was not suited for Parson's process, so he had to import pig iron bars from the United States. In 1826 he was charged by the Canadian Customs Department, with smuggling iron bars into Canada without paying duty. The charge was further complicated when it was discovered that the iron bars were marked with the King's Brand - two arrows in a row, stamped on the bars -indicating that they had been taken from British ships captured on Lake Erie during the War of 1812-14. Prominent citizens in Chippawa attested to Parson's good character, and eventually the authorities dismissed the case, as it was quite legitimate to purchase these iron bars, and because they were of British origin, they were thereby duty free. Parson's Iron Foundry is considered to be Chippawa's first industry.*

It was ship building however, which brought about the period of industrial expansion, which would last for about twenty-five years. There were boom times and periods of depression, still characteristic of the ship building industry today. The shipyard provided employment not only for the carpenters and shipwrights required to cut and shape the timbers for the ships, but also for the blacksmiths and founders needed to build the boilers and forge the hardware and machinery.

* The mills at Bridgewater,(present day Dufferin Islands)though close by and staffed by residents of Chippawa, were not considered part of Chippawa. Ernest Green wrote that in 1829 that besides Parson's foundry the Telferton Steam Flour Mills were also located in Chippawa. There was also a tannery located along this stretch of river bank.

Willoughby Historical Museum

Macklem Foundry

Also known as Chippaway Steam Foundry, Chippawa Foundry and Steam Engine Manufactory and Macklem Iron Works, the foundry was located along the north bank of Chippawa Creek, in front of the present day Niagara Falls Water Filtration Plant. The foundry burnt in 1842, when an "incendiary" - a spark from a chimney - set the foundry's roof on fire. It was immediately rebuilt. In the 1840's, 50's and into the 1860's the steam engine manufactory built vertical beam engines and steam boilers for many of the steamboats built by the Niagara Harbour and Dock Company at their Niagara and Chippawa shipyards. When the market for steamboat engines dwindled, the foundry turned to the manufacture of a wide range of products, including stationary fire engines, parlour stoves, cooking ranges and hot air furnaces.

In 1832 John Lovering established a shipyard at Chippawa. He had contracted to build a steamboat for Robert Hamilton of Queenston. In 1833 the steamboat *Adelaide* was launched at the new Chippawa shipyard, to become part of the *Lake Ontario and Lake Erie Steamboats,* Robert Hamilton's line, which sailed from Buffalo to Detroit. There are no records of other ships being built at Lovering's shipyard. [2]

The Niagara Harbour and Dock Company, which had been building steamboats at Niagara since 1831 purchased 0.8 ha (2 acres) of land from James Cummings (Thomas Cummings' son) in 1840, for a shipyard. [3] As Cummings' land was on the south bank of the Creek, it is presumed that this was the location of the shipyard. Ernest Green wrote that the Dock Company established a shipyard at Chippawa because they had orders for ships to sail on the Upper Lakes. The breadth of these ships would be too wide to go through the Welland Canal, which could accommodate ships with a maximum 7.6m (25 foot) beam. Some parts for the ships built at Chippawa were fabricated at the Dock Company's Niagara shipyard and transported over the Portage Road to Chippawa.

Oliver Macklem's foundry and iron works which were located on the north bank of the river, just east of the bridge, first called the Chippawa Steam Foundry, was equipped to handle the new business which the shipyard would generate. It was not long before Macklem's Iron Works, began to supply the machinery for many of the ships built at the main yard at Niagara, as well as for those built at Chippawa.

---

*

According to the reminiscences of James Cleland Hamilton in his 1893 book *The Georgian Bay*, shipbuilding took place at or near Chippawa as early as 1818. He wrote: "Two vessels, the *Nawash* and *Tecumseh* were built at Chippawa in 1818 and were brought to Penetanguishene in 1819.(2) There was still some activity at this shipyard - a Royal Navy yard -according to Robert Gilkison's diary, twenty years later.

On August 25, 1839 there is this entry: "Received word Captain Harper, Royal Navy, that the Government are determined to build a steamer for Lake Erie and I was to undertake her construction either at Chippawa or Dunnville whichever I deemed the best place for it so it was decided that Chippawa was the place most suited to build the Gunboat *Draught*." According to Lossing's map of the Battle of Chippawa, there was a British Navy Yard and barracks on the Niagara River, about half way between Chippawa and Street's Creek (Ussher's Creek).

"Emerald"

The "Emerald" built at the Niagara Harbour and Dock Company's Chippawa shipyards, was built for James Macklem. This 40.2m (132 foot) by 6m (20 foot) by 2.7m (8 foot 8 inch), 212.5 tonnes (216 ton) wooden hull, paddle wheel steamboat was launched May 20,1844. It sailed for many years between Buffalo, Chippawa and Port Robinson. Original sketch from "Early American Steamers" by Eric Heyl.

In 1844 a wooden hull, side-paddle wheel steamboat was built at the Chippawa shipyard for James Macklem, with a vertical beam engine made by the Macklem Iron Works. Christened *Emerald* this ship made regular runs between Buffalo and Chippawa, where she docked at the *Erie and Ontario Rail Road* dock, located at the intersection of present day Front Street and Norton Street, where the *Emerald* made connections with the *Erie and Ontario Rail Road.* For a time in 1844 the boat also sailed to Port Robinson where passengers could transfer to and from ships passing through the Welland Canal.[4]

A traveller of the time wrote of her *Impressions of Niagara Falls* for the May 1848 edition of the *Ladies Repository:* "On a bright morning in September, I embarked at Buffalo, on the little steamer *Emerald* for Chippawa. The transfer from the steamer to a rail-car at Chippawa was quite speedy."

In 1845 a 48.7m (160 foot) long side-paddle wheel steamboat *Canada* was built in Chippawa for James Macklem. Then in 1846, a a much larger and more luxurious steamboat, *London* was built also for James Macklem, for the lake boat passenger trade between Buffalo and Detroit.

In 1853 an unknown shipbuilder used the Niagara Dock Company's facilities at Chippawa to build a ship for the *Buffalo, Brantford & Goderich Railroad Co.* He built a wooden hulled ship, 48.7m by 9.6m by 3.0m (160 feet by 32 feet by 10 feet),weighing 467 tonnes (474 tons). This ship, christened *International,* had a short life serving as a ferry between Buffalo and Fort Erie. A newspaper account of the ship's demise reported that she caught fire while at her dock on December 3, 1854, was cut loose and allowed to drift downriver. The ship grounded and burnt to the water line. The account also provided an indication of the cost of such a vessel as the loss was estimated at $30,000.

"London"

In 1854 the Niagara Harbour and Dock Company at Chippawa built a wooden hull, side-paddle wheel steamer, for J. Macklem and H. Van Allen. This 49m (160 foot 6 inch) by 8m (25 foot 2 inch) by 2.7m (8 foot 8 inch) steamboat, with machinery built by the Macklem Iron Works, was built to sail the Buffalo to Detroit and Windsor Lake Erie run. Original sketch from "Early American Steamers" by Eric Heyl.

"Clifton"

Shipbuilder Louis Shickluna built the "Clifton" in 1853 at the Chippawa yards of the Niagara Harbour & Dock Company, for Oliver T. Macklem. The "Clifton" was built to replace the "Emerald" on the Buffalo-Chippawa route. In 1857 when the passenger business declined, she was shifted to the Fort Erie-Buffalo ferry service. In 1860 the "Clifton" returned to the Niagara River run, docking at Schlosser on the American side as well as at Chippawa. She had a brief moment of fame when she brought the Prince of Wales from Fort Erie to Chippawa in September 1860.

The *Erie and Ontario Rail Road* which had been operating its horse-drawn railroad between Queenston and Chippawa since 1841, realized that it had to change with the times. In 1852 the company received new capital when Samuel Zimmerman of Clifton, the wealthy Great Western Railway contractor, bought a controlling interest in the *Erie and Ontario Rail Road* company. The company applied for a revision to its charter, to allow the railroad to be converted to steam operation, and to extend the line from Queenston to Niagara. The revision to the charter was granted and a new broad gauge rail line was built, with a roadbed solid enough to carry a steam engine.

The railroad's Chippawa terminus was at the junction of present day Front and Norton Streets. Here a hand-operated turntable was installed so that the one steam engine, *Clifton,* which the railroad owned, could be turned around for the return journey after bringing passengers to Chippawa from Niagara. A steamboat dock was built at the end of the rail line. The *Erie and Ontario* steam line began operating on July 3, 1854. At the same time the horse-drawn rail line ceased operating.

While the construction of the new rail line was going on, Louis Shickluna was building the *Clifton* a 232 tonnes (236 tons) side-paddle wheel steamboat at the Chippawa shipyards of the Niagara Dock Company, to sail the upper Niagara River, between Chippawa and Buffalo in connection with the railroad. Also at the Niagara dockyards the 467 tonnes (475 tons) side-paddle wheel *Zimmerman* was being built to sail Lake Ontario, bringing passengers from Toronto to Niagara. The *Clifton* and the *Zimmerman* operated in conjunction with the railroad, providing a through service between Toronto and Buffalo, from 1854 until 1857. Then, the combination of Samuel Zimmerman's untimely death as a result of the Desjardins Canal train accident on March 12, 1857 and the economic depression which restricted travel, caused the boat service to be discontinued, and the *Clifton* and the *Zimmerman* were assigned to other routes. The *Clifton* was the last known steamboat to be constructed at the Chippawa shipyards.

In the mid 1850's the travelling public abandoned steamships in favour of riding on the new steam railroads, resulting in a drastic loss of revenue for the

James Thompson's Merchandise Account with Robert Kirkpatrick, 1829-31.

Anyone who has made repairs or alterations to his home can appreciate James Thompson's predicament when he had to return to Kirkpatrick's in Chippawa to buy three more pounds of shingle nails on June 12, when the forty-five pounds he bought on May 13 were not enough to finish his roofing job.

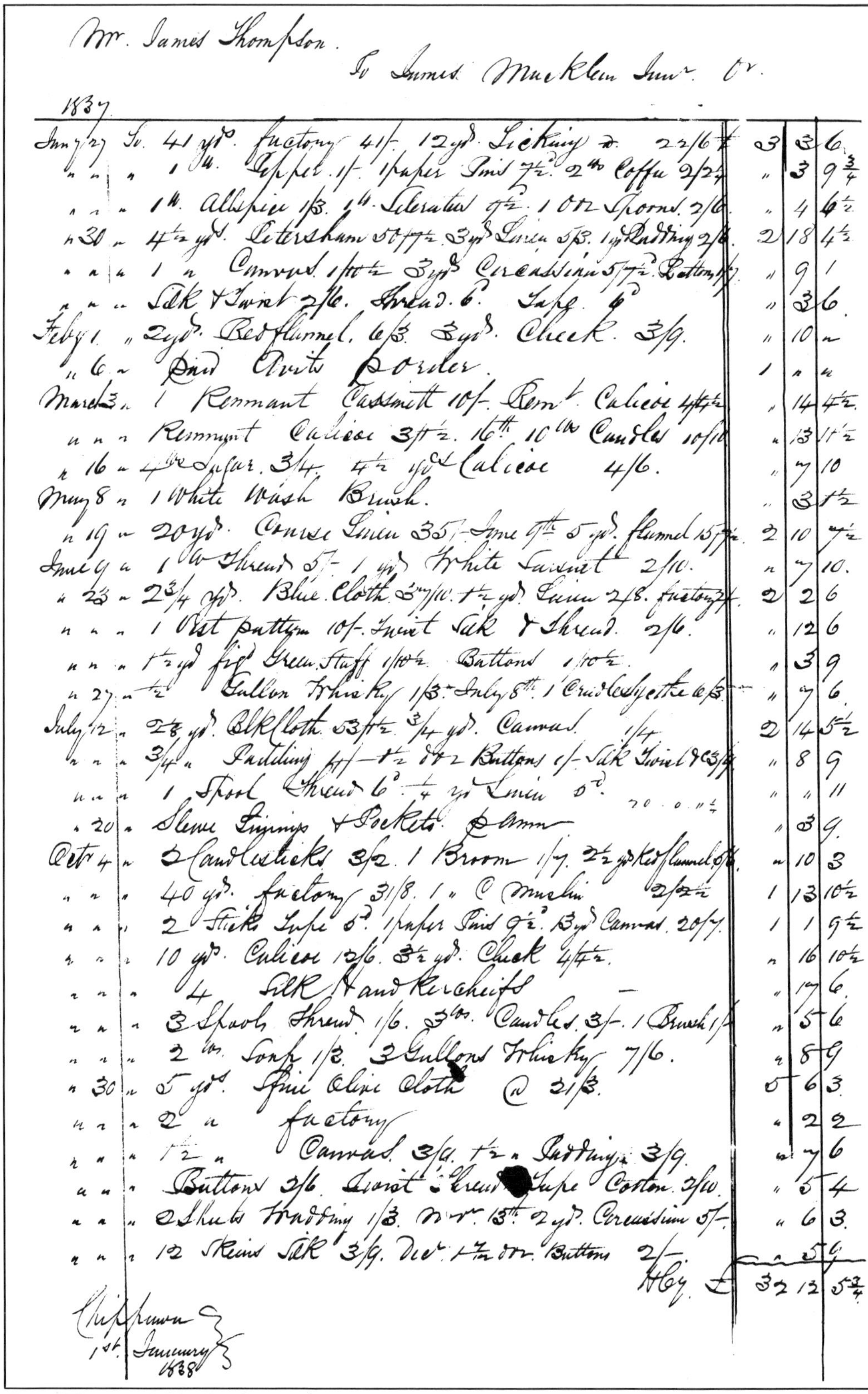
Mr. James Thompson.

To James Macklem Junr. Dr.

1837		£	s.	d.
Jany 27	To 41 yds. factory 41/- 12 yd. Ticking do. 22/6	3	3	6
" "	" 1 lb. Pepper 1/- 1 paper Pins 7½d. 2 lbs Coffee 2/2	"	3	9¾
" "	" 1 lb. Allspice 1/3. 1 lb. Saleratus 9½d. 1 Oz Spoons 2/6	"	4	6½
" 30	" 4½ yds. Petersham 50/7½ 3 yds Linen 5/3. 1 yd Padding 2/6	2	18	4½
" "	" 1 " Canvas 1/10½ 3 yds Circassian 5/7½ Buttons 1/7	"	9	1
" "	" Silk & Twist 2/6. Thread 6d. Tape 6d	"	3	6
Feby 1	" 2 yds. Red flannel 6/3. 3 yds. Check 3/9.	"	10	"
" 6	" Paid Clarks Order	1	"	"
March 3	" 1 Remnant Cassimett 10/- Remt. Calicoe 4/4½	"	14	4½
" "	" Remnant Calicoe 3/1½. 16 lb 10 lb Candles 10/10	"	13	11½
" 16	" 4 lbs Sugar. 3/4 4½ yds Calicoe 4/6.	"	7	10
May 8	" 1 White Wash Brush.	"	3	1½
" 19	" 20 yds. Coarse Linen 35/- Fine 9th 5 yds. flannel 15/7½	2	10	7½
June 9	" 1 lb Thread 5/- 1 yd White Cassinett 2/10.	"	7	10
" 23	" 2¾ yds. Blue Cloth 37/10. 1½ yd. Linen 2/8. factory 2/-	2	2	6
" "	" 1 Vest pattern 10/- Twist Silk & Thread 2/6.	"	12	6
" "	" 1½ yd fig'd Green Stuff 1/10½ Buttons 1/10½	"	3	9
" 27	" ½ Gallon Whiskey 1/3 July 8th 1 Cradle Scythe 6/3	"	7	6
July 12	" 2⅞ yds. Blk Cloth 53/1½ ¾ yd. Canvas 1/4	2	14	5½
" "	" ¾ " Padding 1/- 1½ doz Buttons 1/- Silk Twist &c 3/-	"	8	9
" "	" 1 Spool Thread 6d. ¼ yd Linen 5d. 20. 0. 11½	"	"	11
" 20	" Sleeve Linings & Pockets. Same	"	3	9
Octr 4	" 3 Candlesticks 3/2. 1 Broom 1/7. 2½ yds Red flannel 5/6	"	10	3
" "	" 40 yds. factory 31/8. 1 " C Muslin 2/2½	1	13	10½
" "	" 2 Sticks Tape 6d. 1 paper Pins 9½d. 13 yd Canvas 20/7	1	1	9½
" "	" 10 yds. Calicoe 12/6. 3½ yd. Check 4/4½.	"	16	10½
" "	" 4 Silk Hand Kerchiefs	"	17	6
" "	" 3 Spools Thread 1/6. 3 lbs. Candles 3/- 1 Brush 1/-	"	5	6
" "	" 2 lbs. Soap 1/3. 3 Gallons Whiskey 7/6.	"	8	9
" 30	" 5 yds. Fine Olive Cloth @ 21/3.	5	6	3
" "	" 2 " factory	"	2	2
" "	" 1½ " Canvas 3/9. 1½ " Padding 3/9.	"	7	6
" "	" Buttons 3/6. Twist Thread Tape Cotton 2/10	"	5	4
" "	" 2 Sheets Wadding 1/3. Novr 13th 2 yds. Circassian 5/-	"	6	3
" "	" 12 Skeins Silk 3/9. Decr 1½ doz. Buttons 2/-	"	5	9
	£	32	12	5¾

Chippewa 1st January 1838

James Thompson's Merchandise Account With James Macklem, 1837.

James Macklem was a general merchant who kept an extensive stock of dry goods and dressmaking accessories as this invoice shows. Included in the billing is "1 1/2 yd. fig'd Green Stuff". The whiskey and the white-wash brush on this list seem to be out of place.

Thompson Papers, Isabel Walker Collection

steamboat companies. This competition, coupled with the economic depression which prevailed in 1857, meant that there was no market for steamboats, and the Chippawa shipyard closed. Steamboat companies went into bankruptcy.

The Macklem Foundry felt the loss of the ship engine business, but having a diversified production it survived. An advertisement of the day listed the products of the *Chippawa Foundry and Steam Engine Manufactory*. They were: "steam engines for saw and grist mills; gearing and shafting for grist mills; fixtures for Muley sawmills; boilers; Improved Stationary Fire Engines; iron planing; turning screw cuttings; brass castings." As well, the iron works had diversified into stove manufactory, and advertised a wide range of stoves: "English and American cooking ranges, cooking stoves, office, hall and Fancy Parlour stoves, Hot Air Furnaces."

Niagara Chronicle
September 19, 1839

FAGAN & BOWEN,
Cracker-Bakers,
CHIPPAWA,

WILL attend at Niagara every other week.
September 12th, 1839.

The advertisement described the Foundry's facilities: " the moulding floor covers an area of 10,800 sq.ft.; there are 3 cupolas capable of melting 9 tons of iron per day, and casting of anything within that limit can be supplied." The founders were called on to prove this claim when in 1853 they were asked to cast the 2.9 tonnes (3 ton) iron caps for the towers of the new Railway Suspension Bridge at the Whirlpool Rapids. Stove production was forty per day, and Macklem stoves were shipped and sold all over the Province of Ontario. [5]

James Macklem and W.H.T. Thomas established the Chippawa Distillery, located on Main Street, at the Sodom Road. Nearby was a grist mill, to supply the damp grain used for the distilling process. The brick distillery, built at a cost of about $50,000, employed thirty-five men. Its production was rated as twelve hundred gallons of whiskey a day. Some of the distillery's brand names were Monongahela, XXFamily and Old Rye. No mention was made of whether the product was aged for any specific time or whether it was sold directly to the consumer.

Niagara Chronicle
March 13, 1838

JAMES H. LYONS,
F A S H I O N A B L E
BOOT AND SHOEMAKER,
C H I P P A W A :
(From London, Late from Wall Street, N.Y.)

RESPECTFULLY returns thanks for the very extensive patronage and support with which he has been favoured since his arrival in the Province, and begs leave to call the attention of the Public to his

WATER PROOF HUNTING BOOTS, which, for neatness and durability cannot be surpassed in any part of the World, and which he has confidence in recommending to gentlemen as the very best article that can be procured on this side the Atlantic; He also solicits attention to his

DRESS BOOTS,

which following the Fashions constantly received by him from London and Paris, he forms from the best patterns supplied by the Courts of St. James and the Tuilleries.
Chippawa, March 13th, 1838.

John Bartle established the Chippawa Tannery in 1846, producing sole leather, leather machine belting and other leather products. He employed as many as thirty men and had thirty-eight vats where seven hundred hides of sole leather a week were processed, nine tenths of which were Spanish, the balance domestic. It took three thousand cords of hemlock bark to provide fuel to heat the vats, at a cost of $6.00 a cord. Bartle's tannery was reputed to be the largest in Upper Canada. [6]

In the 1850's the manufacture of potash was an important industry. Potash was used in making soap and glass and there was a waiting market for potash (potassium carbonate) in England. The need for potash was one of the reasons that the first English colonists were sent to Virginia in 1607.

Chippawa had three potasheries. To make potash, wood ashes were put in huge pots, lime was mixed in, and the liquid mixture was boiled and left until it evaporated, producing a dry powder. What was left was potassium carbonate and hydroxide.

The settlers derived income by selling ashes to the potasheries. There were three sources for ashes. The first was the ash left when the land was cleared and the settlers burned the wood where it fell. They

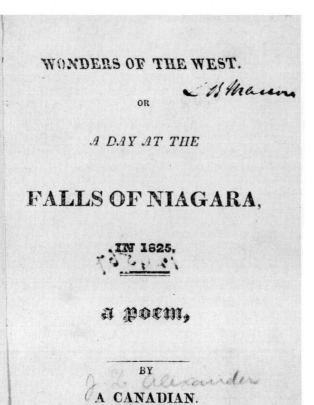

WONDERS OF THE WEST.

OR

A DAY AT THE

FALLS OF NIAGARA,

IN 1825,

a poem,

BY

A CANADIAN.

1825.

A Day at the Falls of Niagara.
A poem by James Alexander, 1825.
James Alexander was teaching school in Chippawa when he wrote this poem in 1824. It was a tale of the adventures of two young French visitors to the Falls of Niagara. In 1825 he persuaded a Toronto newspaper publisher, Charles Fothergill, to print his poem. It was the first book of poetry to be published in the province, and an original copy in the Metropolitan Toronto Library, Baldwin Room, is considered to be one of Canada's rarest books. At about the same time as the poem was published, Alexander received a scholarship, allowing him to enter an Anglican seminary. he became an Anglican clergyman and dedicated the rest of his life to the church. Chippawa has the distinction of having had as a resident and teacher, the author of this poem, the first book of poetry to be printed in Upper Canada.

collected this field ash, and kept it separate from their second source, their stove ashes from cooking and heating fires. The stove ashes which were cleaner were worth more than field ashes. The third source was from the logs themselves. Maple logs were brought to potasheries, where they were burned to ashes.

As more and more of the forest was cleared to prepare the land for agriculture, and as chemical knowledge increased, the production of potash from burning wood declined. This source of income for the settlers, the sale of wood ashes for about four pence a bushel, was a misuse of the trees, as it took about 4 ha (10 acres) of forest to make 1134 kg (2500 pounds) of potash. [7]

Chippawa became the trading centre for the northern part of the peninsula. Ray Corry Bond wrote in her history of Chippawa, *Peninsula Village,* that people even came from Buffalo to shop there. She reported "at least six general stores, several groceries, two bake shops, two butchers, the Ross Dry Goods and tailoring shop, the Amm Tailor shop, a number of cabinet makers, tin-smiths, blacksmiths, wagon makers, gunsmiths, an upholsterer, shoemakers". Thomas's grist mill, Urlocker's furniture factory, T. Davidson's planing mill and John Bartle's tannery were also in operation in the village.

Other historians have mentioned a brewery as well - in fact everything for a self contained community. The 1840's, 50's and 60's were boom days for Chippawa. In 1850, it was the first village in Welland County to be incorporated. It was also, at one time, the largest community in the County. At a time when Chippawa was a booming industrial centre, Clifton and Drummondville, the communities which make up much of present day Niagara Falls, had Russell's Brewery as their only industry.

Chippawa was so prosperous that the first newspaper in Welland County was established there in 1851. It was called *The Chippawa Advocate,* but did not publish for very long. There are no copies of this newspaper in existence, to our knowledge.

The accounts of John Thompson's son James with merchants in the area show that during the 1830's James did business with Robert Kirkpatrick, James Fraser and James Macklem. The Thompson account with Macklem indicated that Macklem kept a wide range of materials and sewing supplies for dressmaking, and domestic sewing. Included were: "factory cotton, ticking, canvas, linen, flannel, calicoe (sic), buttons, padding, thread, sleeve trimmings, pockets," and something described as "1 1/2 yds. fig'd (figured) Green Stuff". During the early 1840's he bought similar merchandise from another general merchant, Hugh Fraser. James Cummings also was in business during those years. Thompson charged other merchandise at Macklem's, ranging from a white-wash brush, silk handkerchiefs, to spoons, knives, brooms and candlesticks.

Chippawa's shoemakers were not only shoe repairers, they made shoes and boots and one of them,

Astrid Akkerman

The North Bank of Chippawa Creek, circa 1880's.

This sketch, made from a discoloured photograph from the late 1880's in the Francis Petrie Collection at the Niagara Falls Public Library, shows the north bank of the Creek, near the area of present day Front and Norton Street (formerly First Cross Street). The wooden pilings visible are the remains of the "Erie and Ontario Rail Road" dock, where the "Emerald", the "Clifton", and the other steamboats of the time docked, to discharge passengers on their way to Niagara Falls, Queenston, Niagara and to Toronto, by way of the Lake Ontario steamboats. The photo was taken from the railway swing bridge, which carried the railway across the Creek. The railway's station would be at the left and just out of the picture. The tall smokestack at the right belongs to Macklem's Foundry. The unidentified stone building in the centre of the sketch is no longer in existence.

H.F. Pierson Photo, Denver, Colorado

Slater's Dock and the "Pilgrim"

Slater's Dock was located at Slater's Point, 2.4 km (a mile and a half) south of Chippawa, just op-posite the northern tip of Navy Island. Dr. Robert Slater settled there in 1832, and built a two-storey frame house which he called "Willoughby Grove". According to Niagara Falls historian Francis Petrie, the Slaters built a warehouse and docks on the point to accommodate steamboats coming from Buffalo with excursionists. After Dr. Slater's death, his son Jonathan continued to operate the dock.

On June 9, 1894, the Niagara Falls Park & River Railway Company received permission from the Queen Victoria Niagara Falls Park Commissioners, to extend its electric car line beyond Chippawa to Slater's Dock. From this point the electric cars would pick up boat passengers from Buffalo. The Richelieu and Ontario Navigation Company placed its new steamer, the "Columbian", 45.7 m (157 feet) long, on this route, to operate in conjunction with the electric railway.

The Niagara Falls Park & River Railway, anticipating the extra passenger business from this arrange-ment, double-tracked the line from Dufferin Islands to Chippawa. This route went into operation on

May 24, 1895, and thousands of passengers from Buffalo travelled by boat and electric car to Niagara Falls. Besides the "Columbian", the "Pilgrim" and the "New York" also sailed the Niagara River between Buffalo and Chippawa making regular daily trips, with special sailings on weekends and holidays. During the Pan American Exposition (similar to a World's Fair) held in Buffalo in 1901, thousands of the Exposition's visitors used the Niagara River boats and the electric railway on their way to Niagara Falls. Boat service was abandoned on October 31, 1905 when the interurban electric line between Buffalo and Niagara Falls, New York went into service. The "Columbian" and the other steamers lost their passenger trade to this new, faster, electric rail line.
This photograph is dated 1896, and shows several of the Niagara Falls Park & River Railway's open-sided motorized cars and several open-sided trailers, standing on the siding, waiting to load passengers. Our only reminder of Slater's Dock and the railway terminus is a plaque set on a stone marker, along the Niagara Parks Recreation Trail to mark their location. The northern tip of Navy Island is seen at centre right.

Navy Island (from the Canada Side), 1838.
A sketch by W.H. Bartlett, engraved by C. Cousen, in "Canadian Scenery", Vol. 1.

Bridge Near Chippawa Creek, circa 1838.
Water colour by Sir James B.B. Estcourt.

While Sir James Estcourt was in this area he made a number of sketches of the unspoiled natural scene in the area from Lundy's Lane to Chippawa Creek. The house and the line of trees in this water colour indicate that the scene could be near the Creek, and the small stream, whose bridge is the artist's subject, could be what was later called Pell's Creek.

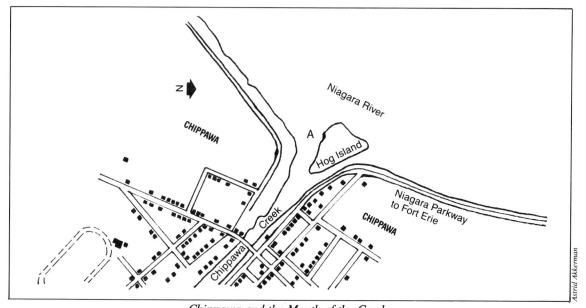

Chippawa and the Mouth of the Creek
This sketch, taken from a Topographical Map of the Niagara Gorge, U.S. Geological Survey, circa 1913, shows the position of Hog Island at the mouth of Chippawa Creek before the Hydro Electric Power Commission of Ontario constructed the intake structure for the Chippawa-Queenston canal. The northern channel, ''A'', was filled in when the intake structure was built, and it is now King's Bridge Park.

The Village of Chippawa from the Air, circa 1923.

This view from the air shows part of the river bed dried off at the mouth of Chippawa Creek, where the Hydro Electric Power Commission of Ontario is installing the intake structure for the Chippawa-Queenston power canal. Only a sliver of Hog Island remains, the rest has been removed to enlarge the intake area. The original channel, where the Creek emptied into the Niagara River, and where the batteaux and other vessels used to enter the Creek, is visible between what is left of Hog Island and the mainland. This old channel was filled in when the intake structure was completed, and it is now part of King's Bridge Park. Navy Island is in the upper centre of the picture, with Grand Island directly above. The huge block of concrete which was the counter-balancing weight for the new bascule ridge over the Creek is discernible.

From Rev'd F. Miller's Balcony. Chippawa Creek, circa 1838.
Water colour over pencil by Sir James B.B. Estcourt.

Reverend F. Miller was the rector of and virtual owner of St. George's Anglican Church which was located in Drummondville on the Portage Road, where the present day parking lot for the Patterson Funeral Home is located on Main Street in Niagara Falls. James Estcourt held the rank of Major when he was stationed here in 1838-39 with the 43d Monmouthshire Regiment. He was a frequent visitor at Mr. Miller's.

Entrance to Chippawa Creek. Pencil Sketch by Alexander Gaviller, circa 1874.

The island between the two channels of Chippawa Creek was originally part of the peninsula which extended from the south bank, two thirds of the way across its mouth. It became an island in 1829 when the Welland Canal Company cut a 102.7m (396 foot) channel along the southern bank to allow shipping to enter and leave the Niagara River heading directly upstream, rather than by leaving the Creek by its natural channel, which led into the downstream current of the river. The pilings were probably put there to keep ships from grounding on the island.

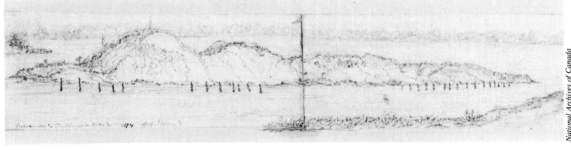

Old Erie Belle in Harbor
Chippawa, Ontario.

F.H. Leslie

Old Erie Belle in Harbor at Chippawa, Ontario, circa 1915.

This postcard view shows the ''Erie Belle'' an abandoned three-masted sailing ship which, according to Ernest Green, was the last sailing ship on the Great Lakes. The ship is tied up at the Niagara Park & River Railway wharf, in the same location where the Government wharf was located during the time that the Niagara portage was in operation.

Laura Secord's Home

Laura Secord bought this cottage from James Cummings in 1841, the same year in which her husband died. Ray Corry Bond wrote that Laura's husband's pension ended with his death, leaving her without any income. She established a private school in her home, which gave her a meagre living. When the Prince of Wales visited the area in 1860, Laura's name was one of those on a petition presented to the Prince, asking for his indulgence, in view of her service to Canada. It was at this time that the story of her walk and her warning to the British at Beaverdams of an American attack became known. The Prince asked about her circumstances and later sent her £100. Laura Secord died in 1868 at the age of ninety-three and was buried beside her husband in Drummond Hill Cemetery.

Residence of Laura Secord, heroine War 1812—14.
Chippawa, Ont., 1835—1855.
For some years she taught private school in this little house.

F.H. Leslie

MOUTH OF THE CHIPPEWA RIVER

Mouth of the Chippawa River. Engraving in "Picturesque Canada", circa 1890.

This pastoral view shows a man and a horse on Hog Island. Tradition says that this island was named after the large log booms, called "hog pens", which were anchored off the island until enough logs had been collected to warrant towing them out into the Niagara River and upstream to the saw mills at Tonawanda on the United States side. During the War of 1812-14 the British set up a gun emplacement there, called a tete-de-pont battery, to protect the King's Bridge.

James H. Lyons, advertised in the *Niagara Chronicle* in March 1838, that he was "From London, Late from Wall Street N.Y.". The London that Lyons referred to was London, England. His message was that his shoe styles were fashionable, after styles in London and New York.

Chippawa's bakers not only baked the staple bakery products, bread, buns, etc., but specialized. Fagan & Bowen who advertised in the September 1839 edition of the *Niagara Chronicle* told prospective customers in Niagara that they were Cracker-Bakers and that they would be in Niagara every other week to sell their crackers. Evidently not every baker was able to bake crackers.

By the late 1870's Chippawa's industrial base had deteriorated. Gone were the shipyards. Macklem's Iron Foundry, burnt in 1842, then rebuilt, was not operating at anywhere near capacity. The Chippawa Distillery, now operated by W.H.T. Thomas was bankrupt with liabilities of over $100,000 and assets of $19,000. A contributing factor to the distillery's

demise might have been that on July 4 of 1877, three months before the distillery went bankrupt, the *Niagara Falls Gazette* reported: "Nearly 100 residents of Chippawa have recently signed the Murphy (Temperance) Pledge". Mr. F. Fischer who operated the Chippawa Brewery bought out Russell's Brewery on the Ferry Road in Drummondville and was hereafter going to carry on the business in the latter place.

Chippawa, which had been made a Port of Customs in 1802, became in 1877 an outport of the Port of Clifton. J. Bartle died and J.F. Macklem bought his tanning business. W.E. Tench of Drummondville and Leonard McGlashan of Lyon's Creek bought the bankrupt distillery and grist mill. The population was decreasing, and by 1881 the census would record only 664 people as residents of Chippawa. Through it all there were things to be thankful for. C. Bosse reported that he had three geese which had laid 260 eggs since the spring!!! [8]

Stamford

Settlement in the area we now know as Stamford Centre began along the Portage Road, at its junction with other roads. The first and largest settlement was adjacent to the junction of the Portage Road and the road to St. David's, the area around present day Stamford Green. A smaller settlement grew up at the crossroads where the Thorold Road, present day Thorold Stone Road, intersected the Portage Road.

In 1792 William Dummer Powell, Justice for the former District of Hesse, came from Detroit to Niagara to take up his position as Chief Justice of Lieutenant-Governor John Graves Simcoe's government of the new Province of Upper Canada. Rather than live in Niagara, Powell chose a lot on the brow of the escarpment, north of the Mountain Road and on the west side of the ravine road leading to St. David's. Here, on the highest point of land along this part of the escarpment, he built a large one storey home, with a centre hall running from front to back along the length of the house. The double living rooms, dining room and bedrooms all had unusually high ceilings. The kitchen was in the basement.

Chief Justice Powell chose this area as the site for his home because he wanted to get as far away as possible from John Graves Simcoe. While Simcoe and Powell were not friendly, their wives, Ann Murray Powell and Elizabeth Simcoe, were friends and Mrs. Simcoe records several visits to the Powell residence in her diary. While Powell was building his home on the escarpment, Simcoe changed the name of the township from Mount Dorchester to Stamford. Powell who was a friend of Lord Dorchester, chose to name his house "Mount Dorchester", to honour Dorchester and to spite Simcoe.

After York (Toronto) became the new capital of the Province of Upper Canada in 1774, Chief Justice Powell remained at Niagara because there were no accommodations for his office at York. He was advised by letter on February 26, 1796 that he was transferred to York. The Powells, with their eight children, left Stamford. Their house, Mount Dorchester, was subsequently destroyed by fire. A depleted sandpit on the west side of the ravine road leading to St. David's marks the location of "Mount Dorchester".

Sir Peregrine Maitland became Lieutenant-Governor of Upper Canada in 1818. His official residence was in York, but he and Lady Maitland did not like the humid summer weather in York, and visited the Stamford area frequently during the summer months, where they found the weather more to their liking. In 1822 they built a summer residence on the brow of the escarpment and thereafter spent the summer season in this area. The Maitlands along with the retinue of military officers who accompanied him, made a lasting impression on Stamford. They and many of our pioneer families are remembered by the houses and buildings which they built which are still in existence.

235

Metropolitan Toronto Public Library

"Stamford Park"

Sir Peregrine Maitland was appointed Lieutenant-Governor of Upper Canada in 1818. He and Lady Sarah found the summer weather at York oppressive, and in 1822 they decided to move to Stamford. Maitland purchased 20.6 ha (51 acres) of land on the northwest corner of the Portage Road and the Mountain Road. He then built a summer residence on the brow of the escarpment which he named "The Cottage". This modest building was gradually enlarged until it had twenty-two rooms. He renamed his estate and called it "Stamford Park".

He was instrumental in having St. John's Church built and tradition says that in order to be able to see the tower and spire of his beloved church from "The Cottage", he had a vista cut through 0.8 km (half a mile) of woods. The Maitlands spent their summers here until his term expired and he moved to take up his new appointment as Lieutenant-Governor of Nova Scotia.

John Cleveland Brown purchased the estate when Maitland left. Ernest Green wrote in "The Niagara Portage Road" recounting comments made by Mrs. Jameson who visited "Stamford Park" in 1837: "It is the only place in Canada combining our ideas of an elegant well-furnished English villa and ornamental grounds with some of the grandest and wildest features of the forest scene. It enchanted me altogether." The "Cottage" burned and was replaced by a more modest structure. The Great Western Railway right-of-way cut through the property, and the expansion of the sand pit on the east side of the ravine road eventually removed all evidence of what had once been an elegant home. For many years the wrought iron entrance gates remained standing at the corner of the Portage Road and the Mountain Road. They were eventually removed to be used at a private residence in St. Catharines.

The "Whirlpool Inn"

Andrew Rorbach who built the building known today as the "Whirlpool House" emigrated to Canada from New Jersey about 1799. He erected this building on the Portage Road and began a saddlery business. His customers were the settlers who hauled the goods along the portage in their ox-drawn wagons. As traffic increased along the road, stage coach drivers began to stop here and the passengers got out to stretch their legs. Rorbach then began to provide refreshments and sanitary facilities and a tavern or inn evolved.

For a half a century the "Inn" was the centre of social and political affairs for the people of Stamford. In 1818 John Gourlay, a man with a revolutionary idea for the time, that of challenging the power of the Family Compact, advertised that he would have a meeting there for all interested inhabitants on April 20. Gourlay came from Scotland in 1817 as a land agent and soon became disenchanted with the autocratic Family Compact which governed this province. His outspoken criticism of the living conditions of the general populace annoyed the members of the Family Compact. His efforts to improve living conditions were described as "...writing to gain popularity amongst the lowest classes, by traducing and abusing almost every respectable body and character in the country."

Thomas Clark, who supported Gourlay when he began his reform crusade, was obliged to recant and warn against Gourlay, at the meeting held at "Rorbach's Tavern" just prior to Gourlay's advertised meeting. Gourlay was subsequently accused of being a seditious alien, tried and found guilty. He was sentenced to banishment and returned to Scotland. His real crime was that, in his campaign to improve the average person's living conditions, he opposed the Family Compact.

"Rorbach's Tavern" was also used as a polling booth during elections. Ernest Green, wrote in "Niagara Portage Road": "Here was the single polling place of the 3rd Riding of Lincoln in the infamous corrupt election of 1834 when Alexander Hamilton stained his fame in an ignoble attempt to save the seat for the (Family) Compact candidate." Elections were rough and ready in those pioneer days. The tavern was the scene of many social affairs and the second floor became a ballroom for these events. According to Isabel Walker an invitation to a ball at "Rorbach's Tavern" is still in existence, written on the blank side of a playing card. The founding meeting of the Erie and Ontario Rail Road Company was held there, as were the annual meetings of the Stamford Agricultural Society. In 1858 a meeting of the Stamford Fair executive was held here to make arrangements for the Fair. A momentous decision was made at that time. For the first time a ladies' committee was appointed: Mrs. John Lemon, Mrs. Robert Garner and Mrs. William Lowell. They were allowed $15.00 for prizes for the ladies section. James Oswald succeeded Andrew Rorbach as proprietor of the tavern and the name was changed to the "Whirlpool Inn".

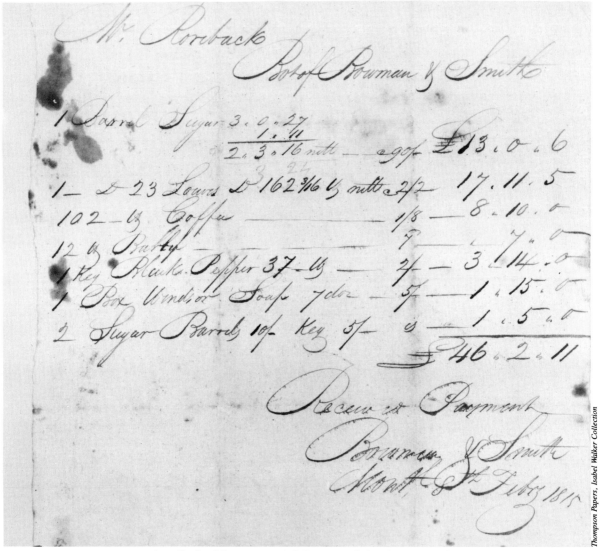

Andrew Rorbach's Account with Bowman & Smith, Montreal.
This account for £46, 2s 11p dated February 8, 1815, is for bulk quantities of merchandise which An-
drew Rorbach purchased for his Tavern, including pepper, coffee, sugar and a box of Windsor soap.

"Whirlpool House" as a Private Residence.
To make the building suitable for a private residence, the second floor which had been used as a ballroom
and a meeting room, was partitioned into bedrooms. Mr. and Mrs. Ross Kenzie became the owners
in 1967 and made additional improvements. The foundation was repaired, the first floor was shored
up, the electrical wiring system was modernized and a new heating system was installed. The covering
on the living room ceiling was removed, exposing the original oak beams. Mr. and Mrs. Reginald Flagg
bought the house from the Kinseys and lived in it until they moved to Grand Manan Island off the New
Brunswick coast.

The "Whirlpool Inn", circa 1920.

As the years passed and other taverns were built in Stamford, the "Whirlpool Inn" lost its place in Stamford's social life. Ernest Green wrote: "In its declining years the old hostelry was the resort of a gang of evil reputation and many dark tales cluster about its neighbourhood." In the 1920's it was in a dilapidated condition and it deteriorated further. Then in the 1940's when it was in such a deplorable condition that it was about to be condemned Mr. and Mrs. Walter Anderson bought it and undertook a major restoration.

Alexander-Robinson House

This house at 3289 St. Paul Avenue adjacent to the Stamford Green was Hugh Alexander's home and store. The centre portion of the house has walls of squared timber lined with brick which are characteristic of construction methods in the early 1800's. Mary Stewart (Mrs. W. Stewart), purchased adjoining land from the Trustees of the Church Lands. In 1879 Puella Morrison bought more land to add to the property. When Almon Atwater became the owner, the property comprised 1.1 ha (2.5 acres). The land remained as one parcel until James Robinson subdivided the property into ten lots in 1953.

Mr. Robinson operated the land as a fruit farm, while working as a foreman at the Wm. Rogers Silverplating plant on River Road. During the 1920's two rooms were added to the south side of the house to provide accommodation for the increasing number of tourists who were travelling on the new King's Highway No. 8, which led from Hamilton to Niagara Falls. The property was bequeathed to W.A. Lorne Robinson when his mother died at the age of 94 in 1968. Lorne Robinson and his wife Jean had the house restored before they occupied it in April 1970. The house was designated on April 6, 1981, under the Ontario Heritage Act of 1974 as being of historical and architectural value.

Early Stamford Schools

The first written reference to a school in Stamford Township was made by Elizabeth Simcoe in her diary. On September 22, 1795 she wrote: "We walked with Francis to the school, where he goes every day, a mile from this house, he carries some bread and butter or cheese for dinner with him and returns in the evening." The Simcoes were staying on Mrs. Tice's property at the corner of the Portage Road and Mountain Road.

The summer of 1795 was oppressively hot and Mrs. Simcoe thought that the weather might be cooler and less humid on the Mountain - the land above the escarpment - so she persuaded Governor Simcoe to camp out or "rusticate" as she called it, there. About the second week of August they set up their tent at Mrs. Gilbert Tice's. From here Governor Simcoe went on trips to Fort Erie and the southern shore of Lake Erie, while Mrs. Simcoe and their son Francis remained camped at Mrs. Tice's.

Their tent was the large marquee they used on their arrival at Niagara in 1797, when their accommodations in Navy Hall weren't ready. This canvas house, as Mrs. Simcoe called it, was bought by the Governor before he left England, at a sale of Captain Cook's effects, the same Captain Cook who made the famous voyage around the world.

The location of the school which Francis attended is not known, but it could have been in St. David's. Walking such a distance, from the corner of Mountain Road and the Portage Road to attend school was a considerable accomplishment for a young boy four years and four months old. [1] It would be just as far to travel to attend one of the other two schools, which could have been established at the time.

According to Ernest Green in *Township Number 2*, there is a note in an old township register about a freeholders' meeting in 1796, "at the school-house near John Row's." Green wrote that John Row was probably living near the Portage Road in Stamford village. As well there was a very early school in "Thompson's Bush," located on what is now present day Thompson Road, just east of Stanley Street. There are no official records of either school.

Teachers were often individuals who were self taught, whose main qualification was their skill in penmanship. They often undertook to teach children privately, either in their homes, or in the homes of their students. One of these early teachers was Francis Goring, who had been an indentured apprentice of a Mr. Pollard, who was a fur trader at Fort Niagara.

Goring spent the whole of the time of the American Revolution working as a clerk for Pollard, and for his successor Captain Robinson. Around the end of 1779 he became a partner in the trading firm of Bennet, Goring and Street, engaged in trading furs at Fort Niagara. When this firm was dissolved in 1781 Goring took a position as secretary to Robert Hamilton, who was in the fur and merchandise business, when Hamilton moved to the Landing on the west bank. [2]

When Goring received a Crown Grant of land he left Robert Hamilton's employment and took up farming. Being an energetic and ambitious man, he soon recognized a need that he could satisfy, teaching his neighbours' children. He was meticulous in keeping a Date Book, or Diary, and it is from this source that we are able to relate his experiences as a teacher and the names of the pupils he taught. [3]

He began a school in 1790 near St. David's. He kept this school until February 1791, when he built a new school house at Six Mile Creek. His Date Book gives the probable reason for his leaving St. David's. In late January of 1791 he wrote: "Kept no school from Nov. 23, 1790 to Jan. 23,1791, gave it up. On account of their not providing a stove and keeping me out of employ." Evidently the parents of the children he was teaching did not live up to their obligation to provide heat for the school and Goring had to suspend classes and suffer a loss of income.

In January 1792, he was employed by Mrs. Gilbert Tice to settle her affairs after the death of her husband, for which he was to be paid 32 bushels of corn. A notation in his Date Book on January 22, 1792 reads: "Received from Mrs. Tice 2 bushels of corn on account. Agreed to teach David her son every Saturday and Sunday morning for which she is to allow me 1/2 bushel of corn every time." Again on February 3 he wrote: "Went to Mrs. Tice's to teach David."

An entry in his Date Book for Monday, December 10, 1792 records the beginning of a school in Queenston: "This day commenced keeping school at the Landing for day scholars." Those attending on the first day were Robert Hamilton's three sons, Robert Jr., George and Alexander. The next day Archibald Fletcher and William Chisholm from the Mountain began to attend school, and on the 17th Sarah Secord became a student. Hugh Alexander's name was entered as having started school on the 12th, but it was crossed out indicating that Alexander may not have continued to attend.

On January 1, 1793 two Queenston girls joined his class, Rachel Vrooman and Sarah Mabey. Sarah evidently did not keep up her attendance as her name was crossed off the list. Then on the 4th of January, Charles Hill started school. He must have had difficulty in keeping up his attendance, because there were notations beside his name: "left 12th, returned 21 st - missed one week - left 16th Feb., returned 25th - week lost - left 9th Mar."

Names of other students recorded in his Date Book as having attended school on January 1, 1793 were: Robert, George and Alexander Hamilton, Solomon Vrooman, Elias Smith, Simon Mabey, George Dorsheimer, George Simpson, John Gold, William Peterson, Peter McEwen, Lewis Bastedo, Thomas Cooper, John Parker, Adam Vrooman, Betsy Murray, Polly Secord, Achmody Farewell, William Farewell.

Others who attended during the rest of the year were: James Allen, Mary Avery, Paul Avery, Samuel Avery, Jacob Birdsall, James Cartwright, John Chisholm, John McMicking, Hugh Rose, William Rose, Ann Smith, Deborah Smith, Robert Smith, Ann Vrooman, Rachel Vrooman, Diana Walker, Peggy Wright, Simcoe Wright.

Robert Hamilton's sons, Robert Jr., George and Alexander did not attend Goring's school after 1793. A stone building was erected on the Tremble property on the River Road north of Queenston which was used as a school for the Hamiltons. Robert Hamilton hired a tutor to teach in this school, but his name is not known. [4]

During 1794 Goring had fewer students. Those listed as attending were: Hugh Alexander, Paul Avery, Samuel Avery, Archibald Fletcher, Benjamin Fox, Daniel Lutz, Oliver Mabey, George Reed, Polly Reed, Polly Secord, Ann Smith, Eleanor Thompson, Frederick Ulman, John Wood, Peggy Young.

Goring also taught the two children of Christian Warner, the pioneer Methodist preacher in this area. Goring's account to Warner for tuition for parts of 1796 and 1797, which included evening classes, totalled £ 7. Warner, who was often paid in farm produce himself, paid Goring's account in wheat, flour, straw and peas. Four bushels of wheat was credited on Goring's account as £4.

In September 1798 James Thompson's eleven year old son, also called James, began to take lessons from Goring. At that time Goring would have travelled to the Thompson farm at the Whirlpool to teach his new pupil. James' copy book, bought from Robert Hamilton's store in Queenston, is still in existence. The price of this book, 4 shillings, is written inside the front cover. The book is full of problems set by Goring. One problem in the copy book is: "How many times doth the wheel which is 18 feet 8 inches round turn between London and York which is 150 miles." [5] Road distances in England were used for these problems as there were no roads in Upper Canada to serve as examples.

James Thompson's copy book is full of other examples of arithmetic problems that Goring posed to his pupils. The front of the book is decorated with elaborate geometric patterns and scrolled drawings, done by Goring himself. These confirm Goring's preoccupation with penmanship and were probably put there to motivate James Thompson to try his skill at matching them.

It is evident from Goring's record of school attendance that his girl students were often absent from school for a week or more at a time. The boys were able to attend on a more or less regular basis during the winter months because farm work slackened during that time. Work never came to an end for the girls. There were always chores to do

In this receipt James McBride acknowledges that he has received money from John Thompson, for tuition, covering any account that Thompson might have incurred with him, "from the beginning of the world to the day of the date of these presents".

around the house, and it is probable that their absence for a week or more was on the occasion of their mother giving birth and so the girls were required to stay at home to help while the mother convalesced.

Without a formal school system parents interested in educating their children eventually banded together to raise a sum of money to hire a schoolmaster, with each paying according to the number of children to be taught. The schoolmaster's meagre pay was augmented by free room and board, the custom being that he would board around with the families of his students during the term of his engagement. The teachers needed no diplomas and most restricted their teaching to the basic subjects of reading, writing and arithmetic.

It was by such an agreement made by a group of Stamford residents that a teacher was engaged in 1799, with James McBride arriving in the area. He agreed to teach their children in exchange for a salary of £55 for the school year. As well McBride was to receive bed, board and washing at the homes of the subscribers, during the course of the school year.

The signatories to this agreement were: Archibald Thompson, John Thompson, John Chisholm, Daniel Rose, Thomas McMicking, William Dorsheimer, Peter Thompson and James Cooper. It was probably at this time that the one room log school house was built on Thompson Road, east of the Portage Road.[6] This school house referred to as the school in Thompson's Bush, was also the school referred to in the old Stamford Township Record Book which recorded a freeholders' meeting, "at the school house near John Rowe's".[7] According to Ernest Green, John Rowe was living on or close to the Portage Road at that time.

Young James Thompson continued to be tutored by Francis Goring until 1804, despite the presence of James McBride. It is thought that some parents chose to send their children to Goring because of his skilled penmanship, in the hope that he would be able to impart this gift to their children. James McBride continued to teach until at least 1810, as there is a receipt in existence dated December 16, 1809, where McBride acknowledges receiving the sum of £1, 10s

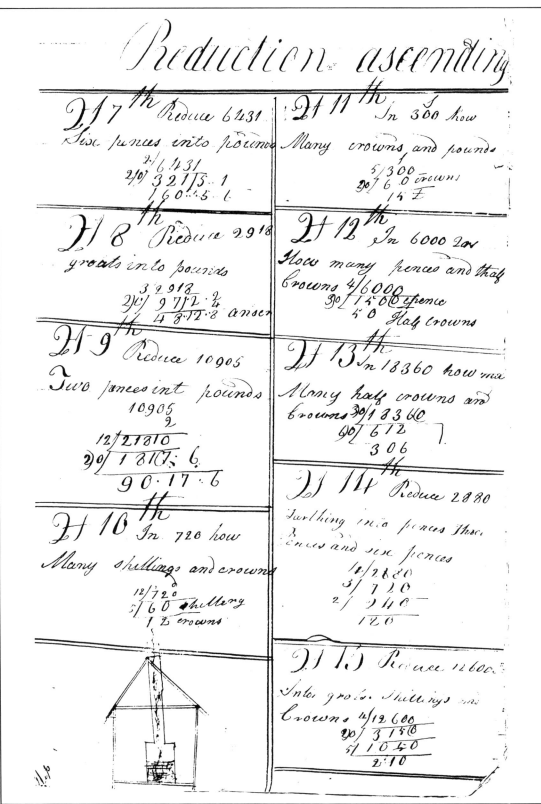

Reduction ascending

7th Reduce 6431

Six pences into pounds

```
  2/ 6431
2/0) 3 2 1 5 . 1
     1 6 0 . . 5 . 6
```

8th Reduce 2918

groats into pounds

```
      3 2918
2/0) 9 7 2 . 2
  1/  4 8 . 12 . 8  ansr
```

9th Reduce 10905

Two pences int pounds

```
       10905
         2
  12/ 21810
2/0)  1 8 1 7 . 6
      9 0 . 17 . 6
```

10th In 720 how

Many shillings and crowns

```
  12/ 7 2 0
  5/ 6 0  shilling
     1 2  crowns
```

11th In 300 how

Many crowns and pounds

```
  5/ 3 0 0
2/0) 6 0  crowns
     1 4 E
```

12th In 6000 2or

How many pences and that
Crowns 4/ 6 0 0 0
```
3/0) 1 5 0 0  pence
     5 0  Half crowns
```

13th In 18360 how ma

Many half crowns and
Crowns 3/0 / 1 8 3 6 0
```
  6/0) 6 1 2
       3 0 6
```

14th Reduce 2880

farthing into pences three
pences and six pences
```
  4/ 2 8 8 0
  3/ 7 2 0
  2/ 2 4 0
     1 2 0
```

15th Reduce 12600

Into groats shillings and
Crowns 4/ 1 2 6 0 0
```
2/0) 3 1 5 0
  5/ 1 0 4 0
     2 . 1 0
```

The mathematical process of calculating the value of British currency and coinage was called Reduction ascending, according to the heading James Thompson wrote at the top of this page from his Ciphering Book. Of particular interest is the doodle at the bottom left, where James in an idle moment drew his version of a fireplace in a house, with smoke rising up the chimney.

and 5d in New York currency for tuition, from John Thompson, for tutoring his children. [8]

The earliest reference to a school at the South End of the Township was made in 1812. On July 23, Lieutenant-Colonel Myers wrote to Captain James Cummings regarding the location of the warning beacons - a system of iron baskets, filled with wood, suspended from poles, which were to be set afire in case of an enemy attack. "You will please examine the rising ground around Lundy's Lane (the school house) and find out whether a beacon from that place could be seen from any part of the high lands of Pelham (Fonthill)." [9]

Before schoolhouses were built classes were often held in the home of one of the students' parents.Whoever had the largest room available, usually provided the space for a classroom. The very first schools were built of logs and usually had two rows of desks, one on each side, with two rows of benches without backs, to sit on. The benches were too high for the younger children and their feet dangled in the air.

At one end of the room was the schoolmaster's desk, usually a table, and a chair. In the middle of the room was a big stove with a wood box to hold a supply of firewood. Part of the teacher's agreement of contract was that every parent would furnish an equal proportion of firewood according to the number of pupils he sent to the school. The firewood was to be delivered to the school to be ready when needed.

There were no blackboards, maps, globes, or other teacher's aids. Quill pens were used for writing and a teacher's ability was gauged by his proficiency in penmanship and his ability to transfer this skill to his pupils. It was a time when teaching children how to read and write was considered sufficient education for ordinary children. The children's hats, coats and dinner pails were hung on pegs driven into logs or on a board hung at the back of the room. Stone ink bottles were used and in the winter the ink would freeze overnight and it would have to be thawed out on the stove before writing could begin. [10]

Whenever there was an annual meeting of the ratepayers, it was customary for the teacher to attend and to be ready to answer questions that the parents might want to ask of him. On one occasion a parent complained that one of his sons, the smartest boy he had, after a year's attendance had not learned a thing and that in his opinion the trustees should get another teacher. The teacher replied that this man's son might be the smartest boy in doing farm chores, but when it came to putting some knowledge into his head he was not a smart boy.

In another case a complaint was made against a teacher who brought a horse into the classroom. The teacher who came from Northern Ireland replied: "It was a very rainy day when this occurred, too wet for the children to go out and have their usual recreation. The poor horse had stood with his back to the schoolhouse, shivering, all day. I thought it would be both an act of humanity and a little divarsion (sic) for the scholars." [11]

The first act of the Parliament of Upper Canada, leading toward the setting up of a system of education was passed in 1798. This act set aside Crown Lands for the establishment of free Grammar Schools in each District. In 1807 the Legislature concurred in the principle that it is the duty of the country to provide free education for its youth. It allocated £800, £100 for each District. Kingston, Cornwall and York took up their share in 1807, and established the first grammar schools (secondary or high schools) in the Province. The Act specified that the Niagara District Grammar School be established in Niagara Township and it opened in 1808.

Reverend John Burns who came to Stamford in 1804 as the third minister of Stamford Presbyterian Church, became the first teacher at Niagara District Grammar School. In 1804 the Burns family moved to Niagara and Rev. Burns preached two Sundays at Stamford Presbyterian Church and the third at St. Andrews Presbyterian Church in Niagara. In 1908 he received an additional sum of £50 a year to conduct the District Grammar School. He taught Latin, Greek and mathematics, until the school was discontinued during the War of 1812-14, and did not reopen until 1820. [12]

The trustees of the Niagara District Grammar School were: Colonel Claus, Robert Ker, James Muirhead, John Symington, The Honourable Robert Hamilton, William Dickson and Thomas Cummings. The first four were from Niagara and the last three from Queenston and Chippawa.

In 1816 the Legislature passed an Act authorizing the inhabitants of any town, township, village or place, to meet together for the purpose of making arrangements for common or primary schools. They could appoint three trustees, provided they had twenty pupils. The trustees in turn appointed and dismissed teachers, and made rules and regulations governing the schools.

An agreement between Richard Secord and the Township of Niagara gives us an insight into the working conditions of a teacher at that time. He was to attend the school from 9 a.m. to 4 p.m., eleven days out of every two weeks; to teach Spelling, Reading, Writing and Arithmetic according to the respective capacities of his students. For this he was to receive 10s currency every three months for each pupil subscribed.

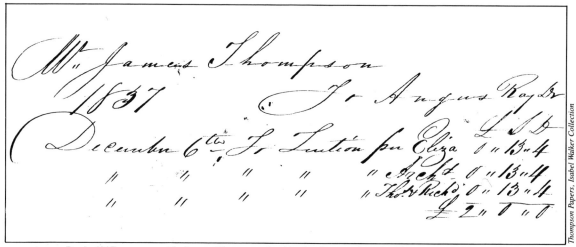

Angus Ray's 1837 account with James Thompson for his fee for tutoring the Thompson children, Elizabeth, Archibald, Thomas and Richard.

The trustees for their part agreed to furnish the school desks, benches, etc., and each subscriber was to furnish an equal proportion of firewood according to the number of pupils covered by his subscription. The firewood was to be delivered to the school to be ready when needed. [13]

The maintenance of the stove was important and the taking down of the stove pipes for cleaning in the spring, and putting the pipes back up again in the fall was fraught with difficulty. No matter how carefully the pipes were marked, they never seemed to fit together again in the fall. Later when women were allowed to teach, they too were expected to look after the stove and the fire.

A woman teacher who taught in country schools for many years, tells of an experience she had with stove pipes. The wires from the ceiling which supported the pipes loosened and the pipes sagged. In her attempt to straighten them out, they came apart and she was covered with soot. While she was trying to put them together again the District Inspector came unexpectedly to make his quarterly visit.

On entering the classroom he looked around, and asked one of the pupils where the teacher was. He had not recognized the soot covered figure, valiantly trying to sort out the mess of the stove pipes. He immediately went over to help. and it was not long before all the pipes fell to the floor raising a cloud of soot. The inspector used several expletives, much to the astonishment of both the teacher and the pupils. One young boy came over to the teacher and said "He swored". The frustrated and angry man, covered with soot, left the school room, telling the teacher to call the trustees to fix the pipes.

In spite of the establishment of schools some people still preferred to have their children tutored privately, as late as 1837, as noted in a statement of account by Angus Ray to James Thompson, for tuition to Elizabeth, Archibald, Thomas and Richard, his children. [14]

In 1847 John McMicking and his wife Susan deeded land for a school on the east side of St. Paul Avenue and Church's Lane in exchange for five shillings. A one room school was built on the property and was used until S.S. No.4 was built on the southeast corner of St. John and St. Peter Streets, now the site of John Marshall School. John Collard was the first teacher, followed by Sylvester Smith, and the last teacher before the school was torn down was Miss Beckie Myers. [15]

After 1846 the Thompson Bush school was replaced by a more substantial structure, which still exists as a residence. It served as a school until a frame building was erected in the 1880's on the site occupied today by the Greek Cultural Centre on the Portage Road at Stanley Avenue. [16]

Early Stamford Churches

Robert Gourlay wrote on November 17, 1817 in his *Statistical Account of Upper Canada* about the churches in Stamford Township. ''It has one Presbyterian Church, built in 1791, by subscription, another church was also built by subscription in 1795, for use of all persuasions. This last was destroyed during the late war, One other church is now building for Methodists. We have one resident Presbyterian clergymen (supported by subscription): also itinerant Methodist preachers who preach once a fortnight; and occasionaly divine service is performed by the established Episcopal clergymen of the neighbourhood, when they see convenient.'' [1]

When Township Number 2 was resurveyed beginning in 1787 -Allan Macdonell's original survey had been found to be faulty -Deputy Surveyor Philip Frey and Surveyor Augustus Jones, set aside eight lots of 40.5 ha (100 acres) each as common lands for the use of the settlers. Included were 44 and 55, which extend along present day St. Paul Avenue, from Riall Street to O'Neil Street. [2]

The first settlers in the area were mostly Scottish. They had been carrying on Presbyterian worship together, in each others homes, for five years when in 1791 they erected a modest kirk on the common lands. It was constructed of logs, over a stone foundation. Having no regular minister, they invited missionaries and preachers of any denomination who were passing through the area, to preach from their kirk's pulpit. [3]

The settlers, right from the beginning, were served by a variety of clergyman. In 1784 Reverend John Stuart, D.D. took care of his Anglican brethren and Reverend John Dun(n) those belonging to the Church of Scotland (Presbyterian). As early as 1784 a travelling Roman Catholic priest visited the soldiers. There were few if any Roman Catholics among the Loyalists who settled in Townships Number 1 and 2. There were Roman Catholics among the Loyalists of German descent who settled in Willoughby and Bertie Township in the southern half of the peninsula. On October 7, 1786, Major George Neal who was converted to Christianity while attending a Methodist meeting in the United States, settled in Queenston and began holding services in settlers' homes. Mennonite and Baptist lay preachers also made frequent visits to the area.

In 1795 a log church was built on Lundy's Lane at the top of Drummond Hill by the joint efforts of Anglicans, Presbyterians, Methodists and Baptists, along with a few families of Lutherans and Quakers. This ''church of all persuasions'' was a community achievement, and served for many years, not only as a house of worship, but as the first school house in the southern part of the Township. Present day Drummond Hill Presbyterian Church is built on the site of this early community church. [4]

This display of ecumenism continued in spite of Governor Simcoe's desire that the Church of England, also known as the Episcopal Church and the Anglican Church, would be the established church in Upper

National Archives of Canada

The Circuit Rider.
This sketch of a Methodist saddle bag preacher as the Methodist circuit riders were known, shows the way in which preachers such as Darius Dunham travelled. Dunham covered the Niagara Circuit, from just east of Toronto to Brantford, then to Long Point on Lake Erie, and the Niagara Peninsula from lake to lake. Charles William Jeffreys, after a long career as a book illustrator and artist, did this artistic conception of a Circuit Rider, one of 600 illustrations in his greatest single achievement, a three volume "Picture Gallery of Canadian History" published between 1942 and 1950.

The Methodists in Stamford Township were led by Christeyan (Christian) Warner, a Loyalist of Swiss ancestry, who was converted during one of George Neal's meetings. Warner was immediately appointed a class leader for the newly organized Methodists in Stamford, and was licensed as a lay preacher. A copy of *The Christian Guardian* in the United Church of Canada Archives, dated April 24, 1833, contains Christian Warner's obituary , which includes the following: "The Methodist class organized by George Neal with Christian Warner as class leader was the first ever organized in Upper Canada." [7]

The Methodist Niagara Circuit was established in 1795 with Darius Dunham as circuit rider - a preacher who would travel from one area to another holding meetings in members' homes. Dunham appointed Warner as the Niagara Circuit's Recording Steward. It was Warner's duty to travel and attend the quarterly meetings throughout the circuit, where he would collect the few shillings his class was prepared to donate to the Circuit Leader. He then had to turn over the proceeds to the travelling preachers for their expenses. If there was money left then Warner, as Steward was required to save it to have it accumulate for the building of a church. [8]

Wilfred D. Warner in *Upper Canada's 1st Methodists, Niagara Circuit 1795-1823,* has compiled a series of original documents,which are excerpts from an old accounts ledger. An interesting entry, part of the entry for February 1798 was "For Wine at Q. Meeting." When Warner had accumulated enough money to build a church,land was purchased from Edmund Horton, near the Warner homestead below the escarpment west of St. Davids.

In 1801 the first trustees of the Warner church were Christian Warner, Benjamin Williams,Philip Shave, Robert McKinley, William Mann and George Keifer. Only the church's cemetery remains today, known as the Warner Cemetery. It is located on the east side of

Canada. To help attain this goal he arranged that up to one seventh of the land in each township would be reserved for the Protestant Church - the Anglican Church. The Clergy Reserves as they were called, were Lots 72, 88, 89 and 104 in Stamford. This allotment of land was considerably less than one seventh of the land in the Stamford Township. [5] Governor Simcoe also had the Legislature of Upper Canada pass an Act in 1793, whereby only members of the Anglican Clergy were authorized to perform marriages.

A Dr. Howison, visited the area and left this comment on churches. "Churches are a rarity in the land...in the whole of the Niagara District but two belonging to the Establishment" (Anglican). At Shipman's (St. Catharines) he followed a crowd into a church where the service was Presbyterian. "The clergyman was dressed in a showy blue coat, white pantaloons, top boots and spurs. There was no more decorum than if it were an inn. They had a flute and a flageolet for music accompanying a hymn, after which the company dispersed. There were many Methodists who met two or three times a week in each other's houses." [6]

Stamford Presbyterian Meeting House circa 1791.
This Meeting House stood on the site of the present church. It was about 13.7m by 17m (45 feet by 56 feet) in size.
The frame timbers were white oak, covered with clapboard. It had cottage style gables, and a wood shingle roof,
with two chimneys. There were six large windows with small panes, two in the east, two in the west, one in the
north and one in the south. The entrance was a small uncovered porch about 0.9m (3 feet) high with three or four
steps. The double entrance doors swung outward. This sketch was drawn by Audrey Johnston from a written
description left by Gilbert McMicking.

the Queen Elizabeth Highway, just north of the Canadian National Railway underpass on what is called Sandpit Hill.[9]

Former slaves who were loyal to the Crown sought refuge as Loyalists and came to the Niagara area as early as 1782. There is a record of only one slave accompanying a Loyalist family, that was Thomas McMicking's young black male slave, Cornelius. Others found their way here, and their status was uncertain until 1793, when Lieutenant-Governor Simcoe had the Parliament of Upper Canada issue a proclamation abolishing slavery, thereby giving them their freedom.[10] Darius Dunham provided spiritual guidance to these former slaves. As more of them came to the area a congregation was organized, under the African Methodist Episcopal Church. The British Methodist Episcopal Church on Peer Street, Niagara Falls South is the direct descendant of John Dunham's congregation.

The Methodists upset the established Anglican Church. There were Anglican churches in large communities such as Newark (Niagara-on-the-Lake), too far away for most of the settlers to attend. The Methodists, realizing that the Loyalists were lonely, brought their message to religious meetings held in homes with neighbours gathered together. Families came, giving young and old a chance to meet and

mingle with their peers. George Neal was so successful that the Commanding Officer of the British forces in the area told him that if he did not cease preaching he would be deported back across the river. The British officer died of natural causes before the date of Neal's deportaton deadline and Neal was not threatened again. [11]

Methodists were subjected to verbal and written abuse because of their ardour. Bishop John Strachan denounced them in a funeral oration: "They are uneducated, itinerant preachers who, leaving their steady employment, betake themselves to preaching the gospel from idleness, or from zeal without knowledge, by which they are inducted without preparation, to preach what they do not know, and which for their pride, they disdain to learn." [12]

An English settler, wrote home to England: "The number of Methodist missionaries is very considerable. Wherever a settlement is formed, there they are to be found. Many of them are excellent men, and all of them apparently are zealous. The Methodists have obtained ascendancy over our infant population. Their habits of domicility, house-to-house visitation, their acquaintance with the taste and peculiarities of the Canadians, their readiness to make long fatiguing rides in the discharge of their self-appointed labours, render them formidable rivals to our easy-going clergy." [13] According to tradition, Anglicans were advised that in the absence of an Anglican Church in their area, they were to worship with the Presbyterians rather than with the Methodists.

As early as 1799 Baptist families began holding prayer meetings in each other's homes, as well as sharing in the worship services at the "church of all faiths" on Drummond Hill. Then in 1809 they were recognized as a sister congregation to an already established congregation in Beamsville. This Baptist congregation was the forerunner of present day Main Street Baptist Church. [14]

It was not until after the Battle of Chippawa on July 5, 1814, when the American Army overran the Niagara Frontier that the churches were damaged. The Presbyterian Church in Stamford had most of its roof blasted away, and the "church of all faiths" on Drummond Hill, was destroyed by artillery fire during the Battle of Lundy's Lane. The post war

period would be a period of reconstruction and progress.

The Presbyterians repaired their kirk and the "church of all persuasions" was rebuilt. The "church now building" in Robert Gourlay's 1817 report, was a Methodist church, the Old Red Meeting House on the northeast corner of Lundy's Lane and Montrose Road. This is the site of present day City of Niagara Falls Recreation Commission Building. The Red Meeting House's trustees were Jacob Garner, Benjamin Corwin, Isaac Howey, James Slaght and Darius Williams. [15]

James Morden, in *Historic Niagara Falls* quoted an extract from Stamford Township records of 1819 which read: "It being proposed to build a Protestant church either at Chippawa or Drummond Hill, it was put to a vote, when it was carried by a large majority that it should be built near where the old log one stood on the Heights." A committee under the direction of Major Leonard, Thomas Clark, John J. Lefferty,

The Interior of Stamford Presbyterian Meeting House, circa 1791.

This sketch by Audrey Johnston, is based on Gilbert McMicking's detailed description of the church. The inside walls were plastered. There were two galleries, which were never used, extending the entire length of the building on the north and south sides. They were supported by two 45.7cm by 76cm (18 inches by 30 inches) oak beams. The pews were box pews - enclosed by a waist high wall, with a door which fastened on the aisle side with a wooden button. Along the top front of each pew was a 15cm (6 inch) slanting book-board which ran the whole length of the pew. The pews between the aisles were double pews and there were six pews at each side of the pulpit. The first pulpit was oval-shaped, set high on the wall with winding stairs leading up to it, and the small platform at the top which had room for only one person, was enclosed and had a door. The building was heated by wood fires set in two immense box stoves located in the centre of the aisles. Candles, placed in holders about 25cm (10 inches) long hung on the walls, were used for lighting.

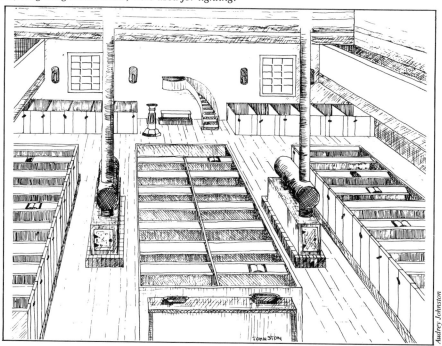

Audrey Johnston

James McLem, and John Hardy was appointed to raise money for the building fund. This would indicate that the "church of all persuasions" was no longer in existence.

Whether as a result of this resolution, or for other reasons, a church, Trinity Anglican Church was begun at Chippawa the next year, 1818. The Anglicans had no church closer than Queenston and it was reported that: "Many members of the Church have been seduced to join dissenting congregations,from the want of a regular missionary." [16] The people of Chippawa wanted a church in their area, it was reported that: "The Principal inhabitants are Presbyterians, yet they have subscribed to the Church. It was at first objected to its being exclusively Episcopalian; but they are now reconciled to it."

On February 10,1818, a petition was forwarded to the Lord Bishop of Quebec, saying that money had been subscribed for a church. The signers were John Hardy, Haggai Skinner, James Thomson. John Bender, John Lycan, Joseph Moore, Christopher Wallis, Thomas Clark, J.P., Thomas Cummings, J.P., Robert Grant, J.P., John Usher, J.P., Crowell Willson, J.P.., Richard Leonard, J.P., James Macklem, J.P., Robert Kirkpatrick, George Maclaurin, John Kirkpatrick, John Howison, Surgeon, Gilbert McMicking, Samuel Street, J.P., Frederick Smith, and William Powell. Samuel Street and Thomas Clark gave the land for the church, and the cemetery, an area of "one acre and eighteen and a half perches."[17]

By 1822 services had begun in Holy Trinity Anglican Church with William Leeming as rector. Leeming was sent to Chippawa by the Society for the Propagation of the Gospel in Foreign Parts of the Anglican Church. The first services were held in the Methodist Red Meeting House in 1818, and the Genesee Conference met there in July with ministers travelling long distances to attend. A cemetery was opened beside the church, present day Lundy's Lane Cemetery, and the first recorded burial was that of Joseph Corwin who died April 19, 1820. [18]

At the northern end of the Township, the Presbyterian kirk was the only Meeting House in the area and Anglican settlers worshipped there. Lieutenant-Governor Sir Peregrine Maitland came to Stamford in 1822, and built a summer residence at the top of the escarpment, east of the St. David's ravine. He and Lady Sarah Maitland worshipped at the Presbyterian kirk until St. John's Anglican church was opened in 1825. [19]

William Lyon Mackenzie, who lived in Queenston, was a member of Stamford Presbyterian Meeting House. In the June 3, 1824 issue of the *Colonial Advocate* he wrote about arriving late for the communion service. "The action sermon, a discourse introductory to the communion, had commenced.

Every corner of the church was crowded to excess, the female part of the audience sat on the left side of the pulpit, the males on the right, which differs from the Scottish, where the sexes sit together indiscriminately. One of the elders, a venerable man with hair as white as snow, sat on the stairs of the pulpit, a temporary table was placed in the middle of the church fronting the pulpit and extending its length towards the church doors about 12 or 14 feet; it was covered with a beautiful white linen cloth and at the upper end was placed the elements. The audience was very attentive. Almost everybody was well dressed, only one woman, however, wore the mutch of plain white linen, which is still to be seen in common use in Scotland.

"The church is a good frame building,was erected by the Scotch on the mountain a good many years ago, and is still unfinished. It contained about 600 (an exaggeration, as the seating capacity was just under 250) persons I should think. All around the church without,and at the windows, and in front, there were many people standing who could not obtain admission." [20] With such a large attendance, it was impossible to use the accepted system of "lifting the offering" - ushers carrying poles about 1.5m (5 feet) in length with a small hoop on the end over which was sewn a dark red velvet bag, directed the bags at the congregation. To collect the offering, plates were set out on tables at the back of the church. [21]

When it became necessary to "re-seat the meeting house" in 1829, it was decided to auction the right to rent the seats or pews, giving the sucessful bidders exclusive seating rights to their personal pews for a limited time - fifteen years - the proceeds to pay the carpenter's bill. There was opposition to this plan,but on May 28, 1830 the pews were offered for sale by auction on the following terms: "The purchasers' right in the pews discontinues at the expiration of fifteen years from the date. The price of each pew not less than Two Pounds...The two pews opposite the pulpit as communion seats, not to be sold, but to be retained for the benefit of the congregation in general, also the pew adjoining the pulpit stairs to be retained as the Minister's pew. Likewise, pews numbered one and three (to be left) for the benefit of the congregation as free seats. Pews number fourteen, fifteen and sixteen, were preferred locations, were to be sold at £2, 10s, by private sale." [22]

Captain Robert Henry Dee, an aide-de-camp to Lieutenant-Governor Sir Peregrine Maitland, accompanied the Lieutenant-Governor when he came to live in his summer residence. Dee purchased property on the Portage Road, built a house and settled here with his wife and family. He felt that there was a need for an Anglican church in the northern part

Ron Kitchen

Restored Old St. John's Anglican Church.
This photo of the restored church, which is to become a columbarium – a depository for cinerary urns containing human remains – was taken in August 1989. The columbarium, which will be non-denominational, will be known as Stamford Green Heritage Columbarium.

In 1971, some fifteen years after it was deconsecrated and five years after its original pulpit and reredos (wall behind the altar) were removed to Upper Canada Village, the church was in bad repair and in danger of being demolished. George Seibel, as chairman of the recently formed Niagara Falls Heritage Foundation took an interest, and as one of the Foundation's first projects, began a move to save the church. Through the co-operation of the Lundy's Lane Historical Society which had been caring for the building since 1957, the Niagara Falls Heritage Foundation placed sheets of plywood over the broken windows to keep rain water out.

The Niagara Falls Heritage Foundation arranged for architect Alice Alison of Toronto, to produce plans for a complete restoration. She received a Canada Council Grant for this work and it became an integral part of the work towards her Masters Degree in Restorative Architecture from Columbia University, New York, New York. She was assisted in her study of the building by Jack A. Sampson who took photographs and John A. Verroche who provided measurements of the building and its architectural features. Although Mrs. Alison's concept for a complete restoration was not used, it served as a first step in the preservation of the church.

By 1976 sufficient interest was aroused amongst citizens who wanted the building preserved, and the Old St. John's Heritage Association was chartered in December. R. Jack Hall was elected its president at the first meeting held in April 1977. Charter directors were: Reginald Flagg, Robert C. Fenwick, W.A. Lorne Robinson, Harry M. Chesher, Reverend Peter J. Darch, Jacqueline A. Dix, Melvyn H. Fiske, Peter E. Jocelyn, Donald J. Keppy, Malcolm S. McLeod, Olive E. Mewburn, Jack E. Niven, Francis J. Petrie, George A. Seibel, and Venerable Archdeacon G.W. Standish.

In the intervening years, as the restoration progressed, there were many changes in the board of directors. Almost 500 groups and individuals contributed towards the restoration with donations and memberships in the Association. Foremost were grants received from the City of Niagara Falls, the Provincial Ministry of Culture and Communications, the Ontario Heritage Foundation and Government of Canada Ministry of Employment and Immigration.

Baird, Sampson, Architects of Toronto, drew up plans for the restoration and the work was done over a period of three years from 1985 to 1988 by Scholts Bros. Construction Co. of Welland, Ontario. The building is open to view during the summer months, and beginning in June 1990 it will have a historical display and audio visual presentation, supplied by the Niagara Falls Heritage Foundation, featuring the history of the Portage Road, the Stamford Green area and the old church's part in this history.

of Stamford Township and he donated a parcel of land for this purpose located on the east side of the Portage Road, just north of the intersection with the road to St. David's, present day St.Paul Avenue. The deed for this property, the present site of Old St.John's Anglican Church, the cemetery and the present St. John's was dated September 20, 1820. [23]

An undated subscription list records the donations of money and materials, which were used in the construction of the church. Sir Peregrine Maitland gave £75 plus the velvet for the altar and the pulpit, and the carpet; Captain Dee, besides giving the land

for the Church and Yard, contributed £25; The Lord Bishop of Quebec £5 and the Silver Service for the Communion Table; The Attorney-General of Upper Canada £50 for the pulpit; L. Tunnahill supplied nails to the value of £2, 10s; George Green contributed 10 days work as a carpenter £2, 10s; William Miller, putty £17, 6s; John Johnston used his horse and wagon to bring lumber to the building site, 10s. The foregoing is only a partial list of the contributions.

The expenditures include: Putman and Lee, masons, for drawing the stone and laying up same,

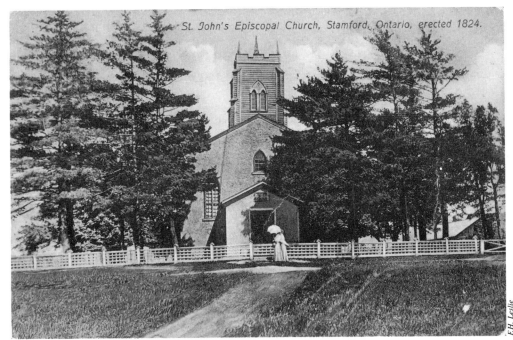

St. John's Episcopal Church, Stamford, Ontario, erected 1824.

F.H. Leslie

Church of St. John the Evangelist, Anglican.
This postcard view dates to the early 1900's.

United Presbyterian Church, Stamford, built 1871.

United Presbyterian Church, Stamford, Ontario.   Built 1871.
First church built 1785. Oldest stone in burial ground dated 1792.

W.A. Lorne Robinson

Metropolitan Toronto Public Library

The Old Red Meeting House.

Charles Green received £12 for the land on which the Red Meeting House stood, the present day location of the City of Niagara Falls Recreation Commission Building at the northwest corner of Lundy's Lane and Montrose Road. The building was 11m by 17m (36 feet by 56 feet) with a clapboard exterior, painted red. It had a high box pulpit at the north end. Women sat on benches located on the west side and the men sat on the east side. There were wooden sheds, along Lundy's Lane and around the corner along the side road, now Montrose Road. These sheds sheltered the horses, who had a long layover between the time they brought their owners to the church and the time they were hitched to the carriages for the return trip home. For most of the members it was a long trip to the church, and so when they were there the services were lengthy. The first burial, according to the earliest death recorded on a gravestone was that of Joseph Corwin in 1820. James Morden, writing in "Historic Niagara Falls", about the sale of the building in 1869, so that the property could be used for a school, said: "The graveyard remained unsold and for the past sixty years (since 1872) has been more or less neglected...most of the time it showed positive neglect and abounded with briars, thorns and weeds." In 1836 the minister, Pastor Jones, used the cemetery as a pasture for his horse. His congregation did not approve and one morning when he went to get the horse he found that it had been tarred and feathered. In 1923 the Lundy's Lane Historical Society obtained a grant of $25.00 from Stamford Township Council, and after adding $25.00 of their funds, they renovated the cemetery grounds. James Morden wrote: "In 1931, the Council spent $122.00 in improving the appearance of this historic spot (present day Lundy's Lane Cemetery) and it is now a credit to the municipality."

This side view of Old St. John's Anglican Church shows the multi-framed windows and the tower restored to their original style. The small window in the vestibule at the front of the church was cut into the stone after the vestibule was built, to enable the ladies of the congregation to look out to see when their husbands were arriving with the horse and carriage to pick them up. Before the restoration this window frame was askew, having been cut by a volunteer. The Ontario Provincial Historic Plaque standing by the side of the church was dedicated on May 26, 1968. Others who have served as directors of the Old St. John's Heritage Association since its incorporation are W.A. Barratt, Emma Bearss, Phyllis Brant, John Burtniak, Basil Clark, Len Fanstone, Evelyn Fenwick, John A. Fordham, M.H. Graham, Barry Kington, J.W. Mitchinson, William Oswald, Carl Overstrom, Arthur Simmons, A.R. Tilbrook, David Williams, Isabel Walker, John Young and Lucy Young.

£130; James Thompson £12, 7s, 6d, for 66 cords of stone and £16, 15s, for 134 barrels of lime for mortar; Scofield and Brown, for the roof, tower and laying the floor £56. Evidently extra help was required to raise the roof and tower, help which was contributed by volunteers, who were aided by 5 1/2 gallons of whisky at a cost of 13s, 9d. On another occasion R.H. Dee received 18s for supplying wine. Other items detail the amounts paid for building the altar, turning the rails which were of black walnut, constructing the cornices, lining the outside of the windows, and putting up the pews.

When the church was ready, money was raised renting the pews. Sir Peregrine Maitland paid £30 for two pews; Captain Gordon £11 for one and Mr. Kirkpatrick £12 for one. Stephen Brown and George Keifer rented a pew each at £10, and Samuel Street, who was a member of Holy Trinity Anglican Church in Chippawa, rented a pew for £5. On September 28, 1825 the Lord Bishop of Quebec, the Honourable Charles James Stewart, consecrated the church, to be known as the *Church of St. John the Evangelist,* with Reverend William Leeming as Rector. The offering taken on the occasion of the consecration amounted to £3, 9s. [24]

When the Clergy Reserves were sold, Lots 72, 88, 89 and 106 in Stamford Township were sold and the proceeds were invested in a capital account, held by the Synod of Niagara. Lot 72 is the land encompassing the corner of present day Portage Road and Thorold Stone Road as far west as Dorchester Road.

The interest from this account is still being paid to St. John's and is used to help pay the stipend of the rector. [25]

Reverend F.W. Miller came to Drummondville in 1830 to act as an assistant to Reverend William Leeming, who was at that time rector of both the Chippawa and Stamford Anglican churches. Not long after his arrival, a disagreement arose between the two men and Miller decided to establish his own church. He purchased land on the Portage Road from John Misener and with the help of his wealthy friends erected St. George's Anglican Church Drummondville.

Miller put a great deal of his own time and money into the construction of the church. He purchased the framework of a building which the Baptists had intended to use for their church. To this framework he added a tower and Gothic windows, He paid for

St. George's Anglican Church.
From a water colour by Lieutenant-Colonel J.B. Estcourt, 1838.
Estcourt made St. George's Anglican Church, Drummondville, the dominant building along the Portage Road
in his water colour which was sketched from the tower of the Presbyterian Church on Drummond Hill. Lieutenant-
Colonel Estcourt of the 43rd Monmouthshire Regiment was a member of St. George's and a friend of the rector,
Reverend F. Miller. The building to the right of the church is the Alanson Ross home and carriage factory, the
location of present day Patterson Funeral Home on Main Street. The American Falls with a column of spray ris-
ing is at the top of the scene, behind the church.

the organ, stoves, lamps and the pews. He used walnut for the pillars of the two galleries, and for the pulpit and the pews. For several years he supplied the wood for the stove fires, which was cut from the bush on his 80.9ha (200 acre) farm on the Chippawa Creek.[26]

The church accommodated 200 people and many of the members were soldiers. When the 43d Monmouthshire Regiment was stationed at Drummondville in 1838, many of the officers, including Lieutenant-Colonel J.B.B. Estcourt and his wife Caroline attended St. George's. In 1828 Estcourt made the only known sketch of St.George's, including it in a panoramic view of the Portage Road, from a perspective on top of Drummond Hill. Miller's church was popular and competed with Leeming's Trinity Anglican Church in Chippawa. Both churches were in the same parish, Leeming's parish, but many

of Trinity's members were attracted to St. George's.

Miller's appeal to the Military came from his previous service as a Chaplain of the 96th Regiment. St.Georges became known as the "chapel of ease", because he was a sportsman and joined with his military congregation in hunting, which was principally pigeon shooting. He also had a theatrical touch and he became known as Priest Miller, for his High Church mannerism of changing his vestments during the service.

Leeming tried repeatedly to take control of St. George's but was unsuccessful as the church stood on Miller's property, and had been built largely with his money. Miller died in 1847 while the church was closed for renovations. It was re-opened and re-dedicated on November 18, 1847, the same day that Leeming finally took possession of the building. He

The Shrine of Our Lady of Peace.

Our Lady of Peace Roman Catholic Church, on the Portage Road at Falls View, celebrated its sesqui-centennial in 1987 by undertaking an extensive renovation and restoration program which cost over $250,000. A new roof was built over the old roof, while maintaining the original roof line. The stucco was removed and the stone walls were tuck-pointed, with the addition of new mortar, and left unstuccoed, leaving the stone work exposed.

A new walk was laid from the front of the church, to facilitate access from the parking lot. In the late spring of 1989 over 2000 daffodil bulbs, donated by the Niagara Parks Commission, were planted on the Canadian Pacific Railway embankment in front of the church. The planting was done by N-Tec, the Niagara Training & Employment Agency, as a Niagara Portage Road Bicentennial project of the Kiwanis Club of Stamford.

Church of Our Lady of Peace, Niagara Falls, Ont., Canada

was not able to acquire the property on behalf of the Anglican Church until July 1856, after which time the church was demolished. The land on which it stood was deeded to John A. Orchard in 1858. The church stood on the lot now occupied by the Pure Nature store, north of the Patterson Funeral Home on Main Street (Portage Road) in Niagara Falls.[27]

As early as 1816 a few Roman Catholic families had settled along the banks of the Niagara River, from Fort Erie to the Falls. They travelled to Kingston to make their Easter Communion until 1826 when a congregation was formed and the first church was built at Niagara. It was not until June 13, 1837 that the church at Falls View, Our Lady of Peace, was dedicated, At that time Father Gordon, who was the parish priest for the whole district - 817 people - paid only semi-annual visits to Our Lady of Peace.[28]

British Methodist Episcopal Church

According to Niagara Falls historian Francis Petrie, the beginning of the B.M.E. church on Peer Street can be traced to August 1814, just one week after the Battle of Lundy's Lane. An old church chronicle records the advertisement of "An Anniversary of the African Emancipation", to be in the form of a public dinner, to be held August 1, 1814 "on the Battle Ground at Drummond Hill". Tickets were one dollar a couple and Thomas H. Brooks, S. Scott and Henry Garrit arranged the event.

As a result of this meeting, the nucleus of a Black Methodist mission was formed at what was to become Drummondville, and it became part of the existing Hamilton, St. Catharines African Methodist circuit. In 1836 a chapel was erected at the intersection of present day Murray Street and Allendale Avenue in Falls View. In 1856, when the British Methodist Church of Canada was founded, largely through the efforts of Oliver Parnell, Burr Plato, who was a member of the local congregation arranged to have the existing building moved to a lot which had been purchased by Oliver Parnell for the purpose, at the south-west corner of Peer and Grey Streets. The B.M.E. church, still stands there 133 years later and its congregation is 153 years old.

The City of Niagara Falls Council passed a by-law on February 6, 1986, designating the B.M.E. church on Peer Street as an historical site. On Sunday, November 20, 1983, the church was rededicated to be known as the R. Nathaniel Dett Memorial Chapel of the B.M.E. Church of Canada. This was in honour of R. Nathaniel Dett, D.Mus., who was a member of this church as a boy, and who went on to achieve considerable fame as a musician and composer in the United States. Dr. Dett, who died in 1943 while on a U.S.O. Tour, entertaining American service men and women, is buried in the family plot in Fairview Cemetery, Niagara Falls, Ontario.

Trinity Church and Sunday School, Chippawa, Ont. Built 1842. First church burned by rebel sympathizers in 1837. King Edward VII, Jennie Lind and Laura Secord have worshipped in the present structure.

An Early Stamford Merchant

Hugh Alexander is the earliest merchant storekeeper of record in the Township of Stamford. Before he began in business in early 1813, the settlers in the northern part of the Township, near present day Stamford Green, travelled to St. David's and Queenston to make their purchases, or barter their produce for food and clothing. They needed sugar, salt, pepper, soap, tallow, saltpetre, tobacco and alcoholic beverages such as Madeira wine, and whisky.

Alexander was born in 1780, and came to this area in 1782 with Thomas McMicking. He attended Francis Goring's school, irregularly, in 1793 and 1794 and then apprenticed as a clerk, probably with one of the merchants who had a warehouse at Fort Erie. In 1797 he was granted 81ha (200 acres) of land in Bertie Township, near Waterloo (present day Fort Erie). He became a merchant trader and was assigned Lot No.5 in the merchant's storehouse and wharf area on the Military Reserve, south of the Fort. [1]

In October 1811, he purchased a sailing ship of 35.4 tonnes (36 tons) burthen, which he named *Chippawa*. He began to transport bulk shipments of salt, pork, flour and whisky between Chippawa, Fort Erie and other Lake Erie ports. [2] The *Chippawa* continued to sail on Lake Erie after the beginning of the War of 1812, but was lost around March 13, 1813, when she became trapped in lake ice.

According to an undated newspaper report from the United States, which read: "Another vessel said to be the *Chippewa* (sic) owned by Mr. Alexander of Fort Erie...being driven out by the wind and being surrounded by cakes of ice...was abandoned." [3]

The Americans recovered the ship and put it into service. The *Chippawa* was "on shore and dismantled" in December 1813, when it was burnt by the British during the attack on Buffalo. [4] Another version has the *Chippawa* captured at the naval battle of Put-in-Bay, but still burnt by the British.

Hugh Alexander and his brother Ephriam were in partnership as early as August 1, 1812, "trading and selling goods and transacting mercantile affairs." [5] They operated under the name of Hugh & Ephriam Alexander. On the morning of May 27, 1813 the American Army crossed the Niagara River and invaded Upper Canada at Niagara, and the next day, May 28, they crossed the upper river at Fort Erie.

They found that the British had abandoned the Fort, and had blown up its magazines. [6] The Alexanders' storehouse, store and a house with eight apartments was also burned and their stock of merchandise was also destroyed. [7] The destruction of the Alexanders' property was the result of the scorched earth tactics carried out by the British Military when they abandoned Fort Erie and retreated from the area.

The *National Advocate* of New York City reported on June 13, 1813: "The American Flag is flying at Fort Erie. All the public property belonging to the enemy consisting of provisions and clothing was burnt...Nothing is to be found in or about the batteries or storehouses but a complete head of ruins...It is stated by the inhabitants...that an immense quantity

James Thompson's Account with Hugh Alexander,
November 1815 to September 2, 1816.

This account shows that the portage was once again in operation and goods were being landed at Queenston. Thompson had a contra account for hauling "34 cwt. of Goods", merchandise for Alexander's store. He also sold Alexander 8 barrels of lime. The notation "At the Kiln" would indicate that Alexander arranged for the transport of the lime from Thompson's lime kiln at the Whirlpool to his store.

John Thompson's Account with Hugh Alexander, March 31, 1813 to March 30, 1814.

John Thompson died on March 30, 1814, and this account which had been outstanding since March 3, 1813, was paid on May 13, of that year. Thompson made his usual purchases of tobacco and brandy. Mrs. Thompson died on January 21, 1813, and the purchases of sewing materials such as olive cloth, skeins of silk and buttons indicate that the Thompson daughters, Marion, Isabel, Sarah and Jeannet were making their own clothing. Hugh Alexander's store was plundered by the Americans after the Battle of Chippawa on July 5, 1814. He was evidently back in Stamford and in business again in May 1815 when he accepted payment in full for this account.

> ## CHOICE GOODS
>
> of almost every description which will be sold for Cash. Also a few chests of excellent Tea for sale by the chest.
>
> Stamford, March 10, 1816
> Hugh Alexander
>
> *St. Davids Spectator*

of provisions was destroyed by the enemy British." [8]

Hugh Alexander was not at Fort Erie when his property was put to the torch by the British Army. He was with the 3rd Lincoln Militia, having joined earlier in 1813 as a Lieutenant. At some time before the destruction of his property in Fort Erie, Alexander had established a store in Stamford. He was in business there on March 31, 1813, as that is the first date on an account entry for purchases that John Thompson made at this store. Thompson bought tea, tobacco, dry goods and liquor. When this account was paid, Thompson paid off part of it by barter, providing Alexander with a barrel of flour. [9]

Hugh Alexander's house and store are believed to have been located south of the corner of present day St. Paul Avenue and Stamford Green Drive - opposite Stamford Green - and just north of the present intersection of St.Paul Avenue and the Portage Road. W. Lorne Robinson and his wife Jean, live in what is believed to be Hugh Alexander's house or store. The centre portion of the Robinson house has solid walls of wood frame filled with brick, after the style of the walls of Butler's Barracks on the outskirts of Niagara-on-the-Lake.

Alexander had the misfortune of having received a large shipment of merchandise from Montreal in June 1814,including dry goods and groceries, just before the Americans again invaded Canada. On July 3, the American Army, led by Major-General Jacob Brown, crossed the Niagara River at Fort Erie. They advanced north, and on July 5 they met and defeated the British, led by Major-General Phineas Riall, at the Battle of Chippawa.

The British withdrew after this battle and left the whole of the Niagara Frontier under American control. It was during this occupation by American forces that the people of Stamford were plundered, not by the regular American forces, but by a force of volunteers and Indians under the command of Colonel Chapin. This volunteer force was not on the American Army payroll and they were expected to get their pay for their services from the plunder they managed to obtain from the inhabitants of Stamford.

There are different accounts of the plundering of Alexander's store by the Americans, on July 9, 1814. Susannah, Alexander's widow, in her Memorial to the War Losses Claims Tribunal in 1824, stated that her husband was taken prisoner on the 9th of July, 1814 and sent to Buffalo. This contradicts the information in a deposition made by Benjamin Willson, Alexander's principal clerk who said that Alexander was present at different times between the 11th and 20th of July, when his Stamford property was being plundered.

Benjamin Willson's deposition said: "...that he, Alexander, was present in the store from the commencement of the plunder, till the store was almost entirely cleared, when he fled from the premises, owing to the threats made by the plunderers, that he should be taken off." [10] Both accounts agree that Hugh Alexander was present and unable to prevent the plunderers from carrying off his property.

After the end of the war, Alexander rebuilt his storehouse and other facilities at Fort Erie, and continued with his store at Stamford. An advertisement in *The Spectator,* published in St.Davids, dated March 16, 1816 announced that: "Hugh Alexander...has on hand a general assortment of Choice Goods of almost every description, which will be sold for cash. Also a few chests of excellent TEA for sale by the chest." [11]

Hugh Alexander died on November 2, 1817 and was buried in Stamford Presbyterian Cemetery. According to his will, dated October 30, 1817, he had a share in a Grist Mill: "...now erecting at Fort Erie" and he owned 90ha (176 acres) of land in Bertie Township and several other lots in Fort Erie. He acknowledged in this will that his brother Ephriam was his partner and as such owned: "one equal half of the dwelling house, out houses, forwarding store and wharf at Fort Erie." [12]

Alexander's widow, Susannah continued to live in Stamford and paid rent on their property, until November 30, 1834. Hugh Alexander's life story has been carefully researched by W.A. Lorne Robinson who lives in what is thought to be Alexander's original house, and by Louis C. McDermott of Fort Erie, In spite of all the research the complete story of Hugh Alexander, Stamford's first merchant has yet to be told.

Stamford Village Plan

When John Frey surveyed Township Number 2 (Stamford Township) in 1791, approximately 324ha (800 acres) of land, were set aside for the benefit of all the settlers. These lots, numbers 5,16, 28,36,44,55 and 61 ran from north to south, along St. Paul Avenue and the Portage Road between Mountain Road and present day Thorold Stone Road. They extended west to present day Dorchester Road. These lots were called common lands.

At a public meeting held on March 7, 1796, to consider ways and means of putting 80.8ha (200 acres) of these lands to use a committee composed of John Reilly, Irish John Wilson, Thomas McMicking, Peter and Archibald Thompson, was appointed to bring back a proposal. The land under consideration was Stamford Township Lot Number 55 which today includes the land between O'Neil Street and Brock Street, running from the Portage Road on the east to Dorchester Road on the west.

The committee decided that the land should be leased, not sold outright, for a term not to exceed nine hundred and ninety-nine years. Each lessee would be required to construct a dwelling on his lot, and allowed to cut firewood and timber as he saw fit. The terms of the leases were one dollar New York Currency, per acre, per year, the rent to begin one year after the lessee received title to the land. This was the origin of the Town of Stamford Plan - the first official subdivision of land in the Township of Stamford. [1]

In 1805 Lot Number 55 and the east half of Lot Number 44, 60.7ha (150 acres) of land, were deeded to the congregation of the Presbyterian Meeting House. Hugh Alexander replaced John Reilly on the Board of Trustees at this meeting.

W.A.Lorne Robinson who has researched this subject thoroughly, says that from the records available, it does not appear that any lands were leased until after the War of 1812-14. His research was made more difficult by the fact that the first four pages of the Board of Trustees Book of Minutes were missing, having been cut out.

On July 17,1816 the St.David's *Spectator* in an ad prepared by trustee Hugh Alexander announced that the Trustees "have laid out a tract of land at the Stamford Meeting House...into suitable lots for buildings of various description, also a number of Park lots, very suitable either for pasture or meadow." [2] The lots were to be "offered for sale on Saturday, the 27th at eleven o'clock a.m., to the highest bidder by a lease for a long term of years - rent to be paid annually and other particulars to be made known at the day of sale." The Trustees said that they would have a map of the plan available for inspection. On July 25, John Knox, John Burch, Ezekiel Woodruff, Hugh Alexander and Reverend John Burns, who had already taken up the lots of their choice on the property , were given the opportunity of signing a lease.

On December 14, leases were approved. Those who acquired building lots at that time were: Thomas Dickson, Hugh Alexander, M.C. Beardsley, James Thompson, Thomas McCormick, Wm. Weishuhn,

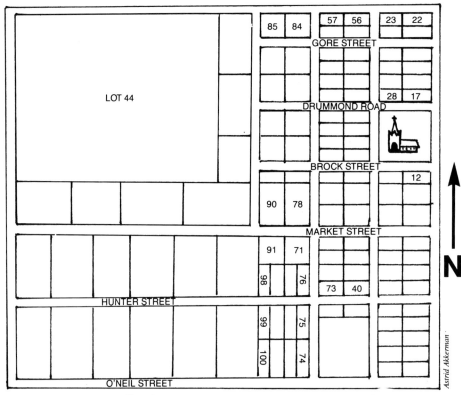

Scale: 12 chains to one inch

Town of Stamford, Plan Number 1791.
Hunter was changed to Russell Street, and Drummond Street to McMicking at a much later date, to avoid confusion with streets of the same name in Niagara Falls.

Dr. J.J. Lefferty, Charles Anderson, Thomas Wilson. Those who leased Park Lots were: Thomas Dickson, M.C. Beardsley, Wm. Weishuhn, Thomas McCormick, John Knox, Dr. J.J. Lefferty, John Burch, Hugh Alexander and James Thompson.

The map or plan which the trustees had prepared so that bidders would know what lot or lots they were bidding on, had street names assigned. The proposed streets running east to west were named after military officers: O'Neil, Hunter, Brock, Drummond, Gore and Riall. The streets running north and south were named Saint Andrew, Saint George, Saint Patrick, and the road to St. David's which served as the eastern boundary of the plan, was named St. Paul. Present day Stamford Green Drive, between Hunter and Brock was named Market Street, because there was a block of land reserved for a market, but never used, on all four corners of the intersection of St. Patrick and Market Streets.

The area of this Stamford Town Plan, Plan Number 1791, presently is the site of many of the historic

homes in the Stamford Green area of Niagara Falls. The land reserved for the Presbyterian Meeting House, between Brock Street and Drummond, present day McMicking Street, is largely taken up today by Stamford Presbyterian Church, the manse and the cemetery.

On December 22, 1870 the congregation of the Presbyterian Church petitioned the Legislature of Upper Canada that they be allowed to appoint a new Board of Trustees - the former Board had all died - and that they be allowed to offer the rest of the land for sale. The petition was granted and John Thompson, David Thorburn, William Parker, William Morrison and Robert Niven were appointed trustees. However, it was not until the building boom after World War II in 1947, that the remaining church lands were sold. The money received was added to the funds of the Stamford Presbyterian Church. The names of the streets and the historic houses located in this area are a reminder of the first organized subdivision of land in present day Niagara Falls.

Stamford Green

Village Greens are found throughout the British Isles. They are plots of land set aside for the enjoyment of all citizens of the community. Agricultural Fairs, election meetings, and festive celebrations are held on these public lands. Niagara Falls has the distinction of having the only village green in Canada, Stamford Green, located at the intersection of St. Paul Avenue and the Portage Road.

This 1.5ha (3 and a half acre) plot of land was formerly the western extremity of the Dee farm. Captain R.H. Dee was aide-de-camp to Lieutenant-Governor Sir Peregrine Maitland. When Maitland came to this area and bought property on the escarpment for a summer residence, Captain Dee accompanied him and purchased land on the Portage Road that was formerly part of one of John Burch's Crown Grants. The house which Captain Dee built was later enlarged and is now 3252 Portage Road.

This piece of property, a wedge between St. Paul Avenue and the Portage Road, was kept open by the Dee family, for the benefit and enjoyment of the public, from 1821 until the mid 1980's. In 1908, Mrs. Percival Prest learned from a conversation with Dr. John Dee, who was then the owner, that he was willing to sell the property for $1,000. This was conditional that the land would always be used as a public park.[1] He further stipulated that the property should be administered by five trustees, and that it should never be fenced, no trees were to be planted and no buildings erected on it.

A public meeting was held on May 5, 1908 and a committee of three men was appointed to raise money for the purchase of the property. Those on the committee were: J.R. McMicking, Thomas Berriman and George E. Russell. At a subsequent meeting on July 15, 1908, five men, Thomas Berriman, Calvin Emmett, William Prest, C.R. Johnson and George V. Russell were elected as trustees.

The public contributed $672.50 towards the cost of the property. The remainder of the money was raised by holding teas, small fairs, and auction sales. By November 3, 1909 enough money had been raised to purchase the property and it was put under the control of the Board of Trustees.[2]

The Green became a sports and recreational centre. At one time there was a ball diamond, with a backstop, and both softball and hardball were played there. It had a tennis court on the southwest corner and then a bowling green. A small clubhouse was built beside the bowling greens, lights were installed and these facilities provided a great deal of enjoyment for lawn bowlers. For many years members of the St. John's Anglican Church held strawberry festivals there.

When the original flag pole was declared unsafe because of wood rot in 1917, a new 22.9m (75 foot) pole was erected through the courtesy of Mr. George Foster, Superintendent of the Niagara Falls Electric Light Commission. In those days the Union Jack was flown, and it was the custom to hoist it on holidays

The aluminum flag pole and the War Memorial at Stamford Green.

and special occasions, and to fly it at half-mast upon the death of dignitaries, both local and national. At one time the flag pole was struck by lightning, and was repaired by the Stamford Volunteer Firemen. In July 1987 a 15m (50 foot) flag pole, costing $4334.72, was donated by the Volunteer Firemen. This flagpole, is equipped with an inside halyard, which keeps the rope out of the weather. [3]

W.A. Lorne Robinson's family home overlooks the Green from the west, and he has been a witness to and a participant in many of the events which took place there. This chapter is based on his research and his recollections. He recalls when the gravel surface on St. Paul Avenue was replaced with cement by the Ontario Department of Highways, and became King's Highway Number 8. When the construction equipment was available near the site, Stamford Council took advantage of the opportunity and arranged with the Department of Highways to have the Green levelled. Then the area was fertilized and grass seed planted, resulting in the level surface we know today. The Township and the Highway Department shared the $1,000 cost for this work.

The Stamford Horticultural Society was given permission to construct a memorial garden at the Green's apex. This memorial recognizes Stamford Township men who died in the service of our country during World Wars 1 and 2. This memorial was dedicated on August 7, 1949. The Horticultural Society continues to maintain the floral garden adjacent to the memorial stone. Some of those who have served on the Board of Trustees are: Hope Rose, Robert Embleton, William Meadows, Hugh Johnson, George Ellis, Dr. Culverhouse, John M. Wallace, Hugh Kerr, Leonard Hawken, Peter C. Calder, Claude Morningstar, and Ewald Oberlein.

This view of the apex of Stamford Green shows the enclosed lawn bowling green and the clubhouse which occupied this portion of the green from 1923 until 1938. The narrow concrete roadway at the right was the new King's Highway Number 8, which ran from the Whirlpool Rapids Bridge, at the foot of Bridge Street, through St. David's and then to Hamilton and points west, until it ended at Goderich.

The Portage Road Oak Tree

The following is an abridged version of the story of the Portage Road Oak Tree written by the Reverend Hugh Appel a former minister of Stamford Presbyterian Church.

"Not far from the church stands an old oak tree. Its trunk is huge and its many arms reach upwards as if they were carrying a heavy load. The tree has suddenly become famous, has had its picture taken and had reporters write stories about it in our local newspaper. In other words the tree has become the centre of attention here in our community lately.

"Imagine that! Old Oak stands on what used to be called Portage Trail. From its viewpoint it has seen and heard a lot over the last some centuries. It saw the settlers move in as they came down the trail in their ox carts, wagons and by foot. It watched the people working from early morning until sundown clearing the land, building their homesteads and securing a future for generations to come. As it stood there along the trail Old Oak served many a traveller as a guide post during the day and provided shade for those who needed a cool place on a hot summer day. It watched the birds seeking a place among its sturdy branches to build a nest for their young. It listened to the songs of the birds praising their Creator.

"As the years slipped by season after season, the oak tree grew stronger and its roots went deeper into the soil, drawing up water from which it grew. It saw a church being built a short distance away. Not a very fancy building, much like others surrounding it, but it was a place the people could meet to worship God who fed them and cared for them...Many things happened as the tree kept watching. The larger and higher it grew the better the view. It saw young brides dressed in beautiful white gowns, escorted by their fathers down the aisle. It watched as little children, like white bundles in the arms of the mothers, were carried in to be baptized into the church. Many a time it saw people gathered around the graveside in the cemetery...standing there with their heads bowed, grieving over one of them, now with the Father.

"Years came and went. The tree was getting older now but stood nevertheless firmly planted in the soil. The community began to change. Automobiles began to replace buggies, while gravel roads were being paved. Wires appeared alongside the tree, carrying electricity into the homes surrounding it. More and more new houses were being built. Farm land changed into shopping plazas and highrise buildings. Not too many people paid attention to Old Oak anymore until that day in 1983 when a group observed the tree and announced its verdict. They made statements that Old Oak was no longer safe, its branches could easily break off causing a lot of damage. They decided that the tree should be cut down for safety reasons.

"The tree was shocked. For more than 300 years it had towered and watched over the community. It had vibrated to the sound of cannonballs flying during the war. How vividly it remembered so many events. Now according to the experts, the days of the tree were numbered. During the long cold winter months it may

The Stamford Green White Oak, circa 1900.
This photograph shows the oak tree along the east side of a one track, gravel Portage Road. Stamford Green is at the left.

 W.A. Lorne Robinson

look as if the tree has lost its life, as if the roots were no longer able to draw up the sap for even the smallest branches. 'Well, thought the tree, if I am not growing anymore does that mean that I cannot longer be alive?'

"People in the community read about the verdict and began to take action to save old Oak. The City Fathers listened and gave in to their request. The tree would have another chance. With medication, proper pruning, support and care it would be able to continue to live. Of course it would cost money. Thousands of dollars, as a matter of fact…Old Oak realized that only sacrificial love could save him, but the people were willing to sacrifice to save the tree. It stands majestic and proud with green foliage, a gift from God. For the first time Old Oak realized that when growth stops, life ends." [1]

An inspection of the tree was carried out by George. W. Dalby Superintendent of Parks, and Ross Wood, Horticultural Coordinator, of Niagara Parks. Their report stated that the cost of preserving the tree, and preparing it to last another fifteen to twenty years was estimated to be $3500.00. [2]

In response to the newspaper publicity and the public concern expressed over the ailing "Stamford Green White Oak", George Seibel, Chairman of the Niagara Falls Heritage Foundation wrote to City Council and offered to pay the stated $3500.00 cost involved in preserving the tree. [3] A newspaper report

on June 21, 1983 headed *Oak Tree Saved* reported City Council's acceptance of the Niagara Falls Heritage Foundation's offer. [4]

The Niagara Parks School of Horticulture Alumni Association then wrote to Mr. Jack Collinson, Chief Administration Officer of the City of Niagara Falls, on July 12, 1983, offering to preserve the tree. They wrote: " Although our financial resources are very limited, we do have through our members, a good deal of expertise and knowledge which could be of valuable assistance in the assessment and the possible planning and implementation of a preservation program." [5] It was understood that they would provide the labour and expertise and the Niagara Falls Heritage Foundation would provide money for other expenses.

The City of Niagara Falls Parks and Cemeteries Department decided that the work should be done under their supervision and so they hired a tree preservation firm to carry out the work. The resulting work increased the tree's life expectancy another 50 to 100 years, cost a total of $7,535.26. The Niagara Falls Heritage Foundation contributed its $3500.00 and the City of Niagara Falls paid the balance. The Portage Road Oak, or the "Stamford Green White Oak" as it was also called, was given a new lease on life, and will continue to be a spectator to the life of the community, for another hundred years.

Drummondville

One of the first roads leading from the Portage Road was the lane through the bush which ran up and over the sandy hill, through the woods, to William Lundy's farm. The junction of this lane with the Portage Road, (present day Lundy's Lane and Main Street) became known as the Crossroads. The settlement which grew up later near the Crossroads was called Drummondville, after Major-General Sir Gordon Drummond who commanded the British forces at the Battle of Lundy's Lane.

The land on the north side of Lundy's Lane was Thomas Millard's Crown Grant and the land to the south adjoining the Lane was James Forsyth's. Settlers in the western half of the Township used the Lane when they brought their grist to John Burch's Mills. It was not long before people settled at or near the Crossroads, to provide those passing by with services, such as an inn, a harness maker's shop, a blacksmith and a carriage and wagon maker's shop.

Whereas the area around the junction of the Portage Road and the road to St. David's had been settled earlier because of its proximity to Queenston and the St. David's area to the north, the area at the Crossroads grew at a much slower pace. In 1795 a church was built at the top of the sandy hill, on the south side of Lundy's Lane, by the joint efforts of Protestants of all denominations. This community church, the "Church of all persuasions" as it was called, had Baptists, Lutherans, Methodists, Presbyterians and Quakers as members. It was also used as a school house during the weekdays.[1]

The first mention of a tavern or inn at the Crossroads was during the War of 1812-14, Lieutenant FitzGibbon captured two Americans from Dr. Chapin's marauding force at a tavern run by a Mrs. Denfield. James Forsyth also kept an inn on the Portage Road, about .8 km (a half mile) south of the Crossroads. It was at times used as a headquarters for the British Army and many British army despatches were issued with Forsyth's as the location of origin.[2]

While there is a record of Austin Morse having bought lumber from Clark and Street at the Falls Mills, on May 2, 1825, and others were also in business at the Crossroads at that time, it was not until 1831 when the village of Drummondville was incorporated, the first community in the Township of Stamford, that we have a business census.

Drummondville was described in the census as a cluster of about a dozen houses near the Crossroads, with others along Lundy's Lane. There were 150 people living there. The businesses listed in the census were: Adam Fralick, hotel keeper; Samuel Falconbridge, postmaster and merchant; Woodruff and Lowell, merchants; William Gurnan, blacksmith; John Misener, wagon maker; Austin Morse, furniture maker and undertaker; Robert Slater, hotel keeper; Andrew Moss, cabinet maker; James Skinner, harness maker.

In 1838 Lieutenant-Colonel J.B.B. Estcourt came to this area with the 43rd Monmouthshire Regiment. This was just after the Mackenzie Rebellion when Americans were protesting the incident of the American Steamboat "Caroline". It had been cut loose from the dock at Schlosser, set afire and left to drift over the Horseshoe Falls. Estcourt and his wife Caroline were both artists and while they were here they did a number of water colours depicting Drummondville and the surrounding area.

In June 1838 he climbed to the observation gallery at the top of the Presbyterian Church on Drummond Hill, and made a sketch of what he saw from that vantage point. Fourteen of the twenty-eight buildings shown in the sketch have been identified by Isabel Walker.

Village of Drummondville, Falls of Niagara...
Battleground Lundy's Lane, June 1838.
A water colour over pencil by Lieutenant-Colonel J.B.B. Estcourt.

No. 1, St. George's Anglican Church

Estcourt drew St. George's Anglican Church out of proportion, making it the dominant building on the Portage Road. St. George's was built about 1835 by Reverend F. Miller, after he had a disagreement with Reverend William Leeming who was the rector of the church of St. John the Evangelist in Stamford and Holy Trinity Church in Chippawa. Miller bought the land on which the church stood, as well as providing his own money to furnish the church with pulpit, pews, organ, lamps and a stove. St. George's was known as the garrison church as its membership at one time was composed almost entirely of members of the 43rd Monmouthsire Regiment, including Lieutenant-Colonel Estcourt. Miller died in 1846 but it was not until 1856 that Leeming was able to gain title to the church. Shortly afterwards he had it demolished.

No. 2, Woodruff's Hardware Store

This building is still standing today, and is recognizable by the ''crow's step'' design of the brickwork at the rear of the building. The double chimneys have long since been removed. Joseph Woodruff acquired the property from William Scott in 1871 and operated there a hardware store, which was later taken over by his son, George C. Woodruff. From 1907 until 1946 it was owned by Cataract Lodge #103, 10OF, and then from 1946 until 1966 by the Serbian Club. During the Serbian Club's ownership extensive renovations were made. It was sold again and has housed various businesses since then.

No. 3, "Pavilion Hotel"

The "Pavilion" was located on the site of present day Oakes Inn. In 1820, William Forsyth took over Mrs. Wilson's Inn, enlarged it and called it the "Niagara Falls Hotel". In 1821 he purchased the property, demolished the hotel and built a new three storey frame building with a white clapboard exterior, which he named the "Pavilion".

Forsyth's hotel had galleries, called piazzas, which ran along the three storeys on the east side, overlooking the Horseshoe Falls and the Upper Rapids. The "Pavilion" was the foremost hotel at the Falls until the "Clifton Hotel" was opened at the end of the Ferry Road in 1835. The "Pavilion" was destroyed by fire on February 19, 1839, rebuilt on a smaller scale and served travellers until April 26, 1865 when this hotel also was destroyed by fire. It was not rebuilt.

No. 4, James Forsyth's House

James Forsyth was among the first ten settlers who came to this area in 1783. His 157ha (388 acre) Crown Grant of land included the area extending south from Lundy's Lane at present day Main Street, to Livingstone Avenue north of Loretto. He built his first house on this site which is now 6218 Main Street. He later added to it to provide facilities for an inn. The British Army used the house as a headquarters during the War of 1812-14. Lord Elgin, who was Governor-General of Canada from 1847 to 1854, lived in this house for a brief period in 1849 when he was forced to leave Montreal.

When Lord Elgin gave Royal assent to the controversial Rebellion Losses Bill, those who opposed the Bill rioted and burnt the parliament buildings which were then located in Montreal. Lord Elgin had to leave Montreal for his own safety and came to Drummondville. The building shown here was destroyed by fire and the present building was built on the site. It was also an inn known as "Duffy's Hotel" and later as "Anderson's Hotel". It is now a two family residence.

No. 5, ''Prospect Hotel''

This hotel, first called the ''National'', was one of the area's most famous landmarks for almost 150 years. It was built in 1827 by Harmanus Crysler, on property he bought from J. Buchner who had bought the land from his father-in-law, James Forsyth, in 1799. When Crysler began building the ''Clifton House'' in 1833, he sold the ''National'' to Richard Woodruff. It subsequently became the property of James C. Woodruff, who sold it to William Ellis in 1871. It then became known as the ''Ellis House''. In 1888, E.J. Fischer, a brewer from Chippawa, bought it and named it the ''Prospect House''. Fischer took this name from a hotel by the same name which had been located on the Front, in what is now Queen Victoria Park, after the Queen Victoria Niagara Falls Park Commissioners had this ''Prospect House'' demolished.

The ''Prospect'' had a colourful history. It was requisitioned by the military and used as a barracks during the Mackenzie Rebellion of 1837-38 during which time it was known as the ''Brick Barracks''. Tradition says that in 1849 when Lord Elgin, the Governor General of Canada took refuge at Niagara Falls, several government cabinet meetings were held at the ''Prospect''.

The ''Prospect was at one time owned by J.P. Slater, who sold it to William and Jack Ward, who were to own and operate it for almost fifty years. Soon after they took over, the interior of the hotel was gutted in a fire on November 20, 1893. The hotel was rebuilt, with oak woodwork and the ceilings on both floors were hand painted by a Danish artist. Jack Ward became the sole owner of the hotel and it was during his tenure that the ''Prospect'' achieved a reputation as a historic site. Ward built up a large collection of guns and memorabilia from the War of 1812-14, which he eagerly displayed to anyone interested. He took a special delight in showing off the ''detention cells'' which had been erected in the basement during the time in 1837-38 when it was used as a barracks.

After Jack Ward died in 1947, George Sainovich purchased the ''Prospect''. In 1957 the hotel was again badly damaged by fire. It was restored and the Sainovichs operated it for another seventeen years until 1974, when it was completely destroyed by fire. The ruins were demolished, and the property sold. The ''Prospect'' stood beside the Portage Road, serving as a social centre for the people of Drummondville, and an overnight resting place for travellers, for over one hundred and forty-seven years.

No. 6, Alanson Ross House and Carriage Factory

In 1820, Alanson Ross, who was a carriage maker, emigrated to Canada from Pennsylvania, and joined John Misener, who had a carriage shop just north of the northeast corner of present day Main and Peer Streets. In 1826 he left John Misener and bought a lot from William Forsyth, at present day 6062 Main Street. Here he built his residence and established his own Ross Carriage Factory in a shop behind the house. From here he carried on an extensive business manufacturing carriages and stage coaches which he sold throughout Ontario. The Alanson Ross house is now owned by Francis Patterson, from which he operates the Patterson Funeral Home.

No. 8, Thorburn Drug Store

The first building on the site was of frame construction. It was occupied in 1854 by G.J. Duncan, a general merchant, who sold boots, shoes, crockery, glass, earthenware, lamps, coal oil, bank deeds, mortgage forms and memorials. He advertised: ''Any article not in stock will be procured on short notice.'' This building was destroyed by fire and replaced by the present brick building, now occupied by Thorburn Drug Store. For many years Theodore Woodruff operated a dry goods store here. After Woodruff's time, the store was known as Darker's and then Purcell's. The addition at the rear of the store was used as a post office and at another time as a police station and jail. In 1899 A.C. Thorburn bought out Smith's Drug Store which was located next door, in the store presently operated by Letha Leonard as a ladies wear store. In 1900 Mr. Thorburn purchased the red brick building on the corner and moved his drug store there. For many years there was a hall on the second floor of the building where the Loyal Orange Lodge, the Carpenters' Union and other organizations held meetings.

No. 9, John Misener's Home and Carriage Shop

John Misener came to this area in 1793 and received a grant of 121 ha (300 acres) of land. A carriage maker by trade he soon purchased land from James Forsyth, at the northeast corner of present day Main and Peer Streets, and built a house and a shop where he built carriages and stage coaches. John Misener died in 1860 and his son John took over the business. According to Newton Misener, who lives in the family home on Peer Street at the corner of Sylvia Place, the second and third generations of the family, Newton's grandfather, his father and brothers built thirteen houses in Drummondville. John Misener's house, shown in this Estcourt water colour was moved and is now at 5491 Robinson Street, making this house one of the oldest in the area. Newton Misener is a fourth generation direct descendant and only surviving male member of this branch of the Misener family.

No. 10, William Russell Home

William Russell was a stone mason building contractor. He settled in Drummondville in 1833. He built a two storey brick home on the Ferry Road, just east of its intersection with the Portage Road. There was a plentiful supply of water coming from a spring at the rear of his property. In 1844 he built a brewery at the rear of his house, and used the spring water in brewing 20,000 gallons of beer annually. At the time the brewery was Drummondville's largest industry. E.J. Fischer bought it in December 1877 and in 1886 W.H. Ferguson became the owner. In the late 1880's it was destroyed in a spectacular fire and was not rebuilt. In 1851 Russell built a stone building on the property adjoining his home on the east. This became known in contemporary times as the Ivy Block and was incorporated in the "Stevens Hotel", known today as the "Concord Motor Hotel".

No. 11, Morse and Son Funeral Home

Austin Morse emigrated to this area in 1821 from Nobleton, New York. He was a cabinet maker and an upholsterer and it was not long before he began in business. His account with Clark & Street, dated May 2, 1825, for sawn lumber he purchased as raw material for his cabinet work, is the first evidence of his being in business. On January 8, 1826 he purchased a lot on the Portage Road from Samuel Street, at the location shown on the Estcourt water colour.With his skill as a cabinet maker and upholsterer, he soon established a reputation for fine craftsmanship, for the fine quality of his wooden furniture and for his upholstered sofas and chairs. A natural extension of the furniture trade in those times was the manufacture of coffins. This in turn led to the provision of an additional service to the family of the deceased. He acquired a team of black horses, and a black suit, and began transporting the deceased from their homes to the cemetery. The buildings shown in this Estcourt water colour were destroyed by fire on November 13, 1891.

Prospect House, Jack Ward, Proprietor, 1951 Main St., Niagara Falls, Ontario. The Old Barracks of 1837.

Niagara Falls Heritage Foundation Collection

National Archives of Canada

*The good woman of colour who with her husband took in and nursed a poor sick
black man who could not pay for his lodging. She lived near us and became a great friend.
A water colour on pencil attributed to Lady Caroline Bucknall Estcourt, 1838.*

*This unidentified black woman has been accorded a place in history for her humanity and compassion. Daniel
G. Hill wrote in ''The Freedom Seekers'': ''There were small Black settlements... at Drummondville and Niagara-
on-the-Lake where at least 14 Black families came as refugees between 1830 and 1840. At the time of the Mackenzie Rebellion, in May, 1838, there were Black companies of Militia stationed at Drummondville and when they
were disbanded many of the soldiers settled here. Over the years a community of Blacks grew up around present
day Peer and Grey Streets. The area was known as ''Pollytown'' after a man by the name of Polly who befriended
the Blacks. They found employment as waiters in the ''Clifton House'', the ''Pavilion'' and the ''Ontario House''.
Others worked as tourist guides for Thomas Barnett at the ''Niagara Falls Museum'' and Saul Davis at ''Table
Rock House''.*

*Daniel Hill wrote about Burr Plato, whom he described as ''a remarkable member of the Black community in
the Niagara District... he fled Virginia with seven other Blacks in 1856. While a slave, Plato had saved $50 in
gold and this money kept the group of fugitives alive until they reached Fort Erie a month later with only five
dollars, a bag of biscuits and a strong desire to work in freedom.'' He settled in Drummondville where he found
employment.*

*''For the next several years Plato worked as a porter and a farm-hand and spent every spare moment learning
to read and write. He saved enough money to buy a home on Stanley Street, where he raised his family of 10 children
and took a very active part in community and political affairs. He was one of the very few Blacks of the 19th century to win elections in municipal office in Canada.''*

*Ernest Green wrote in ''Some Graves in Lundy's Lane'', published by the Niagara Historical Society: ''By thrift
and untiring industry he acquired education and a comfortable property and was so respected as an honest and
God-fearing citizen that he was on several occasions elected as an alderman of the local municipal council by
his white neighbours.'' Burr Plato died in 1905 and was buried in Drummond Hill Cemetery with other members
of Drummondville's early black families, the Allegoods, Fords, Guarries, Littles, Peirmans, Smiths, Suttons and
the Washingtons.*

National Archives of Canada

Cottage in Lundy's Lane which we lived in from Aug. 1838 to Aug. 1839.
Water colour over pencil by Sir James Bucknall Estcourt.

Estcourt gave no indication as to the exact location of this cottage on Lundy's Lane. The cottage is built on high ground, and as the land rises south of Lundy's Lane, it would most likely have been located on the south side of the Lane, between present day Drummond Road and Franklin Streets.

The word "cottage" as we use it today suggests a small house, but the "cottage" in this picture seems to have been quite a large home. It was apparently an English custom to call a house, no matter the size, a cottage. Lieutenant-Governor Sir Peregrine Maitland built his summer home on the top of the escarpment, a twenty-two room home which was named "Stamford Cottage." Captain Creighton built his home on the high bank overlooking the American Falls, south of the Ferry Road, and called it "Clifton Cottage."

In the 1830's a great many English people emigrated to Canada. They included many retired military officers who were people of means. Some of them settled in this area and built fine homes. Major Leonard built a home, just north of Lundy's Lane, which later became Stamford's first grammar school. Among those who built on Lundy's Lane were the Asfords, the Pims, the Nashes and Colonel DeLatre. The "cottage" in the Estcourt water colour could very well have been Colonel DeLatre's house.

Philip Chesneau DeLatre, was a Lieutenant-Colonel, retired, in the British Army. He saw service in the East Indies and was an officer of the Ceylon Regiment in 1818. His residence on Lundy's Lane was "a place of entertainment for visitors of quality from Old England." He was president of the Niagara Harbour & Dock Company and had a residence also at Niagara called "DeLatre Lodge", which is still standing.

Lieutenant-Colonel J.B. Estcourt and other officers of the 43rd Monmouthshire Regiment were stationed in Drummondville in 1838-39, at the time after the Mackenzie Rebellion when tension between Canada and the United States was high. Colonel DeLatre would have been in his element with so many officers and their wives available and eager to attend social gatherings. In the words of Ernest Green "They used to drive out in great style." Drummondville's fling with the military "four hundred" was short lived. When the officers died, their wealth was dispersed to relatives in England and their houses passed into other hands.

George Bailey

Ross-Patterson House

This is the former Alanson Ross house and Ross Carriage Factory, now the Patterson Funeral Home, as it looks in 1989. The accompanying advertisement which appeared in the Drummondville Reporter on April 28, 1855 states that the Carriage Factory, which was in a building attached to the rear of the house, was established in 1826. A subsequent advertisement in the same newspaper, dated April 22, 1857, announced that the Pyper Brothers were the new owners of the Ross Carriage Factory. This house is one of the oldest and best preserved houses on the former Portage Road, at what was formerly Drummondville.

NIAGARA FALLS, C.W.
CARRIAGE FACTORY,
ESTABLISHED IN 1826.

THE subscriber, in returning thanks to his numerous customers for the very liberal patronage which he has always received, announces to them and the public generally, that he has lately much enlarged his establishment in all its branches, and is now prepared to execute orders for Carriages on the shortest notice, and in the best possible style. A large assortment of the very latest styles of highly finished

Carriages, Buggies, Wagons, Sleighs & c. always on hand. Having engaged none but the Best Mechanics, and being possessed of all the other facilities required to do a large business, he is enabled to offer such inducements, by

Selling Cheap, and turning out Good Work. as can not be surpassed by any other establishment in Canada.

                                    ALANSON ROSS.
Drummondville, April 28, 1855.   1tf

George Bailey

John Misener's House

One of the oldest houses in the area, John Misener's house now at 5491 Robinson Street, originally had an attached kitchen and several outbuildings. When the Campaigne Block was built in the mid 1920's (the building between the Government of Canada Employment office at the corner of Main and Peer Streets, and Bickle's Hardware), John Misener's house was moved to Robinson Street.

James Forsyth's Second House

James Forsyth's second house, present day 6103 Culp Street, was built in 1798. Forsyth sold the house to Isaac Culp who operated a farm and present day Culp Street was the lane leading from the Portage Road to his farm house.

Forsyth's original house and Inn on the Portage Road just south of Symmes Avenue (No. 4), was destroyed by fire in April 1875. The "Niagara Falls Gazette" reporting the blaze in the April 17 edition said: "The building destroyed was an old historic landmark. It was built in 1795, and consequently was one of the oldest houses in Drummondville. Originally built and occupied as a hotel, it was at that time the only first class place of entertainment on either side of the river. The building was occupied by (U.S.) General Scott, who made it his headquarters... The property was owned by a Mr. Duckett at the time of its destruction." The British military also used the premises as headquarters and many despatches were issued with "Forsyth's" as the place of origin.

Niagara Falls New York Public Library

Dr. Nathaniel Dett

The Drummondville black community's most distinguished citizen was Dr. Nathaniel Dett, who was born here on October 11, 1882. The Dett family lived on the corner of Ferry and Temperance Streets. They moved to Niagara Falls, New York in 1893 after a tragic occurrence on Halloween night. One of the Dett boys was shot while being involved in a prank and subsequently died as the result of his injuries. R. Nathaniel Dett was then eleven years old, and he continued to attend school in Niagara Falls, Ontario, crossing the border each school day. He continued his education here until he graduated from Niagara Falls Collegiate.

Described as "an average boy – with an extra talent", a musical talent, Dett learned to play the piano and in the evening during his high school years he played the piano at the "Cataract House" in Niagara Falls, New York. There someone recognized his talent and encouraged him. He became a student of Professor Oliver Willis Halstead of Lockport, new York. By 1902 he was an accomplished pianist, and he left the area for further experience. By 1924 he had acquired his Bachelor of Music degree at Oberlin University in Ohio and later his Doctorate of Music.

He then began travelling throughout the world, writing and composing, playing, singing and entertaining. he became a Professor of Music at Hampton University in Virginia and for a time he taught at the Eastman School of Music. During World War II, he travelled with the U.S.O., the United Services Organization, entertaining troops. While he was on a U.S.O. tour in 1943 he died, and was buried in Fairview Cemetery in Niagara Falls, Ontario.

Arlene E. Gray, BSLS, BM, MM, a retired Research Librarian living in Crystal Beach, Ontario, compiled a source book of Dr. Nathaniel Dett's compositions, named "Listen to the Lambs" after his most famous composition. This book was published in 1983 and is a memorial to Dr. R. Nathaniel Dett. In 1982 the Niagara Falls New York Historical Society placed a memorial stone on Dr. Dett's grave in Fairview Cemetery and in 1983 this same organization placed a memorial stone on the grave of Charlotte Washington Dett, Dr. Dett's mother. On August 31, 1986 the Niagara Falls Heritage Foundation placed a more substantial monument to mark the Dett family graves.

The inscription on this monument reads: "The family of Charlotte Washington Dett lived in both Niagara Falls, Ontario and Niagara Falls, New York. Mrs. Dett and her sons Arthur, Nathaniel and Samuel are all buried here. R. Nathaniel Dett Mus.D. was an outstanding black composer, pianist, conductor and poet. Dr. Dett wrote many inspirational religious songs including "Listen to the Lambs."

On February 6, 1986 the City of Niagara Falls passed a by-law designating the B.M.E. church on Peer Street which the Detts attended, as an historical site. At that time the church was re-dedicated as the R. Nathaniel Dett Memorial Chapel of the B.M.E. church.

NOTES

The Falls of Niagara and the East Bank Portage

1   René Bréhant de Galinée, *Explorations of the Great Lakes, 1669-70*, Ontario Historical Society Papers and Records vol. 4, pp. 38-41.

2   Father Louis Hennepin, *A New Discovery of a Vast Country in America Extending about Four Thousand Miles between New France and New Mexico with a Description of the Great Lakes, Cataracts, Rivers, Plants and Animals*, 2 vols. (London: 1699; reprint ed. n.p.n.d.).

3   Thomas Morin, *The Life and Death of Lord Edward FitzGerald*, vol. 1 (London: Longman, Rees, Orme, Brown & Green, 1831), p. 145.

4   The Neutral Indians were one of three tribes inhabiting what is now present day Southern Ontario. Their land was in what is now the Niagara Peninsula, particularly on the north shore of Lake Erie. They were known as the Attiowandoron, meaning people who speak a slightly different language. The French called them Les Neutres or the Neutral Nation because they refused to take sides in the incessant warfare between the Hurons to the north of them and Five Nations Iroquois who lived in what is now the State of New York. In spite of their neutrality, by 1650 they, as well as the Hurons, were annihilated by the Five Nations Iroquois. Archer Butler Hulbert, *The Niagara River*. (New York: G. Putnam & Sons, 1908).

5   Brian Leigh Dunnigan, *The French Castle and Old Fort Niagara* (Youngstown, N.Y.: Old Fort Niagara Association, Inc., 1987), p. 9.

6   Louis Thomas Chabert de Joncaire was born in Provence, near Arles, France, in 1670. He came to Quebec as a soldier in 1687. He was captured along with a dozen others about the time of the Denonville expedition. The captives were held by the Indians. All but Joncaire died on the torture platform. Joncaire broke loose from his captors as he was being held, waiting his turn to be tortured. He rushed a war chief who was standing nearby and with one punch flattened him, breaking his nose. The Indians admired his courage and he was given the opportunity of winning adoption by running the gauntlet. He ran through and became what the Iroquois called a White Indian. He used his influence with the Indians to further the French cause. Robert West Howard, *Thundergate: The Forts of Niagara*. (Englewood Cliffs, N.J.: Prentice-Hall, Inc., 1968).

7   The French Castle was erected by Gaspard de Léry, Louis XV's chief engineer in Canada. He had already built a massive fortress at Quebec and a city wall at Montreal. He used oak beams and granite blocks in its fieldstone construction so that the casemented third story of this cleverly designed and so-called House of Peace could be used as a gun deck for cannon. Brian Leigh Dunnigan, *Siege-1759 The Campaign Against Niagara*, Old Fort Niagara Association, 1986.

8   *Thundergate: The Forts of Niagara.*

9   R.C. *An Account of the English and the French colonies in North America*, Universal Mag. No. 1755.

10   *Thundergate: The Forts of Niagara.*

11   The French were successful in the initial skirmishes of this war, but by 1759 British seapower had throttled New France and affected her ability to resist the steadily mounting British pressure, and the outposts of the French North American empire were nipped off one by one. Philip Mason, *The French in Canada*, in *Niagara Falls Canada, a history* (Niagara Falls: Kiwanis Club of Stamford, 1967).

12   Ibid., *The French in Canada.*

The British Portage on the East Bank

1   Report of Lt. George Demier, October 24, 1762, Amherst Papers, vol. 22, in Wm. L. Clements Library. Quoted in *Portaging Niagara*.

2   Pontiac, the Ottawa Indian chief, consistently supported the French during the Seven Years' War (1756 to 1763). After the final defeat of the French he organized the Indian uprising, sometimes known as Pontiac's Conspiracy, in an attempt to take control of the Northwest from the British. No help was forthcoming from France and the uprising failed. Pontiac made peace with the British in 1766.

3   Captain John Schlosser was a German who served with the Royal American Regiment, stationed at Fort Niagara, as Engineering Officer.

4   Devil's Hole Cave, at the bottom of Devil's Hole Gorge, was visited in 1678 by French explorer LaSalle. Tradition says that he entered the cave despite the warnings of an Indian guide. Thereafter, numerous disasters plagued LaSalle's exploration of America, culminating in his murder in 1687. The Seneca Indians attributed LaSalle's fate to his disturbing of the cave's Evil Spirit. Reported in the *Caves of Niagara County, New York*, Scott A. Ensminger (Niagara Falls, N.Y.: The Niagara County Historical Society, Inc., 1987).

5   Lieutenant-Colonel William Browning to General Amherst, Sept. 16, 1763, Amherst Papers, vol. 22. Quoted in *Portaging Niagara*.

6   Ibid., Browning to Amherst, Sept. 25, 1763, Amherst Papers, vol. 7. Quoted in *Portaging Niagara*.

7   Captain John Montressor in 1763 held the rank of Engineer Extraordinary and Captain Lieutenant. He was stationed at Fort Niagara and constructed the portage road redoubts with a battalion of the Canadian Volunteers. *Thundergate: The Forts of Niagara.*

8   Captain Enys, *Visit to Niagara*, handwritten journal of Captain Enys, 29th Regiment, 1787, National Archives of Canada.

9   Wilkins to Amherst, Sept. 20, 1763, Amherst Papers, vol. 22. Quoted in *Portaging Niagara*.

10   Joseph Hadfield, *An Englishman in America 1785, being the Diary of Joseph Hadfield*. Edited and annotated by Douglas S. Robertson (Toronto: The Hunter-Rose Co. Ltd., 1933).

11   Ralph Izard, *An Account of a Journey to Niagara, Montreal and Quebec in 1765,* (New York: Osborn, 1846), p. 9.

12   General Gage to Colonel John Bradstreet, March 17, 1766, Gage Papers, vol. 49. Quoted in *Portaging Niagara.*

13   *John Lees Journal July 23, 1768,* typed copy in the Burton Historical Collection, John Lees Papers. Quoted in *Portaging Niagara.*

14   Deposition of Francis Goring, February 4, 1824. Buffalo and Erie County Historical Society, John Stedman Papers, A00-560.

15   John Maude, *Visit to the Falls of Niagara in 1800* (London: Longman, Rees, Orme, Brown and Green, 1826).

16   Hazel C. Mathews, *The Mark of Honour* (Toronto: University of Toronto Press, 1965).

17   Inventory, Oct. 19, 1779, Buffalo and Erie County Historical Society, John Stedman Papers, A00-560. Quoted in *Portaging Niagara.*

18   The Jay Treaty or Jay's Treaty, was signed by Great Britain and the United States on Nov. 19, 1794, and named after John Jay, the American diplomat who represented the United States in the negotiations. It provided for the withdrawal of British forces from posts within United States territory – a provision of the Treaty of Paris – and for a survey and commission to settle certain boundary problems.

19   General Sir William Johnson, Superintendent of Indian Affairs for New York in 1755, became a respected friend of the Six Nations Indians. His first wife died, and he married Molly Brant, sister of Joseph Brant, the principal chief of the Six Nations Indians. Johnson commanded the provincial troops under General Prideaux in the expedition against Fort Niagara, and was chiefly responsible for the capture of Fort Niagara from the French. After the Devil's Hole ambush, Sir William extracted reparations from the Senecas who transferred their land along the Niagara River to the British. "The lands from the Fort of Niagara extending easterly along Lake Ontario about four miles, comprehending the Petit Matais (Four Mile Creek) and running from thence southerly about fourteen miles to the creek above Fort Schlosser, or Little Niagara, thence down the river or strait (Niagara River) and across the same at the great cataract, thence northerly to the banks of Lake Ontario at a creek or small lake about two miles west of the fort (Four Mile Creek on the west bank), thence easterly along the banks of Lake Ontario and across the strait to Niagara, comprehending the whole of the carrying place with lands on both sides of the strait, and containing a tract about 14 miles in length to four in breadth."

20   National Archives of Canada Colonial Office Records, M.G. 11, Q Ser., vol. 16, p. 611, Butler to Haldimand, Sept. 20, 1779. Quoted in *The Mark of Honour.*

The West Bank Portage

1   Third Ontario Archives Report, 1905, p. 297. "The Land Board for the district of Nassau, having received from Lord Dorchester instructions to open the Portage on the west side of the river above Niagara, and his Lordship wishing to do this on the most liberal and useful terms for the settlement, directs them to be consulted on this business, and that every proposal they individually or in companies may think proper to make for a contract shall be handed to him; the Board have appointed their second meeting on the second Tuesday in April, when the court sits, at which time they will communicate every particular respecting this business to whoever may apply…".

2   Lieutenant-Colonel E. Cruikshank, *Notes on the History of the Niagara District.* In Niagara Historical Society Publication Number 26 (Niagara-on-the-Lake: n.d.).

3   Isabel Walker, Thompson Papers, John Thompson to Thomas Clark Dr., January 1, 1810.

4   Ernest Green, *The Niagara Portage Road.* Ontario Historical Society Papers and Records, vol. 23 (1926).

5   Ibid., Ernest Green.

Our Early Settlers

1   *Thundergate: The Forts of Niagara,* p. 145.

2   Faye Vernette Whitfield, B.A. (Hons.), Dip. Ed., *The Origin of the Settlement of Niagara-on-the-Lake.* A Thesis to the School of Graduate Studies in Partial Fulfilment of Graduate Studies for the Degree of Master of Arts, McMaster University, June, 1986.

3   Lieutenant-Colonel E. Cruikshank, *Ten Years of the Colony of Niagara,* quoted in Ernest Green, *The Niagara Portage Road.* This area remained Indian lands until May 22, 1784, when by a treaty executed by a grand council at Niagara, the Mississauguas deeded to the Crown the whole remainder of the Niagara Peninsula, and the lands extending along Lake Erie and northward to the Thames, nearly as far as the present city of London.

4   Hazel C. Mathews, *The Mark of Honour,* p. 86. Isaac Dolson and the Secords chose land side by side under the brow of the escarpment, opposite the Lower Landing, Dolson at the lower end of what was to become the portage, James Secord adjoining on the west, (Lots 42, 43, 44 & 50), Peter Secord where the waters of the Four Mile Creek (present day St. David's) tumbling down the escarpment gave him a potential water power source. Samson Lutes adjoined Peter Secord on the south and Michael Showers chose a tract of land beside the river below the landing at Five Mile Meadow.

5   Ernest Green, *The Niagara Portage Road.*

6   Robert Rogers, *A Concise Account of North America…* London: Millan, 1765).

7   Patrick Campbell, *Travels in the Interior Inhabited Parts of North America in the Years 1791 and 1792* (Edinburgh: Guthrie, 1793).

8   Hazel C. Mathews, *The Mark of Honour*.

9   National Archives of Canada: B 168, p. 135. Quoted in Ernest Green, *Township No. 2 - Mount Dorchester - Stamford*. Ontario Historical Society Papers and Records, vol. 25 (1929).

10 Ibid., Ernest Green, *Township No. 2*. There is a difference of opinion as to how Stamford Township got its name. In 1791, John Graves Simcoe became the first Lieutenant-Governor of the newly created Province of Upper Canada. One of his first acts in 1792 was to change geographical names in the area to names in Lincolnshire, England. Stamford would then have been named after the Town of Stamford in Lincolnshire. Ernest Green, one of Niagara Falls' early historians concluded, "There is no evidence that a single person from Stamford in England had settled in the township or had any connection with it." As well, Hazel C. Mathews in *The Mark of Honour*, records that George Chisholm, Daniel Rose, Archibald Thompson, James Park, who were early settlers in this area, all came from the area of New Stamford, Kortright and Harpersfield in New York State. Today this is the area roughly bounded on the north by North Harpersfield, on the south by Bloomville, on the west by Davenport and Fergusonville, on the east by Stamford and Hobart in Delaware County, New York State. Hazel Mathews concluded that Governor Simcoe, who was well acquainted with many settlers on the Mountain, as he frequently visited them, agreed to the Stamford name originating with those settlers from the Head of the Delaware. *The Mark of Honour*, pp. 15, 135.

11 The Bender name was variously interpreted as Painter and Banter. The Indian Ladder was located a little south of the bottom of present day Clifton Hill and led to what is now the Maid of the Mist Landing. It was a tall pine or cedar tree with the branches cut off, leaving stubs about 15.24 cm (6 inches) long at the trunk to serve as steps. The log was then put over the bank and leaned against the face of the cliff, serving as a ladder. On the 24th of August, Mrs. Simcoe wrote: "Mr. Pilkington having been desired to, put one or two short ladders to make the descent easy from rock to rock by the side of the Indian Ladder". These became known as "Mrs Simcoe's Ladders". Elizabeth Posthuma Simcoe, *Diary*, ed. Mary Quayle Innis (Toronto: 1965).

12 Peter N. Moogk, Ph.D., *John Burch, Industrial Pioneer, Niagara Advance, Historical Issue, 1965*.

13 Ernest Green, *Township No. 2*.

14 National Archives of Canada, B109, p. 19.

15 Ernest Green, *Township No. 2*.

16 Hector St. John de Crèvecouer, *Description of Niagara Falls,* in a letter to his son under date of July, 1785. Mag. *American History,* Oct. 1878, vol. 2, pt. 2.

17 Ernest Green, *Township No. 2*.

18 Miss Beatrice Dennis, McMicking Papers.

19 Isabel Walker, *The Thompsons of Whirlpool Farm*, unpub. March 1976.

The Portage Road

1   Ernest Green, *The Niagara Portage Road*, Ontario Historical Society Papers and Records, vol. 23, pp. 265-66.

2   Third Ontario Archives Report, 1905, p. 197.

3   John Clark, *Memoirs of Colonel John Clark, of Port Dalhousie, C.W.* Ontario Historical Society Papers and Records, vol. 7, pp. 173-175.

4   *The Diary of Mrs. John Graves Simcoe,* ed. John Ross Robertson (Toronto: Ontario Publication Co., 1934).

5   Isaac Weld, *Travels through the States of North America, and the provinces of Upper and Lower Canada, during the years 1795, 1796 and 1797* (London: Stockdale, 1799), p. 114.

6   John Milton Holley and Charles Whittlesey, *Early History of Cleveland Ohio,* (Cleveland: Fairbanks, Benedict, 1867), pp. 175-176.

7   Robert Hamilton, Agent for Post Contracts, to Simcoe, 28th April, 1796. Simcoe Papers (Cruikshank), vol. 4.

8   *Early History of Cleveland, Ohio.*

9   Ray Corry Bond, *Peninsula Village A Story of Chippawa* (Chippawa: Village of Chippawa, n.d.).

10 *Niagara Herald,* April 25, 1801, from personal research by Richard Merritt M.D.

11 Thomas Fowler, *Journal of a Tour Through British America to the Falls of Niagara.*

12 Ibid., Thomas Fowler.

13 Edwin C. Guillet, *Pioneer Travel in Upper Canada* (Toronto: University of Toronto Press, 1933).

14 *There is a Tavern in the Town,* uncredited article in *Heritage Magazine* of the New York State Historical Association, vol. 3, No. 2, Nov.-Dec. 1986.

15 Louis Philippe, King of France 1830-48. *Diary of My Travels in America.* Translated from the French by Stephen Becker (New York: Delacorte Press, 1977).

16   *There is a Tavern in the Town.*

17   T.C., *A ride to Niagara, The Portfolio*, July, August, September, 1810.

18   *Upper Canada Gazette,* December 4, 1797.

19   T.C., *A ride to Niagara.*

20   Lieutenant-Colonel E. Cruikshank, *Documentary History of the Campaign of 1812,* Part 1.

Early Pioneer Life

1   Lieutenant-Colonel E. Cruikshank, ed., *The Correspondence of Lieutenant-Governor Simcoe, with allied documents relating to his administration of the government of Upper Canada,* 5 vols. Letters from a gentleman to his friend…, Nov. 20, 1794 (Toronto: 1921-31), vol. 3, p. 191.

2   Hazel C. Mathews, *The Mark of Honour.*

3   Dorothy Van Slyke, *Forest, River, Early Settlers,* (Niagara Falls: Niagara Falls Public Library, 1984).

4   Hazel C. Mathews, from the McMicking Papers, p. 130.

5   John Maude, *Visit to the Falls of Niagara*, p. 24.

6   Hazel C. Mathews, from the McMicking Papers, p. 130, and also from a letter E.J. Crossman, M.A., Ph.D., curator of Herpatology R.O.M. to George Seibel, Dec. 23, 1970. The Timber rattlesnake *Crotalus horridus horridus* and the Massassauga rattlesnake *Sistrus catenatus*, two subspecies of *Crotalus viridus,* make up the only poisonous snakes in Canada at present. The larger Timber rattlesnake is thought to be extinct in the Niagara Peninsula, the last sighting, when the snake was killed, was in 1959 in the Niagara Glen. The smaller and more widely distributed Massassauga prefers swamps and wetlands for a habitat and still exists in some parts of the Niagara and Bruce Peninsulas.

7   John Maude, *Visit to the Falls of Niagara in 1800,* p. 24.

8   McMicking Papers, Miss Beatrice Dennis, as quoted in *The Mark of Honour.*

9   Isabel Walker, *The Thompsons of Whirlpool Farm.*

The Portage Road and the War of 1812

1   Lieutenant-Colonel E. Cruikshank, *The Documentary History of the Campaign on the Niagara Frontier,* Lieutenant-Colonel Robert Nichol to Captain James Cummings, June 27, 1812. Part 3, p. 77.

2   Ibid., p. 126. *New York Gazette,* July 12, 1812.

3   Ibid., p. 221. John Lovett to Alexander Van Vechten, Lewiston, August 28, 1812. Ibid., p. 143. Lieutenant-Colonel Myers to Captain James Cummings, July 23, 1812.

4   Ibid., Part 4, p. 332. Sir Howard Douglas to Lord Bathurst, Dec. 20, 1812.

5   Ibid., Part 1, p. 299. Sir George Prevost to Lord Bathurst, Aug. 1, 1813.

6   Ibid., Part 5, p. 274. *Buffalo Gazette,* June 1, 1813.

7   Ibid., Part 7, p. 154. *Buffalo Gazette,* Sept. 21, 1813.

8   Ibid., Part 7, p. 155. *Buffalo Gazette,* Sept. 24, 1813.

9   Ibid., Part 1, p. 96. Extract from MSS. of William Hamilton Merritt.

10   Ibid., Part 6, p. 173.

11   Ernest Green, *Told by a Grandmother, Elizabeth Hewlett (Fralick) Green, Niagara Falls Evening Review,* Feb. 15, 1930.

12   *Documentary History,* Part 8, p. 188. Major-General Vincent to Major-General D. Rottenburg, Nov. 15, 1813.

13   Ibid., Part 1, p. 135. Captain Alexander Dobbs R.N., to Sir James L. Yeo.

14   Ibid., Part 2, p. 358. Memorial of Lieutenant-Colonel Robert Nichol to Lord Bathurst, Sept. 24, 1817.

15   Ibid., Part 1, p. 106. Extract of a letter Dr. E.L. Allen of the 21st Regiment, July 26, 1814.

16   Ibid., Part 1, p. 87. Sir Gordon Drummond to Sir George Prevost, July 27, 1814.

17   Ibid., Part 1, p. 105. Colonel James Miller to----. July 26, 1814. From the Adjutant-General's Report for New Hampshire for 1868.

18   Ibid., Part 1, p. 104. Dr. Bull to ----, July 31, 1814.

19   Sir J.E. Alexander, 14th Regiment, *Sleigh Ride in Canada West.* A visit to the battlefield of Lundy's Lane in 1843. Clearwater Collection, Niagara Falls New York Public Library.

20 Ernest Green, *Told by a Grandmother*.

21 *Documentary History*, Part 7, p. 99. Thomas G. Ridout to Thomas Ridout at York, Sept. 4, 1813. Also from *Ten Years of Upper Canada* by Lady Edgar, pp. 211-13.

Portage Road Industries – Bridgewater Mills

1 Ernest Green, *Old U.E.L. Mills are Recalled*, Ernest Green Scrapbook, Niagara Falls Ontario Public Library.

2 A.E. Coombs, *History of the Niagara Peninsula* (Toronto: 1930).

3 T.C., *A ride to Niagara*.

4 Mrs. Roy (Esther) Summers, Bond Papers.

5 Simcoe Papers, vol. 5, Petition H 15-1.

6 François Alexandre Frederic La Rochefoucault-Liancourt, duc d'Estiasse, *Travel in Canada, 1795,* ed., Sir David William Smith, Bart. (Toronto: Bureau of Archives, Province of Ontario, 1916).

7 Ibid.

8 War Losses Claims #523. Letter Thomas Clark to William Walton, Secty. to Lieutenant-Governor Gore. National Archives of Canada.

9 Ibid., War Losses Claims #523.

10 Ray Corry Bond, *Peninsula Village*.

11 Ibid., *Peninsula Village*.

12 *Documentary History...* Part 3, p. 42.

13 Ernest Green, *The Niagara Portage Road*, Ontario Historical Society Papers and Records, vol. 23 (1926).

14 *Documentary History...*, Part 2, p. 424.

15 War Losses Claims 1812, #523. Letter Thomas Clark to William Walton, Niagara Falls, January 29, 1816.

16 Ernest Green, *Old U.E.L. Mills are Recalled*.

The Portage Road, Travel, Hotels, Tourism, After the War of 1812

1 Petition of William Forsyth and Proceedings thereon in Council, under dates of 28th and 30th of Nov., 1820. Court of Appeal for Ontario, Appendix A Part 1.

2 *Niagara Patriot*, Buffalo, June 24, 1820. Buffalo Public Library.

3 Copy of notes taken at trial by Presiding Judges, 5th September, 1827, King vs Forsyth, and 22nd September, 1834, Clark and Street vs Bonnycastle, in Court of Appeals for Ontario, Appendix A Part 2.

4 Dr. John Bigsby, *The Shoe and Canoe*, quoted in Edwin Clarence Guillet, *Pioneer Inns and Taverns,* 5 vols. (Toronto: 1954-64), vol. 4, pp. 29-30.

5 Ernest Green, *The Niagara Portage Road*.

6 *Niagara Patriot,* June 5, 1821.

7 Ernest Green, *The Niagara Portage Road*, p. 290.

8 Copy of notes taken by Presiding Judges, King vs. Forsyth. Testimony Captain Philpotts, No. 62 C, p. 195.

9 *Upper Canada Gazette*, Feb. 12, 1827.

10 Ernest Green, *The Niagara Portage Road,* pp. 290-91.

11 James Morden, *Historic Niagara Falls*.

12 William Leete Stone, *From New York to Niagara – Journal of a Tour... to Niagara.* (Buffalo: Buffalo Historical Society, 1919), as quoted in Dow, vol. 1, p. 174.

13 James Morden, *Historic Niagara Falls,* p. 97.

14 Lieutenant E.T. Coke, *A Subaltern's Furlough,* as quoted in *The Niagara Portage Road,* p. 297.

15 James Morden, *Historic Niagara Falls,* p. 36.

16 *Niagara Gleaner,* July 13 and August 3, 1833.

17 Patrick Shirreff, *A Tour Through North America* (Edinburgh: 1835).

18 Ernest Green, *The Niagara Portage Road,* p. 302.

19   *A letter from the Falls of Niagara*, by an officer of the 43rd Regiment, signed *Bugle*, in *United States Journal*, August 1838. Clearwater Collection.

20   Elizabeth McKinsey, *Niagara Falls Icon of the American Sublime* (Cambridge: Cambridge University Press, 1985), p. 179.

21   *A letter from the Falls of Niagara*, signed *Bugle*.

22   Samuel DeVeaux, *The Falls of Niagara – a tourist guide* (Buffalo: 1839).

23   Inventory of furniture, etc., in the *Pavilion Hotel*. Ontario Archives.

24   Sir J.E. Alexander, 14th Regiment, *Sleigh Ride in Canada West, 1843*.

25   Sister M. Maurice O'Heare, *Loretto Convent*, in *Niagara Falls Canada, a history*.

26   *Niagara Chronicle*, October 5, 1848.

27   *Niagara Falls Gazette*, January 24, 1855.

28   William Leete Stone, *From New York to Niagara*.

City of the Falls

1   James C. Morden, *Historic Niagara Falls* (Niagara Falls: Lundy's Lane Historical Society, 1932).

2   Ibid., *Historic Niagara Falls*, p. 36.

3   *The Farmers Journal*, June 7, 1826. St. Catharines Public Library.

4   Ernest Green, *The Old Bath House, Niagara Falls Evening Review*, April 10, 1923.

5   Lieutenant E.T. Coke, *A Subaltern's Furlough*, quoted in Ernest Green, *The Niagara Portage Road*.

6   Sir Richard Henry Bonnycastle, *Canada and the Canadians*, new edition, 2 vols. (Toronto: Canadiana House, 1969), vol. 1.

7   Ernest Green, *The Niagara Portage Road*.

8   *Niagara Falls Evening Review*, Sept. 29, 1951.

The Erie and Ontario Rail Road

1   *Niagara Gleaner*, Nov. 16; Dec. 14, 1833.

2   *Historic Niagara Falls*.

3   Sir Richard H. Bonnycastle, *The Canadas in 1841* (London: Henry Colburn, 1842).

4   Orville Luther Holley, *The Picturesque Tourist: Being a Guide Book Through the Northern and Eastern States and Canada* (New York: J. Disturnell, 1844).

5   John Morley, a York Road resident, whose property abuts the escarpment, in conversation with the author, March 1989.

6   *The Emigrant Churchman*, H. Christmas (1849), vol. 1, p. 132.

7   *Historic Niagara Falls*.

8   Ibid.

9   Sir Richard Bonnycastle, *Canada and the Canadians* (London: 1849).

10   Ernest Green, *The Niagara Portage Road*.

11   National Archives of Canada, RG30, vol. 1.

12   Robert V. Nicholls, *The Erie & Ontario Rail Road*, C.R.H.A. News Report No. 118, January 1961.

13   Letter, George Redford, Superintendent *Erie & Ontario Rail Road* and Steamer *Zimmerman*, to J. Cummings, Reeve of Chippawa, January 11, 1857. Francis Petrie Collection, Niagara Falls Public Library.

14   Robert V. Nicholls, information obtained from Mr. Robert Brown.

15   *Historic Niagara Falls*.

16   Mrs. Roy Williams, Willoughby, Personal Scrap Book of History of Willoughby Township, Niagara Falls Public Library.

Queenston Ferries

1   Thomas Dickson, letter to His Excellency Francis Gore, Lieutenant-Governor of the Province of Upper Canada, York, April 3, 1816, Upper Canada State Papers RG1 E3, vol. 34B, p. 159.

2   Samuel Lewis, letter to His Honour Samuel Smith Esq., Administrator of the Government of the Province of Upper Canada, Queenston, August 6, 1818, Upper Canada State Papers RG1 E3, vol. 26.

3   Thomas Dickson, letter to his Excellency Sir Peregrine Maitland, May 5, 1832, Upper Canada State Papers RG1 E3, vol. 29A, National Archives of Canada.

4   Ibid., Upper Canada State Papers RG1 E3, vol. 34D.

5   Ibid., Upper Canada State Papers RG1 E3, vol. 29A.

6   Ibid., Upper Canada State Papers RG1 E3, vol. 94A.

7   Reverend Wye Smith, *Star Journal,* St. Catharines, January 11, 1906.

8   Upper Canada State Papers RG1 E3, vol. 94A.

9   Ibid., vol. 103.

Niagara Falls Ferries

1   Christian Schultz, *Travel on an Inland Voyage, --- in the year 1807 and 1808,* 2 vols. (N.Y.: Isaac Riley, 1810).

2   Letter, *New York Gazette,* dated Buffalo, July 14, 1812, *Documentary History of the Campaign on the Niagara Frontier in the Year 1812,* Lieutenant-Colonel Cruikshank, Part 3, page 127.

3   A letter from Upper Canada, Drummondville, December 20, 1838, from the *United States Journal.*

4   William H.G. Kingston, *Western Wanderings, or a pleasure tour in the Canadas* (London: Chapman and Hall, 1856).

5   Upper Canada State Papers RG1 E3, vol. 26.

6   Ibid.

7   Thomas Clark, letter to the Secretary to the Governor-in-Council, October 18, 1820, Upper Canada State Papers RG1 E3 vol. 2, No. 97, National Archives of Canada.

8   Executive Council, Administration of Lieutenant-Governor Sir Peregrine Maitland, January 23, 1822, Upper Canada State Papers RG1 E3 vol. 2.

9   Schedule of Leases of Mills and Ferries, Upper Canada State Papers RG1 E3 vol. 47.

10   Representation of 21 Manchester Inhabitants, about John Shutterburgh and Hammond, Archives of Ontario.

11   John Shutterburgh, endorsation of the inhabitants in the vicinity of the Falls as Lessee Ferryman between the Niagara Falls, March 15, 1842. Archives of Ontario.

12   Anthony Trollope, *North America* (London: Chapman and Hall 1862).

13   *Niagara Falls Gazette,* May 18, 1864.

14   Ibid., June 16, 1869.

Fort Erie Ferries

1   Duc de la Rochefoucault-Liancourt, *Travels in Canada in 1795.* Thirteenth Report of the Bureau of Archives for the Province of Ontario, 1916.

2   Charles D. Norton, *The Old Ferry at Black Rock,* a paper given before the Historical Society Club (Buffalo), December 14, 1883, Buffalo and Erie County Historical Society.

3   Upper Canada State Papers RG1 E3, vol. 61, National Archives of Canada. The references quoted in this chapter are in the Niagara Falls and Fort Erie Public Libraries.

4   Letter, James Kerby to Honourable J. Macauley, Inspector-General, Fort Erie, December 19, 1840, Upper Canada State Papers RG1 E3, vol. 43.

5   Charles D. Norton, *The Old Ferry at Black Rock.*

6   Tyrone Power, *Impressions of America during the years 1833 & 1834,* vol. 1 (London: 1836).

7   Upper Canada State Papers RG1 E3, vol. 43.

8   *The Old Ferry at Black Rock.*

9   Ibid.

10   Eric Heyl, *Early American Steamers.*

Queenston

1   Canniff Papers, Fragment of a diary. Quoted in Hazel C. Mathews, *The Mark of Honour.*

2   Janet Carnochan, *Names Only But Much More,* Niagara Historical Society Publication No. 27. n.d.

3   Memorial of Samuel Street to Peter Russell, Administrator of the Province of Upper Canada, August 25, 1787. Court of Appeals for Ontario, Part 1, 1894.

4   National Archives, Series C, vol. 272, page 124, as quoted in *Robert Hamilton* (Buffalo Historical Society, 1903), vol. 6 p. 82.

5   Lieutenant-Colonel E. Cruikshank, *Notes on the History of the Niagara District.*

6   Bruce G. Wilson, *Enterprises of Robert Hamilton* (Ottawa: Carleton University Press, 1983), p. 70.

7   Elizabeth Posthuma Simcoe, *Diary,* ed. Mary Quayle Innis (Toronto: 1965).

8   *Travel in Canada 1795.* Thirteenth Annual Report of the Bureau of Archives for the Province of Ontario. Edited with notes by William Renwick Riddell L.L.D. 1916, page 402.

9   *Enterprises of Robert Hamilton,* page 92.

10 The Military Reserve, or Chain Reserve, was a strip of land adjacent to the river, 66 feet wide, which was reserved for the Crown when the townships were surveyed. Above the escarpment the Reserve ran along the top of the broken bank of the gorge, and along the river's edge to Lake Erie. Below the escarpment it occupied the land from the river's edge to the top of the bank. Samuel Street had evidently established himself on this Reserve without permission of the Crown.

11 *Enterprises of Robert Hamilton.*

12 Ibid., page 71.

13 *Travels in Canada 1795.*

14 John Cousens Ogden, *A tour through Upper and Lower Canada, by a citizen of the United States...* (Litchfield: 1799), pp. 110-112.

15 John Maude, *Visit to the Falls of Niagara 1800.*

16 Christian Schultz, *Travels on an Inland Voyage...*

17 T.C. *A ride To Niagara.*

18 Ibid., T.C.

19 Lieutenant-Colonel E. Cruikshank, *Simcoe Papers,* vol. 1, page 247.

20 Niagara Historical Society Publication No. 25.

21 *Enterprises of Robert Hamilton.*

22 Thompson Papers, Isabel Walker Collection.

23 Lincoln County Surrogate Court Records, *Inventory of all the Goods, Chattels, Rights and Credits... of the late Honourable Robert Hamilton.* As quoted in *Enterprises of Robert Hamilton,* page 92.

Queenston and the War of 1812

1   *The Documentary History of the Campaign on the Niagara Frontier.* Letter Thomas Dickson, Robert Grant, James Kerby, to Messrs. Benjamin Barton, Rufus Spalding, Joshua Fairbanks, April 17, 1812; April 18, 1812, Part 3, p. 55.

2   Ibid., p. 125. The *New York Gazette,* July 24, 1812. Report from their Buffalo correspondent dated July 14, 1812.

3   Ibid., p. 193. Inspector-General Nicholas Frey to Governor Tompkins, August 19, 1812.

4   Ibid., Part 2, p. 97. Major Parmento Adams to General Porter.

5   Ibid., Part 3, p. 138. John Lovett to Joseph Alexander, Buffalo, November 4, 1812.

6   Ibid., Part 4, p. 8. Major-General Stephen Van Rensselaer to the Honourable William Eustis, United States Secretary of War, Lewiston, October 14, 1812.

7   Ibid., Part 4, p. 80. John Lovett to Joseph Alexander.

8   Ibid., Part 4, p. 10. Letter from the *Kingston Gazette* vol. 3, No. 48, Saturday October 18, 1812, sent to Kingston from Brown's Point, October 14, 1812.

9   National Archives of Canada. Major J.B. Clegg to Mr. Wm. Brock, October 14, 1812. Q317, pp. 203-04.

10 *Documentary History...* Part 4, p. 83. Major-General Van Rensselaer to Major-General Brock, October 14, 1812. Quoted in *Bonney's Historical Gleanings.*

11 Ibid., Part 4, p. 127. In *Poulsen's American Daily Advertiser.* November 24, 1812.

12   Ontario Legislative Assembly, Fifty-Eighth Annual Report of the Niagara Parks Commission 1944 (Toronto: 1946) pp. 12-14.

13   *Documentary History... Part 7*, p. 271. ''Observations from Lewiston'' in *Buffalo Express,* February 23, 1813; March 16, 1813.

14   Ibid., Part 7, p. 271. United States General McClure to the United States Secretary of War, December 12, 1813.

15   Ibid., Part 1, p. 176. Sir George Prevost to Vice-Admiral the Honourable Alexander Cochrane, Montreal, July 10, 1814.

16   Ibid., Part 2, p. 324. Account of Homes Burned in the Town of Niagara and on the Niagara Frontier by the Enemy, and the Supposed Valuation Thereof.

Queenston After the War of 1812

1   J.P. Merritt, *Biography of W.H. Merritt M.P.* (St. Catharines: E.S. Leavenworth, 1875), p. 38.

2   *Journal of Captain Richard Langslow,* in Buffalo and Erie County Historical Society Library.

3   E.A. Talbot, *Five Years Residence in the Canadas.*

4   John Howison as quoted in *The Niagara Portage Road.*

5   Stephen Otto, private paper on Francis Hall, 1983, unpub.

6   Colin Troup, *Postal Villages in the Niagara Peninsula,* a paper read at the Second Annual Niagara Peninsula History Conference, April 12-13, 1980 (St. Catharines: Brock University, 1980).

7   Upper Canada State Papers, State Book F.

8   Upper Canada State Papers RG1 E3, vol. 34D.

9   Upper Canada State Papers, State Book F, 25.

10   Ibid., p. 255.

11   Ibid., RG 1 E31, vol. 56.

12   Reverend W. Wye Smith, *Star Journal,* St. Catharines, January 11, 1906.

13   *Colonial Advocate,* Queenston, May 24, 1824, p. 2.

14   Stephen Otto.

15   James C. Morden, *Historic Niagara Falls.*

16   *Early American Steamers,* vol. 2.

17   W. Haldorson, Superintendent, Parks Canada, Niagara Region, *Sir Isaac Brock's Four Funerals,* unpub.

18   J.P. Merritt, *Biography of William Hamilton Merritt.*

19   Upper Canada State Papers RG1 E3, vol. 3.

20   Orville Luther Holley, *The Picturesque Tourist...*

21   Edwin C. Guillet, *Pioneer Travel in Upper Canada* (University of Toronto Press, 1963).

Queenston and the Lake Boats

1   Barlow Cumberland, *A Century of Sail and Steam on the Niagara River* (Toronto: Musson Book Company, n.d.).

2   A. James Rennie, *Niagara Township,* 1967.

3   Toronto *Mail and Empire,* August 8, 1915.

4   John M. Mills, *The Niagara, St. Catharines & Toronto Railway,* Upper Canada Railway Society, May 1967.

Chippawa

1   Ray Corry Bond, *Peninsula Village - A Story of Chippawa.*

2   Francis Parkman, *La Salle and the Discovery of the Great West* (Boston: 1890).

3   Henry R. Howland, quoting from *Diary of Sir William Johnson* in *Navy Island and the First Successors to the Griffon, Buffalo Historical Society, No. 1, 6,* p. 23.

4   From the *National Intelligencer* of Washington D.C., Jan. 1813, probably based on a Memoir of Dr. Tiffany, a former resident of the Province. In *Documentary History of the Campaign on the Niagara Frontier in the year 1813,* Part 1, p. 23.

5   Captain Enys, *Visit to Niagara,* Journal of Captain Enys, 29th Regiment, 1787. National Archives of Canada.

6   *Diary of Joseph Hadfield 1785,* edited by Douglas S. Robertson (Toronto: Hunter, Rose and Co., 1933).

7   Isaac Weld, *Travels Through the States of North America, and the provinces of Upper and Lower Canada, during the years 1795, 1796, and 1797.*

8   Elizabeth Simcoe, *Diary,* ed., Mary Quayle Innis.

9   Rochefoucault-Liancourt, *Travels in Canada 1795.*

10   Charles M. Snyder, ed., *Red and White on the New York Frontier, Insights from the Papers of Erastus Granger, Indian Agent 1807-1819* (Harrison, N.Y.: Harbor Hill Books, 1978).

11   Journals of the Legislative Assembly, Upper Canada, 26 Feb. 1897, Archives of Ontario.

12   *Remembrances of the Past - A Country Merchant,* Eva Elliott Tolan, *Niagara Falls Evening Review,* November 8, 1958.

Chippawa and the War of 1812

1   *Documentary History,* Part 4, p. 41. General Van Rensselaer to General Dearborn, October 12, 1812.

2   Ibid., Part 3, p. 187. From *New York Statesman,* March 29, 1813.

3   Ibid., Part 5, p. 274. From the *Buffalo Gazette,* June 1, 1813.

4   Ibid., Part 6, p. 184. Lieutentant-Colonel Thomas Clark to Lieutenant-Colonel Harvey, July 5, 1813.

5   Ibid., Part 2, p. 329.

6   War Losses Claims No. 1767, John Muirhead, dated Chippawa, 24th October 1815. National Archives of Canada.

Chippawa After the War of 1812

1   DeWitt Clinton, *Journal of a Tour.*

2   Barlow Cumberland, *A Century of Sail and Steam on the Niagara River.*

3   J.P. Merritt, *Biography of William Hamilton Merritt.*

4   Sixth Annual Report of the Grand River Navigation Co., 1841, p. 236.

Chippawa Becomes a Shipbuilding and Industrial Centre

1   Certificate of Erastus Parsons, January 4, 1826, National Archives of Canada.

2   Jesse Edgar Middleton, *The Province of Ontario - a History 1625-1927.* (Toronto: Dominion Publishing Co. Ltd., 1927), vol. 2, chapter 12.

3   Samuel Street Papers. Letter James Cummings to Samuel Street, January 13, 1840. Archives of Ontario.

4   John M. Mills, *Canadian Coastal and Inland Steam Vessels, 1809-1930* (Providence, R.I.: Steamship Historical Society of America Inc., 1932). Also, Eric Heyl, *Early American Steamers* (1956), vols. 1, 6.

5   Ray Corry Bond, *Peninsula Village.* From an advertisement. National Archives of Canada.

6   Ibid., *Peninsula Village.*

7   Hazel C. Mathews, *The Mark of Honour,* p. 21.

8   *Niagara Falls Gazette* files, Niagara Falls, New York Public Library.

Early Stamford Schools

1   Elizabeth Simcoe, *Diary,* ed., Mary Quayle Innis.

2   Hazel C. Mathews, *The Mark of Honour.*

3   Francis Goring's Date Book, Mary Goring Dann.

4   Mrs. Hagen, as told to Isabel Walker.

5   *James Thompson, his Cypher Book, 1798-1804.* Thompson Papers, Isabel Walker Collection.

6   Isabel Walker, *The Thompsons of Whirlpool Farm,* March 1976, unpub.

7   Ernest Green, *The Niagara Portage Road.*

8   Thompson Papers, Isabel Walker Collection.

9   *Documentary History of the Campaign on the Niagara Frontier in the Year 1812,* Part 3, p. 143.

10   Michael Gonder Sherk, *Early Pioneer Life in Upper Canada* (Toronto: William Briggs, 1905).

11   J.M. Crysler, *A Short History of the Township of Niagara, 1793-1893*. In *Niagara Advance*, 1943.

12   Reverend John Burns, from a document in the possession of W.A. Lorne Robinson.

13   *Family History and Early Reminiscences,* Niagara Historical Society Publication No.28.

14   Thompson Papers, Isabel Walker Collection. Angus Ray to James Thompson, December 6, 1837.

15   School Section No. 10, from information supplied by W.A. Lorne Robinson.

16   Grace M. Near, *Victoria School*, in *Niagara Falls Canada, a history.*

Early Stamford Churches

1   Robert Gourlay, *Statistical Account of Upper Canada.* n.d.

2   W.A.Lorne Robinson, *Stamford Presbyterian Church.*

3   Ernest Green, *Township No. 2 - Mount Dorchester, Stamford,* Ontario Historical Society Papers and Records, vol. 25.

4   Reverend Peter J. Darch, *The Protestant Churches*, in *Niagara Falls Canada, a history.*

5   W.A. Lorne Robinson, *Stamford Presbyterian Church.*

6   J.P. Merritt, *Biography of William Hamilton Merritt.*

7   Lorne C. Ball, *George Neal, A Number One Methodist in Upper Canada*, unpub. (1986).

8   Wilfred D. Warner, *Upper Canada's 1st Methodist, Niagara Circuit, 1795-1823,* unpub. (1988).

9   Ibid., Wilfred D. Warner.

10   Reverend Peter J. Darch, *The Protestant Churches.*

11   Lorne C. Ball, *George Neal, A Number One Methodist...*

12   Ibid.

13   Reverend Kenneth Moyer, *My Saddle Was My Study* (Elmira: the author, 1974).

14   Reverend Peter J. Darch, *The Protestant Churches.*

15   James C. Morden, *Historic Niagara Falls.*

16   Louis Blake Duff, *Hundredth Anniversary of Trinity Church, Chippawa 1920* (Welland: Trinity Church, 1920).

17   A.H. Young, Introduction to *Hundredth Anniversary of Trinity Church, Chippawa, 1920.*

18   James C. Morden, *Historic Niagara Falls.*

19   *Stamford Presbyterian Church, 200th Anniversary History.*

20   Ibid.

21   Ibid.

22   Ibid.

23   *150 Years of Christian Witness, a history of the Church of St. John the Evangelist,* 1970.

24   Ibid.

25   Ibid.

26   Reverend Percival Mayes, *The Story of the Historic Church of All Saints* (Niagara Falls: Lindsay Press, 1951).

27   Isabel Walker, *St. George's Anglican Church,* unpub.

28   Arnold A. MacAdorey, *The Roman Catholic Churches* in *Niagara Falls Canada, a history.*

An Early Stamford Merchant

1   Colonel Gother Mann, *Plan Shewing the Situation & Dimensions Proposed for Building Lots for Merchants and Traders in the King's reserve lands at Fort Erie in the Province of Upper Canada, June 1798.* National Archives of Canada.

2   Hugh Alexander to James Sinclair, Fort Erie, October 23, 1813, W.A.Lorne Robinson Papers.

3   *Documentary History,* Part 5, p. 82.

4   Ibid., Part 9, p. 87. From A Statement of the Services of Major-General Richard Say Armstrong.

5   Will of Hugh Alexander, October 30, 1817. W.A. Lorne Robinson Papers.

6   *Documentary History*, Part 5, pp. 263, 267.

7   Lieutenant-Colonel Ernest Cruikshank, *Memorials of Fort Erie and Early Navigation*, October 30, 1817. W.A. Lorne Robinson Papers.

8   *Documentary History,* Part 5, p. 267. *National Advocate,* New York, June 12, 1813. From a postscript to the *Batavia Republican Advertiser.*

9   Thompson Papers, Isabel Walker Collection.

10   *Memorials of Fort Erie and Early Navigation.* Deposition of Benjamin Willson, W.A. Lorne Robinson Papers.

11   *The Spectator*, St. David's, March 16, 1816. Wilfred Woodruff Collection.

12   *Will of Hugh Alexander,* W.A. Lorne Robinson Papers.

Stamford Village Plan

1   *Stamford Presbyterian Church.*

2   *The Spectator,* Richard Cockerell, ed. Printed and Published by the Proprietors at the Village of St. David's, Upper Canada, July 19, 1816.

Stamford Green

1   Francis Petrie, *Captain H. Dee Assured Stamford Green Stays, Niagara Falls Review.*

2   W.A. Lorne Robinson, *Stamford Green.* January 19, 1976, unpub.

3   George Caswell, letter to George Seibel, September 21, 1988.

The Portage Road Oak Tree

1   *Stamford Presbyterian Church.*

2   Letter. George W. Dalby, Superintendent of Parks, The Niagara Parks Commission to J.L. Collinson, Chief Administrative Officer, City of Niagara Falls, June 1, 1983.

3   Letter, George Seibel, Chairman Niagara Falls Heritage Foundation, to Wayne Thomson, Mayor, City of Niagara Falls, June 12, 1983.

4   *Niagara Falls Review,* June 21, 1983.

5   Letter, Lee Shipp, Director of Publicity and Advertising, Niagara Parks School of Horticulture Alumni Association, to J.L. Collinson, Chief Administrative Officer, City of Niagara Falls, July 12, 1983.

Drummondville

1   Reverend Peter J. Darch, *The Protestant Churches.*

2   *Documentary History,* Part 2, p. 228.

BIBLIOGRAPHY

Adamson, Jeremy E. *Niagara – Two Centuries of Changing Attitudes, 1697-1901.* Washington: Corcoran Gallery of Art, 1985.

Alexander, Sir J.E. 14th Regiment. ''Sleigh Ride in Canada West, 1843.'' Clearwater Collection, Niagara Falls New York Public Library.

Antonio, April Petrie, ed. *The Shrine of Our Lady of Peace.* Niagara Falls, Ontario: The Shrine of Our Lady of Peace, 1987.

Appel, Reverend Hugh, et al. *Stamford Presbyterian Church,* Niagara Falls, Ontario: Stamford Presbyterian Church, 1983.

Ball, Lorne C. *George Neal A Number One Methodist in Upper Canada.* Niagara Falls: 1986.

Bigsby, Dr. John. *The Shoe and the Canoe.* London: Chapman and Hall, 1850.

Bond, Ray Corry. *Peninsula Village.* Chippawa: Village of Chippawa, 1963.

----. Bond Papers. J.C. Bond, Ottawa.

Bonnycastle, Sir Richard Henry. *The Canadas in 1841.* London: 1841.

Bradley, A.G. *Sir Guy Carleton.* Toronto: University of Toronto Press, 1965.

Burtniak, John, and Turner, Wesley B. ed. *Villages in the Niagara Peninsula.* Paper from Second Annual Niagara Peninsula History Conference, Brock University, 1980. St. Catharines: Brock University, 1980.

----. *Immigration and Settlement in the Niagara Peninsula.* Paper from Third Annual Niagara Peninsula History Conference, Brock University, 1981. St. Catharines: Brock University, 1981.

----. *Religion and Churches in the Niagara Peninsula.* Paper from Fourth Annual Niagara Peninsula History Conference, Brock University, 1982. St. Catharines: Brock University, 1982.

----. *United Empire Loyalists in the Niagara Peninsula.* Paper from Sixth Annual Niagara Peninsula History Conference, Brock University, 1984. St. Catharines: Brock University, 1984.

Campbell, Patrick. *Travels in the Interior Inhabited Parts of North America in the Years 1791 and 1792.* Edinburgh: Guthrie, 1793.

Carnochan, Janet. ''Inscriptions and Graves in the Niagara Peninsula''. In Niagara Historical Society Publication Number 19. Niagara-on-the-Lake: n.d.

----. ''Names Only But Much More''. In Niagara Historical Society Publication Number 27. Niagara-on-the-Lake: n.d.

Chambers, William. *Things as they are in America.* London: William and Robert Chambers, 1854.

Clark, John. ''Memoirs of Colonel John Clark of Port Dalhousie.'' In Ontario Historical Society Papers and Records, Vol. 7. Toronto: n.d.

Clearwater Collection, Niagara Falls New York Public Library.

Clinton, George W. ''Journal of a Tour, 1826''. In Buffalo and Erie County Historical Society Publication Number 14. Buffalo: n.d.

Coke, Lieutenant E.T. *A Subaltern's Furlough.* London: 1833.

Combe, George. *Notes on the United States of America in 1838-39-40.* Edinburgh: Maclachlan, Stewart & Company, 1841.

Coombs, A.E. *History of the Niagara Peninsula and the new Welland Canal.* Toronto: 1930.

Crèvecoeur, Hector, St. John de. Description of the falls of Niagara in a letter to his son under date of July 1785. *Magazine of American History,* October 1878, pp. 605-613. In Dow, Charles Mason. *Anthology and Bibliography of Niagara Falls.* Albany: The State of New York, 1921.

Cruikshank, E.A. ''Ten Years of the Colony of Niagara.'' In Niagara Historical Society Publication Number 17. Niagara-on-the-Lake: n.d.

----. ''Notes on the History of the District of Niagara 1791-93.'' In Niagara Historical Society Publication Number 26. Niagara-on-the-Lake: n.d.

----. ed. *The Documentary History of the Campaign on the Niagara Frontier – 1812-1814,* Volumes 1-9. Welland: Lundy's Lane Historical Society, 1896-1910.

----. ed. *The Correspondence of Lieutenant-Governor John Graves Simcoe,* 5 Vols. Toronto: Ontario Historical Society, 1923-31.

Crysler, J.M. ''A Short History of the Township of Niagara.'' In *Niagara Advance.* Niagara-on-the-Lake: 1943.

Cumberland, Barlow, *A Century of Sail and Steam on the Niagara River.* Toronto: Musson Book Co., 1913.

Darch, Reverend Peter J. "The Protestant Churches in Niagara Falls Canada." In *Niagara Falls Canada, a history.* Niagara Falls, Ontario: Kiwanis Club of Stamford, 1967.

DeVeaux, Samuel. *The Falls of Niagara – a Tourist Guide.* Buffalo: 1939.

Dimitroff, Terry Curtis. "The Portage Era of the Niagara River Region and the Development of Queenston." A Thesis submitted to the Department of Geography in partial fulfilment of the requirements for the degree of Bachelor of Arts. Brock University, 1968.

Dow, Charles Mason, LL.D. *Anthology and Bibliography of Niagara Falls.* Albany: The State of New York, 1921. 2 Vols.

Duff, Louis Blake. *Hundredth Anniversary of Trinity Church, Chippawa, 1920.* Welland: Trinity Church, 1920.

Duncan, John M. *Travels through part of the United States and Canada in 1818 and 1819.* Glasgow: 1823.

Dunnigan, Brian Leigh. *Siege – 1759 The Campaign Against Niagara.* Youngstown: Old Fort Niagara Association, 1986.

----. "Portaging Niagara". In *Inland Seas,* Vol. 42, No. 3. Cleveland: Great Lakes Historical Society, 1986.

Eccles, W.J. *The Canadian Frontier 1534-1760.* Albuquerque: University of New Mexico Press, 1976.

Encyclopedia Canadiana. Ottawa: The Grolier Society of Canada, 1963.

Ensminger, Scott. *The Caves of Niagara County, New York.* Niagara Falls, New York: The Niagara County Historical Society, 1987.

Enys, Captain. "Visit to Niagara". Handwritten journal of Captain Enys, 29th Regiment, 1787. National Archives of Canada.

Flint, James. *Letters from America.* Edinburgh: W. and C. Tait, 1822.

Fowler, Thomas. *Journal of a Tour Through British America to the Falls of Niagara.* Aberdeen: Smith, 1832.

Galinée, René Bréhant de. *Explorations of the Great Lakes, 1669-1670.* James H. Coyne, transl. and ed. Ontario Historical Society Papers and Records, Vol. 4. Toronto: 1903.

Goring, Francis. "Diary of Francis Goring." In Niagara Historical Society Publication Number 36. Niagara-on-the-Lake: 1924.

Gourlay, Robert F. *Statistical Account of Upper Canada.* London: Simpkin and Marshall, 1822.

Grand River Navigation Co. *Sixth Annual Report.*

Green, Ernest, F.R. Hist. S. "The Niagara Portage Road." In Ontario Historical Society Papers and Records, Vol. 23. Toronto: 1926.

----. "Township No. 2 – Mount Dorchester – Stamford." In Ontario Historical Society Papers and Records, Vol. 25. Toronto: 1929.

----. "Told by a Grandmother, Elizabeth Hewlett (Fralick) Green." In *Niagara Falls Evening Review,* February 15, 1930.

----. "The Old Bath House." In *Niagara Falls Evening Review,* April 23, 1930.

Greenhill, Ralph, and Mahoney, Thomas D. *Niagara.* Toronto: University of Toronto Press, 1969.

Guillet, Edwin C. *Pioneer Travel in Upper Canada.* Toronto: University of Toronto Press,, 1963.

Haldorson, Walter. "Sir Isaac Brock's Four Funerals." In *Niagara Advance.* Niagara-on-the-Lake: 1975.

Heriot, George. *Travels through the Canadas.* London: Richards Phillips, 1807.

Heritage. "There is a Tavern in the Town." In Vol. 3, No. 2. New York: New York State Historical Association, 1986.

Heyl, Eric. *Early American Steamers,* 6 Vols. Buffalo: Erik Heyl, 1953-1967.

Hill, Daniel G. *The Freedom Seekers.* Agincourt: The Book Society of Canada Ltd., 1981.

Holley, John Milton and Whittlesey, Charles. *Early History of Cleveland, Ohio.* Cleveland: Fairbanks Benedict, 1867.

Holley, Oliver Luther. *The Picturesque Tourist.* New York: J. Disturnell, 1844.

Holt, William. ed. *Niagara Falls Canada, a history.* Niagara Falls, Ontario: Kiwanis Club of Stamford, 1967.

Howland, Henry R. "Robert Hamilton, the Founder of Queenston." In Vol. 6 of the Publications of the Buffalo Historical Society. Edited by Frank H. Severance. Buffalo: 1903.

Hulbert, Archer Butler. *The Niagara River.* New York and London: Whitaker, 1823.

Innis, Mary Quayle, ed., *Mrs. Simcoe's Diary.* Toronto: Macmillan, 1965.

Izard, Ralph. *An Account of a Journey to Niagara, Montreal, and Quebec, in 1765.* New York: Osborn, 1846.

Jackson, John N. and Burtniak, John, *Railways in the Niagara Peninsula.* Belleville: Mika Publishing Co., 1978.

Jefferys, C.W. *The Picture Gallery of Canadian History,* Vols. 1-3. Toronto: Ryerson Press, 1950.

Kingston William H.G. *Western Wanderings, or a pleasure tour in the Canadas.* London: Chapman and Hall, 1856.

Langslow, Richard. "Journal of Captain Richard Langslow." In Vol. 5 of the Publications of the Buffalo Historical Society. Buffalo, 1904.

Lees, George. George Lees Journal, July 23, 1768.

Liancourt, la Rochefoucault, François Alexander, duc d'Etaisse. *Travel in Canada, 1795*. London: R. Phillips, 1799.

MacAdorey, Arnold, A. "The Roman Catholic Churches". In *Niagara Falls Canada – a history*. Niagara Falls, Ontario: Kiwanis Club of Stamford, 1967.

McKinsey, Elizabeth. *Niagara Falls Icon of the American Sublime*. Cambridge: Cambridge University Press, 1985.

Martineau, Harriett. *Retrospect of Western Travel*. London: Saunders and Otley, 1838.

Mathews, Hazel C. *Mark of Honour*. Canadian Studies in History and Government, Vol. 6. Toronto: University of Toronto Press, 1965.

Maude, John. *Visit to the Falls of Niagara in 1800*. London: Longman, Rees, Orme, Brown and Green. 1826.

Mayes, Reverend Percival. *The Story of the Historic Church of All Saints*. Niagara Falls, Ontario: Lindsay Press, ˙1951.

Merritt, J.P. *Biography of William Hamilton Merritt*. St. Catharines: E.S. Leavenworth, 1875.

Mewburn, Amy. et al. *150 Years of Christian Witness 1820-1970*. Niagara Falls, Ontario: Church of St. John the Evangelist, 1970.

Middleton, Jesse, Edgar. *The Province of Ontario – a History 1615-1927*. Toronto: The Dominion Publishing Company, Ltd., 1927.

Mills, John M. *The Niagara, St. Catharines & Toronto Railway*. Toronto: Upper Canada Railway Society, Ontario Electric Railway Historical Association, 1967.

----. *Canadian Coastal and Inland Steam Vessels 1809-1930*. Providence, Rhode Island: The Steamship Historical Society of America Inc., 1979.

Moogk, Peter N. Ph.D. "John Burch, Industrial Pioneer." In *Niagara Advance Historical Issue*. Niagara-on-the-Lake: 1985.

Morden, James. *Historic Niagara Falls*. Niagara Falls, Ontario: Lundy's Lane Historical Society, 1932.

----. *Historical Monuments and Observatories of Lundy's Lane and Queenston Heights*. Thorold: Lundy's Lane Historical Society, 1932.

Moyer, Reverend Kenneth. *My Saddle Was My Study*. Elmira: Reverend Kenneth Moyer, 1974.

Near, Grace M. "Victoria School". In *Niagara Falls Canada, a history*. Niagara Falls, Ontario: Kiwanis Club of Stamford, 1967.

Newspapers: *Colonial Advocate, New York Gazette, Niagara Advance, Niagara Chronicle, Niagara Gleaner, Niagara Falls Gazette, Niagara Falls Evening Review, Niagara Herald, Mail and Empire*.

Niagara Escarpment Commission. *Cuesta*. 1986.

Niagara Historical Society Publications. Niagara-on-the-Lake.

Nicholls, Robert V.V. "The Erie and Ontario Rail Road." In *C.R.H.A. News Report*. Toronto: January 1961.

Norton, Charles D. *The Old Ferry at Black Rock*. Buffalo: Historical Society Club, 1863.

O'Heare, Sister M. Maurice. "Loretto Convent". In *Niagara Falls Canada, a history*. Niagara Falls, Ontario: Kiwanis Club of Stamford, 1967.

Ontario. *Third Ontario Archives Report, 1905*. Toronto, 1905.

Otto, Stephen. Private papers.

Owen, David A. *Fort Erie – 1764-1823 – An Historical Guide*. Fort Erie: The Niagara Parks Commission, 1986.

Panko, Andrew, and Bowen, Peter. *Niagara St. Catharines & Toronto Electric Railway in Pictures*. Niagara-on-the-Lake: NiagaRail Publications, Limited, 1984.

Parkman, Francis. *LaSalle and the Discovery of the Great West*. Boston: 1890.

Petrie, Francis. "First a playground, Stamford Green now a site for war memorials". In *Niagara Falls Review*, April 22, 1974.

Philippe, Louis, King of France, 1830-48. *Diary of My Travels in North America*. Translated from the French by Stephen Becker. New York: Delacorte Press, 1977.

Rennie, A. James. *Niagara Township*. Niagara-on-the-Lake: Niagara Township, 1967.

Robinson, W.A. Lorne. Papers and records.

Rogers, Robert, Major. *A Concise Account of North America, 1763*. London: J. Millan, 1765.

Seibel, George A. *300 Years Since Hennepin – Niagara Falls in Art, 1678-1978*. Niagara Falls, Ontario: Niagara Falls Heritage Foundation, 1978.

----. *Ontario's Niagara Parks – 100 Years*. Niagara Falls, Ontario: The Niagara Parks Commission, 1985.

Severance, Frank H. *Studies of the Niagara Frontier*. Buffalo: Buffalo Historical Society, 1911.

Sherk, Michael Gonder. *Early Pioneer Life in Upper Canada*. Toronto: William Briggs, 1905.

Schultz, Christian. *Travels on an inland voyage.* New York: Isaac Riley, 1810.

Shirreff, Patrick. *A Tour through North America.* Edinburgh: 1835.

Snyder, Charles M., ed. *Red and White on the Niagara Frontier.* Harrison, New York: Harbor Hill Books, 1978.

Spectator, The. St. David's: March 16, 1816.

Stansbury, Philip. *A pedestrian tour.* New York: Meyers and Smith, 1822.

Stevens, G.R. *The Incompleat Canadian.* Toronto: G.R. Stevens, 1965.

Stewart, Walter. *True Blue – The Loyalist Legend.* Toronto: Collins, 1985.

Stone, William Leete. *From New York to Niagara – Journal of a Tour.* Buffalo: Buffalo Historical Society, 1910.

Sutcliffe, Robert. *Travels in some parts of North America in the years, 1804, 1805 and 1806.* Philadelphia: B. and T. Kite, 1812.

Talbot, E.A. *Five Years Residence in Canada.* London: Longman, Hurst, Rees, Orme, Brown and Green, 1824.

Thompson Papers. Isabel Walker Collection.

Tolan, Eva Elliott. "A Country Merchant". In *Niagara Falls Evening Review,* Nov. 8, 1950.

T.C. "A Ride to Niagara." In *The Portfolio,* July, August, September, 1810.

Trollope, Anthony. *North America.* London: Chapman and Hall, 1862.

Troup, Colin *Postal Villages in the Niagara Peninsula.* Paper from Second Annual Niagara Peninsula History Conference, Brock University. St. Catharines: Brock University, 1980.

Upper Canada State Papers. National Archives of Canada. Ottawa.

Van Slyke, Dorothy. *Forest, River, Early Settlers.* Niagara Falls, Ontario: Niagara Falls Public Library, 1984.

Van Steen, Marcus. *Governor Simcoe and his Lady.* Toronto: Hodder and Stoughton, 1968.

Vinal, Theodora. *Niagara Portage – From Past to Present.* Buffalo: Henry Stewart, 1948.

Volpi, Charles P. de. *The Niagara Peninsula.* Montreal: DEV SCO Publications Ltd., 1966.

Walker, Isabel. *The Thompsons of Whirlpool Farm.* Niagara Falls, Ontario: 1976.

Warner, Wilfred D. *Upper Canada's 1st Methodist, Niagara Circuit 1795-1823.* Niagara Falls: 1988.

Weld, Isaac. *Travel through the States of North America, and the provinces of Upper and Lower Canada, during the years 1795, 1796 and 1797.* London: Stockdale, 1799.

Whalen, Dwight. "The Restless Tombs of Isaac Brock." In *Canadian Frontier.* Langley, B.C.: 1973.

Whitfield, Faye Vernette, B.A. (Hons.), Dip. Ed. "The Origins of the Settlement of Niagara-on-the-Lake." Thesis in partial fulfilment towards Master of Arts degree, McMaster University, 1986.

Williams, Mrs. Roy. Personal Scrap Book.

Wilson, Bruce, G. *Enterprises of Robert Hamilton.* Ottawa: Carleton University Press, 1983.

Zaslow, Morris, ed. *The Undefended Border – Upper Canada and the War of 1812.* Toronto: The Macmillan Company of Canada Limited, 1964.

Appendix

FAMILY NOTES

The following family records compiled by Ernest Green have been reprinted with the permission of the Ontario Historical Society. They were first published in 1929 in Volume 25 of the Society's Papers and Records.

Supplementary notes to the Ernest Green records have been contributed by Mrs. Roy Summers. Her notes are printed under the heading Notes, at the end of the Ernest Green record for each family.

In addition, Mrs. Summers has contributed material on some families not included in the Ernest Green records. These entries are marked in each case with the bracketed initials, (ES) for Esther Summers.

Mrs. Summers' sources are listed in full in the bibliography which is printed here following Ernest Green's "Reference Code."

REFERENCE CODE

To avoid a multiplicity of foot-notes the following code of references and authorities is used in the succeeding pages.

T - Tradition

LP- Upper Canada Land Petitions in the National Archives Ottawa.

"A" - Upper Canada Land Book "A," National Archives, Ottawa.

"B," "C" and "F" - Upper Canada Land Books, National Archives, Ottawa.

OA3 - 3rd Report, Ontario Bureau of Archives, 1905.

OA13 - 13th Report, Ontario Bureau of Archives, 1916.

DMS - *Diary of Mrs. John Graves Simcoe.*

ECNP - *Early Churches of the Niagara Peninsula* (Carnochan), Ontario Historical Society's Papers and Records, Vol.8, 1907.

HN - *History of Niagara (Carnochan).*

JHT - *Jubilee History of Thorold.*

LAB - *Lincoln at Bay* (Green).

OBF - *Officers of the British Forces in Canada, 1812-1815* (Irving)

NHS17 - *Ten Years of the Colony of Niagara* (Cruikshank). Niagara Historical Society Publications No. 17.

NHS19 - *Inscriptions and Graves in the Niagara Peninsula* (Carnochan). Niagara Historical Society Publication No.19.

NHS22 - Some Graves at Lundy's Lane (Green). Niagara Historical Society Publication No. 22.

NHS26 - *Notes on the History of the Niagara District, 1791-1793* (Cruikshank). Niagara Historical Society Publication No.26.

NHS38 - Records of Niagara, 1778-1783 (Cruikshank). Niagara Historical Society Publication No.38.

NPR - *The Niagara Portage Road* (Green). Ontario Historical Society's Papers and Records, Vol. 23, 1926.

WCH - *Welland County History*

BIBLIOGRAPHY
for Mrs. Esther Summers' Material

Ancaster Township Historical Society. *Ancaster's Heritage.* Ancaster: The Society, 1970.

Annals of the Forty: nos. 3-9: *Loyalist and Pioneer Families of West Lincoln, 1783-1833.* Grimsby Historical Society, 1952-58.

Askin, John. *The John Askin Papers;* edited by Milo M. Quaife. Detroit Library Commission, 1928. 2 vols.

Avery, Joseph. *Visit of Rev. Joseph Avery, 1805.* In Buffalo Historical Society *Publications,* v.6, 1903, pp. 223-30.

Bingham, Robert W. *The Cradle of the Queen City; a History of Buffalo to the Incorporation of the City.* In Buffalo Historical Society *Publications,* v.31, 1931.

Bond, Ray Corry. *Peninsula Village; the Story of Chippawa.* Chippawa: The Author, 1963.

Brown, Mabel (Bacon) Warner and Wilfred D. Warner. *Warner Genealogy.* Niagara Falls, Ont., Wilfred D. Warner, 1987.

Canniff, William. *The Medical Profession in Upper Canada, 1783-1850.* Toronto: William Briggs, 1894.

Carnochan, Janet, ed. *Early Churches in the Niagara Peninsula, Stamford and Chippawa, with Marriage Records of Thomas Cummings and Extracts from the Cummings' Papers.* In Ontario Historical Society *Papers and Records,* v.8, 1907, pp. 149-225.

Corwin, Edward Tanjore. *Corwin Genealogy.* New York: S.W. Green, 1872.

Covell, Lemuel. *Visit of Rev. Lemuel Covell to Western New York and Canada, 1803.* In Buffalo Historical Society *Publications,* v.6, 1903, pp. 207-16.

Cruikshank, E.A. *A Memoir of Colonel the Honourable James Kerby, his Life in Letters.* Welland County Historical Society *Papers and Records,* v.4, 1931.

Cruikshank, E.A., ed. *Petitions for Grants of Land, 1792-6.* In Ontario Historical Society *Papers and Records,* v.24, 1927, pp. 17-144.

Cruikshank, E.A., ed. *Petitions for Grants of Land in Upper Canada. Second series, 1796-99.* In Ontario Historical Society *Papers and Records,* v.26, 1930, pp. 97-379.

Cruikshank, E.A., comp. *The Settlement of the Township of Fort Erie, Now Known as the Township of Bertie.* In Welland County Historical Society *Papers and Records,* v.5, 1938, pp. 18-90.

Crysler, John Morden. *History of the Crysler Family Who Settled in the Township of Niagara.* Niagara Township: *Niagara Advance,* 1936.

Durham, Davis Godfrey, and Mabel Kamfoly-St. Angelo. *James Durham, U.E., of Niagara, and his descendants in the United States and Canada (1740-1987).* Wilmington, Delaware: The Author, 1988.

Finch, Jessie Howell, comp. *The Ancestral Lines of Chester Everts Howell, 1867-1949, of Elmira, New York, U.S.A.* Elmira: Howell Associates, 1965.

Frank, Robert. *A Genealogical Letter of Robert Frank, 1850;* ed. by Faxon R. Dean. In *Ontario Register,* v.4, no. 2, 1971, pp. 113-16.

Green, Kathryn M. *A Nevills Genealogy.* Jackson, Mich.: The Author, 1987.

Historical Society of St. Catharines. *The Mini-Atlas of Early Settlers in the District of Niagara, 1782-1876.* St. Catharines: The Society, 1983.

Hunter, A.F., ed. *The Probated Wills of Men Prominent in the Public Affairs of Early Upper Canada.* In Ontario Historical Society *Papers and Records,* v.23, 1926, pp. 328-59.

Hunter, A.F., ed. *The Probated Wills of Persons Prominent in the Public Affairs of Early Upper Canada. Second Paper.* In Ontario Historical Society *Papers and Records,* v.24, 1927, pp. 381-409.

Kalar, Vincent H. *Kalar Family History and Pedigree Chart;* rev. ed. Camlachie: The Author, 1987.

Morden, James C. *Historic Niagara Falls.* Niagara Falls, Ont.: The Lundy's Lane Historical Society, 1932.

Penrose, Maryly Barton. *Baumann/Bowman Family of the Mohawk, Susquehanna and Niagara Rivers.* Franklin Park: Liberty Bell Associates, 1977.

Perry, Queen M. *The History of the Chambers Family of Niagara Falls, Canada, a Mayflower Family; including Genealogies of Related Families: James Slaght (Slecht), U.E., Nicholas Outhouse (Van Uythuysen), U.E., James Smith, U.E., Rev. James Boyd.* San Antonio: The Author, 1983.

Petrie, Francis. "Historic Farm House Destroyed by Fire – Built by Early Stamford Township Settler." In *Niagara Falls Review,* December 14, 1981, p.5.

Poole, Lilly Blackwell Lundy. *Lundy Genealogy, 1741-1945.* 1945.

Reid, William D. *The Loyalists in Ontario; the Sons and Daughters of the American Loyalists of Upper Canada.* Lambertville, N.J.: Hunterdon House, 1973.

Roberts, Phoebe. *Phoebe Roberts' Diary of a Quaker Missionary Journey to Upper Canada;* ed. by Leslie R. Gray. In Ontario Historical Society *Ontario History,* v.42, no.1, 1950, pp.7-46.

Roebuck, Arthur W. *The Macklems of Chippawa.* Toronto: The Author, 1969.

Russell, Peter. *The Correspondence of the Hon. Peter Russell, with Allied Documents Relating to His Administration of the Government of Upper Canada During the Official Term of Lieut.-Governor J.G. Simcoe while on leave of absence;* collected and edited for the Ontario Historical Society by E.A. Cruikshank and A.F. Hunter. Toronto: Ontario Historical Society, 1932.

Scovell, J. Boardman. *A Short History of the Niagara Portage.* Lewiston; Rotary Club of Lewiston, New York – Queenston, Ontario: 1949, 1951.

Severance, Frank H. *An Old Frontier of France: the Niagara Region and Adjacent Lands Under French Control.* New York: Dodd, 1917. Buffalo Historical Society *Publications,* v. 20 and v. 21.

Scherck, Michael Gonder. *Pen Pictures of Early Pioneer Life in Upper Canada,* by A "Canuck" (of the Fifth Generation). Toronto: W. Briggs, 1905.

Simcoe, John Graves. *The Correspondence of Lieut.-Governor John Graves Simcoe, with Allied Documents Relating to His Administration of the Government of Upper Canada;* collected and edited by E.A. Cruikshank. Toronto: Ontario Historical Society, 1923-31. 5 vols.

Stamford Presbyterian Church, Niagara Falls, Ont. *Stamford Historic Sites Tour, Saturday, June 29, 1985.* Niagara Falls, Ont.: The Church, 1985.

Swiggett, Howard. *War Out of Niagara: Walter Butler and the Tory Rangers.* New York: Columbia University Press, 1933.

United Empire Loyalist Centennial Committee. *The Centennial of the Settlement of Upper Canada by the United Empire Loyalists, 1784-1884; the Celebrations at Adolphustown, Toronto and Niagara, with an Appendix Containing a Copy of the U.E. List, Preserved in the Crown Lands Department at Toronto.* Toronto: Rose Publishing Company, 1885.

Wilson, Pearl. *Irish John Willson and Family, Loyalists.* In Ontario Historical Society *Papers and Records,* v. 31, 1936, pp. 228-42.

Woodruff, Norris Counsell. *Twelve Generations from the Colony of Connecticut in New England and the Province of Upper Canada, 1636-1959; a Woodruff Genealogy.* Hamilton: The Author, 1959.

Yeager, William, and Orrena Buchner Hanley, eds. *Sources in Buchner-Boughner Genealogy.* Norfolk Historical Society *Genealogical Paper,* no. 7, 1977.

Young, A.H., ed. *The Parish Register of Kingston, Upper Canada, 1785-1811;* edited with notes and an introduction for the Kingston Historical Society. Kingston: The Society/British Whig Publishing Company, 1921.

FAMILY NOTES

The following notes, gathered from various sources are intended to supplement the outline story of the settlement of Stamford by giving more intimate particulars concerning some of the pioneer families, and also to provide a guide for the researches of those who may desire to compile genealogical or biographical data. They are given chiefly as "raw material" and little attempt has been made to put them in narrative form.

The chief sources from which the notes are derived are the Upper Canada Law Books and the Upper Canada Land Petitions in the Public Archives of Canada (1989 National Archives) at Ottawa. These collections constitute a veritable mine of information, only the surface of which has been touched by historians.

The Land Petitions are mostly for secondary grants. The settlers were given their original lots on personal application, when their identities and loyalty were vouched for by Colonel Butler and other officers under whom they had served, or on production of army discharge papers. It does not seem to have occurred to the Loyalists that the stories of their services, sufferings and losses were worth telling for their own sakes. Only when they sought additional allottments of land, to complete the grants to which they were entitled under the general rules, or in recognition of special services or unusual family circumstances, did they put their stories in written form. Many of these old statements are awkwardly composed and ill-written, yet in their crude simplicity they have a dignity and convincing force that would probably be lost in more polished recitals.

After reading a number of these petitions, one is tempted to the impression that the demands of the petitioners fully equalled their deserts. They were "good askers." But it must not be forgotten that most of these people had three-fold claims upon the consideration of the government - they had sacrificed properties and improvements to values far in excess of what they might hope to obtain in the form of wild land in Canada, they had given long and extremely arduous service as fighting-men, and they were the settler-founders of a new colony. Any one of these considerations should have entitled the petitioner to a substantial grant. In our day, though virgin land is of much greater value, it is given freely to the war veteran and the immigrant homesteader. We can hardly criticise the old Ranger, who had abandoned a good farm on the Susquehanna, fought the King's battles for seven years and then brought a large family into the new country, if he sought to obtain every acre of good land for which he could put forward a plausible claim. Certainly the deserts of the least of these was greater than those of some of the Family Compact parasites to whom grants were made in terms of, not hundreds, but thousands of acres a few years later.

The Executive Council subjected the petitions to keen scrutiny. Alleged military service had to be substantiated by discharge papers or the evidence of officers under whom the claimant had served; the date of arrival in this province had to be established by certificate from a Justice of the Peace; the uniform loyalty and good conduct of the petitioner and his industry as a settler had to be proved, and he must have taken the oath of allegiance. The son or daughter of a Loyalist had to prove his or her paternity, and, because of the deaths of many parents by war or privation, the scattering of families and former neighbours, and the total lack of registration of births, marriages and deaths,documentary evidence of such characters was often very difficult or quite impossible to procure. Numerous petitions were laid over, or even refused, for lack of some detail of corroborative evidence. Other refusals were based on such grounds as "the petitioner has received all the lands to which he is entitled," "it appears that the petitioner's children are illegitimate," "the U.E. List is closed." etc., etc.

Trivial claims were promptly disallowed. If land previously granted had proved too swampy for cultivation, additional acreage in a new location was sometimes ordered, - the unsuitability of the first grant being proved by magistrate's certificate. In neighbouring townships additional grants were sometimes allowed in lieu of lands broken by the rocky face of the "mountain," and consideration was given to the claims of those whose forested land had been visited by hurricanes and rendered almost impossible to clear by the only means available to the settler.

Two men who had each secured land in two different localities asked for more acreage on the plea that they had not enough good land in either place to make a good farm. They were refused. Having passed examination in all such particulars, land petitions were finally referred to the Crown officers who searched all the records to make sure that no duplication should occur and a claimant be awarded lands twice on the same account.

Well might the recipient of a lot or two of "waste lands of the Crown," although exempt from payment of fees if he were a U.E., consider that he had been put to much inconvenience and anxiety in complying with all the requirements of the regulations! Happily for Stamford people, the seat of government remained at Niagara, until most of them were firmly established in possession of their lands. As in the securing of their final patents, they went to the land office by groups of neighbours, mutually supporting each other with identifications and other evidence. At the foot of one petition may be seen a post script that the petitioner "awaited without the Council door." His state of suspense while that august body was formulating judgment upon the claim that represented a large part - possibly all - of his worldly possession, and his mingled hope and fear that he might be called into the dread presence of the Lieutenant-Governor or Administrator, surrounded by the Chief Justice and other Councillors, may be dimly imagined but cannot be described.

Even a hearing before the Land Board was an ordeal not without its terrors, as the experience of Staats Springsteen (q.v.) indicates. These frontiersmen - farmers of the old colonies, lately trained in savage warfare, with a post-graduate course in forest pioneering, were ill-prepared to render instinctive deference to all the official and personal punctilios of civil and military functionaries, often newly-appointed and hypersensitive to their dignities.

On the whole, the settler usually presented his case with a straightforward truth and simplicity that commanded respect. Those who sat in judgment on his claim included some who had known him in times of war and privation and had, perhaps, been his fellow sufferers. If his petition was ill-spelled and worse written, and, not infrequently, signed with a mark, they knew that he had been handling the axe, the plough and the rifle on the edge of civilization at an age when town boys were dallying with the slate and the primer. Good penmansip there was in those days, and the bundles of old petitions contain many examples of it, but spelling has not been made the exact science that it has since become, and documents from the pens of high and highly-educated officials of the army and State contain variations in orthography that forbid any harsh judgment upon the productions of their less favoured fellows.

Justices of the Peace and others in official positions were ever ready to assist the land-claimants in preparing and presenting their cases. Scores of certificates bear the signatures of William Dickson, Thomas Dickson, John Reilly, Robert Kerr, John Burch, John Warren, David Secord or Ralfe Clench. The first-named was a lawyer and engaged in many cases of disputed titles after the Land Board days had passed and the original''tickets,'' ''certificates'' or ''locations'' were being finally confirmed by, or exchanged for, patents or deeds. His participation in such work - and also another form of difficulty that troubled many settlers - are shown by his memorial to the Executive Council, dated 25 April, 1797.

He sets forth that he is an agent for two men who have deeds of land lying in the Provincial Secretary's office. The Secretary refuses delivery of the deeds because the signatures of the Powers of Attorney differ in orthography from the names in the deeds themselves. One case is that of William Garner, a Loyalist and a veteran of Butler's Rangers who was awarded two hundred acres of land. In the Council order the name was spelled ''Gardiner'' and the deed was made in conformity. On the U.E. roll it was spelled ''Garner,'' as it was also in the Power of Attorney. If the claimant were to simplify the position by waiving the exemption of fees, he might thereby jeopardise his status and that of his family as U.E's, - a proud distinction, highly prized by those who had won it, but strangely unappreciated by their later-day descendants.

Continuing, Mr. Dickson says: ''Your memorialist has to remark that in this country the Ignorance of some, & the many Descendants from the Dutch and other Nations Intermixed will unavoidably occasion many mistakes in the Uniformity of Orthography. The F and V as in the instance of Follick the son, perhaps anglified, prevents him from the Mark of Honour stamped on the Descendants of his Father - Vollick, who adhered to the Unity of the Empire.''

The Secretary of the Province was ordered to issue deeds in cases in which such differences occurred, when he could satisfy himself as to identity, - in other cases to ask the Council for instructions.

ACOR

Lambert Acor served in Butler's Rangers and is described in a Land Petition as ''of Grantham''. He married the daughter of a U.E. In 1786, having previously received 200 acres of land, he was granted an additional 100 acres for his wife. (B) In some old records the name ''Lambert A. Ker'' is found, and in the Welland registry office there are documents in which the name is spelled ''Acre.''

Notes

Lambert Acor of Grantham, married Mary Laraway, daughter of Jonas Laraway, U.E.L. of Louth.

Lambert Ekor, 26 years, 6 months, Mary Laraway, 17 years, 3 months, listed at Niagara 1 Dec. 1783.

AGLOR (ACKLER - AIGLOR - AYCKLER - EGLER - EIGLE)

This uncommon name has many spellings in local records. A note attached to the land petition of ''William Aglor,'' dated 9 May. 1797, says: ''The proper spelling of this man's name is 'Aglor.' He is on the list as 'Ayckler.''' In the petition he asks to be confirmed in his possession of Lot 18 on the 2nd Concession of Stamford, also lands for his wife and four children who were born before 1789.(LP) He was granted 100 acres additional as a settler and 250 acres family lands. (C)

In the U.E. List, "William Egler," is entered as a soldier of Butler's Rangers having a wife and two children, "Provision List, Niagara, 1786."

William "Agler" was in the 2nd Lincoln in 1814. (LAB)

Catherine, daughter of William Ackler,U.E., of Stamford, married Henry Warren of Fort Erie. (LP)

Mary Ayckler married William, son of James Forsyth. (T)

"William Lampman, son of James and Hannah Aglor, Stamford farmer," was baptised 14 September, 1820; and Mary, Elizabeth and John of the same parents, on 18 April, 1825. (ECNP)

Rev. Wm. Leeming's parish register of burials has this entry under date, 18 April, 1823, - "Mrs. Aglor, Stamford, aged about 70 years." (ECNP)

ALEXANDER

Hugh Alexander was granted 200 acres of land as a U.E., in 1797.(B., p.300)

He was one of those who endeavoured to save the goods of John Burch, when the latter fled from Albany, but the rebels detected the attempt and Alexander, and others,were imprisoned. (L.P.)

One Hugh Alexander was a leading merchant in Fort Erie before the war of 1812-14. He was a merchant and trader and owner of the schooner "Chippawa," which was taken over and armed by the government, lost in the battle of Lake Erie and finally burned by the British at Buffalo on 31 December, 1813. Alexander's house and store at Fort Erie were burned during the war. He was appointed a Lieutenant of the 3rd Lincoln militia in 1813.

In Merritt's narrative of the war there is a mention of the plundering of "Alexander's" house in northern Stamford by United States troops in 1813.

After the war, a Hugh Alexander lived and carried on some kind of a commercial business in Stamford.

Notes

Thomas Alexander: Irish John Willson, drowned in 1798. His widow, Elizabeth (Baty?) Willson married 2nd Thomas Alexander and they lived in Stamford.

Auldjo Alexander was a merchant in Montreal who acquired land on Lake Erie and in Niagara. He and James Muirhead traded through Thomas and James Cummings of Chippawa. In July 1798, Elijah Phelps mortgaged Lot No. 2 Niagara township to Alexander Auldjo of Montreal for £ 3448.10.2. David Secord on Oct. 16, 1816, ref. Bargain & Sale No.5281, acquired this lot for £ 4,000 when Phelps defaulted on the mortage. In 1819 Secord sold 24.3ha (60 acres) to Joseph and Adam Brown. Then in 1843 David Secord sold another portion of this lot to Matthew Ottley.

BARNES - BARNS

Jonas Barnes(or Barns) came into this province in 1785 and was given a "ticket" by P.R.Frey for four township lots, but located only one. On 5 October, 1796, on petition, his lands were ordered made up to 400 acres.

In September, 1797, Jonas Barnes, junior, stated, in a petition, that his father had been dead two years and his mother four months. He was the eldest of six children. He asked confirmation in his father's Lot, No. 71. In June 1798, the administrators of the estate secured leave to sell the property to Lawrence Lemon, for the support of the infant family. The administrators were Noah Millard, brother-in-law of deceased, Noah Cook, chosen guardian of his will and Jonas Barnes, the eldest son. Certificates as to the circumstances were furnished by Hon.Robert Hamilton, Thomas Willson and John Reilly. (J.P.)

One Jonas Barns was assessor of Crowland in 1811, and was in the 3rd Lincoln militia in 1812.

Joseph and Jonas Barnes were jurors in the inquisition held at Charlotteville in 1817 into the treason of Andrew Westbrook. (Papers & Records,Vol. 24, p.200).

Notes

Jonas Barnes married Anna Millard.

BENDER

Philip George Bender, a native of Germany, and his wife, born in Holland, emigrated early in the second half of the Eighteenth Century, to New Jersey, removing after a short time to Philadelphia. In the winter of 1776 they formed part of a company of fifty-three Loyalist refugees who, having been driven from their homes, took the wilderness trail towards Niagara. Exhaustion, hunger, cold and disease so beset them that only seven reached Fort

Niagara in the following April, - Bender and his wife being of the number. Some of the others had found refuge with sympathizers along the way, some had sought shelter with the Indians, some had laid down to die in the forest. (T)

Bender enlisted in Butler's Rangers in 1779 and served five years. He was one of the two first settlers in Stamford township and chose his land on the brink of the gorge, facing the Falls. He was granted 300 acres, with family lands added later. His lots now form a large part of the city of Niagara Falls. Two children had been brought from the lost home in Pennsylvania (it is believed that they were left with friends and sent to Niagara some time after the flight of the parents) and three others were born before 1789. (LP) (C). A daughter, Elinor, married John Burch, junior (F).

In the list of farmer-settlers in 1783 the family appears as "Banter" and its members, with their age, are Philip 40, Mary 30, John 8, Mary 5, Sarah 2, (NHS 38).

There are numerous references to Bender's home in Mrs. Simcoe's Diary, but she spells the name "Painter", as does Captain Enys.

The house, which stood where the new factory of the Oneida Community is located (present day site of Maple Leaf Village), was burned by the United States forces during the War of 1812-14. When the old Loyalist couple died, they were buried on the farm, and natural slabs of stone from the gorge were erected at the graves. When the Erie & Ontario railway was built, the remains were exhumed and reinterred on Drummond Hill, but the stones were not replaced. The location of the graves is now not known.

John Bender, son of Philip G., served in 1812-14 in the 2nd Lincoln, in the Niagara Light Dragoons, in Merritt's Provincial Dragoons, and in the militia artillery. He married a Marr and had a family of eleven. Their eldest son, Philip, was a cavalry officer in 1837 and rose to be a lieutenant-colonel of militia. A grandson, Hiram, served in 1866 and was later a major of the 44th Lincoln & Welland regiment; one of his sons Harry, great-grandson of the original settler, was with the Canadian Forces in France in the Great War (1914-18). Thus, five successive generations of this Loyalist family bore arms for the British crown.

There is a tradition in the Bender family that Philip, the Ranger, bought land from the Indians. As the British government recognized no private treaties between white and Indians affecting lands, this has been denied. The explanation of the story lies in a document, now in the National Archives, Ottawa, reading as follows:

"Niagara, 14 May, 1783.

"You may purchase the Ind'n Improvements and allow five or six pounds for the whole below John Hutchinson's which you will be repaid should government think proper to take it from you together for what may be thought reasonable for such improvements as you may make hereafter.

"Mr. Bender"   "John Butler."

The "improvement" purchased by Bender from the Indians had a spring. In 1797 he brought the matter before the Executive Council and asked that a deed be issued to him for Lot 128, on which he said, the spring was located. This was done. A little later he discovered that he had given the wrong lot number, the spring being on Lot 144, adjoining. He asked that No. 144 be given him, but it had already been granted to James Forsyth.

When making his claim before the Commissioners of Claims, Bender stated that he was a native of Germany and came to America when very young; had taken up 320 acres on the Susquehanna; Indians and rebels carried off his live stock and some of his grain; tried to remove his furniture too fast and was found out by the rebels; abandoned everything, including £120 worth of clothing and furniture in the spring of 1777, and joined Col. Butler at Niagara; could not stay any longer without joining the rebels; was discharged from the army in 1782.

His evidence was corroborated by John Depuy. A notation on the Commissioners' record reads. "A very good man - to be allowed as much as we can."

BIGGAR

The Biggars were Covenanters (persons who signed and supported either of the Covenants of the Scottish Presbyterians in the 17th Century) who fled to the North of Ireland about 1660. Between 1730 and 1740 one of them emigrated to Philadelphia. His son James, married Elizabeth Litel, had two sons, John and William, and lost his life in a forest fire.

John and William came to Canada about 1789 or 1790 and settled near Stoney Creek. John married twice (his first wife was a Pettit, the second a Comfort), had twenty-one sons and daughters and died in Trafalgar Township in 1841, aged eighty years. William married a sister to John's first wife, who died, leaving a son, James. William removed to Lundy's Lane where he married, in 1805, Rebecca, daughter of Charles and Sarah Green, who had been born on the Bender farm, 26 September, 1786, eight days after her Loyalist parents reached Canada. They had eleven children.

William Biggar was a sergeant in Captain Burch's company of the 2nd Lincoln and was engaged in several actions in 1812-14. On the morning after the battle of Lundy's Lane his wife, unable to obtain news of him, searched the battlefield, examining the bodies of many of the dead. She then followed the army towards Chippawa, finally finding her husband with his regiment.

William Biggar died in 1858, aged eighty-one years; his wife in 1880, aged ninety-four years.

BOWMAN

There is enough scattered material concerning the Bowmans to make a book, but the family has so many branches and the duplications of names are so frequent that the construction of a connected record would be a task of great difficulty. The name is said to have been originally Baumann. They emigrated from Germany in the reign of Queen Anne and settled at "Bowman's Creek" on the Mohawk.

Petition of Adam Bowman, read in Council 10 August, 1795, states that he was a soldier in Butler's Rangers, was repeatedly taken prisoner and wounded, and had received 300 acres of free land. Attached certificate of John Butler, dated 7 August, 1788, states that Adam Bowman joined the British forces in 1777 and served against Fort Stanwix. He and others then got leave to go to the Susquehanna to bring their families to Niagara, they having been driven from their habitations by the enemy. Bowman was there captured and put in prison and after some time was put in irons and removed to Hartford, Conn., where he was held until the end of 1778. He was then exchanged and sent to New York where he remained until 1780, when he got leave to attempt to join the Rangers. In this attempt he was again made prisoner on the Susquehanna, after receiving three bad wounds. He was conveyed to different parts of the colonies until 1783, when he was exchanged to Canada, rejoined the corps and served until the general reduction in 1784. One of the wounds he received at the Susquehanna was badly attended to, never made a cure, and remained open. Being unable to employ a surgeon himself, he asked to be admitted to one of his Majesty's hospitals where he might receive proper attendance and be restored to health. This Butler recommended.

In 1795 Adam Bowman was granted 200 acres additional. (Text of the petition and certificate will be found in Vol. 24 of these Papers and Records, pages 27-8.)

Adam Bowman, junior, son of a Loyalist, stated that he accompanied his father during the war but was too young to bear arms. He was granted 200 acres on his father's merits. (LP).

George Adam Bowman, in a petition dated 20 July, 1795, stated that he was driven from home because of his loyalty at the earliest stage of the American rebellion and served in Butler's Rangers from its formation. He had a wife and nine children, some of them very young. His service was certified to by Andrew Bradt, "Captain late Rangers, Lt. Col. Militia." Walter Butler certified, (Montreal, 16 January, 1780) that "Adam Bowman" was discharged from service in the preceding spring as he had too large a family to support, with himself, on his subsistence allowance. He had served in an independent company in 1777 under his (Butler's) command, and since in the Rangers. He left a farm on the Susquehanna for his loyalty. (See Papers and Records, Vol. 24, pages 28-9.)

In petitions dated 2 July, 1796, and 26 January, 1797, "George Bowman" of Stamford stated that he came into the province in 1787 with a wife and seven children and settled on Lots 29, 30, 31 and 32. He asks confirmation of possession and 200 acres additional, which was granted. David Secord certified to the facts.

Henry Bowman, by petition of 18 July, 1795, stated that he was private in the colonel's company of Butler's Rangers for seven years and attached his discharge certificate, dated at Niagara, 24th June, 1784, and signed by Colonel Butler. He had a wife and three children and had received 100 acres. He was allowed 200 acres additional and 200 acres family lands. (LP). Abraham Bowman (petition 3 August, 1795) served in the King's Royal Regiment of New York, drew 300 acres, married a daughter of a U.E. and had three children. A grant was made to his wife. (LP).

Abraham and Jacob Bowman, having served through the American was and until the peace, were granted lots in Newark. ("C" p. 310). There was also on the U.E. List a Peter Bowman, who settled in the Home District.

Jacob Bowman (petition, 3 July, 1795) joined Butler's Rangers in 1777, and was in the expedition to Fort Stanwix. He returned as far as Oneida Lake and got leave to go for his family. Was taken prisoner and kept in Hartford gaol until exchanged to New York. In attempting to force his way to his regiment at Niagara, he was taken prisoner on the Susquehanna, being wounded while resisting capture. He was sent to the Provost, loaded with irons, moved from gaol to gaol until he reached "Kats Kiln." Thence, chained by couples, prisoners were removed to Lancaster, where he remained 18 months, 20 weeks of the time in chains. After a further 18 months in Philadelphia gaol he was exchanged to New York, sent to Quebec and thence joined his regiment. He was separated from his family for seven years and his considerable property in the States was forfeited, for which he received no compensation. He had a wife and nine children. (LP).

In Ryerson's "United Empire Loyalists" appears the statement of Mrs. Spohn of Ancaster regarding the experiences of her grandfather, Jacob Bowman. For services in the "French War" he had received 1500 acres on the Susquehanna and settled thereon. A Loyalist, he was surprised one night in November, by rebels and, with his eldest son, aged sixteen years, carried to prison. The house was pillaged and his wife and six young children left without food, clothing or bedding. Another child was born within a few hours. Friendly indians assisted them during the winter, and carried tales of their plight to Fort Niagara. At the commandant's order, they, with other destitute families, were brought into that post in the Autumn. Peter, the second son, then aged about thirteen years, joined Butler's Rangers in 1777, a brother, aged nine, being enrolled as a fifer. Jacob, the father, and the eldest son, being exchanged were re-captured, and the son wounded. Jacob was kept in prison, often in irons, until the end of the war. He was given a year's treatment in a military hospital but never fully recovered. (This tradition would appear to cover the same events as the preceding petition.) Peter Bowman, above-mentioned, married a daughter of Frederick Lampman.

The next generation of Bowmans, who received lands as children of Loyalists, included John Bowman of Thorold, son of Jacob of Butler's Rangers, came into the province in 1788; Jacob, junior, of Thorold, son of George, of Thorold, came 1787; Hannah, daughter of Jacob; and Christine Scott, daughter of Jacob Bowman of Butler's Rangers. (LP).

Inscriptions on gravestones in Stamford Presbyterian cemetery include: Dorothy, wife of Abraham Bowman, senior, born in New Jersey, April 16, 1768, died October 12, 1820; Adam, son of Jacob and Elizabeth Bowman, born on the Mowhawk river, April 22, 1758, died March 13, 1842; Jacob Bowman, died October 10, 1813, aged 77 years, 9 months and 10 days; Elizabeth, wife of Jacob Bowman, died January 28, 1800, aged 61 years; Ann, second wife of Jacob Bowman, died September 5, 1820, aged 80 years, 5 months, 21 days; Mary, daughter of David and Chrstenia Jones, and wife of Abraham Bowman, born March 1, 1770, in New Jersey, died February 10, 1854; Mary Shainholdts, "wife of the late Jacob Sniveley, and late wife of Abraham Bowman, born in Pennsylvania, July 4, 1785, died at St. Catharines, Aril 28, 1846."

In the Anglican cemetery at Port Dalhousie is buried Adam Bowman, died 1865, aged 89 years. (NHS 19).

Christian McDonell, of Gainsboro, late private in Butler's Rangers, married Susanna, daughter of Adam Bowman, formerly of the same corps. (LP).

A "Mr. Bowman," Thorold, buried June 9, 1827, was aged 90 years; Elizabeth, "daughter of Adam and Mary Bowman, Stamford farmer," was baptized May 7, 1821; Abraham Bowman, widower, of Stamford, and Mary Snively, widow, of Willoughby, were married 7 November, 1821. (ECNP).

Lieut. Abraham Bowman of the 2nd Lincoln was wounded in the battle of Chippawa. Adam, Henry, Sergt. John and Sergt. Peter Bowman were in the same regiment. (LAB). (See "Dayton").

BROOKS

Robert Brooks became a resident of this province in 1786 and was allotted 300 acres by P.R. Frey, - the lots being originally numbered 144, 148 and 146, but changed to 163, 164, and 165. His land ticket was a "Queen of Hearts," on the reverse of which was written: "Mountain Township,Robert Brooks No. 144, 148, 146. Board, P.R. Frey."

The numbers have been changed with lead pencil. Brooks had a wife and four children when he secured confirmation of his grant in 1795. (LP).

Robert Brooks is said to have served in Butler's Rangers. His gravestone, in Drummond Hill cemetery, says that he died on August 1, 1846, aged 87 years. His wife Mary, died in 1835, in her 72nd year. They had nine children. Their daughter Abigail, born 1815, married John S. Colbath and survived until 1913. Her grandson, G.H. Colbath, died in the Phillipines in 1901 while serving in the United States Marine Corps.

Thomas Brooks died 1857, aged 68 years. His wife Elizabeth, daughter of Thomas and Abigail Wilson, died 1847, aged 57 years. (NHS22).

One Robert Brooks, probably the original settler, was assessor of Stamford in 1803. The same name appears among the ensigns of the 2nd Lincoln regiment in 1810. Both Robert and Thomas Brooks are on the Lincoln militia rolls of 1812-14. Tradition says that two women of the Brooks family captured a straggler from the United States Army and forcibly carried him to the British just when the troops were forming line of battle at Lundy's Lane

BROWN

William Brown, who had served in the 10th Regiment and in Butler's Rangers, was on the Niagara Provision List in 1786, with a wife and two children.

Township lots Nos. 93,94 and 110, now the heart of the city of Niagara Falls, were patented to William Brown in 1803.The map of 1791 also shows his name on these lots.

The story of the McMicking family, written by James McMicking (see "McMicking" in these Notes) says that Janet McMicking Cooper married "Wullie Broon," a Scot, who had a farm near where the suspension bridge was later built. She died in 1809 and is buried in Stamford Presbyterian churchyard.

James Brown, a Loyalist from New Jersey, settled at first in Stamford but removed to Norfolk in 1800. He had a son, James, born in New Jersey in 1783.

BUCHNER

"Boughner" was the original Dutch(or German) form of this name. Emigrating to America, members of the family took up the first land at what is now New Town, N.J. Christopher, taking the King's side in the Revolution, escaped through the forest to Canada, the party carrying some goods on pack horses. (T).

Christopher Boughner was a wheel-wright for the Stedmans on "the old portage." He stated that he came into this province in 1786 or 1788 with a wife and family. (LP). He married Sarah daughter of James and Eunice Forsyth, and, in 1799, obtained from his father-in-law, by purchase or gift, the property, south of Lundy's Lane now known as "Drummond Hill." He donated the ground for Drummond Hill Cemetery. (NHS22). He and his wife received 80.9ha (200 acres) of Crown land, each (LP).

In 1786 Christopher Buchner sought to secure a mill-site on Patterson's Creek in the Long Point settlement, but it had already been granted to Captain William Francis. (LP).

Christopher Buchner was ensign, and subsequently lieutenant, of the Grenadier company of the 2nd Lincoln, but was lieutenant of Captain Burch's company in 1814. He and his son, John, were in the battles of Chippawa and Lundy's Lane. John was taken prisoner at Lundy's Lane, but soon escaped. John Buchner married Mary Ann Corbett, whose mother was a Johnson. (OBF) (NHS22) (T). Christopher Buchner died 7 September, 1824, aged fifty-nine years. Lieut. John Buchner died 14 April, 1828, aged thirty-four years.

Peter Buchner came into the povince in 1792, having served in Buler's Rangers. He married a daughter of Philip Bender. Each got 80.9ha (200 acres) of land. (LP).

In Drummond Hill cemetery are these inscriptions:
"Peter Buchner, died August 15th, 1848, aged 78 years and one month."
"Mary, wife of Peter Buchner, died March 3rd, 1854, aged 75 years, 4 months and 3 days. She was a member of the Wesleyan Methodist church for 50 years."

Daniel Buchner was a brother of Christopher. (LP). Henry Buchner, who died in 1842, aged eighty-two years is buried in Crowland, as is also Joanna, his wife who died in 1820, in her fifty-fifth year. He was a Loyalist from New Jersey (WCH, p.449), is said to have come to Canada in 1778, and is probably identical with Henry "Boughner", who was captain in the 3rd Lincoln from 1809. (OBF). In this officer's company were Christoper, Peter, Joseph and Henry(junior) Buchner. (NHS22). Martin Buchner was in Captan Muirhead's company of the same regiment.

"Buchners" and "Boughners" are buried at Beamsville. (NHS19).

The land petition of Mathias Bugginer was published in Vol. 24, Papers and Records, page 32-3.

BURCH

John Burch was a native of England and settled in America in 1772. The story of his experiences in the Revolution is fully told in the evidence supporting his claim for losses.

He was residing in New York when the trouble broke out. Being pressed to sign an "Association," he refused to do so and retired to Albany to avoid it. Having a large property on the Delaware, he went there in 1778; the disturbances increased and he could not return to Albany.

Hearing that Colonel Butler was going to attack the Susquehanna country and would need provisions, Burch arranged to supply him, and with forty of his neighbours and 136 head of cattle, joined Butler.

Burch then returned to Delaware, but the rebels, hearing of his activities for the British, plundered his house three times. On the last occasion he escaped to the woods under fire and made his way through the Indian country to Niagara.There he was keeper of the Indian stores in March 1779. (NA B109 p.19).

His property on the Delaware consisted of 5,000 acres, purchased for £ 2500 or more. All his buildings, including a tenant house,were burned and a lot of valuable live stock and grain carried away. He had a saw mill and grist mill machinery and numerous other effects at Marble Town and Woodstock. When he fled from Albany he tried to carry away the contents of his dry-goods store and japanning and tin shop, but the goods were seized on the road and those with them were imprisoned, one of them being Hugh Alexander. Burch's Albany losses exceeded £1,000.

John Burch may fairly be said to have been the leading man in Stamford during the first fifteen years of the settlement. He located at the mouth of the Chippawa and took up land along the Niagara down to the rapids.

In 1786, by permission of Major Campbell, then commanding at Fort Niagara, he built saw and grist mills beside the rapids above the Falls, being bound in the sum of £200 to build them within two years. These mills are the first item in the list of mills in Nassau, 1792, and with the exception of "the King's Mills," near Niagara, built for the government by Lieut. Brass, were probably the first mills in the province. (NHS26)(NPR).

In March 1793, Burch presented a petition for relief by government. He stated that he had been recommended by Colonel "Depyster" and Major Campbell and had secured leave from the Governor at Quebec to erect mills at a place pointed out by Mr. Tinling, engineer, and Colonel "Depyster" as being, in their opinion, suitable. He built the mills at very considerable expense, provisions and labour being at extravagant prices. He risked more than his property in the enterprise. Others now wanted to build mills a mile above, at a place he (Burch) was always in hope of obtaining leave to build on, himself. Building by another would render his present saw mill entirely useless and cut off the greater part of his trade with his grist mill. He had not yet been able to redeem himself for the expense of his undertaking. He had lost a large amount of improved land at Chipaway which had been reserved for government use by Mr. Humphreys and Mr. Coachie. The new mills now proposed by others would bring him to beggary in his old age. If he were permitted to build higher up, on his own farm, he could bring timber to his mill by water, - now he had to "slay" the logs in winter. He would be able to supply the government with boards at 1 shilling per 100 feet less. He had then at Chipaway upwards of £300 worth of timber of which he feared he would not be able to get one-third to his mill that winter, for want of snow. The steep declivity of the hill behind his mills caused him serious difficulty. (For text of this petition see Papers and Records, Vol.24, pp.33-4).

He was not granted the desired permission to build at the upper site. (LP). Canby & McGill built their mills above Burch's in 1794.

Burch approached the Executive Council again on 11 October, 1796 reciting that he was one of the first settlers, that he had been a member of the Land Board until its dissolution, and had served as magistrate. For his public service his land grant was increased to 1200 acres . (LP).

The importance of "Squire Burch" in the neighbourhood, and his mill enterprises are mentioned in Capt. Enys, La Rochefoucault, Capt. Campbell and others. He was one of the company that secured the first contract for carriage of goods over the "new portage." (NHS26) (NPR) (NHS17).

John Burch died 7 March, 1797, in his 55th year and is buried on Drummond Hill. His grave is called the first in that cemetery.

Martha, wife of John Burch, senior, was a daughter of John Ramsay, senior, U.E. She came to Canada with two brothers and a sister in 1778. In 1797 she was awarded 167.9ha (400 acres) as the wife of a magistrate. (LP).

John Burch, junior, was a land surveyor and a prominent Freemason. He died in 1822, aged 38 years. (NHS22). He was lieutenant of the Grenadier Company of the 2nd Lincoln regiment and was promoted to captain in 1814 (DBP). His wife was Elinor, daughter of Philip Bender. (F).

CAIN - COON - KERN

The records of persons described under the above name, with further variations in spelling, are very confusing.

John Coon was a sergeant in Butler's Rangers and came into the province in 1778; his wife and five children came in 1781, and in 1787 he had seven children. (LP).

In 1792 one John Coon asked relief from a hard situation. He had settled on and improved lands nine miles distant from the old French Fort at Toronto, discovering later that the property had been assigned to another. In consideration of his actual military service from the beginning to the end of the Revolution, and of his large family of small children, he asked assistance. His petition was dated at "New Ark," but whether he was living there, or merely wrote as from the seat of government, is not clear. (LP).

Before the Commissioners on Claims, John Coon said that he was a native of America; lived in Albany county, joined the British in 1777 and served seven years as sergeant in Butler's Rangers. He had some leased land and a house of his own on "Rancellor's" Patent; had a share in undivided family estate of which his father and eldest brother remained in possession. When he went off to join Burgoyne the rebels seized and sold his live stock, tools and furniture, his father being unable to save them. John Segar, witness, said that Coon had a house at Norman's "Kits" (Kill?); one of his horses was sold by the rebels for £52.

"Mather Carne" petitioned in 1796 for the balance of his lands as a former Ranger. He had received 150 acres and had cleared 60 acres, On his petition there is a note by T. Ridout, - "The name should have been written Matthew Kern agreeably to his discharge." (LP).

John Caine, senior (Carn), served in Butler's Rangers and had a wife and one child before 1789. He had a son, John. (LP).

John Cain was a private in the 2nd Battalion of the King's Royal Regiment of New York. Robert Kerr, "late surgeon," certified his petition in 1795. (LP).

Peter Caine married a daughter of Christopher Servos, who was "killed for his loyalty" in 1778. (LP).

Barnabus Cain was a sergeant in the Indian Department.

Among the land grants to Loyalists appear the following:

Elizabeth Carns, 200 acres; Jacob Carns, 300 acres; Mary Carns, 300 acres; Jacob Carns, junior, 200 acres. (C).

Members of the Cain family are buried at Virgil, and of the Coon family at Grimsby. Barney Cain was with the 1st Lincoln at Lundy's Lane and carried the corpse of George Coghill away on his back. (NHS19).

Private John Coon, of the 2nd Lincoln, died 2 January, 1813. Mathias Carn was in the same regiment (LAB), also Thomas Cain.

Rev. William Leeming's burial registry has an entry "Mathias Kerns, Stamford, aged 70 years," under date of October 25, 1830. (See "VanEvery").

CAMPBELL

Robert Campbell joined the Royal forces in 1776, and served with credit as sergeant-major in Butler's Rangers. He married Mary, daughter of Frederick Smith, U.E., of the Rangers and had eight children, four of whom were born before 1789. Four of his children were named, James, Margaret, Deborah and Mary. (LP). In 1797, having already received 300 acres, he was granted 200 acres additional for his military service, 250 acres family lands and 200 acres for his wife, as the daughter of a U.E.

While Sergt-Maj. Campbell received land in Stamford, it is not known that he resided in this township. He may be identical with Sergt. Campbell who received several lots in Grantham.

One Robert Campbell was captain of the 2nd Lincoln in 1812, but resigned in 1814. (OBF).

CHAMBERS

One Isaac Chambers, born 1762, died 1805, is buried at Grimsby. It is not known whether this is the Stamford pioneer or not.

Notes

Isaac Chambers married Sarah daughter of James Slaught of Stamford.

CHISHOLM

John Chisholm was a native of North Britain, came to America in 1774, settled in Tryon county, New York, had 60.7ha (150 acres) in Courtright's Patent on perpetual lease, cleared some land, built a house, had some stock, furniture and blacksmith's tools - all of which were lost in the Revolution. He joined the British forces in 1777 and served in the Indian Department to the end of the war. Capt. Joseph Brant certified that he served without pay. (Evidence before Commissioners on Claims.)

A petition from John Chisholm, dated 10 April, 1797, states that on 10 September, 1789, he bought three lots from Lott Regan, late a private in the 84th Regiment. The transfer had been approved by the Land Board.

In the U.E. List, John Chisholm of the Indian Department is recorded as having a wife and two children on the Provision List of Niagara, 1786.

In Stamford Presbyterian churchyard is a memorial inscription to "John Chesholm." born in the parish of Crowand (Croy and Dalcross), shire of Inverness Scotland, 11 March, 1746, emigrated to Canada in 1779, and died on Queenston Heights, 7 March, 1830. His wife and other kin are also buried there.

On August 21, 1825, Rev. William Leeming recorded the burial of "Mrs. Chisholm, Stamford." aged 66 years.

One George Chisholm was a carpenter in Burgoyne's army.

Dumas may write of "Three Musketeers" and Kipling of "Soldiers Three," but Stamford has its true tale of four comrades in arms that, for devoted loyalty and self-sacrifice, outshines the best tales of the romanticists.

John Chisholm, James Park, Archibald Thompson and Daniel Rose were the members of this quartette. No embellishments could add to the dignity and impressiveness of their story as simply told in their petition.

To his Excellency John Graves Simcoe,Esq., Lieutenant-Governor and Colonel commanding His Majesty's Forces in the Province of Upper Canada, etc.,etc.

In Council

The petition of Daniel Rose, Archibald Thompson, James Park and John Chisholm-

Most Humbly Sheweth-

That in the month of July 1777 your Petitioners being then settled on the Head of the Delaware River, took up Arms for the Government, along with several others, under the command of Mr. John Macdonall, afterwards a Captain in the Second Battalion of the King's Royal Regiment of New York-

That in the year 1778 your Petitioners joined Captain Joseph Brandt who commanded a party of Indians on Service on the Susquehanah River, near Tioga point, and from the beginning of May 1778 until October 1779 remained on Actual Service under the said Captain Brandt-

That in October 1779 your Petitioners being come to Niagara, Colonel Guy Johnson informed them that they could only draw pay from the day of their arrival at Niagara - and nothing for their preceding severe and dangerous service of eighteen months - on which your petitioners replied that as they served the Crown from principle not for the sake of Emolument - they would continue to serve without pay during the remainder of the war - Which they did - and they are happy to add,satisfactorily, being almost irremittingly on active service -

That the sufferings of your Petitioners by the war have been as great as their Services-
That your Petitioners are married and have numerous families - to wit -

Daniel Rose	a wife and 7 children
Archd. Thompson	do & 5 do
James Park	do & 3 do
John Chisholm	do & 3 do

That your Petitioners have only drawn as yet a very small proportion of Lands.
Wherefore your Petitioners pray that your Excellency would inquire into their claims & allow them respectively such proportion of the unoccupied lands of the Crown as in your Excellency's Wisdom may seem meet, and as in duty bound your petitioners will ever pray etc. etc. -

Newark 8th July 1795	Daniel Rose Archibald Thompson James Park John Chisholm

We do certify that we have known Daniel Rose, Archibald Thompson, James Park, and John Chisholm now of the County of Lincoln in this Province, since the year 1776, that they served from that period in the Indian Department until the Conclusion of the American War, voluntarily and without receiving any pay for their Services altho they were employed almost without intermission on the most severe and perilous Duty - and that we have always considered them as meritorious Servants of the Crown.

Newark 7th August 1795	John Butler J.McDonell

James Park must have died shortly after the preparation of the foregoing petition, for a second petition, dated October,1796, is in the names of Daniel Rose, John Chisholm, Archibald Thompson and "the widow of James

Park, deceased.'' It recites the story in slightly different form with a few added details, recalling that they joined the Royal Standard at an early period of the late war and ''suffered every extremity of distress in the different expeditions ''conducted by Captain Brandt and the Indians with whom your petitioners volunteered the most dangerous enterprises. That during a period of seven years your petitioners, unpaid, unprovisioned and uncloathed, served his majesty with all the zeal and bravery of Britons. That your petitioners under sentence of death for joining the Indians have escaped from Americans.'' That since the peace they had proved themselves good husbandmen and members of society, as Hon. Robert Hamilton will bear witness. They asked further grants of land such as will ''render them and their families after them Respectable and mark the Honor on them recommended by the Governor-General Lord Dorchester.'' They had suffered large losses of property in the former colonies. The schedule of families attached to this petition indicates that one child had been born in each since the former petition was prepared -

Arch. Thompson, wife and 6 children, 4 born before 1790

Daniel Rose, wife and 8 children, 5 born before 1790

James Park, wife and 4 children

John Chisholm, wife and 4 children

The claims of the four families were, apparently, not finally dealt with until after the war of 1812-14, for the petition of 1796, as filed in the Archives, has attached to it a certificate from Thomas Dickson, J.P., late Lieutenant-Colonel of the 2nd Lincoln Militia, regarding the Rose family, which indicates how they ''persevered in the Fidelity and Conduct so honourable to their Ancestors'' as foreshadowed by Lord Dorchester when he placed the ''Mark of Honour'' upon the original Loyalists and their posterity. ''There was not a more loyal family in the province'' writes Colonel Dickson. Five of Daniel Roses's sons were under his (Dickson's) command at Chippawa on July 5th, 1814, and two of them were wounded in action.

Eventually each of the four claimants, Chisholm, Park, Thompson and Rose, were awarded 1000 acres, with additional family lands.

CHISHOLM (ES)

John Chisholm's will which was dated, Niagara, 23 April, 1828, left his farm, which is now inundated by the waters of the Ontario Hydro Reservoir, to his son George. His eldest daughter, Jane (Silverthorn) and his youngest daughter Janet (Miller) were mentioned in the will.

CLOW

David, Duncan and John Clow presented land petitions in February, 1797, each stating that he had come into the province with his father in 1785. David had resided with his father. John stated that his father died four years prior to his (John's) petition. (LP). It is not stated that these petitioners were brothers. The original list of land grantees includes Peter Clow. Margaret Clow, wife of Daniel Ostrander, died 1824, is buried in the Warner cemetery.

Duncan Clow and Eliza. Smith were married by Rev. Robert Addison, 3 October, 1802.

Notes

Peter Clow died 1795.

Mary Clow married Solomon Hyatt, she died 1835, aged 83 and is buried in the Warner Cemetery.

COOK

Robert Cook, in a petition dated 18 August, 1795, stated that he suffered in the Revolution, came into Upper Canada in 1785, and received 200 acres of land of which he had cleared 71 acres. He had a wife and eight children. He was allowed 200 acres family land. (LP).

On 11 April 1797, Haggai Cook stated that he came in 1786 with his father, Robert, now deceased. (LP). On the same date Calvin Cook stated that he came in eleven years before with his father, Robert, who had lived with him in Stamford. (LP).

A petition dated 3 January, 1791, is signed by Haggai Cook for Noah Cook. It states that Noah Cook came in 1786 with a wife and had one child before 1789. His children, with the months of their births, were: Huldah, July 1788; Charles, July 1790; Robert, May, 1793; Moses, February, 1795; Calvin, December 1796. A certificate of correctness by Dan. Millard, J.P., is dated 1797. (LP).

The Cook family traditon states that Robert came from New Jersey. His wife was Martha Skinner, and they had eight sons and four daughters. Their graves in the cemetery adjoining Lundy's Lane Methodist Church (Lundy's Lane United Church), are unmarked. The gravestone of Haggai, their son, shows that he was born 27 October, 1773, and died 1 November, 1848. His wife Sarah, born 14 April, 1777, died 7 January, 1813. She was a daughter of James and Eve Durham (NHS22). Edna, daughter of Robert Cook, was the wife of Harmanus Crysler.

Noah and Calvin Cook, believed to be of this family, built a grist and saw mill on Lyons Creek at an early date, founding the village of Cooks Mills. (WCH).

"Daniel Cook of Stamford, farmer," petitioning the Executive Council for a grant of land, 14 June, 1806, stated he served in a provincial regiment that was commanded by Colonel Brown and was reduced at St. John, N.B. He came to Upper Canada in 1801, with a wife and seven children. He was not recognized as a "military claimant" as he had not been in the province in 1798. (LP)

Calvin, Robert, Charles, Haggai and John Cook and Noah Cook, junior, were in the 2nd Lincoln in 1814. Other members of the family were in other Lincoln Regiments.

Notes

Calvin Cook: Charlotte Misener, born 1779, daughter of Leonard (Lemard?) Misener and his wife Barbara (Bender), married Calvin Cook.

Ann Cook: Leonard Misener, junior, born 1771, married Ann Cook.

Noah Cook of Stamford at the age of 85 married Mrs. Skinner of Stamford, age 76.

COOPER

In the story of Thomas McMicking, elsewhere in these notes, reference is made to his nephew, James Cooper. In St. Andrew's cemetery, at Niagara, are gravestone inscriptions as follows:

"In memory of James Cooper, born in Scotland, 1770, emigrated to America in 1774, died 1856, in his 86 th year."

"Elizabeth Hixon, his wife, born in the Province of New Jersey, 1773, emigrated to Canada in 1788, died 1855, aged 82."

In Miss Carnochan's (Janet Carnochan) *Inscription and Graves* there is a note to the effect that James Cooper, when a child was a captive among the Indians for several years (NHS19).

James Cooper, lieutenant of a flank company of the 2nd Lincoln, promoted captin in 1812, was present at the battle of Queenston (despatches) and Frenchman's Creek. (OBF).

In Miss Carnochan's *History of Niagara* the following obituary notice is quoted:

"James Cooper, on 24th of March, 1860, at his residence, Queenston Road, Niagara Township, died, aged 86 years. He was one of the few surviving original settlers of U.C., having been brought to this Province as a prisoner by the Indians in 1776. Mr. Cooper was one of the sterling men of the olden time, full of truthfulness, honesty and loyalty. He was a member of the Church of Scotland, and in every relation of life a man greatly esteemed."

There are several graves in Stamford Presbyterian cemetery of members of the Cooper family of Niagara Township.

Notes

According to the register at Niagara, 1 Dec., 1783: Jane Cooper, age 43; Thomas Cooper, age 14; James Cooper, age 11.

CORWIN

The Corwin family in America is traced to John Corwin (or Curwen) who purchased an estate at Sibbertoft, Warwickshire, that was sequestered by Henry VIII. Captain George Corwin, born 10 December, 1610 (son of John), emigrated from Northampton, Eng., to Salem Mass., in company with Hugh Peters, a notable supporter of Cromwell; settled in Salem, 1638, died 1685. His son John (by his first marriage to Elizabeth, daughter of John Herbert, mayor of Northampton), married Margaret, daughter of Governor John Winthrop, jr. of Connecticut. Their son, George, married Lydia, daughter of Hon. Bartholomew Gedney. They had a son, Bartholomew, who married Esther Bart, from which marriage sprang Joseph Corwin, progenitor of the Corwin family in Canada. (Corwin Genealogy.) (Stark's *Loyalists of Massachusetts* differs in several particulars.)

Joseph Corwin was living at Log Jail (now Hackettstown), N.J., before the Revolution and came to Canada with the Loyalists. He had fourteen children some of whom accompanied the parents, but others, including several married daughters remained behind.

Joseph Corwin, senior,died 25 May, 1805, aged 84 years. His wife Elizabeth, died 16 April, 1815, aged 84 years.Their son, Joseph died 7 February, 1807, aged 32 years. (NHS22). His wife was Lydia Swayze and his twin brother, Benjamin, married Penelope Swayze, both daughters of Israel Swayze. (Y). (Chronology).

The will of Joseph Corwin (senior), made 14 March, 1796, is a characteristic document of the early Loyalist type. Although Simcoe's regime was then nearing its close,the old U.E., in his last transcription of business, adhered to the nomenclature of Dorchester, describing himself as "of the township of Dorchester, county of Nassau, and Province of Upper Canada." One of the provisions reflects the intense and undiminishing British spirit that filled the men who "followed the flag" out of the lost colonies. The sum of £10, New York currency is bequeathed to a grandson,Joseph Corwin, "if he becomes a subject and residenture of Great Britain." (According to the Corwin genealogy,Joseph senior,had two grandsons bearing his name. One was a son of Bartholomew, who had remained in New Jersey, and the other was a son of Samuel). The witnesses to the will were Irish John Willson, Thomas Willson and James Nevills.

Naomi, daughter of Joseph and Elizabeth Corwin, married (1) Timothy Hixon, who died in 1792. (2) Henry Johnson. She died 2 March,1825, aged 72 years. (NHS22). (See "Hixon")

Esther, another daughter, married John Silverthorn; Elizabeth married John Robertson; Rachael married Alex. Fletcher; Annie married Adam Spencer. All of these were the parents of Niagara District families. (Chronology).

By marriages in the next generation the Corwin stock became connected with the Moores, Coopers, Cloughs, Hopkins, Emerys, Killmans, Garners, Leffertys, Uppers, Vanderburgs, Wares, Wilsons, Lemons, Ellsworths, Lewis' and other families, many of them also of Loyalist origin.

Samuel Corwin (probably son of Joseph and Elizabeth) came into this province in 1788. (LP). One Samuel, born in New Jersey, 1768, and his wife, are buried at Beamsville. (NHS19).

Samuel, son of Joseph and Elizabeth, married Ann Beam.

One of the first Methodist conferences held in the province met, in 1812, at the home of Benjamin Corwin, near Lundy's Lane.

Benjamin Corwin was in the 2nd Lincoln in 1814.

CRIPS

In a petition for land, dated December 31, 1796, Paul Crips stated that his father served in the British forces in the Revolution. David Secord certified that Paul Crips had been in this province for three years.

Paul Crips owned land on the Holland Road, in Thorold Township, east of Allanburg, in 1803. (*A Century of Municipal History.* Cruikshank, p. 36.)

Paul Crips appears in the roll of Captain James Cooper's company of the 2nd Lincoln in 1814. (LAB).

The deep eddy in the Niagara River at the head of Foster's Flats (recently called "Niagara Glen") was formerly known as "Crips eddy." (Cripps Eddy).

Jacob Cripp was in the 2nd Lincoln in 1812.

DAYTON

Asa Dayton's land petition, dated February, 1797, states that he joined the Royal Standard prior to 1783 and that Major-General Simcoe commanded a troop of horse on Long Island at the time of his joining. He came to this province in 1788, married, Sarah, daughter of Jacob Bowman, U.E., of Butler's Rangers, and had a child before 1789.John Reilly, J.P., certified as to the identity of Dayton's wife.She was granted 200 acres. (LP).

DEE (ES)

Robert Henry Dee, Captain, died Nov. 1832, aged 45, buried in St. John's Anglican cemetery. His wife, Elizabeth, born London, England, 5 Oct., 1796, died 23 Sept. 1876, aged 80, was a daughter of Matthew Ottley.

DICKSON

The well known Dickson family of Queenston and Niagara held land in Stamford but, though more or less associated with the affairs of the township (especially Thomas, who was lieutenant-colonel of militia and member of the Legislature for that part of Lincoln county) it is doubtful if any of them ever resided in it. Much information concerning them may be found in other historical publications and cannot be repeated here.

There is evidence, however, of a "William Dickson," probably of another family, having been a pioneer settler of Stamford. This man, in a petition dated 20 May, 1796, describes himself as "of the township of Stamford, farmer," says he has received and improved 100 acres of land, and asks for more. He had a wife. Another 100 acres was allowed him.

DONALDSON

The story of John Donaldson, told in two petitions over his signature, with certain details certified to by "John Johnson on the mountain" and Barnabas Cain, is one of the most striking among the records of Stamford pioneers.

He was a soldier of the 55th Regiment, in which he served for nine years. At Ticonderoga in "the war of '56," he received three wounds in one day. He was also at the taking of Niagara from the French and at the surrender of Montreal. He later "aided to quell the Indians at Detroit," - presumably in Pontiac's war. During the Revolution he endeavoured to assist the British cause and had gathered a quantity of supplies for General Burgoyne's army. These were seized by the enemy and he was imprisoned and his property confiscated. Altogether, he gave forty years of loyal service to the British crown.

Coming into Upper Canada in 1783, with a wife and five children, he lived in Barnabas Cain's house for six months. His wife was the daughter of a Loyalist who died in New York in 1777. He was awarded four lots by P.R.Frey, his ticket, preserved in the Archives, reading:

Mountain. John Donaldson
Entitled to four Lots by
order of the Board.
P. Frey

He took up 100 acres where the Canadian National Railway yards in Niagara Falls are now located. Muddy Run - a stream of some volume before the forests were cut away and Cook's bog drained, but now reduced to a trickle and confined in a sewer, - ran through his farm, and near where it plunged over the cliff into the gorge, forming a beautiful cascade, he built a sawmill. D.W. Smith, surveyor-general, in his list of mills of the District of Nassau, dated November 7, 1792, records it as follows:

"12. A Saw Mill on a small creek called the Muddy Run, near the Whirlpool in Township No.2, in the year 1791, by John Donaldson." (NHS26)

In Mrs. Simcoe's Diary there are several references to a sawmill near the whirlpool which may have been Donaldson's.

The mill did not fulfil the builder's expectations and he found that he had "hurt himself materially" by the unprofitable enterprise. He "laboured industriously on his farm" but, apparently, was not prosperous and, in 1797, he asked for the remaining 300 acres of land to which he was entitled. He was awarded this amount of "family land" in the Fifth township, and 200 acres to his wife as the daughter of a U.E. No tradition of this family can now be found in the locality. The name appears in old records both as "Donalson" and "Donaldson."

The mill was remembered as a ruin in the middle of the last century. It was the first manufactory of any kind within the limits of the present city of Niagara Falls.

Added at the front of the petition that Donaldson presented to the Executive Council in 1797 are the words "Your petitioner is at the Council Door." - a line eloquent of the humble anxiety of the old soldier to secure his rights and relieve the distress of himself and his family.

DORSHIMER

The spelling "Duchamber," often given for the family name, is probably one of those frequent errors due to mispronounciation. George Dorshimer of Stamford, yeoman, in a petition dated January, 1802, stated that he was a son of Conrad Dorshimer of Stamford who had been settled for fifteen years. David Secord J.P., certified as to his good character, and Stephen Secord, captain of the Lincoln Militia, that he had served in the militia for two years.

Martin "Dershimer" was a sergeant in Captain Cooper's company of the 2nd Lincoln in 1814. John Dorshimer was in Captain Hamilton's company in 1812.

Notes

Martin Dorshimer married Catherine, sister of Andrew Rorbach.
Their son, George, born March 1780, Greenwich, Warren Co., N.J.

DUNBAR

William Dunbar who received a lot in Stamford, is probably identical with William Dunbar, native of the shire of Nairn, in Scotland, who came to Canada in 1787 and bought Lot No. 1 in "Fort Erie Township" (Bertie) from John Gardner (Garner). He cut a raceway through the rocky shore of the Niagara and in 1792, erected mills, but the level of Lake Erie lowered, the race went dry and the mills were useless. He spent nearly £1,000 in this undertaking. His creditors seized his land and left him the mill. In 1795 he asked confirmation of ownership to the mill-site and suggested that his mill-race might be useful as a canal to get boats past the rapids. (See Papers and Records, Vol. 24, p.58.) In 1797 he was granted 200 acres of land. In his petition on February 9, in that year he described himself as "carpenter, of Queenston." (LP).

DURHAM

James Durham, having suffered imprisonment and the confiscation of his property because of his loyalty, took five of his children, left his old home in New Jersey in 1786, and became a settler in Upper Canada in the following year. He received 200 acres of land "near Queenston," which he improved, and endeavoured to establish a home so that he might send for his wife, Eve, and four children that he had left behind him. About four years later he died, whether before or after the arrival of the remainder of the family, in 1791, is not certain. James Durham's sons included James, Edward, Isaac and John. The latter came to Canada with a wife and family in 1794 and received 200 acres, to which another 200 acres was subsequently added. The other three were given a lot each in 1794, (LP). Edward, born 1772, died 1844. (NHS22), He was in Captain Rowe's Company of the 2nd Lincoln in 1812.

According to family tradition, Catherine, daughter of James and Eve Durham, was the second white child born in this district. Sarah another daughter, born 1777, married Haggai Cook.A number of graves of the earliest generations of the Durhams and Cooks in this province may be seen in the cemetery adjoining Lundy's Lane United church, Niagara Falls. (NHS22).

In the Warner cemetery is the grave of James Durham, who died in 1832, aged eighty-five years.

ELLSWORTH

Francis Ellsworth, a soldier of Butler's Rangers, and his wife, were on the Niagara Provision list of 1786. His house was closest to the Falls when Captain Enys visited the locality in 1787. He sold the property of what is now "Falls View" to Charles Wilson in 1811 (NPR).

Francis Ellsworth, aged 38, and Mary Ellsworth, aged 27 years are recorded in the list of farmer settlers in 1783. (NHS38).

In 1795, having improved his original 150 acre grant and purchased 300 acres more from David Bailey, he was granted an additional 200 acres. (B).

FORSYTH

James Forsyth emigrated from near Aberdeen, Scotland, to the Wyoming Valley between 1765 and 1770. Early in the Revolution he and his family endeavoured to reach Niagara but were taken prisoners by the Indians. British soldiers, attacked the Indian camp in the night and the captives were set free. (T).

The list of families settled as farmers in 1783 includes James Forsyth(aged 44), Unis(38), Daniel(11), William(9), John(2) and Sarah(5). (NHS38).

James Forsyth, with his wife and four children, were on the Niagara Provision List of 1786.

James Forsyth built his home on the Portage Road at the site now described as No. 2218 (6218) Main Street, Niagara Falls, and afterwards made it a public house. This was the place frequently referred to in the period of the war of 1812-14 as "Forsyth's." It was army "H.Q." on several occasions. During the Navy Island campaign, 1838, Sir Allan McNab occupied it; Lord Durham stayed there; James Buchanan, long British consul in New York, owned it; Lord Elgin occupied it for a time; at last it was burned. (NHS22),

William, son of James Forsyth, married Mary Ayckler, was noted as the proprietor of the Pavilion Hotel, and had a famous contest with the government of the province concerning rights on the "Chain Reserve."

One James Forsyth, private in the 2nd Lincoln, was killed in action at Chippawa. He left children, of whom William and Hannah Dockstader were guardians. (Pension List). One William Forsyth served in the same regiment. (LAB).

Mme.Celleni, once a famed opera singer, was a great-granddaughter of the original James Forsyth.
See "Buchner."

Notes

George Forsyth who was a merchant and one of the members of the Portage Syndicate, was married 25 July, 1804 to Catherine TenBroeck of Niagara, at Queenston. George Forsyth died before 1809; Catherine died and was buried by Rev. Addison, 17 Feb.,1817.

FRALICK - FRELICK

John Fralick was born in 1775, in New Jersey. (T). He and his wife, Abigail Spencer, (1761-1844), came to Niagara at an early period of the Revolution, and he served in Butler's Rangers. His name is on the "U.E. List" by authority of the "Niagara Stamped Book" and the "Provision List, Niagara, 1786." He was granted 200 acres and his wife a like amount of land as the daughter of a U.E. (C). Later he received an additional 100 acres, and 150 acres as family lands. (B). He died 12 May, 1839, and, with his wife is buried on Drummond Hill.

According to family tradition, the children of John and Abigail(Spencer) Fralick were: John, married to Margaret Rice, had a fulling mill at the Falls; Catherine, married to Aaron Crane; Robert, married Abigail VanWyck; Mary, married James Secord; Lydia, married Hugh Wilson of Thorold; Elizabeth,married Louis Smith; Barnabas, married Sarah Bragwell; Abigail, married Patrick Dowling; Adam, married(1) Eliza Durham, (2) Catherine Finnemore. Some early records mention Benjamin Fralick, son of John. A Benjamin Fralick was a corporal in Butler's Rangers. He had a wife and four children.

One John Fralick was sergeant, and later ensign, in the 2nd Lincoln militia in 1812-14 - whether the elder or the younger man of the name is uncertain. Robert Fralick was in the same regiment. The late Sir William Glenholme Falconbridge was a great-grandson of John Fralick, U.E.

Other branches of the Fralick family settled in New Brunswick and in the Bay of Quinte district.

Before the Commissioners on Loyalists' Claims, Benjamin Fralick stated that he was a native of America; lived near Albany; had been settled ten years on Patroon lands, had cleared ten acres and built a house and barn. He suffered terribly on account of his loyalty before leaving his home. The rebels took his live stock,utensils, furniture and tools and drove his family out. He joined Butler's Rangers in 1778 and served six years as sergeant. Christian Warner corroborated his evidence. Warner Fralick and Jacob Ball were neighbours in their old homes. Benjamin Fralick was living in Louth in 1804. He had a son, John, who was a small boy at Niagara during the Revolution, and who was sometimes confused with John Fralick of Stamford. (F).

GARNER

The records of the Garner family, which played a prominent part in the affairs of Stamford township for a hundred years, are uncertain as regards to earliest generations in this country. John Garner came out from England, where he had met with financial reverse about 1778. He was a widower, with one son, George. In Canada, John Garner married —— Rogers. All the children of this marriage emigrated to Michigan except one son, Thomas, who settled in "the Beechwoods." (T).

George, son of John, married Christeen Killman and had issue as follows: Jacob, married Abigail Corwin; John (1799-1871), married Elizabeth Spencer (1803-1881); Philip married Ann Upper; William married —— "Spausback"(?); Robert, married Libby(Lydia?) Spencer; Elizabeth married —— Adams (no issue). (T).

Jacob and William Garner were in Captain Grant's company of the 2nd Lincoln in 1812-14 and it is said that the father, George, also served. (LAB) (T). James, John and Thomas Garner were in the same regiment (Muster rolls).

Jacob Garner, son of George, was born on Lot No. 87, Stamford; John, Philip, William and Robert were born on Lot No. 118. (T).

Jacob Garner was one of Stamford's early school teachers, and held various municipal offices.* He was a trustee of the "Red Meeting House." He married Abigail Corwin, their children being: Maria, Millicent, Anson, James, Susan, Joseph, Mary Ann and Lydia.

The "Niagara Provision List" of 1786 contained the names of John Garner, a former soldier of Butler's Rangers, then living in Crowland and William Garner, the latter having a wife.

One John Garner first held land in Bertie, fronting the rapids (see "Dunbar"). A man of the same name was living "at Chippeway" in 1796-7. (LP). These may be the same, and identical with the John Garner first referred to. (See Papers and Records, Vol. 24, p. 86.)

One William Garner served in Butler's Rangers. (see introduction to these notes.) "William Garner of Stamford, yeoman," petitoned Council, 25 June, 1805, stated that he was then twenty-two years of age and born in this province. (LP).

Joseph Garner, born in Stamford in 1827, removed in 1849, to Pelham, where he was long prominent. Robert. S. Garner, of Thorold Township, was a native of Stamford. (WCH).

In Drummond Hill cemetery are the graves of Thomas Garner, died 1870, aged eighty years. Catherine, wife of Thomas Garner, died 1864, aged sixty-nine years: Philip Garner, died 1884, aged eighty-three years. William Garner, born 1803, died 1874.

Philip was first buried in a graveyard(now removed)on the Upper farm in Thorold township, facing the Thorold-Stamford line, a short distance south of the Beaverdams Road, where an Episcopal Methodist meeting-house once stood. In the cemetery at th west end of Lundy's Lane are buried George Garner,died 21 July, 1839, aged sixty-six years; Christeen (Christine),wife of George Garner, died 26 April, 1842, aged sixty-four years; Abigail Garner, died 23 June, 1838, aged thirty-five years; Jacob Garner, died 14 September, 1862, aged sixty-six years; Lucretia, wife of Jacob Garner, died 17 June, 1844,aged thirty-three years.

*"In the Garner settlement, a frame or log house stood a short distance west of the present school, Shortly afterwards, a rough-cast school house was built on the road allowance north-ward of the present building. It was here that Jacob Garner taught around 1833. This building being too limited in size, and on the road allowance, was superseded by the stone school-house which was built in 1844." - From a memoir on Niagara Falls (and Stamford) Schools, by Mr. J.C. Morden of this Society (Ontario Historical Society), in *The Niagara Falls Evening Review.* The first school building in this location was in existence in 1803(see order of Commissioners establishing Beaverdams Road,in this memoir). From the "Garner settlement" it took the name "the Garner school." but in later years, "the stone school" was commonly current. The stone building gave place to a brick structure in 1916. The concession road that intersects the Beaverdams Road at this point has lately been officially named "the Garner Road."

Notes

Mary Ann Garner, daughter of Jacob Garner, married Robert Spencer of Thorold, 6 Oct., 1841.

GILMORE

Henry Gilmore came into the province in 1796. He lived for the first few months in John Garner's house "at Chippaway." (LP).

Moses Gilmore of Grantham was a son of Benjamin Gilmore of Grantham an enrolled U.E. (LP).

A Benjamin Gilmore served in the Jersey Volunteers(Loyalist).

Thomas and William Gilmore were in the 2nd Lincoln in 1812.

GREEN

Charles Green was a loyal resident of the "Jersies" who "suffered very considerably, both in person and in property" for his attachment to the Crown. He was imprisoned by the rebels on several occasions and after the battle of Princeton, a price was put upon his head. He gave up the attempt to remain in his home and with his family, took the trail through the Blue Mountains of Pennsylvania towards Canada. Two young children were carried in panniers on the horse ridden by his wife; the husband walked. Evidently they spent some time in some temporary reguge, for they did not cross the Niagara, at Queenston, to take up their home in this province until September 18,1786. (T) (LP). Charles is said to have had a brother, Lawrence, who took the Revolutionary side. (T).

Charles Green's wife is said to have been Betsy(?Sarah) Scritchfield. (T). In 1795 he had a wife and five children (LP). A son Reuben, was in his third year when the family came to Canada. He was the central figure in several dramatic exploits in the war of 1812-14. He married a Fortner. Other sons were William, Henry and Charles - the latter being the youngest. Henry, born about 1780, married Mehitible Johnson. A daughter, Rebecca, born a few days after the family reached Canada, married William Biggar. (q.v.)

Charles Green was described as "a very old man" by Thomas Clark, in 1824, when certifying to his loyalty during 1812-14. Charles Green and his wife were buried in the cemetery "at the end of the Lane," the site of which was part of his original grant of 200 acres. He received a second grant of 200 acres in Humberstone Township.

Charles Green, junior, served in the war of 1812-14 and married Rebecca, daughter of Basnet Dell, U.E. of Crowland (or Willoughby).

Another Reuben Green, of undetermined relationship to the Stamford family, joined the Royal forces in February, 1777, and was a sergeant in the 1st Battalion of New Jersey Volunteers, commanded by Lieut.-Col. Joseph Barton, in Brig.-Gen. Skinner's brigade. He was not able to get his family to Canada until August, 1798. Certificates as to his loyalty and services, signed by Samuel Ryerse and Daniel Hazen are extant. He settled in Norfolk county (LP), and was nominated for a captaincy in the militia in 1806.

GRELINGER

George Greliner was a private in Captain Frazer's company of the 34th Regiment under Lieut.-Col. Hoye during the "American war," was in this province from 1775, received his discharge in 1784 and was entered as a "U.E." (LP).

HALL

Giles Hall came into the province in 1795 and took the oath of allegiance before John Reilly, J.P., in 1797. When he applied for and received a grant of 200 acres of land, subsequent to the war of 1812-14,David Stewart certified that he (Hall) had behaved as a good subject. (LP).

In Stamford Presbyterian cemetery is the headstone of Captain Giles Hall who died on December 2nd, 1816, aged sixty-seven years.

HAGERTY

Hugh Hagerty came into the province in 1786, with his wife. He had two children before 1789 and five before 1797. He was recognized by the Justices in Session as one who had adhered to the Royal Standard before 1783. (LP). He was born in the North of Ireland. His son was named Stephen.

One Hugh Hagerty served in the Jersey Volunteers(Loyalist).

Hugh and Stephen Hagerty were in the 2nd Lincoln in 1814.

Hugh Hagerty was still a prominent resident in 1835 when he headed a petition to the Legislature for financial aid to build a bridge across the Chippawa at the line between Crowland and Willoughby (Montrose bridge). A local subscription had failed to raise sufficient money for the purpose.

Stephen Hagerty married, first, Nancy Fortner, daughter of James Fortner, concerning whose descent from a Scottish Lord Douglas there is a romantic tradition. Their daughter, Catherine, married Edward, son of Stephen Peer of the 2nd Lincoln who fell at Chippawa. By a second marriage, Stephen Hagerty had two sons and a daughter.

HARDEY-HARDY

John Hardy served for eight years as a sergeant in the 84th Regiment. He is also described as a "sergeant of grenadiers." He was one of five brothers, and had a wife and four children. He was granted 500 acres and each of his brothers received 200 acres. (LP).

He is said to be indentical with the John Hardy who was a lieutenant in the Lincoln Artillery in 1803 and captain of the 3d Lincoln in 1809. (OBP). A "Captain John Hardy" is buried in Drummond Hill.

One John Hardy had a tannery on the shore of the Niagara above Cedar Island early in the Nineteenth century.

HEASLIP

James Heaslip came into the province in 1785 and was granted one township lot by F.R.Frey. In 1796 he received an additional 200 acres in Long Point settlement. (LP).

Before the Commissioners on Claims, James Heaslip, late of Albany county, New York stated that he was a native of Ireland; came to America in 1774; settled at Beaver Dam, 20 miles from Albany, on Patroon land; joined Butler's Rangers in 1777, was corporal, served to the end of the war. Col. Butler certified to his loyalty and services. The surgeon of the Corps certified that he has been severely wounded. He lost his house, live stock. crop, furniture, clothes, etc., taken by the rebels.

Catherine, daughter of Thomas Heaslip, U.E., married Adam Young, U.E., of Crowland. (WCH,p.524).

The Heaslips are said to have been of Covenanting stock who fled from Scottish persecution to Co. Cavan, Ireland. James was a surgeon's mate in the war of 1812-14, married Mrs. Eleanor (Elima?)Stephenson, and was buried on Drummond Hill. Joseph, brother of James, also came to Canada as a Loyalist and married Nancy Spink(Spinks). They are buried in Drummond Hill. Thomas, their son, served in the 2nd Lincoln in 1812-14 and died, unmarried, in 1842, aged 59 years. Another son, when a youth was lost in the forest when searching for strayed cattle, went insane and died soon afterwards. Both are buried on Drummond Hill. Catherine, a daughter of Joseph and Nancy Heaslip,married Thomas Reaveley, a native of Northumberland, England, who emigrated to America before the Revolution, was persecuted and maimed because of his loyalty, fled to this province and established a carding mill above the Falls prior to 1790. He was a sergeant in the 2nd Lincoln in 1812-14. (NHS22-T).

HICKSON-HIXON

"Enome" Hickson, widow of Timothy, in a petition dated April, 1797, stated that she came to this province in 1788, with eight children. Her husband drew 200 acres. She was allowed 400 acres family lands. (See"Corwin.")

A petition from Daniel Hixon, date 17 July, 1797, states that he was a house-joiner and carpenter. He was a grandson of Joseph Corwin of Stamford and son of Naomi Johnson, wife of Henry Johnson, then living on the road between Newark and Queenston. He was allowed 400 acres.

Nathan Hixon - probably the son of Timothy Hixon and Naomi Corwin - was in the 2nd Lincoln in 1814. (See "Cooper.")

HOOVER

Henry "Hover," claiming compensation for losses in the Revolution, stated that he was a native of Hanover, came to America in 1753, served in the last French war and was living on the Mohawk river when the Revolution broke out. He had 100 acres under perpetual lease, had built a house and barn, all of which the rebels seized. He did all he could for the King from the first, joined Sir John Johnson's 1st battalion in 1780, having also five sons in that regiment. Major James Gray certified as to his services and those of his sons. Had settled in Stamford Township.

On the first map of Stamford, the name of "George Hover" appears. In Beaverdams cemetery is the grave of George Hoover who died 15 February, 1827, aged ninety years. Catherine, his wife, died 1 June, 1825, aged 76 years. In Rev. William Leeming's burial register are entries evidently referring to both of these interments but stating the ages slightly differently. Both are described as of "Stamford."

One of the Hoovers shared the imprisonment and suffering of Jacob Bowman during the Revolution.

Peter and John Hoover were in the 2nd Lincoln in 1814.

HOWEY

Jonah Howey came into the province on 7 July, 1787, with his wife and two children, because of his loyalty to the British crown. By 1797 he had three sons and one daughter. (LP).

He was a leader of the earliest Methodist organization and a blacksmith by trade; his wife's name was Winifred. He is buried in the cemetery at the west end of Lundy's Lane.

Robert Howey, who had served in the New Jersey Volunteers, is on the U.E. List as a settler in the Home District. Jonah, Stephen, Samuel and Isaac Howey served in the 2nd Lincoln in 1812-14. Stephen was wounded in the battle of Chippawa.

HUTT

According to the petition of Adam Hutt, dated 19 June, 1795, he had then been settled for several years. He had been allowed two lots, but as the town line of Thorold intersected the property it measured only 160 acres. He was granted Lot No. 12 in the Gore 18 acres, an additional 200 acres, and a town lot in Newark. His wife was a daughter of Jacob Ball, U.E. (LP).

Sergt. John Hutt of the 2nd Lincoln was killed in action at Chippawa.

HYATT

Solomon Hyatt's land petition of April, 1797, states that he came into the province in June, 1787, with his wife and three children and purchased land. David Secord certified that Hyatt was in the province in 1790, with a family, as stated, and that he subsequently had a fourth child. He was granted 200 acres. (LP).

It is probable, although definite evidence is lacking, that Solomon was the father of James and John Hyatt who were in the 2nd Lincoln militia in 1812-14.

JOHNSON

John Johnson of Stamford came into the province about 1787. He had a wife and eight children and drew 200 acres of land. (LP).

James Johnson, U.E., was a brother of the above. He went back to the States in July, 1788, via Oswego, and brought his mother, wife and three children to this province. His pass signed "P. Hunter, Lt. Col. 60th" is extant. He drew 200 acres. (LP).

Henry Johnson, Loyalist, came in 1786 and was given a certificate for 450 acres for himself and family by Major Campbell (LP).

Jeremiah Johnson settled on the 20-Mile creek in Clinton. One Henry Johnson had land in Grimsby. Petitioning in 1796, both reported having suffered losses by hurricane a few years earlier. (LP).

(See "Donaldson," "Green," "Hickson," "Millard")

KILLMAN

The Killman (Kuhlmann)family is of Dutch origin.

Jacob Killman, from Pennsylvania, a former soldier in Butler's Rangers, with a wife and five children, were on the Niagara Provision List of 1786. His sons included Jacob, born 1775, Christian and James.

Jacob, junior,married Mary, daughter of Sergeant Joseph Petrie. Petitioning for land, in 1801, she stated that she was born in this province, was then twenty-one years of age, and that her father, formerly of Butler's Rangers, served from 1777 to 1784. John Reilly J.P., certified to her claim and she was awarded 200 acres as the daughter of a U.E. (LP).

In the cemetery at the west end of Lundy's Lane is the gravestone of:
"Mary, wife of Jacob Killman, died, Aug.30, 1858, aged 78 years." One Jacob Killman was a sergeant in Captain Grant's company of the 2nd Lincoln, was taken prisoner at Queenston, 22 July, 1814, and is said to have been wounded and again taken prisoner at Lundy's Lane (WCH). He also served in the Lincoln artillery. Several other members of the family, including Adam, served in the 2nd Lincoln in 1814. (LAB).

Catherine Weishuhn, wife of William Weishuhn of Willoughby, was a daughter of Jacob Killman of Stamford, U.E. (LP).

Philip and John Killman and Adam Killman(said to have been a half-brother of Jacob) were also settlers at a very early time.

One John Killman was killed about 1831, by a falling tree. His widow, Margaret, and her sister, Martha, were drowned 10 June, 1832, when their horse backed their wagon off a bridge into the Welland Canal near Keefer's mill, Thorold. They were daughters of Samuel McKerlie.

In Stamford Presbyterian churchyard are buried Adam Killman, who died 9 May, 1873, in his eighty-third year.Elizabeth, his wife, who died in her eighty-second year, and other members of the family.

LAMPMAN

John, Casper and Frederick Lampman emigrated from Hanover to America about 1750. Frederick, born 1722, a Loyalist, left his home on the North River, went within the British lines on Long Island, and came to Canada at the close of the Revolution, with his wife Katherina. They had seven sons and five daughters. Four sons and two sons-in-law served in the British forces. Frederick died in 1789 and is buried with his wife, on Lot No. 100 Stamford, close to the ruins of their home. Their children included Peter, William, Frederick, John, Matthew (Mathias ?), Elizabeth, Stephen, Abraham. A daughter married Peter Bowman.

Peter Lampman(1749-1834) came to Canada during the Revolution leaving his wife (Elizabeth) Haines, of an English-U.E. family that settled afterwards in Niagara Township). After the war he brought her and two children to this province, where their family increased to ten. William Lampman was killed by the rebels. Stephen Lampman founded Bedford, Que.

A petition from Peter Lampman, dated 11 October, 1796, says that he came to this province in 1783, and received 300 acres. He was allowed 250 acres family lands. A list of his children, certified to by Dan. Millard, J.P., follows: Catherine, born 1778; Jacob, born 1783; Frederick, 1785; Peter, 1787; Adam, 1789; John 1790; Hannah, 1793; Elizabeth; 1794; He was allowed 250 acres family lands. (LP).

Abraham Lampman, petitioning in 1796, said that he had settled "some years." He had four brothers in His Majesty's service during the American war, one of whom was hung by the rebels. He married Hannah, daughter of Samuel Pew, U.E., and had three children. Having received 100 acres, he was allowed 100 acres more, with 200 acres for his wife. (LP).

In the cemetery at the west end of Lundy's Lane lie Abraham Lampman, died 14 September, 1832, aged fifty-six years; also Hannah, his wife, died 30 November, 1832, aged fifty-six years.

Martha, daughter of Abraham and Hannah Lampman, was baptized by Rev. Robert Addison, 22 July, 1792. They had, also, a son named Matthias.

Abraham Lampman, senior, and Abraham Lampman, junior, were soldiers in the "Loyal Rangers."
Frederick Lampman, "of Stamford," petitioning in 1802, described himself as "an enrolled U.E. Loyalist and amongst the first settlers in Stamford." He had received 200 acres and claimed he was entitled to 100 acres more, - also to an allowance for his wife, Mary. (LP).

In the cemetery of the old "German Church," near Thorold, from which the graves have lately been removed to permit canal construction, was a stone with the inscription:

"In memory of Peter Lampman, who died in 1834, aged 86. He came from New York to this Province in 1783 with his family and and has resided fifty years in the township of Niagara. He was always a pious, faithful and respectable member of the German Lutheran Church." (NHS19).

He was buried on December 28 by Rev. William Leeming.

George Keefer, founder of Thorold, married Catherine Lampman, daughter of a U.E., born, 1778, died 1813. (JHT).

At Beaverdams cemetery are buried Frederick Lampman, died 23 March, 1874, in his 83rd year, and Mary Anna, his wife, died 15 August, 1842, aged 65 years.

The Lampmans of Canada are a very numerous family, with repetitions of the same Christian names in the several branches and in successive generations. The preparation of a complete genealogy would be a difficult undertaking.

LEMON

Lawrence Lemon came into the province in 1792. (LP). He is said to have come from Pennsylvania, settled in Bertie and removed to Stamford, where he was town warden in 1800 and held other municipal offices in later years. He died in 1842, aged 71 years, 6 months, 11 days. (NHS22).

Joseph Lemon, senior, was on the U.E.List. He had a daughter who married William Current of Willoughby. (LP).

Jacob Lemon, senior, died 1816, aged 73 years. He was town warden of Willoughby for a number of years. (NHS22).

Mary Lemon, died 1823, aged 76 years. (NHS22).

Mary Willson, wife of Lawrence Lemon, born 1776, died 1868. (NHS22).

Lawrence Lemon was in the 2nd Lincoln in 1812.

Many members of the Lemon Family are buried in the cemetery adjoining Lundy's Lane United Church, Niagara Falls. (See"Barnes.")

LUNDY

William Lundy's land petition states that he came into the province in 1786, with his wife and six sons, "as a matter of conscience." Isaac Swayze's certificate says that Lundy came in 1788 with his wife and five sons and that another son was born before 1789. (LP).

William Lundy came from Pennsylvania. He married Nancy Silverthorn. Their children were Eli (Eliezar),(married Mary Keefer); Azariah,(married Elizabeth Miller): James,(married Mary Anderson); Thomas,(married Catherine, daughter of Daniel Shannon and sister of Lanty Shannon); Benjamin,(married Rachel Shannon), and Joseph. (T).

James Lundy was a sergeant in Captain Burch's company of the 2nd Lincoln in 1814.

Samuel Lundy, a brother of William, who had five sons, settled on Yonge street, and some of William's sons went to the same locality. (T).

Rev. William Leeming's register for 1829 records the burial on September 13, of William Lundy, aged 88 years and 9 months.

The Lundys are said to have been Quakers before coming to Canada.

In the cemetery at the west end of Lundy's's Lane are buried:

"James Lundy, died Nov.20 1867, aged 88 years and 20 days."

"Mary, wife of James Lundy, born in Nova Scotia, Nov.22,1784, died Dec. 18, 1848, aged 64 years.

LUTES-LUTZ

Sampson Lutes is credited with service in both Butler's's Rangers and the Indian Department during the Revolution.

John Lutes came into the province in 1786 with his wife and ten children. One child was born in 1788. (LP).

In 1797 a land petition was filed by Margaret, widow of John Lutz, now wife of Daniel Gleeson. (LP).

Joseph "Lootz" and John Lutz were in the 2nd Lincoln in 1812-14.

The family of Samuel "Louts" who had a wife, four sons and a daughter is listed in the settlers roll of 1783. (NHS38).

MACKLEM

For a hundred years, the Macklems were the leading family in Chippawa. In a petition to the Executive Council of Upper Canada, dated 4 November, 1794, James Macklem stated that he wished to reside in the province and to establish a potash works and lumber yard on the public land at the mouth of the Chippawa. The application was evidently received with favour, for Lieut. Pilkington was instructed to pick out a proper location (LP).

James Macklem, son of William Macklem(or Maclean) of Ardcairn, Donaghley, Tyrone, Ireland, emigrated to Pennsylvania in 1789 and came to Canada in 1791. He married Lydia Smith, of Bertie. (Chadwick).

James Macklem was a captain of the 2nd Lincoln at the outbreak of the war of 1812-14.

McCLELLAN

William McClellan, with his wife and three sons - John, Martin and William - were residents of Cherry Valley before the Revolution. The father was seized by raiding Indians who put rings in his ears and nose. Eventually he escaped and was able to bring his wife and two sons to Niagara. The other son, Martin, born 1771, was carried off by the Indians to Ogdensburg but returned three months later to Cherry Valley, where he was rescued by the whites and sent to join his family at Niagara. (T).

William McClellan, junior, settled at Beaverdams. He served in the 2nd Lincoln in 1812-14 and attained the age of ninety-six years.

John McClellan was married, 22 April, 1802, by Rev. Robert Addison, to Jane Thompson. He bought land in Stamford from the executors of the Tice estate. At the time of one of the invasions during 1812-14, the McClellans abandoned their home and fled as far as Stoney Creek. They conveyed their smaller children by placing an empty straw-tick across a horse and putting some of the little ones on each side, so as to balance the load. Mary, daughter of John and Jane McClellan, born 1808, married William McMicking in 1827. Later John McClellan moved to Caledon. (T).

One John McClellan was lieutenant of the artillery company of the 2nd Lincoln Militia in 1812-14 (OBF).

Martin McClellan was lieutenant of a flank company of the 1st Lincoln Militia and was promoted captain in 1812. (OBF).He was killed in action at the taking of Niagara and Fort George, 27 May, 1813.

According to the family tradition, he visited his wife at "the Cross Roads" (now Virgil) on the day before the battle and placed his watch and pocket book in her hands saying that he had a premonition that his death was near. The bullet that killed him passed through his empty watch-pocket. (T). The pocket-book is now in Memorial Hall at Niagara. Captain McClellan left five small children, greatly reduced in circumstances through property losses in the war.

A branch of the McClellan family remained in th States after the Revolution. General George B.McClellan of Civil War Fame, is said to have been a descendant. (T).

McDONALD

Allan McDonald was a sergeant in Butler's Rangers until the disbandment of the corps. He was employed in survey work by order of General Powell, Colonel Butler and Lieut. Tinling, acting surveyor, but received no remuneration. He had a wife, six sons and two daughters. On his petition of June 11, 1794 he was granted 400 acres. (LP).

MACDONELL

In July, 1793, A. Macdonell applied for lease of a site on the "chain reserve" between the mouth of the Chippawa and a small island in the Niagara River on which he might erect a saw and grist mill. The application was refused.

John and Alexander McDonnell served in Captain Askin's company of the 2nd Lincoln in 1814. Lieut. Christoper McDonnell and Private Alexander McDonnell of the 2nd Lincoln were killed in action at Chippawa. The former left a widow - Susannah.

McEWIN -McEWEN

John McEwin was a native of North Britain, came to America in 1784 and to this province in 1786 - as stated in his petition dated 16 July and 12 August, 1795, and in a certificate signed by Robert Ker, John Reilly, Isaac Swayze and David Secord, which described him as a man of "known industry and spirit of culture." He took up 300 acres of land on the Chippawa creek, cleared and fenced 140 acres, and spent £1,600 on improvements. He called the place "Thornhill Farm." He had three sons, and, on the petition above referred to, was granted an additional 300 acres of land.

In the same year he wrote to Major John Small, Clerk of the Executive Council, stating that he was going to North Britain in the Fall and proposed to bring out a considerable number of immigrants if the government would grant him three townships to assist the new settlers. His scheme was not acted upon at the time.

In his petition of 16 July, 1795, he stated that he had discovered on his premises, a body of bog iron, contiguous to a stream of water sufficient to drive a bloomery. He asked a lease of the ore, on which condition he would erect a bloomery immediately. The petition was ordered to "stand over" and no record of further development has been found. (LP). The deposit of ore referred to was probably situated between the present Montrose yards of the Michigan Central Railway (in 1989, the Canadian Pacific Railway) and the Chippawa Creek.

There was a very lively interest in connection with deposits of iron ore in that vicinity in 1795. The Journal of la Rochefoucault has this entry under date of June 22: "An iron-mine, too, has lately been discovered near Chippaway creek. A company has associated for the working of this mine, and resolved on erecting an iron-forge in the vicinity of the falls. But this they dare not establish without the governor's permission; for the mother country still persists in supplying all its colonies with its own manufactures; and refuses to relinquish a monopoly that has already cost it that part of America which composes the United States. But the company hope to obtain the desired permission." (OA13).

In the same month Joshua Pell petitioned the Governor in Council for a site on the bank of the Niagara between the Chippawa and Benjamin Canby's mills for the erection of "a good forge and furnaces to make hollow ware and 'iron'." He also asked for an acre of land on which to build dwellings for the employees of the proposed works, and also for the right to take iron ore wherever he could find it. Their proposition was considered by Council to be "inadmissable."

Ezra Dean, who with two hundred associated petitioners, had been conditionally granted 20,000 acres of land for settlement somewhere on the Chippawa (probably on its upper reaches) in 1793, also sought the right to build an iron works in 1795. He asked a mill-site or twenty chains frontage on the bank of the Niagara beginning at the first break of the rapids and extending down to within twenty chains of Benjamin Canby's house; also an acre of land in the military reserve at Chippawa, the privilege of building a flume, warehouses and coal houses; also 2000 acres of land on Grand Island to supply "wood coal" - 1000 acres for the founder of the forge and 1000 acres for the founder of the furnace.

The pretentious scheme of "Ezra Dean and Company" was supported by petition from John Wilson, Robert Weir, John Warren, Parshall Terry, Benj. Hardison, Thos. Cummings, Henry Weishuhn and Nathan Raymond. Council could not grant the prayer "for the present" as all minerals were reserved and because Pell's petition had already been filed. (Text of these two petitions appears in Papers and Records, Vol. 24, p.50-52, 100).

An iron forge was susbsequently established by Robert Randall as part of "the Bridgewater Works," which he had acquired from Canby & McGill, and there he claimed to have turned out the first bar iron made in Upper Canada.

In 1798 one John McEwen of Queenston was the owner of a vessel sailing between that place and York. (LP).

One John McEwen was captain of a Flank company of the 1st Lincoln from 1811, was at Queenston(Despatches)and was later taken prisoner and interned at Burlington, Vt. (OBF).

McMICKING

There were apparently two families of McMickings in Stamford in the earliest days - of the same Scotish origin but of undetermined relationship.

Peter McMicking was living in the province of New York at the outbreak of the Revolution. He abandoned considerable property, fled to Niagara, joined Butler's Rangers and served in the company of Major John McDonell, later of the Royal Canadian Volunteers, to the end of the war. No compensation was allowed him for his losses, his petition being received too late and declared informal. He had a wife and six children and was granted 300 acres. In 1795 his allowance was made 200 acres for himself and 400 acres for his family (LP).

Peter McMicking was High Constable of Nassau (or Lincoln), a coroner, and town warden. At a later date he petitioned the Executive Council for recognition of his services in various civil offices without pay. In consideration of his "very spirited and zealous conduct in the office of High Constable" his land grant was ordered increased to 1000 acres. (B., p.231).

At the storming of Fort Niagara, in December, 1813, one of the British prisoners released was Peter McMicking, aged 80 (70? years). ("Drummond's Winter Campaign.")

John McMicking, son of Peter, was granted 200 acres in 1801, as the son of a U.E.

John McMicking was lieutenant of Captain Rowe's company of the 2nd Lincoln in 1814. (LAB). A man of the same name was, in later years, captain of the cavalry troop attached to this regiment.

Elizabeth, daughter of Peter McMicking, married David Bastedo. ("Gilbert Tice, U.E.")

In the Stamford Presbyterian cemetery are the following inscriptions:

"Peter McMicking, a native of Scotland, Are Shire, town of Colmonell, who died in Stamford, April 13, 1823, aged 83 years."

"Agnes, wife of Peter McMicking, a native of Scotland, town of Whigton, who died January 3d, 1827, aged 77 years.:

"Gilbert McMicking, died February 11, 1861, aged 83 years." Gilbert McMicking was Quartermaster of militia on this frontier in 1812-14. One Gilbert McMicking was member of the Upper Canada Assembly for the Fourth Riding of Lincoln, 1835-1840.

Thomas McMicking, one of the two first settlers of Stamford, belonged to the McMicking family of Wigtownshire and Ayrshire. The McMickings (MacMicking or MacMichan) of Killantringan held one of the most ancient baronies of Ayrshire. One of the family lost his life in 1427 when he supported the Lord of the Isles against James I. This family was conspicuous in the Reformation and religious wars and suffered fine and imprisonment in the reign of Charles II. Sir Gilbert MacMichan, ninth in descent from Mahun Rusid, married Agnes Macdonald, daughter of John, son of Angus, Lord of the Isles.

The McMickings are still prominent in political and military life in the Old Country.

Thomas McMicking, the Stamford pioneer, was the fourth in succession of that name. His father, Thomas III, died in 1756, leaving children by two marriages. Thomas IV and John were sons by the second wife, nee Janet Mulwain. Of Thomas III,(II?) it is related that, during the period of religious persecution, he was overtaken on the moors by a party of Claverhouse's dragoons but escaped detection by throwing himself down among the heather. His garments so blended with the colors of the herbage, that the troopers passed within six paces without discovering him.

The life-story of Thomas IV, was written many years ago, by his youngest son, James, for the information of his (James's) children.

Slightly condensed it reads as follows:

"Thomas McMicking (IV) was born in the parish of Stranraer, in the county of Galloway, now in Wigton, on 11th of April 1750(N.S) His father died when he was very young and he was reared in the home of a minister, from whom he received some education. At eighteen he was apprenticed for three years as a mason. Having obtained his trade, but being dissatisfied with that method of making a living, he, with his brother, John, sailed from Port Patrick on the 2nd of June, 1771, and arrived at New York nine weeks later.

"Thomas and John took up land on the west branch of the Delaware, and not far from the Catskill Mountains. Two years later, their mother and two sisters - Sarah and Janet (the latter, widow of John Cooper, being accompanied by her two sons, Thomas and James Cooper) - sailed from the same port. Sarah died and was buried at sea. The captain of the ship lost his reckoning, after being some time at sea, but was set right by the captain of another ship, who also advised him to make all speed to some port as a war had broken out.

"The captain obtained the consent of all the passengers to be landed at the first port they could reach. Your great-grandmother, her daughter and two grandsons were landed at Philadelphia from which place the captain provided them with passage to where Thomas and John McMicking were living, on the Delaware.

"Here they all remained until the war of 1776 broke out, when they were taken prisoners by the Seneca Indians except for your great-grandmother, who had a short time before fallen from her horse and broken her leg. The captors,thinking her too lame to walk, resolved to kill her. Some of the Indians, remaining near the house to let the others get far enough away not to see the murder, were watching them recede with their backs toward her. She took advantage of it and escaped into the woods, where she hid behind a log until they were gone. In the meantime the party detached to do the bloody deed returned to the house, but not finding her they began stamping on the floor, and finding there was a cellar underneath, but could not find the entrance, thought she was concealed therein, set the house on fire and watched it until they were sure she was dead. They then started to overtake the rest of the party.

"She, now seeing her way clear, left her concealment and after travelling several days through field and forest, she found herself on the shores of Lake George. There she found three fellows with a boat. She offered them a guinea to take her in sight of the British shipping which they accepted, and after rowing a short distance rounded a point and found themselves immediately under the guns of the Royal George, a British man-of-war. She then showed a flag of truce. This brought a boat to take her on board. The captain asked her who she was, and how she came there. She related the capture of her son, daughter and grandsons,and how she had escaped and made her way through the woods and of giving the guinea to the fellows to show her the British shipping. The sailors, hearing the story of the guinea, offered to take if from the rascals and restore it to her. She replied, 'Nay, nay; they have fulfilled their bargain; its none o'mine.' She arrived at Niagara some time during the summer, her daughter and grandsons having arrived there the March before.

"We will now follow the other party from their being made prisoners, to the same place. The party consisted of the previously mentioned Janet McMicking Cooper, her two sons, Thomas and James and her brothers, Thomas and John McMicking. They began their journey through the woods towards the Seneca villages and after travelling several days in that direction they were met by a runner,who told of a party of Indians and a boy who had gone southward on a marauding expedition, and had taken three negroes prisoners. On their way homeward they all lay down to sleep, having theirs arms scattered about, but the negroes kept awake and when the Indians were sound asleep got up and seizing the arms killed the three Indians,wounded the boy and made their escape. The boy then went to the village and told the tidings. A runner was then sent to meet the party that had the first-mentioned prisoners, Thomas, John and Janet McMicking Cooper, and her two sons. They halted and held a council which decided that three white prisoners should be killed to compensate for the three braves the negroes had despatched. Your grandfather, Thomas McMicking, was elected as one of the substitutes and condemned to run the gauntlet.

"When they arrived at the village, a day or two later, the arrangements being completed, he was brought near a brush fence with a rude wicket gate, behind which an Indian (who had asked the privilege of killing him) was standing with his tomahawk over his shoulder, ready to strike the fatal blow as the prisoner passed in, but fortunately he slipped by without the young hero observing him, after which the Indian lost ground which he was not able to make up. The fastest runner in the tribe then took up the chase, but was not able to gain on the refugee. A white boy, standing on the fence called out, "Run my man, or they will kill you." He stopped to ask him, "Where shall I run to?" "To some house in the village. Perhaps they will show you." During this dialogue the pursuer gained on him, and as the prisoner started to run, threw his tomahawk which struck McMicking between the shoulders and staggered him, though he did not fall, and again maintained his distance. On reaching the village he entered a house which soon filled with Indians who began beating him, and calling him 'Damn Yankee,' the juvenile rabble striking him with sticks.

"He now for the first time began to think of revenge and if there were enough white men to kill those outside, he would despatch those around him, but that not being the case, he spread out his hands as in swimming, and clearing a passage for himself, gained the open air, when he again set off at full speed. Turning into another house he was more successful, as there were two squaws in it, who seemed to pity him and pointed to a scalp wound on the back of his head, from which the blood was flowing freely, but he did not know how he got it. About that time a chief came in, followed by a rabble who wished to get him out to run again, but the chief said: "He has gained his life, go away." This order they obeyed, and he was left without further molestation, but was still a prisoner.

"I think he was a prisoner four years when he set out with a party on their journey through the wilderness, bound for Niagara, where they arrived after sleeping ten nights in the snow. Each had a sock-foot full of corn, dealt out as the ration for the journey. They killed a racoon, which was distributed among them. On arriving at Fort Niagara they were supplied with new clean garments by the government. The men joined Col.Johnson's Foresters, a fatigue regiment, and remained with it a little over a year. Then they were honorably discharged and given land because they were loyal to the British flag. Each man was given two hundred acres and each of their children the same. The land is situated on the bank of the Niagara River, about a mile from Queenston. (John McMicking returned to Scotland, married, and afterwards lived in the States.)

"Your grandfather now began to clear his farm. He built a log house where they all lived. In 1787 he returned to Scotland to get a wife. He married Isabella Gass, daughter of William Gass, grain merchant. She was born in Annandale, Dumfriesshire,Scotland, in 1767, and married to Thomas McMicking in 1787.

"Your great-grandmother, Janet (Mulwain) McMicking, died about 1794. She was the first one buried in Stamford (Presbyterian) Cemetery.

"Your grandfather continued to improve his farm, which he found to be much better than the first one, as he could raise better crops. He continued to work with the usual varied success until the war of 1812. His home being in the midst of the battlefields, we were sorely put about. We were obliged to go farther from the frontier. We loaded all the furnishings we could on two wagons and found quarters in the Short Hills, near Beaverdams, in the home of a Mr.McGlashan, where our neighbors the Chisholms were also sheltered. When we returned home we found our place plundered and in great disorder.

"Times were exceeding hard for some years after. Grist would be taken twenty,thirty, even forty miles, to a mill, and the owners arranged prices to suit themselves. When they had grain to sell, they would be offered half a dollar per bushel, half cash, half trade. Farm produce was plentiful and difficult to sell at any price. There was a habit at that time that is quite worthy of deprecation - that was that every family kept spirituous liquors in the house and gave to everyone that came in. It was considered an insult if they refused to drink it. The consequence was that many drunkards were reared in such neighborhoods.

"Janet McMicking Cooper, your grandfather's sister, married Wullie Brown, a Scotchman. They owned a farm near where the Suspension Bridge (present day Whirlpool Rapids Bridge) now crosses the Niagara River. She died there a short time previous to the war of 1812.

"Your grandfather brought apple seeds from the Catskill mountains for the purpose of raising trees to plant an apple orchard. He was told to steep them in milk, to make them sprout better. He put them in a cup of milk and placed it on top of the cupboard. A cat found it and ate the seeds, milk and all, showing the futility of human calculation. He must have tried again, for he planted an apple orchard and had the first apples in this vicinity.

"He was Warden of Stamford Township in 1793. He was a man of medium height, stoutly built, hair auburn, had a firm step and was considered of more than ordinary strength and activity, being a fine runner. All he owned was confiscated during the war of 1776. He just got comfortably situated again when the war of 1812 broke out. He fought in the battle of Queenston Heights. He died on the farm he so dearly earned Feb. 19, 1830, is buried in the Presbyterian cemetery at Stamford village, beside the Presbyterian church he helped to organize in 1783, and was a faithful member and ardent supporter of as long as he lived."

Entries in the McMicking family bible include the following:

	Born	Died
Thomas McMicking	31 March 1750 (O.S.)	19 February, 1830
Isabella Gass	4 September, 1767	2 November, 1830

(Married in Scotland, 29 March, 1787)

Children:
 Janet, born 29 March, 1788; died 9 May, 1793
 Eleanor, born 13 February, 1790; died 31 May, 1859
 Margaret, born 12 June, 1792; died 3 May, 1793
 Thomas, born 13 August, 1794; died 29 September, 1857
 Sarah, born 4 July, 1797: died 13 May, 1873
 Jane, born 16 November, 1799; died November 1839
 Mary, born 5 November, 1801; died February 1837
 William, (a), born 6 March, 1805; died 20 August, 1857
 John, born 4 August, 1807; died September 1809
 James, born 27 November, 1811; died 1891
    (a) Married Mary McClellan, 17 May, 1827

The list of farmer-settlers in 1783 gives the "McMicken" family, with ages as follows: Thomas 33, Jane 66, Jane Cooper 43, Thomas Cooper 14, James Cooper 11, Harvay Alexander 3. (NHS38).

Thomas "McMeeking" filed a claim for property losses in the Revolution at the claims office in England. He is described as "late of W. Branch Delaware River, Tyron Co., N. York Province." Evidence was taken by the Commissioners at Niagara on 12 May, 1788.

Claimant swore that he came to America in July, 1774, was living in Tyron county when the war broke out and joined the British army at Niagara in March, 1781. He was desired by Brant to remain in the country in order to get intelligence and to supply British scouts with provisions. He had a large family which he could not remove. His mother lived with him and broke her leg "so as to be an object." He was obliged to take up arms once with the Rebel militia for one night; before that he had been under arms with Capt. T. McDonell of Sir John Johnson's regiment, and was in consequence imprisoned by the rebels. In 1781 he was taken by the Seneca Indians and brought to Niagara where he joined Colonel Guy Johnson's Foresters and served for a year.

On June 5, 1779, a party of British Indians took from his farm stock, etc. valued at £166. He was then in Albany gaol for furnishing provisions to a British party. John Burch and "Sir Wm. Johnson Jnr." certified to these circumstances. On 5th April 1780, he furnished provisions to Brant and his party. Brant certified that McMicking frequently furnished him with provisions and intelligence.

On October 18, 1790, the Senecas took from him stock, etc. valued at £143 and brought him prisoner to Canada. Part of the stock belonged to Peter "McMeeking" of Butler's Rangers. Nothing but his friendship for Great Britain kept him where he was and exposed him to these losses.

Lieut. Joseph Ferris certified that the claimant often furnished his parties with provisions and thought he was plundered of 8 sheep by the Delaware Indians. Lieut. David Brass certified to claimant's loyalty and that he frequently furnished his ("Brass's") parties with provisions.

MARTIN

Thomas Martin who had land in Stamford may be identical with Thomas Martin who was living in Willoughby in 1795, as he had been permitted by the Land Board to transfer his Stamford lands to Robinson in 1791. (OAS). He stated in a petition that he had served five years in the Navy and was taken prisoner at Stoney Point. He came to the country in 1786, with his wife and six children; received a ticket from Frey for 300 acres of land but lost it. He had taken up only 100 acres and asked for Lots 16 and 17 on the 2nd Concession of Willoughby, which was granted. (LP).

METLAR

Philip, John and George Metlar, brothers, were pioneer settlers, the latter locating in Pelham and the two former near Stamford-Thorold line. Philip "Midler" came in 1787 with a wife and two children. (LP). John "Midler," son of John, of Stamford, came in 1788. Philip "Medlar", aged 40 years, from New Jersey, figures in a settlers' roll of 1787.

Philip and Daniel Metler appear in the rolls of the 2nd Lincoln in 1814. (LAB). This Philip was a son of the original settler of that name. The battle of the Beaverdams was commencing when the United States column was passing along the Mountain Road in front of his farm. Philip was seized, while working in his fields, by enemy soldiers who demanded to know where "those damned Indians" were. He was not held prisoner but his horses were taken. (T). Philip Metlar (probably "junior") married Rebecca Fennen, who had walked with her father, from Pennsylvania.

MIDDAUGH

James Middaugh served in the Revolutionary war under Brant, - in what capacity his petition does not state. His aged parents came into this province at the end of th war and James labored on his father's land. In 1795 he asked for a grant of land at Long Point and was allowed 400 acres. The spelling "Middaugh" is established by the well-written signature to his petition. The name appears in various forms in other records. (LP).

Inscriptions in Stamford Presbyterian cemetery, include the following:

"Benjamin Meddough, died August 10,1830, aged 61 years, 5 mo."

"James Middough who departed this life June the 28th, 1839, aged 79 years, 5 months and 15 days."

The Middaughs are connected, by marriages of the next generation, to the Johnsons, Fields,Clements and other families of Loyalist origin.

MILLARD

Isaiah Millard came into the province in 1784, took up 200 acres of land "on Mount Dorchester" and made good improvements. He died in 1793, leaving a widow, Beulah, seven sons and one daughter. Family lands were allowed them on petition in 1795. (LP).

Daniel Millard married Margery, daughter of Peter Secord, U.E., and had five sons. He was a Justice of the Peace. He was awarded 600 acres of land and his wife 200 acres as the daughter of a U.E. (LP). One Daniel Millard was a corporal in the 85th Regiment. He removed in 1799, to the township of Woodhouse and, in 1800, was appointed treasurer of London District.

Jesse Millard served in the 84th Regiment, had a wife and four children and died prior to 14 July, 1796. He was a brother of Daniel. (B).

In the list of farmers in the Niagara settlement in 1783 appears a "Millar" family, which probably should read "Millard."

The members mentioned are Thomas, aged 54, Mary 55, Thomas 29, John 18, Noah 13, Unis 16 and Sarah 12. (NHS 38).

Jason, Dan and Thomas Millard were signers of a petition from the inhabitants near Sugar Loaf in 1793. (Papers and Records, Vol 24, p.136.)

Before the Commissioners on Claims, Thomas Millard gave evidence that he was a native American, always supported the British government and had three sons in the King's service from 1778 to the end of the war. Before the outbreak he lived on 300 acres on the Susquehanna, which he had purchased in 1774. He had also paid £100 on the purchase of other lands. All his family came away with him, abandoning stock, grain and other crops, utensils, furniture, etc. A notation on the Commissioner's record says "Claimt. seems a very fair man." "May be allowed." (This was Thomas Millard,senior, as a son, - one of the three who were in the army, - giving evidence for his father, is described as "Thomas Millard, junior.")

Thomas Millard, senior, had land in Stamford and there is a land petition from Thomas Millard, senior, "of Crowland," who says that he came into the province in 1777.

One Thomas Millard was a sergeant in the King's Royal Regiment of New York.

Mary, daughter of Thomas Millard, junior, married (1) Wareham Johnson, and (2) Ransom VanTassel. Her eldest son by her first marriage was Benjamin Johnson. Wareham Johnson kept an inn on the N.W. corner of Lundy's Lane and the Portage Road. When the battle of Lundy's Lane was beginning, he buried $1500 in gold in the woods east of the Road, but, after the battle, could not locate the spot where it was concealed. He was in the 2nd Lincoln in 1812 and was still living in 1818. He had a brother, Elijah, who was also in the 2nd Lincoln.

Thomas Millard, junior, was in the 2nd Lincoln in 1812. Samuel Millard was in the Niagara Light Dragoons of 1812 and Jesse Millard in Merritt's troop of 1814.

MOLYNEUX- MULLINEAUX

William Molyneux was an employee of Hon. Robert Hamilton of Queenston. Old records indicate, though they do not definitely state, that he married Nancy (Anne), daughter of Charles Anton, a soldier of the 1st Battalion of the 60th Foot(Royal Americans). She, also, was an employee of Hamilton. (LP).

Notes

William Molyneux placed an advertisement in the *Niagara Constitution* which appeared on September 13, 1799. It read:

> "TO BE SOLD In the township of Stamford, a farm situated about five miles from Queenston, containing 100 acres of land of which eighty or ninety are cleared and under fence; the whole being in good order, together with a dwelling house, within twenty yards of a good stream of water; a barn and orchard, also about ten tons of the best of hay, wheat, rye, etc.; a yoke of excellent working cattle, a pair of horses, two cows, one heifer and ten hogs. Also two hundred and eighty acres in the township of Bertie, situated at Point Abineau bounding on Lake Erie. The whole of the above property is free of all mortgages or encumbrances whatever, and for which indisputable titles will be given. Wm. Molyneux, Newark, Sept. 13, 1799."

It is believed that William Molyneux sold out and moved to Molyneux Corners in the United States.

MOORE

A vivid story of the trials and sufferings of the Loyalists during the Revolution, and of their struggles to establish themselves in this province, is told in the petition of Jeremiah Moore.

The first was received by the Executive Council on 21 September, 1792. Petitioner describes himself as of the township of Mount Dorchester, and says that he came from Lancaster county, Pennsylvania, where he had a freehold estate and was in affluent circumstances until the war. He publicly declared his loyalty and harbored and assisted British prisoners held in the stockade there, "who mostly go to New York" (evidently escaped prisoners). There was no proof against him (Moore) but the rebels were much incensed; his moveable property was entirely taken from him and he was burdened with double taxes. He lost heavily in horses and cattle. Finally he had to sell his 225 acres of good land. In 1788 he came with his wife and eight children to Nassau.

Here he would have suffered from want of provisions for his family but for the "humanity and hospitality" of Squire Hambleton (sic) who also assisted him to purchase 100 acres in Mount Dorchester, adjoining the lands reserved for Commons. This lot proving wet, Col. Butler and Hamilton exchanged 50 acres of it for 50 acres of Common land. But still the greater part of his land was too swampy for cultivation and the support of a large family. He asked 200 acres elsewhere.

On 3 August, 1795, "Jeremiah Moore of Stamford" states that he came into the province in 1788; that Col. Hunter and Mr. Hamilton of the Land Board gave him Lot 61 in Stamford; that he has built a house and barns; planted an orchard and made other improvements. He has since discovered that Lot 61 is part of the Glebe. Asks confirmation of his possession of Lot 61 and to be allowed to give up Lot 88 in lieu, it being better in soil and timber.

Attached is a certificate signed by Irish John Willson, Thomas Willson, Samuel Pew, Jonas Barnes and Jacob Killman - "Whereas Jeremiah Moore made application to us his neighbors, inhabitants of Stamford being Freemen of s'd township," - they confirm his statement of the case, Lot 88 is superior to many lots in the township, being well timbered, with much chestnut, very suitable for rails, which adjoining Glebe lot is destitute of. The transfer would do no injury to the Crown or to individuals.

Council referred the case to the Surveyor General. (The patent list indicates that the desired change was made.)

Another petition, date 21 July, 1795 from "Jeremiah Moore of Stamford," states that he came in 1786 with his wife and eight children; that the Land Board gave him a ticket for three and one-half lots, which should have been five and one-half; that he got 200 acres in Stamford; that he had been a great sufferer in the war. Attached is a "nine of hearts" with the following written on the reverse side:

Jeremiah Moore
   is entitle to three lots
   and a half
   by order of the board
   3 1/2   P. Frey

On his petition, a grant of 500 acres was recommended.

A petition in the same name, dated 19 July, 1793, deals with a different matter. Petitioner says that he is "living in Mount Dorchester." There being no lands left in that township he went about fifty miles up the Chippawa, found unclaimed land and built a house 16 by 20. Waited three years for a survey. Contemplated building saw and grist mills. Now learns that Benjamin Canby tanner, of Queenston, has made claim before the Council for his (petitioner's) lands. What action, if any, was taken by Council, is not indicated in the endorsement.

The three petitions are so identical in some details and so contradictory in others that it is difficult to decide whether there were one or two men named "Jeremiah Moore" living in Mount Dorchester at that period.

One Jeremiah Moore was the first town clerk of Stamford.

Solomon Moore, son of Jeremiah, came in 1788, received a ticket for one lot (the eight of hearts) from Frey, improved two lots in Pelham, married, had a family, and was confirmed in possession in 1795. (LP).

An interesting relation of several events in the careers of Jeremiah Moore and his son, Solomon, appears in Vol. 23 of these Papers and Records, under the title "A Story of Early Upper Canada," by Honourable Mr. Justice Riddell.

MUCKLEHONE

Records of this family are very scanty.

The petition of John Mucklehone of Stamford in 1795, says that he came to this province in 1785 with a wife and two children and received 200 acres. Family lands were allowed him. David Secord was his sponsor. There are several petitions from "John Muckle," late of Jessup's corps.

In 1796, John Mucklehone certified that he had no claim on Lot No. 63, the witnesses to his declaration being James Neville, John Johnson, Joseph Lutes, Solomon Hyate and Margaret Clew.

John "Meiklehorn" of Lundy's Lane was buried by Rev. William Leeming, 25 January, 1831, "aged 85 years." (ECNP).

Elizabeth "Macklehone" was buried in 1835.

Notes

Elizabeth Mucklehone of Stamford declared in her will of 1835, that her father was John Jay. (WRO).

NEVILS

James Nevils settled in Stamford in 1787 with his wife and five children. In 1796 he had nine children. In a petition he states that he attended when the Land Board first called the inhabitants together. (LP). That meeting took place in 1790.

James Nevils, was of Irish origin; his wife, Eve De Shired, was German. (WCH, p.439).

In Drummond Hill cemetery are these inscriptions: Isaac Nevels, died July 19, 1852, aged 70 years, 4 months, 4 days."

Rachel Nevills, died October 17, 1874, aged 78 years, 9 months, 27 days."

Six men of the Nevills family were in the Lincoln Militia in 1812-14; Abraham, sergeant of the 2nd Regiment, was taken prisoner at Queenston on July 22, 1814.

By marriage the Nevills family is connected with the Fortners, Wilkersons of Thorold, and Pews.

OLDFIELD

William Oldfield came into the province in 1787 "and settled on lands bounded on the Chipaway lotts not far back from the Falls." - to quote a certificate of John Burch, J.P., dated "Falls Mills," supporting Oldfield's petition of 3 February, 1797. In the next year his wife and one child came. Two other children were born to him. Oldfield received a ticket from Frey, the surveyor, for two lots, which grant was confirmed in 1797 and 100 acres of family land added. (LP).

In 1802, Mary, widow of William Oldfield, stated that the certificates for her husband's two lots had been made out, by mistake, to Nathaniel, a son by a former wife, who had now left the province, resigning the lands to the Crown. William's will had left the property to his son, Joseph, with life rent to the widow. The Council awarded the lands to Joseph. (LP).

Sergt. Joseph Oldfield of the Grenadier company of the 2nd Lincoln was killed in action at Chippawa.

OSTRANDER

The petition of Andrew Ostrander, dated July, 1795, states that he had been ten years in the province, had a wife and seven children, and had received 100 acres of land. Additional 200 acres was granted.

Andrew Ostrander, senior, native of Germany; his wife, Jane Davis (died 1864 aged 104 years) was Scottish. Their son, Andrew (died 1852, aged 57 years), married Agnes (died 1866, aged 74 years), daughter of James Nevils and Eve DeShired. (WCH, p. 439).

In the Warner cemetery are gravestones with the following information:

"Andress Ostrander, died March 4, 1831, aged 71 years, 5 months, 4 days."

"Margaret Clow, wife of Daniel Ostrander, died 1824."

Eleanor Ostrander, daughter of John Clark, Loyalist, who served His Majesty, came into the province in 1788. She was allowed 200 acres as the daughter of a U.E.

William Hooker Lee, brother-in-law to Andrew Ostrander of Stamford, came to the province in July, 1797, with his wife and five children. (LP).

Andrew Ostrander's claims to be ranked as a Loyalist are set forth in the following affidavits of John Hodgkisson and Jacob Vanalstine; the certificate of Colonel Clark shows how the family maintained its loyalty during the war of 1812, while the endorsement indicates further evidence, and the point of view taken by Council.

Upper Canada)   Personally came before me, Thomas Clark, Esquire, one
Niagara District)   of his Majesty's Justices of the Peace for the said District, John Hodgkisson, of the township of Grantham in said District, yeoman, who being duly sworn, maketh oath and saith, That during

the American Rebellion in the year 1777 he joined the British Army under General Burgoine - was taken prisoner at Bennington by the Americans from whom he ran away and went to the West of Albany in February 1778. That in the end of June or beginning of July following, he hearing of a party of Loyalists going off from Albany county to Niagara - he joined this party which consisted of about Forty in number, one of which was Andrew Ostrander now of the township of Stamford in said District - and further says that the whole party proceeded together as far as Schoharie Creek where the party arrived he thinks on the third day in the morning - that at said Creek said Andrew Ostrander and an English lad were sent across the creek to endeavour to secure some provisions - and whilst at a house inquiring for provisions, they were both made prisoners by a party of American rifflemen (sic) who fired upon the party across the creek killing one and wounding two of Hodgkisson's party, who returned the fire, and whilst the firing continued Ostrander & the English lad made their escape, one running up the Creek & the other down, the one that ran down the Creek was Ostrander who again joined Hodgkisson's party - but the Americans proving too many for them his party dispersed, as their pilot was killed - and further says that he went along with Ostrander as he Ostrander knows the country & that they returned together to Norman's Kill where they then parted, and also says that he did not again see Ostrander until he saw him at Niagara about three or four years after the peace of 1783 - And further says that he was acquainted with Ostrander's father and all the family who resided at Norman's Kill from 1777 to 1781 and that they were a loyal family, and further said Andrew did everything in his power to join the British in Canada - and also that he has every reason to believe that said Andrew Ostrander was & always has continued a loyal subject. - He further says that he understood before the peace of 1783 that Ostrander again tried to make his escape to Canada, and was made prisoner, and further the deponent saith not.

Sworn before me
at Stamford the 23rd May   "John Hodgkisson"
1816
 Thomas Clark, J.P.

Personally sworn before me Thomas Clark, Esquire, one of His Majesty's Justices of the Peace for the District of Niagara, Jacob Vanalstine of the township of Grantham in said District, Blacksmith, who being duly sworn - sayeth that in the summer of 1778 he was one of a party of Loyalists between forty and fifty in number, who went off from Norman's Kill near Albany to join the British in Canada, that at Schoharie Creek they were attacked and beat back by a party of American rifflemen (sic), one of his party being a man by the name of Smith, their pilot, was killed and two wounded, upon which his party, one of which was Andrew Ostrander, now of the township of Stamford in said District, dispersed, & made the best of their way back to Norman's Kill where the inhabitants were in general very loyal - That in the end of October or beginning of November following he again set off with a party to join the British, one of which party was said Andrew Ostrander, that this party, about sixty in number joined the British at Auchquaga then commanded by the late Col. Butler - That about a fortnight after having joined the British, he with three others, one of which was said Andrew Ostrander were sent out by the Officers to procure supplies such as provisions & moccasins for the purpose of making an expedition to the German Flats or to Cherry Valley - that the same night on endeavouring to procure supplies, he, Andrew Ostrander and one Andrew Shanklin were made prisoners by a party of seventeen Americans and carried to Cherry Valley & there lodged in jail; he also says that being a blacksmith by trade he was permitted to work at his trade in the day time, he made his escape to Norman's Kill leaving Andrew Ostrander behind, which was in March 1779 and that he did not again see or hear of Andrew Ostrander until he came into Niagara in the year 1785, where Andrew Ostrander has resided ever since - He further says that he knew all Ostrander's family in the States during the American rebellion, that they were all loyal and did everything in their power to assist the British - And further the deponent saith not.

Sworn before me at
Stamford the 23rd May 1816   Jacob Vanalstine
   Thomas Clark, J.P.

* * * * * * * * * * * * * * * * * * * *

Stamford, May 23rd 1816

I certify that during the late war with the United States Andrew Ostrander and his sons behaved themselves as good militia men, that his son James was one of the flank company of men of the 2nd Lincoln regiment, and that I believe the foregoing affidavit to be correct.

   Thomas Clark, Lt.. Col.
   2nd Lincoln Militia

* * * * * * * * * * * * * * * * * * * *

(Written in lead pencil on the back of the sheet bearing Vanalstine's affadavit and Col. Clark's certificate.)

These papers were brought to the Council Office in May,1816, by Ostrander for the purpose of obtaining a Petition to be put on the U.E. List which was not done in consequence of its appearing by his own statement that he was servant to an American officer 3 or 4 last years of the war who obtained his release from gaol in Cherry Valley (where he states he was threatened to be hanged) on condition of serving him.

* * * * * * * * * * * * * * * * * * * *

Isaac, James, Thaddeus and William Ostrander served in the 2nd Lincoln in 1812-14.

(The derivation of the name Ostrander, and further data will be found in "Place and Stream Names of Oxford County, Ontario," by W.J. Wintemberg, published in Vol.22 of these Papers and Records.)

Notes

Andrew Ostrander's wife, Jane Davis, is buried in Page's Cemetery near Brampton, she died in 1864, age 104.

William Hooker Lee (Dr. Wm. Hooker Lee), born 1761 in Connecticut, married Phoebe David in 1787. He practised medicine in the Niagara Peninsula but moved to Southwold, near London, where he died March 30, 1829.

William Hooker Lee's son, Dr. Hiram Davis Lee, born 1791, practised medicine in Chippawa , then moved to London. In 1819 he married Annie Terry, daughter of Parshall Terry.

Ebenezer Lee (1717-1811) married Abigail Bull in 1750. They settled in Oakland near Brantford. Abigail died 1812.

PARK

The story of James Park's services in the Revolution is told in the petitions under the heading ''Chisholm.''

Archibald Thompson and James Park appeared together before the Commissioners on Loyalists' Claims, with John Chisholm as witness. Both were natives of Scotland and came to America in 1773; settled together on John Harper's land in Tryon county; cleared 12 acres, built a house, had horses and cattle - all of which they lost, with their clothes and furniture when they joined the loyal forces under Captain Macdonell in 1777. In 1778 they joined Captain Brant and served to the end of the war. Brant certified that they were volunteers, serving without pay.

In a Land Petition of 1817, concerning a town lot in Niagara, it is stated that James Park of Stamford, then deceased, left a son and daughter.

Notes

There were several men called James Park - Parke in the area.

A James Park died in 1796 according to a petition submitted by a widow Hagar Park.

James Park (1791-1854), married Sarah Shainholtz, daughter of Martin & Elizabeth Shainholtz, in 1806. Sarah married (2) Samuel Birdsall (1785-1864), nephew of Benjamin Canby, and step son of John Darling (Miller) of St. Johns.

The late Dr. Hugh Park of Port Robinson was a descendant of Sarah and James Park.

PETRIE-PETRY

Hanjost Petrie declared before the Commissioners on Claims that he was a native American and lived at Burnets Field, twelve miles from the German Flats, where he had a deed for several hundred acres of land, with buildings worth £600. He was loyal from the outbeak of the Revolution and suffered severely for it. He had to abandon all his stock and effects as he fled through the woods and could not carry it away. He joined the King's troops at Fort Stanwix, and served four years in Butler's Rangers. (See ''Killman'' and ''Reilly.'')

Notes

Hanjost Petrie's will dated 29 May,1804, left assets to his son Joseph Petry, grandson Joseph Hilts and a friend Adam Miller.

PHELPS (ES)

Elijah Phelps was an early settler on the west bank, and was granted Lot No. 2 and Lot No. 5 in Niagara Township. In 1784 he had 20 acres of grain and 8 other acres cleared. By 1816 he was in financial difficulty, as his land was sold when he defaulted on a mortgage.

A malicious letter which was circulated, accused him of being a Jacobin. Jacobins were an extremist political group which advocated egalitarian democracy, and which advocated revolution and violent methods to achieve its goal. Phelps moved to the Short Hills and died 15 March, 1843, age 103.

PUGH-PEW

There are scanty records of this family, who were one of the most numerous in Stamford for many years. They were of Welsh origin, and are said to have been Loyalists from New Jersey and Pennsylvania. Samuel, an original settler, was known as ''Pugh,'' but the modern spelling of the name appears very early.

Two Samuel Pews, also William, Robert, Henry and James Pew, served in the 2nd Lincoln in 1812-14. One Samuel died in service, 10 September, 1813. He left a widow, Mary. A James Pew was in the Niagara Light Dragoons in 1812.

Inscriptions in Drummond Hill cemetery include, William Pew, died 1850, aged eighty-eight years, ten months; Mary Magdalene, wife of William Pew, died 1838, aged seventy-five years; Samuel Pew, died 1869, aged seventy-seven year; Mary Kelly, wife of Samuel Pew, died 1857, aged sixty-two years; Mary, wife of James Pew, senior, died 1848, aged sixty-nine years. There are many others of early dates (NHS22)

The first recorded Methodist baptism in Stamford was that of ''Samuel, son of James and Mary Pew,'' born 6 April, 1806.

Robert Pew, born 1784, died 1822, is buried in Stamford Presbyterian churchyard.

QUICK

Benjamin Quick was a soldier of Butler's Rangers. (B).

Solomon Quick, soldier, with a wife (Fanny) and one child was on the Niagara Provision List in 1786.

RAMSAY

James Ramsay, senior, U.E., lived at Cherry Valley, on the Mohawk early in the Revolution, as certified by George Forsyth, J.P. Two sons and two daughters came to this province in 1778 (LP). (See "Burch.")

In his claim for losses, James Ramsay stated that he was a native of America and lived at Cherry Valley, Tryon county. He remained quiet at the beginning of the revolution. The Americans took some of his stock. When the Rangers and Indians came to that settlement in 1778 he joined them, abandoning all his property. The buildings were burned. He joined the Rangers but was discharged after a year on account of illness. He settled at Detroit, but removed to the Falls of Niagara. A notation on the Commissioners' record says: "Seems a good man; to be allowed, but not to the amount of what he claims."

The wife of Thomas Cummings of Butler's Rangers, called the first settler at Chippawa, was Jenny(Jean) Ramsay. Her brother was a U.E. who came to this province in 1778, and she had two brothers in Butler's Rangers. James Cummings, son of Thomas, was born in 1778. (LP).

Henry Ramsay of Willoughby was a soldier of Butler's Rangers, discharged in 1779.

REILLY

John Reilly was a sergeant in Butler's Rangers during the Revolution, received 200 acres of land, on which he settled, married a daughter of Joseph Petry of the Rangers and had nine children. A petition presented by him in February, 1797, says:

"That your Petitioner served his Majesty during the whole of the American War as a non-commissioned officer - and has received 900 acres - for military and family lands being the whole he is in these respects entitled to -

"That being honoured with an appointment in the Magistracy of this District he is induced to hope your Honor would be pleased to extend his grant to 1200 acres - and praying such indulgence may be conferred on him," etc., etc.

He was granted 1200 acres including what he had already received.

John Reilly was, for many years, one of the most active inhabitants of Stamford, as a magistrate and town officer. Many Loyalist claimants for land were fortified by his certificates. His acquaintance with the early families appears to have been most extensive.

Patrick Reilly was lieutenant in the 3rd, and, later, in the 2nd Lincoln, in 1812-14. Walter Reilly was in the 2nd Lincoln.

Notes

John Reilly's will listed William, Patrick, Daniel, James, Walter, sons; Mary, Margaret, Ann, Catherine, Elizabeth, Hannah, Cordilly, daughters.

John Reilly's second wife was Cordelia Petrie, daughter of Joseph Petrie. In a petition she called herself Delia Reyley.

ROCHE-ROCK

Rodolph Roche was a native of Germany who served six years in the German troops commanded by General Reidesel in the Revolution. He married the widow of Sergeant William Newberry of Butler's Rangers who had been hanged by the rebels on the Mohawk River during the war. Newberry left a son and three daughters, one of whom married Anson Stringer. By her second marriage, to Roche, the war-widow had three more children. In 1796 Roche was awarded 300 acres. (LP).

John "Rock: or "Rocke," who served four years and eight months in the Queen's Rangers was granted 300 acres.

John Rock, senior, enrolled in the 3rd Lincoln in 1812. A John Rock, serving in that regiment, died, 1st December 1812, leaving a widow, Catherine.

RORBACK

Andrew Rorback was a native of New Jersey. On 7 October, 1796, Andrew "Roorbach," a "reduced captain" applied to the Executive Council of Upper Canada for a grant of land. He was allowed 300 acres on condition that he settle in the province. The deed was not to issue for two years. (B). He had a brother, Samuel, and a sister, Hannah, who married George McCarter of Newton, Sussex, N.J.

Elsewhere it is stated that he came to Upper Canada in 1799. He settled at Stamford Village where he kept a store and conducted a saddlery business. For many years he owned the Whirlpool Hotel, and is said to have built it.

He was adjutant of the 2nd Lincoln in 1813-14, became captain in 1814, major in 1831, and lieutenant-colonel in 1839. He commanded the regiment on active service in 1837-38. He was a major of the 10th Provisional Battalion, Upper Canada Militia, in 1839.

He was identified with the Erie & Ontario railway and many other early enterprises, and was one of the donors of land for a road from Stamford village to the Whirlpool. He was a Commissioner of the Court of Requests, 1837; postmaster 1842; collector of rates, 1842.

His first wife, Martha, died 13 December, 1837. His second wife was the widow Brown, who, after his death, married ———- Sniveley. His only son George, died in 1821, aged twenty-two years.

His tombstone in St. John's churchyard, Stamford, bears this inscription.

"Andrew Rorback, a native of the State of New Jersey, who resided in Upper Canada for upwards of forty years and was Lieut-Col., of the 2nd Lincoln, who died in Stamford, August 11th, 1843, in the 70th year of his age."

ROSE (ES)

Daniel Rose, a member of Butler's Rangers, was granted 100 acres of land and family lands in response to his petition of 21 July, 1796. His land, Lot No. 1 in Niagara Township was adjacent to the Stamford Township line. His land was registered in January 1794.(Only Niagara Township could register land, beginning in 1792, the other townships, including Stamford, were not able to register land until 1796.)

According to his will No. 6993, dated 1802, he left his land to his son Daniel. His other sons were Lewis, Peter, Alexander and James. His wife's name was Jane.

ROWE

Records of Butler's Rangers contain many mentions of Sergeant John Rowe. He appears to have been one of the most active and trustworthy non-commissioned officers of the regiment. On its disbandment he was allowed 500 acres of land. In early days he lived at Stamford village and was prominent in local affairs. Most of his land was at Chippawa.

He was captain of the Grenadier company of the 2nd Lincoln militia in 1812-14, was mentioned in Despatches for his services at Queenston Heights, and fell while leading his company at the battle of Chippawa. General Drummond's despatch refers to him as "a brave veteran captain...who nobly fell in gallantly leading his company against the enemy." His son, George, was ensign of the company. (LAB).

Inscriptions in Stamford Presbyterian churchyard include

"Leah, first consort of John Rowe, who departed this life, September 5th, 1793, aged 25 years, 8 months, 3 days."

"Elizabeth Ludlow, wife of George Rowe, who died February 7th, 1853, aged 64 years, 3 months, 27 days."

SEBURN

Stephen Seburn, died 1828, aged seventy years, and Mary his wife, died 1830, aged sixty-five years, are buried at Beaverdams. He came from New Jersey and was settled prior to 1787. Matthew and William Seburn served in the 2nd Lincoln in 1812-14.

Notes

Stephen Seburn's wife Mary's maiden name was Smith. Their children were: John, who married (1) ......Bessey, (2)....... Dolson; Nancy, who married (1) ......Wilkerson,(2) Nathan Hixon; William, who married Jane Lampman; Matthew, who married Betsy Forbes; Margaret, who married (1) one of George Hoover's sons, (2) Jacob Vanderburg; Mary,who married John Hudson; Jacob, who married Hannah Ann Forbes.

SECORD (ES)

James and Peter Secord were Loyalists who came from the Susquehanna. James Secord, aged 47 years, had four children younger than Solomon, Stephen and David who had come with him to Niagara to join Butler's Rangers in March 1777. Peter Secord, aged 53 years, had recently been discharged from the Rangers because of his age. He and his wife Abigail had five children ranging from six to fourteen years. (MH),

On 10 May, 1799 Peter Secord was granted 300 acres of land (Lots No. 90,91,92 of Township No.1 - Niagara Township), but he could not take possession of it as unexpected difficulties had arisen over ownership of the land on the west bank, when the Mississaugua Indians claimed that they had not been party to the treaty of 1764, made between the British and the Senecas. It was another year before a treaty was signed and settlement could begin.

On 4 August, 1780, Francis Goring wrote in his journal that "Secord (Peter) commenced farming over the river." James Secord, Isaac Dolson, Michael Showers, and Samson Lutes and possibly one or two others went over at the same time. The distinction of being the first to settle was claimed by both Peter Secord and Hannah Showers, for her husband. (MH)

The Secords were anxious to make use of the water power available from the Four Mile Creek, build a saw and grist mill. Due to a lack of a grist mill the farmers were required to exchange their wheat for flour at the King's stores, They announced their intention to build a saw and grist mill on the banks of Four Mile Creek on Peter Secord's farm (present day St.David's) and begged permission to be allowed to purchase the mill stones and iron work in Canada and to have them sent up in the King's bateaux. They were refused permission as General Haldimand "would not permit anything of the kind as Private Property." The British Army built mills at the upper end of Four Mile Creek, where the Creek widened into a Pond and the banks were low. These government mills were called the King's Mills, and the farmer-settlers were required to haul their logs and grain to these mills. (MH).

Peter Secord's lots which were below the escarpment, and included the Four Mile Creek, were registered 10 May,1799. He then sold them to David Secord, junior, on 2 July, 1799. This transaction was witnessed by Francis Goring, John Smith and Noah Millard. (ES)

David Secord,junior, was the son of Peter Secord,senior, He married May Mabee.

Peter Secord,junior, born 1764, married Sarah Millard, daughter of Isaiah and Beulah Millard.

Lucy Secord, born 25 Aug. 1765, married Francis Goring, son of Abraham and Ann (Lloyd) Goring, born 1755, died 1842. Lucy Secord died Jan. 1801, had 11 children.

SILVERTHORNE

In July, 1797, Johanna Silverthorne,"widow of Thomas Silverthorne, senior, late of the township of Stamford," stated in a petition that she came into the province in 1787 with her husband and one son. They had improved 200 acres of land. David Secord, J.P. certified that she came into the province in 1787 with one child, that her husband had died since and that she was a poor widow. Council granted 100 acres to "heirs of deceased." (LP).

Thomas "Silverthorn," evidently "junior," of Stamford petitioned the Executive Council, on 11 October, 1797, to be placed on the U.E. List, stating that he had been settled for ten years.

In support of the petition he presented an affidavit from Mathias Boughner, of Willoughby, who declared that at the outbreak of war he lived near Sussex court house in "the Jersies" and that the Silverthorns were neighbours. The family were loyal, the father being heavily fined and imprisoned and put in irons. Thomas had enlisted but "the affair at Trenton" prevented him from joining. He was fined by the rebels.

Council decided that Thomas Silverthorn was not a U.E.L and that the list was closed.

The name "Thomas" was evidently used in three successive generations of the family, as Thomas Silverthorn who died in 1808 was described as "senior." He must have been the "junior" of the Revolutionary period.

John Silverthorn and Mary Steinhoff were married by Rev. Robert Addison on 10 August, 1806. John and William Silverthorn were in the 2nd Lincoln in 1812.

See "Lundy."

Notes

Thomas Silverthorne, husband of Joanna (Newman) died before 1797.

Thomas Silverthorne's widow, Rachel, in a will dated 30 Jan. 1800, probated 4 March, 1800 stated she had two sons, Jonathan and William, a son-in-law, Jonah Howey and four daughters, Winnifred, Rachel, Susanna and Hannah.

SKINNER

Thomas Skinner emigrated from Colchester, England, to Colchester, Connecticut, in the reign of Charles I. He had six sons - Benjamin, Daniel, Joseph, Nathaniel and Ebenezer - and died at the age of 103 years. His son, Ebenezer, married —- Leuvedone and had three sons who became heads of families —- Ebenezer (II), Gideon and Joseph (II.) He died in Colchester, aged about seventy years.

Joseph (II) married Martha Keene and was killed by the Indians at Colchester, on the Delaware, in 1755. The children of Joseph (II) and Martha were - Joseph (died, aged 17 years), Benjamin, Abner, Timothy, Huldah, Martha, Calvin, Josiah, Joseph, Haggai and Lydia. Several members of this family came to Upper Canada as Loyalists and it is probable that some of the descendants of Ebenezer (II) and Gideon also entered the province at that time.

Haggai (son of Joseph(II) and Martha), was born at "the Nine Partners," 5 March, 1750, and married (23 December, 1773) Elizabeth Westbrook (born 27 February, 1751).

(All the foregoing is from the Skinner genealogy and family tradition, unverified by documentary references.)

Haggai took the loyal side in the Revolution but, in endeavouring to join the British forces in 1778, was made prisoner by the rebels and kept in custody until the end of the conflict, a period of more than four years. He came to Canada in 1785, bringing a wife and five children. Another child was born before 1789. John Reilly and Isaac Swayze were his sponsors when he asked the Council for land, and Allan McDonald, the surveyor, certified that he had known "Haggiah" Skinner since 1775 and that he was a loyal subject. (LP).

In 1813, when invading United States forces held the Niagara Peninsula, the ancient grudge of the revolutionists against this old Loyalist family was again in evidence. Haggai Skinner, sixty-four years of age, exempt from militia duty and peacefully working in his fields, was seized by a raiding detachment of cavalry and carried away. He languished in a war prison at Greenbush for six months and was repatriated in July, 1814, landing at Sugar Loaf at the very time when the battle of Lundy's Lane was being waged on the border of his homestead. Elizabeth Westbrook, wife of Haggai Skinner, senior, died 3 April, 1812. On November 12, 1812, he married Elizabeth Shaneholt. He died 8 October, 1823, aged 73 years and was buried on Drummond Hill. (NHS22)

The children of Haggai and Elizabeth were: Levi (born 23 February, 1775; died at Lewiston, Mifferland county Pennsylvania, 18 January, 1808); Magdalene (born 5 March, 1777; married 20 June, 1797; drowned 3 May, 1798); Haggai,junior,(born 22 January, 1780, died 28 June, 1844); Huldah (born 5 October, 1782); Lydia (born 13 August,1785(: Alice (born 25 August, 1788); Joel (born 12 April, 1791); Rachel (born 25 March, 1799). (T)

Haggai Skinner, junior, married Susannah——-. Several of their sons served with the Union armies in the Civil War.

Another authority on the Skinner genealogy names Calvin, Timothy, Haggai, Daniel, William and Joseph Skinner, all brothers, with sister, Huldah (married ———Connell). Calvin lived in Washington county, New York. Timothy, Haggai and Huldah came to Canada with the Loyalists. (T).

One Job Skinner was in Butler's Rangers

Benjamin Skinner suffered confiscation of his property and was imprisoned by the rebels. He came to Canada in 1785 with ten children and was allowed 550 acres. He did not appear before the Commissioners of Claims and his later petition to Council for compensation for his losses was not allowed. (LP).

Benjamin Skinner, junior, son of the above, also suffered for his loyalty to the Crown. (LP).

Jeptha Skinner, another son of Benjamin, senior, was loyal in the war and assisted two families, numbering 14 persons, to reach the British lines. He came to the province in 1794 with a wife and two children and was allowed 200 acres. (LP).

Timothy, Henry and Josiah Skinner were among the Loyalist refugees at Fort Niagara in 1784. Timothy filed a claim for property losses in the revolution.

In 1800 Timothy Skinner sought permission to erect mills on the bank of the Niagara in front of Lot 174,not to interfere with the property of the heirs of John Burch, also in front of the south half of Lot 160. He submitted plans for a saw-mill 26 by 12 feet in size and a grist mill 28 feet square, but his application was refused. (LP).

Benjamin Skinner was assessor of Stamford in 1793 and Timothy Skinner in the following year. Haggai Skinner held the office in 1804.

The rolls of the Lincoln militia, 1812-14, contain the names of Benjamin, Colin, Ebenezer, Gideon, Haggai, Job, Joel, John, Noah, Stephen and Timothy Skinner.Private Timothy Skinner, of the 2nd Lincoln, was killed in action at Chippawa.

The numerous duplications of names in the various branches and generations of the Skinner family make identifications very difficult.

SMITH

Frederick Smith left his former home during the war, with his wife and six children. His wife died on the road but he reached Niagara with their children and joined Butler's Rangers in 1777. (LP).

Elias Smith received a land ticket from P.R. Frey, the certificate being written on the back of a "six of diamonds." (L.P).

(See "Campbell.")

Notes

In a will probated in 1819, Elias Smith's wife was named Catharine. He had sons, William, John, Elias, and daughters, Deborah (Middaugh), Ann (Turney), Phebe (Adams), Mary (Durham), Elizabeth (Clow), Sarah (Clement).

His grandchildren were (John), Richard, William, Thomas, Elias, Catharine; (Elias), Solomon, William, Mary; and Philip Secord.

SPENCER

Robert Spencer, senior, served his Majesty for fifteen years, including eight years in Butler's Rangers and brought his wife and six children into the province in 1785. He was then allowed 100 acres, but in 1797 received 200 acres more to complete his military lands and 350 acres as family lands. (LP). His wife's name was Hannah. They came from the Mohawk Valley.

Adam Spencer and Robert Spencer, junior, of Stamford, were sons of Robert Spencer, senior. When they petitioned for land, David Secord certified that they were "good men and subjects, as their father and friends were before them." (LP).

One Adam Spencer married Annie Corwin.

Sarah Spencer, wife of John Fralick, is said to have been a sister (?daughter) of Robert Spencer, senior.

In the cemetery at the west end of Lundy's Lane is buried Ann Spencer, died 30 August, 1864, aged ninety-two years.

Notes

Sarah Spencer, daughter of Robert & Sarah (Rice) Spencer, died October, 1826. She was the wife of John Hodgkinson and they lived on Lot 11, Con.2, Grantham.

SPRINGSTEEN

Staats Springsteen served in Butler's Rangers for six years and seven months and brought nearly a hundred men into the British service during the war. He brought a wife and two children into this country. He settled upon and improved three lots in Township NO.2, known as Nos. 21,22 1nd 23 on the 5th Concession, - later described as Lots 6,15 and 21 in the township of Stamford. Peter McMicken and Peter Medaugh having encroached on his land, a hearing was held before the Land Board. According to Springsteen's statement "petitioner having unguardedly let some expressions to fall from him which gave undesigned offence to two gentlemen of the Board, Mr. Hamilton and Mr. Kerr, a spirit of animosity against your petitioner was set loose." Arbitrators were appointed who cut his land up by new lines and gave some of it to Medaugh. He offered to give up the three lots to McMicken and Medaugh if they would pay him for his improvements. The whole matter was laid before Council in a petition dated 14 August, 1795. Endorsement does not indicate what action, if any, was taken.

In 1793 Springsteen improved some land on Murphy's Creek, in the Long Point settlement, but his petition to be confirmed in possession was rejected.
(See Papers and Records, Vol.24, p. 131.)

STEINHOFF

John Steinhoff came into the province in 1785 with his wife, eight sons and six daughters, Frey gave him a ticket for five and one half lots and he settled near Chippawa creek. In 1795 his occupancy was confirmed and 200 acres added. (LP).

Leo Steinhoff, son of John, got 200 acres at Long Point. Andrew Steinhoff born in New Jersey, 1773, also asked a grant at Long Point, as he had friends there.)LP).

Emanuel Steinhoff, son of John, complained, in 1796, that his lands in Thorold township were full of windfalls and swampy. He asked 200 acres at Long Point, but the grant was not recommended. (LP).

Frederick Steinhoff received patent for lands in Stamford in 1798.

Jacob Steinhoff was a trooper in the Niagara Light Dragoons.

The name is often mis-spelled in old records, appearing sometimes as "Stoneheap."
(See "Silverthorn.")

STEVENS

John Stevens' story of sufferings and service is told in his own petition as follows:

"The petition of John Stevens, an Inhabitant of the County of Lincoln, most Humbly Sheweth-

That your Petitioner at the commencement of the American War was an Inhabitant of the County of Sunbury on Susquehanna River in the Province of Pennsylvania was Possessed of One Thousand Acres in said County, was severely Persecuted by the Revolted Americans for his attachment to His Majesty, he was dragged by a Rope fixed about his Neck across the River Aforesaid at the stern of a Canoe because he would not subscribe his name to a Paper, drawn up in the form of an Oath, which he thought tended to Rebellion, after suffering everything but Death at their hands he made his Escape to Niagara, served Seven Years in the Corps of the Rangers at this Place, never made any return of his loss to Commissioners as he could not swear his property was confiscated, therefore only drew the Lands allotted to a Private in said Corps aforesaid, without any allowance for his Wife and Daughter; and as the whole of his Estate was Confiscated and he never received any compensation from Government, hopes your Excellency will consider his case and Grant him an addition of Lands, as he has faithfully employed his time in Cultivation since the Corps to which he belonged were disbanded, or grant him such other relief in the Premises as your Excellency may seem meet.

Newark, 10th Sept. 1792   John Stevens"

In a further statement, dated 9 September, 1797, he stated that he came into the province in 1778 with his wife and seven children and had received 300 acres. He was awarded 400 acres family lands. (LP).

On 24 February, 1797, he reminded Council that he joined the Royal Standard in 1777, served in Butler's Rangers until the peace and "suffered more in person and property by his loyalty than any one in the province in his station in life, and neither applied for nor received any compensation." His youngest daughter was now of age.

John Stevens, junior, son of John Stevens, U.E. in Butler's Rangers, served in Sir John Johnson's corps. He was granted 200 acres which he desired to have located at Long Point. (LP).

Aaron Stevens joined the Royal Standard in 1778 and served until 1785. He was a commissary in the Indian Department and married Maria, daughter of Adam Crysler, lieutenant in the Indian Department. His father, Nicholas Stevens, and his brother, John Stevens, were interpreters in the Indian Department and both died in the service after the peace. (LP).

(See "Van Every.")

William and Simon Stevens were in the 2nd Lincoln in 1812.

SUTTON

Anne Sutton was the widow of John Sutton, U.E., and came into the province about 1796 with her two sons and three daughters, bringing also some cattle. On her petition of 30 September, 1796, certified to by Isaac Swayze, she was allowed 400 acres "on account of her large family." (LP).

Aaron, Benjamin and John Sutton were in the 2nd Lincoln in 1812-14.

Notes

Benjamin Sutton of Stamford married Jane, daughter of Hugh Haggerty of Stamford.

THOMSON-THOMPSON

Archibald Thomson, a native of Hawick, Roxburghshire, Scotland, emigrated to America and settled on the Delaware before the Revolution. His experiences and services in that struggle are described in the petitions quoted under the headings "Chisholm" and "Park" in these notes. Archibald's children included two sons - Benjamin, born 1796 and John. Both were in Captain James Cooper's company of the 2nd Lincoln. John, a sergeant, was mortally wounded in the battle of Chippawa, 5 July, 1814 and died in his brother's arms. His body was among those buried by the enemy.

James and John Thomson, brothers of Archibald, came out from Scotland in 1785. In the Old Country the name was spelled without the "p" but the land-granting officials in this province added the letter to the name when preparing documents and the family adopted the changed form as a matter of convenience. (WCH).

James was granted 200 acres "on the mountain" and, in 1797, was given 100 acres additional as family lands. He made his home in the locality known as "Montrose," that name being chosen by his son Archibald, many years later, for the post office there. He had seven sons and three daughters.

James, junior, was ensign in the Light company of the 2nd Lincoln and was wounded at Lundy's Lane. (OBF). David, a brother, was adjutant of the same regiment, and was wounded at Lundy's Lane. He afterwards settled in Haldimand and was a member of Parliament, as were his son and grandson after him. Archibald, son of James, senior, born 12 December, 1800, served in the rebellion of 1837 and rose to be a lieutenant-colonel of militia. He was a Justice of the Peace and member of the Niagara District Council, and in 1858, contested the Welland county seat in the Parliament of Canada with Gilbert McMicken, but was defeated by a small majority. He died, 1 March, 1892, and was buried in the Presbyterian churchyard in Stamford village. His first wife, Jane Fitch, bore him five daughters and three sons, and died 22 January, 1845, aged 41 years and 26 days. Subsequently, he married twice, (WCH).

James, senior, the original Montrose settler, died 22 November, 1831, aged seventy-nine years. His wife, Margaret, died 1830, aged sixty years.

John Thompson, another brother of Archibald, served in Scotland in the "Edinburgh Volunteers" and came to America at the peace to settle beside his relations. He lived eleven years on Lots 41 and 58, granted to him by the Land Board, but in 1797 he had a dispute with the widow Park over a "broken front" lot. Archibald Thompson, in evidence before Council stated that the lot in dispute had been given to him in 1782 by General Powell, then commandant at Niagara. General McLean had ordered Allan McDonald, surveyor, to "run it out" for him. When James Thompson came out from Scotland, Archibald gave the lot to him. When the land was re-surveyed by Augustus Jones, part of the lot fell to Peter Thompson and part to John. James gave up his rights to Peter and John. Council ended the confusion and dispute by awarding B.F Lot No.41 to John Thompson. (LP). The incident is illustrative of the difficulties experienced by the settlers in getting their lands properly marked out and their titles fully established.

"John Thompson of Stamford, late corporal in the 80th Regiment" came from Scotland, spent six years in His Majesty's service in America and settled about 1785. He had a wife and six children in 1795. His original allotment 180 acres, which he had much improved, and on which he lived, was increased by a grant of family land. (LP). Whether he is identical with the preceding is uncertain.

Peter Thompson was forced to leave the States at the beginning of the war and his property, which was considerable, was confiscated. He served in the Rangers and received 200 acres of land as a military claimant. Neglecting to send in an estimate of his losses to the Commissioners of Claims, he received no compensation. He laid his case before the Council in 1795, stating that he had a rising family for whom he would "incline" to make provision. He was given an extra 100 acres as military land and 200 acres as an old settler. (LP). In another petition he is described as "Peter Thompson on the Mountain" and it is stated that he had a wife and one child before 1789 and a second child before 1797.

Peter Thompson died 23 February, 1839, aged eighty years. An obituary notice stated that he emigrated from Scotland before the Revolution, came to Canada in 1783, and was an elder of the Presbyterian church for more than thirty years. "He has left no enemy."

The graves of numerous members of the various branches of the Thompson family are to be found in the Stamford Presbyterian cemetery at Stamford. Colonel James Thompson born "near the Whirlpool," 29 June, 1786, died October 24, 1850.

Jannet, daughter of James Cooper and wife of James Thompson, born 9 July, 1797, died 29 September, 1832 (1852?).

Richard Thompson of Waterloo, Bertie, merchant, third son of James Thompson, senior, born in Stamford 25 October, 1797, died 21 June, 1832. (He married, in 1828, Sarah Hardison of Bertie.) (ECNP). There are many other inscriptions, some with early dates.

TICE

The story of Major Gilbert Tice is pretty fully told in Vol.21 of the Papers and Records of the Ontario Historical Society. Since the publication of that memoir it has been established that Tice died in 1791. His full allowance of Crown lands was 3000 acres, of which he had drawn 1,100 acres before his death. The remainder was ordered assigned to his widow in 1796. (B) (F). David Bastedo, nephew of Mrs. Tice, was granted 400 acres, and his wife (daughter of Peter McMicking) received 200 acres as a child of a Loyalist, in 1796. (LP).

Notes

Gilbert Tice's will dated 8 Dec. 1790 leaves estate to David Bastedo who lived with him after the death of his (Bastedo's) wife, but to be shared with son-in-law Ebenezeer Batchler if he comes to Canada.

Christina Tice, nee VanSlyck, widow of Gilbert, died 14 August, 1814.

Sir Peregrine Maitland bought most of the Tice-Bastedo land near the top of St.David's hill and built his summer residence, "Stamford Cottage" there.

VAN EVERY

The record of the Van Every family is remarkable in many respects. McGregor VanEvery had five sons and served in Butler's Rangers. The father's name was not included in the U.E. List because he was in the province before it was made up. (Apparently it was compiled as a roll of Loyalists as they came in from the revolted colonies.) The old Ranger's name was added in 1802 on petition of his son, Andrew. (LP).

Evidence on the claim for property losses in the Revolution by McGregor VanEvery "late of Schohary, N.Yorke" was heard at Niagara, 15 May, 1788. David VanEvery, the oldest son, stated that his father died at Niagara in September, 1786, leaving a wife, Mary and seven children. He had attempted to join the British army early in the Revolution but was seized and imprisoned, so that he could not enlist until 1781. Five sons were in the King's service from the beginning of the war. The widow stated her husband was in gaol for six months. They were plundered of live stock, farm implements and furniture. Captain John McDonnel of the Rangers certified to the service of McGregor VanEvery and his five sons.

David VanEvery, a son of McGregor, was a sergeant in the Rangers, married the daughter of a Ranger, had two children before 1783 and eventually a family of six sons and a daughter. He removed to Flamboro. (LP).

Samuel, another son, married, Hannah, daughter of John Coon of the Rangers. (LP).

Henry VanEvery was a Ranger; Andrew was too young to serve, he married the daughter of John Stevens of the Rangers. They had two children before 1788. He received 150 acres of family lands in 1796 and 200 acres was granted "Elizabeth VanEvery" (probably the wife), as the daughter of a Loyalist. (LP). William VanEvery, died 1832, aged sixty-seven years, and Elizabeth, his wife, died 1857, aged ninety-three years, are buried in the Warner cemetery. (NHS19).

On 16 July, 1794, Council received petition from Elizabeth VanEvery, former wife of Frederick Dochstader who served in Butler's Rangers from the commencement of the war and died on expedition in 1781, leaving his widow and one child in distressed circumstances. (LP). She was later granted 1200 acres. (I). Her second husband was John VanEvery. Her daughter by her first husband, Catherine, married Captain John DeCou. (Further information will be found in "John DeCou, Pioneer" in Vol. 22 of these (Ontario Historical Society) Papers and Records.)

(See "Warner.")

Notes

Gregory VanEvery born 22 April, 1723, died 25 September, 1786, age 63.

Elizabeth VanEvery, wife of William and widow of Fred Dochstader was granted 1200 acres in Ancaster of which lots 13, 14 and 15 were given in 1805 by William & Elizabeth to Catherine Decou.

Mary Wilcox, daughter of William, born 29 April, 1736, buried in Warner cemetery.

John VanEvery (1795-1862), wife Margaret McKinlay (1799-1841) buried in Warner cemetery.

VAN WYCK

The VanWycks were anciently lords of Wyk, in Holland, but lost their estates during the Spanish occupation and found shelter in the colony of New Amsterdam about 1660. (T).

Samuel VanWyck came into this province about 1797 with a wife and two children. His father had been a captain in the Long Island militia before the Revolution. (LP). He located in York and owned a sailing ship on Lake Ontario. This vessel was lost, after which he came to Stamford, settled near what is now the corner of Victoria avenue and Morrison street in Niagara Falls. Their place was plundered by the Indians during the war of 1812-14 and the family fled towards the Short Hills for safety during the Lundy's Lane campaign. Samuel VanWyck died about 1815. His wife, Sarah, daughter of Weart Banta, U.E., died 1857, aged eighty-two years. (T).

The children of Samuel VanWyck and Sarah Banta were: Hiram Seabury, died in New York, aged three years; Gilbert, served in the 2nd Lincoln in the war of 1812-14, married Nancy Brooks of Lundy's Lane and received lands in Chinguacousy; Abigail (1799-1858) married Robert, son of John and Abigail Fralick, U.E. (q.v.); Veart, married Nancy Blaine; Cornelius, served in 1812-14, married Matilda Forsyth, settled in Chinguacousy; John, married Jane Shaw; Hiram, died unmarried; Daniel, married Nancy Killman; Maria, married John Killman. (T).

Weart Banta joined the King's troops in New York at the beginning of the Revolution and served as lieutenant in the King's Militia volunteers. He was badly wounded while fighting in New Jersey. He came to Canada in

1795, was granted 2000 acres of land, and died prior to October, 1796. His wife's name was Elizabeth and their children were: John; Sarah, married VanWyck; and Elizabeth, married Isaac Davis. (LP). "Wyart" and "Bonter" variations of spelling in the old records.

There was a Samuel VanWyck in the 2nd Lincoln in 1812.

WARNER-WANNER

"Warner" has long been the spelling of this name, but the signatures to some of the earliest documents were plainly "Wanner" - nevertheless, there is always the possibility of error due to mispronunciation or to careless penmanship.

Michael Warner came to this province in 1781, joined the Royal forces at Niagara, and died in 1783. Christian Warner, his only son and heir, served as a sergeant in Butler's Rangers for seven years. His application for a land grant on his father's account was refused. (LP).

Christian Warner's claims on his own behalf are set forth in his petition, dated 1 May, 1797.

To the Honourable Peter Russell, Administrator for the Government of the Province of Upper Canada. In Council.

The petition of Christian Wanner, Loyalist, Humbly Sheweth:

That your Petitioner in the year 1777 then resided in Albany County, and hearing that Gene'l Burgoyn wished that all the Loyalists would join him at Still-water - Your petitioner with others went to him to know the certainty of it, but he advised that they would still remain neutral till he would send them word. I then joined Colo'l Peters corps there, and was then employed (with two others) by Goven'rr Scheen (Skene) by order of Gene'l Burgoyn to go down the North River till we could hear with certainty if Gene'l Clinton ment to come up the North River, which I performed with great difficulty and hazard of my own life, for which service I was promised at my return great reward,but on returning was informed that Gen'l Burgoyn was captured, which made it impracticable for me to get him word,and then was taken prisoner and detained in Albany prison three months, but as soon as I could make my escape came to this place and joined Colo'l Butler's Corps in which I served as as Serjeant (sic) until the corps was disbanded. Likewise your Petitioner in the years 1780 and 1781 was employed by Col'l Butler three different times to go into the States for intelligence and bring in all Recrutes I could get, which I performed and helped to bring in at different times upwards of sixty men, for which services I was promised, but never received any recompense.

Now your Petitioner most humbly begs your Honour will please to take his case into consideration and if his Services merit any reward, that you will please grant to him what quantity of land you may think proper.

And your Petitioner as in Duty bound will ever pray.

(signed) Christ'n Wanner, Capt. Militia.
(endorsed)

In consideration of the Petitioners very meritorious services & the Respectable Recommendations which support him the Board orders 200 acres in addition.

(accompanying certificate)

We do hereby certify that Christian Warner late Sergeant in Butler's Rangers did in the beginning of the American war take a decided part in favor of the Crown, that in the year 1777 he went to General Burgoyn's camp then at Still Water, at the request of us the subscribers and in behalf of considerable number of Friends to Government who were desirous to show their Loyalty by joining his Majesty's forces if he desired and practicable, this service he performed at great risk, as this happened but a few weeks before Gen'l Burgoyn surrendered, and that he for this act put in Albany jail where he remained the Winter following and in the Spring of 1778 he joined Butlers Rangers and served in said Corps to the end of the War - during his services in the Rangers he was always Ranked among the most active was very usefull in Bringing of men on which business he went several times from here to the North River and was very successfull in his undertaking - at the end of the war he settled in the township of Newark where he has made large improvements and has in every respect behaved himself as a good industrious inhabitant.

Given under our hands.
(sgd) P. Ball J.P & Lieut.

Newark May 1st 1797

Late Ranger Christian Warner had a son, Peter, who married Mary, daughter of William VanEvery, U.E., and was allowed 200 acres. Christian also had a son named Michael, (LP).

On August 28,1823, Rev. William Leeming recorded the burial of "Mrs Warner, Thorold, aged about 70 years."

WEAVER

Peter Weaver "of Stamford" came into the province in 1786 with his wife and three children. The family later increased to five children. He settled in 1787 on Lots 8 and 9 on the 7th Concession of Pelham, built a house and cleared ten acres. In 1791, before the land had been surveyed, his improvements were destroyed by a hurricane. On his petition of 23 June, 1795, supported by John Warren and David Secord, these lots were confirmed to him and 200 acres of family land added, - the latter in Oxford county. (LP). Before the Revolution he lived in New Jersey.

The headstone of Peter Weaver at Beaverdams cemetery states that he died 7 March, 1801, aged 52 years, 7 months and 10 days. (JHT).

Paul and William Weaver were in the 2nd Lincoln in 1812.

WILLSON

Thomas Willson and Abigail, his wife,(said to have been a daughter of Judge Pettit) fled from "the Jersies" with the Loyalists. The wife rode a horse which also carried their two small children. They drove a cow with them, and its milk, thickened with flour, in a brass kettle, was the chief article of their diet. They crossed the Niagara at Queenston and took up land three-quarters of a mile north of Lundy's Lane. They secured and sowed wheat, but their food supply failed before the new crop was ripe and some of it had to be gathered while still immature. (T). The children of Thomas and Abigail Willson were: Margaret (married——Pew); Mary (married——Helliwel); Elizabeth (married——Brooks); Abigail (married——Pettit): John; Nathaniel; Thomas; Sarah; Rachel (married——Ross). (T).

In the cemetery adjoining Lundy's Lane church, Niagara Falls are the graves of Thomas Willson, born 22 January, 1768, died 31 May, 1845; also Abigail Willson, born 8 May, 1764, died 15 August, 1854.

WOODRUFF

Ezekiel Woodruff was a Loyalist from Connecticut. He settled in Stamford township and followed the occupations of school teacher, conveyancer and town clerk, holding the latter office for twenty-two years. He died in 1837, aged seventy-three years, and is buried in the Methodist churchyard at St. David. He had three sons, Richard, Henry and William, and one daughter, Sarah, who became the wife of Judge DeVeaux, the founder of DeVeaux College, Niagara Falls, N.Y. Richard and William were members of Parliament. Richard, who was locally known as "King Dick." from his leadership in many enterprises, married Nancy Clement, and had five sons and two daughters. The youngest daughter Margaret, was the first wife of Samuel Zimmerman, the railway builder, who is called the founder of Clifton, - now Niagara Falls, Ont. (WCH).

Ezekiel Woodruff was enrolled in Grant's company of the 2nd Lincoln in 1812.

The Woodruff family was always identified with the locality of St David and with Clifton and Drummondville.

WRONG

John Wrong who had land in Stamford, was a Loyalist who settled in Gainsboro. His wife, Phoebe, the widow of Jeremiah Johnson, came into this province at the close of the Revolution with her eight children. She got 450 acres of land (LP) (B).

STAMFORD PRESBYTERIAN CHURCH CEMETERY

The burial ground adjacent to Stamford Presbyterian Church was called God's half-acre when it was opened in 1784. The first burial was that of Janet Mulwain, mother of Thomas McMicking, one of the founders of the original congregation. This cemetery is resting place of many of Stamford's earliest settlers and the list of burials is included in this book as a help to those engaged in genealogical research. It was intended that a similar list of burials in the other church cemeteries along the Portage Road be included in this book, but this information was not available.

Audrey Johnston began to uncover and record the headstones over the burials in the cemetery as a Bicentennial Anniversary Project for Stamford Presbyterian Church. She carried on unassisted, probing the turf where a depression indicated a stone might be buried under the sod, then removing the sod to uncover the headstone. Audrey walked to the cemetery, carrying her tools until she was joined by Allan Brand who picked her up in his car and brought her to the project, where they both worked at the task of uncovering, then deciphering the names and dates in the inscriptions on the stones.

Until the chart and list of burials was printed in the brochure *Stamford Historical Sites Tour* as part of the Bicentennial Celebrations of Stamford Presbyterian Church in 1985, there was no complete record of the burials in this cemetery. Don Millar typeset the material for this brochure, and it has been photographed and reproduced here in the same form as it appeared in the brochure. Audrey Johnston also enhanced the brochure with her sketches of the first church and the burial ground. This material is reproduced here with the permission of The Heritage Group of Stamford Presbyterian Church.

CHART SHOWING THE LOCATION OF THE BURIAL PLOTS LISTED ON THE FOLLOWING PAGES

BURIALS IN STAMFORD PRESBYTERIAN CHURCH

Letters and numerals in question have been underlined and maiden names of women are shown in parenthesis ( ). In a few cases known historical facts have been added to the information taken from the stones. Some obvious spelling errors in transcription were not corrected but appear exactly as inscribed on the stones.

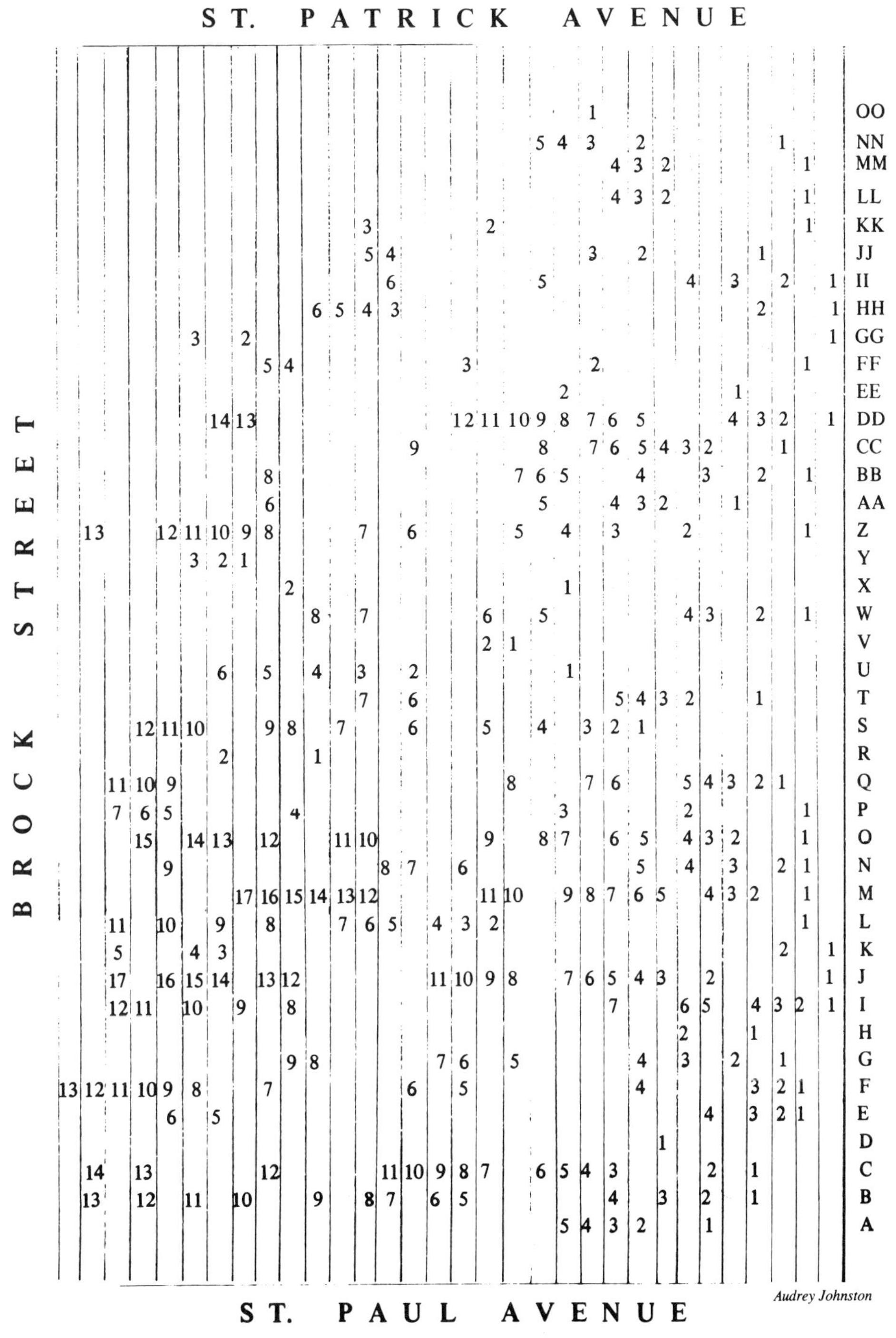

ST. PATRICK AVENUE
BROCK STREET
OO
NN
MM
LL
KK
JJ
II
HH
GG
FF
EE
DD
CC
BB
AA
Z
Y
X
W
V
U
T
S
R
Q
P
O
N
M
L
K
J
I
H
G
F
E
D
C
B
A
Audrey Johnston
ST. PAUL AVENUE

Plot	Name	Date
M13	Alexander, Dolly	1819
M17	Alexander, Ephram	1818
M15	Alexander, Hugh *U.E.L.*	1817
M14	Alexander, Marth Jane	1814
	dau. of Hugh & Susana Alexander	
M16	Alexander, Susan	
	widow of Hugh Alexander	
G6	Allen, David	
LL3	Bacon, Abraham	1925
LL4	Bacon, Harry C.	1971
	husb. of Elsie Church	
LL2	Bacon, Margaret	1948
	wife of Abraham Bacon	
C14	Baker, Stanley	1906
	son of T. & M. Baker	
L7	Bastedo, Susanna	1839
	wife of John Bastedo	
L1	Bell, Mina	
Q7	Bliss, Martha	1860
E2	Bowman, Adam	1818
	s of Jacob & Elizabeth Bowman	
F3	Bowman, Ann	1820
	2nd wife of Jacob Bowman	
E3	Bowman, Dorothy	1820
	wife of Abraham Bowman	
F1	Bowman, Elizabeth	1800
	wife of Jacob Bowman	
F2	Bowman, Jacob	1815
NN1	Britt. Emeline	1910
	wife of John Britt	
NN1	Britt, John	1923
O12	Brown, Janet (McMicking)	1809
	(Cooper) *wife of Wm. Brown*	
JJ2	Burns, Sarah J. (Farrow)	1914
	wife of William Burns	
JJ2	Burns, William	1916
S3	Butts, Eudora	1860
	dau. of ___ J.C. Butts	
U6	Carnoghan, Andrew	1858
X1	Carson, Alex	1820
BB8	Carter, Amy (Thompson)	1930
	wife of Charles H.Carter	
W3	Chamberlin, Catharine	1851
	wife of Joel H. Chamberlin	
P4	Chisolm family	
P6	Chisolm, Catharine	1823
	cousin of John Chisolm	
P5	Chisolm, John *U.E.L.*	1815
P7	Chisolm, John *U.E.L.*	1830
L8	Church, Archibald	
	son of Murray Church	
HH6	Church, E.A. Kate (Collins)	1935
	wife of M.K. Church	
AA6	Clark, Janet (Morrison)	1890
	dau. of Thos. & Elizabeth Morrison	
HH5	Collins, Catharine J.	1909
HH4	Collins, George	1904
HH3	Collins, Sarah J	1881
	wife of Albert Collins	
MM1	Cooper. Earl Delos	1907
	son of Horatio & Sarah Cooper	
L10	Cooper, John	
MM1	Cooper, John E.	1911
	s of Haratio & Sarah Cooper	
DD13	Craigie, Cora R.	1934
DD14	Craigie, David T.	1914
DD13	Craigie, Georgina M.T.	1879
DD14	Craigie, Grace M.	1957
	wife of Lewis R. Craigie	

Plot	Name	Date
DD13	Craigie, John	1887
DD13	Craigie, John D.	1920
DD14	Craigie, Lewis R.	1962
DD13	Craigie, Margaret (Thorburn)	1903
	relict of John Craigie	
DD14	Craigie, Robert C.	1956
	son of Lewis & Grace Craigie	
Q5	Crawford, Bartholemew	1832
Q3		
Q5,Q1	Crawford, Eliza. (Shaw)	1859
	dau. of John & Margaret Crawford	
Q5	Crawford, John	1909
Q5	Crawford, John	1862
Q5	Crawford, Margaret	1832
Q5,Q4	Crawford, Margaret A.	1884
	wife of John Crawford	
C12	Davidson, James	1923
C12	Davidson, Jane	1904
	wife of John A. Davidson	
C12	Davidson, John A.	1896
S11	Davis, Anna	1848
	wife of William Davis	
FF5	Dawson, Alexander R.	1894
FF4	Dawson, Henrietta	1868
	wife of John Dawson	
S11	Dawson, John	1896
KK2	Dougan, Alexander	1867
C11	Dunning, Alfred B.	1895
II6	Embury, Albert W.	1929
II6	Embury, Lottie (Gunter)	1925
	wife of Albert W. Embury	
Z2	Emmett, Calvin D.	1934
Z2	Emmett, Jennie	1880
	wife of Calvin D. Emmett	
Z1	Emmett, Mary	1883
	wife of James Emmett	
JJ3	Farrow, William	1939
AA1	Fisher, Adeline	1883
	wife of John C. Fisher	
AA1	Fisher, John C.	1874
M10	Fitch, David	1832
	son of Henry & Jane Fitch	
Q8	Fitch, Henry	1852
M9	Fitch, Nathan	1832
DD3	Foote, Milton H___e	1887
	son of Rev.J.G. & Sarah L. Foote	
DD3	Foote, Sarah Leona	1887
	wife of Rev. J.G. Foote	
M12	Gilchrist	1873
S6	Gownlock, Jane	1837
M11	Green, Mary Margaret	1847
	(Thompson) *wife of Jonas F.Green*	
	dau. of Arch. & Jane Thompson	
S5	Hall, Juley Ammorette	1834
	wife of Woren Hall	
P2	Heaton, Mary Jane	1850
	wife of Andrew Heaton	
P3	Henry, Charles	1849
	wife of Wm. & Elizabeth Henry	
A2	Hess	
A5	Hess, Albert	1918
A4	Hess, Flora (Donaldson)	1959
	wife of William Hess	
A3	Hess, William M.	1955
CC9	Hill, Amoret (Kilman)	1895
C7	House, Mary	1964

Plot	Name	Date
O10	Hugoe, Diana Hillery	1858
	wife of Thomas Hugoe	
O11	Hugoe, Thomas	
H2	Hutt, Mary	1865
	wife of William	
L5	Jeffery, John	1854
AA2	Johnson, Bertha (McMicking)	
	wife of Calvin Johnson	1916
	dau. of James R. &	
	Margaret McMicking	
AA5	Johnson, Eva (McMicking)	1955
U7	Johnson, John	1854
C10	Johnson, Linda	1974
D1	Johnston, Euphemia	1838
	wife of James Johnston	
E1	Jones, Mary (Bowman)	1854
	dau. of David & Christinia Jones	
	wife of Adam Bowman	
W7	Keith, Daniel	1824
	died from fall from Gen. Sir	
	Isaac Brock's monument	
E5	Killman, Adam	1818
E6	Killman, Elizabeth (Near)	1820
	wife of Adam Killman	
F12,	Killman, Ellen & Elizabeth	1853,
F13	*twin dau's. of Adam*	1851
	Killman & Elizabeth Near	
CC9	Kilman, Jacob	1868
CC9	Kilman, Josiah	1870
	son of Jacob & Amoret Kilman	
F5	Knox, John	1842
F5	Knox, Margarett	1811
	wife of John Knox	
W4	Kohles, Emma	1861
	dau. of John & Catharine Kohles	
T7	Law, John	1882
T7	Law, Margaret (White)	1849
	wife of John Law	
KK3	Lawrence, John	
DD13	Lyon, Isabel T. (Craigie)	1939
	wife of G.H. Lyon	
F4	J M	
C9	MacIntyre, Kenneth	
JJ5	Mastin, George Albert	1865
	son of Wm.G. & Caroline Mastin	
JJ4	Mastin, William G.	1873
LL1	McCarthy, Dennis	1875
LL1	McCarthy, Elizabeth	1887
	wife of Dennis McCarthy	
Y1	McClive	
II2	McClive, Blanche	1892
	dau of George & M.E. McClive	
II3	McClive, Eliza	1886
II2	McClive, Frederick	1882
	son of George & ME. McClive	
GG1,Y3	McClive, Hugh	1822
GG1,II1	McClive, Isabella	1872
	dau. of John & Mary McClive	
GG1	McClive, James	1914
GG1	McClive, Jane	1819
GG1	McClive, John	1883
Y2	McClive, M	1813
GG1,X2	McClive, Margaret	1840
GG1	McClive, Maria	1827
GG1	McClive, Mary (Pew)	1880
	wife of John McClive	
II2	McClive, Mary Edna	1894
	wife of George McClive	
II2	McClive, Nellie	1891
	dau. of George & M.E. McClive	

Plot	Name	Date
II4	McClive, William H.	1872
W1	McConnell, John J.	1868
K5	McCredie, Isabel	1854
	dau. of Everand & Jannet McCredie	
L11	McCredie, Janet	1841
	wife of Everand McCredie	
K3	McCredie, Jennet	1849
	dau. of Wm. & Margaret McCredie	
K4	McCredie, William	1819
	son of Everand & Jennet McCredie	
U5	McDowell, Janet	1880
	mother of the late A. Carnoghan	
U2	McKay, Elizabeth	1855
	wife of Henry McKay	
U3	McKay, Elizabeth	1849
	dau. of Henry & Elizabeth McKay	
T6	McKenzie, Donald	1882
I6	McKenzie, William	1843
I4	McMicking, Agnes	1827
	wife of Peter McMicking	
K1	McMicking, Agnes	1815
	dau. of Susan & John McMicking	
BB7	McMicking, Eleanor	1880
	wife of James McMicking	
I5	McMicking, Gilbert	1861
I2	McMicking, Gilbert	1847
	son of Agness & Peter McMicking	
O14	McMicking, Isabella	1830
	wife of Thomas McMicking IV	
AA2	McMicking, James Russell	1917
O15	McMicking, Jane	1839
	dau. of Thom. & Isabella McMicking	
	wife of Russell	
AA2	McMicking, Margaret A. (Shugg)	
	w of Jas. R. McMicking	1929
AA3	McMicking, Martha	
K2,K1	McMicking, Mary	1821
	dau. of Susan & John McMicking	
BB6	McMicking, Mary (McClellan)	
	w of William McMicking	1873
I3	McMicking, Peter U.E.L.	1823
I1	McMicking, Rhoda	1875
	wife of Gilbert McMicking	
K1,J1	McMicking, Susanna	1821
	wife of John McMicking	
AA4	McMicking, Thomas	
	son of __ r ___ McMicking	
O13	McMicking, Thomas IV	1830
	s of Thomas McMicking III	
	and Janet Mulwain	
BB5	McMicking, William	1857
	son of Thos. & Isabella	
G2	Meddough, Benjamin	1830
G5	Meddough, Deborah	1850
	w of Benjamin Meddough	
H1	Meddough, Eleanor	
H1	Meddough, Gilbert	
G1	Meddough, Margaret	1830
	w of Peter Meddough	
G3	Middaugh, Mary	1863
	wife of James Middaugh	
I7	Middough, Ann Elizabeth	1866
	wife of Smith Middough	
I7	Middough, Deborah	1862
	child of Middough	
I7	Middough, James	1848
	child of Middough	
G4	Middough, James	1839
I7	Middough, Phillias	1858
	child of Middough	

Plot	Name	Date
I15	Ramage, Andrew	
W2	Ramage, Margaret Mary	1839
MM3	Robbins, Allen A.	1934
MM2	Robbins, Annie T.	1963
MM4	Robbins, Edith A.	1911
B1	Roberts, Calvin	1938
B1	Roberts, Elizabeth (Thompson)	
	w of Calvin Roberts	1972
A1	Robinson, James George	1953
A1	Robinson, Mary (Donaldson)	1968
	wife of James Robinson	
I6	Rodgers, Jessie	1875
Q10	Rose, Adam B.	1846
	s of Hugh & Eunice Rose	
Q9	Rose, Eunice	
	wife of Hugh Rose	
Q11	Rose, Hugh	1848
L4	Roskelley, Ann	1857
	wife of Wm. Roskelley	
L3	Roskelley family unreadable	
L6	Roskelley, Elizabeth A.	1852
	dau of Wm.& Ann Roskelley	
L2	Roskelly, William	1881
S12	Rowe, Elizabeth (Ludlow)	1853
	wife of George Rowe	
S10	Rowe, William	1847
Z3	Russell, Grace (Clark)	1858
	only dau. of Rev. Henry Clark	
	Widow of Rev. John Russell	
Z4	Russell, Rev. John D.D.	1854
O9	Scott, George	1852
	s of George & Catharine J. Scott	
O1	Scott, Harriet	1854
	wife of James Scott	
O9	Scott, Harriet	1831
	dau of Geo. & Catharine Scott	
O9	Scott, Thomas E.	1851
	s of George & Catharine Scott	
P1	Sharp, Donald	1873
P1	Sharp, Margaret	1881
Q5,Q1	Shaw, Eliza. (Crawford)	1859
	wife of John Shaw	
Q5,Q2	Shaw, John	1843
C1	Shrimpton, Albert	1916
C1	Shrimpton, Martha	1905
	wife of Albert Shrimpton	
DD2	Shugg, Adam K.	1922
DD1	Shugg, Annie B.	1892
DD4	Shugg, Catharine	1870
	wife of John Shugg	
DD2	Shugg, James Coulter	1966
DD4	Shugg, John	1888
DD1	Shugg, Susan	1932
	wife of Adam K. Shugg	
FF1	Siggs	
EE1	Siggs, Elizabeth	1865
	N. & J. Siggs	
FF2	Smith, Carlton	
	s of Charles & Agnes Smith	
FF2	Smith, Ellsworth	
	s of Charles & Agnes Smith	
B13	Smith, Jane E. (Hammond)	1899
	w of Sylvester Smith	
B13	Smith, Sylvester	1922
B13	Smith, Thomas O.	1946
FF2	Smith, William	
	s of Charles & Agnes Smith	
E4	Sniveley, Mary (Shainholdts)	1846
	w of Jacob Sniveley	
	(Bowman) *w of Abraham Bowman*	

Plot	Name	Date
NN5	Staroster, Jacob	1935
NN3	Staroster, Jimmy	1936
OO1	Staroster, Mary	1933
NN4	Staroster, Nicholas	1936
NN2	Staroster, Lena	1961
Z10	Start, Elizabeth	1907
Z9	Start, William	
B12	Stevens, Eliza	1905
Z6	Symons, Mary E.T.	1872
V1	Thomas, Elizabeth	1820
	wife of Matthew Thomas	
V2	Thomas, Matthew	1847
JJ1	Thompson, Amelia	
	wife of John Thompson	
BB8	(Thompson), Amy Carter	1930
	w of Charles H. Carter	
M6	Thompson, Ann (Shipton)	1857
	w of Archibald Thompson	
C13	Thompson, Anna Maria	1899
	dau of Arch. & Martha Thompson	
C13	Thompson, Amelia	1927
	w of Archibald Thompson	
HH2	Thompson, Archibald Alfred	
		1942
C13	Thompson, Archibald	1909
DD7	Thompson, Barbara	1888
	dau of John & Isabella Thompson	
HH2	Thompson, Benjamin F.	1910
BB8	Thompson, Catharine	1917
	dau of Archibald Thompson Sr.	
GG2	Thompson, Daniel	1912
FF3	Thompson, Daniel L.	1866
	s of Archibald & Susan Thompson	
DD10	Thompson, Elizabeth	1867
	dau of James & Jennet Thompson	
B11	Thompson, Elizabeth	1899
O7	Thompson, Harriet	1844
	dau of Archibald&Susan Thompson	
DD9	Thompson, Isabella	1872
	wife of John Thompson	
DD11	Thompson, James	1867
	s of James & Jennet Thompson	
O4	Thompson, James	1868
N5	Thompson, Colonel James	1850
N1	Thompson, Jeannet (Nixon)	1813
	w of John Thompson	
DD8	Thompson, John	1886
	s of James & Jennet Thompson	
N2	Thompson, John	1814
	s of Archibald Thompson	
N2	Thompson, John	1865
	s of John Thompson	
O5	Thompson, Lydia Emily	1851
	dau of Archibald&Susan Thompson	
BB8	Thompson, Lydia	1924
	dau of Archibald Thompson Sr.	
GG2	Thompson, Margaret	1911
GG2	Thompson, Phoebe	1912
	wife of Daniel Thompson	
N6	Thompson, Richard	1832
	s of James & Jennet Thompson	
HH2	Thompson, Ruth (McIngraham)	
		1971
DD6	Thompson, Sarah Augusta	1889
	3rd dau of John & Isabella Thompson	
DD12	Thompson, Thomas	1882
	s of James & Jennet Thompson	
DD5	Thompson, Walter	1902
	s of James & Jennet Thompson	
O6	Thompson, Walter	1852
	s of Archibald&Susan Thompson	

Plot	Name	Date
O3	Thomson, Archibald *UEL*	1821
M7	Thomson, Archibald Sr.	1892
	s of James Thomson Sr.	
O3	Thomson, Benjamin	1885
O3,O2	Thomson, Eleanor	1832
	dau of Margaret & Benjamin Thomson	
N4	Thomson, Hugh	1825
	son of James Thomson	
M4	Thomson, James Sr.	1832
M8	Thomson, Jane (Fitch)	1845
	w of Archibald Thomson Sr.	
N4	Thomson, Jennet (Cooper)	1832
	dau of James Cooper	
	wife of James Thomson	
M2	Thomson, Margaret	1830
	w of James Thomson Sr.	
O3,N3	Thomson, Margaret Rose	1836
	w of Benjamin Thomson	
M1	Thomson, Mary	1812
	dau of James Thomson	
M5	Thomson, Richard	1832
	s of James Thomson Sr.	
M3	Thomson, Thomas	1810
	son of James Thomson	
Z7	Thorburn, Catharine	1918
Z7	Thorburn, David	1836
Z7	Thorburn, David	1862
Z7	Thorburn, Isabel	1881
	wife of David Thorburn	
Z7	Thorburn, Mary	1914
Z7	Thorburn, Richard M.D.	1900
Z7	Thorburn, Sarah	1872
DD13	Trowbridge, Alice T.	1899
	(Craigie) *w of F.E. Trowbridge*	

Plot	Name	Date
R1	Walker, Ellen	1889
	wife of James Walker	
R1	Walker, Katherine	1837
T3	Wallace, Agnes	1863
	wife of Robert Wallace	
T2	Wallace, Alexander	1863
B2	Wallace, Andrew Earle	1945
T1	Wallace, Jennet	1835
	wife of Alexander Wallace	
T5	Wallace, John	1826
	s of Robert & Agnes Wallace	
B3	Wallace, John M.	1934
B3	Wallace, Mary (Turner)	1902
	wife of John Wallace	
B3	Wallace, Minnie (Blackmer)	1939
	sec. w of John Wallace	
T4	Wallace, Robert	1865
B2	Wallace, Viola M.	1980
B4	Wallace, Zella May	1889
	dau of John & Mary Wallace	
F7	Wesley, Jane	
S2	Willson, Mary Jane	1830
	dau of James & Jannet Willson	
R2	Wilson, Agnes	1833
	dau of James & Janet Wilson	
BB3	Wilson, Ann	1868
BB3	Wilson, Samuel	1868
BB2	Wilson, Samuel	1884
BB1	Wilson, Sarah J.	8
	wife of Samuel Wilson	
CC3	Wood, Agnes	1882
J2	Woodman, Mary Ann	1836
	(Hegeman) *w of J. Woodman*	
B9	Young, Amelia (McCombs)	1914
	wife of Gilbert Young	
B9	Young, Gilbert	1901
B9	Young, Gilbert L.	1958
B9	Young, Jeannette (Barbeau)	
	wife of Gilbert L. Young	

Biographical Sketches

George Bailey

GEORGE SEIBEL

George Seibel was born in Kitchener, Ontario in 1919 and came to Niagara Falls at the age of 6. He attended Simcoe Street School and Niagara Falls Collegiate Vocational Institute. At the age of 8 years he was taking American tourists, who stayed at his parents' tourist home, on sightseeing trips, for one dollar a day. He read everything he saw in the newspapers on Niagara Falls, and its history and was particularly interested in Albert Tiplin's series of geological columns which appeared in the Niagara Falls Evening Review in 1938 and 1939.

George and his wife Olive worked as a team to produce this book on the Niagara Portage Road. As in the past, when *Ontario's Niagara Parks - 100 Years* was being written from 1983 to 1985, and during 1987-88 when *Our Romantic Niagara* was underway, George did the writing and Olive was editor and proofreader.

Olive Haine was born in Niagara Falls in 1920, and was educated at Lundy's Lane Public School and Stamford Collegiate. She received her Bachelor of Arts degree from McMaster University in 1942. In May 1943 George and Olive were married and went to live in Nova Scotia, where George was stationed with the Royal Canadian Air Force. While there she taught school in Florence, Nova Scotia. She taught English, French and History - Canadian, British and Modern European - to Grades 9, 10 and 11, and Latin and the Geography of Nova Scotia to Grade 9 and acted as vice-principal, all for $800 a year.

In early 1966 George Seibel was appointed chairman of the Kiwanis Club of Stamford's Centennial Project Committee. He convinced the club that they should publish a history of the City of Niagara Falls, as a Centennial project. A year and a half later on July 27, 1967, the book was ready for sale. *Niagara Falls Canada, a history* was an anthology with contributions from forty-two different writers.

In 1971 George formed the Niagara Falls Heritage Foundation, whose aim was to foster the historical heritage of Niagara Falls and the surrounding area.

Over the next ten years, with the aid of a number of Federal Government Job Creation Grants, and grants from Wintario, and other organizations, several books of which he was the author were published. They were *Three Hundred Years Since Hennepin - Niagara Falls in Art,* and *Visitors' Guide to Ontario's Niagara Parks.* A twenty minute, 35 mm film, entitled *Niagara Falls - 300 Years Since Hennepin* was also produced.

In 1981 The Niagara Parks Commission asked George Seibel to write a book for the 100 th Anniversary of the Parks, *Ontario's Niagara Parks 100 Years,* published in 1985. In July 1988 *Our Romantic Niagara,* a book which included Albert H. Tiplin's original geology columns from the *Niagara Falls Review* was published. George Seibel edited the Tiplin columns and added additional material on geological events which had taken place since the columns appeared in the newspaper.

There is another book to be written. The Niagara Falls Bridge Commission has asked George Seibel to prepare a book, tentatively entitled, *The Bridges Over the Niagara Gorge,* for the 50th Anniversary of the Rainbow Bridge in 1991.

George is able to draw from the thousands of pictures of Niagara Falls, which he has collected over the past eighteen years, and to refer to the extensive library of historical research material collected from libraries, and archives in Canada, the United States and England. At present there are no plans for a book beyond 1991.

George Seibel has been active in community work. He is a charter member, and a life member of the Kiwanis Club of Stamford and a member of the Kiwanis Legion of Honour. He has been recognized for his community work through Kiwanis, having been named Kiwanian of the Year for the Stamford Kiwanis Club in 1960, 1964 and 1967. In 1965 he received the Fred McAllister Award as the outstanding Kiwanian in the Ontario, Quebec and Maritimes Division.

He was the recipient of a Canada Centennial Medal in 1967; the Ontario Bicentennial Medal in 1984; a Certificate of Appreciation for his contribution made during the celebration of the 75th Anniversary of the City of Niagara Falls in 1979. He has been honoured three times by the Niagara Falls Visitor and Convention Bureau, receiving a "Special Misty" award in 1980 and a "Murie Misty" award in 1983 and 1985.

In 1981 the Rotary Club of Niagara Falls recognized his contribution to local history, by making him a Paul Harris Fellow. He was appointed Niagara Parks Historian in 1984 and City of Niagara Falls Historian in 1985. In September 1989 the

Sertoma Club of Niagara Falls honoured George and Olive Seibel when they were given the Sertoma "Service to Mankind Award". At the same time Mayor William S. Smeaton presented George and Olive Seibel with a "Key to the City" in recognition of their contribution to the preservation of our local history.

ERNEST A. CRUIKSHANK

Lundy's Lane Historical Museum

Ernest Alexander Cruikshank was born in Bertie Township on June 29, 1853. After his graduation from university he returned to Fort Erie and in 1874 was appointed Ensign in the 44th Battalion. He was appointed assessment officer for Bertie Township in 1875 and two years later he became Treasurer of Fort Erie. He resigned this position when he was elected Reeve of the village of Fort Erie. He served from 1878 to 1881, then for two more terms. During that time he was elected Warden of Welland County. He was appointed a Justice of the Peace in 1883 and became Bertie Township Engineer in the same year. He served on Welland County Council until 1904.

While devoting his energies to public office, he still had time to research and write about his favourite subjects, military history and the history of the Niagara Frontier. During his lifetime he wrote 400 books and pamphlets. In 1905 he was recognized as an established historian when he was appointed a Fellow of the Royal Historical Society of Canada.

In 1904 he left Fort Erie to live in Niagara Falls, where he became Magistrate. He bought an acre of land just north of the Whirlpool and lived there, calling his property "Whirlpool Heights." He moved to Ottawa in 1908 to take charge of military documents in the Public Archives. Throughout the years he progressed steadily through the military ranks, and his writings show his progress from Captain, to Major, to Lieutenant-Colonel, and then Brigadier-General. His major historical work was the nine volume *Documentary History of the Campaign on the Niagara Frontier of the War of 1812-14*. These volumes were published by the Lundy's Lane Historical Society from 1896 to 1910.

His articles were published by the Ontario Historical Society, Niagara Historical Society, Welland County Historical Society, and the Lundy's Lane Historical Society. Ernest Cruikshank was a meticulous researcher. He was appointed to the newly created Dominion Historic Sites and Monuments Board in 1919. At its first meeting, he was elected chairman. In the ensuing years he was the directing genius and took part in the assessment, research and erection of more than two hundred bronze tablets commemorating events, people and places important in Canadian history. He died on June 23, 1939 at the age of 86. He was active to the very end of his life and had just returned from an extended trip made to secure sites for historical markers. A sentence in his obituary summed up his devotion to history: "Few historians have been found so trustworthy."

ERNEST GREEN

Ernest Green would be second only to Brigadier-General Ernest Cruikshank if we were to rank the outstanding historians of Niagara Falls, but he most certainly is first as a local historian. Both of these men were dedicated to the principles of research, and adhered to the maxim "If it isn't the truth, it isn't history." Ernest Green was born in Stamford Township on January 30, 1881. After completing high school he was a reporter, news editor, and correspondent for various newspapers, including the *Niagara Falls Evening Review, Niagara Falls Gazette, Toronto Globe, Toronto News, Buffalo Express,* and a contributor to magazines and labour publications.

The first series of his articles to appear in the *Niagara Falls Evening Review* was on the Battles of the War of 1812-14. Then in 1913 his first local history articles, under the pseudonym "The Old Timer" were published in the *Review*. These appeared until 1914, and it was not until 1920 that another series appeared under the name "Recollections of an Old'Un". This series was

followed by a column entitled "Do You Know", containing interesting historical items. Dozens of other articles appeared over the years, with titles calculated to entice the reader. Some of them were: "The Crime That Never Was Committed"; "Pre-Toonerville Trolley Days in Niagara Falls"; "Told by a Grandmother - Traditions and Reminiscences of Early Days in Stamford and Drummondville". Most of these newspaper columns are available for reference in the Local History Collection of our Niagara Falls Public Library.

Ernest Green was a Civil Servant in the Dominion Government Department of Trade and Commerce, and in 1929 he was transferred to Ottawa, where he worked as a statistician in the Dominion Bureau of Statistics. While in Ottawa he had access to the

Lundy's Lane Historical Museum

material in the Public Archives, and he continued his research and writing. The authenticity of his research and the quality of his writing was recognized by the Ontario Historical Society and twelve of his articles were published in their Papers and Records. In particular "The Niagara Portage Road" and "Township Number 2 - Mount Dorchester - Stamford," were consulted in depth during the compilation of this book. Seven of his articles were published in the Welland County Historical Society Papers and Records and two were chosen for Niagara Historical Society Publications. He was honoured for his historical expertise when he became a Fellow of the Royal Historical Society of Great Britain in 1928. He also served as President of the Ontario Historical Society, Honorary President of the Lundy's Lane Historical Society, President of the Welland County Historical Society, and Regimental Historian of the 2nd/10th Dragoons, and of the 176th Battalion.

Ernest Green died in Niagara Falls on November 5, 1947 and was buried in Fairview Cemetery. An editorial in the *Niagara Falls Evening Review* which appeared before his death, had these commendatory words: "Niagara Falls is indebted to Ernest Green for his inimitable articles on this city and the district." One of his last public appearances was at the unveiling of a plaque at the Welland County Courthouse in memory of Brigadier-General E.A. Cruikshank, in October 1947. His obituary said "Many mourned his passing, not only because he was a great historian, but because he was a true friend and a Christian gentleman."

RAY CORRY BOND

Ray Corry was born in 1885 to Walter and Sarah Corry of Stamford Township. Her father died while she was a young girl but her mother ensured that she received an education. She attended both Stamford Collegiate and Niagara Falls Collegiate and Vocational Institute. After graduation from Trinity

James C. Bond

College, Toronto, and a year later from Teachers College in Goderich, she taught in secondary schools in Newcastle and Caledonia.

In 1914 she married James R. Bond and they had one son, James. The Bonds settled in Chippawa where her husband was employed as an engineer by the Queen Victoria Niagara Falls Park Commission. Mrs. Bond developed a keen interest in the history of Chippawa and of Holy Trinity Church. She used her interest in history to produce a variety of tableaux, playlets and exhibitions, which involved young people. She was an active member of the Imperial Order Daughters of the Empire and served as librarian and regent of the Chippawa Chapter.

It was through her efforts that the Archaeological and Historic Sites Board of the Provincial Department of Travel and Publicity erected commemorative plaques at the site of Laura Secord's home in Chippawa, April 1960, and Fort Chippawa in June 1960. In 1966 she compiled a history of the Village of Chippawa, which was published as *Peninsula Village.* The proceeds from this book were donated to the building of a library in Chippawa. She contributed a chapter, entitled *Early Settlers - Early Mills,* to the Kiwanis Club of Stamford's Centennial History, *Niagara Falls Canada, a history.*

Mrs. Bond was recognized and honoured for her historical endeavours when she was awarded a Canada Centennial Medal in 1967. She continued to live in her bungalow, "Riverview Cottage", on the banks of the Chippawa River, until her death in 1970.

JANET CARNOCHAN

Janet Carnochan's parents, James and Mary Carnochan, emigrated from Colmonell in Ayrshire, Scotland in 1830, and settled in Stamford Township where James worked as a carpenter. On November 14, 1830, Janet was born. Two years later the Carnochans moved to Niagara, present day Niagara-on-the-Lake. Here Janet attended school and acquired enough education to become a teacher when she was sixteen. She later attended Toronto Normal School and received a First Class Certificate. She was a school teacher and a school principal for 39 years retiring in 1900.

She had an interest in history and when the Lundy's Lane Historical Society, the first historical society in the Province of Ontario, was formed through the leadership of Canon George Bull of All Saints Anglican Church in Niagara Falls, Janet became a member. In 1892, at the request of Canon Bull she wrote an article *Niagara One Hundred Years Ago: The Ancient Capital and Its Vicinity.* The Lundy's Lane Historical Society published it as a thirty-five page pamphlet. In 1914 she published her *History of Niagara,* a full length book which sold for $2.25 a copy.

Although she had never attended college, nor had she received formal training in historical research, she had a clear grasp of local history, and told its story with liveliness and feeling. She wrote other articles and pamphlets including: *Two Frontier Churches, Centennial St Andrew's Niagara, 1794-1894, The Count de Puisaye: A Forgotten Page of Canadian History,* and contributed articles to several of the Niagara Historical Society Publications series and to the Ontario Historical Society's Papers and Records.

She was instrumental in the formation of the

Niagara Historical Society

Niagara Historical Society. William Kirby, a prominent Niagaran, author and editor of the *Niagara Mail* had begun a historical society in 1892, but interest had waned. Janet Carnochan, in 1895, took up the challenge, accepted the position of President, and succeeded in reorganizing it. The Niagara Historical Society became one of the most active in the Province. On June 4,1907 the Society had the official opening of the museum building which was to house its historical artifacts. Janet Carnochan was the driving force in raising the money and completing the project.

She was a loyal worker in St. Andrew's Presbyterian Church, as a Sunday School teacher and

member of the Women's Missionary Society; honourary Regent of the Newark Chapter, Order of Daughters of the Empire. A newly formed group of Daughters of the Empire in the Toronto area decided to name their chapter after her. She was a member and secretary of the Niagara Public Library Board; a senior member of the Ontario Historical Society, a vice-president and then an honourary member; instrumental in arranging for the installation of at least eight historic markers in Niagara-on-the-Lake. On March 31, 1926, Janet Carnochan died, bringing an end to a remarkable life which was devoted to her church, her teaching and to the prservation of our local history.

MRS. EMMA AUGUSTA CURRIE

Emma Augusta Harvey was born in Niagara (Niagara-on-the-Lake) on November 18, 1829. She received private tuition from William Kirby, author of *The Golden Dog,* in Niagara until the family moved to St. David's when her father, Ursen Harvey, bought a tannery there. She attended school at St. David's until she was 12 years old. Her parents, at the urging of a cousin in East Bloomfield, New York sent her there to attend the East Bloomfield Academy. While she was there her cousin, who was Mrs. Parke Godwin, a daughter of William Cullen Bryant, gave her drawing lessons. She next attended Canandaigua Ladies Academy.

Astrid Akkerman

Her education gave her an interest in history, literature and the arts. She married the Honourable J.G. Currie in 1865 and lived in St. Catharines. Here she was active in the I.O.D.E. and the W.C.T.U. However it was through the Women's Literary Club of St. Catharines that she made her contribution to the preservation of our history.

Mrs. Wm. Tuttle of Niagara Falls who was almost 100 years old in 1967, told George Seibel in a private conversation how the Women's Literary Club came into being. There were women at that time, the turn of the century, who wanted to become involved in political matters. Their husbands disapproved of women organizing a club for such a purpose, but they did not have any objection to women meeting to discuss culture, books, and the arts. It was on this premise that Mrs. Currie and other like minded women founded the Women's Literary Club of St. Catharines, while at the same time they intended to discuss other things besides book reviews.

Mrs. Currie, became president of the Women's Literary Club. Through her efforts the story of Laura Secord was drawn to the attention of the public, when she wrote, in 1900, *The Story of Laura Secord and Canadian Reminiscences.* She had the Women's Literary Club place a commemorative stone at the site of Laura Secord's home in Queenston. In 1911 she was instrumental in securing a grant from Parliament towards the erection of the memorial to Laura Secord on Queenston Heights.

At her urging, the Women's Literary Club erected the commemorative monument "Sheaffe's Path to Victory", located on York Road, between St. David's and Queenston. Prior to the erection of this monument there was no recognition of Major-General Roger Hale Sheaffe's part as the victorious general at the Battle of Queenston Heights. Brock's Monument commemorated only the General who died before victory over the Americans was achieved.

Mrs. Currie was described as "Always a Reformer; has ever believed that the women of Canada are entitled to the same political privileges as the men; they have earned them by industry and self-sacrifice."

BRIAN LEIGH DUNNIGAN

Brian is a native of Michigan who came to Western New York in 1979 as Executive Director of the Old Fort Niagara Association. He received his B.A. in history from the University of Michigan in 1971 and his M.A. from the same institution in 1973. In 1979 Mr. Dunnigan was awarded an M.A. from the History Museum Training Program of the Cooperstown Graduate Programs. Before coming to Old Fort Niagara he was Managing Director of Historic Fort Wayne in Fort Wayne, Indiana.

After taking over as Executive Director of Old Fort Niagara, Mr. Dunnigan used his skills as a researcher and a writer to further public knowledge of the history of the Fort and of the Niagara Portage on the east bank of the Niagara River. He is the author of four publications on the history and architecture of Old Fort Niagara. His well researched article *Portaging Niagara* was an invaluable reference for our chapter about the east bank Portage.

In addition to his duties at Old Fort Niagara, Mr. Dunnigan belongs to a number of local and national historical and museum organizations. He is an Adjunct Assistant Professor of Anthropology at the State University of New York at Buffalo, and sits on the boards of the Western New York Association of Historical Agencies, the Landmark Society of the Niagara Frontier and the Friends of Fort George. He is a Fellow of the Company of Military Historians. Brian Dunnigan is an accomplished public speaker, and imparts his love of the history of Old Fort Niagara and the Niagara Frontier to his audiences.

R. JACK HALL

Jack Hall was born in Hamilton on November 26, 1921, and has lived in Niagara Falls since 1927. His father, Cecil, was a farm manager and Jack and his three brothers and two sisters grew up on the Calvert Farm on the Portage Road (now inundated by the water of the Ontario Hydro Reservoir). Jack attended Victoria School at the Stamford Halfway and Stamford Collegiate, graduating in 1939.

He worked at the Niagara Wire Weaving Co. from 1939 until 1974 and was Corporate Secretary when the plant closed. After the Niagara Wire Weaving Co. ceased operations, Jack worked almost twelve years for the East Niagara Housing Authority as project manager administering senior citizens' apartments and low income family homes. He retired in 1986.

Jack Hall is a very active member of St.John's Anglican church on the Portage Road. He attended St. John's Anglican Church and Sunday School since he moved to this area. He has been a member of the church choir since 1933, was a Sunday School teacher and Sunday School Superintendent for many years. He is currently on Parish Council and is Lay Delegate to the Synod. He began assisting in the church service when he was 17 and later became a lay reader. He has also served a term as people's warden.

After the new St. John's Church was built beside the old church in 1957 there were no funds to maintain the old church. The old church's furnishings and memorial windows were removed, and the building was left to deteriorate. In 1971 the Niagara Falls Heritage Foundation led by George Seibel, boarded up the windows and began a movement to restore the church. It was not difficult for George Seibel to persuade Jack, who had a love for the old church, and was interested in history, to organize a local committee to consider its restoration.

In 1975 this committee was incorporated as the Old St. John's Heritage Association and Jack was elected president. Under his leadership, plans were made, funds were raised. With the aid of a dedicated board of directors, and donations from 500 individuals and groups, Jack Hall saw the project through to a successful restoration. During the ten years it took to complete the project, Jack served as president, handled most of the correspondence and the contacts with the Associations members. The restored church will be a columbarium, a repository for cinerary remains. Historic Old St. John's has been restored under Jack's dedicated leadership and its history, and the history of the area will be displayed in a room set aside for the purpose in the front of the building. The church will be open to view to those interested in its history and the history of the Portage Road.

Jack Hall's dedication to the Old St. John's restoration project was acknowledged when he received a City of Niagara Falls Good Citizen Award in 1988 and a Fifteen Year Volunteer Service Award from the Ministry of Culture and Communications.

JEAN HILL HUGGINS

Jean Hill was born in Woodstock, Ontario in April 1895 and attended school there. She lived there until 1918, when at the age of 23 she moved to Queenston to become a teacher at Laura Secord School. At the time this was the newest school in Lincoln County, with indoor toilets, water fountains and modern desks. Her salary as a teacher was fifty dollars a month.

She developed a love of history and it was her favourite subject in school. When she married Arthur Huggins in July 1930 she gave up teaching and kept herself busy by researching the history of Queenston. She wrote historical articles for *The St. Catharines Standard,* and the *Niagara Falls Evening Review,* took photographs of the village, the dock and the lake boats. Many of these photographs have been reproduced in this book.

She served on the former Niagara Township Council in 1958 and 1959 and she was chairman of the Niagara Township School Board. She was active in the Local Council of Women in Niagara Falls and Queenston's Women's Institute, as well as being an active member of Queenston United Church.

Mike Conley St. Catharines Standard

FRANK H. LESLIE

Frank Leslie was born in 1877 in Bruce County, where he was educated and became a school teacher. He left teaching and became a newspaper publisher when he purchased the weekly Tavistock *Gazette.* He came to Niagara Falls in 1904 and purchased the *Review,* a weekly newspaper. On October 5, 1914 he began publishing the *Evening Review* as a four page daily newspaper. Shortly afterwards he purchased the rival *Daily Record,* and amalgamated the two newspapers so that the *Evening Review* was the only newspaper in town.

Mr. Leslie was active in Niagara Falls affairs. He headed the Board of Trade, the forerunner of to-day's Chamber of Commerce. During the days of the depression he was a member of a triumvirate, Niagara Falls men appointed by the Provincial Government as a supervising group and guiding advisors for the city of Niagara Falls which was in financial difficulties at that time because so many of the citizens could not pay their taxes. He was a member of the Temple Male Choir, and an active officer of the Niagara Falls Soccer Association. He donated the property for the F.H. Leslie park which is adjacent to the Valley Way Swimming Pool.

She liked to recount that her great-grandfather, Levi Hoyt Perry, was a first cousin to two famous American naval commanders - Oliver Hazard Perry who was the successful commander of the American fleet at the Battle of Lake Erie in the War of 1812 and Matthew Galbraith Perry who led the naval expedition that opened up United States trade with Japan. Levi Hoyt Perry was also Woodstock's first doctor.

In August 1989 after a long life which was dedicated to her family and her community, Jean Huggins, Queenston's unofficial historian, died. She loved Queenston and her school pupils. She was there when Queenston got its first street lights and municipal water; when the Queen Victoria Niagara Falls Park Commission built the Niagara Parkway, making it possible to take a more gradual route up the escarpment rather than the steep ascent of the old Portage Road; when the Mackenzie House and the Laura Secord House were restored. She cheerfully contributed items from her voluminous collection of historical material and photographs to this book. It is regretted that she did not live to see her material published. Jean Huggins will be missed but she will be remembered.

He was interested in local history, and wrote numerous articles. His greatest contribution to the cause of local history was giving newspaper column space to local history articles. Beginning with Ernest Green's "Old Timer" columns which began after the

1914-18 War, thousands of columns written by Ernest Green, James Morden, Eva Elliott Tolan and Francis Petrie, appeared regularly in his newspaper. Without his co-operation in giving space for these columns, interest in our local history would not have been the same.

Mr. Leslie contributed to *Niagara Falls Canada, a history,* the Kiwanis Club of Stamford's Centennial History of Niagara Falls in 1967, with his "Reminiscences of the Fourth Estate", a history of newspapers in Niagara Falls. He maintained his interest in history and was still writing the occasional column when he was over ninety years of age. He died in 1969 at the age of ninety-two.

DONALD S.LOKER

Donald Loker has had a life-long interest in local history, in particular Niagara's past - Niagara on both shores of the Great Falls and River. He has a degree in History and spent many years as the Head of the History Department at DeVeaux School, Niagara Falls, New York. While at the school he researched and published the biography of Judge Samuel DeVeaux, who was a founder of the community of Niagara Falls, New York.

Mr. Loker is a member of many of the historical societies along the Niagara Frontier, and has served as an officer in several of them. He is a sought after

speaker and has given talks on a wide variety of local subjects. He is the author of several published titles in Local History as well as numerous articles which have appeared in the *Niagara Falls Gazette.*

He is a member of Phi Alpha Theta, the National Honorary Fraternity, and he is listed in *Who's Who In the East.* He is at present President of the Niagara Falls, New York, Historical Society Inc. He is also Niagara Falls, New York,City Historian and Local History Specialist in the Niagara Falls , New York, Public Library. It is in this latter capacity that he excels in providing information, guidance and encouragement to those who come to his department to do research. The author of this book has reason to be grateful to Don Loker for the assistance, co-operation and encouragement he has so willingly given him over the past eighteen years.

JAMES C. MORDEN

James Morden was born in Hastings County, in 1869. His family moved to Niagara Falls when he was five years old. He taught school in Stamford for more than 50 years, during which time he was principal for two years at the Old Stone School at Falls View, seventeen years as principal of Barker Street School, and principal of the Falls View Consolidated School, on the site of present day Cavendish Manor, where he served continuously for 24 years until he retired in 1941.

He was active in Stamford Township politics and was a councillor from January 1922 until 1944, except for a two year break. During that time he was Stamford Township's representative on the Welland County Council. He was several times Deputy Reeve and Reeve of the Township.

His political activities did not keep him from pursuing his interest in local history. He was a leading member of the Lundy's Lane Historical Society and was for many years secretary-treasurer of that organization. He wrote many articles on local history which appeared in the *Niagara Falls Review.* In 1932 his book, *Historic Niagara Falls* was published by the Lundy's Lane Historical Society. A much sought after speaker by local social organizations, he used hand coloured slides and a lantern slide projector in his historic presentations. The lantern slide projector was the forerunner of later 35mm slide projectors.

When he died in October 1944, an editorial comment in the *Niagara Falls Evening Review* said: "He made a lasting contribution to the lore of the Niagara district, the result of indefatigable study and research." In 1951 he was honoured and recognized for his years as a teacher and a school principal when a new school on Dorchester Road north of McLeod Road was named J.C.Morden School.

FRANCIS PETRIE

Francis James Petrie was born in Niagara Falls, Ontario, July 19,1920. He attended Maple Street School and Niagara Falls Collegiate and Vocational Institute, and was employed as a research technician at Cyanamid of Canada's Welland Plant for 40 years. Francis was a devoted father to his four children.

His passion, however, was history. In his *History in the News* newspaper column, he presented local history in an informative and interesting way. His first column appeared in 1970 and at the time of his death, September 23, 1983, column number 1,092 had just been published. He was a sought after speaker and provided interesting local history programs for those who were fortunate enough to obtain his services. His public speaking was sponsored for many years by Lincoln Trust and then by their successor Canada Trust.

Niagara Falls Review

Francis Petrie was appointed City Historian for the City of Niagara Falls in 1970. He served as a Director of the Niagara Falls Board of Museums, historian for the Niagara Region Historical Council, executive member of both the Ontario Historical Society, and the John Graves Simcoe Memorial Foundation. He also belonged to ten historical societies in the Niagara Peninsula, including the Lundy's Lane, Thorold, Beaverdams and Willoughby Historical Societies. He was the first chairman of Niagara Falls Local Architectural Conservation Advisory Committee; a member of the Niagara Peninsula Conservation Authority Advisory Committee;, and a member of the Niagara Falls Library Board.

He wrote articles and provided historical information to the St. Lawrence Seaway Authority, The Niagara Parks Commission, City of Niagara Falls, and the Niagara Peninsula Conservation Authority. In 1978, he was honoured by the Niagara Falls Tourist and Convention Bureau, when he was presented with the ''Murie Misty.'' This honour is accorded each year to the person who best promotes Niagara Falls without being connected with the tourist industry.

Francis Petrie's interest in local history began when he was 12 years old. Over the years he accumulated a massive collection of photos, clippings and postcards, all of them related to the history of Niagara Falls and other localities in the Niagara Peninsula. This collection, called the Francis Petrie Collection is now in the Niagara Falls Public Library and it serves as a reminder of his devotion to the history of our area and to sharing his knowledge with everyone who would read or listen.

WILLIAM A. LORNE ROBINSON

Lorne Robinson was born in Montreal on May 22, 1904. His parents were James G. Robinson and Mary M. Donaldson. His great-great-grandfather, Lancelot (Lanty) Robinson and wife Rebecca Hesket, with ten children, emigrated from King's County Ireland, leaving Cork on May 24 , 1819, the day Queen Victoria was born. They landed at Three Rivers, Quebec and obtained seigneurial land near Maschouche.

In 1912 the Robinson family moved to Stamford and lived on the Hess farm which is now part of the present day Stamford Green Plaza. In 1913 James Robinson purchased 1.01ha (2.5 acres) of land opposite present day Stamford Green from Thomas Berriman.

Ken James

Mr. Robinson attended S.S.No.6 for six years, and graduated from the Commercial Department at Stamford Collegiate in June 1920. He then joined the staff of the Imperial Bank of Canada, Stamford Centre Branch. During his career with the bank he served in fourteen different branches, retiring as manager of the Fergus, Ontario branch after 49 years of service, in 1969.

He married Jean S. Milling, U.E., on May 5, 1927. Jean's maternal grandfather, Gilbert Young, was a descendant of the Young family who came to Canada at the time of the American Revolution. Several of the family belonged to Butler's Rangers and they also fought in the Battle of Queenston Heights on October 13, 1812. Mrs. Robinson died on July 31, 1989 after a long illness.

Lorne Robinson was active as a community volunteer. He was a member of Rotary in Bolton and Fergus. While he was in Fergus he was also a member of the Chamber of Commerce and Chairman of the Fergus Highland Games. He is a member of Stamford Presbyterian Church and he and Isabel Walker co-operated in the *Stamford Historical House Tour* booklet which was published by Stamford Presbyterian Church in 1984. He also contributed to the 200th Anniversary Book which the church published to mark the occasion. He has been a member of the Local Architectural Conservation Advisory Committee.

The central part of his home is thought to be the remains of Hugh Alexander's house and store, dating before the War of 1812. Lorne has made a detailed study of the life of Hugh Alexander, the enterprising portage trader, who was Stamford's first merchant. Lorne's material on Hugh Alexander, his own property adjacent to Stamford Green, and on Stamford Presbyterian Church has been used in this book.

Lorne Robinson was a founding director of Old St. John's Heritage Association and served as a director and as treasurer of that organization for eleven years. His service to the community was recognized when he received a city of Niagara Falls Good Citizen Award in 1988.

ESTHER RALPH SUMMERS

Esther Ralph was the fifth child of eight children born to Alton and Kristin Palmason Ralph. She was born in 1913, near Earlton, Ontario. The Ralphs moved to Niagara Falls in 1919 where Esther attended Stamford Collegiate, and then Hamilton Normal School. She taught school in Thorold and Allanburg until her marriage to Roy Summers in 1934.

Esther Summers has been an active church worker, Sunday School superintendent and Bible class teacher at historic Beaverdams United Church. Her real love is local history, genealogy in particular. She helped reorganize the Beaverdams, Pelham and Thorold Historical Societies, and is also a member of other historical societies, including the Lundy's Lane Historical Society and the St.Catharines Museum.

She was officially appointed Thorold's historian in 1983, and is historian for the Niagara Regional Historical Council. She is a life member of the Niagara Branch Ontario Genealogical Society and the DeCew Falls Women's Institute.

She has been a source of information for authors, and radio and television producers, who are looking for local history and genealogical material. She has been given credit for her assistance in more than two dozen books, including *The War of 1812-13* and *Flames Across the Border* by Pierre Berton; *Peninsula Village* by Ray Corry Bond. Ruth McKenzie dedicated her book *Laura Secord the Legend and the Lady* to Mrs. Summers.

She has answered thousands of genealogical information requests at her own expense. She has been honoured for her efforts, and received an Ontario Bicentennial Medal in 1984; two Ministry of Culture Volunteer Service Awards; was written up in *Women of Action* for International Women's Year, 1975. The Town of Thorold is presently naming a street after her.

Genealogy is Esther's forte. She says that helping others and sharing her knowledge makes life interesting, exciting and rewarding.

EVA ELLIOTT TOLAN

Mrs. Tolan was born in Woodstock, Ontario, the eldest daughter of Rev. Otho Christopher Elliott, a Baptist minister. Her mother Sophronia Stokes was of United Empire Loyalist ancestry. Because of her father's transfer to various pastoral charges, Mrs. Tolan received her education in elementary and secondary schools in Peterborough, Belleville, Stratford and St. Thomas . She came to Niagara Falls in 1919.

She was interested in local history for most of her adult life and accumulated a library of more than 300 books and an extensive collection of clippings and other information relating to the history of the Niagara Frontier. In October 1952 her first local history column, entitled "Reminders of the Past" appeared in the *Niagara Falls Evening Review.*

For the next seven years her columns appeared weekly. Her articles which averaged 900 words, took up to six hours to research and write. During the same period she was sought after as a speaker for clubs and social organizations. For many years she was a correspondent for several out-of-town newspapers, including 17 years as the Stamford correspondent for the *Niagara Falls Gazette.* She wrote articles on Niagara Falls, Welland, Welland County and communities with a population of 500 or more in the county, for the 1957 revised version of the Grolier *Encyclopedia Canadiana.*

During her long career as a historian she was twice president of the Lundy's Lane Historical Society, a member of the Toronto Branch of the Canadian Authors Association, the (American) Association of Professional Women Writers, and the Ontario Historical Society. Eva Elliott Tolan died on June 27, 1967 at the age of 75 years.

DOROTHY VAN SLYKE

Dorothy Van Slyke was born in Perth, Ontario, the daughter of Rev. and Mrs. J.G. Van Slyke. She attended schools in Perth and Niagara Falls, graduating from Stamford Collegiate, and holds degrees in Arts from McMaster University and in Library Science from the Univeristy of Toronto.

She joined the staff of the Niagara Falls Public Library in 1951, and has been Chief Librarian since 1972. She has served on the executives of many library associations, and on advisory committees for Niagara College and the Niagara Region regional library system.

She has been active in church work, and as a member of many local associations, including the Niagara Falls Local Architectural Conservation Advisory Committee, has served on the executive of Niagara Concerts, and is a member of various associations in the conservation and humane fields.

Her interest in local history and the preservation of its records has led her to assist in several books. She has served on the Advisory Board and was a contributing editor and index co-ordinator for the book, *Niagara Falls Canada, a history,* published by the Kiwanis Club of Stamford. She was also index co-ordinator of *Ontario's Niagara Parks: 100 Years,* published by The Niagara Parks Commission, and assisted with editing and was index co-ordinator of *Our Romantic Niagara: A Geological History of the River and the Falls,* by A.H. Tiplin, published by the Niagara Falls Heritage Foundation. She wrote a children's book, *Forest, River, Early Settlers - A Little History of Early Settlement of the Area Now Within the City of Niagara Falls, Ontario, to the year 1800,* which was published by the Niagara Falls Public Library in 1984. This book is being reprinted by the Niagara Falls Heritage Foundation, to be used in the schools during the Niagara Portage Road celebrations.

Dorothy Van Slyke has a special interest in Niagara Falls art - art with Niagara Falls as the subject. Her co-operation with George Seibel in the compilation of *300 Years Since Hennepin - Niagara Falls in Art 1678-1978,* was acknowledged when the Niagara Falls Heritage Foundation dedicated the publication to her.

ISABEL ROBERTS WALKER

Isabel Roberts was born in Niagara Falls, Ontario, the daughter of Calvin and Elizabeth (Thompson) Roberts. On her mother's side she is a direct descendant of John Thompson of Whirlpool Farm, who was her great-great-grandfather. She attended school in Niagara Falls and graduated from Niagara Falls Collegiate. She then attended Ontario Ladies College in Whitby, Ontario and after graduation worked for the Ontario Provincial Government as a dietician. She married Canon A.H. Walker, who was rector for many years of the Church of St.John the Evangelist on the Portage Road at Stamford Green.

George S. Butt

Mrs. Walker is a charter member of the Stamford Chapter of the I.O.D.E., a member of the Lundy's Lane Historical Society and a member of L.A.C.A.C. She is a recognized authority on the historic houses in Niagara Falls and has contributed her knowledge freely on this subject. The chapter "Historic Houses" in *Niagara Falls Canada, a history,* published in 1967 by the Kiwanis Club of Stamford was written by Mrs. Walker and Dorothy Van Slyke. *Stamford Township - Our Old Buildings,* published by the Lundy's Lane Historical Society contains much of her material. The *Stamford Historical House Tour* published by Stamford Presbyterian Church in 1984 is a joint effort with W.A.Lorne Robinson.

Mrs. Walker has assisted a number of prominent authors when they were researching information in this area. When C.W. Jefferys was doing sketches for his three volume *The Picture Gallery of Canadian History,* he stayed with Canon and Mrs. Walker when sketching, and returned to the Walker home in time for supper. Hazel C. Mathews consulted the Thompson papers which Mrs. Walker has in her possession, while she was researching *The Mark of Honour.* Mrs Walker is willing to share her knowledge and is a constant source of information for owners who call on her when they are researching the history of their houses.

JOHN BURTNIAK

John Burtniak was born in Manitoba but grew up in Thorold Township. He attended schools in Allanburg and Welland, and then the University of Ottawa (B.A.) and the University of Toronto (B.L.S. and M.L.S. degrees in Library Science). He joined the Brock University Library staff in 1965, and over the years has had responsibility for cataloguing and acquisitions in the Technical Services Division, while maintaining overall supervision of the Library's Special Collections. John now holds the full-time position of Special Collections Librarian and University Archivist. Over the years, he has developed a superb Niagara Collection, recognized as such on both sides of the Niagara River and throughout Canada.

John has had a life-long interest in Niagara Peninsula settlement history and has been actively involved with various heritage-related organizations on a local, provincial and national level, as well as a member of professional library organizations. He is Past-President, Ontario Genealogical Society and currently, Vice-President, Canadian Canal Society. As a member of various historical and heritage-related organizations and museums on both sides of the Niagara, he is currently President, Lundy's Lane Historical Society, and Secretary, Old St. John's Stamford Heritage Association, and Past-Chairman, Niagara Regional Historical Council, Past-President, Thorold and Beaverdams Historical Society and Past-Chairman, St. Catharines Historical Museum Board. For his involvement in local history, he received a Bicentennial medal in 1984.

He is co-organizer of the University's annual Niagara Peninsula History Conferences, co-editor of its published papers, co-author of a celebrated Niagara Peninsula railway history, and author of various papers and a frequent speaker on local history topics.

John also collects the Niagara Peninsula in all its printed and pictorial forms. Some of his other interests include the history of Ukrainian settlement in Canada, Canada's printing history, Canadian woodcuts and linocuts, Canadian Christmas books, Big Band music, Art Deco, the Avanti, and glass canes.

GENERAL INDEX

Numerals in italics denote illustrations

The Mark of Honour